THE CAMBRIDGE
HISTORY OF JUDAISM

VOLUME ONE

THE CAMBRIDGE HISTORY OF JUDAISM

EDITORS

W. D. Davies   L. Finkelstein

ADVISORY EDITORIAL BOARD

THE
CAMBRIDGE
HISTORY OF JUDAISM

EDITED BY

W. D. DAVIES, D.D., F.B.A.
LOUIS FINKELSTEIN, D.Litt., D.H.L.

VOLUME ONE

INTRODUCTION; THE PERSIAN PERIOD

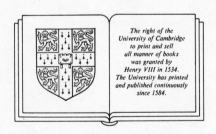

The right of the
University of Cambridge
to print and sell
all manner of books
was granted by
Henry VIII in 1534.
The University has printed
and published continuously
since 1584.

CAMBRIDGE UNIVERSITY PRESS

CAMBRIDGE

NEW YORK   NEW ROCHELLE
MELBOURNE   SYDNEY

Published by the Press Syndicate of the University of Cambridge
The Pitt Building, Trumpington Street, Cambridge CB2 1RP
40 West 20th Street, New York, NY 10011-4211, USA
10 Stamford Road, Oakleigh, Victoria 3166, Australia

First published 1984
Reprinted 1988, 1991

Printed in Great Britain by the
University Press, Cambridge

Library of Congress catalogue card number: 77-85704

British Library Cataloguing in Publication Data
The Cambridge history of Judaism.
Vol. 1: Introduction; The Persian period
1. Judaism – History
I. Davies, W. D.   II. Finkelstein, Louis
296'.09'01   BM165

ISBN 0 521 21880 2

07672733

PREFACE

Critical study of Judaism, by which is meant the form which the religion of Israel assumed in and after the Babylonian exile, is of comparatively recent origin.

It began seriously among Jews about the middle of the last century. It has been continued by a number of great Jewish scholars, and sustained by the growing self-awareness and self-expression of the Jewish people. For over 80 years Gentile studies have established the rootage of the Christian religion in Jewish Apocalyptic, and first-century Judaism as the matrix of Christianity. In short, Judaism has now become a shared object of historico-critical research by Jews and Gentiles, in Europe, in Israel, and on the American continent. Historical works dealing with its formative period from the Babylonian exile to the codification of the Mishnah have appeared in many languages. Why, then, should another series of volumes be devoted to this period now?

We begin by observing that most of the historical work – certainly in English – was done by Jewish and Gentile scholars working individually and independently. Great as has been their achievement, historians of Judaism have not always been able to escape the constraints, limitations and even distortions of their respective religious and social traditions. No historical writing can achieve full impartiality, of course: partiality, indeed, may have its own valuable insight. But as the study of Judaism is peculiarly open to emotive interests and unconscious influences which make it highly susceptible to hurtful misinterpretation, no effort to get rid of the blinkers of tradition and prejudice may be deemed superfluous.

The editors have therefore sought to enlist contributors from various religious and non-religious backgrounds, and from various countries, so that the work may be truly ecumenical and international. They have particularly sought to bring together the two seas of Jewish and Gentile scholarship which have hitherto been too little intermingled. No effort has been made to reconcile contributors' differing points of view. Different approaches to and interpretations of the same sources will be found here, and even contradictory treatments of certain events

and movements. Such differences of viewpoint and emphasis witness
to the intrinsic difficulty of the whole enterprise; they can be mutually
and enrichingly corrective.

The dimensions of this difficulty have been greatly enlarged by new
sources of knowledge gained in this century. Their impact is a second
reason for undertaking this history. We have to look afresh at the
history of Judaism in the light of new data provided by archeology,
new knowledge of the Apocryphal, Pseudepigraphical, Qumranic and
Gnostic writings, and recent critical work on the Rabbinic sources.
The large space which we have allotted to archeology and literary
sources illustrates the historian's new opportunities and the complexity
of his task.

Hence the necessity of adding descriptions of non-Jewish backgrounds to certain themes, as in the chapters by Dr Boyce, Dr Bresciani, and Dr Dandamayev. Hence, too, certain hesitancies on the part of
contributors which may seem to be characteristic of this work. Some
urge that in certain areas the necessary preliminary textual and other
critical studies for anything like an adequate treatment have not yet been
fully done. Others point to irresolvable complexities and inconsistencies
in the sources. Unlike many historians in the past, they hesitate to
present with any confidence a 'story' of chronologically and causally-
related events. The reason for this hesitancy (according to Professor
Chaim Tadmor, whom circumstances alone prevented from contributing) is mirrored by our disjointed times. Living historians have
constantly to live with contemporary problems which are recognized
to be inescapable and largely beyond solution. Resigning themselves to
acceptance of the insoluble, they feel induced to a like passivity in their
examination of sources. Be that as it may, this 'hesitancy' is certainly
bound up with our contributors' frequent recognition that much textual
and exegetical work remains to be done before Judaism can be
satisfactorily interpreted. This simply affirms that historians are more
than ever aware that a 'definitive' *History of Judaism* (or of any other
phenomenon) is an impossibility. Indeed, the very notion of such a
History should be buried.

The editors have the pleasant duty of recording their indebtedness.
They are grateful to the advisors and relieved that the questions which
had to be put to them were few. To two scholars their gratitude is
inexpressible. From beginning to end the late Professor Elias Bickerman and Professor Morton Smith, both of Columbia University, have
given their expertise readily and freely. In the structuring of the
volumes, the spacing of the various themes, the choice of contributors
and in other uncountable ways, they have proved highly effective

instruments for the fashioning of this history. Though the editors recognize that such effective help in no sense diminishes their final responsibility for the finished work, they are proud and grateful that the imprint of Elias Bickerman and Morton Smith is heavy upon it.

The editors are also indebted, specially and deeply, to all the contributors. For many reasons beyond their control the time taken over publication has been far longer than was anticipated. They deeply regret this and here pay tribute to the patience and forbearance with which contributors have responded to unavoidable delays.

The editors also acknowledge with the keenest appreciation the generosity of the two institutions which they serve, and which has made this supplementary work possible: namely, the Jewish Theological Seminary of America, New York, and Duke University, Durham, North Carolina. Above all they name especially two Deans of the Divinity School of Duke University: Dr R. E. Cushman and Dr T. A. Langford. It is no exaggeration to claim that without their understanding co-operation and support this *History* would not have seen the light of day. Our warmest thanks go also to Mr Michael Farris, the indefatigably devoted Librarian of the Duke Divinity School, and to his staff for constant and unfailingly courteous help, and to two secretaries who have worked on this history untiringly, Mrs Patricia Haugg in the earliest stages, and then through most of the work Mrs Sarah Freedman to whom our debt is immeasurable. In addition, the editors gratefully record the valuable assistance given to the project in its later stages by the National Endowment for the Humanities.

We would like to acknowledge warmly the help given in various ways by Professor Steven Katz of Dartmouth College. A number of sometime graduate student-assistants shared in the work at different stages. These were Dr G. Stemberger, Father Benedict Viviano, Dr Joseph Trafton, Dr Gerd Lüdemann, Mr Menachem Mor, Dr Dale Allison, and Mr Lynn Tatum. The staff at the Cambridge University Press in New York, the editors, readers, subeditors and printers of the Cambridge University Press in England gave of that skill and devotion which it would be an impertinence to praise. The final word goes to Mrs Eurwen Davies, who shared in this work with informed enthusiasm and selflessly endured the many difficulties that such an enterprise involves.

W. D. D.

L. F.

3 February, 1982

CONTENTS

Preface   *page*   v

List of abbreviations   xi

Frontispiece   xvi

INTRODUCTION

1   The geography of Palestine and the Levant in relation to
    its history   1
    by DENIS BALY, Department of Religion, Kenyon
    College, Gambier, Ohio

2   Numismatics   25
    by URIEL RAPPAPORT, Department of Jewish His-
    tory, University of Haifa

3   Calendars and chronology   60
    by ELIAS J. BICKERMAN†, Department of History,
    Columbia University, New York

THE PERSIAN PERIOD

4   The Persian empire and the political and social history of
    Palestine in the Persian period   70
    by EPHRAIM STERN, Institute of Archeology, The
    Hebrew University of Jerusalem

5   The archeology of Persian Palestine   88
    by EPHRAIM STERN

6   Hebrew and Aramaic in the Persian period   115
    by JOSEPH NAVEH, Institute of Archeology, The
    Hebrew University of Jerusalem and JONAS C.
    GREENFIELD, Department of Semitic Languages,
    The Hebrew University of Jerusalem

7   The Jewish community in Palestine in the Persian period   130
    by PETER ACKROYD, King's College, University of
    London

8   Prophecy and Psalms in the Persian period   162
    by GUNTHER WANKE, Seminar für Geschichte und
    Exegese   des   Alten   Testaments,   Universität
    Erlangen-Nürnberg

9   Wisdom literature in the Persian period   189
    by HARTMUT GESE, University of Tübingen

10 Jewish religious life in the Persian period   219
    by MORTON SMITH, Department of History,
    Columbia University, New York

11 Persian religion in the Achemenid age   279
    by MARY BOYCE, Department of the Near and Middle
    East, School of Oriental and African Studies, University
    of London

12 Iranian influence on Judaism: first century B.C.E. to second
    century C.E.   308
    by SHAUL SHAKED, Faculty of the Humanities, the
    Hebrew University of Jerusalem

13 The Diaspora   326
    A. Babylonia in the Persian age   326
    by M. DANDAMAYEV, Institute for Oriental Studies of
    the Academy of the U.S.S.R., Leningrad

    B. The Babylonian captivity   342
    by ELIAS J. BICKERMAN†

    C. Egypt, Persian satrapy   358
    by EDDA BRESCIANI, Istituto di Storia Antica e
    Antichità Classische 'Ippolito Rosellini', Pisa

    D. The Jews in Egypt   372
    by BEZALEL PORTEN, Faculty of the Humanities, The
    Hebrew University of Jerusalem

Bibliographies   401

Index   447

Chronological table   462

ABBREVIATIONS

AAA	*Annals of Archaeology and Anthropology*
AASOR	*Annual of the American Schools of Oriental Research*
AB	Anchor Bible
ABR	*Australian Biblical Review*
AcOr	*Acta orientalia*
ADAJ	*Annual of the Department of Antiquities of Jordan*
AfO	*Archiv für Orientforschung*
AHHI	*Alon Hahevra Hanumismatit Le'Israel*
AION	*Annali dell'istituto orientali di Napoli*
AJBA	*Australian Journal of Biblical Archaeology*
AJS Review	*American Journal of Jewish Studies Review*
AJSL	*American Journal of Semitic Languages and Literature*
ALUOS	*Annual of Leeds University Oriental Society*
ANET	J. B. Pritchard (ed.), *Ancient Near Eastern Texts Relating to the Old Testament*, 3rd edn. Princeton, N.J., 1969
ANS Museum Notes	*American Numismatic Society Museum Notes*
AOS	American Oriental Series
ArtAs	*Artibus Asia*
AS	*Assyriological Studies*
ASAE	*Annales du Service des Antiquités de l'Egypte*
ATD	Das Alte Testament Deutsch
ATR	*Anglican Theological Review*
AUSS	*Andrews University Seminary Studies*
AVTR	*Aufsätze und Vorträge zur Theologie und Religionswissenschaft*
BA	*Biblical Archaeologist*
BAR	*Biblical Archaeologist Reader*
BASOR	*Bulletin of the American Schools of Oriental Research*
BETL	Bibliotheca ephemeridum theologicarum lovaniensium
BHT	*Beiträge zur historischen Theologie*
Bib	*Biblica*
BibOr	*Biblica et orientalia*
BIE	*Bulletin de l'Institut d'Egypte*

BIES	*Bulletin of the Israel Exploration Society*
BIFAO	*Bulletin de l'institut français d'archéologie orientale*
BJRL	*Bulletin of the John Rylands University Library*
BKAT	Biblischer Kommentar: Altes Testament
BMB	*Bulletin de Musée de Beyrouth*
BO	*Bibliotheca orientalis*
BOT	De Boeken van het Oude Testament
BR	*Biblical Research*
BSac	*Bibliotheca Sacra*
BSOAS	*Bulletin of the School of Oriental and African Studies*
BWANT	Beiträge zur Wissenschaft vom Alten und Neuen Testament
BZ	*Biblische Zeitschrift*
BZAW	Beihefte zur Zeitschrift für die alttestamentliche Wissenschaft
CAP	A. Cowley, *Aramaic Papyri of the Fifth Century B.C.* Oxford, 1923.
CBQ	*Catholic Biblical Quarterly*
CIS	*Corpus inscriptionum semiticarum*
ClassPhil	*Classical Philology*
CRAIBL	*Comptes rendus de l'Académie des inscriptions et belles-lettres*
CTM	*Concordia Theological Monthly*
DJD	*Discoveries in the Judaean Desert of Jordan*, ed. P. Benoit *et al.* Oxford, 1961.
EncJud	*Encyclopaedia Judaica*, ed. C. Roth and J. Wigoder, Jerusalem–New York, 1971
ERE	*Encyclopaedia of Religion and Ethics*
ET	English translation
ETL	*Ephemerides theologicae lovanienses*
EvT	*Evangelische Theologie*
EV(V)	English version(s)
ExpTim	*Expository Times*
FRLANT	Forschungen zur Religion und Literatur des Alten und Neuen Testaments
HAT	Handbuch zum Alten Testament
HKAT	Handkommentar zum Alten Testament
HomBib	*Homiletica en Biblica*
HR	*History of Religions*
HSCP	*Harvard Studies in Classical Philology*
HTR	*Harvard Theological Review*
HUCA	*Hebrew Union College Annual*
ICC	International Critical Commentary
IDB	G. A. Buttrick (ed.), *Interpreter's Dictionary of the Bible*
IDBSup	Supplementary volume to *Interpreter's Dictionary of the Bible*

IEJ	*Israel Exploration Journal*
ILN	*The Illustrated London News*
INJ	*Israel Numismatic Journal*
Int	*Interpretation*
IntNumConv	*International Numismatic Convention, Jerusalem, 1963,* ed. A. Kindler, Tel Aviv–Jerusalem, 1967.
IOS	*Israel Oriental Studies*
ITQ	*Irish Theological Quarterly*
JA	*Journal Asiatique*
JAOS	*Journal of the American Oriental Society*
JBL	*Journal of Biblical Literature*
JBR	*Journal of Bible and Religion*
JCOI	*Journal of the K. R. Cama Oriental Institute*
JCS	*Journal of Cuneiform Studies*
JHS	*Journal of Hellenic Studies*
JJS	*Journal of Jewish Studies*
JNES	*Journal of Near Eastern Studies*
JQR	*Jewish Quarterly Review*
JSOR	*Journal of the Society of Oriental Research*
JSOT	*Journal for the Study of the Old Testament*
JSS	*Journal of Semitic Studies*
JTS	*Journal of Theological Studies*
KAI	H. Donner and W. Röllig, *Kanaanäische und aramäische Inschriften.* 2nd edn. Wiesbaden, 1968
KAT	Kommentar zum Alten Testament, ed. E. Sellin.
KD	*Kerygma und Dogma*
Leš	*Lešonénu*
MDOG	*Mitteilungen der deutschen Orient-Gesellschaft*
MIO	*Mitteilungen des Instituts für Orientforschung*
MPAIBL	*Mémoires présentés à l'Académie des inscriptions et belles-lettres*
MVAG	*Mitteilungen der vorderasiatisch-ägyptischen Gesellschaft*
NC	*Numismatic Chronicle*
NNM	*Numismatic Notes and Monographs*
NTS	*New Testament Studies*
OIP	Oriental Institute Publications
OLZ	*Orientalische Literaturzeitung*
OrAnt	*Oriens antiquus*
Or	*Orientalia* (Rome)
OTS	*Oudtestamentische Studiën*
PAAJR	*Proceedings of the American Academy of Jewish Research*
PEFQS	*Palestine Exploration Fund, Quarterly Statement*
PEQ	*Palestine Exploration Quarterly*

PJ	*Palästina-Jahrbuch*
PW	Pauly-Wissowa, *Real-Encyclopädie der classischen Altertums-wissenschaft*
PSBA	*Proceedings of the Society of Biblical Archaeology*
QDAP	*Quarterly of the Department of Antiquities in Palestine*
RAL	*Rendiconti Accademia Nazionale de Lincei*
RB	*Revue biblique*
RE	*Realencyklopädie für protestantische Theologie und Kirche*
REg	*Revue d'égyptologie*
REG	*Revue des études grecques*
REJ	*Revue des études juives*
RES	*Répertoire d'épigraphie sémitique*
RevQ	*Revue de Qumran*
RGVV	Religionsgeschichtliche Versuche und Vorarbeiten
RHR	*Revue de l'histoire des religions*
RLA	*Reallexikon der Assyriologie und vorderasiatischen Archäologie*
RN	*Revue Numismatique*
RSO	*Rivista degli studi orientali*
RSR	*Recherches de science religieuse*
SAW	*Sitzungsberichte der österreichischen Akademie der Wissenschaften*
SBO	*Studia Biblica et Orientalia*
SBT	Studies in Biblical Theology
ScEccl	*Sciences ecclésiastiques*
SchTU	*Schweizerische theologische Umschau*
SCO	*Studi classici e orientali*
SE	Seleucid Era
SEÅ	*Svensk exegetisk årsbok*
SH	Studia Hellenistica
SJT	*Scottish Journal of Theology*
SPAW	*Sitzungsberichte der preussischen Akademie der Wissenschaften*
ST	*Studia Theologica*
ThZ	*Theologische Zeitschrift*
TLZ	*Theologische Literaturzeitung*
TPQ	*Theologisch-Praktische Quartalschrift*
TRu	*Theologische Rundschau*
TRev	*Theologische Revue*
TWNT	G. Kittel and G. Friedrich (eds.), *Theologisches Wörterbuch zum Neuen Testament*
TynBull	*Tyndale Bulletin*
TZ	*Theologische Zeitschrift*
VD	*Verbum domini*
VDI	*Vestnik Drevnei Istorii*

VF	*Verkündigung und Forschung*
VT	*Vetus Testamentum*
VTSup	*Vetus Testamentum*, Supplement
WMANT	Wissenschaftliche Monographien zum Alten und Neuen Testament
WO	*Die Welt des Orients*
WZKM	*Wiener Zeitschrift für die Kunde des Morgenlandes*
WZLeipzig	*Wissenschaftliche Zeitschrift der Karl-Marx Universität, Leipzig*
ZA	*Zeitschrift für Assyriologie*
ZAS	*Zeitschrift für ägyptische Sprache und Altertumskunde*
ZAW	*Zeitschrift für die alttestamentliche Wissenschaft*
ZDMG	*Zeitschrift der deutschen morgenländischen Gesellschaft*
ZDPV	*Zeitschrift des deutschen Palästina-Vereins*
ZKG	*Zeitschrift für Kirchengeschichte*
ZKT	*Zeitschrift für katholische Theologie*
ZST	*Zeitschrift für systematische Theologie*
ZTK	*Zeitschrift für Theologie und Kirche*

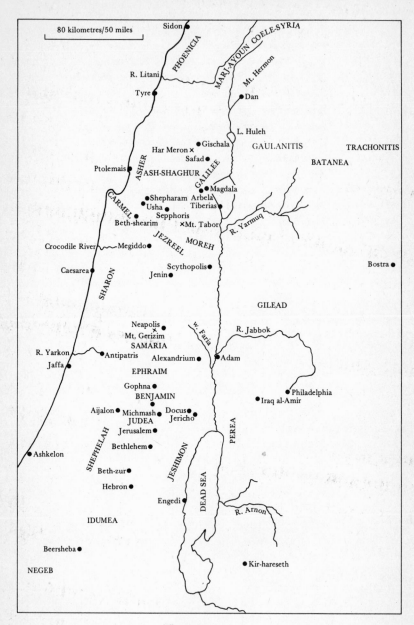

The Palestine area.

INTRODUCTION

CHAPTER I

THE GEOGRAPHY OF PALESTINE AND THE LEVANT IN RELATION TO ITS HISTORY

Geography has been defined as the study of space relationships, and it is in this sense that the geography of Palestine must be considered, for upon these relationships very much of its history depends. They are threefold in nature and involve the relation of each region within the country with the other internal regions, of Palestine with the Levant coast of which it is a part, and finally the relation of the Levant with the larger outside world. This world was enormous indeed, for it was in York in England that Constantine was first proclaimed emperor, an event which was to alter the face of Palestine and bring much grief upon the Jewish people, and it was the rich Asian trade, ranging as far as the East Indies and China, which made the Romans so determined to maintain the Provincia Arabia.

In this context two facts are of fundamental importance: the centrality and the extraordinary smallness of Palestine. The entire Middle East is dominated by three great barriers to settlement and easy movement: the towering mountain chains of central Europe and Asia, the dry, forbidding deserts, and the penetrating fingers of the seas, which hold the whole area in their grip. This constriction has determined both the main concentrations of population and the course of the major routes, followed for century after century by both merchants and warriors. Although the notable trading cities of Tyre, Damascus, Palmyra and Petra lay just beyond the Palestinian borders, the routes they served crossed its territory; for here at the south-western end of the Fertile Crescent the desert, closing in upon the Mediterranean, brings cultivation to an end, and all the roads from Asia to Egypt came together at Gaza, where also the opulent caravans from southern Arabia, bringing the riches of the East to Rome, finally reached the sea. For the whole of the long period under review Palestine may be said to have had, properly speaking, no internal history; everything that happened

I

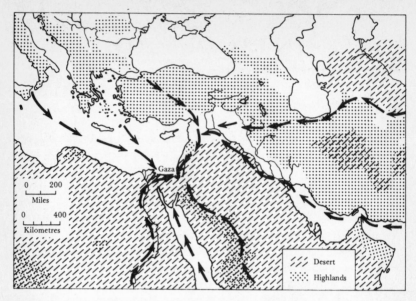

Fig. 1. Strategic position, showing how the major land and sea routes converge on Palestine. (Figs. 1, 3, 4 and 5 are reproduced from Professor D. Baly's book, *The Geography of the Bible* (Harper, N.Y., 1957).)

there was in some sense conditioned by the fact that it was the prisoner of its position at this crossroads. There was in theory an independent state for less than ten per cent of the time, and even much of that independence was illusory.

In relation to this vast and often menacing world Palestine proper, that is, the area of effective Jewish settlement, was amazingly tiny. From Dan in the north to Beersheba in the south is only a little over 150 miles as the crow flies and from the port of Joppa to the Jordan no more than 45. Even if we extend our view over what may be called the whole 'Palestine area', it is no more than 250 miles from Dan to Ezion-geber on the Red sea and 75 miles from Jaffa to the desert's edge at Philadelphia (modern Amman). Nevertheless, by reason both of structure and climate, this restricted area is remarkably varied and strongly compartmentalized, and the endless torments of Palestinian history derive no less from inescapable internal conflicts than from the stranglehold of the foreign powers. The two forces acted and reacted upon each other: imperial governments used the internal conflicts for their own purposes and the Palestinian communities in their desperation sought again and again the help of foreign authority to resolve their problems, only to find that they had solved nothing at all. So persistent has been this pattern of Palestinian history, not merely for centuries but for millennia, that it would not be wrong to speak of it as geographically determined. The pattern is demonstrably no different today.

THE STRUCTURAL PATTERN

The most immediately obvious feature of the Levant is its division into four longitudinal zones: the narrow lowlands along the coast, widening only in the south, the western highlands, the central rift valley, and the eastern plateau. This alignment of the highlands and lowlands parallel to the coast has sharply restrained the penetration inland of the winter rainfall, and therefore of cultivation, and has made of the Levant an extended bridge between the desert and the sea, deflecting all major movement of traffic northwards and southwards in accordance with the dominant lines of relief. In the ancient struggle between Egypt and Mesopotamia this was the bridge across which the armies were obliged to move.

But these divisions are imposed upon a more complicated structural framework with which the four north–south zones are only partially in agreement. The Levant rests on the edge of the solid Saharo-Arabian platform, which was washed on the north by the long sea of Tethys, of which the present Mediterranean, Black sea, Caspian sea and Persian gulf remain as fragments. To the north of this again was the platform of Angaraland, which included the present Russian and Siberian plains. In the Levant the coast ran more or less north and south, not far from where it is now. In periods of transgression parts, or the whole, of the Palestinian–Syrian region sank beneath the sea and received deposits of marine sediments, mainly limestone and chalk; and in the intervening periods of regression dry land emerged and terrestial sandstones were laid down. Very generally speaking we may distinguish three major layers: the lower, or Cambrian, limestone; the middle, or Nubian, sandstone; and the upper limestones and chalks laid down during the transgression which lasted from the Jurassic through the Eocene periods. These three layers are clearly evident in the Lebanon mountains. In Transjordan the Nubian sandstone is widely exposed in the south, and in the region south of Petra the pre-Cambrian granite platform has been thrust up to the surface. In Palestine proper, however, only the uppermost layer is exposed, the most important components being the hard Cenomanian limestone at the bottom, the soft Senonian chalk, and at the top the chalk and limestone of the Eocene period.

The Levant received only the 'ground swell' of the storm which produced the high mountain ranges of Anatolia and Persia, and here the sedimentary rocks, which were in any case restrained by the massive platform beneath them, were folded and warped only moderately. Nevertheless, the intense pressure shattered the underlying platform to create the complicated system of faulting and rift valleys which extends all the way from the borders of Anatolia through the Red sea and East Africa to beyond lake Nyasa.

So powerful was this faulting in the Levant that the highlands, though the sediments of which they are formed are usually warped or folded, are essentially block mountains with more or less level, plateau-like summits and steep, even precipitous, sides. In Cis-jordan, notably in the ancient territories of Judea, Ephraim, Upper Galilee and the headland of Carmel, the highlands are composed of hard Cenomanian limestone, whose formidable cliffs reinforce the difficulties of ascent. In Transjordan the same is true of much of Gilead, while in the drier centre and south the Nubian sandstone, exposed along the edge of the Rift valley, stands up in dizzy precipices, cleft by narrow and forbidding gorges.

The dominant alignment of the surface folds is roughly from south-west to north-east, clearly visible in the Lebanon and Anti-Lebanon mountains and those parallel folds which form the Negeb uplands of southern Cis-jordan. Extended and profound faulting often follows the same direction, especially in the Lebanon and Anti-Lebanon region. In the Palestine area, however, the dominant faulting is from north to south, with the result that the great central Rift valley has here cut right across the north-east–south-west folds. Consequently, the structural continuation of the highlands of Judea is Gilead, east of the Jordan, and not as the physical map would suggest the region of Samaria which, despite the uplifted heights of Ebal and Gerizim, is structurally a basin rather than an upfold. This difference is important, for the high plateau of Judea is protected on the west, not only by the rocky Cenomanian limestone slopes, but by the fact that the soft, easily eroded Senonian chalk interposes a sunken moat between it and the Eocene limestone hills of the Shephelah to the west. Samaria, however, has no such protection, since here the soft chalk lies inside the basin and its valleys lead to the very heart of the region.

Considerable faulting has occurred at right angles to the two main alignments already mentioned, that is, from north-west to south-east and from west to east. A prolonged down-faulted depression extends south-westward from Sidon and Tyre, cutting off abruptly the heights of Lebanon and Anti-Lebanon, along the wadi Sirhan in eastern Transjordan through al-Azraq to al-Jauf in Arabia. Parallel to it is the lowland corridor from Ptolemais to Scythopolis and the much smaller, but important, wadi Faria connecting Samaria with the central rift and dominated at its lower end by the Maccabean, and later Herodian, fortress of Alexandrium. Other north-west–south-east faulting has formed the steep scarps which interrupt the plateau of Moreh south-west of the lake of Galilee, and in Transjordan characterizes the plateau edge south of the Arnon gorge.

At right angles to the north–south faulting are the west–east depressions. In the north the long Homs–Palmyra corridor extends to Dura-Europos and the Euphrates, which alters its course eastward upon entering it. Throughout its length this corridor was a trade route of major importance, especially after the eclipse of Nabatean power by Trajan in 106 C.E. In the west, where the corridor divides the high Lebanon from the Nuseiriyeh mountains to the north, it is somewhat obscured by the basalt outflows between Emesa (modern Homs) and the coast. Here is the river Eleutheros (Nahr al-Kabir), which was of such importance in the struggles between the Seleucids and Ptolemies, each seeking to gain complete control of the coast.

South of the Lebanon mountains is the complicated Galilee–Hauran (Batanea) depression, which includes both the present Haifa bay and the lake of Galilee. The northern limit in Cis-jordan is the sharp ash-Shaghur fault dividing Upper from Lower Galilee, where other minor west–east faults have created the basins which so facilitated the movement of trade towards Ptolemais. Further north another important west–east fault, cutting across the central rift at Dan, separates the low-lying Jordan valley from the upland central valley of Lebanon, which is moreover, aligned from south-west to north-east, the line of the Jordan fault running out apparently at the headland of Ras Beirut. The complexity of the Galilee–Hauran region is increased by its intersection with the north-west–south-east Sidon–wadi Sirhan depression and by widespread outflows of volcanic basalt which have erupted through the fissures. Most striking of all is the high mountain country of Jabal Druze, which extends north-westward into the tormented landscape of Trachonitis and south-westward into the rugged volcanic highlands which lie all along the eastern side of the wadi Sirhan. This formidable barrier of brutal rock so seriously impeded movement that all caravans were diverted into the wadi Sirhan, which became a vital routeway for the Nabateans. Also volcanic are the *tulul*, those extinct cones which enhance the strategic effectiveness of Gaulanitis (modern Golan heights), the plateau of Moreh, and the filling of the Jordan valley to create lake Semechonitis (lake Huleh) and the marshy wastes to the north of it.

The third major west–east depression is that of Beersheba, extending across the rift into the Zered valley of Transjordan, and dividing the high plateau of Judea from the much lower Negeb uplands to the south.

A fourth depression, of much less magnitude, is the saddle of

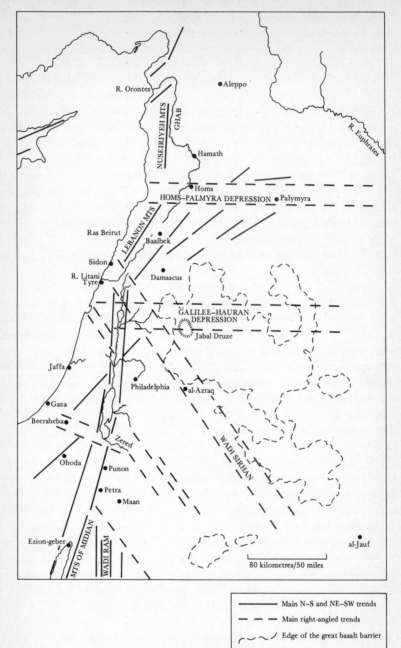

Fig. 2. The structural pattern.

Benjamin, which in the days of the Israelite monarchy separated Judah from Ephraim. Here two hinge faults curve back into the highlands from either side. On the west is the vitally important valley of Aijalon (the ascent of Beth-horon), which throughout history has provided an easy approach to Mizpah and Jerusalem and was always the Achilles heel of the Judean defences. On the east is the impressive fault scarp of Quruntul, dominating the oasis of Jericho and crowned by the fortress of Docus. From here the two routes led up into the hill country, on by the Ascent of Blood to Jerusalem and the other along the foot of the scarp to Michmash.

The peculiar significance of these transverse depressions is not merely that they facilitate movement from west to east, which they certainly do, but that they leave on either side less easily penetrable regions which tend to develop ways of life of their own, characterized by a marked separatism and disinclination to co-operate politically with the neighbouring regions. Consequently they often serve as administrative divisions.

In the days of the Israelite monarchy the long Homs–Palmyra corridor was the limit of David's, and later Jeroboam II's, empire, and in the period with which we are concerned it constituted the northern boundary of the territories of Phoenicia and Coele-Syria, as it is today the boundary of Lebanon. The cultural separation between the north and the south is still very apparent, between the Alouites on the northern side and the Maronites on the southern, between the Hamath steppe, with its characteristic beehive villages, and the arid district of Damascus.

The cultural distinction between Syria and Palestine can be traced far back into prehistory and has persisted throughout the subsequent millennia, but the complexity of the dividing region, where two zones of weakness cross and interfere with each other, makes any clear-cut division impossible. However, the southern limit of the Roman province of Syria lay in its central section close to the present north Israeli frontier and it is exactly in this region of easy west–east movement that the kingdoms of Herod the Great and Herod Agrippa extended farthest across the Jordan to include even Trachonitis.

The Beersheba depression also retained its importance as both a cultural and an administrative boundary, because it marks the end of the cultivated hill country to the north and the beginning of the arid Negeb in the south. Here was the northern limit of the Nabatean kingdom and the southern boundary of Idumea and here also at a later date were the *limes Palestinae*.

The four north–south zones, therefore, are far from simple and their roles in history are often unexpected. It is doubtful, for instance, whether it is altogether correct to speak of a 'coastal plain', for to the north the mountains rise almost straight out of the sea and in the south a barrier of sand dunes and low limestone (*kurkar*) ridges separates the plain from the coast itself, which forms a region apart. The political division between north and south was marked persistently, not by the impressive headland of mount Carmel, but by the Crocodile river eight miles to the south of it. Here the land of Phoenicia came to an end, for the sodden Crocodile marshes were a greater obstacle to traffic than the cliffs of Carmel, and they marked, moreover, the southern limit of the 'Phoenician' type of narrow, rocky coast with frequent harbours, represented in Israelite terminology by the name Asher, which was a descriptive, regional word long before it took on a tribal connotation. South of the Crocodile river the plain suddenly opened out, although until the Yarkon had been crossed the forests and marshes of Sharon still presented a formidable obstacle. Only in the short stretch between Jaffa and Gaza, the ancient Philistia, was communication with the interior plain at all easy, though even here it was strictly limited by the extensive sand-dunes. After Gaza the desert began.

The sharp distinction between the actual shoreline and the land behind it explains the great importance of such cities as Ptolemais, Tyre, Sidon and Tripolis, for here the west–east depressions opened up the possibility of communciation with the distant interior. Yet none of these routes could be described as actually easy. Travellers along all of them had to cope with the recurrent problem of marshland where the short coastal rivers were blocked on their passage to the sea, and with the complications of terrain caused by cross-faulting and volcanic outflows. The coastal cities consequently developed a life of their own and often maintained considerable independence, or at least semi-independence, in which they were assisted, of course, by the fact that their location on the seaboard enabled them to withstand prolonged sieges from the land.

During the lengthy struggle between the Seleucids and the Ptolemies after the death of Alexander the shoreline became for the first time in history a major strategic land route all the way from Cilicia to Egypt. Sections of it had always been important, as the inscriptions at the Dog river north of Berytus (Beirut) bear witness,[1] but there is no precedent for the continual movement of armies to and fro along its entire length.

[1] J. B. Pritchard, *ANET* (2nd edn. 1955) 2, n. 255, gives an example of one of these famous inscriptions.

Previously the road north and south along the Levant bridge had lain for the most part inland, since the coast north of Joppa was impeded by so many obstacles. Now, however, the strategic situation was altered. First, the capital of the empire controlling the northern end of the bridge was close to the sea at Antioch instead of far inland. Second, the Ptolemies were determined to re-establish the control that in the distant past Egypt had maintained over the Phoenician coast, to ensure a regular supply of timber from the Lebanon mountains, but the Seleucids were equally determined to prevent them. Consequently, control of the coastal cities became of prime importance. Third, Alexander had introduced into warfare the strategy of an army and a navy working in close co-operation and thereafter both Seleucids and Ptolemies used this technique, with which each had remarkable success. Indeed, one of the striking features of the history of this period is the speed with which the Egyptians were able to penetrate as far north as mount Casius on the borders of Cilicia, and the Seleucids as far south as that other minuscule mount Casius close to the delta of the Nile.

The arrival of Pompey in Syria in 63 B.C.E. completely altered the pattern of external relationships, and henceforward the Levant's historic role as a bridge between the desert and the sea, linking the Nile valley with the Mesopotamian and Anatolian powers, gave place to a new role, that of a beach-head for the West in its struggle with the East. It was to continue to play this role, though often with considerable reluctance, until the Muslim conquests once more shifted the kaleidoscope and brought about a completely new pattern of relationships.

The western highlands are divided by the west–east depressions into five sections: the Nuseiriyeh mountains, the high Lebanon, the central shattered section, the Palestinian highlands, and the Negeb uplands. The Nuseiriyeh mountains form a long tilted block, aligned from north to south. The more gradual western slopes are deeply seamed by narrow gorges and were in the past thickly forested, but on the east a steep scarp descends suddenly to the Orontes valley. It is a remote and isolated region, very difficult of access, which in the time of the Crusaders sheltered the notorious Assassins.

South of the river Eleutheros rise the massive mountains of Lebanon, with a remarkably level, uninterrupted crest 8,000 feet or more above sea-level. Terminated on the east by a towering fault scarp, the mountains are sharply folded downwards on the west, where the heavy rains have carved tremendous gorges. The rocky Cenomanian limestone is exposed in the lower sections, but above this is the sandstone, crowned again by the older Jurassic limestone which forms the grey and denuded summits. At the junction of the upper limestone with the

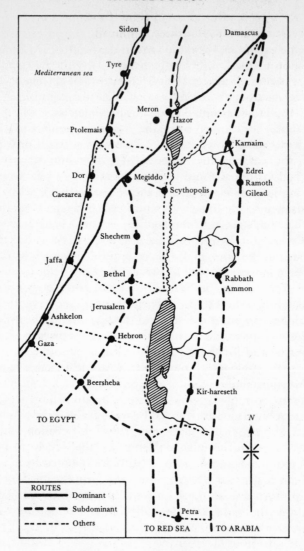

Fig. 3. The routes of Palestine.

sandstone is a series of prolific springs, about 4,000 feet above sea-level, many of them sacred in antiquity and today supplying abundant water for an important line of town and villages. This whole section of the Levant, it should be noticed, is a vast, uplifted block, and even the central valley between the Lebanon and Anti-Lebanon is at its central point 3,000 feet above sea-level.

This block is brought to an end by the cleavage of the Sidon–wadi Sirhan depression and the western highlands are interrupted by a shattered zone extending from the sudden descent of the Lebanon just south of Sidon to the borders of Samaria. Only the massif of Upper Galilee rises above 3,000 feet (Har Meron, or Jabal Jarmaq, is 3,963 feet), for both the region behind Tyre to the north of it and the hills of Lower Galilee to the south are everywhere much lower. In the north a west–east fault has enabled a coastal stream to cut back and capture the river Litani, which flows to the sea through a curiously straight and narrow gorge. In the south this central section comes to an end with the low-lying corridor, never more than 300 feet above the sea, which connects Ptolemais with the Jordan valley at Scythopolis. The north-western entrance to Haifa bay is almost closed by the near approach of the Lower Galilee hills to the fault scarp of Carmel, hindering the flow of the Kishon; and the central part of the corridor tends to be very marshy in winter. It is crossed, however, by a low causeway of hard basalt from Tabor to Megiddo, no less a cause of the strategic importance of Megiddo than the narrow exposure of soft Senonian chalk which made possible the famous pass of Megiddo across the Carmel ridge. In the south-east the valley of Jezreel, only three miles wide, leads down to the central rift.

The highlands of Palestine must be divided into four parts. First comes the basin of Samaria, with open chalk valleys enclosed within a rim of Cenomanian limestone. At its centre the younger Eocene rocks, here a hard resistant limestone, have been preserved and also elevated to form the twin heights of Ebal and Gerizim which enclosed in the gap between them the city of Neapolis (Nablus). South of this basin is the broad Cenomanian dome of Ephraim, slightly over 3,000 feet at its highest, and south of this again the saddle of Benjamin.

Still further south the plateau once more rises to the windswept plateau of Judea, some 40 miles long by 20 miles wide, of which the eastern half is the wild and desolate wilderness of Jeshimon. A considerable area of land round Hebron is over 3,000 feet and Hebron indeed is the true centre of the region. Somewhat to the north and west of it is Beth-zur (Khirbet at-Tubeiqeh), which played so significant a part in the Maccabean revolt. An important road ran northward along the water-parting between the eastward and westward streams, but the towns all lay to one side where the beginnings of the steep-sided valleys gave them necessary protection.

The Negeb uplands south of Beersheba consist of a series of relatively low ridges, hardly more than 2,000 feet in height, and rising to over 3,000 again only on the border of Sinai. They are cleft in the middle by the broad sickle-shaped Biq'at Zin, which was followed by the important highway known in Arabic as Darb as-Sultan and controlled in the classical period by the city of Oboda on the uplands. The western slopes are gentle and receive in winter a little rainfall, though it is erratic and unpredictable. This was the region of the cities, first founded by the Nabateans and surviving, though not continuously, until the Arab conquests. Their existence in this arid region was made possible only by the most careful use of the available water and the great economic stimulus of the trans-Arabian trade. The dry eastern slopes to the Arabah are rocky and desolate.

The central rift valleys, though very obvious on the physical map and enclosed for so much of their length between towering mountain or plateau walls, provide neither the easy north–south communication nor the obstacles to west–east movement that one might at first expect. Of course, roads from north to south did exist, but they were not continuous. In the far north the Ghab, lying at the eastern foot of the Nuseiriyeh mountains and occupied by the central Orontes, was so ill-drained and marshy that no road ran along it at all. Further south the valley was filled with basalt and the Orontes was here deflected eastward on to the plateau near Emesa (Homs).

Between the Lebanon and Anti-Lebanon the central valley, or Baqa'a, is not a true rift valley, for only on the west is it limited by a fault scarp. On the east rise the steep, uptilted slopes of the Anti-Lebanon, the lower ridges of which disrupt the valley floor, especially in the south, where they are crowded close against the Lebanon scarp. Movement, therefore, was far from easy and though the Baqa'a did provide a route between the high mountains for the armies which sought to bypass Damascus, the great caravans normally kept to the much drier but more level plateau east of the Anti-Lebanon.

Between the lake of Galilee and the Dead sea the rift valley was open and on both sides a road followed the springline at the foot of the scarp; but in the north passage was interrupted both by the basalt dam, which fills the valley south of lake Huleh, and by the impassable Huleh marshes which forced the road to cling closely to the lower slopes of Galilee.

The precipices along the side of the Dead sea seriously impeded movement and in the east forbade it altogether, though on the west a road came down from Hebron to the strong springs at Engedi and then followed the shoreline southward to the Arabah. Here the double road began again and took on great importance, for here at the foot of the scarps there was water in the desert and to the east were the copper mines in the Nubian sandstone.

The steep scarps which bordered the central rift were, of course, an obstacle, but the political frontiers frequently ran across the rift instead of along it. Thus the Baqaʻa, despite the mighty barrier of the Lebanon mountains, was included administratively with the Phoenician coast, as it still is today, and the dividing line was the Anti-Lebanon. In the Galilee–Hauran region the kingdom of Herod the Great extended far across the valley to Trachonitis, and the Decapolis on the eastern plateau included also Scythopolis, west of the Jordan. Again, south of the Dead sea the Nabatean kingdom was firmly established across the Arabah to include the whole Negeb within its domain.

Nor is the eastern plateau a unity. In the north it is of only moderate height and divided from the arid steppe around Damascus not only by the Homs–Palmyra corridor but also by the long limestone ridges which splay out north-eastward from the Anti-Lebanon like the spokes of a fan. Damascus in fact owes its importance not only to its magnificent water supply from the river Barada in an otherwise semi-desert region, but also to the fact that all routes are directed towards it, from the north by these converging ridges, and from the south by the long barrier of basalt which in Trachonitis closes in upon the Anti-Lebanon.

Between Trachonitis and the edge of the Jordan valley the plateau of Batanea is a broad and fertile tableland, though diversified by the lines of volcanic cones which cross it in a south-eastward direction. Movement here is almost everywhere extremely easy.

The level surface extends for some miles south of the Yarmuq gorge, but then the land rises steeply to the dome of Gilead, which is cut in two by the broad valley of the Jabbok (Zerqa). This rises at Philadelphia (Amman) and flows first north-eastward before swinging round in a great curve to cut its way westward and join the Jordan close to the entrance of the wadi Faria from the other side. The whole of Gilead formed part of the Decapolis, of which Philadelphia was the most southerly city. This dome is the structural continuation of the highland of Judea and continues south-westward towards the Dead sea in a triangle of dissected westward-facing slopes known in the Israelite monarchy as the Abarim. After the Exile it became the territory of the Tobiads, with their centre at Iraq al-Amir, and with the coming of the Romans the administrative district of Perea.

Behind Perea was the smooth and level tableland, once known as the Mishor, which had been the territory of Moab, whose chief city was south of the canyon of the Arnon at Kir-hareseth (Kerak) later known as Charachmoba. The rainfall is less here than it is to the north and this is mainly excellent sheep-rearing country. It is divided from the wadi Sirhan by a wide stretch of barren flint-strewn desert known as Ardh as-Suwan.

South of the gorge of the Zered which cuts down to the south-eastern corner of the Dead sea, the plateau edge, which has been climbing steadily along the side of the Dead sea, has been forced up even higher and for 75 miles it is well over 5,000 feet in height. This ridge, which slopes off steeply to the eastern desert and on the west drops in terrifying precipices to the Arabah, is divided into two parts by the Punon embayment, where a number of faults have cut back into the plateau. At their foot were the valuable copper mines of Punon (Feinan). Petra lay to the south of this embayment.

Well to the south of Petra the plateau edge is again shattered by faulting and the true plateau edge in fact now swings back south-eastward, the edge of the Arabah being continued southward by the uplifted granite block of the mountains of Midian. Behind this, and south of the plateau, is an extraordinary archipelago of rock, where towering sandstone islands stand up out of a sea of sand. Between them are deep, extended corridors, of which the most famous is the wadi Ram, and through these the Arabian caravans came to Petra.

The north–south road system along the Levant bridge was controlled by Damascus, where the routes from Aleppo and Palmyra converged. From Damascus they opened out again across the level plateau of Batanea. The main route to Egypt divided, one branch crossing the Jordan just south of lake Huleh, and then turning southward. It left the lake of Galilee at Magdala and followed the valley up to Arbela on the plateau of Moreh, and thence went round Tabor to Megiddo. The other branch made use of the Yarkon valley and crossing the Jordan south of the lake of Galilee, went to Scythopolis and up the valley of Jezreel to Megiddo, or turned aside at Ginae (Jenin) for Samaria. From Megiddo the road hugged the edge of the hills, avoiding the Sharon marshes, as far as the source of the Yarkon at Antipatris, and then made its way toward the coast and Gaza by way of Gazara (ancient Gezer), and from Gaza along the edge of the sea to Egypt.

From Damascus also, as we have seen, an important route followed the edge of the basalt into the wadi Sirhan and then along it south-eastward to al-Jauf. Two other routes went more directly southward to the Red sea, the ancient 'king's highway' from one stronghold to another along the edge of the plateau, despite the obstacles created by the deep river canyons; and the other along the line of the present Hejaz railway, that is to say keeping to the level land behind the valleys and on the very edge of the desert. They came together near Ras an-Naqb south of Maan. After 106 C.E. the Romans developed and used both these roads.

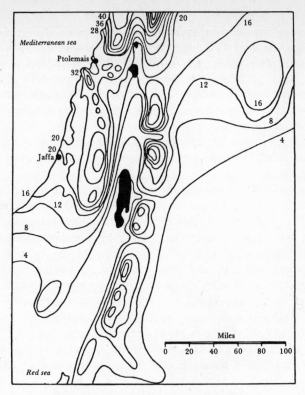

Fig. 4. Average annual rainfall (in inches).

THE CLIMATE OF THE LEVANT

The nature of the Palestinian climate also helped to compartmentalize the country, which lies close to the southern limit of the Mediterranean climate belt. The whole Levant is characterized by hot, dry summers and mild, wet winters, and also by the alignment of the main highlands across the path of the winter cyclones, which move in from the west. Consequently there is everywhere a marked difference between the wetter westward slopes and the much drier lee slopes to the east. The central valley throughout its length is in a marked rain shadow. Another consistent feature of the Levant climate is the tendency of the rainfall to decrease, more or less steadily, from north to south.

Within this general climate similarity, however, we must notice considerable regional differences. In two areas the winter rain sweeps very much further inland than it does elsewhere. One is in the north

of Syria, where the rainfall is in any case greater and where there is only
one mountain barrier, the Nuseiriyeh mountains. The low plateau to
the east forms, therefore, the relatively well-watered Hamath steppe,
extending all the way to the Euphrates. The other area is the broad
Galilee–Bashan depression. The low hill-country south of the ash-
Shaghur fault, never as much as 2,000 feet in height, and cut by
down-faulted west–east basins, offers little hindrance to the eastward
movement of the cyclones which carry their rain far into the interior
of the Batanea plateau; and in the east the rise of the land towards the
heights of Jabal Druze more than counteracts the increasing distance
from the sea.

Between these two regions, however, the tremendous elevation of
the Lebanon and Anti-Lebanon interposes a double climate obstacle and
most of the cyclonic rainfall is deposited on the western slopes of the
Lebanon to nourish the forests of cedar, cypress and pine for which they
were famous in ancient times. The rainfall of the central valley is
decidedly less, and is anomalous in that it decreases markedly from 35
inches annually at Marj-ayoun in the south to less than 8 inches in the
north-east, where the rain-shadow effect is greatest, since the rain-
bearing winds sweep in from the south-west. Baalbek, although more
than 3,000 feet above sea level, has only 16 inches.

The full force of the cyclonic storms having been spent on the
Lebanon mountains whose higher regions have almost everywhere
more than 48 inches annually, much of it as heavy snow, the Anti-
Lebanon are, for all their great height, surprisingly dry. Even the ridge
receives less than 28 inches a year and only mount Hermon in the
south, which by reason of the Sidon–wadi Sirhan depression is exposed
to the influence of the sea, has over 40 inches. The lee slopes of
the Anti-Lebanon are consequently dry and the arid steppe laps the
foothills, Damascus having on average no more than 8 inches of rain
a year.

Within the Palestinian area the climate becomes more and more
marginal, and the unreliability of the rainfall increases with the
continuing decrease of the average annual total towards the south as
well as eastwards away from the sea. Two very striking features are the
long gulf of drought thrusting up the Rift valley from the south and
bringing desert conditions as far as the narrow 'Jordan waist', and the
parallel peninsula of moisture extending southward along the plateau
edge of Transjordan to beyond Petra. Here in the south the low Negeb
uplands offer little obstacle to the passage of the erratic cyclones, which
are forced to drop their rain upon the huge Edomite wall more than
5,000 feet above sea-level. This southward extension of the winter rains

along the exalted edge of the eastern plateau made possible a narrow line of settlement, well protected from attack by its precipices, and having at its feet the rich copper mines of Punon (Feinan) in the Nubian sandstone. The narrowness of the cultivable area, with only a single line of towns and villages, forced those who settled here, as it were, to export men, sending them out to seek their living elsewhere. From this necessity grew the powerful trading kingdom of the Nabateans who, it should be noticed, were normally careful not to seek to extend their authority into the territory of the 'Sown', where they would come into contact with the concentrations of settled populations, but contented themselves instead with developing their hegemony along the broad trackways, sometimes as much as 100 yards wide, which their caravans followed through the desert wastes and arid steppes. At one time, it is true, they did bring the Mishor, the tableland south of Gilead, under their control but later their boundary was the deep Arnon gorge. The only major exception was their penetration northwards from al-Azraq in the wadi Sirhan to bring the vitally important caravan city of Damascus under their authority; but Damascus, as we have seen, was itself a piedmont oasis on the very edge of the desert. Palmyra, which had taken over Petra's role as mistress of the great caravan routes, was much closer to the settled agricultural world, with its many villages and cities, and was forced to be less discreet. Her imperial pretensions in the mid-third century C.E. were short-lived. Any expansion along the trade routes brought her quickly from the desert into the Sown, which a desert oasis, however wealthy, was ill equipped to control; and though for a time her empire included all the Levant, Mesopotamia, Egypt and much of Anatolia, its splendour endured for no more than a generation.

The marginal character of the rainfall means that great importance attaches to aspect and orientation, the western and northern slopes of even the tiniest hill being always greener than the eastern and southern slopes. This is an absolute rule. Increased effort, as it were, such as strong convectional currents on the hot plains or forced ascent of the air up the mountain slopes, is needed to precipitate the desperately longed-for rainfall. Even a moderate rise may achieve this, but once the summit is reached the descent of the air on the further side suddenly and inexorably reduces the rain, sometimes almost to zero. It follows that the difference between the western and eastern slopes of the Palestine highlands is exceedingly pronounced and the crest marks an immediate change from agriculture to pastoralism, villages extending only a very short way over the edge. In Judea the transition is most dramatic, for here the eastern slopes, where the air plunges down into the deepest part of the Rift, are composed of the soft and thirsty Senonian chalk

which absorbs immediately such little rain as there is. Beneath the
Senonian chalk is the hard Cenomanian limestone which, once exposed,
forms steep and terrifying gorges. This is the wilderness of Judea, the
Jeshimon of the Old Testament, less than ten miles wide as the crow
flies, but so desolate that even at the present day the unwary may easily
be lost there and die of thirst. To go westward from the gates of
Jerusalem, Bethlehem or Hebron was to pass through the vineyards and
orchards of Judah, even so only a narrow zone, for they were limited
by the steep cliffs of the western slopes; but to go out of the eastern
gate was to step almost straight into the desert.

MINOR REGIONS OF PALESTINE

The effect of all that has been written so far about structure and climate
is to divide Palestine into a large number of tiny regions, of the kind
known to geographers as *pays*, after the name given to such regions in
France by Vidal de la Blache. All the Israelite tribal regions were *pays*
of this kind, distinguished from each other by the nature of the farming
methods made possible by the soil and climate, and therefore marked
by differing agricultural rhythms. Although the tribal organization
disappeared after the Exile, these regional distinctions did not
disappear, though of course they were considerably modified by new
methods of agriculture, introduced particularly during the Roman
period, and by the opening up of the country by Roman roads, such
as the five roads which were built to cross the previously largely-
deserted Sharon in order to supply the new and artificial port of
Caesarea. Nevertheless, the underlying rock does not alter and,
whatever fluctuations in the climate there may have been in the course
of more than a thousand years, the general pattern remained.[1] Palestine
did not then, nor has it ever, become a culturally unified and
harmonious country.

[1] That climate does continually fluctuate and that these fluctuations can have disastrous
effects especially in marginal regions is now absolutely beyond question. The shifting
of the general wind and pressure patterns in the upper atmosphere since 1960,
bringing less rain to western Europe but more rain to the Mediterranean region, has
caused a tragic decrease in rainfall on the southern edge of the Sahara, with appalling
consequences for the people who live there. We do not, unfortunately, have the
evidence to allow us to determine the nature of the climatic fluctuations in Palestine
between 539 B.C.E. and 636 C.E. All that can be said, but it must be said emphatically,
is that climatic fluctuations must have occurred during this long period, and that we
can no longer rule out the possibility that such fluctuations influenced changes in
patterns of settlement, even if they may not have been the major cause. For fuller
discussion of this question see D. Baly, *The Geography of the Bible*, 2 (New York, 1974),
ch. 9.

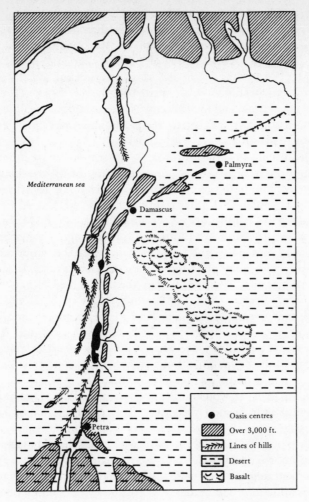

Fig. 5. Regions of difficulty.

An important distinction must be made in Palestine between regions of settlement and regions of difficulty, where villages were few or non-existent and where the land was still untamed. Most of this untamed land constituted what in biblical terminology was described as *midbar* or *ya'ar*, normally translated as 'desert' and 'forest', though these two terms are misleading. *Midbar* was any kind of rough country beyond the village fields where the natural vegetation was mainly confined to winter grasses and flowers and included anything from quite respectable steppe-land to almost complete desert. *Ya'ar* merged into this, but indicated that type of landscape where the vegetation was of a kind to impede easy movement. It could range, therefore, from arid scrub through *maquis* and open woodland to the magnificent forests of Lebanon. The common feature of both *midbar* and *ya'ar* was their roughness. The bushes of the *maquis* and scrubland which formed so much of the Palestinian *ya'ar* were tough and thorny, exceedingly difficult to penetrate, and the *midbar* was increasingly arid, almost always littered with boulders, and often precipitous and rocky. An even greater obstacle was marshland, so great indeed that biblical Hebrew has no clear word for it, an indication that it lay entirely apart, unused even by the herdsmen with their sheep and goats. Such marshlands were naturally few, but there was an extensive stretch filling the Jordan valley north of lake Huleh and other semi-permanent marshes in the Sharon plain and, especially in winter, at certain points along the Mediterranean streams where rocks or sand impeded the drainage. Permanent marsh prohibited all movement and settlement and even the temporary winter marshes of the Kishon valley and other river valleys turned the traveller aside and drove all settlement up on to the higher land. When the winter marshes of Esdraelon and the basins of Lower Galilee dried out, however, they provided excellent land for grain and consequently do not belong to the true 'regions of difficulty'. The combined marshes and *ya'ar* of the very ill-drained Sharon plain must certainly be included because, until the development of Caesarea necessitated the building of roads across it, Sharon was largely uninhabited.

Increasing urbanization and the growth in the Palestinian population in the centuries following the return from the Exile naturally pushed back the edges of both *ya'ar* and *midbar* and brought more and more land under the plough. This process was hastened by the new technological skills and improved husbandry of the Roman period and the demands of imperial strategy, which called for an efficient network of roads and the establishment of new settlements for the better control of an always troublesome country.

That it was always troublesome was in no small measure due to the fact that regions of difficulty continued obstinately to exist even in the heart of the country. The difficulties were a product of the underlying rock or of climatic factors, or sometimes of a combination of both. Except in Batanea, where the layers of basalt are thin and break down fairly easily into a rich and fertile soil, volcanic regions with their hard and brutal rock were always to be avoided if possible and especially in the savage volcanic deserts east of the wadi Sirhan. Even the much less formidable plateau of Moreh south-west of the lake of Galilee and the basalt dam to the north of it must be counted among the difficult regions. The Cenomanian limestone is another hard and problematic rock, but it breaks down into the valuable *terra rossa*, and so on the more level plateaux the forests and *maquis* were gradually cleared and olives and vines took their place. Nevertheless the higher, more thickly-forested, regions and the steep hillsides remained a nearly permanent obstacle in Judea, Ephraim, Carmel, Gilead and Upper Galilee. It should be noticed how often in such regions the roads are forced to shun the stream beds, which are confined in narrow gorges. Also avoided by the farmer was the much softer, often chalky, Eocene limestone of the Shephelah between Judea and the Philistine plain, the central (Umm al-Fahm) section of the Carmel range, and the south-western part of Lower Galilee, the Allonim hills of modern Israel. These are all only moderately high hill country without precipitous slopes, but the surface tends to be formed of a hard cap of limestone accretions known as *nari* which inhibits agriculture, and here the tangled, uncleared scrub was left to the nomadic shepherd.

The soft Senonian chalk which lies between these two major limestone layers is not particularly fertile, but the absence of boulders makes it easy to dig and to plough and, wherever exposed, it is at once eroded into those smooth valleys which provide so many of the routeways of Cis-jordan. It is therefore normally settled. Only in Jeshimon, where the desert imposes itself on the too-porous chalk, does it form a region of difficulty, but here it is very difficult indeed.

The whole vast region with an average annual rainfall of less than eight inches, that is to say all the south and east as well as the great gulf of drought extending up the Jordan valley as far as Adam (Damiyeh), is altogether part of the 'great and terrible *midbar*', and therefore without permanent settlement save only in the small oases.

The historical significance of these regions of difficulty, even though those within the settled farmlands of Cis-jordan were very small indeed, is that they were permanent regions of dissidence, always of refuge and often of revolt. No part of Palestine lacked, as it were, a back door into the *midbar* or the *ya'ar*, and in times of trouble the dissatisfied and oppressed had always somewhere close by to which they could flee. A very regular pattern of such movement was eastward into the wastes of Jeshimon on the very borders of Judea, down into the Jordan valley, where the badlands and the jungle of Jordan provided added protection, and even further afield to Gilead and the distant eastern pleateau. The rugged Trachonitis (al-Leja or 'the Refuge' in Arabic) was very evidently such a region and so also was the Jabal Druze, the mountain of Bashan. The Negeb in the south was another place of refuge for the fugitives, but so also were the very much smaller regions of difficulty in the midst of Palestine proper. Indeed, without such rude sanctuaries it is doubtful whether Palestinian Jewry could have survived either the determination of Antiochus Epiphanes to suppress it or the prolonged time of tragedy which followed 70 C.E. The Maccabean revolt would probably have been crushed at the start if there had not been conveniently at hand the forested Cenomanian highlands above Gophna (Jifna) to provide an immediate place of escape, and the stern hillsides of Judea to offer such advantages to the guerilla fighters and so many obstacles to the chariots and elephants of the regular army. A very important feature of the limestone was the existence of caves which gave the refugees living quarters hidden both from the enemy scouts and from the ferocity of the weather. In the Cenomanian regions the deep caverns are natural, but in the Eocene regions they have been carved out of the softer chalk which underlies the hard *nari* capping, as in the great necropolis at Beth-shearim in the Allonim hills.

These caves were a hide-out for the discontented at all times and only a strong central government could ensure that the roads of the country were free from brigandage. Certain routes, indeed, became notorious for their danger, such as the roads from Jerusalem to Jericho and from Bethel to Shechem across the high limestone country of Ephraim. Another dangerous passage was the road leading up from Magdala on the lake of Galilee to Arbela. Herod the Great was not the only ruler who was compelled to send an army there to suppress the robbers.

Though Galilee and Jeshimon are famous in Jewish history for fanatical resistance against the ruthless might of the Romans, it must not be thought that all flight to the *midbar* or *ya'ar* was for purposes of armed defiance. Many came to them seeking peace and security and the possibility of living what they understood to be the true way of life free from all molestation. Prominent among such people was the Qumran community, at variance with the religious authorities in Jerusalem. At a later date the regions of refuge in *ya'ar* of Galilee played an important part in the survival and development of the Jewish community after the double blow of the destruction of Jerusalem in 70 C.E. and the crushing of Bar Kochba's revolt 65 years later. After 70 C.E. many from Jerusalem and Judea fled, as refugees so often do, to the cities, where there is hope of earning some kind of a living, and by the end of the century there were important Jewish communities in such places as Caesarea, Ptolemais and Scythopolis. After 135 C.E., however, we find the Sanhedrin moving to Usha, Shepharam and Beth-shearim, all in the Allonim hills, where it remained until improved conditions made possible the move to the cities, first to Sepphoris and then Tiberias. The extension of agriculture in Upper Galilee must certainly be dated to the same period, since Josephus seems to use the name 'Galilee' to mean only what we today would call Lower Galilee, together with the more approachable but smaller eastern section of Upper Galilee where the road to Tyre led up from the lake past Gischala and Safad. The rest of Upper Galilee apparently lay outside his purview. Then, however, it provided a secure refuge, where for many life could begin again, though slowly, for the great Galilean synagogues belong apparently to the fourth century c.e.[1]

A final feature of the historical geography of the Palestine area in the millennium following the conquests of Alexander is the unparalleled development of Transjordan, the result of the new pattern of relationships between East and West. It started with the establishment of the Greek colonies of the Decapolis, which were to contribute so much to the Hellenization of the region and to provide an important centre of opposition to the Maccabean revolt; and with the growth of the wealthy trading empire of the Nabateans. With the conquest of Petra and the creation of the province of Arabia in 106 c.e. the centre of gravity was firmly established at Bostra, previously a caravan post of only moderate importance, but now destined to rival Damascus. From this centre, with its efficient system of strongly constructed and carefully maintained roads, it proved possible not only to control, but even to 'civilize', the normally rebellious and separatist basalt regions of the Jabal Druze and Trachonitis, for example Philippopolis and Canatha, as evidenced by the ruined Roman and Byzantine cities, in whose buildings stone replaced wood for almost every purpose. The brief episode of Palmyrene expansion provoked even further emphasis on Roman authority, which reached its greatest heights under Diocletian at the end of the third century. This extraordinary development of power in a region that had never known such greatness before, and was never to know it again, resulted in part from the fertility of Batanea, which became one of the granaries of the Roman empire; in part also from the legendary value and importance of the caravan trade with the East; and from the fact that the Syrian desert was the ill-defined dividing line between the empires of Rome and Parthia (later the Sasanids). All this stimulated Rome to bend every effort to establish, not only a beach-head on the Levant coast, but also a great military stronghold on the threshold of the desert. It was indeed a remarkable achievement, for though the wealth of the Transjordan cities was to decline after Diocletian, the Christian history of the region is evidence of its continued significance.

[1] E. M. Meyers, T. Kraabel and J. F. Strange, 'Archaeology and the Rabbinic Tradition at Khirbet Shemaʿ: 1970 and 1971 Campaigns', *BA*, 35 (1972), 2–31.

Bostra was still important in the days of Muhammed and the small town that survives there is known to this day among the Arabs as Bosra-eski-Sham, that is, Bosra the old Damascus.

This chapter was written in 1973. The maps were added at the suggestion of the editors in 1977.

CHAPTER 2

NUMISMATICS

Since the eighteenth century the careful, scientific study of ancient Palestinian coinage struck by both Jewish and non-Jewish authorities has been recognized as an important adjunct to the study of classical Jewish history. The careful recording of coins, the exact cataloguing of the numismatic evidence found in archeological excavations (neglected until well into this century), the systematic and detailed description of coin hoards and the methodology relevant to their study, the comparison of dies and the sequence of coins, have all shed new light on classical Jewish history. In addition, the application of related studies in epigraphy, religion, art and architecture, chronology, prosopography, metallurgy and economics have all contributed to our understanding of ancient coinage and, conversely, have increased the light that the study of numismatics can shed on these other disciplines as well as on the study of history in general.

THE PERSIAN PERIOD

Coinage was first introduced into the economic life of Palestine during the sixth and fifth centuries B.C.E. as part of the extended growth of coinage in the Mediterranean world. The two oldest coins which have so far been found in Palestine were minted in Greece in the sixth century, one from Thasos, found at Shechem, and the second from Athens, found in Jerusalem. But as isolated finds they do not allow any definite conclusions. Later on, in the fifth and mainly in the fourth centuries, Phoenician coins as well as local coins came into circulation, though Greek coins continued to be in use.

The Greek, mainly Athenian, coins attest mercantile relations with Greece, which are corroborated by the archeological finds of Greek pottery. The Phoenician coins found reflect the economic activity of Phoenician merchants in the inner parts of Palestine in that period and their control of its coastal regions. The Phoenician coins found in Palestine were minted in the first place in Sidon and also in Tyre.

During the Persian period a local Palestinian coinage also sprang up,

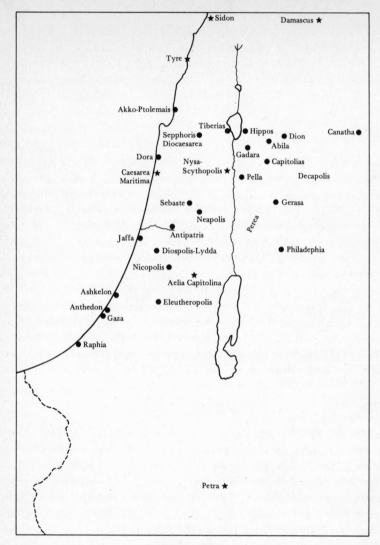

Fig. 1. Mints.

imitating in style the Attic coinage, which was the most popular coinage
of the day and well known throughout the East. Moreover, the recovery
of Greek coins and their local Palestinian imitations corroborates what
we already know from other sources of the considerable Greek
economic and cultural influence in Palestine even before the Macedonian
conquest.

Of the local coinage which has been found, most is traceable to Gaza, then the most important harbour south of mount Carmel. Gaza served as an outlet for the Arabian incense trade and was in close contact with the Arabian kings of Qedar who ruled the desert areas bordering Egypt and Palestine. This significant commercial activity encouraged, or even required, the issue of an indigenous coinage. It is probable, however, that at least some of the coins of this type, known variously as Philisto-Arabian, Egypto-Arabian, Greco-Persian or Greco-Phoenician, were minted elsewhere than in Gaza and by some other authority, for example, Persian officials.[1] However, at the time of writing there is no scholarly consensus on the matter. It is interesting to note that these coins are extremely varied in their representations of divine images, animals and mythological figures. Many coins of this group are imitations of the Athenian coins, which were the main international currency in the East under Persian rule. On other coins of the same group Phoenician, Egyptian, Cyprian and Anatolian influences are noticeable, in addition to Athenian influence.

A subdivision of the group of local coins mentioned above is the coinage of Judea. The attribution of the coins in this subdivision is validated by their legend: *Yehud* (lit. Judea, an Aramaic form of *Yehuda* in Hebrew). These coins show a variety of representations among which are the falcon, fleur-de-lis (lily, pl. I, 3), owl, and human figures both facial (pl. I, 4) and complete. The single most complete composite representation appears to be a god in a chariot. These Judean coins clearly reflect the influence of Attic coinage.

These coins were struck by the *Peḥa* (lit. governor) of Judea, as has lately been confirmed by a new reading on a group of these coins, which is *Yeḥezqia/o Ha Peḥa* (lit. Yehezqia the governor: pl. I, 4), instead of a former reading, *Yeḥezqia Yehud*. On the basis of this new reading we can fairly assume that the other coins struck with the legend *Yehud* were also struck by holders of the *Peḥa*'s office. In any case the legend *Yehud* on those coins is unusual, because as a rule only names of governors, dynasts or cities appear, if at all, on coins minted within the Persian empire. It should be noted that although many, if not all, of the governors of Judea were Jews, they did not obey the traditional biblical interdiction on images (compare Exod. 20: 4, Deut. 5: 8). Either they felt themselves, as state officials, free from its legislative force, or more

---

[1] E. Stern, *The Material Culture of the Land of the Bible in the Persian Period* (Jerusalem, 1973, in Hebrew), p. 221, proposes that the so-called Philisto-Arabian coins were struck by officials of the Persian administration. He points to similarity between the emblems on the coins and those on officials' seals known from other parts of the Persian empire.

probably the application of this interdiction to coins, as well as to gems and seals, was not yet rigidly fixed or authoritative.

Most of the coins struck with the legend *Yehud*, though minted in silver (bronze coinage not being widely known in Palestine and the East before the Hellenistic period) represent small denominations only and were probably struck primarily for local use.

With regard to the coinage of this period, it is interesting to note that besides the Greek and Phoenician coins and the local creations already discussed, almost no Persian imperial coins, nor any coins from Egypt, Cyprus or Asia Minor, are recorded as having been found in Palestine.[1]

ALEXANDER AND THE HELLENISTIC DYNASTIES

Alexander's victories between 334 and 331 B.C.E. brought Palestine under Macedonian rule by 332 B.C.E. In such circumstances Palestine shared the same monetary system as other regions with which it shared the same, that is, Hellenistic, government. Thus in the time of Alexander and the Diadochi the enormous minting of new imperial coinage – the *Alexandreis* – also made its presence felt in Palestine (pl. I, 5). The existing situation of mints in Palestine was altered. Thus Gaza, which had shown fierce resistance to Alexander, ceased minting altogether for a time. But a new mint was opened in Akko, probably begun initially

[1] See Stern, *Material Culture*, pp. 224–5 and n. 45a on p. 278.

PLATE I

1. AR; Tyrian didrachm; fourth century B.C.E.; Melqarth on winged sea-horse / owl and date: year 32.
2. AE; Gaza; second century B.C.E.; (obverse, not reproduced here: head of Zeus); two jugate cornucopias, 'Demou Gazaion'.
3. AR; Judean obol; fourth century B.C.E., enlarged; fleurs-de-lis / falcon, 'Yehud'.
4. AR; Judean obol; second half of fourth century B.C.E.; head full face / owl, 'Yehezqiya/o Ha Peha'; enlarged.
5. AR; tetradrachm; end of fourth century B.C.E.; head of Herakles / Zeus seated, 'Alexandrou' and Phoenician legend 'AK(o) year 39'.
6. AR; Ptolemaic half-obol; about 300 B.C.E.; head of Ptolemy I / eagle, 'Yehuda'; natural size and enlarged.
7. AE; dilepton of Antiochus VII; lily / anchor, 'Basileos Antiochou Euergetou', year 182 S.E. = 130 B.C.E.
8. AR; Ptolemaic tetradrachm; 247 B.C.E.; Ptolemy II. (Mint: Ioppe.)
9. AR; Tyrian shekel; *circa* 19 C.E.; head of Melqarth / eagle.
Key: AE = bronze   AR = silver

The author of this chapter wishes to thank Mr A. Kindler, Director of the Kadman Numismatic Museum, Tel Aviv, for producing these plates.

in relation to Alexander's long siege and eventual conquest of Tyre and to the interruption of its coinage (pl. I, 1) for some twenty-five years. Nevertheless, Akko continued to strike coins, even after Tyre's mint was reopened. These new coins, now in circulation in Palestine, should not however be considered local issues, though struck locally, but rather as a part of the 'imperial coinage' which was organized and supervised by the central Hellenistic authority.

After a generation of political upheavals following Alexander's death and the resulting struggle for succession, Palestine became part of the new Ptolemaic empire centred in Egypt. As a province of the Ptolemaic empire (301–200 B.C.E.) Palestine was also brought into the Ptolemaic monetary system. However, a recent find suggests that before the complete absorption of Palestine into the Ptolemaic system there was an intermediate period of transition reflecting the political uncertainty of the era. This find is composed of small silver coins similar in denomination to the *Yehud* coins of the Persian period discussed above. They bear on their obverse a portrait, in all probability that of Ptolemy I, and on their reverse an eagle standing on a *fulmen*. Their legend is *Yehuda* (pl. I, 6) (in Hebrew *Yhdh*, not Aramaic *Yhd*, as on the *Yehud* coins).[1] These coins, attributed to the first quarter of the third century B.C.E. are, then, representative of a transitional step between the former monetary pattern and the new one just coming into being. Their existence may help to shed light on the political administration of Judea in this poorly-documented period.

After this brief interlude Ptolemaic coinage became the standard coinage of Palestine. Ptolemaic bronze began to be used in large quantities, and typical of it are its large denominations, ranging all the way up to 100 grams. Likewise, Ptolemaic silver replaced other silver coins in the country and archeological finds reflect the near-monopoly of Ptolemaic coinage in third-century Palestine. The exclusion of other coinage resulted not only from natural monetary processes but also as a consequence of the monopolistic monetary policy of the Ptolemies, who strove to exclude all foreign coinage from their dominions. Among the most significant devices used to achieve this exclusive situation was the introduction of an alternative standard of value to that operative in other states, that is, the substitution of the so-called Phoenician (or Ptolemaic) standard (with a tetradrachm weighing about 14.20 grams) for the Attic standard which became the accepted currency in the Hellenistic world through Alexander's coinage (a tetradrachm of which was supposed to weigh 17.26 grams).

[1] See A. Kindler, 'Silver Coins Bearing the Name of Judea from the Early Hellenistic Period', *IEJ*, 24 (1974), 73–6; D. Jeselsohn, 'A New Coin Type with Hebrew Inscription', *IEJ*, 24 (1974), 77–8.

Many of the Ptolemaic coins found in Palestine were minted in Alexandria, though there is significant coinage from certain other mints in the Ptolemaic empire, especially those in Phoenicia or in Palestine itself. The Palestinian minting took place in Akko (now renamed Ptolemais), in Gaza (which recovered from its destruction by Alexander) and also in a new mint in Ioppe (= Jaffa) (pl. I, 8). As formerly, this coinage was imperial no matter where it was struck.

With Ptolemy V Ptolemaic rule in Palestine came to its close, and with it ended the regular use of Ptolemaic coins in Palestine. In their place, coins of the new ruling Seleucid dynasty, who finally and permanently replaced their Ptolemaic adversaries in 198 B.C.E., were introduced.

The Seleucids continued to mint in Akko-Ptolemais and to a lesser extent also in Gaza, while the Ptolemaic mint at Jaffa was discontinued. Alternatively, a new mint was opened in Ashkelon which was to become an important centre in the course of the second century, supplying much of the currency of Judea, while Akko remained a source of supply for the north of Palestine. Some numismatists also contend that in the second century there was a Seleucid mint in Jerusalem itself which struck for Antiochus VII (138–129 B.C.E.), because a certain type of his bronze coinage (pl. I, 7) has been found with great frequency in and around the city.[1]

Seleucid coinage was predominant in Palestine almost to the last quarter of the second century B.C.E., and its gradual disappearance was a corollary of the gradual decline of the political influence of the Seleucid empire. In some regions the last prominent Seleucid coins are of Demetrius II Nicator (145–139/8; 129–125 B.C.E.) and of Antiochus VII (138–129 B.C.E.), the last two Seleucids to exert real power in Palestine. However, in those few areas of the country where Seleucid influence continued to be exerted somewhat longer, we continue to find coins of later Seleucid rulers. During this period of declining Seleucid influence we also witness the emergence of autonomous coinage minted by different cities. This process, which had begun much earlier, came to full effect in the last quarter of the second century with completely autonomous coins being minted in both bronze and silver, and bearing differing dates reflecting the alternative eras of the various cities. So in Tyre autonomous coinage began in 126–125 B.C.E. and in Ashkelon a local era began in 103 B.C.E. The autonomous coinage of Akko-Ptolemais began some time between these dates, and that of Gaza ceased simultaneously with the city's destruction by Alexander Janneus.

[1] Against this opinion see U. Rappaport, 'The Emergence of Hasmonaean Coinage', *AJS Review*, 1 (1976), 171–86; *idem*, 'Ascalon and the Coinage of Judaea', *Meḥḳarim, Studies in the History of the Jewish People and the Land of Israel*, 4 (1978), 77–88.

THE HASMONEANS

The new Hasmonean state, which was advancing continuously towards independence from the troubled period of Antiochus IV (167 B.C.E.) onwards, also began to issue bronze coins of its own minting. These bronze coins replaced in direct sequence the coins of Antiochus VII who, as noted above, was the last Seleucid ruler to exert influence in Judea. From 129 B.C.E. onwards Judea became fully independent (Josephus, *Antiquitates Judaicae* XIII.273) and as a result the ready supply of Seleucid bronze came to an end. As a consequence a shortage of 'small money' began to be felt in Judea since bronze coins were usually struck for local supply only. The responsibility for remedying this situation fell to John Hyrcanus I (135/4–104 B.C.E.), the Hasmonean ruler of the day. That Hyrcanus fulfilled this obligation is attested by a series of coin finds in various excavated Judean sites, especially the one in Beth-zur.

Though meeting his obligations, Hyrcanus I probably did not welcome the opportunity to mint his own coins because he was unable either to match the quality of the coins of his contemporaries in appearance or to use his coins fully as an instrument for personal and dynastic propaganda as was the custom in the Hellenistic world. The primary obstacle in the way of this second objective was the Jewish abhorrence of any human or zoological representation, which had become current by this time. The strength of this anti-iconographic sentiment is clearly in evidence now, in all probability drawing its new momentum from the Antiochene persecutions, the resultant Maccabean revolt and the religious and cultural revival which then ensued.

This religiously-dominated outlook, which seems to have been shared by the Hasmoneans themselves, determined the appearance of Jewish coins from this period onwards. Those authorities, whether Jewish or non-Jewish, who minted coins in Judea were expected to abide by this disposition and seem usually to have done so. Taking this restriction for granted, the Hasmoneans did not see their coinage as a vehicle for propaganda or as a major advantage to their regime and were quite indifferent to its production, fulfilling the role of minters only out of necessity. Consequently, Hasmonean coinage is relatively dull in appearance and negligent in execution. Usually the coins bear Hebrew legends in the older Phoenician script, which again served to limit their communicative value, and carry neither dates nor any reference to specific historic events. For example, even the first coins of the Hasmoneans were not related to the achievement of their independence, but were struck only after it had already been well consummated. In addition, Hasmonean coinage was struck only in bronze (lead coins are exceptional and will not be discussed here), whereas it was silver coins which were generally considered to have political significance.

Unlike bronze coins, which became scarce with the departure of the Seleucids, silver coins were always present in sufficient quantity in Judea, since they were not limited in circulation to their place of origin. As a result, even though silver coins were seen to have much more political significance than bronze ones, they were never struck by the Hasmoneans, who were reluctant to produce a poor issue of silver (without portraits and with a very limited choice of symbols) and preferred instead to refrain from minting silver coins altogether. It is superfluous to look for any further political or legal reasons for the failure of the Hasmoneans to issue silver coins since no contemporary foreign power interfered with their complete sovereignty to mint in silver. Their issue of bronze coins was totally independent. They could have struck silver coins simultaneously had they wished to do so.

Hasmonean coins usually show either the obverse and reverse bearing symbols, or the reverse bearing a symbol and the obverse an inscription surrounded by a wreath. The symbols used, remembering the limitations under which they were produced, are the cornucopia, palm-branch, lily, helmet (rare), anchor, star, and pomegranate (as a secondary symbol with the cornucopia) (pl. II, 1–6). Certain other symbols on the coins of Mathathya Antigonus will be discussed separately below.

Attempts have been made to explain the meaning and significance of these symbols in political or religious terms, for example the anchor in relation to maritime policy, or the star in relation to theological meaning. Such attempts are not persuasive, however, for, although some specific significance might have been attached to this or that symbol, it must be emphasized that basically the symbols were merely an imitation and continuation of those found on the former Seleucid bronze coins which were in wide usage in Judea (compare pl. I, 7). The Hasmoneans merely imitated former coins. The supply of coins now became their responsibility, and they deviated from the older issue only in respect of the new legend, which suited the new political realities, and by the avoidance of any human representation. What little innovation did take place can be seen, for example, in the replacement of a caduceus by a pomegranate between the two horns of the cornucopia (pl. II, 3, 4), or again, in the presence of a star of very obscure origin on the coins of Alexander Janneus (pl. II, 5).

JOHN HYRCANUS I

The most complicated problem which arises in dealing with Hasmonean coins concerns their sequence. Thus, for example, while the former attribution of some Jewish coins to Simon Maccabeus has been decisively discarded, of late a new hypothesis has been brought forward which suggests that Hasmonean coinage began only with Alexander Janneus and attributes all other Hasmonean coins exclusively to Judah Aristobulus II and to John Hyrcanus II. However this thesis, too, seems unacceptable, given the present state of our knowledge, and the opposite, more generally accepted view still appears correct.[1]

Accordingly, it seems proper to argue that Hasmonean coinage began with John Hyrcanus I who, some time after the débâcle of Antiochus VII in 129 B.C.E. when a shortage of 'small money' began to be felt in Judea, struck the first Hasmonean coins. His first coins were probably

[1] For this debate see A. Ben-David, 'When did the Maccabees begin to strike their First Coins?' *PEQ*, 104 (July–December 1972), 93–103; A. Kindler, 'Hoard from the Second Half of the Second Century B.C.E.', *AHHI*, 4 (1970), 41–6 (in Hebrew); Y. Meshorer, *Jewish Coins of the Second Temple Period* (Tel Aviv, 1967) and 'The Beginning of the Hasmonean Coinage', *IEJ*, 24 (1974), 59–61; U. Rappaport, 'Pure Numismatics', *Beth Mikra*, 31 (1967), 112–18 (in Hebrew), and *AJS Review*, 1 (1976), 171–86; R. S. Hanson, 'Toward a Chronology of the Hasmonean Coins', *BASOR*, 216 (1974), 21–3; D. Barag and S. Qedar, 'The Beginning of the Hasmonean Coinage', *INJ*, 4 (1980), 8–21.

PLATE II

1. AE; trilepton; John Hyrcanus I, 135/4–104 B.C.E.; helmet / two jugate cornucopias.
2. AE; lepton; John Hyrcanus I, 135/4–104 B.C.E.; flower / palm-branch.
3. AE; dilepton; John Hyrcanus I, 135/4–104 B.C.E.; double cornucopias / legend surrounded by wreath.
4. AE; dilepton; Judah Aristobulus, 104–103 B.C.E.; double cornucopias / legend surrounded by wreath.
5. AE; dilepton; Alexander Janneus, 103–76 B.C.E.; star surrounded by diadem and Hebrew legend / anchor, 'Basileos Alexandrou'.
6. AE; lepton; Alexander Janneus, 103–76 B.C.E.; flower / palm-branch.
7. AE; *dichalkous*; Mathathya Antigonus, 40–37 B.C.E.; double cornucopias, Hebrew legend / wreath, 'Basileos Antigonou'.
8. AE; dilepton; Mathathya Antigonus, 40–37 B.C.E.; shew-bread table / seven-branched candlestick.
9. AE; *chalkous*; Herod I, 37–4 B.C.E.; *thymiaterion* / tripod, 'Herodou Basileos'.
10. AE; lepton; Herod I, 37–4 B.C.E.; eagle/cornucopia, 'Basi Hero'.
11. AE; trilepton; Herod Archelaus, 4 B.C.E.–6 C.E.; two jugate cornucopias, 'Herodou' / galley, 'Ethnarchos'.
12. AE; dilepton; Herod Archelaus, 4 B.C.E.–6 C.E.; bunch of grapes, 'Herodou' / helmet, 'Ethnarchos'.
Key: AE = bronze

the helmet-cornucopia coins which bore the legend ' *Yehohanan HaKohen HaGadol Rosh Hever HaYehudim*' (lit. John the High Priest Head of the community of the Jews) (pl. II, 1). These coins reflect a noticeable, if rudimentary, attempt to avoid the portrait habitually seen on the obverse of Hellenistic coins. Now the portrait is replaced by a spacious helmet which covers the whole field of the obverse, as is usually done by the portrait. On the reverse, the inscription and the symbol are left untouched. It should be noted that symbols are also to be found on both sides of former Seleucid coins.

This first, exceptional, coin may have been followed by the other '*Rosh Hever HaYehudim*' coins or even by the '*Rosh Hever HaYehudim*' and the '*VeHever HaYehudim*' coins, which may have run simultaneously. These coins were struck in two denominations, *peruta* (= dilepton) and half-*peruta* (= lepton, the smallest bronze coin), whereas the very first coin, the helmet-cornucopia, was a trilepton. The half-*peruta* coins followed the same pattern as that of the helmet-cornucopia, that is, the obverse has a flower (the lily) covering the whole or most of the face of the coin and the reverse a palm-branch and inscription (pl. II, 2). However, an improvement over the former coins can be seen in the superior arrangement of having the inscription along both sides of the narrow vertical palm-branch rather than letting it inconveniently encircle the cornucopia as it has done earlier.[1]

For the *perutoth* a more sophisticated and developed aniconic arrangement was arrived at. Instead of the two-symbol pattern (where one symbol was used to avoid the habitual portrait) the portrait was replaced by an inscription which was placed spaciously in the field and encircled by a wreath (pl. II, 3r.). Thus only one symbol was needed for the other side. It is interesting to notice that as a consequence of this change an alteration in the obverse–reverse order took place which, once established, was also employed on the coins of Judah Aristobulus I and Alexander Janneus. The result of this change was that the reverse (now the side with an emblem but without a legend) was adorned with cornucopias but in a new form. As the inscription was transferred to the obverse, the double cornucopia with the parallel horns (in the helmet-cornucopia coins) was replaced by cornucopias covering the whole face of the coins, with two extended horns and a pomegranate between them (pl. II, 3l.). In this form it became the most common and representative symbol on Hasmonean coins.

On the coins of John Hyrcanus I two legends appear (we ignore here minor differences and incomplete renderings): (*a*) *Yehohanan HaKohen*

---

[1] It is interesting to note that the encircling legend is typical of Ptolemaic coins and the vertical one of Seleucid coins.

HaGadol Rosh Ḥever HaYehudim (lit. John the High Priest, Head of the community of the Jews), and (*b*) *Yehoḥanan HaKohen HaGadol VeḤever HaYehudim* (lit. John the High Priest and the community of the Jews). Two questions arise with regard to these legends, one about their meaning and the other about their sequence (or their interrelationship). As to their meaning, the prominence of the Hasmonean rulers as high priests is well known, but what is the *Ḥever HaYehudim* which is referred to on the coins and hence what office is being referred to as *Rosh Ḥever HaYehudim*? In all probability the phrase *Ḥever HaYehudim* refers to the Jewish people of which Hyrcanus I was the head or *Rosh*, like his father Simon before him (compare 1 Macc. 14: 47). In addition, the phrase *VeḤever HaYehudim* suggests the notion that the whole people of Israel was associated with Hyrcanus I in the ultimate sovereignty of the nation. This expressed sense of partnership between ruler and people is seen also in some documents of this period and reflects certain political and ideological realities of the early Hasmonean state. Consequently, we should not consider the difference between the two legends to be a decisive chronological criterion but rather a likely reflection of the existing contemporary constitutional situation.

To sum up: the 'helmet-cornucopia' trilepta with the legend '. . . *Rosh Ḥever* . . .' are to be assigned to the beginning of John Hyrcanus I's coinage. They were either followed or accompanied by two denominations, the *peruta* with wreathed inscription and cornucopia (the legend usually, but not always, *VeḤever* . . .) and the half-*peruta* with lily and palm-branch (usually the legend is *Rosh Ḥever*, but there are exceptions). Moreover, *Rosh Ḥever* does not necessarily refer to a later phase of Hyrcanus' reign in which there was tension between Hyrcanus I and the Pharisees and some usurpation of power by him. Had this been a reflection of a changed situation in the later stages of his reign it seems likely that his successor, Judah Aristobulus I, would have adhered to it; but there is no evidence of this at all. Finally, no prosopographical identification is possible concerning the monogram A (or certain other letters) which appears on some coins of John Hyrcanus I. There is no evidence to support the claim, tempting though it is, that the A is the initial of Antipater, the vizier of Hyrcanus II, and that consequently those coins are to be attributed to him. There is even less reason to credit several other, even more far-fetched, identifications. Who or what figured behind the A will remain obscure as long as our knowledge of Hasmonean prosopography remains as preliminary and meagre as it is.

John Hyrcanus I was succeeded by his son Judah Aristobulus I who ruled for only one year (104–103 B.C.E.). The only known evidence of his coinage is of *perutoth* which bear the legend *Yehuda (Ha)Kohen (Ha) Gadol VeḤever HaYehudim* (lit. Judah the High Priest and the community of the Jews) (pl. II, 4). This inscription does not seem to support Josephus' statement (*Ant.* XIII.301) that Judah Aristobulus I was the first Hasmonean ruler to proclaim himself king, and though it does not conclusively exclude this possibility it renders Strabo's account (XIV.2, 40) that Janneus was the first Hasmonean king more plausible.

ALEXANDER JANNEUS

The most copious and varied Hasmonean coinage was issued under Alexander Janneus (103–76 B.C.E.) although there is no consensus about its sequence. Janneus' coinage reflects a variety of influences: in some respects it bears a resemblance to his predecessors' coins (the *perutoth* with wreathed legend and double cornucopia and the half-*perutoth* with lily and palm-branch with legend: pl. II, 6), as well as sharing some resemblance to former Seleucid coins (especially the anchor–lily coins: pl. I, 7). However, certain aspects of his coinage are derived from a more obscure and uncertain ancestry as, for example, the star mentioned above.

More innovative than the designs of the coins are their legends which attest to Janneus' kingship in no less than three languages: *Yehonathan HaMelech* (Hebrew, lit. Jehonathan the king); Αλεξανδρου Βασιλεως (Greek, lit. of King Alexander); *Alexandros Malka* (Aramaic, lit. Alexander the king). It would certainly appear that the Janneus coins that bear the more traditional legend *Yehonathan... VeḤever HaYehudim* were struck before those coins which announce Janneus' kingship, but this is not free from difficulty because of coins bearing the title king and supposedly overstruck by *VeḤever HaYehudim*. In trying to deal with the implications of these overstruck coins it is reasonable to assume that they either reflect some compromise between Janneus and his adversaries as a result of which he modified to some extent his claim to kingship, or, and this seems even more probable, the overstriking took place posthumously.[1] In any case, the only certain dating appears on an extremely poorly-executed series of anchor–star coins whose legend has only recently been satisfactorily read as: *Alexandros Malka Shenath Kaf He* (lit. Alexander the king, year 25).[2] Besides the unique appearance

---

[1] Such a possibility has already been mentioned. See, for example, B. Kanael, 'Literaturüberblicke der griechischen Numismatik-altjüdischen Münzen', in *Jahrbuch für Numismatik und Geldgeschichte*, 17 (1967), 154–298, under no. 160 (last paragraph).

[2] See J. Naveh, 'The Dated Coins of Alexander Janneus', *IEJ*, 18 (1968), 20–6 and A. Kindler, 'Addendum to the Dated Coins of Alexander Janneus', *IEJ*, 18 (1968), 188–91.

of an Aramaic legend on a Hasmonean coin, we have here one of the rare occasions when a coin is precisely dated – year 25, which is 78 B.C.E. It should be noted that 78 B.C.E. is very near the end of Janneus' reign and yet he still seems to bear his royal title, making it unlikely that he had at the same time acquiesced to the overstriking of his own coins with the 'king' legend. The supposition that the overstriking of Janneus' 'king' coins occurred posthumously thus appears much more probable.

Outstanding among Hasmonean coins are Janneus' bilingual coins. On one side they bear a Hebrew and on the other a Greek legend, both of which have the same content: Yehonathan (or, in Greek, Alexander) the king. The Greek legend was directed towards the Greek-speaking population which found itself under Janneus' rule, and a comparable purpose was behind the Aramaic legend mentioned above which was directed towards the Aramaic-speaking population. It is somewhat curious that this awareness on the part of Janneus regarding the spoken language of part of the population did not affect the presentation of the Hebrew legends which are always in the relatively antiquated Phoenician script. This script, though not in vogue at that period, had a strongly entrenched position relative to coins and was used instead of the 'modern' Aramaic script right up to the end of ancient Jewish coinage.

Janneus' immediate successors, his widow and two sons, do not seem to have struck any coins at all in their own name. We do not possess a single coin from the reign of Queen Salome Alexandra (76–67 B.C.E.). It seems that the copious coinage under Janneus rendered any additional 'small money' unnecessary,[1] though some posthumous coinage in his name might have been struck under her rule. It is also probable that Janneus' abundant coinage rendered superfluous any additional minting during the short reign of John Hyrcanus II, who ruled for only three months in 67 B.C.E., and the somewhat longer reign of Aristobulus II, who ruled for some three years amid war and civil discord.

In 63 B.C.E. Aristobulus II was deposed by Pompey and as a consequence of Roman intervention Judea lost its independence and a considerable part of its territory. John Hyrcanus II was appointed as a maimed ruler over a disabled Judea and serious doubts are to be cast on the attribution of any *Yehohanan* coins to him.

MATHATHYA ANTIGONUS

Hasmonean coinage was temporarily renewed under the rule of Mathathya Antigonus (40–37 B.C.E.), a son of Aristobulus II. Interestingly, the very precariousness of the position he held manifests itself

[1] For references see Rappaport, *AJS Review*, 1 (1976), 180, n. 43.

in certain innovations in his coins, which were to be the last example
of Hasmonean coinage.

Antigonus, like his predecessors, did not mint in silver, but nevertheless he was the only Hasmonean to use his coinage for overt
propaganda. This use of his coinage came about in the following
manner. Antigonus, a protégé of the Parthians, was left alone to face
Herod and Rome after the Parthians were repelled from Syria by the
Roman legions. In this circumstance, Antigonus used his coins to make
a direct appeal to his own people for support. One of his coins bears
two completely new symbols (pl. II, 8): one is the seven-branched
menorah (lit. candelabrum) which stood in the Temple, the image of
which was intended to awaken religious–national emotions and most
probably to recall the spirit of the Hasmonean rebellion. As is well
known, the menorah was henceforth to become one of the most popular
emblems in Jewish art and the most representative of all Jewish
symbols. The second symbol found is an object composed of a
horizontal line from which four vertical lines are projected. It is often
explained as the shewbread table, one of the sacred objects in the
Temple. If this dubious interpretation (or any other along the same
lines)[1] is correct it would suggest that the symbol served the same broad
purpose as that intended by the menorah.

Besides these two new symbols, Antigonus' coins bear the cornucopia
and a wreathed inscription (pl. II, 7), but unlike former coins of similar
fashion these new coins were now struck in different denominations.
Some weigh as much as 14.00 grams, by far the heaviest Hasmonean
coins we possess. Their legends also reflect their new and quite different
historical situation: they are in Greek and in Hebrew but, in contrast
to Janneus' bilingual coins, the contents of the inscriptions in the two
languages are not identical. Whereas the Greek reads Βασιλεως
Αντιγονου (lit. of King Antigonus), the Hebrew reads *Mathathya
HaKohen HaGadol VeHever HaYehudim* (lit. Mathathya the high priest
and the community of the Jews). This asymmetry would suggest that
whereas Antigonus considered himself king for the non-Jews, he was
content with a lesser position in relation to his own people. *Vis-à-vis*
the Jews he renounced the larger claims of kingship and contented
himself with the traditional office of high priest, probably hoping
through this action to create popular support.

[1] The proposal of D. Sperber in 'A Note on a Coin of Antigonus Mattathias', *JQR*,
54 (1963–64), 250–7, seems to me very doubtful, but his passing suggestion that this
symbol may be a four-branch menorah, though rejected by himself (ibid. 250), seems
to me the most probable among all the suggestions made so far.

HEROD AND ARCHELAUS

In the year 37 B.C.E. Herod conquered Jerusalem and Antigonus was executed. However, Herod's first striking of bronze coins (the Romans never allowed him to strike in silver) occurred even before these events. These first Herodian coins are especially interesting because they are the only series of his which are dated, and all of them are dated to one and the same year, the year 3. Their emblems are the *thymiaterion* (pl. II, 9l.), circular shield, pomegranate, palm-branch and tripod on the obverse; on the reverse are found, respectively, tripod with *lebes* (pl. II, 9ł.), helmet, caduceus, *aphlaston* and cross within a wreath. All the reverses bear the same legend, date and monogram. The inscription reads Βασιλεως Ηρωδου; the monogram ₽, which is not yet explained satisfactorily and the date LΓ (year 3) must refer to the third year of Herod's reign since his enthronement in Rome, that is, the year April (= Nisan) 38 to March 37 B.C.E. The year ending in March 37 B.C.E. had concluded before Herod conquered Jerusalem from Antigonus, so that these first coins were struck somewhere else, most probably either at Ashkelon or at Tyre.

It is difficult to ascertain the meaning and purpose of the symbols on these first coins. Some of them are martial (shield, helmet); some represent the typical plants of Palestine (pomegranate, palm); others are of non-Jewish or even idolatrous meaning (caduceus, *thymiaterion*, tripod with *lebes*); one is of a maritime character (*aphlaston*, which is typical of Ashkelon) and one still remains meaningless to us (the cross within a wreath).[1] Some of these coins are of greater denomination than the later coins of Herod, and for the most part they are of better workmanship. As they were issued outside Judea they may not have been prepared specifically for use by the Jewish population.

Besides these early coins many other coins were continuously minted, usually in *peruta* and half-*peruta* denominations. It is impossible to arrange them in any exact chronological order. For the most part Herod's coins accommodate themselves to Jewish aniconic attitudes (that is, without human forms), and their symbols are either similar to those on Hasmonean coins (for example, anchor, cornucopia, palm-branch) or are new ones which are equally inoffensive (for example, ship, tripod). In only two recorded cases was Jewish sensitivity on this matter ignored. In the first case we have a coin which pictures a standing eagle (pl. II, 10l.) and, in the second a coin which pictures a caduceus between the horns of the cornucopia rather than the traditional pomegranate which appears in a similar position on Hasmonean coins. It is hard to

[1] Cf. R. H. Smith, 'The Cross Marks on Jewish Ossuaries', *PEQ*, 106 (1974), 53–66.

say whether Jewish feelings were intentionally ignored in these two instances; but in any case Jewish practice was less strictly observed by Herod than it had been by the former Hasmonean rulers. Another unique Herodian departure from Hasmonean usage was the sole use of Greek on his coinage. This complete rejection of Hebrew inscriptions became a practice adhered to by all Herod's successors. Only under the two great revolts, of 66–70 C.E. and of Bar Kochba (132–135 C.E.), did Hebrew regain its position on Jewish coinage.

Following Herod's death, Palestine was divided into three separate principalities each of which had its own supply of bronze coinage. Rule over the three provinces of Idumea, Judea and Samaria fell to Herod's son Archelaus, who ruled as ethnarch under the aegis of Augustus from 4 B.C.E. to 6 C.E. Archelaus introduced only minor changes into his father's coinage. The ship, which is relatively rare on Herod's coins, is quite common on his (pl. II, 11l.), and there are scholars who think that it is intended to emphasize that he – and not his brothers – inherited his father's main harbour of Caesarea and his navy. Among his new symbols we find the helmet (different from the one on Hyrcanus I's coin) and the bunch of grapes (pl. II, 12). The legend is Ηρωδου Εθναρχου (lit. of Herod the ethnarch), in various abbreviations. The coins are not dated.

ROMAN GOVERNORS

Archelaus was deposed by Augustus in 6 C.E. and Judea was incorporated into the Roman provincial system. Following this arrangement Judea's Roman governors were in charge of the minting of bronze coinage for the province. Under their lead new symbols were introduced into the provincial coinage of Judea, but these usually conformed with Jewish practice and offensive symbols were avoided. Among the new symbols we may notice the palm-tree, ear or ears of barley, vine leaf, and the representation of different jugs (amphora, *kantharos*). Some of these symbols continued to be used in later Jewish coins.

Within this framework there are, however, several coins which conspicuously broke the rule of not giving offence. Thus two injurious symbols, *simpulum* and *lituus* (pl. III, 5l., pl. III, 4l. respectively), appear on coins issued by Pontius Pilate, the prefect of Judea in 26–36 C.E. This intentional injury of Jewish feelings accords well with our knowledge of both Pilate's callous treatment of his Jewish subjects and contemporary Roman policy towards the Jews, moulded at that time under Sejanus' negative influence.[1]

[1] Doubts about this exposition which followed E. Stauffer's work ('Zur Münzprägung und Judenpolitik des Pontius Pilate', *La Nouvelle Clio*, 9 (1950), 495–514), were

Exceptions to the normal rule might also be seen in a caduceus between cornucopias (pl. III, 2r.) on a coin from the time of Valerius Gratus (15–26 C.E.), for which there is nevertheless a forerunner in a coin of Herod (see above) and in a coin from the time of Antonius Felix (52–60 C.E.) on which two crossed shields and two crossed spears are depicted (pl. III, 6r.). Though in this latter case no religious hurt can be detected, some insult to national pride can be inferred. These coins, struck only in bronze, usually bear the names of the ruling emperor and the date according to their regnal years. No mention is made of any governor. Their minting place was either Jerusalem or Caesarea, where the governor's residence was.

The coins of the Roman governors were issued irregularly. As all the coins are dated we do know that in certain periods they were minted repeatedly while in other periods long interruptions occurred. It seems that usually the minting of these coins was dictated by the demand for a fresh supply and by the governor's awareness of this need. It is probable that the minting of bronze was likewise irregular in other periods, but as both Hasmonean and Herodian coins are undated this fact is not easily noticeable.

HEROD ANTIPAS AND PHILIP

Simultaneously with Judea's Roman coinage the other two remaining successors of Herod also issued coins, Herod Antipas for Galilee and Perea and Philip for the north-eastern parts of Herod's former kingdom, that is, Gaulanitis, Trachonitis and Batanea.

Herod Antipas' first coins were struck only after he had reigned for some twenty years, probably on the occasion of the inauguration of his new city on lake Gennesaret, founded in honour of Tiberius and named Tiberias. The obverse of the coins bears a plant, the legend Ηρωδ[ου] Τετραρ[χου] (lit. of Herod the Tetrarch) and the date ΛΚΔ (year 24, which is 19/20 C.E.); and the reverse Τιβεριας within a wreath (pl. III,

expressed by L. Kadman ('The Development of Jewish Coinage', *Dating and Meaning of Ancient Jewish Coins and Symbols*, Publication of the Israel Numismatic Society, vol. 1 (1954), p. 100, n. 2) and by G. Le Rider ('Les Ateliers Monétaires de la côte syrienne, phénicienne, palestinienne, égyptienne et cyrénéenne', *Relazioni*, vol. 1 of the Congresso internazionale di Numismatica (Rome, 1961), pp. 67–109), following new dates proposed formerly by A. Kindler ('More Dates on Coins of the Procurators', *IEJ*, 6 (1956), 54–7). Nevertheless, as Kindler's readings were rejected convincingly by Meshorer, *Jewish Coins*, and by Stauffer himself (in a later book, *Jerusalem und Rom* (Bern, 1957), p. 136, n. 7), Stauffer's thesis seems to hold the ground. Nevertheless, D. Hennig, *L. Aelius Seianus*, Vestigia, vol. 21 (1975), p. 176 and n. 54, tries to refute it, mainly arguing against any connection between Pilate and Sejanus.

7). The plant on the obverse is usually interpreted as a palm-branch, though the suggestion that the reed, common to the area of Tiberias, is represented here might be correct.

After this issue there are no coins of Herod Antipas until the thirty-third year of his reign (28/29 C.E) when a new series began. The new coins bear the palm-branch, the legend Ηρωδου Τετραρχου and dates (33, 34, 36, 37 C.E.) on the obverse, and on the reverse Τιβεριας within a wreath.

Another group bears the date LMΓ (year 43) which corresponds to the last year of Herod Antipas' reign, 38/39 C.E. These coins bear on the obverse various representations of the palm (palm-branch, palm-tree, bundle of dates), a most important fruit tree in the region of Tiberias, and the usual legend 'of Herod the Tetrarch'. On their reverse they bear an inscription within a wreath, reading: Γαιω Καισα[ρι] Γερμα-νικω (lit. To Gaius Caesar Germanicus) (pl. III, 8).

To sum up: Herod Antipas' coins, unlike the ornamentation of his palace at Tiberias (compare Josephus, *Vita* 65–7), adhere to the aniconic features of Jewish coinage. As almost all of his subjects were Jews he had no wish to alienate them unnecessarily. He produced only bronze coins which were minted in Tiberias and were monotonous in

---

PLATE III

1. AE; dilepton; Roman procurator Marcus Ambibulus; ear of barley / palm-tree, 'Year 39' (of Augustus).
2. AE; dilepton; Roman procurator Valerius Gratus; wreath, 'Kaisar' / two crossed cornucopias, 'Tiberiou year 3'.
3. AE; dilepton; Roman procurator Valerius Gratus; vine leaf / *kantharos*; 'Year 4' (of Tiberius).
4. AE; dilepton; Roman procurator Pontius Pilate; *lituus*, 'Tiberiou kaisaros' / wreath, 'Year 18' (of Tiberius).
5. AE; dilepton; Roman procurator Pontius Pilate; *simpulum*, 'Year 16' (of Tiberius) / three ears of barley.
6. AE; dilepton; Roman procurator Antonius Felix; palm-tree, 'Year 14' (of Claudius) / crossed shields and spears.
7. AE; Herod Antipas; reed, 'Year 24' (of Antipas) / wreath, 'Tiberias'.
8. AE; Herod Antipas; palm-branch, '43' (of Antipas) / wreath, 'Gaio kaisar Germani (Ko)'.
9. AE; Philip; (on left) head of Augustus / (on right) head of Philippus (1/2 C.E.).
10. AE; Agrippa I; bust of Agrippa I/goddess standing.
11. AE; Agrippa I; canopy, 'Basileos Agrippa' / three ears of barley, 'Year 6' (= 42/43 C.E.).
12. AR; denarius; Tiberius; bust of Tiberius / Livia as Pax seated.

Key: AE = bronze   AR = silver

pattern. Their denominations are large (up to 16.00 grams), which is more in line with the coins minted by Philip and Agrippa I and II than with those struck at Judea.[1]

Herod's third successor, Philip (4 B.C.E.–34 C.E.), ruled a mainly non-Jewish population and this is reflected in his coins, which have nothing in common with Jewish coinage. They not only bear human portraits, but his first series (dated year 5 = 1 C.E.) seems to bear his own portrait (pl. III, 9r.), which makes him the first Herodian whose features are known to us. On the reverse of this and other coins of his there is a tetrastyle temple, while on his later coins imperial portraits are figured. The legend reads 'of Philip the Tetrarch' and mentions the names of Augustus and Tiberius as well. The denominations of Philip's coins resemble those of Herod Antipas. Philip's mint was, in all probability, at Panias which he rebuilt and renamed Caesarea (Philippi). In relation to this enterprise he is named Κτισ[της] (lit. founder) on one of his coins.

Philip's fully pagan coinage indicates that it was only the apprehension of Jewish reaction that in all probability restrained the other Herodians, as well as the Roman governors, from similar coinage. The moment these authorities were free of the restraints imposed by Jewish sensibilities, as Philip was, their coinage imitated a non-Jewish pattern.

AGRIPPA I AND AGRIPPA II

Not only did Herod's sons strike coins but so, too, did his grandsons and great-grandsons. Two of these Herodians, Agrippa I and his son Agrippa II, were closely associated with Palestine, while two, Herod of Chalcis, Agrippa I's brother and his son and successor Aristobulus, ruled beyond its borders.

Agrippa I's meteoric rise to power (37–44 C.E.) was accompanied by varied coinage. Already as king of the petty principality of his uncle Philip he struck coins with his own portrait and title on the obverse, while on the reverse was the figure of his son and future successor, Agrippa II, riding a horse and bearing the legend Αγριππα υιου βασιλεως (lit. of Agrippa the son of the king). This disregard for Jewish scruples was in line with the conduct of his predecessor, his uncle Philip,

---

[1] The entangled subject of bronze denominations and their interrelations cannot be discussed here. It is obstructed, especially in the case of the Roman eastern provinces, including Palestine, by the unstable weight of bronze coins, the fluctuation of their copper content, different systems of denominations, absence of denominational marks, and contradictory literary sources. For literature see the section on Herod Antipas and Philip in the bibliography (p. 404).

in the same region and sprang from the fact that the majority of the population was not Jewish. The same principles served him in minting for various other regions of his later larger kingdom (41–44 C.E.), and though he was a very considerate Jewish ruler, most of his coins are inconsistent with Jewish practice. His coins depict, among other things, a portrait of the Emperor Claudius and scenes with human figures, connected most probably with events in his own career. The legend on this coinage reads Αγριππας Φιλοκαισαρ Βασιλευς Μεγας (Agrippa, Caesar's friend, Great King), and also mentions his treaty with Rome or Caesarea with its harbour named Sebastos.

For his Jewish subjects Agrippa struck one coin only, though in ample quantity, which took account of Jewish sensitivities. Its obverse shows a 'royal' umbrella or canopy, that in all probability is a symbol of kingship and bears an inscription Βασιλεως Αγριππα (lit. of King Agrippa). Its reverse shows three ears of barley and carries the date, year 6 (42/3 C.E.) (pl. III, 11).

Agrippa I's coins were minted in at least three places: in Caesarea Philippi (a coin from year 2 could not have been minted elsewhere); in Jerusalem (the umbrella–ears-of-barley coin of year 6); and in Caesarea Maritima where the coins with the legend Καισαρια η προς τω Σεβαστω λιμενι (lit. Caesarea at the Harbour *Sebastos*) were certainly minted, in addition, in all probability, to many other coins of Agrippa I. It is less clear whether or not the mint at Tiberias was active under him. It should also be noted that all the coins of Agrippa I were struck in bronze, for even though he was held in high regard by both Caligula and Claudius and enjoyed their friendship and benevolence, he was not authorized to mint coins in silver.

The copious coinage of Agrippa II was minted during the entire length of his 45-year career (50–95 C.E. approximately). His coins bear no affinities to traditional Jewish coinage and were produced only in bronze, normally in large denominations. They usually bear portraits of the Roman emperors and figures of goddesses, for example, Tyche or Nike. They bear dates of various eras, one of which began in 56 C.E. and another in 61 C.E. (probably in relation to the renaming of Panias Caesarea-Philippi Neronias).

CURRENCY IN PALESTINE TO ABOUT 70 C.E.

For its silver coinage Palestine drew on outside supplies. Tyre has already been mentioned as a source of silver currency in the Persian and Hellenistic periods and Tyrian silver coins were commonly used and highly regarded in Palestine (pl. I, 9). For example, the Temple authorities in Jerusalem preferred them for payments due to them (primarily the half-shekel contribution). This is all the more remarkable when one realizes that these Tyrian shekels (= tetradrachms) and half-shekels (= didrachms) bore idolatrous images (Melqarth-Herakles and an eagle) which were considered repulsive by Jews. However, both archeological and literary evidence point to their predominant place in the currency of Palestine and to their universal acceptance by Jews. The issues of Tyrian shekels run from 126/5 B.C.E. to about 60 C.E.[1] In addition to the Tyrian currency there was also an influx of other silver, struck at Antiochia, among other places. Two denominations are discernible in these coins: the drachm and the denarius (pl. III, 12), the first a continuance of the Hellenistic system of denominations and the second the basic silver coin in the Roman system. As the tetradrachm was reduced in weight under the principate to about 15 grams, it became exchangeable with four denarii, that is, a denarius of about 3.50 to 4.00 grams was nearly equal to a drachm.

Bronze coinage was not limited to the local Roman provincial coins and the dynastic coinage of the Herodians. There was regular minting in some veteran mints, such as Akko-Ptolemais and Ashkelon, and also in some newer ones, such as Sepphoris, whose earliest coins are dated to the last year, the fourteenth, of Nero's reign (67/68 C.E.); Tiberias, which was already active under Herod Antipas and minted under Claudius; Caesarea which, as well as 'procuratorial' coins and those of Agrippa I, also struck local money under Claudius and Nero; and Beth-shean, that is, Nysa-Scythopolis, which produced coins under Caligula, Claudius and Nero. This modest 'municipal' coinage was expanded considerably in the last quarter of the first century and thereafter (see below).

THE COINS OF THE FIRST REVOLT

A new abundant minting of genuine Jewish coinage occurred as a corollary of the first revolt against Rome (66–70 C.E.). This revolutionary coinage broke away from all Jewish precedents and was in itself an open challenge to foreign domination over Israel. Most significantly, it was the first silver coinage issued under Jewish authority and there can be no doubt that it was motivated by political reasons – in addition to serving an economic function. Through the issue of these silver coins

[1] For the date, see A. Kindler, 'The Mint of Tyre – The Major Source of Silver Coins in Ancient Palestine', *Eretz-Israel*, 8 (1967), 322; A. Ben-David, *Jerusalem und Tyros, Ein Beitrag zur palästinensischen Münz- und Wirtschaftsgeschichte, 126 a.C. – 57 p.C.* (Basel–Tübingen, 1969), p. 4 and bibliography in the notes.

the rebellious Jewish government announced its independence and sovereignty. The issuing of bronze coins would not have conveyed this message with anything like the same force.

The political intent to be independent which prompted this coinage is obvious in both the legends and the symbols which they carry. The silver shekels bear on the obverse the inscription *Sheqel Israel* and a date (year 1 to 5) and on the reverse *Yerushalaim HaQedosha* (lit. Jerusalem the holy) or *Yerushalaim Qedosha* (lit. Jerusalem holy) (pl. IV, 1–2). The first inscription is an obvious declaration of sovereignty, and the second, which can be compared to similar inscriptions – ιερα και ασυλος – on some autonomous coins of Hellenistic cities, has the impact of a slogan stressing the aim of the revolt, that is, to protect and purify the holy city which was a symbol of Jewish political, as well as religious, even messianic, hopes. In the ideology of the rebels, according to which the rebellion had messianic significance, Jerusalem the holy was inseparably connected with the consummation of their theo-political hopes concerning the war.

The bronze coins of the revolt (dated only to the years 2, 3 and 4) (pl. IV, 4–5) bear inscriptions which are even less formal and more emotional, stating both the objects and the convictions of the rebels. They read *LeHeruth Zion* and *LeGeulath Zion*. The term *Geula* signifies the messianic redemption and appeared only on the bronze coins of year 4, whereas the term *Heruth* (freedom) appeared only on the coins of years 2 and 3. (No bronze coins of either year 1 or of year 5 have been found.) Probably this change from *Heruth* to *Geula* signified the ascendancy of Simon bar Giora in Jerusalem and with it the strengthening of the messianic element in the rebellion.

The symbols on these coins generally reflect the same ideological purpose. Judea is represented by typical fruit-bearing trees, like the palm-tree and palm-branch, the vine leaf and the pomegranate. The sanctity of Jerusalem and the Temple is expressed by the representation of the Temple's utensils (as the chalice and the amphora are generally interpreted) and sacred objects (the *ethrog* and *lulab*).

The coins of the first revolt are also exceptional among Jewish coins because of their systematic denominational arrangement and its relation to the legends and symbols. Almost all the silver coins are of one pattern. They have a chalice, date and denomination (either *Sheqel Israel*, or *Hazi HaSheqel* or *Reba' HaSheqel* = half-shekel or quarter of a shekel respectively) on the obverse and a bunch of three pomegranates (with the legend 'Jerusalem the holy') on the reverse (pl. IV, 3). The weight of the shekel, half-shekel and quarter of a shekel was 14.00 grams, 7.00 grams and 3.5 grams respectively, which closely approximated to the

weights of Tyrian silver. The coins were also similar to Tyrian silver ones in size and silver content. Likewise the bronze coins, though of lesser importance and of more varied forms, are also systematically arranged.

The rebels were able to strike their silver coins during the entire duration of the revolt, from the first year of rebellion, year *Aleph*, April 66 to March 67, up to and including the fifth and last year, year *He*, which began in April 70, a few months before Jerusalem fell. These coins show a certain cohesiveness and continuity in the government of Jerusalem in those turbulent years, in contrast to the testimony of our literary sources. It is to be noted that study of this revolutionary coinage gives a deeper insight into the events, and their motivating passions, which were to alter the entire course of Jewish history.

THE COINS OF THE SECOND REVOLT

The last stage of Jewish coinage in ancient Palestine was created as a corollary of the second and last major Jewish revolt against Rome, which took place under the leadership of Bar Kochba in 132–135 C.E. The rebellious government struck coins in both silver and bronze with several motives in mind. Foremost among these was to announce its sovereignty, disseminate the names of the rebellion's leaders and third,

---

PLATE IV

1. AR; shekel; Jewish War; chalice, 'Sheqel Israel year 1' (66/7 C.E.) / three half-ripe pomegranates, 'Jerusalem the holy'.
2. AR; shekel; Jewish War; chalice, 'Sheqel Israel year 5' (70 C.E.) / three half-ripe pomegranates 'Jerusalem the holy'.
3. AR; half-shekel; Jewish War; chalice, 'Half a sheqel year 3' (68/9 C.E.) / three half-ripe pomegranates, 'Jerusalem the holy'.
4. AE; dilepton; Jewish War; amphora, 'Year two' (67/8 C.E.) / vine-leaf, 'Freedom of Zion'.
5. AE; semis (one-eighth of a *sestertius*); Jewish War; chalice, 'For the redemption of Zion' / *lulab* and two *ethrogs*, 'Year four' (69/70 C.E.).
6. AE; *sestertius*; Vespasian; bust of Vespasian / palm tree with emperor on left and captive Jewess on right, 'Judaea Capta'; 71 C.E. (Mint of Rome.)
7. AE; Titus (under Vespasian); head of Titus / trophy, on its left, below captive Jew. (Mint: Caesarea (?).)
8. AR; tetradrachm; Bar Kochba war; Temple façade, above star, 'Shim'on' / *lulab* and *ethrog*, 'Year two for the freedom of Israel' (133/4 C.E.).
9. AR; denarius; Bar Kochba war; bunch of grapes, 'Shim'on' / kithara, 'For the freedom of Jerusalem' (134/5 C.E.).
Key: AE = bronze   AR = silver

but not least, to encourage the rebellious spirit of the people and fortify their resolve to achieve independence from Roman oppression.

The coins of the second revolt were exceptional in that they were not struck on new blanks but on older coins, which were overstruck after their former features had been erased by hammering. It appears that this procedure was adopted not only because of the technical considerations of saving time and labour, but also from a desire to erase the idolatrous features of the pagan coinage then circulating. We can also detect that in this period the effacing treatment was likewise administered to objects other than coins, presumably for the same reason.[1]

As a result of this procedure the denominations of 'Bar Kochba's' coins reflect the currency in use in Palestine in the period immediately preceding the revolt, and thus his coinage does not form a consistent monetary pattern of its own. In silver it combines both tetradrachms and denars, while its bronze coinage can be roughly divided into large, intermediate and small denominations.

All the tetradrachms bear a tetrastyle building on their obverse together with a bundle of the *Arba'a Minim* (lit. four species), namely *lulab, ethrog, hadas* and *'arava* (lit. young palm-branch, citron, myrtle and brook-willow, respectively) on their reverse (pl. IV, 8).[2] The tetrastyle building may or may not have a palisade beneath the pillars, and it may or may not have a star above the roof. The legend is sometimes *Yerushalem* and sometimes *Shim'on*. On the reverse we have the date, *Sh(ana) B(eth) LeHeruth Israel* (lit. year 2 to the freedom of Israel), or *LeHeruth Yerushalem* (lit. to the freedom of Jerusalem), or, very rarely, *Shenath Ahath LeGeulath Israel* (lit. year 1 to the redemption of Israel).

The tetrastyle building is in itself an innovation on Jewish coins which until this time did not bear any representation of an edifice, though such an image was very common on non-Jewish coins of this period. It is clear that the edifice is meant to represent the Temple or some prominent part of it. Nevertheless, this representation does present several historical problems. Did the insurgents at any time conquer the holy city or not? If they did conquer the city, did they attempt to reconstruct the Temple to any extent, and did they attempt to offer sacrifices at this reconstituted Temple site? Numismatically the interesting question is whether the building represented was a copy of an actual edifice which stood at the time of minting, or whether it was

[1] For the most recent treatment see, with further references, V. Sussman, 'Early Jewish Iconoclasm on Pottery Lamps', *IEJ*, 23 (1973), 46–7.

[2] See D. Sperber, 'Iyunim be-Matbeot Bar-Kochba', *Sinai*, 55 (1964), 37–41 (in Hebrew).

merely an 'imaginative' representation of an edifice no longer in existence, presented as an expression of pious hope rather than as a copy of an actual structure to be revered and defended. This question awaits its solution from further historical and archeological research on the matter.[1]

The 'four species' which are pictured on the coins have a religious significance as sacred objects, especially in their specific relation to the feast of Tabernacles. It is interesting to note that a similar concern with the 'four species' is also shown in the Bar Kochba documents from the Judean desert, though the exact meaning of these symbols in this context, apart from some obvious general association with religious and political freedom, is uncertain.

Leaving the legends for a moment, let us consider the other symbols found on these coins. These include the representation of different vessels (amphora: pl. V, 3r., ampulla and chalice) which according to many scholars are a symbol of the Temple service. Represented also are the palm-tree (pl. V, 2l., which reminds us of the same symbol on the *Judaea capta* coins: pl. IV, 6r.), the palm-branch, the vine-leaf (pl. V, 2r.) and the vine-grape (pl. IV, 9l., V, 1l.). Interestingly, one also finds a completely new group of symbols representing musical instruments. Among those included are the lyre (of various sorts) (pl. IV, 9r.) and the trumpet (pl. V, 1r.), which are probably pictured to recall the musical performances which accompanied the services of the Temple. Even without exhausting the material represented on this coinage it is clear that the symbols are associated with two dominant motifs: the land (palm-tree, etc.) and the Temple, the two most powerful symbols of Jewish hopes for autonomy.

The legends on these coins may be divided into two categories: the minting authority on the obverse and the date on the reverse. The minting authority, at least in one case, is the leader of the revolt, Shimeon ben Kosba (that is, Bar Kochba), who is designated on the coins *Shim'on Nesi Israel* (lit. Shimeon, President of Israel), or in shorter forms *Shimeon* or *Shma'*. In addition to Shimeon we also find the minting authority attributed to one *El'azar HaCohen*, an otherwise unknown historical figure, who at least in the first stages of the revolt held a prominent position of leadership, either actually or formally, as high priest (*HaKohen*). The name 'Yerushalem' also appears on the coins. Whether this is the expression of an institutional function of 'Jerusalem', for example, the assembly of the people in the liberated city, or is merely an expression of hope, is uncertain.

[1] See the negative conclusion of L. Mildenberg, 'Bar Kokhba Coins and Documents', *HSCP*, 84 (1980), 311–35.

The dates on the coins are as follows: first, there is *Shnath Aḥath LeGeulath Israel* (lit. year 1 to the redemption of Israel), which indicates the first year of the revolt (April 132 to March 133), counted as if the messianic era had already begun. The second date reads *Sh(nath) B(eth) LeḤer(uth) Israel* (lit. year 2 to the freedom of Israel), which would be the year April 133 to March 134. This time the era is not referred to as that of redemption (*Geula*) but rather as that of freedom (*Ḥeruth*), thus stressing the actual political liberation rather than the period of divine salvation. It is probable that this change, as other changes which cannot be discussed here, reflects actual historical developments which are up to the time of writing unknown.

The third inscription in the same position on the reverse is *LeḤeruth Yerushalem* (lit. to the freedom of Jerusalem). Here the concept of 'freedom' used on the coins minted in the second year is retained, but instead of referring to Israel the reference is to Jerusalem and no date is given. Most numismatists assume that this inscription was produced in the third year of the rebellion and that it is somehow meant to replace a fuller inscription, for example, 'year 3 for the freedom of Jerusalem'. Though not fully convincing this explanation is the most reasonable one that has so far been advanced.

Where the rebels minted is uncertain, that is, whether in Jerusalem or in Beithar. This depends on whether Jerusalem was occupied by the insurgents and, if so, for how long.

PLATE V

1. AR; denarius; Bar Kochba war; bunch of grapes, 'Shim'on' / two trumpets, 'Year two for the freedom of Israel' (133/4 C.E.).
2. AE; *dupondius*; Bar Kochba war; palm tree, 'Shim'on' / vine-leaf, 'For the freedom of Jerusalem' (134/5 C.E.).
3. AE; *sestertius*; Bar Kochba war; wreath, 'Shim'on prince of Israel' / amphora, 'Year one for the redemption of Israel' (132/3 C.E.).
4. AE; as; 218–222 C.E.; Neapolis; bust of Elagabalus / mount Gerizim.
5. AE; as; 130/1 C.E. *Gaza*; bust of Hadrian / city-goddess; Phoenician *Mem* to its right.
6. AE; Akko-Ptolemais; Severus Alexander (head of) / the river Belus reclining (222–235 C.E.).
7. AE; Aelia Capitolina; bust of Hadrian / foundation ceremony of the city (COL AEL KAPIT COND(ita)).
8. AR; *Antoninianus*; Aurelianus, 270–275 C.E.; bust of Aurelianus, radiated / Jupiter handing victory to the emperor, 'Concordia exercitus'.
9. AV; solidus; Phocas, 602–610 C.E.; bust of Phocas, full face / Victory, full face. (Mint: Constantinopolis.)
10. AE; *follis*; Ommayad emission of the seventh century C.E.; caliph standing full face, 'Mohammed is the apostle of god' / large M (= 40 *nummia* = *follis*), 'Filastin–Iliyah (= Palestine–Aelia (Capitolina)).
Key: AE = bronze   AR = silver   AV = gold

MUNICIPAL COINAGE AND CURRENCY IN PALESTINE
(*circa* 70–250 C.E.)

The suppression of the two great Jewish revolts in Palestine gradually changed the ethnography of the land and shifted the balance in favour of the non-Jewish elements. This represented a decided shift in the make-up of the population as it had existed in the Hasmonean period, and this change, as one would expect, is reflected in the contemporary Palestinian coinage. The coins now begin to bear testimony to the diffusion of pagan culture in many Palestinian cities and to the different pagan cults of the day in which oriental, Hellenistic and Roman elements all flourished.

The coinage of Palestine in this period now fits generally into the larger framework of the Roman East, especially as represented by Syria. Culturally there is nothing Jewish about it, and even distinct local traits are only partially found. The obverses bear imperial portraits and legends, while the reverses bear the city's name and titles and some widespread type, the most usual being the different pagan deities in various positions. Only in small details and incidentally are local particularities noticeable. Such instances of local distinctiveness can be seen, for example, in the representation of the river Belus (modern Naaman) on the coins of Akko-Ptolemais (pl. V, 6r.); an inscription which relates Caesarea to its harbour (Sebastos); the figure of Hygieia (related, probably, to the warm baths) on the coins of Tiberias; a special attachment to Alexander the Great in the Decapolis (coins of Gerasa and Capitolias bear his portrait); the image of mount Gerizim on the coins of Neapolis (pl. V, 4r.); and scenes from Dionysian myths on some coins of Nysa-Scythopolis (Beth-shean).

There are also specific symbols connected with certain cities as, for example, the dove with Ashkelon, or the peculiar swastika-like shape with Gaza (pl. V, 5r.) – which is in fact a Phoenician *Mem*, standing for the local deity, Marnas. Indeed, Marnas himself appears on some Gazean coins.

Though dull, these coins offer important data and especially help us to supplement our knowledge of an otherwise poorly-documented period of Jewish history. As we have done above, we shall limit our survey mainly to listing the mints active at that time, among which the following should be noted: Akko-Ptolemais, the most durable mint and probably also the most important in Hellenistic–Roman Palestine, minted until 268 C.E.; the mint at Sepphoris ended with Elagabalus (218–222 C.E.); Tiberias' last coins also date from the reign of Elagabalus; the mint at Panias was active for a short time from Marcus

Aurelius to Elagabalus; Dora minted from the time of Nero probably until that of Elagabalus; Caesarean coinage ended with Volusianus (253 C.E.) after a rich minting and almost feverish activity in its last decade; a coin of Elagabalus is also attributed to Antipatris; Diospolis-Lydda minted briefly under Caracalla: Jaffa minted briefly under Elagabalus; Neapolis, founded by Vespasian and called by him Flavia, minted until Volusianus; Scythopolis was irregularly active and its coinage ended with Gordian III (238–244 C.E.); Sebaste minted irregularly – it became a *colonia* under Septimius Severus and ended its coinage with Elagabalus. Aelia Capitolina, one of the most interesting mints, began its coinage at the time of its foundation by Hadrian (pl. V, 7) and ended it under Valerian (253–260 C.E.); Ashkelon, one of the more constant and important mints, had a copious minting up to the time of Maximinus (234/5 C.E.); Anthedon minted briefly under Severus Alexander; the mint at Eleutheropolis (on the site of Beit-Govrim near ancient Mareshah) was active from the reign of Septimius Severus until that of Elagabalus; Gaza possessed an active mint until Gordian III; Nicopolis (Emmaus) minted erratically and its coinage ceased with the reign of Elagabalus; Raphia began minting with Commodus (180/1 C.E.) and ended with Philip the Arabian (244–249 C.E.).[1]

In addition, the coinage of Transjordan should also be mentioned here, if only cursorily. With the Roman annexation of the Nabatean kingdom in 106 C.E., many of the cities of Transjordan were incorporated into the new Provincia Arabia and their coinage was produced steadily up to the time of Valerian and Gallienus (253–268 C.E.). Generally speaking, the coinage of the Transjordan cities does not differ significantly from that of other Palestinian and Syrian coins of that period. Nevertheless, we should note that they give an indication of prosperity during the era of the Antonines and Severans. The importance of the attachment to Rome is also highlighted on these coins, especially on those of the cities of the Decapolis, many of which used Pompeian eras.

The end of municipal coinages in Palestine occurred at the same time as in Phoenicia, Syria and Asia Minor. This demise is usually explained by reference to the severe inflation of the third century, which caused the price of bronze to rise so high that it even rose above the official value of the minted bronze, and so turned the minting of bronze into an unprofitable venture for the cities. In the course of one generation almost all the cities of this region ceased minting, never to begin again.

---

[1] These data are susceptible to frequent changes, because of the publication of new coins. See the recent volumes of M. Rosenberger, *City-Coins of Palestine*, The Rosenberger Israel Collection, I (1972), II (1975), III (1977), the results of which are not discussed in this section.

The economic reforms which were later introduced to re-establish some economic equilibrium all favoured the centralistic and autocratic tendencies of the late Roman empire, thus militating against any renewal of local minting.

Besides its own municipal bronze, Palestine was dependent for its silver, both tetradrachms and denarii, on the principal mints of the East. The supply came mainly from the mints of Antioch and Tyre, as well as from other eastern centres. A sporadic issue of tetradrachms also took place in Palestine under Caracalla, though these seem hardly to have been used in the country itself. Regarding bronze, in addition to the local municipal coinage we should also mention those coins which bear the Greek rendition of *Judaea capta*, reading Ιουδαιας Εαλωκυας, which were probably struck at Caesarea (pl. IV, 7), as well as those bronze coins minted in the vicinity of Palestine.[1]

The country was certainly affected by the factors which affected the Roman monetary systems in general at that period, namely: the decline of the intrinsic value of silver coinage; changes in the ratio between copper, silver and gold coinage; and the tremendous inflation. Similarly, new regulations and policies, as well as new denominations, (for example, the introduction of the *Antoninianus*, pl. V, 8, by Caracalla) left their mark on the numismatic history of Palestine.

THE CURRENCY OF PALESTINE IN THE LATE ROMAN AND BYZANTINE PERIODS

The monetary situation in Palestine in the subsequent period assumed a new aspect, since there were no longer active mints in Palestine and all coins had to be supplied from external sources. The production of coinage was now restricted to a number of official mints – approximately a dozen in the whole of the empire – and the currency in use in Palestine consisted of coins provided by a number of these production centres. Under such circumstances, our main concern here is to enumerate those central minting centres whose coins have been found in Palestine, and to describe the overall monetary and financial situation which existed in Palestine in this particular period.

We cannot here discuss the many changes and reforms which occurred in this period, which runs approximately from Diocletian to the time of the Arab conquest in the seventh century, nor the broader economic history of the era. Instead we must content ourselves with

---

[1] The coins in circulation in Palestine during the period under disussion are illustrated by H. Hamburger in 'A Hoard of Syrian Tetradrachms and Tyrian Bronze Coins from Gush Halav', *IEJ*, 4 (1954), 201–26, with additional references.

the brief note that the supply of coins in this period was copious, and finds indicate that coins from various imperial mints were in circulation. The influx of coins into the region came through trade, payments to soldiers and administration, and so on. In the later period under the Christian emperors another source was also developed: allocations and donations for building churches and monasteries and the growing traffic of pilgrims to the Holy Land.[1]

According to the available information it seems that in the later Empire (from approximately 250 to 491 C.E.) coins minted in Antioch were the most numerous in Palestine, while in the Byzantine period (491 C.E. to the Arab conquest) the mint at Constantinople (pl. V, 9) became predominant. At the same time, coins from other mints also figure in the findings from this period (mid third century onwards), among them coins minted at Alexandria, Nicomedia, Cyzicus and Thessalonica.

We may conclude this survey by referring to Arabic–Byzantine coins, that is, those coins which in a way served as a link between the Greek coinage of Palestine, which had been used for almost a millennium both in Palestine and in other parts of the Orient, and the new, very different Muslim coinage which was on the verge of coming into being. This change took place only gradually and the Arabic–Byzantine coins (pl. V, 10), a problematic group in themselves, represent the transitional phase from one epoch in Middle Eastern history to another.

[1] Cf. M. Avi-Yonah, *The Jews of Palestine, A Political History from the Bar Kokhba War to the Arab Conquest* (Oxford, 1976), p. 221.

CHAPTER 3

CALENDARS AND CHRONOLOGY

The Babylonian conquest changed both the civil calendar and the reckoning of years in Judea. 2 Kings 25 illustrates this transformation: first there are two datings after the regnal years of Zedekiah, the last Davidic king. But, after the capture of Jerusalem in 587 B.C.E., the events, even the burning of the Temple, are dated after the regnal years of Nebuchadnezzar. From 586 on, the Jewish computation of years consistently followed the succession of gentile overlords of the chosen people: 'In the second year of Darius the king' (Hag. 1: 1), 'in the second year of Nero Caesar'.[1] A Mishnah explicitly stated that a bill of divorcement (and, certainly, other documents) with an irregular dating would lack legal force.[2] Accordingly, the documents from the desert of Judea, drafted under the Roman rule, just as the documents of the same kind written in the province of Arabia, were dated after the regnal years of the Roman emperors. 'The name of the ruler is in the beginning (of a bill of divorcement).'[3]

Under the Hasmoneans, from 134–132 B.C.E. on, and under the Herodians, Jerusalem dated by the year of her own kings, as for instance the coins of Alexander Janneus show.[4] During the two rebellions, that of 66–72 C.E. and that of Bar Kochba, coins and documents bore the dates of the respective freedom eras: 'Freedom of Jerusalem' and similar slogans in the first rebellion (years 1 to 6), and 'Redemption of Israel' *vel simile* under Bar Kochba (years 1 to 3).[5]

The regnal years, however, must differ from the fixed civil years. A

---

[1] *DJD*, 2, 18. Cf. Mekilta on Exod. 19: 1 (2, p. 193, ed. J. Lauterbach).

[2] *m. Git.* 8.5. As such illegitimate reckonings the Mishnah names that 'of the Greek kingdom' (the Seleucid era), that of the 'Median Kingdom' (the Arsacid era), that of the building of the Second Temple and that of its destruction. According to *b.Git.*80b the rule was formulated by R. Meir (*c.* 150 C.E.). *t.Git.*6(8).3 also admits datings by the provincial era and by the Roman consuls. Cf. S. Lieberman, *Tosefta-ki-fshutah*, 8 (New York, 1973), p. 890.

[3] *m. Yad.* 4.8.

[4] J. Naveh, 'The Dated Coins of Alexander Jannaeus', *IEJ*, 18 (1968), 20–6.

[5] Y. Meshorer, *Jewish Coins of the Second Temple Period* (Tel Aviv, 1967), pp. 154–69; E. Koffmann, *Die Doppelurkunden aus der Wueste Juda* (Leiden, 1968), pp. 37–41.

king who ascends the throne on 1 January will hardly lose it on exactly 31 December. As the Babylonians had a fixed civil year, beginning on Nisannu (Nisan) 1, about the time of the spring equinox, they counted the time from the accession of a new monarch to the next Nisan 1 as 'the beginning of the kingship', while the first and the following regnal years coincided with civil years. Two oracles of Jeremiah were spoken in the *reshut mamleket* of Zedekiah, that is, in 597.

Persian administration used the same device. Thus, a papyrus of Samaria bears the date 'year 2' (of Arses) which is also the 'beginning of the kingship' (of Darius III), a date which corresponds to the year 336/335 B.C.E.[1] Alexander the Great and the Ptolemies, when they ruled Palestine in the third century B.C.E., reckoned the regnal years from the day of accession to its return in the Macedonian lunisolar calendar. We do not know the style of reckoning under the Hasmoneans and the Herodians. Under the Roman emperors the period from the accession to the next New Year's day in the local calendar was counted as the first year, even if this period did not last more than a couple of days.[2] It is probable that the Jews used the same reckoning for the years of 'Freedom', during the great rebellions of 66–71 and 131–134 C.E.

From 200 B.C.E. until 143/2, the official reckoning in Jerusalem was that of the Seleucid dynasty, the so-called Seleucid 'era', that is, the continuous numbering of the regnal years of Seleucus I, the founder of the royal line, even after his death. This reckoning had two forms, which may be called the 'Macedonian' and the 'Babylonian' modes. The first, used by the court and by the royal administration as well as by the Greek cities throughout the empire, was reckoned from the early autumn of 312 B.C.E. The other, employed in cuneiform documents and probably by the natives elsewhere, had as its starting point the Babylonian New Year's day (see below p. 63), Nisannu 1 of 311 B.C.E. (= 3 April Julian). This form was also used in Jerusalem. To obtain the Julian year of a date given according to the Seleucid reckoning, the Seleucid figure should be deducted from 313 according to the 'Babylonian' form. Thus the year 150, Seleucid era, is: 313 minus 150 = 163/2 (from autumn to autumn) or 312 minus 150 = 5 April 162 B.C.E. The computation of Seleucid years from the spring of 312 B.C.E., postulated by some modern authors, never existed.

---

[1] F. M. Cross, 'Papyri of the Fourth Century B.C. from Dâliyeh' in *New Directions in Biblical Archaeology*, ed. D. N. Freedman and J. Greenfield (Garden City, 1969), p. 44.

[2] *b. Ros. Has.* 2a; *b. B. Bat.* 164b. Cf. Th. Mommsen, *Roemisches Staatsrecht*, 3rd edn. vol. 2, p. 802; C. B. Welles, *Excavations at Dura-Europos*, Final Report 7, 1 (Yale, 1959), p. 130; J. Goldstein, 'The Syriac Bill of Sale from Dura-Europos', *JNES*, 25 (1969), 1–13.

The obvious convenience of Seleucid reckoning brought about its continuous use in Syria and Babylonia even after the end of the house of Seleucus.[1] R. Papa (died about 375 C.E) presumed that in Babylonia any public scribe would know which was the current year 'of the Greek kingdom'.[2] From Babylonia this computation later became adopted by the whole Oriental Jewry. It was used, for instance, by Maimonides in Egypt. The epoch of this 'era of contracts,' as the Seleucid era became known, was Tishri 1.[3]

As a matter of fact, while the first day of Nisan was the New Year's day 'for kings' and for counting the months, in business contracts the scribes of Roman Jerusalem, following the rhythm of the agricultural year, counted the months from Tishri and not from Nisan.[4] Whether this usage, attested to by Josephus, was also practised after 70 C.E. remains unknown. But the statement of Josephus may help to explain the dating difference between the 'simple' and the 'double' document, a point which was already obscure to the rabbis toward the end of the second century C.E.[5]

The official reckoning of years, of course, did not exclude other computations. Ezekiel dated his oracles by the years 'of our exile', that is, from 597 B.C.E.[6] After the destruction of the second Temple by Titus, some people in Palestine took this event as the commencement of a dating era.[7] The reckoning also appears on some tombstones in Palestine about 370 C.E.[8]

With the Babylonian domination came also the Babylonian calendar and the Babylonian names of the months, first attested in Zech. 1: 7, 'the eleventh month which is the month of Shebat' (Bab. *Sabbatu*).[9] The Babylonian calendar, like the biblical one, was lunisolar, and in both

---

[1] L. Bernhard, 'Zur Chronologie der Syrer', *SAW*, 264,3 (1969).

[2] See the discussions in *b. Abad. Zar.* 9a–10a.

[3] E. Mahler, *Handbuch der juedischen chronologie* (Leipzig, 1916; repr. Hildesheim, 1967), p. 137; E. Frank, *Talmudic and Rabbinical Chronology* (New York, 1956), p. 144. According to *b. Abod. Zar.* 10a, this was the computation of 'gentile kings', that is, of the Sassanids.

[4] *m. Ros. Has.* 1, 1; Josephus, *Ant.* 1. 81.

[5] *b. B. Bat.* 164b. Cf. L. Fischer, 'Die Urkunden im Talmud', *Jahrbuch der Juedisch-Literar. Gesellschaft* 9 (1912), 23; M. R. Lehmann, 'Studies in the Murabbaat and Nahal Hever Documents', *RevQ*, 4 (1963), 57.

[6] K. S. Freddy and R. B. Redford, 'The Dates in Ezekiel', *JAOS*, 90 (1970), 462–85.

[7] Mahler, *Handbuch*, 149–52; Frank, *Chronology*, 37–42; S. Baron, *Social and Religious History of the Jews* (Philadelphia, 1952), p. 116; J. Finegan, *Handbook of Biblical Chronology* (Princeton, N.J., 1964), pp. 123–5.

[8] These inscriptions are reprinted in B. Z. Wacholder, 'The Calendar of Sabbatical Cycles', *HUCA*, 44 (1973), 180.

[9] The Babylonian calendar, of course, was also introduced in other territories of Palestine conquered by the Babylonians. For instance, see the Aramean ostracon in J. Naveh and Y. Aharoni, *Beer-Sheba*, 2 (1973), 79.

calendars the beginning of a month depended on the observation of the new crescent.[1] As the twelve lunar months are shorter by approximately eleven days than the solar year of 365 days, the Babylonian kings from time to time ordered the intercalation of a month to bring the lunar year into agreement with the solar year and thus with the agricultural seasons. By the time of the fall of Jerusalem (587 B.C.E.), the intercalation became more or less regularized.

With some exceptions, a cycle of twelve common and seven leap years harmonized the course of the sun and the lunar years. From about 380 B.C.E. the position of leap years became fixed: a month was intercalated in the years 3, 6, 8, 11, 14, 17 and 19 of every cycle.[2] As 235 lunar months practically equal 19 solar years, the place of the New Year's day, on Nisannu (Nisan) 1, now fluctuated no more than 27 days within a cycle, from 26 March to 22 April Julian. Thanks to the excellence of this calendar we are able to express any date in late Babylonian texts in the terms of the Julian year with the margin of one or two days of possible error. Therefore, we can say that the capture of Jerusalem on Adar 2 of the seventh year of Nebuchadnezzar occurred on (or about) 15 March 597 B.C.E. and that the Temple, desecrated by Antiochus Epiphanes, was re-dedicated by Judas Maccabeus (1 Macc. 5: 52) on or about 7 December 163 B.C.E.

The calendar situation in the Roman province of Judea, before and after the destruction of Jerusalem in 70 C.E. remains obscure. The Jewish civil year continued to run from Nisan to Adar, as coins and documents show.[3] But we do not know whether the traditional names of the months referred to lunisolar units. The Julian solar year became accepted in the whole Roman Levant, often without change in month names. For instance, in Roman Arabia the month Nisan (in Greek Xanthikos) now meant the Julian solar month which ran from 22 March to 20 April.[4] Josephus, in his history of the Jewish war, sometimes used the Tyrian (Julian) calendar. We do not know why.[5]

---

[1] Cf. B. Z. Wacholder and D. B. Weisberger, 'Visibility of the New Moon', HUCA, 42 (1971), 227–42.

[2] R. A. Parker and W. H. Dubberstein, Babylonian Chronology, Brown University Studies 19 (Providence, 1956), p. 3.

[3] B. Kanael, 'Notes on the Dates used during the Bar-Kochba Rebellion', IEJ, 21 (1971), 411.

[4] The Julian (and consular) date in DJD, 2, 115 which disagrees with the lunisolar month date in the same document is probably purely ornamental. Roman soldiers in Palestine (DJD, 2, 114) and the Roman colony Aelia Capitolina naturally followed the Julian calendar. Cf. A. Alt, 'Die Zeitrechnung von Jerusalem im spaeteren Altertum', PJ, 30 (1934), 78.

[5] E. Schürer, Geschichte des juedischen Volkes im Zeitalter Jesu Christi (3rd edn., Leipzig, 1901), vol. 1, pp. 756–8. Mahler, Handbuch, pp. 433–9.

In the Diaspora, the Jews naturally followed the local time reckoning. Thus, a decree of the Jewish community at Berenice (Libya) voted 'at the feast of Booths' was dated Paophi 25, year 55 (of local era, that is, 22 October 25 C.E.). Again, R. Nahman says in Babylonia that 'it is taught' that the era 'of the Greek kings' (the Seleucid era) is to be used in the Exile, namely, in Babylonia.[1]

Besides the civil year, the Jews of course had various other forms of the year, for instance, the tax year, the agricultural year (see above p. 62), or the sabbatical year[2] which, too, ran from autumn to autumn and theoretically was to be observed every seventh year.[3] This year of fallow was naturally better known to the farmers than the regnal years of the far-away emperor. Accordingly, the Jewish criminal court, in cross-examination of the witnesses, asked them to give the date of the delict as the year of the septennial sabbatical period, month and day.[4] But as a chronological unit the sabbatical septennate is not attested to before the second half of the fourth century C.E.[5] Its usage for dating probably imitates the dating by the year of indiction, a tax reassessment period of fifteen years, a fashion which became popular at the beginning of the fourth century C.E.

So far we have written of the civil year. Let us now consider the religious year. It was punctuated by the hallowing of every new month, and its course and length were determined by the date of Passover. It began in Nisan and thus paralleled the civil lunisolar year; but neither its months nor its length were pre-calculated and known in advance.

To begin with the moon, the first sighting of the new crescent signalled the beginning of a new month: 'Blow the trumpet at the new moon' (Ps. 81: 3).[6] Accordingly the priests and, after the destruction of the Temple in 70 C.E., the rabbinic *beth-din*, examined the witnesses who had seen the new moon and, if satisfied, proclaimed the beginning of the new month on the evening of the 29th or 30th of the preceding month. (In the present Jewish calendar the new month begins on the pre-calculated day of mean conjunction.)[7]

[1] E. Gabba, *Iscrizioni greche e latine per lo studio della Bibbia* (Turin, 1958) no. 19 + = J. Also G. Roux, 'Un décret du polyeuma juif de Bérénice', *REG*, 62 (1949), 283; *Abod. Zar.* 10a.

[2] *DJD*, 2, 18; 24 E and 24 F.

[3] Baron, *History*, vol. 2, pp. 116, 376, n. 33. Wacholder, *Calendar*, pp. 153–96; A. Rothkopf, *Encyclopedia Judaica* (New York, 1971), 14, 584.

[4] *m. Sanh.* 5.1.

[5] The inscriptions quoted in n. 8, p. 62.

[6] B. Zuckermann, 'Materialen zur Entwicklung der altjuedischen Zeitrechnung im Talmud', *Jahresbericht des juedisch-theolog. Seminar in Breslau*, 1882, pp. 26–9. S. Gandz, 'Studies in the Hebrew Calendar', *JQR*, 39 (1948–49), 239–80.

[7] Cf. S. Gandz, 'The Astronomy of Maimonides and its Sources', *Archives internationales d'histoire des sciences*, 13 (1950), 839–44.

The decisions of the *beth-din* were discretionary, and days were intercalated as a matter of expediency, for instance to prevent the falling of the Day of Atonement on Friday or Sunday.[1] Witnesses could be coaxed or coerced, or their testimony appreciated according to the astronomical knowledge of the examiners.[2] No wonder that some calendar decisions of the patriarch and his *beth-din* provoked the violent opposition of other sages.[3] It could happen that at the end of Elul people did not know when the new month, and thus the New Year on Tishri 1, would arrive. Yet, the rabbis professed that God Himself was observing the festivals according to the rabbinic calendar.[4]

Further, the main Jewish feasts are tied to agricultural activity. The Passover must be celebrated in the lunation when the barley is in the ear. But the growth of crops depends on climatic conditions, which are not the same every year. Accordingly the authorities of Jerusalem and later the patriarchs from time to time intercalated a month before the Passover month (Nisan), taking into consideration such variables as the ripening of barley or even the fitness of the roads for pilgrims.[5] Therefore, there was no fixed sequence of leap years, and it is futile to try to calculate the date of the Crucifixion on a purely astronomical basis.[6]

The improvised empirical year was unavoidable as long as the Temple stood with its sacrificial service and pilgrimages. After 70 C.E. the tradition, economic interest, and later the power of the patriarchs, who naturally disliked losing the prerogative of fixing the calendar, prevented its reform for almost three centuries.[7]

As to the Diaspora, the great Muslim scholar al-Biruni (*circa* 1000 C.E.) observed that the Jewish religious calendar did not take into account the time-lag between the conjunction in Palestine and in the countries outside the Holy Land.[8] In the absence of telecommunications, the

[1] Zuckermann, 'Zeitrechnung', 45–8.
[2] Zuckermann, 'Zeitrechnung', 52–7; Mahler, *Handbuch*, p. 342.
[3] *m. Ros. Has.* 2.8.
[4] See, for example, *m. Erub.* 3.7. Cf. S. Gandz, 'Studies in the Hebrew Calendar', *JQR*, 40 (1949–50), 261. [5] Zuckerman, 'Zeitrechnung', 39.
[6] Cf., for example, G. Amadon, 'Ancient Jewish Calendation', *JBL*, 70 (1942), 227–80; Finegan, *Biblical Chronology*, pp. 285–98.
[7] L. Finkelstein, *The Pharisees* (Philadelphia, 3rd edition, 1962), pp. 602, 643. The story of disagreement between the leading rabbinic authorities about the order of leap years in the nineteenth year cycle, reported by a medieval author, is unreliable. S. Gandz, 'The Calendar of Seder Olam', *JQR*, 43 (1952–53), 253.
[8] al-Biruni, *The Chronology of the Ancient Nations*, trans. E. Sachau (London, 1879), p. 146. al-Biruni (p. 68) says that the Jews learned to calculate the difference between conjunction and the new crescent and the lunisolar cycles about 200 years after Alexander, that is 200 years after the beginning of the Seleucid era, about 110 B.C.E. How are we to understand this curious tradition?

communities in Babylonia or, say, in Asia Minor could not know, for instance, whether the month Elul in the given year had been declared hollow or full in Palestine. Thus it could happen, to quote an incident related in the Talmud, that the Day of Atonement, Tishri 10, as celebrated in Nehardea on the Euphrates, was already Tishri 11 according to the decision of the calendar court in Galilee.[1] Again, the ripening of barley did not come in Egypt or Babylonia at the same date as in Palestine.

To synchronize the dates of festivals in Jerusalem and in the Diaspora, the authorities of Jerusalem as early as 124 B.C.E. (2 Macc. 1:9) sent messengers to the lands of the Dispersion. Fire signals were also used. Later, probably in the second century,[2] the doubling of every festival day, except the Yom Kippur, was introduced in the Diaspora. In this way, the Diaspora Jew could be reasonably certain that either on the first or on the second day of their feast, their prayers went to heaven in the same time as the supplications in the Holy Land. But, as R. Johanan in the middle of the third century, quoting Ezekiel 20: 24–25, caustically stated, the observance of the second day in the Diaspora was a punishment inflicted on those whose ancestors had profaned the one-day feasts in the Holy Land.[3]

In the course of time, and surely willy-nilly, the Diaspora freed itself from the calendrical tutelage of Palestinian authorities. Even in the Holy Land communities unable to learn in time whether the current month was to be hollow or full simply alternated months of 29 and 30 days. The Tosefta tells us that the practice of the Diaspora was already the same in the second century C.E.[4]

Similarly, communities of the Diaspora sometimes made years leap or ordinary independently of the decisions taken in Palestine. Such prominent sages as R. Hananiah, R. Meir and R. Akiba proclaimed leap years outside the Holy Land.[5] The Babylonian Jewry, of course, was headed by the exilarch appointed by the kings of Persia, and the

---

[1] b. Ros. Has. 21a (about R. Levi). Cf. Zuckermann, 'Zeitrechnung', 45–7.

[2] R. Jose in b. Erub. 39b. Cf. Lieberman, Tosefta-ki-fshutah 3, p. 366. (I owe these references to Professor S. Lieberman.) On the two-day celebration of the New Year on Tishri 1–2 in the Holy Land and in the Diaspora, see Gandz, JQR, 40 (1949–50), 256–63.

[3] pal. Erub. ch. 3 ad finem. (I owe the knowledge of this passage to Professor S. Lieberman.)

[4] t. Arak. 1, 8. Cf. Galenus, Opera 17, 23, ed. Kuhn; quoted in Schürer, Geschichte, vol. 1, p. 750.

[5] Meg. 18b, m. Yebam. 16, 7. On the intercalation by R. Hananiah, see J. Neusner, A History of the Jews in Babylonia, (2nd edn. Leiden, 1969), pp. 125–30. The intercalation outside the Holy Land was illegal and invalid according to the Palestinian view (Mahler, Handbuch, p. 376; Zuckermann, 'Zeitrechnung', 12–13). Yet R. Akiba did it and came back to the patriarch (R. Gamaliel II) without being reprimanded.

patriarchs in Palestine found it expedient to send their calendrical messages to their counterparts in Babylonia. Yet in the Babylonian Diaspora the intercalated month (second Adar) could sometimes have 29 days and sometimes 30 days, though the Palestinian authorities in about 230 C.E. informed the head of the Exile that second Adar should consist of 29 days only.[1] But even within the Roman empire, the order of the calendar of Palestinian authorities could be ignored. Thus, at Antioch from 328 to 342 C.E., Passover was celebrated at full moon in March, and the date of the feast oscillated between 2 March and 30 March. Likewise in Egypt at the beginning of the fourth century, the date of Passover fluctuated between 25 February and 25 March in a common year and between 27 March and 25 April every third year which was a leap year.[2] In Palestine, however, the leap year was declared in order to prevent the full moon of Nisan, on account of the lateness of the spring, from occurring before the spring equinox (21 March). This was the calendar secret communicated by R. Huna b. Abin to the Babylonian Jews.[3]

Again S. Julius Africanus, a well-informed Christian writer, about 230 C.E. stated that 'the Jews and Greeks' used the eight-year cycle with three leap years.[4] In fact, in his time the patriarchs themselves based their choice of leap years on pre-calculation.

At last, allegedly in 358–359 C.E., the Patriarch Hillel II made public the secret of the Passover cycle.[5] It was simply the cycle of the Jewish (that is, of the Babylonian) civil calendar. Thus the present Jewish calendar continues the order of leap years of the late Babylonian calendar (see above, p. 62).

Needless to say, the revelation of the 'secret' failed to establish the unity of the calendar of Israel. The ancestral calendrical customs continued to be followed in Alexandria and probably in other communities.[6] As late as the end of the first millennium C.E., Palestine and Babylonia disagreed about the sequence of leap years.[7]

---

[1] b. Ros. Has. 19b. On the messages sent to the exilarch Mar Uqba see pal. Meg. 1.5(7), p. 71a, and Neusner (History), pp. 29, 132. Professor L. Finkelstein informs me that the passage does not exclude the possibility that similar communications about the calendar could have been sent to other authorities in Babylonia.

[2] Ed. Schwartz, 'Christliche und Juedische Ostertafeln', Abhandlungen d. Goettingen Gesellschaft d. Wissenschaften, N.F.8, 1905, 122–5.

[3] b. Abod. Zar. 9b. Cf. the passages quoted in Schürer, Geschichte, vol. 1, p. 753.

[4] Eusebius, Dem.ev. 8, 2, p. 377, ed. I. Heikel; according to Schürer, Geschichte, vol. 1, p. 751, n. 13; Mahler, Handbuch, pp. 441–8.

[5] Mahler, Handbuch, p. 461.

[6] Mahler, Handbuch, pp. 455–6.

[7] al-Biruni, according to S. Poznanski, ERE, 3, 122. Cf. Baron, History, vol. 8, pp. 202–21; Z. Ankori, Karaites in Byzantium (New York, 1959), index, s.v. calendar.

Some split groups, such as the Dead Sea sectarians in the first century
C.E. and the Mihawites in the twelfth century,[1] frustrated by the
uncertainty of the official religious calendar, based their time-reckoning
on the Sabbath, the only holy day that remained independent of the
whimsy of calendar makers.[2] They abandoned the lunisolar calendar
altogether for a schematic year of 52 weeks, 12 months (8 of 30 and
4 of 31 days) and 364 days. In this system all feasts always kept their
place in the course of years and were always celebrated on the same
weekday. The idea for this calendar went back to the author of an
astronomical, or according to our view a pseudo-astronomical, work
which was later included in the Ethiopic Book of Enoch.[3]

We can here end our survey. We considered chronology and
calendars; yet we were unable to refer to any absolute date given in the
terms of Jewish reckoning. To have any absolute date, we must use
Persian, Greek or Roman chronology. For instance, the Julian date cited
for the publication of the standard calendar 'translated' the date 670
of the Seleucid era, which is transmitted by Hai Gaon (died in 1038 C.E.).
Why did not the Jews use their own reckoning? The author of Jubilees,
writing about 200 B.C.E., compiled a biblical chronology based on
Jubilee and sabbatical year periods. We learn from him, for instance,
that Jacob and Esau were born in the year (corresponding to) 2046 after
the Creation. The era from the destruction of the second Temple was
already used by some people in the second century C.E. (see above, p.
62).

Yet the whole rabbinic tradition, including the chronological work
Seder Olam, offers only relative indications of time: 'The Temple was
restored 70 years after its destruction and was destroyed again 420 years
after its rebuilding'; 'Rome began to rule over Israel 180 years before
the destruction of the Temple'; 'the confusion of languages took place
340 years after the Flood'. The only absolute date which is given in
Talmudic tradition comes from messianic calculations and refers to a
future event: the messianic woes shall begin in the year 4231 after the
creation of the world.[4]

---

[1] Ankori, *Karaites*, p. 377.
[2] Cf. Mekilta III, p. 203, ed. J. Lauterbach.
[3] O. Neugebauer, 'Notes on Ethiopic Astronomy', *Or*, 33 (1964), 58–61. The
newly-published scraps of Aramaic mss. of the 'astronomical' work of Enoch show,
however, that 'Enoch' suggested a lunisolar (synchronized) calendar: J-T. Milik, *The
Books of Enoch* (Oxford, 1976), pp. 274–97. This idea differs from the calendar in
Ethiopic Enoch and disagrees with the thesis of Jubilees (6: 36) that the moon
disturbs the times and seasons. The problem of 'Enochic' calendars and of the
calendary practice of the Dead Sea Scrolls sectarians now requires a fresh
investigation.
[4] *Abod. Zar.* 9b. (I owe the explanation of this passage to Professor S. Lieberman.)

But let us not marvel at the rabbinic mentality. The New Testament offers no absolute date for Jesus' life and the activity of his disciples. Again, Plato never gives a chronological reference, though he tells us twice that Socrates died on the day when an Athenian festival ship returned from Delos. (We know the year of Socrates' death from a later Greek chronicler.) In the same way, the Talmud and the New Testament abound in relative datings: when Festus came into his province; when R. Dimi came (from Palestine to Babylonia); Akiba intercalated three years at once when he was imprisoned; R. Hanina was nephew of R. Jose. Such relative datings enabled Maimonides to establish the succession of the sages of the Talmud.

Why this unhistorical attitude? The plain fact is that it corresponds to our inward awareness of time, which is selective and for this reason relative. As Plotinus saw, time, psychologically speaking, is correlated to successive activities of our soul. That is, as Augustine says, when we measure time, we measure the impressions which things as they pass make on our memory. Seneca complains that the Roman ladies of his time counted the years by their successive husbands and not by the annual consuls. But he himself in his *Moral Essays* mentions consuls but not consulates and gives no chronological references. In fact, the relative indications of time in Seneca or in the Talmud are parts of the reported events. The voyage of the Athenian ship referred to by Plato delayed the execution of Socrates; the coming of Diocletian to Tyre, reported by the Talmud, was a fact necessary to introduce a legal precedent established on this occasion by R. Hiya b. Abba. Accordingly Eunapius, a Greek author who wrote about 410 C.E., emphatically denied the value of chronology in the appreciation of Socrates' wisdom or of Themistocles' shrewdness.

The absolute chronology which disposes events on the same time-scale, independently of their magnitude, is an artifice of the historian. He needs this scaffold since he is not a doer but a reconstructor of history.

THE PERSIAN PERIOD

THE PERSIAN EMPIRE AND THE POLITICAL AND SOCIAL HISTORY OF PALESTINE IN THE PERSIAN PERIOD

OUTLINE OF HISTORY

When in 539 B.C.E. Babylon fell to Cyrus, the Achemenid king of Persia (559–530 B.C.E.), Persia was raised to the position of a world empire, which encompassed the whole Near East. In contrast to the Assyrians and Babylonians, however, who had based their rule on large-scale deportations of peoples and a reign of fear, Cyrus from the outset adopted a much more lenient policy, which included resettling exiles in their homelands, reconstructing their temples, and in general presenting himself to the conquered as a liberator. This policy gained him the goodwill of almost the entire ancient world.

Within the framework of this policy, Cyrus issued a proclamation to the Jewish exiles in Babylon, urging them to return to Jerusalem and rebuild their Temple there. The first Jews to return from Babylon, headed by Sheshbazzar 'the prince of Judah' (apparently Shenazzar, the son of Jehoiachin, the former king of Judah), encountered numerous difficulties in their attempt to re-establish the national and religious centre of the Jewish people. On their arrival, they found on the outskirts of the destroyed city a small community of the Am ha-Ares, the descendants of the poor, who after the destruction of the first Temple, had continued to dwell in the almost desolate land. This remnant and their neighbours, the Samaritans, Ashdodites, Edomites and Arabs, did not view the repatriates with favour, and used all means in their power to obstruct them, until they finally succeeded in putting an end to the building activities in Jerusalem.

Throughout this period, Cyrus was engaged in military expeditions in order to consolidate the borders of the new empire. He fell in battle in 530 B.C.E. in the area east of the Caspian sea.

Cyrus was succeeded by his son Cambyses II (530–522 B.C.E.), whose chief accomplishment was the conquest of Egypt and its annexation into

70

the Achemenid kingdom in 525 B.C.E. He gathered his troops in Akko (Strabo, XVI.2.25; Diodorus Siculus, XV.41.3) and achieved victory through the help of Arabian–Qedarite tribes who supplied the Persian army with water during their advance across the Sinai desert. In the spring of 522 B.C.E., when Cambyses was still in Egypt, a revolt broke out in Persia. The king set out to suppress it, but died on the way home. In the course of Cambyses' reign, the condition of the Jewish community in Palestine underwent no changes.

The death of Cambyses was followed by a series of revolts in Persia and a power struggle for the throne, which was finally won by Darius I (522–486 B.C.E.), also a member of the Achemenid royal family. His assumption of the kingship set off widespread rebellions throughout the vast empire. The first uprising took place in Elam and was swiftly put down. Another rebellion broke out in Babylon, led by Nebuchadnezzar III, the son of Nabonidus, the last of the Babylonian kings. Darius quelled this rebellion as well, and by 519 B.C.E. he seems to have pacified the entire kingdom, strengthened his rule, and even extended his empire to hitherto unknown frontiers by annexing parts of India and eastern Europe. During the rest of his reign, he waged wars mainly on the western border, in Anatolia and Greece. In 512 B.C.E. he crossed the Bosphorus and conquered Thrace and, according to Herodotus, he also engaged the Scythians in battle at the mouth of the Danube.

Of major importance for the future of the Persian empire was the rebellion of the Greek cities of Anatolia and Cyprus in 499 B.C.E. Although it was put down harshly, it brought about a major confrontation between the Persians and the Athenians. The hostilities continued over a long period of time and ended in the complete routing of the Persian army at the battle of Marathon in 490 B.C.E. This was the Persians' first serious defeat. According to Herodotus, Darius intended to wage a further war against Greece, but in 486 B.C.E. an uprising led by Khabasha took place in Egypt, and Darius died during the preparations for a campaign against the Egyptians.

The main accomplishments of Darius were in the realm of imperial administration. He consolidated the empire, which during his lifetime reached the largest extent ever attained by any empire in the Near East. He organized it into twenty satrapies, and in order to maintain efficient control over even the remotest governors in the realm he developed a new and sophisticated road and postal system. He also exercised control over the activities of the governors and took the Persian armies out of their jurisdiction. Darius carried out a reform of the laws in the different satrapies, initiated a new system of tax collection and also an efficient administrative organization. His name is also connected with the new imperial system of coinage – the daric. The king also devoted much effort to large-scale building projects. The main palaces in the capitals of the empire are attributed to his reign.

In the early days of Darius' reign, there was a steady increase in the stream of people returning to Palestine from the Babylonian exile. Some historians consider that one of the reasons for the great numbers of returning exiles was the great turmoil in Babylon caused by the revolts of Nebuchadnezzar III (522 B.C.E.) and Nebuchadnezzar IV (521 B.C.E.), which were suppressed with great cruelty, and by the economic crisis which followed in their wake. The repatriates may also have been encouraged by Darius' new imperial organization. It can be assumed that Judah was made an independent 'state' (*mᵉdînâh*) for the short period during which Zerubbabel, the son of Shealtiel and the grandson of Jehoachin, served as governor (*peḥah*) of the province by Darius' appointment. In any event, the Bible records that 42,360 persons returned to Judah from Babylon in those days. They included a large number of priests, headed by Jeshua, son of Jozadak, high priest of the house of Zadok. Darius ordered that all obstacles placed in the way of the returning exiles by the enemies of Judah be removed. The king reaffirmed Cyrus' edict in a letter to Tattenai, the governor of the Abar Nahara (Beyond the River) satrapy. In the second year of Darius' reign, Zerubbabel began to rebuild the Temple with the support of the prophets Haggai and Zechariah. Zerubbabel developed commercial relations with the Phoenicians, who supplied him – as they had Solomon – with cedars of Lebanon for the construction of the Temple, through the port of Jaffa.

For some unknown reason, perhaps because Darius suspected that Zerubbabel was plotting an uprising, the governor – the last of the Davidic line – disappeared suddenly only a short time after construction work began. How the Jewish community was governed thereafter is unknown. N. Avigad may be correct in suggesting that Zerubbabel was replaced by other Jewish governors.[1] In the opinion of the present writer, however, the province may have been ruled by Persian governors from their seat in Samaria (see below, p. 80). A third possibility is that the leadership of the community passed to the priests and the landed oligarchy. By 515 B.C.E., nevertheless, the reconstruction of the Temple was completed and Jerusalem again assumed its position as the Holy City.

In 486 B.C.E., the year of the death of Darius I and the accession to the throne of his son and heir Xerxes I (486–465 B.C.E.), another revolt

[1] N. Avigad, 'Bullae and Seals from a Post Exilic Judean Archive', *Qedem*, 4 (Jerusalem, 1976).

broke out in Egypt headed by Khabasha (see above). This revolt was crushed in 483 B.C.E. only with difficulty and after heavy fighting. Some authorities believe that the letter of 'accusation against the inhabitants of Judah and Jerusalem' (Ezra 4: 6) was written at this time, and that it was in some way connected with the Egyptian insurrection. At the end of the same year, another revolt broke out in Babylon in which the satrap of Babylon and the Abar Nahara (Beyond the River) satrapies, Zopyrus, was killed. Xerxes suppressed the rebellion cruelly and severely punished the king and the population. Babylon henceforth was separated from the Abar Nahara satrapy and the latter appears as an independent unit (see below, p. 78).

In 480 B.C.E., Xerxes undertook an expedition against the Greeks and suffered major defeats in the famous battles of Salamis and Mycale. The Greek campaign ended when the Persian fleet was totally destroyed in the battle of Eurymedon, and the Persians were evidently driven out of the area of the Aegean sea.

After his defeat, Xerxes retired to his palace, and several years later he was murdered by his vizier Artabanus, who sided with Xerxes' son, Artaxerxes I Longimanus (465/4 – 424/3 B.C.E.), in his bid for the throne. As a result, the Egyptians again rose in rebellion, this time led by Inaros, the son of Psammetichus, and aided by an Athenian fleet. Only after a prolonged effort were Megabyzus, satrap of Abar Nahara, and Arsames, satrap of Egypt, able to crush the rebellion (455 B.C.E.). They also destroyed the Athenian fleet which had unsuccessfully laid siege to Kition and Salamis in Cyprus. In 448 B.C.E., Megabyzus himself rebelled against the Persian king with the support of his two sons, Zopyrus and Artyphius. Although Megabyzus later expressed regret for his action, he was nevertheless driven from his post.

In Judah, a period of expansion and population growth characterized the time from the death of Darius I to that of Artaxerxes I. At the same time, owing to the lack of a strong leadership, the national and religious laws were no longer observed: intermarriage undermined the religious and national uniqueness of the Jewish community, and the farmers were harshly oppressed by the landed oligarchy.

Conditions changed when Artaxerxes attained the throne. A new wave of Jews from Babylon left to resettle in Palestine, this time headed by a strong religious and political leadership. According to the Bible, Ezra the priest and scribe came from Babylon in the seventh year of the reign of Artaxerxes (458 B.C.E.), who had appointed him to repair the Temple and to establish the laws of the Torah as the religious and social authority of the Jewish community. His plans collapsed, however, when confronted with the problem of intermarriage and the enmity of

the local Jews and their neighbours. Lacking political power, he failed
to achieve his aims.

Some time later, Artaxerxes accepted the appeal of a court official,
Nehemiah, the son of Hacaliah, and appointed him governor of
Jerusalem. Despite the hostility of Judah's neighbours, Nehemiah
immediately undertook the rebuilding of the walls of the city (which
were probably destroyed in the revolt of Megabyzus). He also
strengthened the town by increasing its population. He enacted new
social and economic laws beneficial to the priests and the oppressed
farmers, who had suffered both from the former governors as well as
from the Jewish landlords. In the religious sphere, Nehemiah and Ezra
forbade further acts of intermarriage, and strengthened the observance
of the Sabbath.

It appears that Nehemiah at this time also re-established the 'state
of Judah' (*yᵉhŵd mᵉdîntha*') as an independent political unit after a long
period – since the days of Zerubbabel – in which the province had been
ruled by the governors of Samaria (see below, p. 82).

By these actions Ezra and Nehemiah laid the foundation for the future
way of life of the Jewish people. However, they also provoked the final
division between the Jews and the Samaritans, the latter abandoning
the centre at Jerusalem and establishing a separate temple on mount
Gerizim.

Thereafter the Bible and other Jewish sources make almost no
mention of the Jewish province, and only Greek sources and archeological finds throw light on its history. The history of the Persian empire
is also known largely from the Greek writers in their descriptions of
the Persian–Greek wars, whereas the Persian and Babylonian sources
are scarce.

On the death of Artaxerxes I, a crisis arose within the empire which
ended when Darius II seized the throne (423–404 B.C.E.). During his
reign new revolts erupted in Media, Anatolia and Syria. The satrap of
Egypt, Arsames, was sent to pacify these regions, but during his absence
from Egypt serious disturbances broke out there as well. From this
period there are two extant letters from the year 408 B.C.E., which were
sent by Jewish mercenaries in the Persian–Jewish garrison at
Elephantine (Yeb).[1] They wrote to Bagohi, governor of Judah, and to
Delaiah and Shelemaiah, the sons of Sanballat, governor of Samaria, to
complain of the destruction of their temple by the Egyptian rebels. From
this time there is also evidence of a similar military colony of Qedorite

[1] A. Cowley, *Aramaic Papyri of the Fifth Century B.C.* (Oxford, 1923), pp. 108–22, nos.
30–1.

Arabs at Tell el-Maskhuta in the area of the eastern delta. At this site an inscription was found of the 'Qainu Bar Geshem, King of Qedar',[1] that is, the son of Geshem the Arabian, one of Nehemiah's rivals (see below, p. 89).

The Persians met with success when the satraps Tissaphernes and Pharnabazus and Darius' younger son Cyrus gave assistance to the victorious Spartans against Athens during the Peloponnesian war.

Artaxerxes II Memnon (404–358 B.C.E.) succeeded to the throne after the death of Darius II. His rule was challenged by his younger brother, Cyrus, who raised an army and marched to Babylon. There they met in battle at Cunaxa, and Cyrus was killed. This war is described vividly in the *Anabasis* of the Athenian writer Xenophon.

During the reign of Artaxerxes II, the process of the disintegration of the Persian empire began. During the war between the two brothers, the Egyptians again rose in rebellion, headed by Pharaoh Amyrteus (404–399 B.C.E.) of the twenty-eighth dynasty from Sais. This time they succeeded in throwing off the Persian yoke for some 60 years (until 343 B.C.E.). During their revolt the Egyptians destroyed the Jewish–Persian military colony at Elephantine and the Arab colony at Tell el-Maskhuta.

Shortly after their successful rebellion, the Egyptians set out on an expedition against the Persians. The route of their campaign was through the Sinai desert and the coastal plain of Palestine. It appears that they gradually occupied this territory. At Gezer a stamp impression and a broken stone tablet bearing the name of Pharaoh Nepherites I (399–393 B.C.E.) were found,[2] the last king mentioned in the Elephantine records and the first king of the twenty-ninth dynasty from Mendes. This inscription indicates that Nepherites conquered at least the southern part of the Palestinian coastal region. His advance was apparently made possible by the war between the two brothers, which continued until 396 B.C.E. Nepherites' successor Pharaoh Achoris formed alliances with the Cypriot king of Salamis, Evagoras I, and with the Athenians. They seized the northern part of the coastal plain of Palestine and for a brief period also held Tyre and Sidon. Two inscriptions of Achoris have been discovered, one at Akko and one at Sidon.[3]

In 385 B.C.E. when Abrocamus was the satrap of Abar Nahara, peace

---

[1] I. Rabinowitz, 'Aramaic Inscriptions of the Fifth Century B.C.E. from a North-Arab Shrine in Egypt', *JNES*, 15 (1956), 1–9.

[2] R. A. S. Macalister, *The Excavation of Gezer* (London, 1912), vol. II, p. 313, fig. 452.

[3] A. Rowe, *A Catalogue of Egyptian Scarabs in the Palestine Archaeological Museum* (Cairo, 1936), p. 295; pl. XXXVIII; W. V. Landau, 'Die Inschrift von Achoris, König von Ägypten', *MVAG*, 9 (1904), 342–7, pl. XII.

was concluded with Athens and the Athenians withdrew their armies. Abrocamus joined forces with the satraps Pharnabazus and Tithraustes and together they expelled the Egyptians and Cypriots from Phoenicia and Palestine. By 380 B.C.E. they had completed this task.

One year later Pharnabazus, satrap of Cilicia, began mustering mercenaries in Akko for a fresh attack on Egypt. By 375 B.C.E. he had assembled 300 ships and about 12,000 Greek mercenaries and a large number of native soldiers. But even before it engaged in its first battle, logistic problems and disease had decimated the force and it was thoroughly routed by the Egyptians (Isaeus *Nicostrat*, 7).

From 366 to 360 B.C.E. the whole of the Persian Empire was endangered by what is generally known as the 'revolt of the satraps'. In 360 B.C.E. when Pharaoh Tachos came to the throne, he assembled a large Egyptian army, as well as Greek mercenaries, and renewed the Egyptian occupation of the coastal plain of Palestine and Phoenicia. During this campaign the Egyptians were actually assisted by the Phoenicians. As Tachos was marching to join the revolting satraps, his own nephew Nekht-har-hebi rebelled against him in the camp and Tachos was forced to surrender to the crown prince Artaxerxes III at his headquarters in Sidon. After a short time, Nekht-har-hebi himself was forced to return to Egypt because of an internal crisis and Persian rule was gradually restored to Abar Nahara as one by one the rebels were captured or surrendered.

In 358 Artaxerxes died and the throne was inherited by Artaxerxes III Ochus (who reigned until 336). After succeeding in putting down the satraps' revolt, the new king set out to conquer Egypt. After a full year of hard fighting (351–350), he abandoned the attempt. This failure was the signal for the rebellion of the towns of Phoenicia led by Tennes, king of Sidon, with the aid of Pharaoh Nectanebo II (359–343 B.C.E.). The uprising encompassed a large area and caused turmoil in the empire in the west. Belsys and Mazeus, the satraps of Abar Nahara and Cilicia respectively, tried in vain to reconquer the Phoenician towns (Diodorus Siculus, xvi.40–6).

At the beginning of 345 B.C.E., Artaxerxes himself assembled a huge army in Babylon and marched against Sidon. The inhabitants of the town made preparations for a lengthy siege but their leaders betrayed them to the enemy and the whole town was razed to the ground (Diodorus, xvi.45.1–9). The Persians then directed the satrap Bagoas to continue the pursuit into Egypt itself. In 343 Bagoas finally succeeded in restoring Egypt to the Persian yoke. Shortly after the end of the Phoenician revolt, Mazeus was appointed satrap of Abar Nahara, a post he held until the satrapy was conquered in 332 by Alexander the Great.

Did Judah take part in the revolt of the Phoenician cities? According to Eusebius (*Chronicon*, ann. Abr. 1657, ed. Schoene, p. 112) and Josephus Flavius (*Contra Apionem*, 11.134), there was a rebellion in this province in the days of Artaxerxes III, and in a punitive action many Jews were exiled to Hyrcania on the coast of the Caspian sea. A reference to the destruction of Jericho should perhaps also be attributed to this period. Some historians believe that an extensive wave of destruction swept through the whole of Palestine.[1] Others see a connection with the story related in the book of Judith. But, in the opinion of the present writer, recent archeological discoveries (see also chapter 5) indicate that the main Palestinian towns were only destroyed some years later by Alexander and his successors.[2]

In 338 B.C.E. the satrap Bagoas, the conquerer of Egypt, poisoned Artaxerxes III. The brief reign of Arses (337–336) ensued, followed by Darius III Kodomanus, the last king of the Achemenid dynasty (336–330). Darius was defeated by Alexander at the battle of Issus and fled to the eastern part of his realm, where he was killed. The whole of the Persian empire was annexed to Alexander's kingdom.

In Phoenicia and Palestine Alexander met fierce resistance at Tyre and Gaza before continuing to Egypt. Later, in the year 332, he also had to put down a Samaritan rebellion, traces of which have been found recently.

As was mentioned above, there are almost no literary references to Judah and Samaria in the fourth century B.C.E. (apart from the possible allusion to a revolt in the days of Artaxerxes III). It can nevertheless be assumed, judging from the fact that all the governors of Samaria belonged to the same family, as is revealed by new records found at wadi Daliyeh, that these provinces did not suffer damage in the continuous warfare that took place in the coastal plain throughout the century. It is even possible that these provinces took no part in them whatsoever.[3]

---

[1] D. Barag, 'The Effects of the Tennes Rebellion on Palestine', *BASOR*, 183 (1966), 6–12.

[2] E. Stern, *The Material Culture of the Land of the Bible in the Persian Period, 538–332 B.C.E.* (Jerusalem, 1973), pp. 250–1 (in Hebrew).

[3] F. M. Cross, 'The Papyri and their Historical Implications', in P. W. Lapp and N. L. Lapp, *Discoveries in the Wadi ed Dâliyeh*, *AASOR* (Cambridge, Mass.) 41 (1974), pp. 17–29.

THE SATRAPY OF ABAR NAHARA AND THE PLACE OF PALESTINE IN THE POLITICAL ORGANIZATION OF THE PERSIAN EMPIRE

During the Persian period Palestine was included in the territory of the satrapy of Abar Nahara (Ezra 4: 10, 11, 16, 17, 20; 8: 36; Nehemiah 2: 7, 9), a term derived from the Assyrian administration (*ebir-Nâri*), established in the days of Esarhaddon or even much earlier (compare 1 Kings 4: 24). Pseudo-Scylax refers to the area as Coele-Syria, which is a translation of the Aramaic term *kol-Swryya'*, an early name for the interior of Syria. Although the borders of the satrapy paralleled those of the Assyrian period on the whole, they underwent a number of changes in the Persian period until they became fixed.

In the days of Cyrus the whole area captured from the Babylonians (including Babylon itself) and the region of Abar Nahara were united into a single satrapy ruled by the satrap Gobryas. At the beginning of the reign of Darius I, the Persian satrapial administration underwent a thorough reorganization and, according to Herodotus (III.88–95), the empire was divided into twenty satrapies. Babylon was separated from Abar Nahara and was combined with Assyria into one satrapy (the ninth), whereas Abar Nahara (the fifth satrapy) included Syria, Phoenicia, and Cyprus (Herodotus, III.91). This division is not confirmed in documents known from the time of Darius I. In three of his extant inscriptions (at Behistun, Naqsh i-Rustam and Persepolis), which list the satrapies established by him, the satrapy of Abar Nahara does not appear. In the Behistun inscription the order of the satrapies is as follows: 3 Babylon, 4 Assyria, 5 Arabia, 6 Egypt. This order is repeated in the Naqsh i-Rustam inscription (nos. 15–18), whereas the list at Persepolis reads: 3 Babylon, 4 Arabia, 5 Assyria, 6 Egypt. It can therefore be assumed that in the days of Darius I the Abar Nahara satrapy was still included in the larger unit of 'Babylon' and the list of satrapies as recorded by Herodotus, although attributed to Darius I, dates from a somewhat later period, probably from the reign of Xerxes I (486–465 B.C.E.), since Babylon was separated from Abar Nahara only in 482 after the town's revolt and destruction (see above, p. 73). In any event, it is certain that when Ezra and Nehemiah arrived in Judah (*circa* 450), the Abar Nahara satrapy already existed. It can be assumed that these changes in the satrapy were not the last ones. In 400 B.C.E., when Egypt succeeded in freeing itself from Persian rule and the satrapy of Egypt became an independent kingdom, there were further changes as the Egyptian army moved inside the territory of Palestine and Phoenicia. Furthermore, some of the coins of the last satrap of this region, Mazeus, are inscribed with his title: 'Who is over the country Beyond the River and Cilicia.'[1] The coastal region of Cilicia (that is, the southern coastal region of Anatolia) seems to have been incorporated in this satrapy at the end of the Persian period. One of the main problems is that almost all the contemporary sources which deal with the boundaries of the satrapy mention only places along the coast and completely lack a description of the eastern borders. According to Herodotus (III.91), its northern border was at Poseideion which can be identified with al-Mina at the mouth of the Orontes or with the promontory of Basit some 25 kilometres farther to the south;[2] and its southern border was located at lake Sirbonis (Bardawil lake), near mount Casius (Herodotus, II.6; III.5).[3]

Pseudo-Scylax, who seems to be about a hundred years later (circa 350 B.C.E.) designates the boundaries of the satrapy in terms of 'stadia' from Tapsahos in the north to the city of Ashkelon in the south. Galling was of the opinion that Tapsahos should be located somewhere in the Orontes region, since he assumed that Scylax listed only settlements along the coast. But the analogy with 1 Kings 4: 24 is all too clear and in both cases the settlement in question is apparently to be located near the Euphrates. In any case, it seems strange that its southern boundary ends at Ashkelon and not at lake Sirbonis, as in the days of Herodotus. It is probable that Scylax omits the whole area under Arabian rule.

The vicissitudes on the borders and in the organization of the fifth satrapy have an important bearing on the history of the state of Judah. If within so brief a period so many major changes occurred in the overall organization of the large satrapy, in the smaller subdivisions of the satrapy there must have been almost continuous adjustments in the government and in the make-up of the territories, and at times even more basic changes. It is generally accepted that at the time of the Persian conquest of Palestine, the country was already divided into designated political units which had been formed in the Assyrian and Babylonian periods. Among the units inherited by the Persians two were of special importance: Judah and Samaria. Proof of their existence is provided in the Bible where Sheshbazzar is called 'the prince of Judah' and Zerubbabel is referred to as 'the governor of Judah', the title used later by Nehemiah. And, as was already stated, a letter from Elephantine mentions a governor of Judah called Bagohi who governed after

---

[1] G. A. Cooke, *A Text-book of North-Semitic Inscriptions* (Oxford, 1903), p. 346.

[2] P. J. Riis, *Sukas I, The North-East Sanctuary and the First Settling of Greeks in Syria and Palestine* (Copenhagen, 1970), pp. 137–8.

[3] M. Dothan, 'An Archaeological Survey of Mt. Casius and its Vicinity', *Eretz-Israel*, 9 (1969), 47–54 (in Hebrew).

Nehemiah. A group of coins from the end of the Persian period found at Beth-Zur and Tell Jemmeh bear the legend: 'Jehezekiah the governor'.[1] It has also been suggested by Y. Aharoni, J. M. Grinz, Y. Kutscher, and later by N. Avigad that the private names found on the *Yehud* stamp-impressions should also be interpreted as names of Jewish governors of the fifth and fourth centuries B.C.E.[2]

That Samaria was an independent political unit is also beyond question. Although Sanballat the Horonite, one of Nehemiah's rivals, is not designated as a governor, the newly-discovered papyri from the wadi Daliyeh cave included a *bulla* inscribed with the name Sanballat (which belonged to a descendant of the original Sanballat of Nehemiah's time) with his full title: '...iahu son of [San]ballat, governor of Samaria.'[3]

If, as we have seen, the existence of the states of Judah and Samaria during the Persian period is certain, how then was the rest of Palestine organized? M. Avi-Yonah[4] suggested that Palestine was divided into three types of political entities: (1) national 'states', that is, units whose borders coincide with the various ethnic elements dwelling in the country, such as Judah and Samaria, Megiddo, Ashdod, and the Edomite province around Hebron as well as Ammon and Moab; (2) the Phoenician commercial cities along the coast; and (3) the tribal system of the Arabs. Avi-Yonah was of the opinion that Akko and Gaza were ruled directly by the Persians.

It appears that the Arab settlement was basically tribal, while that of the Phoenicians was urban. Nevertheless it is difficult, from the standpoint of the Persian satrapal organization, to accept Avi-Yonah's proposal that 'free Phoenician cities' existed in Palestine, which were under self rule. The king of Sidon, for example, was himself known to be governed directly by a resident Persian satrap (Diodorus, XVI.41: 5: his palace was excavated and was found to be built in a pure Achemenid style)[5] who had his own Persian garrison troops. If the king of Sidon was under direct Persian control, the entire concept that the coastal cities

[1] L. Y. Rahmani, 'Silver Coins of the Fourth Century B.C.E. from Tel Gamma', *IEJ*, 21 (1971), 158–60.

[2] Y. Aharoni, *Excavations at Ramat Raḥel (1959–1960)* (Rome, 1962), pp. 56–9; E. Y. Kutscher, '"PHW" and its Cognants', *Tarbiẓ*, 30 (1960–61), 112ff (in Hebrew); Avigad, *Qedem*, 4 (1976).

[3] F. M. Cross, (*AASOR*, 41 (1974), Pl. 61).

[4] M. Avi-Yonah, *The Holy Land From the Persian Period to the Arab Conquest* (Grand Rapids, 1966), ch. 1.

[5] C. H. Clermont-Ganneau, 'Le Paradeisos royal Achéménide de Sidon', *RB*, 30 (1921), 106–9; G. Contenau, 'Sculptures provenant de la ville', *Syria*, 4 (1923), 276–8.

in Palestine enjoyed political independence under the supervision of the king becomes doubtful. However, it does seem as though these cities did possess commercial freedom. Moreover, in another contemporary source, that of Eshmunazar II, king of Sidon, in the late sixth or early fifth century B.C.E., the region indicated coincides perfectly with the boundaries of the Assyrian–Persian province of Dor.[1]

The same seems to have been the case in the southern region of Palestine, the area personified in the Bible by 'Geshem the Arabian'. In recent excavations a number of military fortresses have been unearthed, for example, at Tell Jemmeh, Tell el-Fara' (south), Beersheba, Arad, Kadesh-Barnea, and Tell el-Kheleifeh. Ostraca found at some of these sites indicate the presence of garrison troops. Two ostraca from Arad even designate the unit by name, 'degel' (standard), which is the name of a Persian military unit also mentioned in the Elephantine papyri.[2] In the opinion of the present writer, this entire area was under the direct rule of a Persian governor, assisted perhaps by Arab soldiers.

In summary, Palestine in the Persian period was apparently organized into a number of provinces or 'states' ($m^e dinôth$). Each unit was ruled by a dynasty of governors, generally of a local family: Samaritans in Samaria (according to the wadi Daliyeh papyri) and Arabs in the south (according to the Tell el-Maskhuta inscriptions), and possibly also in Judah (as is suggested by stamp impressions, *bullae*, and coins of Jehezekiah). These governors had small courts, imitating those of the satraps, and they stood at the head of small administrative organizations. One of the titles of their officials is also preserved in the Bible (Neh. 5 : 17) and in the Daliyeh papyri: *seganim*. They were probably in charge of small military garrisons and were allowed to keep official stamps of the 'state' in their possession, one of the most frequent finds of that period at sites excavated in the province. The governors also seem to have been permitted to strike the small silver coins, which are now known as 'Palestinian' coins.[3] Thus far the inscriptions of four of the provinces are clearly legible: Samaria, Judah, Ashdod, and Gaza. The provinces were subdivided into 'parts' (*pelek*; Neh. 3 : 9, 17).

---

[1] Cooke, *North-Semitic Inscriptions*, pp. 30–40.

[2] B. Porten, *Archives from Elephantine* (Berkeley and Los Angeles, 1968), pp. 28–35; J. Naveh, 'The Aramaic Ostraca from Tel Arad', in Y. Aharoni, *Arad Inscriptions* (Jerusalem, 1975, 32, no. 12; 179 no. 18) (in Hebrew).

[3] E. Babelon, *Les Perses achémenides, les satrapes et les dynasties tributaires de leur empire* (Paris, 1893); G. F. Hill, *Catalogue of the Greek Coins of Palestine* (London, 1914); A. Kindler, 'The Greco-Phoenician Coins struck in Palestine in the times of the Persian Empire', *INJ*, 1 (1963), 2–6; 25–7.

Within this general political organization, the province of Judah did not differ basically from the others in Palestine. It too had a governor and the usual bureaucracy, the right to strike coins, official stamps and so on. Its borders encompassed the area of Jewish settlement.

THE PROVINCE OF JUDAH

When was the province of Judah actually established? We shall not deal here with the problem of the return and resettlement of the Jewish exiles but shall limit this question to the framework of the Persian satrapal organization, namely, when was the independent unit known as the province (or state = $m^e d\hat{\imath}ntha'$) of Judah officially established and recognized? From what time do we possess records of its existence?

Sheshbazzar was at this time already known by the title of 'prince of Judah' (Ezra 1: 8) and Zerubbabel had also apparently been appointed a governor (see above, p. 74). These two descendants of the Davidic dynasty served as governors of the state. There seems to have been an attempt at the time of the first return in the days of Cyrus to re-establish the state of Judah under the royal family. However, from 515 to 445 B.C.E., that is from the first return to the days of Ezra and Nehemiah, there are no written sources testifying to the existence of an independent state in the region. Furthermore, it appears that, on his arrival in Judah, Nehemiah stepped into a political vacuum. There seems to have been no organized rule; there is no mention of a previous governor. It must therefore be concluded that even if there was an effort to restore the Jewish state under the royal family at the beginning of the Persian period, it was short-lived.

The archeological finds from the various excavated sites in the region from the initial stage of the state (515–445 B.C.E.) which are of value for our discussion comprise two groups only. There are two types of stamp impressions which shed light on the nature of the political system. The first group are 'neutral' stamps which bear only place names, for example, the 'Moṣa' stamps.[1] The second group, which is common in the period under discussion only in the area of Judah, is most instructive. It consists of uninscribed stamp impressions, on which various animals – mainly lions – are depicted, as well as pagan emblems such as the Persian 'fire-altar'.[2] A comparison of these impressions with those in use in other Persian satrapies, from Persepolis to Egypt, reveals

[1] N. Avigad, 'New Light on the MṢH Seal Impressions', *IEJ*, 8 (1958), 113–19; N. Avigad, 'Hebrew Inscriptions on Wine Jars', *IEJ*, 22 (1972), 1–9.
[2] E. Stern, 'Seal Impressions in the Achaemenid Style in the Province of Judah', *BASOR*, 202 (1971), 6–16.

that they fit organically into the official Achemenid repertoire of stamp impressions, although their execution is of provincial standard. There is nothing in the archeological finds from the first part of the Persian period which distinguishes Judah from the other 'provinces' of Palestine or the other parts of the Persian empire. In our opinion, there is no historical or archeological evidence of the separate existence of a Jewish province in this period.

The situation, however, is completely different for the second part of the period, from the end of the fifth century B.C.E. onwards. At this time there is a sudden appearance of large numbers of seal impressions of various types, all of them bearing the inscription *Yehud*, the Aramaic name of Judah. Some are written in Aramaic and some (perhaps from the very end of the period or even later) in Hebrew.[1]

Together with these seal impressions, new small silver coins begin to appear. These are also inscribed with the name of the state (one found is in Aramaic and all the others are in Hebrew). Although some of these coins may date from the end of the fifth century B.C.E. onwards, the majority are to be attributed to the last decades of the fourth century.[2]

The fact that the stamps with Achemenid motifs were replaced by seals inscribed only with the name of the province (often accompanied by schematic symbols) may indicate that a reform was effectuated in the administration of Judah during the second half of the fifth century B.C.E. A. Alt[3] was of the opinion that during the days of Nehemiah (*c.* 445–432), Judah rid itself of Samaria's control and became an independent province. The use of the *Yehud* stamps and the minting privileges of the Judean province may also be connected with its acquiring independence, probably during the days of Nehemiah and his successors.

The predominant characteristic of the province of Judah as reflected in the Bible and archeological finds is the close connection between the province of the Persian period and that of the Judean kingdom of the pre-exilic period. The strong desire to maintain continuity and bridge the interval between the two periods can be deduced from the biblical sources dealing with the boundaries of the Persian province. Some five

[1] F. M. Cross, 'Judean Stamps', *Eretz-Israel*, 9 (1969), 20–7; Avigad, *Qedem*, 4 (1976).
[2] J. Meshorer, 'A New Type of YHD Coin', *IEJ*, 16 (1966), 217–19; *idem, Jewish Coins of the Second Temple Period* (Tel Aviv, 1966), 15–18 (in Hebrew); A. Kindler, 'Silver Coins Bearing the Name of Judea from the Early Hellenistic Period', *IEJ*, 24 (1974), 73–6.
[3] A. Alt, 'Die Rolle Samarias bei der Entstehung des Judentumes', *Festschrift Otto Procksch zum 60. Geburtstag* (Leipzig, 1934), 5–28; = *Kleine Schriften* II (München, 1953), 316–37.

lists are contained in the books of Ezra and Nehemiah, four of them
(Ezra 2: 21–35; Neh. 7: 25–38, 3: 2–22, 12: 28–29) seem to be factual
descriptions and reflect the actual borders of the province of Judah. The
fifth list is a roster of the people inhabiting Judah (Neh. 11: 25–35).
Its contents are strange – at least at the beginning. It opens with a
number of settlements which in no way could be considered part of the
Jewish province in the Persian period. Towns far away from Judah,
such as Ziklag, Beersheba, and eight towns in the vicinity of Beersheba,
are listed as being inhabited by people of Judah. Further along the list
appear Hebron (under its archaic name Kiriath-Arba) and Lachish, two
towns which also did not belong to the Persian province of Judah. The
list concludes with the statement 'Thus they occupied the country from
Beersheba to the Valley of Hinnom', which is an exact description of
the borders of the Judean kingdom in its last days.

As to the date of this list, some historians (Y. Aharoni, Z. Kallai)[1]
attributed it to the last days of the Judean kingdom and regarded it as
a list of peripheral settlements whose inhabitants were not exiled. New
archeological evidence, however, allows us to trace the development
of Edomite settlement in the Negeb. The excavations of N. Glueck at
Tell el-Kheleifeh indicate clearly that the Edomites inhabited the site
as early as the seventh century B.C.E. (stratum IV). While it is true that
this is a rather remote site, Late Edomite pottery (seventh century B.C.E.)
has also been uncovered recently in the excavations at Tel Malhata and
Aroer in the Beersheba valley. Furthermore, a seventh-century ostracon
from Arad contains a warning sent to the Jewish garrisons in the
fortresses of Arad, Kinah and Ramath-Negeb of an impending Edomite
attack.[2] All this evidence can be interpreted as proof of the beginning
of Edomite rule of the Negeb and the region of Beersheba during the
last part of the Judean monarchy, and prevents us from attributing
Nehemiah's list to the late pre-exilic period. In any case, Edomite
names are mentioned in ostraca from the Persian period recently
discovered at Arad and Beersheba.[3]

There are also a number of historians who ascribe the list in chapter
11 of Nehemiah to the Hellenistic period, claiming that it reflects the
situation in Palestine in the Hasmonean period. This proposal, as well,

[1] Y. Aharoni, *The Land of the Bible* (London, 1968), pp. 356–65; Z. Kallai, *The Northern
   Boundaries of Judah* (Jerusalem, 1960), pp. 82–94 (in Hebrew).
[2] N. Glueck, 'Some Edomite Pottery from Tell El-Kheleifeh', *BASOR*, 188 (1967),
   8–38; A. Biran and R. Cohen, 'Aroer 1976', *IEJ*, 26 (1976), 138; Y. Aharoni, 'Three
   Hebrew Ostraca from Arad', *BASOR*, 197 (1970), 16–28.
[3] J. Naveh, 'The Aramaic Ostraca from Tel Arad', 167 no. 1; 174 no. 10; 180 nos.
   20–1; 185 no. 32; 166 no. 33; 194 no. 43; 'The Aramaic Ostraca from Tel Arad'
   in *Beer-Sheba I*, ed. Y. Aharoni (Tel Aviv, 1973), 80 no. 8; 81 no. 14.

is untenable, since according to the Zenon papyri of the mid-third century B.C.E. – the earliest Hellenistic source – the town of Mareshah near Lachish was already entirely Edomite at that time. Moreover, this same source records that the two main towns of the region are Mareshah and Edoraim (and not Hebron) and that both are populated by Edomites (Diodorus 19; 25.2; 98.1). All other evidence from the Hasmonean period clearly testifies that the direction of the expansion of the Jewish settlement was towards the north. In 145 B.C.E., for example, three new areas inhabited by Jews were incorporated into Judah: Lod, Ramataim and Ophra.

Thus if this list dates neither from the end of the Judean monarchy, nor from the Hellenistic period, and its borders – as we have seen – do not coincide with those of the Jewish province from the Persian period, we can conclude that it belongs to an earlier period in the history of the Judean kingdom, perhaps the end of the eighth or beginning of the seventh century B.C.E. The list was added to the Book of Nehemiah not as a realistic rendering of the *status quo* but as a utopian ideal of the area where the returned exiles *should* settle. These borders would naturally encompass the former area of the Judean kingdom from Beersheba to Jerusalem – the historical territory belonging to Judah.

Archeological finds can also confirm the striving to maintain continuity with the earlier kingdom. This can be seen in the reintroduction of a number of early royal emblems on stamps of the Persian period, and the appearance of ancient names on official weights. The most striking manifestation of this attempt to link the two periods is, in the opinion of the present writer, the revival of the archaic Hebrew script. Although many authorities (F. M. Cross Jr., J. Naveh etc.)[1] attribute this phenomenon to the Hellenistic period, it seems to have begun as early as the Persian period. This script is already found, as we have seen, on the *Yehud* and 'Jehezekiah' coins, which are generally considered to date to the fourth century B.C.E., that is, to the Persian period.

An altogether different picture of the actual boundaries of the *Yehud* province emerges from the study of the biblical lists and archeological evidence. As was mentioned above, the books of Ezra and Nehemiah contain five lists which enumerate names of settlements. We shall not deal with them separately here. Notwithstanding the slight differences between them, their additions and omissions, on the whole the lists of settlements belong to five closely situated regions, which form a clear

[1] F. M. Cross Jr., 'The Aramaic Script of the Late Persian Empire and the Rise of the National Script', in: *The Bible and the Ancient Near East. Essays in Honor of W. F. Albright*, ed. G. E. Wright (Garden City, 1965), pp. 174–213; J. Naveh, 'Hebrew Texts in Aramaic Script in the Persian Period?', *BASOR*, 203 (1971), 27–32.

territorial continuity. These regions include the territory of Benjamin, the Jordan valley (from Jericho to Engedi), the northern part of the Judean hills (from Jerusalem to Beth-Zur), and two districts in the Shephelah, Lod and Adulam.

Since we lack a comprehensive list of the borders of the Judah province, it is not surprising that the date and significance of these lists is still a subject of dispute, but it seems that they can safely be attributed to the Persian period and that they are complementary.

We now possess two new archeological criteria to verify the authenticity of these biblical rosters and to draw more accurate boundaries. One criterion is the distribution of the *Yehud* stamps and coins which, without going into a detailed analysis, were found to range from Beth-Zur in the south, Tell en-Nasbeh in the north, Jericho and Engedi in the east, and Gezer in the west. The distribution of these stamps and coins, which are imprinted with the official stamp of the Jewish province in the Persian period, corresponds exactly with the boundaries as recorded in the various lists in Ezra and Nehemiah.

The second criterion is the result of new surveys conducted by L. Y. Rahmani in the Adulam region and by M. Kochavi in the Hebron hills.[1] These surveys uncovered a line of forts erected by the Jewish province in the Persian period. In the west they defended Judah from the province of Ashdod and in the south from the southern Hebron mountain region which was populated at this time by the Edomites. In the west the defensive line started at Yarmuth, Azeka and Adulam, and in the south at Beth-Zur (which was already excavated in the 1930s). W. F. Albright ascribed the earliest fortress uncovered at Beth-Zur to the Persian period 'when the relations between Judah and Idumea were tense'.[2] This fortress was later rebuilt by Judas Maccabeus when relations again became strained (1 Macc. 4: 61). Between Beth-Zur and Engedi there are at least two other main fortresses on the defensive line, one at Khirbet el-Qatt and the other at Khirbet el-Zewiyye. Thus there is a continuous line of Judean forts which demarcates the southern and south-western boundaries of the province of Judah and this line corresponds exactly with the borders mentioned in the biblical lists and with the distribution of the stamps. These borders appear to be much smaller than the ideal ones sought by the repatriates.

[1] L. Y. Rahmani, 'A Partial Survey of the Adulam Area', *BIES*, 28 (1964), 209–31 (in Hebrew); M. Kochavi (ed.), *Judea Samaria and Golan, Archaeological Survey 1967–68*, (Jerusalem, 1972) (in Hebrew).

[2] W. F. Albright, *The Archaeology of Palestine* (Harmondsworth, 1960), p. 152.

SUMMARY

With the conquest of the Babylonian empire in the days of Cyrus, the satrapy of Abar Nahara, which was at that time an integral part of the Babylonian empire, was annexed as a whole to the young Persian empire. Cyrus inherited from the Babylonian kings the unstable organization of this large region on the south-west border of the empire, which included many kingdoms, provinces, nomadic tribes and commercial towns.

The historical process which later exerted so strong an influence on the country's destiny is already evident in these days. On the one hand, the Phoenicians were expanding in Galilee and on the coastal plain, and establishing towns and colonies along the length of the coast near the river's mouth and in the natural bays. They obtained from the various Persian kings special economic, and perhaps also political, concessions in the harbour towns in the provinces of Dor and Ashdod. In their wake came Greek merchants, and later also soldiers who started settling on the coast as early as the seventh century B.C.E.

The Arab desert tribes, on the other hand, first the Qedorites and later the Nabateans, were spreading into the eastern and southern regions. The pressure of these tribes forced the Edomites out of their traditional homeland on the eastern side of the Jordan and they settled in the southern area of deserted Judah.

In the interior of the country the destruction of the Israelite monarchy and the presence of a foreign population settled there by the Assyrians and the Babylonians brought about the emergence of a new people – the Samaritans.

In the south, the Judean state was re-established first by the descendants of the royal family and later probably by a dynasty of local governors. While in the religious sphere it was headed by priests and scribes and had autonomy, it seems that politically the Judean state did not differ from the many other political entities in Palestine.

CHAPTER 5

THE ARCHEOLOGY OF PERSIAN PALESTINE

CLASSIFICATION OF THE MATERIAL

Between the years 545 and 538 B.C.E. the whole of the Middle East – including Palestine – was conquered by the Achemenid kings of Persia. At that time the Persian empire, the largest of the empires of the ancient world, extended from North Africa to southern Russia and from Asia Minor to India. In the days of Darius I (522–486 B.C.E.) its borders were consolidated and its interior division was determined. According to this division some twenty satrapies were established, each of which was divided into numerous sub-provinces (see the description in the book of Esther 1: 1 'from India even unto Ethiopia, over an hundred and seven and twenty provinces').

The whole of Palestine constituted only a tiny part of one of these satrapies, namely the country 'Beyond the River' (Ezra 4: 10–11), a term which was borrowed from the former Assyrian administration and perhaps from an even earlier period (see 1 Kings 4: 24). The province of Beyond the River included, in addition to Palestine, Syria, Phoenicia and Cyprus. According to Herodotus (III.5) its northern border was in Poseideion (now al-Mina at the mouth of the Orontes) and its southern border was at lake Sirbonis (Bardawil lake).[1]

The sub-division of Palestine appears to have been based on the older divisions of the Assyrian and Babylonian administration, probably related to the territorial boundaries of the various peoples living in the country during that period. The best known of these provinces were Megiddo, Dor, Samaria, Judea, Ashdod and Gaza. At the head of each

[1] R. N. Frye, *The Heritage of Persia* (London, 1966), pp. 119–37; K. Galling, 'Syrien in der Politik der Achämenider,' *AfO*, 28 (1929); O. Leuze, *Die Satrapieneinteilung in Syrien und im Zweistromlande* (Halle, 1935); A. T. Olmstead, *History of the Persian Empire (Achaemenid Period)* (Chicago, 1948); A. F. Rainy, 'The Satrapy "Beyond the River"', *AJBA*, 1 (1969), 51–78; E. Stern, *The Material Culture of the Land of the Bible in the Persian Period, 538–332 B.C.E.* (Jerusalem, 1973), pp. 243–9 (in Hebrew); A. J. Toynbee, *A Study of History* (Oxford, 1955), vol. 7, pp. 580–689; S. S. Weinberg, 'Post Exilic Palestine. An Archaeological Report', *The Israel Academy of Sciences and Humanities Proceedings* (Jerusalem, 1969), vol. 4, no. 5.

province was a Persian governor or a local representative who was responsible to the satrap of Beyond the River for its efficient administration, payment of taxes and the like. This state of affairs lasted for some two hundred years in Palestine, from 538 to 332 B.C.E., in which year the entire Middle East was conquered by Alexander the Great.

In the history of Palestine, the Persian period is one of the more obscure periods, despite the fact that archeologically it is relatively recent. The information provided by the Bible, our major literary source for the Israelite period, gives anything but a clear picture, and even this does not go beyond the middle of the fifth century B.C.E. The same is true of the following period with regard to the information provided by Greek literature (Herodotus, Pseudo-Scylax), and the Apocrypha.[1]

In time, some epigraphic sources were added. These provide, directly or indirectly, more evidence on the history of the country. We may mention the inscriptions of Darius I found at Persepolis; the inscriptions of the Phoenician kings discovered at Sidon;[2] and the important archive of the Jewish military colony from Elephantine in Egypt.[3] Mention should also be made of the inscriptions found at Tell el-Maskhuta in Egypt where a similar Arab military base existed.[4]

In Palestine, too, some outstanding discoveries were made. Of prime importance are the Samaritan papyri discovered in a cave at wadi Daliyeh which dates from the years 375 to 332 B.C.E.[5] Also important are some Egyptian steles found at Gezer and Akko.[6] But the main epigraphic material in Palestine is the ostraca, discovered at many sites

---

[1] K. Galling, 'Die Syrische–Palästinische Küste nach der Beschreibung bei Pseudo-Skylax', *ZDPV*, 61 (1938), 66–96.

[2] M. Dunand, 'Remarques épigraphiques', *BMB*, 5 (1941), 74–85; *idem*, 'Nouvelles inscriptions phéniciennes du Temple d'Echmoun A Bostan Ech-Cheikh, près Sidon', *BMB*, 18 (1965), 105–9.

[3] A. Cowley, *Aramaic Papyri of the Fifth Century B.C.* (Oxford, 1923); E. G. Kraeling, *The Brooklyn Museum Aramaic Papyri* (New Haven, 1953); B. Porten, *Archives from Elephantine* (Berkeley–Los Angeles, 1968).

[4] W. J. Dumbrell, 'The Tell el-Maskhuta Bowls and the "Kingdom" of Qedar in the Persian Period', *BASOR*, 203 (1971), 33–44; I. Rabinowitz, 'Aramaic Inscriptions of the Fifth Century B.C.E. from a North-Arab Shrine in Egypt', *JNES*, 15 (1956), 1–10.

[5] F. M. Cross, Jr., 'The Discovery of the Samaritan Papyri', *BA*, 26 (1963), 110–21; *idem*, 'Papyri of the Fourth Century B.C. from Dâliyeh', in *New Directions in Biblical Archaeology*, ed. D. N. Freedman and J. C. Greenfield (Garden City–New York, 1971), pp. 45–69; and in P. W. Lapp and N. L. Lapp, *Discoveries in the Wâdī ed-Dâliyeh*, *AASOR*, 41 (1974), 17–29. See also the Judean stamps in N. Avigad, *Qedem*, 4, Jerusalem (1974).

[6] R. A. S. Macalister, *The Excavation of Gezer* (London, 1912), vol. II, p. 313; A. Rowe, *A Catalogue of Egyptian Scarabs in the Palestine Archaeological Museum* (Cairo, 1936), pp. 295–6, pl. 38.

and written in Aramaic, Hebrew and Phoenician.[1] They mostly contain lists of proper names (Hebrew, Phoenician, Arabic, Babylonian, Egyptian, etc.), or receipts for consignments of food, merchandise and so on. Though they give no indication of contemporary events, they are of considerable importance for our knowledge of the everyday life of the period. They also contain evidence as to the form of the country's military and fiscal organization, and indirectly shed light on the composition of the population. Short inscriptions, some of office-holders with their titles, were also discovered on seals and seal-impressions (see above, p. 81).

The combined literary and epigraphic sources give but little information as to the history of Palestine during the Persian period, and the overall picture which emerges is still meagre. Unfortunately, our knowledge of the material culture of the country was also for many years unorganized, and fell short of that of the previous periods. This was brought about by several factors peculiar to this period: on many of the local mounds, the Persian levels are the uppermost or the latest on the site; in other tells these levels are found beneath massive Hellenistic and Roman structures. So the Persian remains have suffered, either from exposure or from later building activities. In either case such remains are few, or are mixed with earlier or later material.

It is only recently, thanks to excavations of the 1970s, that abundant finds of the Persian period have been made, largely in clear stratigraphic or homogeneous contexts (at Hazor, Shikmona, Tel Megadim, Engedi, to mention but a few).[2] These discoveries also make possible a new examination and classification of the material found previously.

ARCHITECTURE

Turning to the structural remains from the Persian period found in Palestine, we must first point out the surprising sparseness of building remains, in contrast to the number of sites containing other finds of this period. This situation was interpreted by some scholars as indicating a decided reduction in urban population in the period, following the

---

[1] F. M. Cross, Jr., 'Jar Inscriptions from Shiqmona', *IEJ*, 18 (1968), 226–33; J. Naveh, 'Hebrew Texts in Aramaic Script in the Persian Period?', *BASOR*, 203 (1971), 27–32.
[2] M. Broshi, 'Tel Megadim – A Phoenician City and Roman–Byzantine Road-Station', *Qadmoniot*, 2 (1969), 124–6 (in Hebrew); J. Elgavish, *Archaeological Excavations at Shikmona; The levels of the Persian Period, Seasons 1963–1965* (Haifa, 1968, in Hebrew); B. Mazar and I. Dunayevsky, 'En-Gedi. Fourth and Fifth Season of Excavations (Preliminary Report)', *IEJ*, 17 (1967), 133–43; Y. Yadin, *Hazor*, The Schweich Lectures of the British Academy, 1970 (London, 1972).

extensive destruction at the time of the fall of the Judean kingdom.[1] However, the evidence drawn from recent excavations shows quite clearly that this destruction was actually limited to the Judean hills alone, the other regions indicating no such change. Indeed, in most of the other areas it was a period of building activity. This was especially so in Benjamin[2] and the coastal plain, as is shown by the remains of planned urban settlements discovered at Tell Abu Hawam, Shikmona, and recently also at Tel Megadim.[3] It should also be mentioned that in the neighbouring lands, settlements of this period were built according to a plan, such as the Hippodamic plan which was then coming into use. Among these settlements al-Mina, the port at the mouth of the Orontes, is an outstanding example.[4]

Most of the city fortifications so far uncovered in the Persian period levels in Palestine are located in two regions: one includes the small settlements along the coast and the other the towns near Jerusalem. Their walls were not especially strong and no truly impressive defence system is on record. No city gates have been recovered, with the exception of that of Lachish, and possibly a fortified area near the older gates of Megiddo.[5] However the evidence provided by these discoveries is fragmentary and can hardly provide a complete and representative picture. Moreover, such a picture is also in contrast with what is known from the literary sources, such as the story of the lengthy siege laid by Alexander against Tyre and Gaza, or what is known of siege-warfare as practised in this period.[6] Since Palestine was a battleground throughout the fourth century B.C.E. the picture is even more uncertain.

On the other hand, our knowledge of the typical dwelling is considerably clearer. A great majority of the houses of this period were built according to a surprisingly uniform plan (whether for a simple

[1] Stern, *Material Culture*, pp. 51–64 (in Hebrew); W. F. Albright, *The Archaeology of Palestine* (Harmondsworth, 1960), p. 142; K. M. Kenyon, *Archaeology in the Holy Land* (London, 1960), pp. 296–302; C. Watzinger, *Denkmäler Palästinas* (Leipzig, 1935), vol. 2, p. 3.
[2] N. Avigad, 'Two Hebrew Inscriptions on Wine-Jars', *IEJ*, 22 (1972), 9; P. W. Lapp, 'Tell el-Fûl', *BA*, 28 (1965), 9–10; A. Malamat, 'The Last Wars of the Kingdom of Judah', *JNES*, 9 (1950), 226–7.
[3] Broshi, *Qadmoniot*, 2 (1969), 124–6 (in Hebrew); Elgavish, *Shikmona*; R. W. Hamilton, 'Excavations at Tell Abu-Hawam', *QDAP*, 4 (1935), 2–5.
[4] C. L. Woolley, *A Forgotten Kingdom* (Harmondsworth, 1953), pp. 172–88.
[5] R. S. Lamon and G. M. Shipton, *Megiddo. I: Seasons of 1925–34.* (OIP 42, Chicago, 1939), pp. 88–91; p. 101, fig. 177; O. Tufnell, *Lachish III: The Iron Age* (Oxford, 1953), pp. 98–9.
[6] J. H. Iliffe and T. B. Mitford, 'New Light on Ancient Siege-warfare from Unique Cyprus Discoveries', *ILN* (April, 1953), 613–16.

dwelling or for a complex public building).[1] This plan comprised an internal open courtyard surrounded, or almost surrounded, by rows of rooms, and is known as the 'open court' plan. It is of Mesopotamian–Assyrian origin, and had already been adopted in Palestine by the end of the Israelite period, continuing without change through the Babylonian and Persian periods.[2] This is further clarified by the building technique of several of the structures having walls of *terre pisée* plastered with a clay plaster, a practice common in Mesopotamia, but generally quite rare in Palestine.[3]

The plan of one building only, the 'Lachish Residence', differs from this basic plan, since it has, in addition to the court, two entrances of the *ḥilani* type. It seems that Y. Aharoni's definition of the building as a combination of the '*bit-ḥilani*' plan of Syro-Hittite origin and the 'court house' of the Assyrian type should be accepted.[4] Another aspect which should be pointed out is the similarity of the Lachish Residence with the provincial Achemenid palaces, which are noticeable mainly for several architectural innovations, such as drum columns in the Greek fashion, monumental flights of stairs and vaulted roofing – all late elements common in the monumental structures of the Persian period in neighbouring lands. We must also note that, while pure Achemenid architecture is generally confined to the four imperial capitals (together with Sidon[5]), in the other parts of the empire it was combined with local practice, for example, the 'open court' house of Mesopotamia, the 'megaron' house of Anatolia, and the mixed Mesopotamian–Syrian style in Palestine. Traces of the Persian imperial style in such outlying areas are restricted, as in the Lachish residence, to the appearance of new architectural elements added to the local tradition.

Methods of construction in this period followed older Phoenician methods, for example, the use of rough boulder walls supported at regular intervals by ashlar pillars. This technique is especially preserved in the coastal settlements.[6] But new technical innovations were also in

[1] E. Stern, 'The Architecture of Palestine in the Persian Period', *Eretz-Israel*, 11 (1973), 265–76 (in Hebrew).

[2] R. B. K. Amiran and I. Dunayevsky, 'The Assyrian Open-court Building and its Palestinian Derivates', *BASOR*, 149 (1958), 25–32.

[3] P. L. O. Guy, 'Ayelet Hashahar', *Bulletin of the Department of Antiquities of the State of Israel*, 5–6 (1957), 19–20 (in Hebrew); W. M. F. Petrie, *Gerar* (London, 1928), pp. 8–9.

[4] Y. Aharoni, 'The "Persian Fortress" at Lachish – An Assyrian Palace?', *BIES*, 31 (1967), 80–91 (in Hebrew); Tufnell, *Iron Age*, pp. 131–41.

[5] C. H. Clermont-Ganneau, 'Le Paradeisos royal Achéménide de Sidon', *RB*, 30 (1921), 106–9.

[6] Hamilton, *QDAP*, 4 (1935), 2–5; E. L. Sukenik, 'Tell esh Shuni (Tell el-Kudâdi)', *QDAP*, 8 (1938), 167–8.

use. We have already mentioned some of them: the use of drum columns[1] and the use of vaulting;[2] finally, we have to add the introduction of cement (usually ascribed to the Hellenistic period). Cement permitted considerable advances in cistern and even pool construction,[3] as well as the improvement of drainage systems. In general it can be said that the structures of this period, especially the dwellings, were built symmetrically and with pleasing proportions. It should further be noted that the structures of the Persian period are larger than the average in earlier periods. Columns and vaulting were only used in a few instances, but generous space was also achieved by means of longer but still narrow rooms.

BURIALS

During the period from the sixth to the fourth century B.C.E. there were various types of tombs in use in Palestine. There were three main types, differing both in plan and in contents: the Intermediate type which dates from the sixth century; the Cist type, from the end of the sixth century to the end of the fifth century; and the Shaft type, of the fifth and fourth centuries B.C.E.

The Intermediate type was generally built according to the plan typical of the tombs from the end of the Iron Age, that is, a single burial chamber surrounded with benches.[4] Such tombs often contain local pottery, as did tombs at the end of the Iron Age, though new elements are apparent which are common in the later tombs. These tombs are peculiar to Palestine and should be interpreted as belonging to the local population.

In contrast, the two other types of tombs found here, the Cist and Shaft types, comprise only a small part of such tombs scattered over the entire ancient East. The distribution of these two types reveals that they are peculiar to specific regions: the Cist type, with its variations,

---

[1] J. L. Kelso, 'The Second Campaign at Bethel', BASOR, 137 (1955), 5–10; L. A. Sinclair, 'An Archaeological Study of Gibeah (Tell el-Fûl)', AASOR, 34–5 (1960), 35, pl. 35; Tufnell, Iron Age, p. 132, fig. 11, pl. 22: 6–7; N. Avigad, 'Excavations at Makmish 1958', IEJ, 10 (1960), 91.

[2] Guy, 'Ayelet Hashahar', 19–20 (in Hebrew); Tufnell, Iron Age, p. 131, pls. 22: 1–2, 120.

[3] Elgavish, Shikmona, pl. IX; Lamon and Shipton, Megiddo, p. 89, fig. 99; E. Stern, 'Excavations at Gil'am (Kh Er.-Rujm)', Atiqot, 6 (1970), 35, pl. VIII: 1 (Hebrew series).

[4] Stern, Material Culture, pp. 71–95 (in Hebrew); E. Grant and G. E. Wright, Ain Shems Excavations (Haverford, Pennsylvania, 1939), vol. V, pp. 144–5; R. A. S. Macalister, 'Some Interesting Pottery Remains', PEFQS, 5 (1915), 35–7.

is common only in the east (Persia, Mesopotamia, and the interior of Syria);[1] whereas the Shaft type, in which burial in anthropoid coffins is exclusively found, is definitely western (Phoenicia, Palestine and Cyprus).[2] Not a single Shaft tomb has been found in the east, though several examples of Cist tombs of the eastern type have been found in Phoenicia and Palestine (but not in Cyprus), and it seems that this is of special significance. The division of tomb types into eastern and western is also reflected in their contents: whereas the Shaft tombs contain an abundance of Greek pottery, Greek and Phoenician coins, as well as jewellery and cosmetic utensils in Greek, Phoenician, Cypriot or Egyptian styles, the Cist tombs are peculiar because of the Achemenid style of their metal vessels and weapons. With the exception of the local vessels, which are peculiar to each individual area, there is an evident similarity of finds in the eastern type of tomb in all the lands where they are found, from Persia to Palestine, just as there is a similarity of finds in the Shaft tombs at the various sites. Moreover, it seems possible to distinguish the local pottery used in the two types of tombs. This leads to the conclusion that these differences indicate various ethnic elements buried in the respective tomb types.

From the distribution of the Shaft tombs in Palestine, Phoenicia, Cyprus and across the Mediterranean, and mainly from the unique practice of burial in anthropoid coffins within them, it is evident that this type of tomb belonged to the Phoenician population; and in this connection it should be noted that most of the Shaft tombs in Palestine have been discovered near coastal settlements.

It is more difficult to come to a conclusion concerning the ethnic identity of the users of the Cist tombs. On the basis of the great similarity in the manner of burial in these tombs to tombs located geographically quite far away (from Persia to Palestine), and of the fact that many such tombs have been defined in neighbouring lands as

---

[1] Macalister, *Gezer*, vol. I, pp. 289–99; A. Abel and A. G. Barrois, 'Fouilles de l'Ecole Archéologique Française de Jérusalem, Effectuées à Neirab', *Syria*, 9 (1928), 187–206; 303–19; H. J. Iliffe, 'A Tell Far'a Tomb Group Reconsidered; Silver Vessels of the Persian Period', *QDAP*, 4 (1935), 182–6; E. Speiser, 'Reports on the Tell Billah and Tepe Gawra Excavations', *BASOR*, 46 (1932), 8–9; F. Thureau-Danjin and M. Dunand, *Til Barsip* (Paris, 1936), pp. 75–80; C. L. Woolley, 'A North Syrian Cemetery of the Persian Period', *AAA*, 7 (1914–16), 115–29.

[2] E. Gjerstad, *The Swedish Cyprus Expedition, vol. 3: Results of the Excavations in Cyprus 1927–1931* (Stockholm, 1937), pp. 298–339; Hamdey-Bey and T. Reinach, *Une Necropole Royale à Sidon* (Paris, 1892), 2 vols.; C. N. Johns, 'Excavations at 'Atlit 1930–1931; The South-Eastern Cemetery', *QDAP*, 2 (1933), 41–104; E. Kukahn, *Anthropoide Sarkophage in Beyrouth* (Berlin, 1955); C. C. Torrey, 'A Phoenician Necropolis at Sidon', *AASOR*, 1 (1920), 1–27.

'Achemenid' or 'Persian', we may accept Culican's assumption that they belonged to Persian occupation troops.[1]

From the above it is evident that there are, as yet, no clear examples of Jewish or Samaritan tombs from the fifth and fourth centuries B.C.E.[2]

POTTERY

Examination of the pottery vessels in use in Palestine in the Persian period shows that they are generally made of three different clay compositions.[3] Two of these are common in the coastal regions and the third is peculiar to the mountainous areas of Judea and Samaria. In the coastal regions most of the vessels are made of two clays, one yellowish-greenish and the other reddish. No special significance has been found for this difference (which, incidentally, is found in the pottery of later periods as well). In many cases, one and the same pottery type is found in several examples within a single locus made in the two different types of clay. Generally the vessels are rather crude in form, the clay not being properly washed, and poor firing, to the point where the material is often quite crumbly, is typical. Moreover, many such vessels are characterized by air pockets, either trapped within the clay or having exploded and broken the surface of the vessel. Another characteristic of these vessels (the larger types) is imperfect smoothing of the walls, which have many bumps and dips in them. In form, the vessels are of poor proportions, giving the impression that they were hastily and carelessly made.

In contrast, most of the vessels from the mountainous areas of Judah and Samaria are made of a different clay, mostly of a brown–grey colour, clearly continuing Iron Age pottery traditions. The firing of these vessels is generally better, and their form is pleasing.

The pottery of the Persian period is generally scanty in decoration. In the first phase there are still several vessel types which are decorated with a burnish similar to that of Israelite vessels, though the burnish differs slightly in form and colour: the lines of the burnish are very broad and their shade is light red. This burnish is to be seen on several types of bowls, craters and lamps. Painted decoration is rare and limited to several types of juglets, jugs and bottles. Even then, it shows little variety: the vessels are generally painted only with several horizontal

[1] W. Culican, *The Medes and the Persians* (London, 1965), pp. 146–7.
[2] E. Stern, 'A Burial of the Persian Period near Hebron', *IEJ*, 21 (1971), 25–30.
[3] Stern, *Material Culture*, pp. 96–144 (in Hebrew); P. W. Lapp, 'The Pottery of Palestine in the Persian Period', in *Archäologie und Altes Testament, Festschrift für Kurt Galling* (Tübingen, 1970), pp. 179–97.

bands of reddish-brown. Other vessels have been knife-pared. A new feature in decorating the surface of Persian-period vessels is the use of ribbing. This is not yet the sharp, regular ribbing of the Hellenistic period and later, but rather a broad, flat ribbing. Mention should also be made in this context of an ornamentation impressed with a reed, common on one family of vessels in this period. But decoration in any form is generally quite meagre and rare in this period; most vessels are plain and simple. It would seem that the need for finer and decorated vessels was met by imports, especially the various Greek wares, which were more pleasing in appearance and incomparably finer in quality.

Gathering the various pottery types of the Persian period and examining their origins permits their division into three major groups, each of which stems from a different source of influence: (a) the local group of vessels which continue Iron Age traditions; and imitations of imported ware, in which can be distinguished: (b) vessels imitating imported eastern archetypes, and (c) those imitating imported western archetypes.

(a) Some of the pottery vessels of the Persian period comprise a continuation of the local ware produced in the Iron Age. Within this group are most of the bowls, cooking-pots, hole-mouth jars, an important part of the store-jars (mainly those continuing the 'lamelekh' type), most of the flasks, certain types of jugs and juglets, lamps, double vessels, funnels and stands. Much of this group was very close to the earlier ware in form. Since their geographical distribution is generally limited to the Judea and Samaria region, we may conclude that in these areas the Israelite pottery traditions were maintained for a longer period.

Even so, a detailed analysis of several of these types reveals that there is a fairly clear development among them. Whereas the earlier vessels (from the end of the sixth century and the beginning of the fifth century B.C.E.) are still quite close to the Israelite ware, later in the Persian period (mid fifth century B.C.E. onwards) several of these types disappear and are replaced by other types in which new features closer to the Hellenistic ware are evident. A good example of this is the three types of flask. While the earliest form is little different from the Iron Age flask, the latest form is already quite similar to the Hellenistic flasks.

In the later part of the Persian period there are other characteristic features appearing within this group of vessels, such as the sack shape taken on by many of the closed types; the flat bowls tend to have wide shelf-rims, similar to those of the Hellenistic period. The date of transition between the local types still similar to the Iron Age types and those of the 'new look' is the mid fifth century B.C.E.

(b) The second group comprises local imitations following eastern archetypes. It may be subdivided into groups of Assyrian, Persian, Phoenician and Egyptian influence. The Assyrian ware, especially the 'Palace ware' from the end of the seventh century, is now well known from the excavations at Nimrud (Calah). The first appearance of these vessels and their imitations in Palestine was almost contemporary with their first general appearance.[1] In the Persian period Palestinian potters continued to imitate these forms, which in the meantime had taken their place in the local repertoire. However, the imitations were mostly rather crude and quite far from the originals. Most of the vessels ascribed to this source of influence were carinated bowls thought to imitate Assyrian metalware;[2] bowls of this type are quite common in the Assyrian repertoire in pottery as well. All the types of bottles can readily be ascribed, especially those of 'carrot' shape which can clearly be traced back to an Assyrian 'Palace ware' origin. But again, the Persian vessels differ from the Assyrian and their late Israelite imitations, both in their crude shapes and, even more, in their lack of the typical painted decoration.

The Achemenid pottery was generally quite meagre and not common beyond the borders of Persia proper, so it was seldom imitated. In the repertoire of Palestinian pottery only two or three vessels have been ascribed as direct Achemenid imports.[3] In contrast, the splendid Achemenid metal vessels most certainly were an important source of inspiration for the Palestinian potters, and there were many pottery imitations of them. The most outstanding are the various rhytons found in several places.[4] We believe that the form of decoration of impressed wedges and reeds, common in a large group of Persian-period vessels in Palestine, is actually an imitation of a design on the metal vessels.[5] Several other vessels found in Palestine should be ascribed to a Phoenician source, mainly on the basis of their continuing the form of earlier Phoenician types from the end of the Iron Age, or of vessels common in Phoenician sites and tombs of the Persian period. The influence of these is felt mainly among the jugs and juglets, though possibly some types of store-jars and lamps should be added.

Egyptian influence on the Palestinian pottery of this period is evident

[1] R. Amiran, *Ancient Pottery of the Holy Land from its Beginnings in the Neolithic Period to the end of the Iron Age* (Jerusalem, 1969), p. 291; J. Oates, 'Late Assyrian Pottery from Fort Shalmaneser', *Iraq*, 21 (1959), 130–46.

[2] R. Hesterin and E. Stern, 'Two "Assyrian" Bowls from Israel', *IEJ*, 23 (1973), 152–5.

[3] J. W. Crowfoot, *Samaria-Sebaste, III: The Objects* (London, 1957), p. 216.

[4] Stern, *Material Culture*, p. 134, figs. 211–12; W. M. F. Petrie, *Gerar* (London, 1928), pl. 15: 5–7.

[5] J. C. Wampler, 'Triangular Impressed Design in Palestinian Pottery', *BASOR*, 80 (1940), 13–16.

in one type of vessel only, the lug-handled alabastron, undoubtedly imitating an alabaster archetype.

(c) The influence of western wares on Palestinian pottery is most evident in the Persian period. This influence can be subdivided into Eastern Greek, Cypriot and Attic.

It should first of all be noted that in contrast to 'eastern' wares, which were almost always imitations made in a period later than their archetypes, the 'western' wares were either actual imports or local imitations of the same date. Included under the designation of imported wares are vessels of Eastern Greek origin, mostly painted bowls with horizontal handles, jugs painted black on their upper parts, 'wild goat' types such as those found at Mesad Hashavyahu, and so on.[1] Also included are imported Cypriot vessels, differing from the local imitations in their clay, firing and, mainly, in their richly-coloured ornamentation. Considerable attention must be paid to the imported Attic ware in its various forms: 'black-figure', 'red-figure' and lustrous black slip-ware. It seems that, as in the other lands of the ancient east,[2] in Palestine too the sources of imported pottery changed during the Persian period. At the end of the seventh century and in the sixth century B.C.E. Eastern Greek and Cypriot wares held the upper hand. From the beginning of the fifth century B.C.E. to the end of the Persian period Attic ware was the most prominent.[3]

The pottery imported from the west attracted many local imitations, mainly because of their fine shape; the exquisite painting was, of course, beyond the abilities of the local potters. We can assume that the small bowls and craters with horizontal handles, quite common in Palestine in the Persian period, are derived from similar Eastern Greek bowls. There is no doubt that the closed lamps, made of a rough clay which has not received the typical slip, are also local imitations of the Attic type. At Tel Megadim a juglet was found to have a great similarity to the Attic *lekythos*.[4]

In all these cases, the distinction between imported and local imitations is readily apparent. Thus it is not difficult to ascertain the origins of the imitations. In contrast, it is most difficult to analyse the

[1] J. Naveh, 'The Excavations at Meṣad Ḥashavyahu, Preliminary Report', *IEJ*, 12 (1962), 96–113.

[2] J. Boardman, *The Greeks Overseas* (Harmondsworth, 1964), pp. 29–30; E. Gjerstad, *The Swedish Cyprus Expedition*, vol. 4, part 2: *The Cypro-Geometric, Cypro-Archaic and Cypro-Classical Periods* (Stockholm, 1948), p. 317; Woolley, *Forgotten Kingdom*, p. 184.

[3] C. Clairmont, 'Greek Pottery from the Near East,' *Berytus*, 11 (1954–55), 85–139; *idem*, 'Greek Pottery from the Near East, II: Black Vases', *Berytus*, 12 (1956–58), 1–34; J. H. Iliffe, 'Pre-Hellenistic Greek Pottery in Palestine', *QDAP*, 2 (1932), 15–26.

[4] Stern, *Material Culture*, p. 126, fig. 192.

fairly large group of vessels with shapes almost identical with the three above sources, and because they lack the typical ornamentation, it is impossible to determine whether they are imported or made locally. This group includes the 'Persian' bowls with flat bases, a large family of store-jars, basket store-jars and the amphora type which is the prototype of the Rhodian amphorae of the Hellenistic period. All these were types used for transporting goods by sea and they are common along the entire Eastern Mediterranean shore. It would be possible to reach more definite conclusions only by mineralogical and petrographical examinations. But one thing is definite: whether it turns out that most of these bowls, store-jars and amphorae were locally manufactured or not, the origin of these types and the source of their distribution was undoubtedly the Eastern Greek islands and Cyprus. For they appear there earlier than in Palestine, and their origin in the Eastern Mediterranean is connected with the early Greek trading colonies such as al-Mina, Tell el Sukas, Mesad Hashavyahu, Naucratis and Daphne.[1]

Thus we may conclude that in the Persian period Palestine was divided, as far as pottery production is concerned, into two separate regions: (1) Galilee and the coastal plain, where mainly Greek and Cypriot imports and their local imitations were in use. These forced out the older wares at the beginning of the Persian period, and possibly even earlier. (2) The mountainous regions of Judea and Samaria (and presumably also eastern Transjordan), where at first the vessels continued Iron Age forms or imitated eastern archetypes (mainly Assyrian, Achemenid and Egyptian). In the latter part of the Persian period the types changed as well, being replaced by shapes closer to the Hellenistic repertoire; these changes were, of course, quite slow and gradual.

OBJECTS OF METAL, ALABASTER AND FAIENCE

Dealing with the metal, alabaster and faience vessels, we shall divide our discussion according to their use: (a) daily ware (bowls, jugs, ladles and strainers); (b) cosmetic utensils (mirrors, kohl pots and sticks, alabastra); (c) jewellery; (d) weapons.

These vessels and utensil types suddenly appear at the beginning of the Persian period in large quantities and become standard equipment in tombs both in Palestine and the ancient East in general, from Persia to Egypt. Many of them, however, were discovered in occupation strata.

[1] Naveh, *IEJ*, 12 (1962), 89–113; W. F. M. Petrie, *Naukratis I* (London, 1886); *idem, Tanis II* (London, 1888); P. J. Riis, *Sukas I, The North-East Sanctuary and the first Settling of Greeks in Syria and Palestine* (Copenhagen, 1970); C. L. Woolley, 'Excavations at Al-Mina, Sueida', *JHS*, 58 (1938), 1–30; 133–70.

It seems to the present writer that most of them are imports from various sources: Phoenician, Achemenid, Egyptian and Greek. Each source generally specialized in one particular category, in which production reached a reasonably high level of workmanship and beauty. These imports of luxury items tended to stifle local production and to prevent its development. Only a minor percentage of the objects can be considered as being of local manufacture, and even then they are mostly poor imitations exhibiting crude craftsmanship.

(a) The bronze and silver bowls of the Persian period found in Palestine and Syria are all from contexts associated with the first part of the period (end of the sixth century and the fifth century B.C.E.). Most are of a style quite similar to those discovered in Persia proper, in Persepolis, Susa and Ecbatana. We may assume, following many scholars,[1] that some of these bowls may even have been imported from production centres in Persia, where there was advanced metal production, the successor of older Assyrian and Urartian production. But there is little doubt that most were made in the Phoenician production centres on the Syrian coast, centres also having a considerable tradition behind them. It appears that in the Persian period these centres mostly copied Achemenid patterns rather than the Assyrian or Egyptian patterns, as in earlier periods. The other metalware can be ascribed to the same source: the jugs, ladles and strainers are in a similar style and their chronological context is similar.[2]

(b) Of the cosmetic utensils, the most common type are the mirrors. These began to be widespread in women's tombs at the end of the Iron Age, though the majority of them come from Persian-period tombs. Two types of mirror can be distinguished, one flat and round with a short simple tang, and the other with the joint of the tang and disc decorated with volutes forming braces clasping the disc.[3] It appears that the former group is of Egyptian origin, whereas the latter is from Cyprus.

Other cosmetic utensils often found in the tombs of women are kohl pots and sticks made of various materials: bronze, bone, wood or glass paste.[4] Only in rare instances have the bottles been found, the sticks alone being preserved. These were all of bronze. Their distribution and

[1] P. Fossing, 'Drinking Bowls of Glass and Metal from the Achaemenian Time', *Berytus*, 4 (1937), 121–9; R. W. Hamilton, 'A Silver Bowl in the Ashmolean Museum', *Iraq*, 28 (1966), 1–17; H. Luschey, *Die Phiale* (Bleicherode am Hartz, 1939); Stern, *Material Culture*, pp. 144–58.

[2] R. Amiran, 'Achaemenian Bronze Objects from a Tomb at Kh. Ibsan in Lower-Galilee', *Levant*, 4 (1972), 135–8; Iliffe, *QDAP*, 4 (1935), 182–6.

[3] Johns, *QDAP*, 2 (1933), pls. 23: 551; 27: 712.

[4] Avigad, 'Excavations at Makmish, 1960: Preliminary Report', *IEJ*, 11 (1961), pl. 44: 1; Johns, *QDAP*, 2 (1933), pls. 27: 711.

dating indicate that they are common throughout the Persian period. We consider them to be of Egyptian manufacture on the basis of the fact that in that country there had been a long tradition of manufacture of such utensils.

In the tombs of the Persian period many tens of alabaster vessels of two types have come to light: alabastra with lug handles and bowls. Alabastra of various sizes and body shapes have been found, ranging from long and narrow to squat; these were probably intended as measures, and indeed on several the measure was marked on the outside. They had apparently been used for kohl, spices, and so on. It is commonly accepted that the sources of these vessels were invariably the well-developed production centres in Egypt. According to a study by I. Ben-Dor,[1] production was renewed in Egypt towards the end of the Babylonian period, after having come to a standstill during the Iron Age. In his opinion, most of the vessels found in Palestine are of Egyptian manufacture, and only a small proportion were made of local alabaster, these being crude in form. The local production was evidently restored following the Egyptian.

Alabaster bowls, which are less common, were apparently intended for the grinding of spices, and they evidently replaced the Iron Age limestone bowls decorated with geometric motifs. Similar vessels were made in other materials, for example, glass, pottery and bone. The provenance of the latter is difficult to ascertain, though they seem to be local imitations; their dating and distribution are similar to the above.

(c) Most of the jewellery is of faience, in Egyptian relief motifs, and was probably imported from Egypt. Of the other types, in metal, one group (ear-rings and bracelets) is in pure Achemenid style.[2] As for their place of manufacture, it is difficult to determine whether they are imports or the products of Phoenician and Egyptian smiths who copied the original Persian work; the second possibility is the more probable, since moulds for casting and repoussée work for such jewellery have been found, both at Byblos and in Egypt.[3] Another group of ear-rings of a coiled pattern, also found in several Persian period tombs in Palestine, are definitely Cypriot imports, on the strength of abundant parallels from that island.[4]

[1] I. Ben-Dor, 'Palestinian Alabaster Vases', *QDAP*, 11 (1945), 93–112.

[2] M. Dothan, 'Ashdod II–III, The Second and Third Seasons of Excavations, 1963, and 1965', *Atiqot*, 9–10 (1971), p. 65, pl. XXI: 2; Macalister, *Gezer*, vol. 1, p. 293, fig. 154: 3.

[3] H. Frankfort, 'A Persian Goldsmith's Trial Piece', *JNES*, 9 (1950), 111–12; H. J. Kantor, 'Achaemenid Jewelry in the Oriental Institute', *JNES*, 16 (1957), 1–23; J. Lefebre, *Le Tombeau de Petasiris* (Cairo, 1923–24); A. Roes, 'Achaemenid Influence upon Egyptian and Nomad Art', *ArtAs*, 15 (1952), 7–30.

[4] Johns, *QDAP*, 2 (1933), 52, fig. 5; 53–4, fig. 10; pls. 17: 408–9, 25: 643.

Glass amulets are also common; they are usually in the form of human (male or female) heads, sometimes grotesque. These, too, are a fairly common find in the tombs and strata of the Persian period. On the basis of their distribution along the Syro-Palestinian coast, in Egypt, Cyprus, Sardinia, Carthage and Spain, we may assume that they are of Phoenician manufacture. This assumption is further supported by the fact that the ethnic types portrayed are definitely oriental, for example, the males are bearded.[1]

(d) Among the weapons, we should mention especially the arrowheads, which are the most important type in this category for classification in the Persian period. Here, too, three groups may be distinguished, of differing origins: local, Irano-Scythian and Greek. A statistical analysis interestingly revealed that in the Persian period bronze arrowheads predominated over iron ones by a ratio of 4 to 1. In other words, this is exactly the opposite of the situation in the Iron Age. We may explain this phenomenon by the fact that they were more complex in form than the Iron Age arrows, which made them difficult to cast in iron.[2]

Another type of object found in Palestine directly connected with weapons are the horse bits found at Gezer (though not in a stratigraphical context), which may also be assumed to be Irano-Scythian, and evidently in use among the Persian cavalry,[3] on the basis of close parallels from Persepolis and Deve-Huyuk.

Except for these, few other weapons have been recovered in Palestine. One important discovery was that of a Greek bronze helmet recovered from the sea near Ashkelon.[4]

SANCTUARIES AND CULT OBJECTS

Of the temples of the Persian period only meagre remains have been discovered (at Makmish and Lachish),[5] but many others are known from Cyprus and Phoenicia.[6] Comparing the Palestinian temples with those

[1] Avigad, *IEJ*, 11 (1961), 97–8, pl. 25: b–c; Mazar and Dunayevsky, *IEJ*, 17 (1967), pl. 31: 3–4; Petrie, *Gerar*, p. 24, pl. 66: 1–3.

[2] Crowfoot, *Samaria-Sebaste, III*, pp. 453–7; Johns, *QDAP*, 2 (1933), 53–7, pl. 20; 14, pl. 24; E. F. Schmidt, *Persepolis, vol. 2: Contents of the Treasury and other Discoveries* (Chicago, 1957), pp. 97–101, pl. 76.

[3] Culican, *Medes and Persians*, pp. 147; 14, pl. 24; Macalister, *Gezer*, vol. 11, pp. 13–14, fig. 214; Schmidt, *Persepolis*, p. 100, pls. 78: 2–4, 79: 7–9.

[4] G. Radan, 'Helmet Found Near Ascalon', *IEJ*, 8 (1958), 185–8.

[5] Y. Aharoni, 'Trial excavation in the "solar shrine" at Lachish', *IEJ*, 18 (1968), 157–64; Avigad, *IEJ*, 10 (1960), 90–6; Stern, *Material Culture*, pp. 64–70 (in Hebrew); Tufnell, *Iron Age*, pp. 141–5.

[6] M. Dunand, 'Encore la stèle de Yehavmilk Roi de Byblos', *BMB*, 5 (1941), 57–73; Gjerstad, *Swedish Cyprus Expedition*, vol. 4, part 2, pp. 12–23; 234–8.

of Cyprus and Phoenicia it becomes clear that by chance the two temples found here represent examples of the two major temple plans of this period: (1) the long type, made up of three areas along a single axis; in these temples the cult centred upon the *debir* or innermost part; (2) the broad type with one or more chambers, where the cult centred largely around an enclosed court at the front of the temple.

Examining these plans and the few decorative architectural remains discovered in temples in Phoenicia and Cyprus, it must be concluded that both plans are Phoenician in origin. The former is the earlier and it is possible that the latter form was renewed in this period. This conclusion also agrees with the picture revealed by the cult objects discovered within these temples.

Turning to the cult objects themselves, it seems that the finds of this period comprised mainly two types: (*a*) statuettes and figurines; (*b*) incense altars.

STATUETTES AND FIGURINES

As most of the statuettes and figurines in Palestine come from *favissae*, all chronological discussion must be centred on typological comparisons.[1] The stone statuettes may be chosen as a basis for this, for the following reasons: they are generally considered to be of Cypriot origin; they are not mass produced like the clay figurines, and it is thus easier to trace styles; the Swedish Cyprus Expedition succeeded in distinguishing detailed stylistic groups of a clearly delimited chronological period.[2] Comparison of such finds in Palestine and Cyprus thus enables absolute dates to be ascribed for the first group. These are of considerable value in analysing the other figurines. Comparison reveals immediately that all the stone statuettes found in Palestine are of the Cypriot styles called 'Sub-Archaic Cypro-Greek 1–2' and that they date to between 500 and 380 B.C.E. Among the stone statuettes are also some of Egyptian manufacture, which can only be dated generally to the fifth to fourth centuries B.C.E.[3]

In contrast to the relatively homogeneous stone statuettes, mainly from Cyprus, the pottery figurines of the Persian period in Palestine

---

[1] Avigad, *IEJ*, 10 (1960), 90–6; M. H. Chehab, 'Les Terres cuites de Kharayeb', *BMB*, 10 (1951–52); 11 (1953–54); A. Ciasca, 'Un deposito di statuette di Tell Gat', *OrAnt*, 2 (1963), 45–63; M. Dunand, 'Les Sculptures de la Favissa du Temple d'Amrit', *BMB*, 7 (1944–45), 99–107; O. Negbi, 'A Contribution of Mineralogy and Palaeontology to an Archaeological Study of Terracottas', *IEJ*, 14 (1964), 187–9; Stern, *Material Culture*, pp. 159–81 (in Hebrew).
[2] Gjerstad, *Swedish Cyprus Expedition*, vol. 4, part 2, pp. 93, 119–24.
[3] Avigad, *IEJ*, 10 (1960), 94.

comprise a heterogeneous collection displaying many different stylistic influences: Phoenician, Persian, Egyptian, Cypriot, Rhodian and Greek. However, it is in general possible to divide them into two families: (*a*) eastern style and (*b*) western style. The first group was distributed mainly in Phoenicia, Palestine and, to a more limited extent, Cyprus; individual examples have been found in Mesopotamia and Egypt as well. Not one has been found in the Aegean islands or in Greece proper. In contrast, the distribution of the second group is found to cover not only Phoenicia, Palestine and Cyprus, but also Rhodes, western Asia Minor, Greece and, sparsely, the western Mediterranean.[1] It seems that most examples are of Eastern Greek origin, and some are from Greece proper. The two groups are clearly differentiated according to style: whereas the first group comprises many stylistic elements which can be considered as of Canaanite, Egyptian and Mesopotamian–Persian influence mingled together, in keeping with the best of the Phoenician artistic tradition, the second group is much more uniform, and the origin of the type is much more readily ascertained.

Comparison of the western type of figurines with their parallels in the lands of origin (that is, Rhodes, Cyprus and Greece) reveals that, like the stone statuettes, most are to be dated to the end of the sixth century and the fifth century B.C.E. alone. Only a few types continue into the first half of the fourth century B.C.E.[2]

The dates of the eastern group, most of whose types are found only in Palestine and Phoenicia, are less firmly established. The chronological range determined for most of them is from the end of the sixth century down to the fourth century B.C.E. Since, however, they were found together with Cypriot and western figurines, it is evident that they are all of the same period, though their production in Palestine may have continued later into the fourth century B.C.E., down to the end of the Persian period.

As to the origin of the figurines, mineralogical and petrographic examinations carried out on the Tel Sippor finds revealed that three different clay compositions were used: (1) a type common in the Syro-Palestinian coastal region, of which about 70 per cent of the figurines were made; (2) a type found in the hilly region around Tel Sippor, of which about 25 per cent of the figurines were made; and (3) a Rhodian clay, of which about 5 per cent of the figurines were made.[3]

[1] N. Breitenstein, *Danish National Museum, Catalogue of Terracottas, Cypriot, Greek, Etruscan, Italian and Roman* (Copenhagen, 1941).

[2] F. N. Pryce, *Catalogue of Sculpture in the Department of Greek and Roman Antiquities of the British Museum* (2 vols.), vol. 1, part 3: *Cypriot and Etruscan* (London, 1931).

[3] Negbi, *IEJ*, 14 (1964), 187–9.

Thus, not more than 25 per cent of the Tel Sippor figurines were made in the immediate locality. The remainder had been imported from workshops in the densely-populated Phoenician regions along the coast, except for those belonging to the western group, which were either truly imported or made locally from imported moulds modelled in imitation of western ones. If this is the case with the western type figurines, it is even more true of the eastern group. The distribution of the latter indicates that they were made in the region along the Phoenician–Palestinian coast. This is further supported by their peculiar style, mixing Egyptian, Mesopotamian and Persian elements together. The facts stated confirm the generally-accepted assumption that such figurines are to be ascribed to the Phoenician population;[1] this is not contradicted by the finding of several examples on Cyprus, for there was a large Phoenician element on that island.

As for bronze figurines, most of those found in Palestine come from a single site, Ashkelon. All are of Egyptian style. Two, however, are of definite Canaanite style, continuing a very old tradition. This may indicate that the entire group was made by a local metalworker, using Egyptian patterns similar to those of some of the pottery figurines. The date of these bronze figurines is the fifth to fourth century B.C.E.[2]

In general it may be stated that at the beginning of the Persian period the usual figurines of the previous period (the Canaanite and Israelite types such as the Astarte pillars, and horses and horsemen of a particular type) were still common. Later in the Persian period (possibly at the end of the sixth, or the beginning of the fifth century B.C.E.) figurines and moulds in Cypriot and Eastern Greek styles were imported, being far superior both artistically and in quality. These types were dominant in Palestine and Phoenicia during the entire Persian period and were replaced only at the beginning of the Hellenistic period by figurines in the Attic style.

With the appearance of the latter, local craftsmen (Phoenicians) produced new figurine types, both by imitating the new Greek techniques (hollow moulding) and by improving their artistic standards. Among these appear the older patterns (fertility goddesses, etc.) in new guise, but displaying clearly contemporary influences, especially in minor details such as costume and jewellery.

[1] Avigad, *IEJ*, 10 (1960), 96; Ciasca, *OrAnt*, 2 (1963), 61.
[2] J. H. Iliffe, 'A Hoard of Bronzes from Askalon', *QDAP*, 5 (1935), 61–8.

INCENSE ALTARS

The limestone altars of the Persian period found in Palestine are of four major types: (1) those with geometric ornamentation, and painted patterns of human, animal and floral motifs; (2) those ornamented solely with geometric designs; (3) those ornamented in relief or with sculpture; and (4) plain.[1]

The typological development of two groups only can be established. Each of these groups may be subdivided into three phases of development: (1) in the first phase these two groups were decorated with rich and exact patterns; (2) in the second phase, the former patterns were executed in a careless manner; (3) in the third phase only the degenerate patterns of the first groups appear. This degeneration is evidenced mainly in the ornamentation, but also in the basic form. Examining the archeological contexts of the finds, it seems that dates may be ascribed to the three phases, as follows: (1) end of the sixth century and the fifth century B.C.E.; (2) and (3) second half of the fifth century and the fourth century B.C.E., phase 2 being of the first part of this period and phase 3 being of the second part, though it may have extended even into the Hellenistic period.

In addition to the altars from Palestine, similar incense altars are known in three other centres: Cyprus, South Arabia and Mesopotamia.[2] Various scholars have attempted to connect the Palestinian finds with each of the above groups.[3] But it seems that the Cypriot altars do not comprise a homogeneous type of uniform style, but rather individual finds with with chronological gaps between them. The more abundant assemblage from South Arabia, too, cannot suggest an origin for the Palestinian altars, for they are later (fourth to first centuries B.C.E.).[4] The

[1] N. Glueck, 'Incense Altars', *Eretz-Israel*, 10 (1971), 120–5 (in Hebrew); Macalister, *Gezer*, vol. II, pp. 442–5; Petrie, *Gerar*, pp. 18–19, pls. 40–1; Stern, *Material Culture*, pp. 181–94; E. Stern, 'Limestone Incense Altars', in *Beer-Sheba I, Excavations at Tel Beer-Sheba, Seasons 1969–1971*, ed. Y. Aharoni (Ramat-Gan, 1973), pp. 52–3; Tufnell, *Iron Age*, pls. 68–71.

[2] G. Caton-Thompson, *The Tombs and Moon Temple of Hureidha* (Oxford, 1944), pp. 47–60; R. L. Cleveland, *An Ancient South Arabian Necropolis; Objects from the Second Campaign (1951) in the Tymna Cemetery* (Baltimore, 1965), pp. 118–20; Gjerstad, *Swedish Cyprus Expedition*, vol. 4, part 2, pp. 178–9; L. Legrain, *Terracottas from Nippur* (Philadelphia, 1930), p. 36, pls. 65–7; C. L. Woolley, *Ur Excavations*, vol. 9; *The Neo-Babylonian and Persian Periods* (London, 1962), pp. 127–30, pl. 36.

[3] W. F. Albright, 'Some Recent Publications', *BASOR*, 98 (1945), 28; M. Forte, 'Sull 'origine di alcuni tipi di altarini sud-arabici', *AION*, 17 (1967), 97–120; K. Galling, 'Gerar', *ZDPV*, 52 (1929), 247–8; L. Ziegler, 'Tonkästchen aus Uruk, Babylon und Assur', *ZA*, 47 (1942), 224–40.

[4] R. L. Bowen and F. P. Albright, *Archaeological Discoveries in South Arabia*, part 1: *Archaeological Survey of Beihan* (Baltimore, 1958), pp. 149–53.

beginnings of the Mesopotamian altars, however, lie in the latter part of the seventh century B.C.E, and most are of the sixth to fourth centuries B.C.E., that is, they are older than the Palestinian ones.[1] Thus, it can be concluded – in the present writer's opinion – that the sudden appearance of such limestone altars in Palestine in the Persian period is an imitation of the common Assyrian practice. But there is no doubt that all the altars were made in Palestine, for several reasons: the Palestinian altars are all of local limestone, and not of pottery as in Mesopotamia; and the fairly uniform ornamentation of altars found far apart points to what could almost be called a single 'school', differing in many details from those of the other regions. This brings us to the further conclusion that the altars, like most of the other cult objects of the period, were also made by Phoenician craftsmen. Two of them (from Lachish and Tell es-Saidiye[2]) bear Phoenician inscriptions, and others were found within the Phoenician sanctuary at Makmish.[3]

SEALS AND SEAL IMPRESSIONS

The seals and impressions from the Persian period found in Palestine fall into two major groups: (*a*) private seals and (*b*) official seals connected with the administration of the provinces of Judea and Samaria.

(*a*) In the first group, distinction must be made between seals imported from various sources (Babylon, Persia, Egypt and Greece) and the local seals in mixed style, generally imitating one of the four imported seal types in form or motif.

The *Babylonian* seals are of two types: cylinder seals and octagonal conoid stamp seals.[4] Analysis of the context of their finds indicates that they first appeared in Palestine in the seventh century, were used especially in the sixth century, and continued in use in the fifth century B.C.E. The *Achemenid* seals are of identical form, though the motifs on them are different from the previous types; they date from the fifth to fourth centuries B.C.E.[5] The *Egyptian* seals in the form of actual scarabs

---

[1] W. F. Albright, 'Some Recent Publications,' *BASOR*, 132 (1953), 46–7; Stern, in *Beer-Sheba I*, pp. 52–3.

[2] J. B. Pritchard, 'The Palace of Tell es Sa'idiyeh', *Expedition*, 11 (1968), 20–2; Tufnell, *Iron Age*, pp. 358–9, pl. 49: 3.

[3] Avigad, *IEJ*, 10 (1960), 95.

[4] F. J. Bliss and R. A. S. Macalister, *Excavations in Palestine 1898–1900* (London, 1902), p. 41, figs. 16, 153; R. Dajani, 'A Neo-Babylonian Seal from Amman', *ADAJ*, 6–7 (1962), 124–5; C. N. Tohus, 'Excavations at Atlit 1930–1931; The South-Eastern Cemetery', *QDAP*, 2 (1933), 104; Mazar and Dunayevsky, *IEJ*, 17 (1967), 133–43; Petrie, *Gerar*, pl. 19: 29.

[5] Cross, *BA*, 26 (1963), 114–15; Crowfoot, *Samaria-Sebaste*, III, pl. 15: 42; E. Stern,

generally contain names of the kings of the twenty-seventh and twenty-eighth dynasties.[1] The *Greek* seals are oval, depicting typical Greek motifs such as the owl, the head of Athena, Heracles, etc. Sealings of this type were, of course, common in the Hellenistic period and later, though an examination of the contexts of several of those found in Palestine and other places in the East reveals that they began to appear at the end of the fifth century, and in the fourth century B.C.E. they were quite widespread.[2]

The *local* seals imitate the forms of the first group as follows: octagonal conoids of Babylonian origin; scarabs of Egyptian style; oval seals of Greek origin. However, none were found in cylindrical form, and the scaraboid form is quite common, it being the usual form in Israelite times. Local seals differ from imported ones in containing mixtures of motif (for example, Persian–Greek, Persian–Egyptian, etc.) and inconsistency between form and motif, for example, a Greek motif on a scarab, or a Persian motif on an oval seal. Generally, the foreign motifs have taken on a slight change in form, and the details of the originals are blurred.

Most of the seals of the local group are ascribed to Phoenician workmanship, which habitually mixed styles in this manner; this ascription is suggested by the fact that some of the sealings of this type contain typically Phoenician personal names in Phoenician or Aramaic script.[3]

(*b*) Official seals of the second group include several sealings which may be interpreted as those of Persian administrative officials in the province of Judea, used in the gathering of taxes in kind. This is supported by their verbal content and by their pattern. As for the former, the *yhud* group, in all its variations, may be divided into those containing the name of the satrap, his title and the name of the province, and those containing only the name of the province in various degrees of abbreviation, in Hebrew or Aramaic script, or in a mixed Hebrew and Aramaic script. The *yhud* group of impressions can further be ascribed on the basis of their limited distribution within the borders of

'Seal Impressions in the Achaemenid Style in the Province of Judah', *BASOR*, 202 (1971), 10–11, n. 22; G. E. Wright, *Shechem, The Biography of a Biblical City* (New York–Toronto, 1965), p. 168, fig. 94.

[1] Johns, *QDAP*, 2 (1933), pl. 14: 499, 553, 659; B. Porter and R. L. B. Moss, *Topographical Bibliography of Ancient Hieroglyphic Texts, Reliefs and Paintings* (Oxford, 1951), vol. 7, p. 381.

[2] Y. Aharoni, *Excavations at Ramat Raḥel (1961–1962)* (Rome, 1964), p. 23, pl. 18: 12; Cross, *BA*, 26 (1963), 115; Elgavish, pl. 61: 147–8; Stern, *Material Culture*, p. 197, fig. 310.

[3] Broshi, *Qadmoniot*, 2 (1969), 126 (in Hebrew); Johns, *QDAP*, 2 (1933), 44–5. pl. 14.

this province.[1] Another type contains only a monogram which can be connected with similar monograms used in Judea at the end of the Israelite period. This group may also be interpreted as impressions made by the satrap.[2]

To this group may also be added those impressions that bear names of locations, for example *mwsh*, *yrslm*, and so on, because the present writer believes that these are the impressions of officials overseeing royal estates at these places.[3] The same interpretation may be applied to the group of impressions depicting various animals (for example, lions, griffins, bulls). These impressions contained the symbols of the overseeing officials, certifying the products of their estates or some other sub-district of the satrapy under their control. There is, however, a clear and great similarity between the designs on these impressions and those on the Achemenid impressions found at Ur and Persepolis, and elsewhere in the administrative centres of the Persian empire.[4]

Of the sealings of the province of Samaria, two come from the hoard found in wadi Daliyeh.[5] These include the names of the satraps (one mentions the title 'satrap of Samaria'); the others have not yet been published, and they may include anepigraphic sealings which should be ascribed to the same province. In any event, the group of impressions containing only monograms and numbers, so far unique to Shechem, should be interpreted in a manner similar to those from Judea; that is they are connected with the gathering of taxes in kind within the province.[6]

WEIGHTS AND COINS

The use of the unit of silver by weight in financial transactions was common in Palestine and neighbouring countries throughout the sixth to the fourth centuries B.C.E., alongside the use of coins.[7] The types of weights which are supposed to have existed, on the basis of literary sources and archeological finds, are as follows: (1) the royal Persian

---

[1] N. Avigad, 'New Light on the MSH Seal-Impressions', *IEJ*, 8 (1958), 113–19; F. M. Cross, Jr., 'Judean Stamps', *Eretz-Israel*, 9 (1969), 20–7; G. Garbini, 'The Dating of the Post-Exilic Stamps', in Y. Aharoni, *Excavations at Ramat Raḥel, Seasons of 1959–1960* (Rome, 1962), pp. 61–8; E. Y. Kutscher, '"Pḥw" and its cognates', *Tarbiz*, 30 (1960–61), 112ff (in Hebrew); P. W. Lapp, 'Ptolemaic Stamped Handles from Judah', *BASOR*, 172 (1963), 22–35; Stern, *Material Culture*, pp. 200–5.

[2] N. Avigad, 'Yehûd or Ha'îr', *BASOR*, 158 (1960), 23–7; Cross, *IEJ*, 18 (1968), 226–33; idem, *Eretz-Israel*, 9 (1969), 20–7.

[3] Avigad, *IEJ*, 8 (1958), 113–19; H. N. Richardson, 'A Stamped Handle from Khirbet Yarmuk', *BASOR*, 192 (1968), 12–16.   [4] Stern, *BASOR*, 202 (1971), 6–16.

[5] E. Eitan, ed., *Inscriptions Reveal, Documents from the time of the Bible, the Mishna and the Talmud. Israel Museum Catalogue, no. 100* (Jerusalem, 1973), p. 66.

[6] Lapp, *BASOR*, 172 (1963), 22–35; Wright, *Shechem*, p. 167, fig. 192.

[7] Stern, *Material Culture*, pp. 213–25 (in Hebrew).

standard, divided thus: 1 *karsha* = 10 *sigloi* = 40 quarter *sigloi* = 400 *ḥlrn*; (2) the local Palestinian standard, which preserved the Hebrew names of Israelite times, though the standard itself was entirely different from the earlier one; (3) the Egyptian standard; (4) the Phoenician–Punic standard.

The use of coins in Palestine, on the basis of the finds, began at the start of the Persian period (the end of the sixth century B.C.E.);[1] from this early period only very few coins are extant, and this is true also of the first half of the fifth century B.C.E.; thus we may assume that the use of coins was common only from the end of the fifth century, and mainly during the fourth century B.C.E.

The coins in use in this period were all minted in three principal standards: the Persian, the Phoenician and the Attic. The first was based on the gold daric which weighed 8.4 grams and was divided into 20 sigloi (shekels) of silver, each of which weighed 5.5 grams. The Phoenician standard was based on the silver stater of 13.9 grams, divided into many sub-values, the principal one being the half-stater of 6.5 grams. The Attic coinage was based on the silver tetradrachm of 17.5 grams which was divided principally into drachms of 4.2 grams.

An examination of the Greek coin types of the Persian period discovered in excavations reveals that most come from Athens and a few from Thasos and Aegae. But the assemblage of coins of this period found in Palestine is quite meagre and probably does not reflect reality either in extent or in origin, on the strength of comparison with the neighbouring lands. Hoards of Greek coins of the Persian period from the Syro-Phoenician coast and in Egypt contained thousands of coins from all the known mints in the Greek world.[2]

The published finds of Phoenician coins from Palestine are also quite meagre. In the various excavation reports, only several hundred are recorded, almost all from Tyre and Sidon; very few are from Aradus and there are none from Byblos.[3]

During the Persian period there were also coins in use in Palestine, called today 'Philisto-Arabian' and 'Philisto-Egyptian', which should be regarded as local coinage.[4] What is unique in these coins is the

[1] J. Meshorer, 'An Attic Archaic Coin from Jerusalem', *Atiqot*, 3 (1961), 185; Wright, *Shechem*, pp. 168–9, fig. 95.

[2] S. P. Noe, 'A Bibliography of Greek Coin Hoards', *NNM*, 78 (1937).

[3] Cross, *BA*, 26 (1963), 116–17; A. Kindler, 'The Mint of Tyre–The Major Source of Silver Coins in Ancient Palestine', *Eretz-Israel*, 8 (1967), 318–24 (in Hebrew).

[4] G. F. Hill, *Catalogue of the Greek Coins of Palestine* (London, 1914), pp. 83–9; A. Kindler, 'The Greco-Phoenician Coins struck in Palestine in the times of the Persian Empire', *INJ*, 1 (1963), 2–6, 25–7; C. Lambert, 'Egypto-Arabian, Phoenician and other Coins of the Fourth Century B.C. Found in Palestine', *QDAP*, 2 (1932), 1–10.

abundance of types; there are very few duplicates, at least of examples with the two sides corresponding. We suggest that the privilege of minting these coins had been granted by the Persian authorities to the officials appointed over the various satrapal treasuries in Palestine (in Judea, Samaria, Gaza, etc.) for local business. The minting was done by the treasury officials, each using the device of his own seal. This would explain: (1) the abundance of types, for the officials were changed every so often; (2) the abundant motifs on these coins, all taken from those common on seals of Persian officials at each site. As for date, it is agreed that they begin at the end of the fifth century and that the bulk are from the fourth century B.C.E.

A special branch of the local 'Philisto-Arabian' family consists of those coins bearing the name of the province of Judea.[1] It seems that, like the others in this group, they were also minted by the royal officials in charge of the treasury in Judea (not necessarily of Persian race) who were permitted to coin small silver denominations for day-to-day business needs within the province. New and quite surprising evidence strengthening this hypothesis was discovered only recently when some coins bearing a Hebrew name, with the title 'the satrap', were found in Tell Jemmeh.[2] The '*yhud*' coins are contemporary with the other Philisto-Arabian coins, which are dated in the last part of the fifth century and the fourth century B.C.E. It seems that all these coins were for normal business transactions, like the other coins used in Palestine in this period.

The other types of coins in use in Palestine were those common in the Persian period in neighbouring lands to the north, south and east of Palestine, and even though some types have not yet been found in excavations there, it is not illogical to assume that they had been in use in Palestine as well. These can be grouped as follows: (1) Persian coins of large denomination from the central imperial mint: *darics* and *sigloi*, which were common throughout the empire;[3] (2) Cypriot coins, many of which have been found in Syria and Egypt, but have not yet come to light in Palestine. In this connection it should be noted that the motifs on some of the Philisto-Arabian coins are imitations of Cypriot coins; (3) Egyptian coins, struck in Egypt during the brief period of independence (400–344 B.C.E.); we assume that at the beginning of this period Egypt controlled large parts of the coastal plain, and, further, that the Egyptians may have issued their own coins in this region.[4]

[1] Y. Meshorer, 'A New Type of YHD Coin', *IEJ*, 16 (1966), 217–19.
[2] L. Y. Rahmani, 'Silver Coins of the Fourth Century B.C. from Tel Gamma,' *IEJ*, 21 (1971), 158–60.
[3] A. U. Pope (ed.), *A Survey of Persian Art*, vols. I–IV (Oxford, 1938); F. Zayadine, 'Samaria-Sebaste Clearance and Excavations', *ADAJ*, 12–13 (1967–68), 77–80.
[4] Stern, *Material Culture*, p. 225, fig. 369.

It should also be mentioned that the privilege of minting in gold was retained for the Persian imperial mint alone. In this manner the Persian authorities could control the economy of the areas under their rule. It also seems that the privilege of minting granted to various cities and vassal states was closely controlled and inspected in respect of the amounts minted and the standard used.

THE CHARACTER OF THE MATERIAL CULTURE

A study of the material culture of Palestine reveals that the country was already divided into two regions at the beginning of the period: on the one hand the mountainous area of Judea and Transjordan (and to a lesser extent also Samaria) and on the other, Galilee and the coastal area. The border between these two cultural areas is at times very sharp – almost like a border dividing two countries. Without an understanding of this division of Palestine it is almost impossible to understand the material development of the culture of the period.

An analysis of the culture of these two regions demonstrates that the mountain culture is basically 'eastern' in character. It is made up of a local culture which continues the Israelite tradition, and eastern influences (Assyrian, Babylonian and Egyptian). In the coastal culture on the other hand, which is basically 'western' in nature, Eastern Greek, Cypriot and Athenian elements can be observed. It is therefore probable that the Greek material culture considerably preceded the Macedonian conquest. At the same time there is no doubt that this was exclusively an external conquest, that is to say, Greek cultural products were used without acquiring the significance they had in their native land; they were adapted to local traditions and customs. It appears that the main bearers of this new culture in Palestine were the Phoenicians and only in the second instance Greek soldiers and settlers.

We thus believe that Albright's definition of 'Iron III' for the culture of this period,[1] is justified in so far as it is restricted to the mountain region of Judea and Benjamin. It is not, however, suitable for other regions of the country. Moreover, it is now evident that the difference between the 'coastal' culture and that of the 'mountain' region is not a difference in time, as proposed by Albright, but rather a question of influence of the 'eastern' or 'western' cultures over these areas.

From all that has been said so far, the astonishing fact emerges that in the case of the material culture in Palestine one cannot distinguish any influence of the Persian material culture – the culture of the rulers – by whose name we identify the entire period. The scanty

[1] Albright, *Archaeology*, p. 142.

Persian influence was mainly expressed by isolated types of ceramics; by a small number of ornaments and Achemenid style metal objects, which also appear to have been made by the Phoenicians; and a few clothing accessories on some Phoenician figurines.

The main influence of the long period of Persian rule in Palestine can only be felt indirectly in all the spheres directly connected with foreign rule, such as administration, military organization, money and taxation. In each of the few inscriptions from wadi Daliyeh so far published, the dates given are according to the royal years of the Persian kings and the officials are those of the local Persian administration. Information about military organization is contained on the ostracon recently discovered in Arad;[1] it mentions an individual who belongs to a certain 'standard' (that is, a Persian military unit which is also known from Elephantine in Egypt). The military strongholds and many granaries discovered at nearly all the large sites in Palestine reflect the Persian military system, and – most important – a large part of the weapons and several chariot accessories found in the tombs of that period are of the Scytho-Iranian type, just like those found in the guard-rooms at Persepolis. It was already supposed that some of the tombs at Gezer were in fact the graves of Persian soldiers.

But the area where Persian influence is most conspicuous is that of taxation and money. In contrast to the liberal approach of the Persian rulers towards the conquered people in matters of cult and administration, in questions of economy and taxation it was rather severe. The taxes levied on the various provinces were determined according to their size and prosperity, and had to be paid in precious metals only. The seal-impressions on the handles of vessels from Judea which give evidence of the taxation system, and whose motifs were taken from the range of Achemenid royal motifs, prove that initially matters of administration and finance in Judea were conducted by officials of the Achemenid empire. The stratigraphic context proves that these impressions date from the end of the sixth to the end the fifth century B.C.E. only. Subsequently these Achemenid seals were changed for seals written in Aramaic, bearing the name of the province, *yhud*. This seems to point to a reform in the administration of the province at the end of the fifth century B.C.E., maybe at the time of Nehemiah or a little later. Alt surmised that Nehemiah, in fact, freed Judea from its subjection to Samaria and turned it into an independent province.[2]

---

[1] Y. Aharoni, 'The Second Season of Excavations at Tel Arad', *BIES*, 28 (1964), 153–75.

[2] A. Alt, *Kleine Schriften zur Geschichte des Volkes Israel*, 3 vols. (München, 1953); vol. 2, pp. 316–37.

OUTLINE OF HISTORY

Archeological excavations have contributed greatly to our knowledge of the history of the settlement of Palestine in this obscure period. A detailed study of the results of excavation of the sites of this period in Palestine allows us to conclude with some measure of certainty that there were two waves of destruction during the Persian period.

About the first we learn through the excavations in Benjamin. Here it seems that a large number of the towns which had been spared the destruction wrought upon Judea at the fall of the monarchy were destroyed about a hundred years later (about 480 B.C.E.). No historical explanation was found for this destruction, though it may be assumed that it occurred in connection with some minor war, such as that which threatened Judea in the days of Nehemiah.[1]

The picture is different concerning the second wave of destruction, one which affected only the coastal regions and the Negeb; this evidently occurred around 380 B.C.E. This destruction is connected with the Egyptian struggle for independence (circa 404 to 400 B.C.E.), which spread two decades later to the lowlands of Palestine. This assumption is strengthened by two important finds: an inscription of Nepherites I (399–393 B.C.E.), at Gezer, and steles of Achoris (393–380 B.C.E.) at Akko and Sidon.[2]

The final wave of destruction which hit the settlements of the Persian period in Palestine is irregular and evidently connected with several events, the most significant of which were: the Sidonian revolt in 351 B.C.E., which brought about the destruction of the province of Dor;[3] the wars within the territories of Tyre and Akko, on the one hand, and Gaza on the other, in the days of Alexander; and the Samaritan revolt against Alexander which brought about the destruction of many major cities in these regions, such as Megiddo, Akko, Tell Abu Hawam, Samaria and Gaza.

Several cities may have been destroyed even as late as the wars of the Diadochi (Shiqmonah, Tel Sippor), as is proved by the coins of Alexander the Great which were uncovered within the destruction levels of the Persian period.[4]

[1] Lapp, BA, 28 (1965), 9–10; Weinberg, 'Post Exilic Palestine'; G. E. Wright, 'The Water Systems of Gibeon', JNES, 22 (1963), 210–11; idem, Shechem, p. 167, n. 33.

[2] Macalister, Gezer, vol. 2, p. 313; Rowe, Scarabs, pp. 295–6, pl. 38.

[3] D. Barag, 'The Effects of the Thennes Rebellion on Palestine', BASOR, 183 (1966), 6–12; E. Stern, 'Archaeological Aspects of the History of the Coastal Regions of Palestine during the Fourth Century B.C.E.' in Bible and Jewish History, Studies dedicated to the Memory of Jacob Liver, ed. B. Uffenheimer (Tel Aviv, 1971), pp. 207–21 (in Hebrew).

[4] This chapter was completed in 1973. For additional bibliography see E. Stern, The Material Culture of the Land of the Bible (Warminster, 1982, forthcoming).

CHAPTER 6

HEBREW AND ARAMAIC IN THE PERSIAN PERIOD

Hebrew and Aramaic were the two main languages in use among the Jews during the Persian period. They are both north-west Semitic languages but while Hebrew belongs, together with Phoenician, Moabite and Ammonite, to the Canaanite branch, Aramaic forms a branch apart. Hebrew was the native tongue of both Judah and Israel during the monarchic period, although there were dialect distinctions between the north and the south. Among the Canaanite dialects, Moabite seems to be particularly close to Hebrew, but our documentation for these dialects is relatively meagre. After the dissolution of the northern kingdom, speakers of other languages were introduced into various parts of the country to replace exiled Israelites.

Aramaic was the language solely of the Arameans gathered at first in tribal units and then in city-states and petty kingdoms in Syria and Mesopotamia. In the eighth century it became the lingua franca of the Assyrian empire, especially in the provinces 'Beyond the River' (Euphrates). The complicated cuneiform writing system of the Assyrians was replaced by the relatively simpler alphabetic Aramaic script, at first in those provinces where alphabetic writing was already in use and then in Assyria proper. Aramaic was introduced for commercial and administrative purposes and Aramaic scribes were employed alongside Assyrian ones, since expansion to the west brought about the absorption of many Aramaic speakers into Assyria proper. Aramaic was used for diplomatic purposes in lands outside the Assyrian empire (see, for example, 2 Kings 18: 26, Isa. 36: 11) and subsequently also for communication within the Assyro-Babylonian area (*KAI* 233). During the Neo-Babylonian period, with a Chaldean dynasty in control of the Babylonian empire, followed by Nabonidus, a ruler of Aramean ancestry, the importance of Aramaic grew. Akkadian was replaced by Aramaic as the main language spoken throughout the land, and the increased role of Aramaic may be traced, although Akkadian (Neo-Babylonian) remained in use for centuries to come. The Saqqara papyrus (*KAI* 266) sent, probably, from Philistia to Egypt about 600 B.C.E., attests the continued role of Aramaic in the international sphere.

Cyrus and Cambyses maintained the use of Aramaic in the royal chancery alongside Babylonian and Elamite. Darius I was, it would seem, responsible for the invention of the Old Persian script.[1] Although this was a cuneiform script, it was not, like the Elamite, based on the Sumero-Akkadian tradition, but was rather inspired, in all likelihood, by an alphabetic (Aramaic) model. The Old Persian script was a somewhat artificial means of writing royal inscriptions and was not intended for daily use; alongside the various national languages and scripts that were used in the Achemenid period – Babylonian, Egyptian, Elamite, Greek, Lydian, Lycian, Phoenician – Aramaic was used throughout the empire for all aspects of written communication and records. In the west we have remnants of this use in Asia Minor, Palestine, North Arabia and Egypt. Aramaic papyri have been found at various sites in Egypt (Elephantine, Saqqara, Hermopolis, etc.). In the east, besides the various types of inscriptions at Persepolis and dockets on Neo-Babylonian tablets, it is clear from the continued use of Aramaic as far east as Afghanistan and the Indus valley, and the continuation of the Aramaic scribal tradition in Sogdiana and other parts of the Persian empire in later periods, that Aramaic was already widely used there.[2] A unique method evolved in the Persian chanceries which allowed for this widespread use of Aramaic: the document was dictated in Persian to a scribe who wrote in Aramaic; it was then read aloud at its destination by a scribe or another properly trained person in Persian or another of the languages used throughout the empire. This is what is meant by the term *mephorash* (Ezra 4: 18), the equivalent of Persian (*h*)*uzvarišn*.[3]

Aramaic absorbed many influences. In the earlier periods, the Canaanite dialects in the west and the Akkadian in the east left their traces on the vocabulary and grammatical structure of the language. During the Persian period, Aramaic adopted a great number of Iranian loanwords and it is not surprising to find some Egyptian loanwords in the texts from Egypt. The division of Aramaic into Eastern and Western dialects, usually drawn for the later periods, is already discernible in the Persian period. Official Aramaic – the dialect used in the chanceries and

---

[1] J. Lewy, 'The Problems inherent in Section 70 of the Bisutun Inscription', *HUCA*, 25 (1954), 188–208; H. H. Paper, 'The Old Persian/L/Phoneme', *JAOS*, 76 (1956), 24–6; W. Hinz, *Neue Wege im Altpersischen* (Wiesbaden, 1973).

[2] W. B. Henning, 'Mitteliranisch', in *Iranistik, Handbuch der Orientalistik*, I: 4: 1 (Leiden, 1958), pp. 21–58; cf. A. Dupont-Sommer, 'La stèle trilingue récemment découverte au Lêtôon de Xanthos: le texte araméen', *CRAIBL* (1974), 132–49.

[3] H. H. Schaeder, *Iranische Beiträge* (Halle, 1930), pp. 1–14; H. J. Polotsky, 'Aramaische *prš* und das *Huzvaresch*', *Le Muséon*, 45 (1932), 273–83; in *Current Trends in Linguistics*, 6 (The Hague, 1971), pp. 393–9.

courts of the Achemenid empire – was essentially an Eastern dialect but it was never entirely uniform since it was surely influenced by the spoken language of the scribes. Both dialects can be discerned in the relatively plentiful corpus of Aramaic documents found in Egypt. The letters of Arsames, the Persian governor of Egypt, written on leather, were found in Egypt, but had been sent there from Babylon and Susa and are in the Eastern dialect,[1] as are his letters on papyrus written in Egypt. It is not surprising that these letters are particularly rich in Iranian loanwords, especially *CAP* 26. The official letters of the Jews of Elephantine are also written in the Eastern dialect but the distinctive features of this dialect such as the use of Akkadian and Iranian loan-words and certain syntactic and morphological traits are less frequent in their private correspondence. The Hermopolis letters, late sixth century, are in a Western Aramaic dialect.[2] The legal texts of the Jews of Elephantine are also in Official Aramaic, with elements from a variety of traditions: Neo-Babylonian and earlier Akkadian – *dyn wdbb* = *dīnu u dabābu* (case and lawsuit); *rḥmn* = *remūtu* (gift) etc.; Persian – *'ẓt* = *azata* (free), *ḥnbg whngyt* = *hanbaga* and *hangaitha* (partners), and so on; Hebrew – *'dh* = *'ēdāh* (community), *tkwnh* (ready cash); and are clearly based on earlier formulary combining West Semitic, Aramaic, Neo-Assyrian and Judaic material.

The literary texts also show similar dialect distinctions. The fragmentary Aramaic version of Darius' Behistun inscription is in Eastern Aramaic; the same is true for the framework story of the Proverbs of Ahikar, while the proverbs themselves are written in a dialect which may be considered Western.[3] The only other Aramaic legal texts from the Persian period are those from the wadi Daliyeh cave. Their language shares some of the features of the Elephantine texts but is closer in vocabulary to later Palestinian material.[4] Alongside the Official Aramaic used in legal documents and administrative material, a literary dialect emerged, which may be called Standard Literary Aramaic.[5] It is probable that annals and chronicles were written in this dialect and that even political tracts and court novels were composed in it, as well as

[1] G. R. Driver, *Aramaic Documents of the Fifth Century B.C.* (abridged and revised; Oxford, 1965), pp. 8–12.
[2] J. C. Greenfield, 'The Dialects of Ancient Aramaic', *JNES*, 37 (1978), 93–9; E. Y. Kutscher, 'The Hermopolis Papyri', *IOS*, 1 (1971), 103–19.
[3] J. C. Greenfield, 'Dialect Traits in Early Aramaic', *Leš*, 32 (1968), 364–5; Kutscher, *IOS*, 1 (1971), 108.
[4] The authors thank Professor F. M. Cross for permission to study these documents before publication.
[5] Cf. J. C. Greenfield, 'Standard Literary Aramaic', *Actes du Premier Congrès International de Linguistique Sémitique et Chamito-Sémitique* (The Hague, 1974), pp. 280–9.

translations or adaptations of Sumero-Akkadian literary and religious texts. Biblical Aramaic is now considered by most scholars as part of Official Aramaic, on the basis of morphology, syntax and vocabulary. The Aramaic portions of Ezra and Daniel are composed in it. Ezra is a historical record quoting official letters and documents; modern discoveries have verified that the phraseology and terminology typical of such documents are used, but the orthography has been modernized.

Daniel in its present form is a product of the Hellenistic age; it is more literary than Ezra, consisting of both poetry and prose, and its language is richer than that of Ezra, but it surely contains quotations from earlier literary works. The place of composition and redaction of works such as Daniel in Palestine does not affect the fact that the author wrote in an essentially Eastern dialect. It is in this Standard Literary Aramaic that the Qumran Aramaic texts were composed. Of these, texts such as Tobit and the Dream of Nabonidus may very well be compositions of the late Persian period.[1] Standard Literary Aramaic was also used at a later date for the 'official' Targums – Onqelos and Jonathan – and for such works as the *Megillat Ta'anit*. Its influence may be seen in the orthographic patterns of Syriac and perhaps other Aramaic dialects.

Although Western Aramaic was surely influenced by Canaanite in the early period of their contact in the Syro-Palestinian area, there are few traces of this in the Aramaic of the Persian period beyond certain loanwords in the legal sphere (see above, p. 117) and certain words of religious significance such as *khny'* (priests) and *mzrqy'* (basins) at Elephantine or designating Judean institutions such as *šptyn* (judges; Ezra 7: 25). The root *špt* occurs also in *CAP* 52, one of the earliest texts found at Elephantine. The possibility has been raised that some Elephantine fragments are in Hebrew, but it is clear that the Jews of Elephantine used Aramaic as their language. In the later Palestinian dialects of Aramaic – Jewish, Christian and Samaritan – clear signs of Hebrew influence are present.

Hebrew was the major language in Judah until the Babylonian conquest. It is impossible to assess the linguistic situation in Israel from the time of the Assyrian conquest in 721 B.C.E. since material is lacking, but the main language of the various groups implanted in Judah by the Assyrians was in all likelihood Aramaic. It is clear from passages in 2 Kings and Isaiah referred to above (p. 115) that Aramaic was known by some members of Hezekiah's court at the time of Sennacherib's

---

[1] A list of published Aramaic texts from Qumran will be found in J. A. Fitzmyer, 'The Contribution of Qumran Aramaic to the Study of the New Testament', *NTS*, 20 (1974), 404–6.

campaign in Judah (701 B.C.E.). This is not surprising since Judah was under strong Assyrian influence during the reign of Ahaz. It is clear from the same passages that the populace as such did not know Aramaic. This situation held until the end of the monarchy, although one may assume that, with the rising importance of Aramaic as the lingua franca in both Assyria and Babylonia, an ever-growing number of people in Judah were familiar with Aramaic. The event that was to be crucial for the history of the Hebrew language was the Babylonian Exile, for with the dissolution of the monarchy, the exile to Babylon of a large segment of the population encompassing the governing and artisan classes, the flight of many to Egypt and other neighbouring countries, the scribal schools must also have been deeply affected. The traditional modes of transmitting the language and the institutions that served as a strong guard for its integrity were eroded. The biblical and other sources do not inform us of the Babylonians transferring other population groups to Judah – indeed it was not their policy to do so; it may be assumed that the vacuum left by the deportations to Babylon was gradually filled by the encroachment of neighbouring peoples. It is from Ezra and Nehemiah that we learn of the foreign wives taken by many highly-placed Judeans, and of the fact that many could not speak Hebrew, called here (Neh. 13: 24) *yĕhūdīt*, as in Isa. 36: 11. The number of rural people who moved into Jerusalem also affected the language, for they brought with them their own dialect. For those who returned after Cyrus' edict and for the groups which returned later, Hebrew was no longer a mother tongue; they were surely Aramaic speakers. This, together with Aramaic's official status throughout the Achemenid realm, strongly influenced the linguistic situation in the land. The need to translate the law into Aramaic (for that is surely the meaning of *mephorash*, Neh. 8: 8; compare Ezra 4: 18) bears witness to the widespread use of Aramaic among the Jews of Jerusalem during this period.

Yet Hebrew, to judge from the sources available to us, remained as both a literary and a spoken language in Judah and perhaps in other parts of the country too. Our sources for the period are epigraphic and literary. The epigraphic sources are very slight and will be surveyed below. The literary remains are considerable and varied. Although we learn from Nehemiah of the struggle to keep Hebrew as the spoken language, the literary remains as such cannot prove anything beyond the continued use of Hebrew as a literary language – for prayers and hymns, writing chronicles and recording prophecies. It is from the analysis of Late Biblical Hebrew and the detection of vernacular elements in that literary language that conclusions may be drawn. Also, the continued use of Hebrew in Judea as a spoken language for the following 600 years and the gradual emergence of the vernacular dialect as a new literary language – that is, the replacement of Biblical Hebrew by Mishnaic Hebrew – is important. The use of this dialect in the letters and legal documents from the Bar Kochba caves attests to its vitality up to that period;[1] the language of ordinary conversation recorded in Tannaitic sources, as well as the concreteness and earthiness of the language, attests to its not merely being the product of the schoolhouse.

The literary remains of the Persian period may be divided into the following groups: (a) poetry and prophecy: the Song of Songs, some late Psalms, Haggai, Zechariah and Malachi; (b) prose tales: Jonah, Esther and perhaps also Ruth; and (c) historical works: Ezra, Nehemiah and Chronicles. Three distinctive elements may be detected in Late Biblical Hebrew: Classical Biblical Hebrew, Aramaic and vernacular Hebrew. It may be said in general that the works in categories (a) and (b) prove that some writers were very skilful at using Classical Hebrew forms and giving to their work an antique flavour, but even in these works the choice of words and elements of syntax show that the influence of Aramaic and vernacular Hebrew was strong. New words appear during this period: some are clearly loanwords from Aramaic, Akkadian or Persian; others must have been part of the vernacular vocabulary and are now used for the first time in literature, the same words being found at a later date in Mishnaic Hebrew. Words known from Classical Hebrew occur with new meanings in these texts. The syntax of both prose and poetry has undergone change. The relatively easy, flowing style of the pre-exilic texts has become more complex, for even though sentence structure has become simpler, the syntax is less flexible than in Classical Biblical Hebrew, and in some books, such as Chronicles, the prose style is cumbersome and lacking in elegance. Among the outstanding changes are: (1) the tenses emerge with definite functions, the perfect as a past, the imperfect as a future and the participle as a present tense; (2) there is fuller use of the *waw*-consecutive with the past and future tenses and consequently a much more limited use of the so-called '*waw*-conversive'; (3) a narrative of frequentative past develops with the use of the past of *hyh* (to be) with the participle, for example, *hāyū 'ômĕrīm* (they said) (Neh. 6: 19); (4) few subordinate clauses without relative particles (under the influence of Aramaic *zy/dy*, *'ašer* and *še* replaced *kī*) and greater use of various conjunctions; (5) in the morphology of the noun, greater use of the patterns *qittūl*, *qattālāh*, *taqtīl*; (6) spelling and phonology were affected, plene writing became

---

[1] E. Y. Kutscher, 'The Languages of the Hebrew and Aramaic Letters of Bar Cochba and his Contemporaries', *Leš*, 26 (1962), 7–23 (in Hebrew).

usual; for example, the name David was written *dwyd* rather than *dwd*, the name of Damascus was written and pronounced *Darmeśeq* rather than *Dammeśeq*. These and other changes are found in varying degrees in different books.[1]

The author of Jonah wrote, on the whole, in an acceptable Classical Hebrew style, but in his choice of words he reveals his period, for example: *hit'aśśēt* (to think) for *ḥāśab*; *minnāh* (to appoint) for *hifqīd*; *hetīl* for *hiślik* (throw, cast), *śataq* for *heḥriś* (be silent). The strange *beśellemi* (because of whom) and *ba'ăśer lĕmī* is a calque on Aramaic *bĕdīleman* (Jonah 1: 8).

The author of Esther displays great narrative skill and stylistic ability. He was a master of Classical Hebrew style and used such typical elements as the '*waw*-conversive', the interrogative *he*, and the infinitive absolute with finesse. However, even though he carefully writes *hammelek 'ăḥaśvērōś* (King Ahasuerus) rather than *'aḥaśvērōś hammelek* (Ahasuerus the king), the later Aramaizing form, he cannot avoid using the late *malkūt* (realm) rather than *mamlākā* for kingdom. In addition, the numerous loanwords from Aramaic: *yĕqār* (honour), *'ābdān* (loss), *'ānas* (restrain), *śalaṭ* (rule) – and from Persian: *partĕmīm* (nobles), *patśegen* (copy), *pitgām* (decree), *dāt* (law), *'ăḥaśdarpĕnīm* (satraps) etc., the many neologisms and the use of new nominal patterns also reveal the date of composition. In the late Psalms it is the choice of words, as well as turns of phrase and certain stylistic subtleties, that serve as identifying marks.[2] If the author(s) of Ezra and Nehemiah shared the Babylonian birthplace of the protagonists of these books or made extensive use of their diaries and records, the extensive Aramaic influence on the vocabulary and syntax of these books would be self-explanatory. He was surely a scribe trained in the writing of Aramaic documents. As has long been noted, a sentence such as Neh. 2: 7 can only be written by one for whom Aramaic was the normal means of written communication. These books do reveal certain signs of vernacular Hebrew usage that will be familiar in Mishnaic Hebrew. Chronicles shares many parallel texts with earlier historical books and it is possible to assess the many linguistic divergences and the style of Chronicles. Despite the adoption of many antique phrases from its sources, it reveals, for this period, the strongest Aramaic influence and

---

[1] Cf. A. Ben-David, *Biblical Hebrew and Mishnaic Hebrew* (Tel Aviv, 1971), vol. 2, pp. 60–80 (in Hebrew); and the discussion in S. R. Driver, *Introduction to the Literature of the Old Testament* (repr. New York, 1956) in connection with the various biblical books.

[2] Cf. A. Hurwitz, *The Transition Period in Biblical Hebrew* (Jerusalem, 1972; in Hebrew) for a thorough analysis of the language of these Psalms.

is the weakest link in the continuity of biblical syntax. This has led to the statement that 'hardly a verse occurs, written by the Chronicler himself, which does not present singularities of style'.[1] Among the elements that foreshadow Mishnaic Hebrew is the widespread use in the Chronicles of the double plural: *ḥărāšē 'ēṣīm* for *ḥărāšē 'ēṣ* (carpenters), or *gibbōrē ḥăyālīm* for *gibbōrē ḥayil* (heroes). Recent research has used the term Late Biblical Hebrew for the Hebrew of the Persian and Hellenistic period and this seems to be an adequate designation.

These tendencies in the language of the Persian period were continued in the language of the following Hellenistic period. Ecclesiastes and the Hebrew parts of Daniel reveal the strong influence of Aramaic and some scholars have gone so far as to consider these as translations from the Aramaic.[2] The non-Biblical Hebrew texts among the Qumran scrolls show a diversity of styles, some writers skilfully continuing the classical style while others show the growing influence of Aramaic and spoken Hebrew.

There is both Hebrew and Aramaic epigraphic material from the Persian period in Palestine, the Aramaic material being more plentiful than the Hebrew. The indisputable Hebrew material consists of some coins from Tell Jemmeh on which the legend *yḥzqyw hpḥḥ* (Yeḥizqiyahu the Governor) is found. The same text also occurs on another coin discovered previously at Beth-Zur.[3] This coin legend as well as another, *yhd* (Yehud), the official name of the province, was written in the paleo-Hebrew script in the latter part of the Persian period. Aramaic deeds written at Samaria between 375–365 and 335 B.C.E. were found in a cave at wadi Daliyeh. Among the *bullae* which sealed these papyri, two stamps bearing Hebrew texts were discovered; the clearer one reads: [. . .]*yhw bn* [*sn'*]*blṭ pḥt šmrn* '[. . .]yahu son of [San]ballat, governor of Samaria'. It is reasonable to assume that this is the official seal of the governor of Samaria.[4] A seal from about the same period, discovered at Tel Mikhal (Makmish) near Herzliyah, is inscribed in paleo-Hebrew characters *IX bn Y* (belonging to X son of Y) but it is difficult to say whether this seal is Judean or Samaritan in origin.[5]

The corpus of epigraphic Aramaic texts from Palestine during this

[1] Driver, *Introduction*, p. 539.

[2] Cf. in particular the works of H. L. Ginsberg on these books: *Studies in Daniel* (New York, 1948), and *Studies in Koheleth* (New York, 1960).

[3] L. Y. Rahamni, 'Silver Coins of the Fourth Century B.C. from Tel Gamma', *IEJ*, 21 (1971), 158–60, pl. 31.

[4] F. M. Cross, Jr., 'Papyri of the Fourth Century B.C. from Daliyeh' in *New Directions in Biblical Archaeology*, ed. D. N. Freedman and J. C. Greenfield (Garden City, New York, 1969), pp. 42–3, figs. 33–4.

[5] To be published by N. Avigad. Cf. Cross, 'Papyri', p. 59, n. 47.

period is richer but the number from Judea proper is still meagre. The sole coin bearing the legend *yhd* in Aramaic script[1] seems to antedate the above-mentioned coins with the paleo-Hebrew legend. Jars were impressed with seals bearing the Aramaic inscriptions: *yhwd 'wryw* (Yehud Uriyau),[2] *yhwd ḥnnh* (Yehud Hananah), *yhwd yhw'zr phw'* (Yehud Yehoezer the official), *'ḥzy phw'* (Ahzai the official) and also the abbreviated forms *yhwd*, *yhd*, *yh*.[3] These stamps, impressed in all likelihood by government officials, may certify the capacities of wine jugs. Similar stamps, inscribed *mṣh/mwṣh*, were used in Mozah for the same purpose, the jugs containing wine of local production.[4] In Judea proper, mention should be made of two, as yet unpublished, ostraca from En Gedi, a jar fragment from Gibeon inscribed 'Zephaniah', and another fragment from Horvat Dorban, south-west of Jerusalem, on which there is part of a Yahwistic personal name.[5] In the above-mentioned seal impression *yhwd yhw'zr phw'*, the reading *phr'* (potter) was preferred by some scholars.[6] However, more recent finds of *bullae* of unknown provenance, but in all likelihood from Judea, have confirmed the reading *phw'*.[7] This find consists of 65 clay impressions (*bullae*) which served as sealings on papyri; two seals were also found. The seals read: (*a*) *yhd* (Yehud) and (*b*) *lšlmyt 'mt 'lntn phw'* ([belonging] to Shlomit, maid-servant of Elnathan, the official). The sealings read: *yhd* (two different seals); *yhwd ḥnnh* (two different seals); *l'lntn phw'* (of Elnathan the official); *lyrmy hspr* (of Jeremy the scribe); *lbrwk bn šm'y* (of Baruch ben Shimi); *lyg'l bn zkry* (of Yigael ben Zikri); *l'l'zr bn nḥm* (of Elazar ben Nahum); *lš'l bn nḥm* (of Saul ben Nahum); *l'l'zr* (of Elazar); *lmykh* (of Micah). The translation 'official' for *phw'* is based on the fact that the usual Aramaic word for governor is *phh* (absolute form), *pht'* (determined form); *phw'* may be a back-formation from *phwt'* which occurs in the Migdol papyrus for lower governmental officials.[8] These texts were clearly from an archive which belonged to Shlomit who was

---

[1] Y. Meshorer, *Jewish Coins of the Second Temple Period* (Tel Aviv, 1967), no. 4.

[2] N. Avigad, 'A New Class of Yehud Stamps', *IEJ*, 7 (1957), 146–53.

[3] Most examples of this type were found at Ramat Rahel; cf. Y. Aharoni, *Excavations at Ramat Rahel, Seasons 1959–1960* (Rome, 1962); *Seasons 1961–1962* (Rome, 1964).

[4] N. Avigad, 'New Light on the MṢH Seal Impressions', *IEJ*, 8 (1958), 113–19.

[5] J. Naveh, 'Hebrew Texts in the Aramaic Script in the Persian Period?', *BASOR*, 203 (1971), 31, nn. 25, 26, 29.

[6] F. M. Cross, Jr., 'Judaean Stamps', *Eretz-Israel*, 9 (1969), 22–6; J. Naveh, *The Development of the Aramaic Script* (Jerusalem, 1970), pp. 60–1.

[7] N. Avigad, *Bullae and Seals from a post-exilic Judaean Archive* (*Qedem* 4; Jerusalem, 1976).

[8] E. Bresciani, 'Papiri aramaici egiziani di epoca persiana presso il Museo Civico di Padova', *RSO*, 35 (1960), 13–14; cf. J. A. Fitzmyer, 'The Padua Aramaic Papyrus Letters', *JNES*, 21 (1962), 19. For the 'back-formation' cf. E. Y. Kutscher, '*PHW*' and its Cognates', *Tarbiz*, 30 (1961), 112–19 (in Hebrew).

the maidservant/concubine of Elnathan. The sealings belonged either
to the participants in the affairs recorded in the papyri or to the
witnesses. The *yhwd* sealings reflect the interest of the government in
these proceedings and therefore we find among the participants
Elnathan 'the official'. There is no need to assume that this was an
official archive.

Hebrew names also occur in Aramaic texts from various sites which
were not within the bounds of Judea proper, that is, the name Hashub
is found on a jar-fragment from Tell Abu Zeitun on the Yarkon[1]; the
names of Jehonathan, Aqabiah, Jaddua, Eliashib and Anani, and so on
(beside Edomite and proto-Arabic names) on the ostraca from Arad[2];
Zebadiah on the ostracon from Tel Ashdod[3]; Dalluy on one of the
Beersheba ostraca[4]. The name Nahum bar Hilqiyau is engraved on an
Aramaic seal of unknown provenance.[5]

The number of Aramaic ostraca found in Palestine and its environs
has increased in the last decade. About a hundred sherds containing
Aramaic writing were counted by the excavators at Tel Arad, but only
half of them are partially legible. These deal with supplies of grain,
mainly barley, for the horsemen and their mounts, and also for their
asses. It seems likely that these riders served in the Persian post station
as described by Herodotus (VIII.98), although passing caravaneers and
local residents (including Jews) may be listed on the ostraca. Those from
Beersheba are dockets with exact dates (most probably from the
accession of Artaxerxes III in 359 B.C.E.) while an ostracon from Tel
el-Fara in the northern Negeb refers to a large quantity of barley for
sowing in two fields.[6] A Phoenician name – Ba'alṣid – occurs on an
Aramaic ostracon from Nebi Yunis near Ashdod.[7] A Phoenician
ostracon was found in Elath[8] and a jar inscription in Bat Yam.[9] Mention
should also be made of Aramaic ostraca from Tell es-Saidiye in the

[1] J. Kaplan, 'Excavations at Tell Abu Zeitun', *BIES*, 22 (1958), 97–9 (in Hebrew).
[2] J. Naveh, 'Aramaic Inscriptions from Arad,' in *Arad Inscriptions*, ed. Y. Aharoni
    (Jerusalem, 1981), pp. 153–77.
[3] J. Naveh, 'An Aramaic Ostracon from Ashdod', *Ashdod II–III*, *Atiqot, 9–10* (1971),
    200–1, pl. XIII.
[4] J. Naveh, 'The Aramaic Ostraca' in *Beer-Sheba* I, ed. Y. Aharoni (Tel Aviv, 1973),
    pp. 200–1, pl. xiii; 'The Aramaic Ostraca from Tel Beer-Sheba (Seasons 1971–76)',
    Tel Aviv, 6 (1979), 182–98.
[5] N. Avigad, 'Seals of the Exiles', *IEJ*, 15 (1965), 222–32, pl. 40F.
[6] J. Naveh, 'Two Aramaic Ostraca from the Persian Period,' in *Bible and Jewish Studies
    Dedicated to the Memory of Jacob Liver*, ed. B. Uffenheimer (Tel Aviv, 1972), pp. 184–6
    (in Hebrew). For Arad see above, n. 2; for Beersheba, see n. 4.
[7] F. M. Cross, Jr., 'An Ostracon from Nebi Yunis', *IEJ*, 14 (1964), 108–10, pl. 41H.
[8] J. Naveh, 'Hebrew Texts', *BASOR*, 203 (1971), 27–30.
[9] J. B. Peckham, 'An Inscribed Jar from Bat-Yam', *IEJ*, 16 (1966), 11–17, pl. 4A–B.

Jordan valley. The much-discussed inscription on a small altar from Lachish[1] should be mentioned here, as well as a large soapstone stamp seal inscribed *šlmy/hʿd*.[2]

The use of Aramaic for legal and administrative affairs, known from other parts of the Persian empire, is attested to by the previously-mentioned papyri from wadi Daliyeh. Remains of a great many papyri were found in the caves; of these only twenty pieces were considered worth numbering, and these too are highly fragmentary. The largest number are slave documents, while others deal with loans, sales of property and perhaps marriage. The papyri came from the end of the Persian empire (*circa* 375/365 to 335 B.C.E.) and were written in Samaria (*bšmryn štrʾ znh ktyb*). It is difficult to draw conclusions from the material but it indicates a preference for the use of Aramaic in administrative and commercial contexts. The extant Hebrew epigraphic material, the coin legends and seal inscriptions, belong to this time; it is possible that they were struck after the Tennes rebellion shortly after the middle of the fourth century B.C.E. and reflect a national awakening in Judea and Samaria. This assumption would explain the Hebrew coin legend naming the governor of Judea and the interesting fact that a Hebrew text was engraved on the official seal of the governor of Samaria. This presages the use of paleo-Hebrew *yhd* and *yršlm* jar stamps in the early Hellenistic period as well as the Hebrew legends on Hasmonean coinage and that of the later Jewish revolts.

Although traces of dialects can be demonstrated in the Aramaic of the Persian period, there is a remarkable uniformity in the Aramaic script as used throughout the Persian empire.[3] No regional scripts developed, although Aramaic script was used by peoples of various cultural backgrounds throughout the lands under Achemenid rule. The same script was used in the territories extending from Central Asia to North Arabia. The differences that do exist are of a stylistic nature – both a lapidary and a cursive style coexisted during the Persian period and were used in the various provinces; for example, the same lapidary script can be seen in inscriptions from Egypt, from Asia Minor, from Teima in North Arabia and in the Judean jar-stamps. In the course of the Persian period cursive writing prevailed and by the third century B.C.E. lapidary

---

[1] A bibliography for this inscription may be found in A. Lemaire, 'Un nouveau roi arabe de Qedar dans l'inscription de l'autel à anciens de Larish', *RB*, 81 (1974), 63 n. 2.

[2] Cross, *Eretz-Israel*, 9 (1969), 26–7, pl. V: 3–4.

[3] See J. Naveh, *The Development of the Aramaic Script* (Jerusalem, 1970) for detailed treatment of the Aramaic script during the Persian period.

Aramaic disappeared. Writing was not limited to professional scribes and this cursive script can be subdivided into three substyles: (a) formal cursive – the handwriting of the professional scribes: naturally conservative – represented by the Arsham letters and to a smaller degree by most of the Elephantine legal documents; (b) free cursive – that of the educated person – represented by private letters; (c) vulgar cursive – that of the person of limited schooling – represented by various signatures of the witnesses to deeds. Although many of the short daily messages found on the Elephantine ostraca were written by the same scribe, the great number of individual signatures attests to a degree of literacy even when the signatures are rather clumsy. Despite the uniformity of the script, internal change can be traced over the two hundred years of its use. The materials on which writing, during this period, was recorded were papyrus, leather, ostraca, pottery, stone, wood, bone and even pebbles.

The uniformity of the Aramaic script gradually disappeared in the Hellenistic age when Greek replaced Aramaic as the official language throughout much of the same area. The Aramaic tradition was too deeply implanted to be uprooted, but the cohesive force of a central government no longer existed to preserve the uniformity of the Aramaic script. Therefore, during the third and more so during the second century B.C.E., distinctive scripts developed in the various national, cultural and geographic units. It was at this time that the Jewish script developed in Palestine.

The adoption of the Aramaic script by the Jews and its gradual development into the Jewish script raises some interesting questions. In the pre-exilic period one can distinguish between the three independent script traditions of Phoenician, Hebrew and Aramaic on the one hand, and the derivative scripts of the Ammonites (from neighbouring Aramaic Damascus), of the Moabites (from Hebrew under Israelite hegemony and cultural influence) and the Edomites (under the suzerainty of Judah) in the tenth to ninth centuries B.C.E. on the other hand. What was the status of the Hebrew script during and after the Persian period? What were the circumstances which led to the replacement of the Hebrew script by the Jewish script as seen clearly in the Hellenistic period?

The traditional view assumes that the change took place during the Persian period. This is based on Talmudic remarks such as: 'Originally the Torah was given to Israel in Hebrew script and in the holy language; later, in the time of Ezra, the Torah was given in the Assyrian script and the Hebrew language. They selected for Israel the Assyrian script and the Hebrew language, leaving the Hebrew script and the Aramaic language for the *hedyoṭot* (ordinary people?)' (b. *Sanhedrin* 21b). This passage, as well as subsequent passages (*b. Sanh.* 22a; parallels in Tosefta *Sanh.* 4, 7 and Palestinian Talmud *Megilla* 1, 12, 71b–c), indicate that the rabbis were aware of the changes of scripts and were intrigued and troubled by the problem. Rabbi Judah the Prince (*Yehudah ha-Nasi*) ventured the opinion that the Torah was originally given in the 'Assyrian script'. The term 'Assyrian' refers to the Aramaic script and may be reminiscent of the fact that it was during the period of Assyrian domination that Aramaic script and language received official status; the use of *Assyria Grammata* by Greek writers has a similar origin.[1]

The problem is more complicated than appears from Talmudic tradition. It can be assumed that the relationship between Hebrew language and script remained strong; the few clearly Hebrew epigraphic texts from this period – the seal impression from the Daliyeh cave, the seal from Tel Mikhal and the coin legends – were written in the paleo-Hebrew script. This assumption seems to be contradicted by the sealings on *bullae* from a Judean site mentioned above. Most of these *bullae*, and also the Shlomit seal, bear letters in an archaic Aramaic script which may be dated to the late sixth or early fifth century B.C.E. In these texts the Hebrew word *bn* (son) and the title *hspr* (the scribe) occur. Some scholars have also claimed that the inscription in Aramaic lapidary script on the small altar from Lachish and the soapstone stamp reading *šlmy/h'd* may contain Hebrew texts. In the altar inscription the word *bn* occurs, while the stamp has the word *h'd* (the witness) with the article *h-* common to the Canaanite dialects, including Hebrew. These two items may possibly be explained as follows; the altar inscription (early fifth century) is Edomite, since Lachish was in Edomite territory, and the seal may be either Edomite or Ammonite. It is quite possible that in this period and place, when Hebrew was still widely spoken, the use of *bn* in names, or of a professional designation such as *hspr* or *h'd*, did not reflect upon the assumed language of the remainder of the text. However, when on a seal the word *br* (not *bn*) occurs, the script is always Aramaic. Although the material is still slight and it may be premature to draw conclusions, the following scheme may be ventured: when the language was considered Hebrew, the script used was paleo-Hebrew; when only the title or connecting word (such as *bn*) was Hebrew, the script was Aramaic; when the language was Aramaic, the script was Aramaic. No certainty is possible since literary texts in Hebrew from this period have not been unearthed, but it is plausible that Jews did not as yet write Hebrew texts in Aramaic script since it was identified as a foreign script. The fact that scribes were surely bilingual leaves open

---

[1] C. Nylander, 'Assyria Grammata, Remarks on the 21st Letter of Themistokles', *Opuscula Atheniensia*, 8 (1968), 119–36 discusses the use of this phrase in Pseudo-Themistokles and elsewhere.

the possibility that they may not have been limited to one or another script.

With the disappearance of a unifying Achemenid chancery style, the particularly Jewish script was able to develop from the Aramaic script; it acquired distinctive identifying features in the course of the late third and second centuries B.C.E. This may be discerned in the earliest biblical MSS. from Qumran and the Nash papyrus (discovered in Egypt).[1] A variety of formal and cursive hands developed in this Jewish script which are now well known from Qumran and other epigraphic finds; the formal script is the ancestor of the square Hebrew of later times.

Although the Jewish script prevailed, the paleo-Hebrew script continued in sporadic use among Jews until the Bar Kochba revolt. It is found in the early Hellenistic period on coins with the legend *yhdh*[2] and jars inscribed *yhd* or *yršlm*; on Hasmonean coins and in the paleo-Hebrew MSS. from Qumran. The evolution of this script can be traced to the end of the second Temple period with a monumental (but alas very fragmentary) inscription from the Temple mount,[3] a name on an ossuary[4] and the Abba funerary cave inscription from Giv'at ha-Mivtar.[5] Among Jews, use of the paleo-Hebrew script came to an end with the brief archaizing revival on the coins of the Bar Kochba revolt. It has continued in use among the Samaritans until this day.

The epigraphic finds have made clear the dominant role of Aramaic in the commercial, legal and administrative spheres. The official name *Yehud* for Judea, rather than the traditional *Yehuda*, known from earlier and later periods, is the best example of the pervasiveness of the impact of Aramaic on the Jews. *Yehud* was probably created in the chancery of the Achemenid empire on the basis of the gentilic *Yĕhûdāyye* > *Yĕhûd*, a back-formation on the analogy of *Bablayye* > *Babel*, *Ela-*

---

[1] Cf. W. F. Albright, 'A Biblical Fragment from the Maccabaean Age: the Nash Papyrus', *JBL*, 56 (1937), MS. 167; N. Avigad, 'The Palaeography of the Dead Sea Scrolls and Related Documents' in *Aspects of the Dead Sea Scrolls*, SH 4 (Jerusalem, 1958), pp. 56–87. F. M. Cross Jr., 'The Development of the Jewish Scripts', in *The Bible and the Ancient Near East*, ed. G. E. Wright (Garden City, New York, 1961), pp. 133–202.

[2] Cf. the articles by A. Kindler, 'Silver Coins Bearing the Name of Judea from the Early Hellenistic Period', *IEJ*, 24 (1974), 73–6; and D. Jeselsohn, 'A New Coin Type with Hebrew Inscription', *IEJ*, 24 (1974), 77–8, pl. 11.

[3] B. Mazar, 'Archaeological Excavations near the Temple Mount', in *Jerusalem Revealed*, ed. Y. Yadin (Jerusalem, 1975), pp. 25–40.

[4] M. Rosenthaler, 'A Palaeo-Hebrew Ossuary Inscription', *IEJ*, 25 (1975), 138–9.

[5] See the articles by E. S. Rosenthal, 'The Giv'at ha-Mivtar Inscription', *IEJ*, 23 (1973), 72–81; and J. Naveh, 'An Aramaic Tomb Inscription written in Palaeo-Hebrew Script', *IEJ*, 23 (1973), 82–91, pl. 19.

mayye > *Elam*, etc. It was also used by the Jews on coins, stamp-seals and official documents (Dan. 2: 25; 5: 13; Ezra 5: 1, 8; 7: 14; *CAP* 30: 1; 31: 18). One may assume that in the cities, especially Jerusalem, the populace was bilingual, but that in many villages Hebrew was the chief language. The basis was set in this period for the coexistence of Aramaic and Hebrew in the Jewish tradition.

CHAPTER 7

THE JEWISH COMMUNITY IN PALESTINE IN THE PERSIAN PERIOD

The function of this chapter is a limited one, confined to the consideration of the small Jewish (Judean) community itself, the sources for our understanding of its history, and an attempted reconstruction of the essential elements of that history in the Persian period. The wider background of the Persian empire and the information available to us regarding the position of the political units within the Palestinian area under Persian rule have been considered in chapter 4. The evidence provided by archeology is set out in chapter 5. Inevitably some points of overlap and of difference of interpretation must appear between the present discussion and what has preceded, especially since at many points there are great problems in the interpretation of the relatively meagre evidence. Nor can the history of the Palestinian community be satisfactorily understood without awareness of its relationship to those in Babylonia and in Egypt; the main stages of the history are associated with new figures who appear from Babylonia, and relationship with one particular Jewish group in Egypt, that of Elephantine, raises questions about both the chronology of the Palestinian community and the way it regarded itself, though no direct allusion to this Egyptian group is to be found in the biblical material. Discussions of these other areas are to be found in chapter 13. Clearly too the internal life of the community cannot be adequately considered without an awareness of its expression in religious writings such as are discussed in the two chapters that follow on 'Prophecy and Psalms' and on 'Wisdom literature' (chapters 8 and 9); and in the more general treatment of the religious life of the period there must be overlap and some differences of interpretation from what is here indicated (see chapters 10 and 11).

JEWISH HISTORIOGRAPHY IN THE EXILIC AND PERSIAN PERIODS

It is evident that the disaster of 587 B.C.E., the collapse of the kingdom of Judah with all its attendant misfortunes and the exiling of a prominent section of the population, produced sharp reactions. Of these, the one relevant to our present concern is the reassessment of the significance of the past history of the kingdoms and indeed of traditions concerning the earlier stages of the Israelite community's existence in the light of what had happened; this was undertaken both with a view to interpreting the events themselves and with an interest in assessing how the future life of the people should be organized. The earlier stages in formation of the major historical work of this period, the so-called Deuteronomic History, consisting of the books from Deuteronomy to 2 Kings, are not here our concern. The degree to which earlier writings were modified in the exilic age is a matter of discussion, as is the question of the number of stages of Deuteronomic revision which the work underwent. But whether, as is often held, little more than small adjustments were made, together with the addition of the evidently later ending in 2 Kings 25: 27–30 (not earlier than 562 B.C.E.), or more far-reaching modifications, designed to draw out the significance for the new situation of older and already familiar material, it is clear that once the older material was provided with even a minimal exilic reference, set in a context in which the description of disaster was followed by the short statements on Gedaliah (2 Kings 25: 22–26) and on Jehoiachin (25: 27–30), it could no longer be read in the same way as before the disaster. To the sensitive reader, and more still to the exponent of a religious interpretation of Israel's experience, the whole of this wealth of earlier material took on a new meaning.

The significance of this for our concern with the accounts of the Persian period becomes clearer when we observe the degree to which subsequent presentations make use of parts of this particular work, or draw upon its theological assessments, in order to explicate the nature of the community's position in a new political order. The writings of the Chronicler, of which more must be said, include a very substantial part of the earlier work, though with differences which throughout shed light on the changed situation and the different purposes of the writer; even where little or no change is made, the material must now be read in the light of a new situation. The re-presentation of the earlier stages of the history in the Priestly Code, essentially Genesis to Numbers, provides another line of approach to the understanding of the contemporary situation. This offers no direct account of the period in which it took its final form – and there are differences of assessment of this, with a general probability that the sixth to fifth century B.C.E. is a reasonable date; yet our understanding of that period, particularly so far as its thought is concerned, may be in some measure illuminated by our tracing of the ways in which material covering the Exodus and wilderness (and settlement) periods in that work differ from the abbreviated and often allusive use of the material in Deuteronomy and in Joshua. The theme belongs inevitably more to the consideration of the thought of the period than to the reconstruction of its history.

The discussion of the work of the Chronicler is undertaken more fully elsewhere (see pp. 143–7), with the assumption that its final form belongs to the Greek period. Definitions of date are notoriously difficult for such a work. I would myself place its essential material (but not including the Nehemiah sections) in the later Persian period rather than the Greek; but some modifications in the lists at a later date and the inclusion of the Nehemiah material must, it is true, place the final form in that later period. There is some degree of unreality in too precise a designation of date, since the most that we can do is determine the probable stages in the formation of such a work and in particular here its relationship to its main predecessor, the Deuteronomic History. Its relationship to the Priestly Code, though of a different kind, must also be in mind.

The discussion of this raises questions about the precise form in which particular texts have been preserved. It is now clear that for a number of biblical books (most notably Samuel and Jeremiah) divergent, in some respects very markedly divergent, texts existed side by side and are attested by the Masoretic, Septuagint and Qumran forms. The fixation and canonization of a particular text-form are the result of complex processes. For the works which we are considering, there is evidence of this kind available, indications that the Chronicler, for example, used a text-form of Samuel which was in some respects nearer to that of the Septuagint (and some Qumran material) than to the Masoretic text. Alongside such evidence we may also note the existence, actually within the biblical corpus itself in its Masoretic form, of alternative forms of the same material, providing evidence of divergent editions. Thus the differences between the parallel texts of 2 Kings 18 to 20 and Isa. 36 to 39 point to a long and complex textual history in which we may glimpse early forms which have not survived (probably without references to the prophet Isaiah), the two forms here preserved, in which the latter reveals a substantial move in the direction of the glorification of Hezekiah, and beyond these, in the Chronicler's own form of the material in 2 Chron. 29 to 32, we may detect further stages of development. Of this section we may say securely that we know three clear editions, and can suspect not only an earlier one now lost but at least also the possibility of some non-surviving links between the last two, though it is also conceivable that the Chronicler's highly-coloured presentation is the result of his own imaginative and expository handling of the Kings and Isaiah forms. Similarly, we may observe that material found in the last section of 2 Kings (roughly 24: 17 to 25: 30), appears in a close but not identical form in Jer. 52; in a related but much longer and deviant form in Jer. 37 to 44; and in a very much re-interpreted form in 2 Chron. 36.[1] The evidence of the Isaiah and Jeremiah alternatives points to at least the possibility of a new edition of some part of the Deuteronomic History – perhaps covering the history of the surviving kingdom of Judah after the collapse of the northern kingdom in 722 – in which the significance of that kingdom's fortunes was more fully described and discussed than in the relatively uncommented and sober account of 2 Kings 18 to 25. That such a further development is possible may be seen from the comparable situation which exists, equally difficult to explain fully though here actually attested by a full text, for the latter part of the Chronicler's work; an alternative form of 2 Chron. 35 to Neh. 8: 12(13) (lacking the Nehemiah material and with other major differences) exists in the apocryphal 1 Esdras. Attempts have been made in recent years to identify stages in the evolution of the Chronicler's work, intermediate between the form of the material familiar in the Deuteronomic History and that found in the final completed work. It may be doubted whether they can be demonstrated in detail. But, in spite of this, it is inherently probable that the work of the Chronicler represents the result of a development not all in one stage from the earlier material; and in view of the Chronicler's almost entire concentration upon the southern kingdom of Judah, a first stage might well be some extension of the purely Judah narratives covering the period from 722 to 587 B.C.E.

That part of the work of the Chronicler which covers the Persian period gives some indication of the source material available to the compiler. It remains the prevailing view that the books of Ezra and Nehemiah belong to the same large work, though the recognition that the Nehemiah material is separate and probably a later addition has won a considerable measure of acceptance. Strong doubt has, however, been expressed about this unity of the whole work, and linguistic, stylistic and theological evidence has been adduced to question the supposition that there is one eventual compiler responsible for the whole.[2] Linguistic evidence is extremely difficult to assess; the presence within the Chronicler's work of large extracts, more or less verbatim,

---

[1] Cf. P. R. Ackroyd, 'Historians and Prophets', *SEÅ*, 33 (1968), 18–54; 'An Interpretation of the Babylonian Exile: A study of 2 Kings 20, Isaiah 38–39', *SJT*, 27 (1974), 329–52.

[2] Cf. H. G. M. Williamson, *Israel in the Books of Chronicles* (Cambridge, 1977); S. Japhet, *The Ideology of the Book of Chronicles and its Place in Biblical Thought* (Jerusalem, 1973, in Hebrew).

from the Deuteronomic History and from other known parts of the Old Testament (notably in the lists with their close links to the Priestly Code), makes it less easy to be sure where the Chronicler's own vocabulary and style are to be found. In so far as it may be observed that sources are equally used in the books of Ezra and Nehemiah, this same problem is present. Where there are indications of substantial reshaping or of original composition, the evidence is by no means clear that there is a sharp difference between Chronicles on the one hand and Ezra–Nehemiah on the other. The theological differences which have been detected depend very much on considerations of the degree to which a new interpretation has been placed on already existing material, and fuller study of such questions still needs to be undertaken. T. Willi, who has offered one of the fullest discussions of this area, concludes that the two are to be separated, but he associates them with the same author.[1] R. Mosis, in a comparably detailed study, directed to the theology of the Chronicler, sees so many points of linkage that he remains persuaded of their unity.[2] Indeed the similarities are such that even if separate composition or authorship is maintained, it is necessary to recognize such a degree of closeness within a developing tradition of thought that the matter becomes in a large measure academic.

For our present purposes it is more important to observe the freedom with which the source materials are handled, though we have to recognize the uncertainties about what sources precisely are used. Both within Ezra 1 to 6 and within the Ezra narratives to be found in Ezra 7 to 10 and Neh. 8 (9, 10), there are clear indications of divergent material now brought together. Disorder in the Nehemiah narratives and amplifications of these may also be detected. In each case too we have evidence in alternative forms of the material (in 1 Esdras and in Josephus) and in different valuations of the traditions (for example, in 2 Macc. and in 2 Esdras), that the literary material could be differently handled and the historical reconstruction differently undertaken.

These underlying literary problems must be kept clearly in mind in the discussion of the historical development. However near we may seem to get to the events in the biblical material and in the alternative presentations, it is evident that even the earliest of these stands at some distance from the events, that what we have are selections and arrangements of particular elements. Consideration of the other biblical evidence which is much less precise sheds some further light on the complexity of the problems, but can hardly be said to resolve them. The

[1] T. Willi, *Die Chronik als Auslegung*, FRLANT 106 (Göttingen 1972).
[2] R. Mosis, *Untersuchungen zur Theologie des chronistischen Geschichtswerkes*, Freiburger theol. Stud. 92 (Freiburg, 1973).

prophetic material in Haggai and in Zechariah 1 to 8 offers insights into attitudes but hardly enables the reconstruction of events, important as the evidence is; the present form of these two collections itself raises questions about the way in which their information may satisfactorily be used.[1] Other prophetic material – Joel, Isaiah 56 to 66, Zechariah 9 to 14, Malachi, and possibly some other passages – is so notoriously difficult to date (even Malachi, which has often been used as a fixed point in the early fifth century B.C.E.) that the dangers of arguing in a circle are particularly acute. We are more able to get general insights into aspects of post-exilic thought and life than to find clear indications of historical developments from such material. The same must be said about the Priestly Code; the presence of allusions to contemporary conditions, while most probable, is of such a nature that we are again all too easily arguing from suppositions about date to the meaning of particular passages, and from the latter to imagined confirmation of the date assigned to the work. That much general light is shed on the atmosphere of the period must be clear, but again no precise historical information can be extracted, however many attractive theories are propounded.

THE HISTORY OF THE RETURN

The main chronological framework for the reconstruction of the history of the Jewish community in Palestine from 538 to 331 B.C.E. is provided by the reigns of the Persian rulers (see chronological table, pp. 462–4). For one part of that history, namely the period of the restoration and the rebuilding of the Temple (roughly 538 to 515 B.C.E.), the names of the rulers, Cyrus and Darius, but not Cambyses, appear in the biblical material. Josephus (*Antiquities* XI) gives somewhat fuller background information. For the remainder of the history, the problems of chronology are exceedingly difficult to handle, for while there are references to named Persian rulers, the identification of these rulers is at the most vital points uncertain, with the result that alternative chronologies have been proposed and in particular the chronological placing of both Nehemiah and Ezra remains in some degree uncertain. That of Nehemiah is most generally agreed as mid fifth century B.C.E.; that of Ezra is still a wide-open question. But even Nehemiah's date is inferred rather than fully demonstrated: the evidence for three Sanballats (see below) is an indication of the problems of identification.

The result of these uncertainties and of the purely hypothetical reconstruction of any historical elements for other parts of the period

[1] Cf. p. 142, n. 1.

is that the writing of a straight historical account in sequence must either assume a prior scheme into which the various moments are to be fitted or set out the alternatives at each stage. The method adopted in the discussion which follows represents an attempt at meeting this unsatisfactory dilemma by treating the significant and recognizable moments separately, with only the obvious proviso that the period of restoration is described first. The activities of Ezra and of Nehemiah are treated in that order, not because this can be demonstrated to be the correct chronological sequence, but because the available sources either place them so (so Josephus) or interweave them in that order (so Ezra 7 to 10; Neh. 1 to 13), with the exception of 1 Esdras which omits any mention of Nehemiah at all. The existence of these alternative treatments argues strongly for not attempting a chronological solution initially, but examining the nature of the material and the evidence for a 'period', independently of the discussion of the actual sequence. To these three major moments is added some comment on others that have been postulated on the basis of biblical and other evidence, moments for which the inferences must be regarded as ranging from the possible but tentative to the very improbable.

This description of the main moments is then followed by a review of the chronological information and of the attempts which have been made, particularly in most recent discussion, at resolving the problems. Historical reconstruction is clearly desirable if there is to be an adequate understanding of the period; but in so far as such historical reconstruction is not possible on the basis of the evidence available to us, there may be greater significance in concentrating on how particular moments were interpreted, and on how later compilers thought they were to be integrated in their endeavour to give a coherent view of those elements in the period which they believed to be important. At the very best, our evidence remains incomplete and our knowledge limited to certain themes.

THE RESTORATION AND THE REBUILDING OF THE TEMPLE
(*CIRCA* 538 TO 515 B.C.E.)

The main source for the history of this period is Ezra 1 to 6; it lacks continuity and consists of elements in Hebrew and in Aramaic. Ezra 1, overlapping the last verses of 2 Chron. 36, relates the authorization by Cyrus of the rebuilding of the Jerusalem Temple and the return of the Temple vessels to Sheshbazzar, described as 'leader' or 'prince' (*nāśî*) of Judah. It is further stated that Sheshbazzar took the vessels 'along with the return of the exiles from Babylon to Jerusalem' (Ezra 1: 11; the text of this clause is problematic). No further information is provided in the Hebrew material concerning Sheshbazzar. He is mentioned in the Aramaic section (5: 1 to 6: 18), where it is similarly stated that the vessels were committed to him, that he was appointed as governor (*peḥāh*) and instructed to take the vessels to Jerusalem and rebuild the Temple (5: 14f). It is further stated that Sheshbazzar laid the 'foundation' ('*uššāyā*) of the Temple, and that the work continued, apparently without interruption but unfinished, until the date of the report to Darius (that is, 522 or later, but before 515). This account gives a clearer official status to Sheshbazzar and implies a greater activity, though no information is offered regarding the period of his governorship. From the way he is mentioned – 'a man named Sheshbazzar', 'this Sheshbazzar' – he evidently belongs to the past and indeed we should otherwise expect a precise reference to him in Darius' reply. The 'governor of the Jews' in 6: 7 (*peḥāh*) is unnamed. The context as it now stands (5: 2) implies Zerubbabel, but the absence of his name here is perhaps to be seen as significant.

A number of problems arise in regard to this first account of the restoration. There is an evident lack of proper continuity between Ezra 1 and Ezra 3 where the narrative purports to resume after the list of chapter 2. As the text stands, a chronological continuity is implied, though the reference to 'the seventh month' (3: 1) does not attach to any detailed date in chapter 1; but it shortly appears to be implied though not stated that the activity of chapter 3 belongs to the period of Darius, though even this is really based more on inference from the precise chronological information of Haggai where the start of the rebuilding under Zerubbabel and Joshua is linked to Darius' second year. The absence of any clear chronological note in either chapter 3 or its apparent continuation in 6: 19–22 suggests that either this material contained no precise dating (the evidence of 4: 1–5 must be seen as problematic) or the compiler suppressed it in the interests of his view of a continuous activity culminating in the dedication of the restored building (6: 19–22). The Hebrew material thus implies rather than states that restoration began with Sheshbazzar and continued without break under Zerubbabel and Joshua; the delay in the completion of the Temple, which is now evident from its dating in the Aramaic source to the sixth year of Darius, is explained by the opposition material of 4: 1–5 and 4: 6–23, with its resumptive comment in 4: 24. But clearly there is no proper correlation of these different pieces of evidence.

On the other hand, the indications of chapter 3 taken together with the evidence of Haggai and Zech. 1 to 8 strongly point to there having been a completely new start on the rebuilding work at the beginning of the reign of Darius. Thus, on this basis, a clear distinction needs to be made between the activities of Sheshbazzar, the duration of whose office remains quite unknown, but is not necessarily so brief as is sometimes assumed (so Ezra 5: 15), and those of Zerubbabel. The precise date of the latter's arrival in Jerusalem remains a further point of uncertainty.

The second problem in relation to Ezra 1 arises from the presence of a Hebrew form of the decree of Cyrus which differs from that found in Aramaic in Ezra 6: 2–5. While the two forms are evidently related, their differences make it clear that the one in Hebrew is not a translation of the Aramaic, though it is not impossible to see both as related to a now non-existent original. The general tenor of both forms is sufficiently credible when set alongside comparable material in Persian sources, particularly the Cyrus cylinder and the evidence regarding policy towards the Jewish community at Elephantine in the fifth century. But the points of difference strongly suggest adaptation in both forms. It is then important to attempt to distinguish what particular point the compiler of each narrative is making in his use of the material. It is clear that the Hebrew form in 1: 2–4, close in some respects to the style of the Cyrus cylinder, concentrates on the divinely chosen status of Cyrus, the exhortation to those who are so minded to return – the text of verse 3 is probably to be rendered 'whoever among you, from among all your people, Yahweh his God being with him, let him go up...', thus emphasizing the divine choice of those who are to return (compare the narrative in verse 5) – and the theme of rebuilding supported by gifts from 'the men of his particular place', which, as interpreted in verse 6, suggests support from non-Jews, bringing out a theme associated with the Exodus (so Exod. 12: 35f). In this context, the emphasis on the enumeration of the Temple vessels and on their due transmission to Jerusalem represents a continuity theme, guaranteeing that the rebuilt Temple will have the validity of its predecessor.[1]

The third problem here is the status of Sheshbazzar, described only as 'prince of Judah'. He is not here given the title of governor (*peḥāh*) which appears in chapter 5; nor is there any suggestion in the narrative that he should be identified with Shenazzar the Davidic descendant.[2] He is never denoted a Davidide, whereas this is made quite clear for Zerubbabel; the title *nāśî'* has a wide range of uses, so that its precise significance here cannot be determined. If 5: 14 is right in describing

---

[1] P. R. Ackroyd, 'The Temple Vessels – a continuity theme', *VTSup*, 23 (1972), 166–81.

[2] Cf. W. F. Albright, 'The Date and Personality of the Chronicler', *JBL*, 40 (1921), 108–10; repeated by, for example, F. M. Cross, 'A Reconstruction of the Judean Restoration', *JBL*, 94 (1975), 12 n. 43 = *Int*, 29 (1975), 195 n. 43, without any note taken of the demonstration by P. R. Berger, 'Zu den Namen *ššbṣr* and *šn'ṣr*', *ZAW*, 83 (1971), 98–100, that the identification is wrongly based.

him as *peḥāh*, then we can only observe that the narrator of this account in chapter 1 either did not know of this use of the title or chose to ignore it.

The Hebrew account of the restoration, as we have seen, continues first by giving a list in chapter 2 which serves to undergird the impression created by chapter 1 of a full-scale return. It is clear that this must be related to the Chronicler's view (2 Chron. 36: 17, 20f) that the land lay empty during the seventy years prophesied by Jeremiah. Chapter 3 continues the account, as if without interruption, and relates the setting up of the altar in its proper place or perhaps 'on its platform'. It is emphasized that, although sacrifices could thus be initiated, 'the Temple of Yahweh was not (yet) founded' (*ysd*). Such a statement – for so the text is normally rendered – apparently conflicts with 5: 16; but the matter is not so simple. The root *yāsad* is rather broader in meaning than 'found', and may be better understood as 'build, rebuild, repair'.[1] Thus, 3: 6 would mean that the building had not yet been carried out. The sense of *'uššayyā* in 5: 16 is also uncertain, and it has been argued that it denotes the preparing of the levelled area on which the building can be erected, this being effected by the clearing of rubble from previous buildings, and possibly the building of retaining walls for a 'platform' on which the new one can be set up.[2] A similar difficulty arises in Hag. 2: 18 which seems to refer to a precise moment of the laying of the foundation; and it has been argued that some ceremony connected with this is to be seen in the allusion to the special stone in Zech. 4: 7. But the precise sense is in neither passage completely clear. The Haggai passage may represent an attempt at giving precision to the moment at which divine blessing is to begin, and this could well be the moment of completion rather than the initial stage. The Zechariah passage has been interpreted in many different ways, of which perhaps the most attractive is that which suggests an analogy with other ancient building practice in the inserting in a new, or particularly a rebuilt, temple (or other formal building) of a stone taken from the previous one, the procedure being designed to guarantee the continuity of the new or rebuilt building with its predecessor.[3] Since the theme of continuity is evidently a vital one to the restoration period, this fits

---

[1] Cf. F. I. Andersen, 'Who built the Second Temple?', *ABR*, 6 (1958), 1–35 (see 10–22); A. Gelston, 'The Foundations of the Second Temple', *VT*, 16 (1966), 232–5.

[2] Cf. the discussion by C. G. Tuland, "*Uššayyā*' and '*Uššarnâ*: A Clarification of Terms, Date and Text', *JNES*, 17 (1958), 269–75.

[3] Cf. D. L. Peterson, 'Zerubbabel and Jerusalem Temple Reconstruction', *CBQ*, 36 (1974), 366–72; R. Ellis, *Foundation Deposits in Ancient Mesopotamia* (New Haven, 1968).

in well with other indications. A major difficulty in determining how these various passages should be interpreted lies in our lack of information about the years between the destruction of Jerusalem by the Babylonians and this period of restoration. The archeological evidence for destruction in the city is clear, but none is available for the Temple. Even if the Temple was substantially destroyed, as the 2 Kings account indicates, it may be questioned whether it would have been left untouched for 50 years. Some have argued that a previous restoration was regarded as illegitimate by the returning exiles but there is no direct indication of this in Ezra 3.[1] Arguments from the references to the need to obtain timber for rebuilding in Hag. 1: 8 are also inconclusive, since the existence of substantial quarries in the Jerusalem city area itself would suggest that stone lay near to hand, even if stones from the older building could not be used. The narrators and interpreters of this period are so set on two points – the newness of the building and therefore its freedom from contamination, and the continuity of the new with the old – that they do not provide the kind of detail which enables us to say with any precision just what happened.

It would seem entirely proper to interpret Ezra 3 as a complete account of the rebuilding of the Temple, whatever that involved; it reaches its climax in a great religious celebration in 3: 10–13, and the natural sequel to this is to be seen in the fragment of Hebrew narrative which concludes the whole section in 6: 19–22. A possible chronology is contained in the reference to a seventh month (3: 1), presumably of the first year of Zerubbabel's and Joshua's activity; the second month of their second year (3: 8) when full arrangements for the rebuilding were undertaken; a celebration of the completion of the building, undated (3: 10–13); a celebration of the Passover in the first month of an unspecified year (6: 19–22), which cannot be earlier than their third year but might be later. There would seem to be no reason why this account should not be regarded as providing a comprehensive narrative, probably depicting the rebuilding as occupying the minimum appropriate period. If the completion in 3: 10–13 is, like that of the Solomonic Temple, associated with the Feast of Tabernacles in the seventh month (see 2 Chron. 5: 3 as also in the earlier account in 1 Kings 8: 2), then the rebuilding is regarded as extending over a calendar year, from one seventh month to the next, and the celebration of Passover which marks the climax in 6: 19–22 may be understood by the narrator to be the next available feast. This looks very much like a stylized presentation, in which the initiatory and final moments of the rebuilding are associated with the autumnal feast, and the Passover marks the beginning of the

[1] Cf. E. Janssen, *Juda in der Exilszeit* (Göttingen, 1956), pp. 102f.

first new year of the Temple's existence. The absence of any reference to Darius in this account, and the close association of it with the Sheshbazzar narrative of Ezra 1 suggests a concept of restoration which involved the total rebuilding of the Temple within the shortest possible space of time. The theological significance of such a view is clearly much greater than its historical value.

An alternative account is provided by 5: 1 to 6: 18 (Aramaic). This attributes the initiative for the rebuilding to the activity of the two prophets Haggai and Zechariah in the reign of Darius. Its primary stress lies on the divine protection of the enterprise – so especially 5: 5 – and its successful completion in the sixth year of Darius. The work of rebuilding under Darius is seen as the proper culmination of what is described (5: 16) as having been under way from the time of Shesh-bazzar's activity through to the moment of the enquiry to Darius. It makes use of the Temple vessel theme, as does Ezra 1, as a guarantee of continuity with the previous Temple, and clearly its concern is to show, as does the Hebrew account, that the first task of the returned exiles was to rebuild. It is clearly related to information provided by yet another source, namely the book of Haggai. In a narrative or at least annalistic presentation of the activity of the prophet, the particular sayings are associated with the precise moments in the rebuilding, given a clear chronological base – though the material is not completely in order – and depicting Haggai as the prime mover in bringing about a change of attitude in leaders and people in the reign of Darius. It is clear that this presentation, in which Hag. 1: 12–14 provides the narrative of the response, is concerned to relate the rebuilding of the Temple to the changing fortunes of the people and in particular to the dawning of a new age in which Zerubbabel of the Davidic house is to occupy a primary position. Two passages in Zech. 1–8 are related to this. An isolated fragment in 4: 6b–10a stresses the full part to be played by Zerubbabel in the rebuilding; this is quite explicit, but its relationship to its context and indeed to the remainder of these chapters of Zechariah remains very uncertain. Zech. 6: 9–15 is also directed to the rebuilding, but neither here nor in the related 3: 8–10 is there any mention of Zerubbabel by name. That there may be an allusion to him in 6: 12 in the expression *mittaḥtāw yiṣmaḥ*, linked to the meaning of Zerubbabel's name as 'shoot of Babylon' is possible. But the meaning of the Hebrew is by no means clear. Does it mean 'he will shoot up from the ground' (so NEB), or perhaps 'where he is there will be new growth'? The term *ṣemaḥ*, 'branch' (compare 3: 8), linked to this and found also in Jer. 23: 5; 33: 15 (and Isa. 4: 2, probably in a different sense), is perhaps the source of the idea, meaning that it will be the Davidic descendant who will both build the Temple and restore well-being and fertility. The non-mention of Zerubbabel by name in these Zechariah passages may suggest subsequent editorial modification, directed perhaps towards generalizing specific references to Zerubbabel, or may indicate that to Zechariah the particular hopes centring on Zerubbabel and fostered by Haggai were less acceptable. The eventual presentation of Haggai and Zech. 1–8 shows clear marks of updating, so that the probably divergent attitudes of these two prophets have been conformed and utilized for the purpose of recalling a subsequent generation to faith and obedience (so especially Zech. 8: 9f).[1] In this respect the presentation has some resemblances to the Aramaic source in Ezra 5: 1 to 6: 18 where the two prophets are represented as speaking with a single voice. If this is so, then we may tentatively go one stage further by suggesting that the Aramaic account which mentions Zerubbabel and Joshua in 5: 2 only – their non-mention in the subsequent narrative has given rise to speculation about their removal by the Persians for rebellious activities – has been conformed to the Haggai–Zech. 1 to 8 presentation and to the Hebrew narrative of Ezra 3 by the inclusion of their names in 5: 2 where the original form of the material may have contained no mention of them.

Such an approach suggests that in the biblical material we can trace three different styles of interpretation of the years of restoration. They have been given further integration by the inclusion of the material of Ezra 4, a major part of which is clearly chronologically out of place. Here are gathered fragments of 'opposition' narratives, belonging to various situations. In conflict with 5: 16, 4: 1–5 describes how opposition led to a cessation of building through the reign of Cyrus and on to the reign of Darius. A further moment of opposition in the reign of Ahasuerus (Xerxes) is recorded in 4: 6, and in 4: 7 yet another in the reign of Artaxerxes. These are all in Hebrew. In Aramaic, 4: 8–23 also belongs to the reign of Artaxerxes; it is concerned with opposition to the rebuilding and fortifying of Jerusalem. Its appearance in a quite different position in 1 Esdras (2: 16–30) reveals the artificiality of its use. The link verse 4: 24 picks up the content of 4: 5 and paves the way for the narrative of 5: 1 to 6: 18. Clearly this opposition material, whatever its original context and purpose, has been here built together into an overall presentation of the difficulties which met the Jewish community on its return. The long interval between the decree of Cyrus

---

[1] Cf. W. A. M. Beuken, *Haggai–Sacharja 1–8*, Studia Semitica Neerlandica, 10 (Assen, 1967); L. A. Sinclair, 'The Redaction of Zech. 1–8', *BR*, 20 (1975), 36–47; R. A. Mason, 'The Purpose of the "Editorial Framework" of the Book of Haggai', *VT*, 27 (1977), 413–21.

and the completion of the Temple in 515 (according to 6: 15) is thus bridged and explained.

The difficulty of recovering precise indications of the events is clear from this discussion. It is even more apparent when we observe the way in which the themes are later handled. Josephus has a much more integrated but elaborate account of the process, utilizing the biblical account, but transforming the main opposition theme of Ezra 4 into an account of what happened under Cambyses (so *Ant.* XI.2). 1 Esdras, followed by Josephus, plays up the part of Zerubbabel by showing how he was chosen for favour by Darius (I Esd. 3 to 4; *Ant.* XI.3). The account in 2 Macc. 1: 18 to 2: 15 attributes the building of 'temple and altar' to Nehemiah, stressing the continuity of the new Temple with the old by its story of the preservation of the Temple fire. While not making any precise statement about rebuilding, 2 Esdras clearly sees Ezra as the preserver of this continuity, doing this both by projecting him back into the exilic age (so 3: 1) and by stressing the restoration of the ancient sacred books (so chapter 14). It is evident that no assessment, even of the more sober materials of Ezra 1 to 6, will be adequate which does not take account of the motives for presentation which affect the authors and compilers; the biblical material has itself already moved towards the later even more stylized interpretations.

EZRA

The direct sequel to the restoration, as this is set out in Ezra 1 to 6, is the narrative of Ezra. This covers Ezra 7 to 10 and is continued in Neh. 8; the sequence appears thus in 1 Esdras, whereas in the Ezra–Nehemiah form the narrative is broken by part of the Nehemiah material. It is a matter of debate how much more belongs to the Ezra narrative; Neh. 9 is very closely linked, and Neh. 10 may be so, though this is often associated with Nehemiah. The 1 Esdras form is either deliberately or accidentally broken off at a point corresponding to the opening words of Neh. 8: 13: 'They gathered together' (1 Esd. 9: 55b), corresponding to '(Now on the second day) there were gathered together (the heads of families)...' (Neh. 8: 13). The Josephus account (*Ant.* XI. 5) follows 1 Esdras but adds a note of the death of Ezra in old age; the account of Nehemiah follows without cross-reference.

The chronological questions are considered below. We must here observe that the narrator, whom we call the Chronicler for convenience, saw an immediate link between the restoration and the work of Ezra. The degree of historical disorder in Ezra 1 to 6 prepares us for this. That Ezra was active under a king named Artaxerxes is stated at the outset (7: 1), and the fact that this is set in the seventh year makes a natural link with the last mentioned date, the sixth year (of Darius) in 6: 15. Furthermore, the priestly genealogy of Ezra is given in a form which shows Ezra as direct successor – in a theological, not a historical, sense – to Seraiah, the high priest taken captive by the Babylonians (2 Kings 25: 18, and compare 1 Chron. 6: 14).[1] The significance of Ezra's work as understood by the narrator is clearly in terms of his being the true restorer of religious life after the break of the Exile; what had already happened could be seen as a preliminary stage towards this.[2] The move towards the more unrealistic chronology of 2 Esdras is already observable.

Ezra is shown as commissioned by the Persian ruler to bring about a new and fuller acceptance of the Jewish law in the whole area of the Persian province of Beyond the River, and this conjoined with renewed support for the Jerusalem Temple and a further supply of Temple vessels to emphasize the continuity with what has gone before. The Aramaic commission in 7: 12–26 is cited in this form to give authenticity and authority to what Ezra is doing. We may recognize the reality of Persian policy in its protection for a small subject people, as well as acknowledging a probable background in the desire of the Persians to keep open the lines of communication to Egypt, so often a cause of anxiety during the period. The support for religious institutions and the recognition of the special coherence of the Jewish community in relation to the law are also clear. Here too we may detect an important political element in what the Persians are doing by giving Ezra authority to bring together all who acknowledge themselves to be members of that community within a much wider area than the small unit of Jerusalem/Judah itself. The recognition of the politico-religious problem is important, for the presence of members of the Jewish community in areas occupied by a largely non-Jewish population is here acknowledged, and an attempt is made at giving it a satisfactory organizational basis. Other methods of dealing with this problem are to be traced in the Greek and Roman periods. In the event, the description of Ezra's activity which follows does not show us anything of the implementation of this policy. It is not to be deduced from this that Ezra failed; we may more properly see the interests of the compiler as setting the reforms carried out in Judah and Jerusalem within this wider context. The account of Ezra's journey, of his refusal of military protection, of his concern for the presence of Levites, and of his committing of the new vessels to proper authorities in Jerusalem, all

[1] K. Koch, 'Ezra and the Origins of Judaism', *JSS*, 19 (1974), 173–97 (see 190).
[2] Cf. Mosis, *Untersuchungen*, pp. 227ff.

reveal a highly theological interpretation of the events. The narrator is concerned to draw out from the material at his disposal the meaning of Ezra's coming, and it is clear that, in parallel with his presentation of Exodus themes in Ezra 1, he sees the journey of Ezra as a kind of new Exodus, a ceremonial, processional, move, a pilgrimage of return of Jerusalem.[1]

Ezra 9 to 10 relates Ezra's activity on foreign marriages. The material is complex, and the duplication between these two chapters strongly suggests that more than one source has been utilized, with the possibility that the second, traceable in 10: 1–4, contains elements not originally associated with Ezra at all. The purification of the community by the exclusion of foreign wives and hence of alien religious influence is clearly designed to point forward to the reading and acceptance of the law which follow in Neh. 8. The comparability of the account of this event, with its celebration of the Feast of Tabernacles 'as they had not done since the days of Joshua bin Nun' (8: 17, and compare 2 Chron. 35: 18, modified from 2 Kings 23: 22), with that of Josiah's reform, clearly shows how the narrator understood the work of Ezra. What Josiah was too late to achieve, in view of the impending disaster, is now being brought about. (The presentation of 1 Esdras, beginning with Josiah's reform and ending here, has a coherence which suggests that it is a deliberate extract from the larger work rather than an accidentally fragmented section.) What follows in Neh. 9 is discontinuous with what goes before. The LXX identification of Ezra as spokesman of the long prayer is an understandable harmonization which simply takes further what the Hebrew text implies. But in fact we have here another account of a law-reading, not associated with Ezra, but probably utilized by the compiler both to underline the significance of this moment and to relate it to the theme of the possession of the land which is the central element in the prayer. That the people do not at this moment possess the land of ancient promise is a source of distress (see especially 9: 36f.); the implication is that the renewed acceptance of the law described in chapter 8 and also in 9: 1–4, following on Ezra's 'Exodus' journey and the purification of the people, paves the way for a renewed possession of the land. It is appropriate that the immediate sequel, as the material now stands, is a covenant renewal celebration described in 10: 1–40 (EVV 9: 38 to 10: 39), where the list of verses 2 to 28 (EVV 1 to 27) is probably intrusive. It is true that the association of this with the Ezra material remains uncertain; but the grounds for associating it with Nehemiah – the use of Deuteronomic material and the overlap in

[1] Koch, *JSS*, 19 (1974), 184ff; P. R. Ackroyd, 'God and People in the Chronicler's Presentation of Ezra', BETL, 41 (1976), 145–62 (see 149ff).

the covenant terms with points of reform attributed to Nehemiah in chapter 13 – are hardly sufficient to prove that it was originally a Nehemiah passage. The natural sequel to the Nehemiah material of Neh. 1 to 7: 5 is not here but in chapters 11 to 13.

The degree to which the Ezra material has been handled by the compiler and its presentation in so stylized a form make the reconstruction of his actual work very difficult to undertake. The datings implied in Ezra 7 to 10 and Neh. 8 suggest that a more probable order is to place the law-reading before the foreign marriage action: the re-ordering can be seen to be due to the desire to show a purified community accepting the law. Doubts about Ezra's historicity are out of place; but uncertainty about when he operated and precisely what he did inevitably remain. We can see him only through the eyes of a compiler for whom his work represented a climax to the process of restoration. Our uncertainty about the precise historical place of the Chronicler inevitably makes it equally difficult to assess the degree of interpretative slant imparted to the material.

The political context of Ezra's activity has already been suggested; a contribution towards the stability and peace of the Palestinian area would be effected by a greater degree of coherence and order for the Jewish community, though the only specific point to which the narratives invite our attention is that of the foreign marriages with their religious consequences. Applied more generally, such a policy suggests an endeavour to define more closely the boundaries of the Jewish community and to enable it both in Judah and in other areas to be identified as a separate and legally recognized entity. Since Ezra came from Babylonia we may suppose this line of policy to have been influenced by whatever precise *modus vivendi* had been worked out in practice by the Jewish community there: to live under the rule of the law, accepted as the mark of the Jew, was to be of enduring importance in later years. We may recognize similar problems in the Jewish military colony at Elephantine, and see there the degree to which compromise was necessary in dealings involving Jews and non-Jews. Definition of the community in Judah itself may be understood further in relation to the stages of development – not known to us precisely – by which the status of that particular administrative area was organized, the degree of self-determination which it was permitted, points which may be detected in the evidence for governors of the area and for the minting of coinage. The carrying through of this commission by Ezra is described only in the reading and acceptance of the law in Neh. 8(9) and possibly also in the covenant renewal of Neh. 10. If we ask what law Ezra read, we must recognize that the narrator offers no information, any more than is done in the case of Josiah's reform. In the latter case we may see a relation between that law and Deuteronomy, as the foundation of the interpretation of the history offered in Deuteronomy to 2 Kings. For the Chronicler, two centuries later and already making substantial use of material from the Tetrateuch (Genesis to Numbers) as well as from the Deuteronomic History, the inference would naturally be that he thought that both Josiah and Ezra maintained the same law, and that this was the law already largely defined in the five books attributed to Moses. This is what we are intended to believe, since we should no more assume that the reaction of the people to Ezra's law-reading points to a new and unknown law than we should in the case of Josiah. The response is a formal, liturgical one, representing a proper acceptance of responsibility and of the consequences of disobedience. From the context in Neh. 8 to 9 we might infer a less than complete Pentateuch from the lack of mention of the Day of Atonement on the tenth day of the seventh month (compare Lev. 16: 29; 23: 27; Num. 29: 7); but such an inference depends both on an unsatisfactory argument from silence and from the assumption that chapters 8 and 9 are to be read as consecutive accounts rather than as separate entities.

Suggestions that Ezra failed are inappropriate in view of the problems of evidence, as are also endeavours to suppose that he was associated with activities which brought Persian opposition to the Jewish community, though proposals of this kind have been made. What is more significant is the sequel to these narratives in the glorification of Ezra as the re-founder of the Jewish community and rehabilitator of Jewish faith. Later tradition was to exaggerate the influence and achievement of Ezra so that he outranks all his predecessors with the exception of Moses, but this process is already in its initial stages in the biblical presentation we have been examining.

Our basis for a more realistic assessment can only be in the consideration of the narratives here offered, along with the recognition that the contribution of Ezra and his associates to the stabilization of the Jewish community and to its resilience under attack is to be seen in the period which followed when under Greek rule the Jewish community was subjected to major stresses. Both the positive and the negative sides of that period's reactions can be in part associated with the attitudes and achievements of Ezra and those who shared his understanding of the religious tradition. Josephus, as we have seen, has no further information to add except the affirmation that Ezra died in old age and it is doubtful if this is more than an ascription to him of the propriety of the reward of long life to so exemplary a character. The achievement of Ezra remains unclear.

NEHEMIAH

The activity of Nehemiah is described in the narratives of Neh. 1 to
7: 5 to which is appended an alternative copy of the list found in Ezra
2; and continued in chapters 11 to 13, with the further possibility,
already noted, that chapter 10 may belong to the Nehemiah
material. The narratives are not in completely chronological order:
thus the contents of chapter 5 cover a much longer period than can be
dovetailed into the building of the wall. The first period of Nehemiah's
governorship is given as twelve years (5: 14); more must have
happened in those years than is recorded. A second period as governor
is described in 13: 4ff (see verse 6), but neither its precise starting point
nor its length is noted.[1]

The character of the Nehemiah material has been much discussed;
clearly it has its affinities both with ancient royal inscriptions and with
votive texts (recalled especially by the invocations of 5: 19; 6: 14; 13:
14, 22, 29, 31; and see also such a passage as 3: 36f [EVV 4: 4f]). Some
features of the material suggest that Nehemiah is being presented in the
guise of a royal personage, a builder of the city, a giver and upholder
of the law and a religious reformer; others suggest that he is seen as
a prophetic figure, notably in 1: 1; 3: 33–37 (EVV 4: 1–5); chapter 5;
and 6: 10ff. This is no straight autobiographical account: it is a narrative
written to present Nehemiah heroically, with reminiscences in the style
of presentation of narratives of other such great figures. It marks the
first stage in the evolution of the Nehemiah tradition, taken further in
Ecclus. 40: 13 when he appears as the last figure in the long historical
survey, followed only by allusions to names from the remotest past and
by the author's contemporary, the High Priest Simon. The absence of
Ezra in this material suggests that here, as in 2 Macc. 1 to 2, we have
evidence of a line of thought which saw in Nehemiah the true restorer
of the Jewish community in the post-exilic period.[2]

This impression is further underlined when we consider the opening
of the Nehemiah material. The stimulus to his activity is described as
stemming from a report of the unhappy condition of Judah and
Jerusalem. The wording used is significant: 'The survivors who were
left over from the captivity there in the province (*m^{e}dînāh*) are in great
disaster and distress, and the walls of Jerusalem are breached and its
gates burnt' (1: 3). Attempts have been made to find a specific event

---

[1] The phrase *l^{e}qēṣ yāmîm* in Neh. 13: 6 has been interpreted (e.g. by S. Talmon, *IDBSup*
320) as meaning 'after one year'; but is more probably to be understood as a typically
vague chronological note 'after some time'.

[2] Cf. U. Kellermann, *Nehemia: Quellen Überlieferung und Geschichte*, BZAW 102 (Berlin,
1967).

immediately preceding the activity of Nehemiah to which this refers, and the natural inference has been that Ezra 4: 8–23 describes this (see verse 23: 'they stopped them by military force'). No reference is made in that account to destruction and burning of walls or gates, but we should not expect precise correspondence. Ezra 4: 8–23 has no precise date, but since it is associated with Artaxerxes and Nehemiah's governorship began in the twentieth year of Artaxerxes (not certainly the same ruler), the inference of a connection has seemed clear to many scholars. On the other hand, we need to consider both the nature of the description given in Neh. 1 and the presentation of Nehemiah himself. If, as has been suggested, this presentation already shows moves towards the depicting of him as the real restorer of Judaism after the Exile, then it is much more probable that we should see the allusions of 1: 3 as being to the condition of the province from the time of the Babylonian destruction. The narrator is not concerned with immediate chronology, but with the interpretation of Nehemiah's activity. And this seems clear also from the wording which speaks in terms of 'survivors in the province', left over when others were taken into captivity, or possibly 'left over as survivors there from among those taken into captivity', which would suggest a returned group still living among the ruins of the city. In either case there is no suggestion of any previous rebuilding: Nehemiah is the initiator.

It is with this in mind that we must assess the other elements in the account of Nehemiah. He is depicted as the skilful leader who by courage and discretion overcomes the stratagems of the opposition, both within the city and from outside (see 2: 11–20; chapter 4; chapter 6). Opponents within the community are depicted as allied to the aliens without (so especially in 6: 17–19). Military threats and force are met with both determined action and prayer (chapter 4). Into the account of the rebuilding is woven a detailed description of the work on different parts of the city walls (chapter 3) in which Nehemiah is not mentioned (though another Nehemiah appears in verse 16): the possibility that this is an independent document must be entertained. Rebuilding of the walls and the rededication (2: 12 to 4: end; 6: 15f; 7: 1–3; 12: 27–43) are associated with an interwoven account of the repopulating of the city (7: 4f; 11: 1 to 12: 26 in which various lists are also incorporated). Other opposition elements in chapter 6 are also woven into this, as is a detailed depiction of Nehemiah as the good governor, who protects the poor (chapter 5), by contrast with his unnamed predecessors. He is also shown as the reorganizer of the ordering of the Temple (both in the account of 12: 44–47 which clearly does not concern only Nehemiah's activity, and in the incorporated lists in chapters 11 and 12 which also suggest reflections of a much longer period). In chapter 13

Nehemiah is associated with a reading of the law and removal of aliens from the community (verses 1 to 3 in which Nehemiah is not in fact mentioned), and then with other aspects of purification and religious reform in 13 : 4–31, which is set in the second period of his governorship, and concerns the purification of the Temple, the ordering of levitical portions, the observance of the Sabbath, and again the foreign marriage issue. In particular 13: 28 associates this last with the involvement of a member of the high-priestly family with the opponent Sanballat, and the material of the earlier chapters is thus recalled in this final section. The repeated use of the invocatory refrain in this last chapter strongly suggests a supplement to the main narrative, and it is noteworthy that whereas the primary reference in the earlier chapters is to the walls and the city and to more political matters, here Nehemiah becomes much more clearly a religious reformer. In view of the degree of parallel between the activities of Ezra and of Nehemiah as now presented, it must be at least possible that there has been some magnification of Nehemiah's activity to give him a more evidently religious status than he actually had, even though separation of political and religious elements cannot be undertaken very precisely.

An assessment of the work of Nehemiah can only be undertaken in the light of such an examination of the nature of the account. The rebuilding of the walls and hence the establishment of security, and the repopulating of Jerusalem which would point to the same aim, can be seen as involving an endeavour to bring about the rehabilitation of the Jewish community as a political entity. Conflict with outside forces raises questions about the precise political situation. Sanballat, associated in 3: 34 (EVV 4: 2) with Samaria, though not described as governor, can most naturally be regarded as the first of the governors of this name now known to us (see below), though we cannot necessarily be absolutely sure of this. That he is not described as governor may well be simply the narrator's way of suggesting his insignificance; he treats Tobiah similarly, as an 'Ammonite slave', though probably the title *'ebed* denotes official and important status. The analysis of the various opposition narratives suggests the possibility that the three main opponents, Sanballat, Tobiah and Geshem,[1] were not in reality quite so closely associated as now appears; we may in fact be dealing with

[1] Or conceivably four, if the text is emended to read 'Tobiah and *'bd* the Ammonite' (cf. W. F. Albright, 'Dedan', in *Geschichte und Altes Testament*, BHT 16 (Tübingen 1953), pp. 1–12, especially p. 4). This opens the way to conjectures identifying *'bd* with 'Abd, Persian governor of Dedan, and Geshem with Gašm king of Qedar (see Cross, *JBL*, 94 (1975), 7 and n. 21 = *Int*, p. 190 and n. 21). But such conjectures are very tenuously based.

a number of political problems faced by Nehemiah, having a more *ad hoc* quality than is now implied by the depiction of these three as an unholy alliance against Jerusalem. The influence of passages (such as Ps. 2) which depict a conspiracy of the nations must be allowed. Tobiah's position clearly owed much to the strong support of 'nobles in Judah' (6: 17); according to 13: 4 Eliashib the (high) priest was closely connected (nearly related – *qārôb* – perhaps by marriage) with Tobiah; and 13: 28 tells of a marriage connection with Sanballat. We can only surmise what manoeuvres for political control and for royal favour were going on, and can appreciate the delicacy of Nehemiah's position as a royal favourite and of the problems confronting opponents who must avoid the risk of royal displeasure. When a comparison is made with the internal conflicts of the second century B.C.E. or of the first century C.E., we may get some clue to the complex situation in which Nehemiah actually operated, and sense also the degree to which the presentation of him in the book of Nehemiah has been turned to make of him the great hero of the day.

OTHER MOMENTS WITHIN THE PERSIAN PERIOD THOUGHT TO BE REFLECTED IN THE LITERATURE

It is clear that two or probably three distinct moments are indicated in Ezra 4: 6–23. They are given datings simply in relation to particular Persian rulers, but without more precise chronological indications. In 4: 6 (Hebrew) an accusation is noted against the people of Judah and Jerusalem at the beginning of the reign of Ahasuerus (Xerxes), who reigned from 486 to 465. Since no detail is given, we can deduce nothing further from this; a more elaborate conjecture is briefly considered below. In 4: 7 (Hebrew) the writing of a letter is similarly noted. The text is not entirely clear, but the names of two personages appear: Mithredath and Tabeel, and with the latter are associated 'colleagues'. The occasion is dated in the reign of Artaxerxes, though we do not know which king of this name is meant. It has usually been supposed that it is Artaxerxes I (465–424), but this is solely an inference from the order of the materials here and from the relating of this to the next section. If Tabeel were to be regarded as somehow linked to the Tobiah of the Nehemiah narratives,[1] then a picture of provincial governors operating together against Judah would appear here too. The third passage, 4: 8–23 (Aramaic), is introduced by the reference to the Aramaic rendering of the second letter in verse 7; the last word, 'Aramaic', is a marker to indicate the point at which the Aramaic text

[1] Cf. B. Mazar, 'The Tobiads', *IEJ*, 7 (1957), 137–45, 229–38.

begins. The letter of complaint and its reply in verses 8 to 23 refer to
two personages by name: Rehum and Shimshai. It is gratuitous to
suppose that in reality these are the same personages as are mentioned
in verse 7, and it is much more natural to see here a quite separate
occasion. It is also dated to the reign of Artaxerxes, and is the only one
which provides any details. The complaint concerns the rebuilding of
the city of Jerusalem and is indicated as coming from the high officials
of the remaining areas of the province Beyond the River, with particular
reference to Samaria. It argues the dangers which threaten Persian
control of the whole province. It is possible to read this at an intelligible
political level. Governors of areas neighbouring Judah might well
resent the re-establishment and growth of its power, and it is a
well-known device of subject rulers to complain about the rebellious
activities of their neighbours, sometimes by way of diverting attention
from their own dubious actions. But we must observe that the text is
written at a very different level. The complaint refers back to the
previous history of Judah and to its long tradition of rebellion against
higher authority, suggesting that the re-establishment of Jerusalem will
lead to total loss of control of the whole province. While this may be
seen as the hyperbole of political accusation, the same can hardly be said
of the reply. This not only reiterates the references to the past; it also
states that 'powerful kings were over Jerusalem and had authority over
the whole province Beyond-the-River' (verse 20). Clearly this is a
reference to the Davidic–Solomonic empire, accepting as literal the poetic
claims that that empire extended from the sea to the river (for example,
Ps. 89: 26, EVV 25). It looks in effect towards the total restoration of
the greatness of Israel's past and may be understood as an oblique
presentation of that hope of universal rule, expressed frequently in
psalm and prophecy, an ideal which appears in narrower political terms
or in colourful imagery in later biblical and post-biblical writings. The
account shows how this hope is frustrated by those who are opposed
to the Jewish community; set as it is in its present context, it shows
how under divine protection the Jewish community will nevertheless
complete its Temple and thereby re-establish the religious centre which
represents the point from which God will in due course rule the whole
earth.

The precise historical moments reflected in these passages are no
longer discoverable; the interest in them lies rather in their typifying
of the theme of opposition to the divine purpose of restoration of Judah
and Jerusalem. It has often been thought (see above, pp. 148f) that the
main section must be related to the rebuilding activities of Nehemiah,
and, by placing it in the years before his arrival – that is, between 465

and 445 – the reason for his coming is thought to be made more precise. We have seen reasons for doubting such a narrow interpretation of the opening verses of Neh. 1. The most that can be said is that, since it is likely that more than one attempt at restoring the city was made between Cyrus' accession to power and Nehemiah's activity, this passage may ultimately be based upon such an incident. The correlating of these is, however, a matter of conjecture. Even more conjectural is the assumption that Ezra, assuming him to have come to Jerusalem in 458 under Artaxerxes I, was involved in this attempt at rebuilding the walls. Since there is no reference to any such activity in the Ezra narrative – though its absence could be assumed to be due to the Chronicler's idealization of Ezra – and no date is provided for the account in Ezra 4: 8–23, there is no basis on which this can properly be advanced.[1] The most that we may infer from this accumulation of 'opposition' material, as also from the comparable material in the Nehemiah narratives, is that the whole period was one in which relationships between Judah and her neighbours were delicate and attempts at recovery were in various ways resisted.

The dating of Ezra 4: 6 to the beginning of the reign of Xerxes provides a starting point for the assumption that there was an involvement of Judah in a major upheaval at that moment, and that this is reflected in many passages of the biblical writings, notably in obscure passages of prophecy. The possibility that with the accession of a new ruler over Persia there were widespread disturbances is reasonable enough; the reign of Xerxes was to be a troubled one in view of the conflicts with Greece. But anything beyond this is conjecture. The theme has been worked out with great elaboration and increasing improbability by J. Morgenstern,[2] for the more material is found which, it is claimed, may be interpreted against such a background, the more unlikely does the hypothesis become. It is true that major political moments – such as the accession and conquests of Alexander the Great – find no clear reflection in the biblical writings, though many suppositions have been put forward. A major disturbance in 485 B.C.E could have occurred without there being any overt reference. But the whole argument of the case relies far too heavily on dubious inference and becomes virtually circular, as the detail of the disturbance is constructed from the assumption that the texts refer to it and indeed give precision to it. The same is true of various other suggestions made

---

[1] Cf. W. T. In der Smitten, *Esra: Quellen Ueberlieferung und Geschichte*, Studia Semitica Neerlandica, 15 (Assen, 1973), pp. 105–48, placing this in 446(?) B.C.E.

[2] 'Jerusalem – 485 B.C.', *HUCA*, 27 (1956), 101–79; 28 (1957), 15–47; 31 (1960), 1–29. He also associates Isa. 61 with events in 440 B.C.E. (*HUCA*, 40–1 (1969), 109–22).

by the same writer, discovering other moments of high significance; and this applies equally to endeavours at finding evidence for details of the period from psalms which have been dated, often on very slender grounds, to these centuries. We have to be content with recognizing the possibility of allusions which we are unable to make precise.

A similar hypothesis of disturbance in the reign of Artaxerxes III Ochus (358–336) was put forward some years ago by W. O. E. Oesterley,[1] associating some biblical texts with Jewish involvement in a rebellion reconstructed out of rather obscure allusions in later Greek historians. Recently this has been revived and linked to archeological evidence of destructions of sites in the Palestinian area.[2] The method of reconstruction leaves much to be desired. The evidence of destructions on sites is by no means sufficiently precise to allow it to be claimed that they really all belong to one crisis; and the statements from the historians are themselves in need of very careful study before they can be used satisfactorily to reconstruct the events of the mid-fourth century B.C.E.[3]

CHRONOLOGY

The sequence of Persian rulers provides the primary framework, and within that sequence it is possible to mark out the main stages of conflict between Persia and Greece, Persia and Egypt. The latter conflict, with its repercussions on Palestine, and the involvement in these of the position of the satrap of the province Beyond the River, may be said to be of particular importance. When we look for Persian motivations for action in regard to the Jewish community, these may be expected to lie in the area of protecting lines of communication, and finding greater security in periods of particular conflict. Here it is evident that the middle of the fifth century, with the upheavals in the province and the rebellion of its satrap Megabyzus, himself much involved with Egypt, marks a period when we might expect to find Persian action in regard to Judah; and it is here that both Ezra and Nehemiah traditionally belong, though Nehemiah in 445 falls a little late. The stages by which Egypt moved to independence at the end of the fifth century, providing a background to the later years of the Elephantine community, also provide a moment at which Persian action towards

[1] W. O. E. Oesterley and T. H. Robinson, *History of Israel* (1932), vol. II, pp. 140f.

[2] D. Barag, 'The Effects of the Tennes Rebellion on Palestine', *BASOR*, 183 (1966), 6–12; accepted as proved by Cross, *JBL*, 94 (1975), 12, n. 42. = *Int*, p. 195, n. 42. Cf. also Morton Smith, *Palestinian Parties and Politics that Shaped the Old Testament* (New York, London, 1971), pp. 60, 185.

[3] For a careful critique cf. G. Widengren in *Israelite and Judaean History*, ed. J. H. Hayes and J. M. Miller (Philadelphia, London, 1977), ch. 9, section I, D.

Judah might be expected. But it must be said that such fitting together of events, where we have outline rather than detailed knowledge, is only hypothetical.

Providing a historical sequence internally is difficult, but a number of important clues are available. The evidence for the governors in Samaria becomes clearer. The Elephantine papyri reveal (*circa* 410 B.C.E.) that a governor named Sanballat had been succeeded by his son Delaiah, mentioned together with his brother Shelemaiah as active at that point; and he is associated with Bagohi (Bagoas?) governor of Judah in encouraging the rebuilding of the Elephantine temple. The Samaria papyri provide further information, suggesting that Delaiah was followed by another Sanballat (II), and he in his turn apparently successively by his two sons Yeshayahu and Hananiah. If the evidence of Josephus for a Sanballat in the time of Alexander the Great is accepted – and this needs careful consideration, since his association of it with the foundation of the Samaritan temple must raise questions about its reliability – we should then have yet another governor of the name, Sanballat III. The numbering is based on the assumption that the first of these was the founder of the line; if he is identified with the Sanballat of Nehemiah's narrative, as is most probable but not fully provable, then his designation there as 'the Horonite' rather than with reference to his father might indicate that he was the first holder of the office. Allowance must however be made for the fact that that narrative, as we have seen, tends to treat Nehemiah's opponents in a derogatory manner, and this may account both for Sanballat not being called governor and for this description of him which might be designed to suggest that his position was inferior. We have no evidence for governors of Samaria earlier than this date, but Ezra 4: 10, 17 points to the presence there of a number of officials, with Rehum as $b^{e\cdot}\bar{e}l$ $t^{e\cdot}\bar{e}m$ 'high officer, chancellor, controller', with no mention of either *peḥāh* or *tiršātāh*.

The status of the governor of Samaria is one which it is not easy to define, and it ties in with questions about the position of Judah. Here the evidence is fragmentary, but gradually becoming clearer; further discoveries may fill in the many gaps which exist at present. For the period immediately after the restoration, we have Sheshbazzar, not described as governor in Ezra 1, but given the title *peḥāh* in 5: 14. Zerubbabel is so described in Haggai (1: 1 etc.), but not in Ezra. The term is used in that context (5: 3) for Tattenai as governor of the province Beyond the River, and its use in the books of Kings and Ezekiel 23 points to a fairly wide range of meaning. It is doubtful if any clear argument can be based on the use and non-use of the term for Sheshbazzar and Zerubbabel. It may be argued that they were officers appointed for a specific purpose rather than governors with a term of office, but we have no means of determining this. The only further direct clue in the relevant texts is the mention of an unnamed *peḥāh* in Ezra 6: 7. If this is Zerubbabel, the absence of his name is curious; but we have seen that the presence of Zerubbabel's name at all in this section may be questioned. The supposition that he had been removed from office is without real foundation. If he was still operating, then it could be argued that he was not the governor but held a special office alongside the governor, but this appears less probable. It is simplest to assume that both Sheshbazzar and Zerubbabel were governors of Judah, though this does not necessarily fully define the status of that area.

For the years that follow to Nehemiah and Ezra we have no direct evidence in the biblical texts. If Malachi is dated in this period, as is commonly done, then the reference to a *peḥāh* in 1: 8 points to the existence of such an official in the first half of the fifth century; but this evidence is very fragile. Nehemiah 5: 15 appears to indicate that Nehemiah as governor had been preceded by others described as *peḥāh*; but the assumption normally made that this proves that there were governors immediately preceding Nehemiah does not take sufficient account of the nature of the narrative. It would seem entirely possible that we have here an example of the common rhetorical device of the glorification of an official by contrasting his conduct with the undesirable ways of his predecessors. The title is used of Nehemiah in 5: 14 and 12: 26. In 5: 14 and 18 reference is made to the 'governor's allowance'. Elsewhere in Nehemiah the term is used of the 'governors of the province Beyond the River' (2: 7, 9), and in a very important passage, in reference to the 'seat (throne) of the governor of Beyond the River' (3: 7). If, as appears most natural, this refers to a governor's residence in Jerusalem, then this may be understood as the place in which he resided when visiting the administrative district of Judah. An alternative interpretation associates the reference with the two areas of Gibeon and Mizpah described as 'belonging to the jurisdiction of the governor of Beyond-the-River', but this appears to be in conflict with subsequent statements about Mizpah in verses 15, 19. If Neh. 3 does not belong to the Nehemiah material originally, then the account could reflect a situation in which the administration was differently organized. But these are purely speculative suggestions.

In Neh. 10: 2 Nehemiah is described as *tiršātāh*, and his name has been added to the text at Neh. 8: 9 where the 1 Esdras text refers to the governor without naming him. This term also appears in the two forms of the list of Ezra (2: 63) and Nehemiah (7: 65), and also in 7: 70 (not in the parallel). Since this document refers to a whole series of officials concerned with returns to Judah, including Zerubbabel and Jeshua and Nehemiah and other men whose names can in some instances be paralleled elsewhere (Ezra 2: 2 and the divergent parallel Neh. 7: 7), we cannot satisfactorily date its reference but simply observe that the existence of a governor of Judah is attested for some other moment as well.

The discovery of a series of bullae and seals, and certain other evidence provide some further names. The evidence – which may well be amplified with the consideration of further comparable materials already known – has been published and given preliminary discussion by N. Avigad[1] and dated by him to the late sixth and early fifth centuries B.C.E. The names which appear are Elnathan (*phw'*), mentioned also in association with 'Shelomith maidservant (*'āmāh*) of Elnathan the governor'; Yehoezer (*phw'*); Ahzai (*phw'*) – along with others which have simply *yhwd phw'* without a governor's name; Bagohi (Bagoas?) (*pht yhwd*, Elephantine papyrus 30: 1), dated to 408 B.C.E.; Yehezqiyah (*hphh*, coins, dated to the end of the Persian period on iconographic evidence). It will be observed that only one of these is dated by chronological statement – Bagohi. Of the others, in some instances the stratigraphic evidence of the excavations and that of the coinage provide a fairly clear but not by any means absolute dating. The bullae and seals are without stratigraphic evidence and are dated by Avigad solely on the basis of epigraphy.[2] We know of the appointment of Gedaliah in Judah after the fall of Jerusalem in 587; the term *pehāh* is never used of him, and indeed no actual description is given of his office other than the statement that 'he was appointed' (hiph. of *pqd*, 2 Kings 25: 22; Jer. 40: 5, 7). It is reasonable to see him as a governor; he had a 'residence' or 'palace' (*bait*, Jer. 39: 14), and also apparently had charge of the 'royal women' (*benôt hammelek*, 41: 10). This phrase could denote the royal harem and raises the question whether he was simply to guard them and thus seek to prevent their being claimed, as they evidently were, by a member of the royal house (the mention of them is in connection with Ishmael, a royal claimant), or whether he was regarded

---

[1] *Bullae and Seals from a post-exilic Judaean Archive, Qedem* 4 (Jerusalem, 1976).

[2] Cf. E. Stern, *The Material Culture of the Land of the Bible in the Persian Period* (Warminster, 1982), ch. 7; idem, 'The Province of Yehud: the Vision and the Reality', *The Jerusalem Cathedre–1981*, 9–21, who promises a fuller discussion of the chronology and favours a late fifth century date.

by the Babylonians as taking over the royal functions, since he was clearly a prominent member of the Judean 'aristocracy'.[1] After his assassination no information is given about the arrangements made for Judah by the Babylonians. The hypothesis that Judah was put under the control of the governor at Samaria is an attractive one and provides answers to some of the problems of the subsequent period. The new evidence providing further names of governors could give a clue to the subsequent situation in Judah; but whether any of the names now available could be fitted into the unknown years of Babylonian rule must depend on the fuller analysis of the chronology.

In any event, the new evidence does provide a clearer picture of certain moments within the period of Babylonian and Persian rule, a few further figures to fill the long gaps left by the biblical evidence. It has been thought that this refutes the hypothesis of rule from Samaria, whether that is envisaged as beginning after Gedaliah or after Zerubbabel.[2] Certainly it makes that hypothesis less likely or in need of modification. But we still have to deal with the indications of claims made from Samaria in relation to Judah, and to assess the problems confronting the Jewish community under Persian rule in relation particularly to this northern neighbouring district. While some elements in the biblical text as it now stands may be the result of later anti-Samaritan polemic, this seems insufficient to account for the clear indication in Ezra 4: 8–23 of the lead taken by the authorities in Samaria against the redevelopment of Jerusalem. Are economic motives sufficient to explain this? Nor do we have a satisfactory explanation for the firm denial by Nehemiah of any rights for the neighbouring governors in Jerusalem – the terms used are explicit – *ḥēleq*, territorial rights; *ṣ'dāqāh*, legal rights; *zikkārôn*, traditional rights (this is a difficult term to explain here but may be understood to refer to rights established by custom or time). It is true that as the text stands the affirmation refers to the three opponents, Sanballat, Tobiah and Geshem; but it may be that we have here a first example of the process of combining different opposition elements. The primary reference could well be to Sanballat and to claims from Samaria. A similar point may emerge from the recognition that the appeal of the Elephantine Jews is made to both Jerusalem and Samaria. How far this is to be interpreted at the political

---

[1] A suggestion made by N. Lohfink orally.
[2] A. Alt, 'Die Rolle Samarias bei der Entstehung des Judentums', in *Festschrift O. Procksch* (Leipzig, 1934), pp. 5–28 = *Kl. Schr.* 2 (Munich, 1953), pp. 316–37. Cf. the criticism in Morton Smith, *Palestinian Parties*, pp. 193–201, and the more judicious analysis by Avigad, *Bullae and Seals*, pp. 33f; S. Talmon, 'Ezra and Nehemiah' *IDBSup.* (Nashville, 1976), 325; Widengren, *History*, section II, B.

level – the recognition of some degree of double authority, and how far at the religious – both Judah and Samaria claiming the same religious allegiance, must again be uncertain. But there is a possible indication of a more complex situation than would exist if it were in fact the case that Judah had been treated as a separate administrative unit throughout the period of Babylonian and Persian rule. Alt's hypothesis, for it can be no more, is unproven; but the points which it seeks to explain are still problems for the historian, and the possibility that there is at least some element of truth in his view must remain open.

The sequence of high priests for the post-exilic period also provides some information about different moments (see Neh. 12: 10f, 22f) and the same may be said of Davidic genealogies (see 1 Chron. 3 10–24; Ezra 8: 2–14). But the use of such material is problematic. There are no chronological indications in such lists. Cross[1] has made an attempt at defining the chronology and also at filling out the lists: but his assumptions about probable ages and papponymy and periods of office are all hypothetical; they involve the assumption of a double haplography in the lists, thus enabling the insertion of extra names and the provision of what is then set up as a more satisfactory chronology to be used for historical reconstruction. The nature and purpose of such genealogical information must be carefully investigated.[2] Modification of lists in different circumstances, the degree of padding which is often evident within them, the possibility of omissions, the particular functions which they are designed to perform, must all be taken into account. We have already noted that the genealogy of Ezra in Ezra 7: 1–5 does not include any name between Ezra and the Seraiah of the period of the fall of Jerusalem: were no other evidence available, a totally spurious historical and chronological sequence could be constructed on the basis of this omission.

The internal arguments from the Ezra and Nehemiah narratives for their chronological placing have been many times rehearsed. None is conclusive. The clearest point remains the indication that the high priest of the time of Nehemiah was Eliashib (Neh. 13: 28); that Johanan (Jehonanan) appears in the Ezra narrative (Ezra 10: 6) as son of Eliashib, though he is not there described as high priest; that Johanan

---

[1] Cf. Cross, *JBL*, 94 (1975), 9–11 and 17 = *Int*, 192–4 and 203; largely accepted by Talmon, *IDBSup* 327. Cross can point to evidence of papponymy in Samaria, in Qedar and in Ammon (cf. also Mazar's views on the Tobiad family). But there is no evidence at all of papponymy in the Davidic line, as Cross observes; nor is it clear in the genealogies of the high priestly line. Cf. also the criticisms by Widengren, *History*, section II, A.

[2] Cf. R. R. Wilson, *Genealogy and History in the Biblical World* (New Haven, 1977).

appears in Neh. 12: 22 in a list of priests as grandson of Eliashib, and
that a Johanan appears in the Elephantine papyri in the last years of
the fifth century as high priest in Jerusalem. In view of the use of these
names for other persons in the period, positive identifications cannot
be made; but the high-priestly status affirmed or implied is an important
additional factor. The lack of description in Ezra 10: 6 could be
explained as the result of the Chronicler's view that Ezra, as direct
successor of the high priest of the moment of exile, was the more
important figure of the period. We may note too that Neh. 13: 4
describes Eliashib simply as 'the priest', though this clearly implies
'high priest'.

Josephus, as we have seen, places the account of Nehemiah after that
of Ezra (*Ant.* xi, 5). It appears that he is utilizing the 1 Esdras form
of the material in which there is no place for Nehemiah between the
restoration and the activity of Ezra. If the Nehemiah narrative was
known to him as quite separate from that of Ezra, then it would be
natural for him to place it thus. Josephus names the Persian king of
Ezra's and Nehemiah's time as Xerxes; he follows the account with the
Esther narrative, placing this in the reign of Artaxerxes; he offers an
account, following this, of the murder by the high priest Johanan,
grandson of Eliashib, of his brother Joshua, claiming that the latter had
been supported by one Bagoses, general of Artaxerxes' army (possibly
to be linked with Bagoas, Bigvai, governor of Judah).[1] The next high
priest is named as Jaddua and Josephus connects the marriage of his
brother Manasseh with a daughter of Sanballat, and then links all this
with the advent of Alexander and the building of the temple on Mount
Gerizim. That Josephus has here reminiscences of the period in general
is clear enough; but it is also clear that no satisfactory chronological
sequence can be derived from such evidence, and that the order of Ezra
and Nehemiah given by Josephus does not support or refute the biblical
evidence.

Unsatisfactory as it may be from a historian's point of view, the
indeterminate chronology for Ezra and Nehemiah remains. The
traditional dating in the reign of Artaxerxes I gives 458 for Ezra and
445 for Nehemiah; they may then be understood to have worked in that
order and separately, or to have overlapped, though the latter accords
ill with the texts. An emendation of the year of Ezra's journey to the
thirty-seventh year, giving 428, is pure conjecture and does little to
resolve the problems. The alternative of dating Nehemiah in 445 and
Ezra in the reign of Artaxerxes II (404–358 B.C.E.) in 398 has much to

---

[1] For Bagoas, Bigvai, see nn. 1, 2 on p. 157.

commend it. It must be allowed that a later dating for Nehemiah under Artaxerxes II can still be entertained, especially now that we have fuller evidence for the governors in Samaria. If credence is given to Josephus, this alternative cannot be ruled out. There is some swing back among scholars to the acceptance of the conventional order, but it must be admitted that this order presents its own problems.

Insufficient attention still seems to be given to the literary problems, and in particular to the quite separate nature of the Nehemiah narratives. If, as may be indicated by Josephus, the Nehemiah material originally stood after the Ezra material (and was in its turn followed by the Esther narrative), then we may most naturally suppose that the conflation of the Ezra and Nehemiah material is the result of a late editorial process, deriving from the belief that the two leaders were contemporaries. If there had already come to be some degree of assimilation between the two, so that they had become a pair in tradition, such harmonization is as intelligible as it is also in the cases of Elijah and Elisha and of Haggai and Zechariah. Indeed a more notable parallel still can be seen in the pairing of Moses and Aaron, the figures of Nehemiah and Ezra then offering counterparts to the prophetic leader and almost royal figure of the former and to the priestly figure of the latter.[1] Any penetration behind the present stylized presentation must rest content with a lack of clear chronological information; for much in the appreciation of the influence of Ezra and Nehemiah on the development of Jewish life and thought, and of the degree to which they reflect differing but overlapping areas of concern within the Jewish community, this more precise historical evidence would be useful but its lack is not disastrous.

[1] Cf. P. R. Ackroyd, *The Age of the Chronicler*, Supplement to *Colloquium* – The Australian and New Zealand Theological Review (1970), pp. 25f.

CHAPTER 8

PROPHECY AND PSALMS IN THE
PERSIAN PERIOD

An account of the prophecy and Psalms of the Persian period – that is, the two hundred years of Persian rule over Palestine from 538 to 330 B.C.E. – is fraught with the same difficulties as any other history of prophecy and Psalms within a given period. The problems arise first from the peculiar way in which the literature of the Old Testament psalmists and prophets was handed down, and secondly from the particular circumstances in which the literature of prayer came to be written.

Thus in the first instance written prophecies and prophetic testimonies were rapidly collected into small anthologies; these were then put together to form larger collections and whole books. In the course of this anthologizing process, what were originally anonymous prophetic utterances were very frequently attributed to named prophets, either because within the oral tradition the sayings of well-known prophets had already been enriched by the addition of anonymous material, or because an attempt was made thereby to give authority to anonymous utterances as pseudo-epigraphic literature. The result of this whole process is that most prophetic books represent, not the sole product of a single author, but a complicated tapestry of utterances from a variety of sources. This means that scholars have to deal with an abundance of anonymous and pseudo-epigraphic texts which can be dated and placed in historical order only through an indirect approach. We must find and interpret evidence that will help us place the texts in the right order and we must produce arguments to establish which indeed are the pseudo-epigraphic texts. In carrying out this task Old Testament scholarship has come up with completely contradictory results in relation to one and the same text, precisely because of the above-mentioned problems and difficulties. Lack of agreement over dating the texts is particularly marked in the case of post-exilic literature, that is the literature of the Persian and Hellenistic periods, during which a great many anonymous texts were written.

Although one can still find in the anonymous or undated prophetic texts at least some evidence that helps us to place them historically, this is almost completely lacking in the case of the Psalms. Therefore the evaluation of individual Psalms, and above all the task of arranging them in the correct chronological order, proves extraordinarily difficult. Scholars thus disagree far more over the dating of the Psalms than over the dating of the prophetic texts. The reason lies in the peculiar circumstances in which the Psalms originated. In the first place, Psalms are an expression of a particular kind of piety in the form of a prayer. As individual prayers they reflect the moods, situations, emotions, demands and attitudes of individuals, which are easy to locate in a general human context but very difficult to place in their historical circumstances. Secondly, these prayers were also employed in religious services, or were indeed in some cases destined to be used in this way from the start; they thus became general formulae of prayer, thereby again losing almost all trace of their historical origin.

These difficulties and the conflicting opinions to which they have given rise must always be borne in mind. The reader should not labour under the impression that the following account is based on more or less generally accepted findings. But he can rest assured that a majority of scholars do agree in their assessment of certain evidence. In examining the Psalms and prophecies of the Persian period – with few exceptions, such as Haggai – one cannot hope to achieve results possessing more than a moderate degree of probability.

PROPHECY IN THE PERSIAN PERIOD

The utterances of the great Exile prophet Deutero-Isaiah (Isa. 40–55), above all his proclamation that judgement was at an end and that salvation was about to be vouchsafed to Israel, and the linking of both these things with the figure of Cyrus the Great, created a mental climate in Israel during the early post-exilic years that we can term the matrix of post-exilic prophecy. All the prophets after Deutero-Isaiah had to take a position in regard to this expectation of impending salvation. These include (for the Persian period) the known prophets Haggai, Zechariah and Joel, together with a number of anonymous prophets whose words have come down to us in the book of Malachi and – interspersed throughout the text – in the books of the pre-exilic prophets Isaiah, Jeremiah and Micah. What was said in the introduction above with regard to the problem of dating is particularly relevant to the prophetic texts included in the books of the pre-exilic prophets. We also have to reckon with the possibility that there are texts preserved in other books such as Amos or Zephaniah, for example, which do not properly belong to those prophets and ought to be attributed to a later period. The individual prophets who stand behind these texts are no longer identifiable. All that remains is their message.

PROPHETS AND PROPHETIC TEXTS

Haggai

The prophet Haggai, about whom the Old Testament gives us no personal details except his name[1] seems, like the prophet Zechariah, to have belonged to that group of exiles who returned to Jerusalem from Babylon with Zerubbabel and Joshua the high priest around 521 B.C.E. The precise cause of their return can no longer be divined. At all events the building of the Temple in Jerusalem had by this period come to a halt, or perhaps had not even begun. At the same time in the Persian empire the death of Cambyses II (ruled 529–522) triggered off disputes over the succession. Darius I (521–486) established his claim to the throne only with difficulty after suppressing a series of revolts among the subject peoples. These troubles obviously aroused new political hopes among the vassals of the Persians and stimulated a desire for independence. It is quite possible that even Judah and Jerusalem were not impervious to this development and that this kind of mood found a precipitate in the pronouncements of the prophet Haggai. What is clear is that in this politically somewhat unstable period he proclaims the rule of God as imminent and declares a decisive turning point in history to be at hand. As Ezra 5: 1 and 6: 14 confirm, he advocates the building of the Temple.

The period of his activity in Jerusalem can be deduced with reasonable confidence from the text itself: Haggai proclaimed his message between the first day of the sixth month and the twenty-fourth day of the ninth month of the second year of the reign of Darius I, that is between August and December 520 B.C.E.

The words of Haggai, amplified by one or two editorial additions, are transmitted in the book of Haggai, together with two narrative passages. The sayings are essentially in chronological order. Only at one point can we discern a discrepancy: the date now standing isolated in Hag. 1: 15 is most probably to be taken together with the utterance in 2: 15–19.[2]

Haggai's proclamation links up with the prophecies of Deutero-

---

[1] Apart from the book of Haggai, in Ezra 5: 1 and 6: 14.

[2] Thus Rothstein, but K. Galling, 'Serubbabel und der Wiederaufbau des Tempels in Jerusalem', *Rudolph-Festschrift* (Tübingen, 1961), p. 79 and K. Koch, 'Haggais unreines Volk', *ZAW*, 79 (1967), 52ff, disagree.

Isaiah, announcing the impending eschatological rule of the Lord. Deutero-Isaiah still saw the dawn of redemption as being connected with the return of the Israelites to Palestine. In Haggai's day the return of the Israelites had already taken place, though clearly it was not interpreted in the sense of Deutero-Isaiah as an all-embracing redemption of miraculous character. On the contrary, the tribulations of the Exile had been replaced by the problems of reconstruction and resettlement in Palestine. These difficulties made the promises of the Exile prophet appear as yet unfulfilled. Salvation had still not ensued after the period of judgement. The fact that the eschatological turning point had not yet been reached was associated in Haggai's eyes with the failure to accomplish the rebuilding of the Temple. Thus Haggai threw all his authority behind the plan to build the Temple, in the belief that the last days were at hand.

In 1: 2, 4-8 he takes to task those citizens of Jerusalem and Judah who live in solid houses themselves but refuse to acknowledge that the time has come to build the house of Yahweh. He tries to make clear to them that the dearth of food, drink, clothing and economic success is due to God withholding his blessing. They deny to Yahweh what they themselves enjoy. Not until the Temple is completed will Yahweh's blessing be upon them once again. What is more, Yahweh will graciously accept their offering in the form of the Temple and reveal himself in all his glory. The time to build the Temple has come.

With other men the situation is different: Haggai must here show that in their concern to put up their own houses they have simply forgotten about the house of God. Therefore, Haggai tells them in 1: 9-11 that all their efforts are doomed to failure. Since Yahweh's house still lies in ruins and nothing is being done about it, Yahweh has visited upon them punishment and judgement. This will come to an end only when they begin to rebuild the Temple.

A short note in 1: 12-14 informs us of the success of the prophet's proclamation: Zerubbabel, Joshua the high priest and the people obeyed the prophet's summons and began to build the Temple of Yahweh. Clearly in connection with this the word of the Lord came again to Haggai (1: 15 and 2: 15-19), saying that the laying of the foundation stone of the Temple marked the end of material straits and the beginning of Yahweh's blessing. As work proceeded, it rapidly became clear that the resources available were scarcely adequate to erect a building worthy of Yahweh, corresponding to Solomon's Temple. Faint-heartedness at the impoverished scope of the building must have greatly hampered the progress of construction. Once again Haggai intervenes, about four weeks after work had commenced, with the comforting promise of 1: 15 to 2: 9. The structure which at present looks so meagre should calmly be completed, for in a short while God's rule will be established. Accompanied by the shaking of heaven and earth and all nations, Yahweh himself will fill the house with splendour and glory and adorn his Temple with the riches of the nations, so that it will be even more wondrous than the Temple of Solomon.

Whether there were disputes over who should participate in the building of the Temple, in which Haggai took a hand with his statement in 2: 10–14, has not yet been ascertained. For a long time it was held that the prophet's parable-like, priestly admonition about 'clean and unclean' implied an intention to exclude the Samaritans or other Jewish groups from the task of building the Temple, in order to ensure the purity of the Jerusalem congregation.[1] Recently, some commentators have interpreted this passage as applying to the congregation itself, whose sacrificial offerings are here represented as remaining unclean until such time as the Temple is completed.[2]

In his final utterance at 2: 20–23 the prophet refers to Zerubbabel, a descendant of David, who had played a key role in the construction of the Temple; Haggai promises him in a cryptic manner the messianic sovereignty when the last days are come. Whereas Jeremiah had used the image of the signet ring in order to express the rejection of Coniah the son of Jehoiakim of the house of David,[3] Haggai now inverts this into a promise of election. He anticipates the re-establishment of the rule of the house of David during the last days in the person of Zerubbabel.

From all this it becomes clear that in Haggai the more general announcement of salvation to be found in Deutero-Isaiah is now narrowed down to Judah and Jerusalem in such a way that concrete events and figures are linked through an intensified eschatological expectation with the onset of the last days. An expectation of this kind could have only a limited temporal validity.

Zechariah

Zechariah is identified in Zech. 1: 1, 7 as a son of Berechiah and grandson of Iddo, although according to Ezra 5: 1 and 6: 14 the prophet was not a grandson but the son of Iddo. Which of the two versions

---

[1] Thus the majority of Old Testament scholars since J. W. Rothstein's *Juden und Samaritaner* (Leipzig, 1908).

[2] E.g. Koch, *ZAW*, 79 (1967), 52–66.

[3] Jer. 22: 24.

is correct can no longer be decided with certainty.[1] We may assume, however, that Zechariah's origins were in some way associated with the Iddo family, a family of priests mentioned in Neh. 12: 16. The prophet was thus of priestly stock, like Jeremiah and Ezekiel before him.[2]

Zechariah was a contemporary of Haggai and like him belonged to the group of men who, together with Zerubbabel and Joshua the high priest, energetically urged the people to press ahead with the reconstruction of the Temple.[3] But Zechariah's message resembles that of Haggai not only in his concern to see the Temple completed but also in the expectation of eschatological redemption that he associates with the rebuilding of the house of God.

Since dated utterances are recorded in the book of Zechariah, we can delimit the period of his activity with reasonable certainty. Zechariah made his appearance between the eighth month of the second year of the reign of Darius I, in other words while Haggai was still active, and the fourth day of the ninth month of the fourth year of the reign of Darius I. The period in question is roughly from October 520 to November or December 518 B.C.E. Any texts that might post-date the consecration of the Temple in 515 are no longer extant.

The literary precipitate of the prophet's career is confined to the first eight chapters of the book of Zechariah. The other material handed down under his name comprises collections of the utterances of anonymous prophets which probably go back no further than Israel's Hellenistic period.[4]

The principal sections of Zechariah's message consist of the so-called night visions. These are accounts of the visions of a single night, interspersed with a small number of interpretative comments.[5] There are eight such accounts altogether. With the exception of 3: 1–7 they are all narrated according to the same structural pattern.[6] All these

---

[1] L. Bertholdt, *Historischkritische Einleitung in sämmthiche kannonische und apokryphe Schriften des Alten und Neuen Testamentes* (Erlangen, 1812–19) assumed that the discrepancy between the two pieces of information goes back to a combination of the details in Ezra 5: 1 and 6: 14 with those in Isa. 8: 2.

[2] If the Zechariah named in Neh. 12: 16 is identical with the prophet, we must reckon with the possibility that Zechariah began his prophecy as a very young man and subsequently became a priest, reaching moreover a ripe old age.

[3] For the circumstances at this time, see what was said earlier in connection with Haggai (p. 164).

[4] Zech. 9–11 and 12–14, separated from chapters 1 to 8 by independent titles, were later added to the Zechariah texts, like the book of Malachi.

[5] Zech. 1: 7 to 6: 8.

[6] Depiction of the vision; a question from the prophet; an answer from the *angelus interpres*.

visions refer to the impending dawn of the period of salvation and to the events associated with it.

In the vision of the horseman[1] it is made clear to the prophet that although the nations of the world are again at rest Yahweh will yet transform the fate of Judah and terminate the period of wrath. The approaching salvation has already been prepared by Yahweh. Likewise the fate of the nations which scattered Judah is already sealed, according to the vision of the horns.[2] The vision of the man with a measuring line[3] shows the prophet that, contrary to certain efforts to rebuild the walls of Jerusalem, the city should remain without external defences since Yahweh himself will be a wall of fire around her. The vision of the high priest[4] demonstrates to the prophet that despite the enmity of a satan[5] Joshua will be cleansed and reconsecrated as high priest. Moreover, the vision of the candlestick[6] allows the prophet to behold the pattern of sovereignty in the last days: the two anointed ones denote Zerubbabel and Joshua as representatives of priestly and secular power. Finally, the guilt which the people of God have incurred will be taken away from them; the curse of Yahweh will overtake those who have unlawfully appropriated the property of others and borne false witness,[7] while iniquity will be swept away out of Israel altogether.[8] The final vision, the vision of the chariots,[9] returns to the image of the first vision, thus rounding off all these accounts into a structured whole. It tells of the chariots that go forth in all directions and traverse the earth. The purpose of this vision cannot be clearly interpreted. It seems as if the intention is to extend the eschatological events to cover the whole world. Such a reading is supported by the utterance in 2: 10–12 which predicts that in the last days many nations will turn to Yahweh.

The implications of the individual visions are explained in more detail in a series of utterances which either form a framework for the account of the visions[10] or are collected together and appended to them.[11] Zechariah sees himself standing at the turning point of history. He can survey the past as a time of calamity and disobedience. The past is a warning to the present generation to mend their ways and return to God.[12] The future, on the other hand, is already planned by Yahweh as the period of redemption which is now at hand.[13] There redemption, peace and prosperity shall reign, the Temple will stand completed and

---

[1] 1: 7–15.
[2] 1: 18–21.
[3] 2: 1–5.
[4] 3: 1–7.
[5] = adversary.
[6] 4: 1–6a, 10b–14.
[7] Vision of the scrolls, 5: 1–4.
[8] Vision of the ephah, 5: 5–11.
[9] 6: 1–8.
[10] 1: 1–6; 6: 9–15.
[11] 7: 1–3; 7: 4 to 8: 17; 8: 18–19.
[12] 1: 1–6.
[13] 8: 9–13, 14–15.

Jerusalem will become the centre of the worship of Yahweh.[1] A special place in these eschatological events is reserved for Zerubbabel and Joshua. Zerubbabel, who began the construction of the Temple and who, it is promised, will also complete the work,[2] is symbolically designated the messianic ruler[3] with Joshua at his side as priestly representative. In the prophecy of Zechariah, therefore, we encounter for the first time the notion of the two Messiahs, the priestly and the secular Messiah, which will later recur in Qumran.

Zechariah differs from Haggai in so far as his depictions of the last days are much more concrete and comprehensive. Conversely, the building of the Temple does not have such a central importance as in Haggai. Moreover Zechariah takes up the message of the pre-exilic prophets in that he sees their predictions of calamity as having been fulfilled in the Exile and tries to make clear that the demand of the prophets for obedience and certain ethical norms retain their validity even in the time of transition leading up to the period of redemption.[4]

The concrete detail in the message of this prophet, namely the connection between his eschatological hopes and the personalities of his own day and age, eventually led to the collapse of these hopes. This is doubtless the reason for the absence of any further account of Zechariah, Haggai and Zerubbabel in the subsequent Old Testament tradition.

Trito-Isaiah

Ever since Bernhard Duhm[5] separated chapters 56 to 66 of the book of Isaiah from Deutero-Isaiah and attributed them to another prophet, the term 'Trito-Isaiah' has been adopted among scholars to denote these chapters. The differences between Deutero-Isaiah and Trito-Isaiah are so pronounced that nowadays few authorities subscribe to belief in a common authorship for Isaiah 40 to 66. Whereas for instance Deutero-Isaiah presupposes the Exile as the context of its prophecy, chapters 56 to 66 suggest the existence of the Temple congregation of the post-exilic period with its attendant problems.

Nevertheless the name Trito-Isaiah for this book is a little misleading. It encourages the assumption that we are here faced with a uniform prophetic book, deriving from a single author. This idea is indeed

---

[1] 1: 16–17; 8: 3.   [2] 4: 6b–10a.

[3] The account in 6: 9–15 was revised, obviously after the dashing of the hopes attached to Zerubbabel, in such a way that Joshua's name was inserted instead of Zerubbabel's.

[4] 7: 7–14; 8: 16–17.

[5] *Das Buch Jesaja* (Göttingen, 1892; 4th edn. 1922).

maintained by a number of scholars who believe the prophet in question to have lived in the fifth century or to have been a pupil of Deutero-Isaiah.[1] Yet it must be pointed out that in the case of Trito-Isaiah we very probably have before us an anthology of the utterances of various anonymous prophets, some of whom may very well be seen in association with Deutero-Isaiah. Different utterances presuppose totally different situations; they are concerned with quite different things and reveal no common themes which might suggest a single author. Not all the utterances in the Trito-Isaiah collection even belong to the period of Persian rule. Some pronouncements are probably of a later date,[2] some of an earlier date.[3] The main parts doubtless belong to the period between the building of the Temple and the appearance of Ezra and Nehemiah. For all these reasons it is expedient in the ensuing section to discuss the diverse utterances individually.

Isaiah 66: 1–4 takes us into the period of Haggai and Zechariah. Clearly the linking of eschatological expectation with the rebuilding of the Temple, such as was represented by Haggai and Zechariah, did not remain completely uncontested. For Isa. 66: 1–4 brings a rationalistic criticism to bear upon the over-inflated hopes connected with the Temple. Whether this prophecy was also intended as a fundamental criticism of the Temple and rituals of sacrifice is no longer quite clear.

The three announcements of redemption in Isa. 60 to 62 have a different purport altogether. They place at the heart of their prophecy rapturous descriptions of the renewal of Jerusalem and its inhabitants, the reconstruction and glorious adornment of the city and the Temple. The coming of the last days is passionately longed for. These utterances, which probably stem from one and the same prophet often employ the familiar proclamations of Deutero-Isaiah.[4] Admittedly, at the core of Isa. 60 to 62 is less the action of God than a depiction of the material rewards of redemption and an emphasis on the central importance therein of Jerusalem. The proximity to Deutero-Isaiah on the one hand, and the tense expectation of the last days on the other, indicates that these proclamations of redemption probably date from the time of Haggai and Zechariah. They take up the theme of expectancy and give it even greater urgency in the light perhaps of the recent completion of the Temple.

---

[1] E.g. K. Elliger, *Die Einheit des Tritojesaja* (Stuttgart, 1928), and W. St. McCullough, 'A Re-Examination of Isaiah 56–66', *JBL*, 67 (1948), 27–36.

[2] Isa. 65; 66: 5–24 from the Hellenistic period.

[3] Isa. 63: 7 to 64: 12 from the Exile period.

[4] Cf. 60: 4a with 49: 18a; 60: 9b with 55: 5b; 61: 8 with 55: 3; 62: 10b with 40: 3; 62: 11b with 40: 10b; and other examples.

When the eschatological hopes remained unfulfilled even after the completion of the Temple, and with the establishment of the Jerusalem congregation at the end of the sixth and the beginning of the fifth century, the faith saw itself confronted with new problems. Some of these difficulties figure in other texts by anonymous prophets in Trito-Isaiah. Isaiah 56: 1–8 concerns itself with the question of who should participate in the Temple rites, an issue which had become particularly acute within the post-exile community. The problem was whether anyone else apart from the racially pure Judeans could and should take part in Temple services. On this point the prophet of Isa. 56: 1–8 opted for a generous universalism. Yahweh's house represents for him a house of prayer for all the nations. Therefore all strangers, even all eunuchs,[1] may belong to the congregation of Yahweh in so far as they base their lives on the religious and ethical precepts of the faith.

It was also still an open question why the last days had not ensued. The prophet of Isa. 59 provides an answer by referring to the iniquity and guilt of the members of the Jerusalem congregation. Their sinful conduct is the reason for salvation remaining in abeyance. The prophet is clearly pointing to conditions that had gained ground among the community after the consecration of the Temple, roughly from 500 B.C.E. onwards, and which were themselves perhaps the result of disillusionment after the collapse of intense eschatological expectations. The worship of Yahweh, the administration of justice and the social order seem to be in decline as a result of being treated in a particularly lax and thoughtless manner. The leaders of the people are attacked for their despicable and careless conduct in the extensive prophetic liturgy of Isa. 56: 9 to 57: 13, which belongs roughly to the same period prior to the reforms of Ezra and Nehemiah. What is especially striking about this text is its criticism of orgiastic sexual rites which the pre-exilic prophets Hosea, Jeremiah and Ezekiel had already castigated as apostasy from the Lord. These alien cults had obviously found numerous adherents once again through the agency of Judeans who had stayed behind and the alien peoples who had migrated into the land. Even the members of the new ruling class in Jerusalem could not evade these cults.

Besides these abuses there are bound to have been other circles in Jerusalem which distinguished themselves by their zealous piety. It is they who are addressed in Isa. 58: 1–12. The author of this utterance tries to make it clear that the fasting on which these people obviously prided themselves counts for naught in the eyes of Yahweh as long as it satisfies nothing but the dictates of religious ritual. Rather it should

[1] Partly against the dictates of the deuteronomic law, Deut. 23: 1–8.

be combined with a particular kind of charitable conduct: feeding the hungry, giving shelter to the homeless, clothing the naked and so forth. The promise of Yahweh is meant for those who behave in this manner. Isa. 58: 13–14 likewise deals with the observance of one of the Lord's commandments; it promises salvation to him who keeps holy the Sabbath. This prophetic utterance indicates a certain entrenchment of ritual law during this period.

Viewed as a whole, the prophetic words belonging to the Persian period that are collected in Trito-Isaiah revolve around the decisive problems facing the post-exilic congregation of Jerusalem between the rebuilding of the Temple and the reforms of Ezra and Nehemiah: whether to cut the community off from the outside world or to open it up; the question of the rigorous upholding of religious ordinances; syncretism and alien cults; social abuses; and the problem of the eschatology that had not been fulfilled. Precisely this last issue led to very different responses. On the one hand we note an intensification of hope, while on the other an attempt is made to elucidate the reasons for postponement. A similar conflict characterizes the way in which the significance of ritualistic observances is dealt with. If fasting comes in for sharp criticism, the obligation to keep the Sabbath holy is obeyed in an almost rigoristic fashion. In all this we recognize the beginnings of the polarization which was to become familiar in the course of the subsequent development of Israel and the religious community – the conflict between the rigoristic groups that were bent on sealing themselves off and the less strict groups that were concerned to forge links with the outside world.

Malachi

According to the title of the last prophetic scripture in the book of the Twelve Prophets, this text was written by a prophet called Malachi. In spite of the name, however, it must be assumed that we are here concerned with an originally anonymous scripture. The name Malachi is probably borrowed from Mal. 3: 1, where the term 'my messenger' (= *malachi*) was taken to be a proper name. Even the Greek version, in its introduction to the book, speaks not of a prophet called Malachi but of '*his* [that is, Yahweh's] messenger', thus leaving the book anonymous. Since moreover the title of the book corresponds to a large extent with the titles of Zech. 9 to 11 and Zech. 12 to 14, it is probable that the book of Malachi was first included in the prophetic canon as an appendix to the book of Zechariah, and only later, when 'my messenger' came to be interpreted as a proper name, did it become a separate book. The book of Malachi thus represents an anonymous prophetic text whose utterances may nevertheless still derive from a single author. It is perhaps expedient to follow tradition and call him Malachi.

The prophet's message presupposes the existence of the Temple and the establishment of public worship. He must therefore have appeared at a later point than Haggai and Zechariah. Furthermore he censures those abuses which had already been attacked in part in the utterances of Trito-Isaiah and which Ezra and Nehemiah set about eradicating. Malachi was therefore very probably active shortly before the appearance of Ezra in Jerusalem, perhaps even at the same time as Ezra, so that he might in fact have been supporting the latter's campaign for reform. At the very least Malachi helped to prepare the way for Ezra's reforms and therefore belongs to the periods around 455 B.C.E.

The words of the prophet are couched in the form of a debate. They spring from an energetic argument between the prophet and his contemporaries. The sayings mention in each case the reason for the discussion, the objections of his interlocutors and the prophet's rejoinder, together with a detailed explanation. Altogether there are six utterances in the book of Malachi which can be traced back to the prophet. They reflect the situation within the congregation prior to the coming of Ezra and Nehemiah.

Malachi 1 : 2–5 tries, through the example of the fate of the Edomites, to impress the reality of Yahweh's love upon the Judeans who are losing faith in God's grace. Just as in days gone by Yahweh favoured Jacob rather than his brother Esau, so too at the present time he has shown Israel his love but rejected Edom. In the prophet's opinion no one should doubt God's will to bestow salvation even though the last days have not yet materialized.

Yet doubt does seem to have prevailed, particularly among the priests. So Malachi in 1 : 6 to 2 : 9 criticizes the neglect of priestly duties, such as is evinced above all in the sacrificing of unclean and unworthy beasts, when the priests more than anybody else might be expected to trust in the Lord and carry out their tasks in a responsible fashion.

The population at large has shown itself lax over marital issues. Malachi censures above all the thoughtless termination of marriages.[1] Unfortunately the reasons for the frequency of divorce can no longer be discerned.

In 3 : 6–12 the prophet calls upon the people to turn back to the Lord, for then the community will be assured of rich and abundant blessings.

---

[1] Mal. 2: 10–11a, 13b–16. This utterance was amplified by a comment directed against mixed marriages 2: 11b–13a, which reverses the tendency of Malachi.

Their present need has its root cause in their flouting of Yahweh's commandments, especially their inadequate observance of the tithe law. In the light of this situation within the community the people have naturally grown increasingly doubtful of Yahweh as the God of judgement. But the prophet seeks to counteract this with 3: 1 where he proclaims the day of judgement. Clearly this means the eschatological day of judgement, not an earthly, immanent retribution for godless behaviour. For in the utterance 3: 13 to 4: 3, those who despair of God's justice because the wicked prosper far more than the righteous are confronted with the promise of transcendental retribution on the day of judgement. On that day the difference between the godly and the ungodly will be made clear and manifest.

The prophet Malachi was addressing a community whose intense eschatological expectation had not been fulfilled and who had now succumbed to scepticism with regard to God's justice. This is also the reason for the failure to observe religious rites and laws with due care. Malachi protests against this attitude by proclaiming the last judgement but without linking it to a definite point in time as Haggai and Zechariah had done with the coming of the last days. The day of judgement will certainly come and should be seen as a means of retribution. The community should prepare for it by obeying the law and observing the rituals in all their purity.

It is noteworthy that here, in the case of Malachi, the prophetic announcement of impending salvation is associated with trust in Yahweh, obedience to his precepts and laws, and the love which Yahweh shows to Israel. In this respect there is an obvious relationship between Malachi, the pre-exilic prophets and Deutero-Isaiah.

It was not long before people began to consider this reduction of eschatology to a matter of faith and obedience to the will of God as unsatisfactory. There is at least a partial attempt to meet this criticism by supplementing the prophetic scripture with the eschatological utterance 4: 5–6. In these verses the prophet Elijah is announced as harbinger of the day of the Lord.

Joel

The book of Joel gives in its title only the name of the prophet: Joel ben Pethuel. Nothing is documented of the period or the locality of his prophecy, so we are thrown back on indirect indications in the scripture. It should, of course, be remembered that the interpretation of such evidence is dependent upon the evaluation of the book of Joel itself.

Ever since the unity of the book was called into question, above all by Bernhard Duhm,[1] there has been a continuing argument as to whether chapters 1 to 2: 27, 2: 28–32 and chapter 3 of the book of Joel derive from one or more authors.[2] If we accept that the language and style of chapters 1 to 2: 27, 2: 28–32 and chapter 3, together with the uniform dependency of these chapters on older prophetic texts,[3] do not contradict the notion of single authorship, we may assume that at least chapters 1 to 2: 27, 2: 28–32 and chapter 3 of the book stem from the prophet Joel[4] and can therefore attempt to find a common dating for these chapters.

The occasionally mooted theory that Joel was the earliest scriptural prophet[5] or that he at least belonged to the pre-exilic period,[6] is contradicted by a series of indications which point to the Persian period as the most probable dating. The supplementary passage Joel 3: 4–8, which Wolff[7] attributes to the period prior to the destruction of Sidon (351–343) by Artaxerxes III Ochus, proves the other Joel passages to be considerably older. The mention of the walls of Jerusalem[8] and the probable reference to the proclamation of Malachi[9] take us into the period after the career of Nehemiah, in other words the decades after 433 B.C.E. The self-evident mention of the Temple indicates that a fairly lengthy interval has elapsed since the Exile period, while the interspersing of the language with new Hebrew words points to the early fourth century rather than the middle of the fifth. In the later period, moreover, the rituals of sacrifice and other religious observances would indeed have been as firmly established as is presupposed in the text of Joel.

However, it is not only the uniformity and dating of the book that are problematic but also the interpretation, particularly of the first two chapters in conjunction with the fourth.[10] Chapter 1 and chapter 2: 1–27 deal with drought and plagues of locusts; chapter 2: 28–32 and chapter 3 deal with eschatological events in and around Jerusalem. The question

---

[1] 'Anmerkungen zu den Zwölf Propheten. X. Buch Joel', *ZAW*, 31 (1911), 184–8.
[2] We need not go into details of modifications to the two basic positions.
[3] Isa. 13; Jer. 4 to 6; Ezek. 38f.; Obad. 17a; Zeph. 1f; Mal. 3.
[4] Whether Joel 3 can also be ascribed to the prophet must remain an open question. But we may regard the section Joel 3: 4–8 with a fair degree of certainty as a later addition.
[5] E.g. M. Bic, *Das Buch Joel* (Berlin, 1960).
[6] A. S. Kapelrud, *Joel Studies* (Uppsala, 1948).
[7] H. W. Wolff, *Dodekapropheton 2. Joel und Amos* (Neukirchen-Vluyn, 1969), p. 3.
[8] Joel 2: 7, 9.
[9] Compare Joel 2: 11 with Mal. 3: 2.
[10] The dividing of the book into four chapters derives from the Bombergiana of Jakob b. Chajjim (1524/25), while the Vulgate and the Septuagint nowadays follow the division into three chapters adopted by Stephen Langton in 1205.

soon arose whether chapters 1 and 2: 1–27 should not be interpreted metaphorically, so that they would take on a similar eschatological meaning to chapter 2: 28–30 and chapter 3. This theory is supported by the fact that chapter 2: 1–27 depicts the plague of locusts in terms of war imagery and all the chapters in the book are bound together by the unifying motif of 'the day of the Lord'. Nevertheless, it is advisable to reckon with the possibility that the first two chapters refer to actual historical catastrophes.

Chapter 1 describes impressively the terrible devastation caused by a plague of locusts in the Orient. It summons the people to declare a day of penance and fasting and prescribes the prayers of lament that should be offered on that day. Chapter 2 again describes a plague of locusts, this time in war images; and in the face of this the prophet bids the people turn back to Yahweh and express their remorse in a day of penance; in response to a prayer of petition, Yahweh's favour is promised; and the second chapter closes with thanksgiving and the announcement of salvation. Because of their artistic structure and the use of various literary genres above all from the religious sphere, we can call these two chapters prophetic liturgies. In both chapters the existing or impending calamity is interpreted as 'the day of the Lord'. 'The day of the Lord' is thus a day of calamity which one can only escape through repentance and atonement.

Chapter 2: 28–30 and chapter 3 of the book of Joel introduce the 'day of the Lord' in an eschatological sense; on that day Israel and Jerusalem shall see salvation, while God's judgement is visited upon the nations in the valley of Jehoshaphat. The coming of the Holy Spirit over Israel,[1] cosmic convulsions, the eschatological onrush of the nations and their destruction, together with the preservation of Israel on Zion, are the characteristic features of the eschatological 'day of the Lord'.

If we look at the two sections of Joel's message together, it becomes clear that the prophet undergoes a development which leads him from the adoption of prophetic proclamations of the day of the Lord[2] and their application to concrete catastrophes (chapters 1 and 2) to an eschatological interpretation of this notion in chapter 2: 28–30 and chapter 3. The intensification of the theme of 'the day of the Lord' into a vision of the last days may have been determined in Joel's case by his adherence to the pronouncements of his predecessors.[3] Their proclamation of the impending judgement had not yet been fulfilled; catastrophes which the

---

[1] Provided that chapter 2: 28–30 stems from the prophet Joel, 'all flesh' in 2: 28 must refer to 'everyone in Israel' and must not be interpreted in a universal sense.
[2] Zeph.; Isa. 13; Ezek. 30; Obad.; Mal. 3.
[3] Deutero-Isaiah, Haggai, Zechariah, Malachi and Trito-Isaiah.

prophet witnessed and which he interpreted as the effects of a day of calamity ordained by Yahweh doubtless came to be viewed as a sign that the end was at hand. This he now interpreted as the last judgement and the realization of the prophetic promises.

What strikes us in the case of Joel is that in contrast to his immediate predecessors Haggai, Trito-Isaiah and Malachi he does not give any reasons for the judgement having remained in abeyance. He speaks, it is true, of repentance but not of a specific guilt of the Israelites which has led to a postponement of salvation or which is alleged to have been the cause of the plagues of locusts. The only suggestion of a criticism of the people of Jerusalem may be contained in 2: 12f, where too intensive an orientation towards external ritual can dimly be perceived as a cause for lament. Obviously Joel, who has a very positive attitude to public worship, protests against a tendency to be content with ossifying rituals and the failure to give due attention to the living word of Yahweh as proclaimed by his prophets. The prophet desires to make the Jerusalem congregation newly aware of the eschatological message through the adoption and employment of cultic forms. And he wants to drive home the idea that despite their disappointment in the past they may still look forward with certainty to the day of the Lord.

In proclaiming a universal disaster that will overtake all nations and in reserving salvation for the righteous Israelites, Joel becomes a harbinger of early Jewish apocalyptic teaching.

Anonymous prophetic texts

Apart from the anonymous texts or scriptures which have already been discussed and which are eventually given a name, such as Trito-Isaiah and Malachi, some other selected texts deserve to be mentioned. They can be found predominantly in the form of amplifications or supplements to the books Isaiah (1 to 39), Micah and Jeremiah. The difficulty in dating them has already been discussed in the introduction to the present section. It is probable that the texts dealt with below originated in the Persian period, although it is not impossible that one or two texts derive from the neo-Babylonian or Hellenistic era.

These texts include in the first instance a few utterances addressed to other nations, which were added to the books of Isaiah and Jeremiah. In Isa. 15 and 16 and Jer. 48 are collected prophecies concerning Moab which all refer to the devastation of Moab. This has been linked with a campaign of Nebuchadnezzar in 582 B.C.E., attested only in Josephus;[1] but on the basis of Ezek. 25: 4, 5, 10f we do better to think in terms

[1] *Ant.* x. 9, 7.

of Arabian tribes who from the sixth century onwards were bringing ever greater pressure to bear on the Palestinian heartland and probably did bring about the destruction of Moab and Ammon in the Persian period. Moreover, Isa. 16: 4 indicates that the events took place at a time when Jerusalem herself had to some extent consolidated her position. What is remarkable about the utterances is that the words handed down in Isa. 15–16 reveal a positive attitude full of compassion, while the texts preserved in Jer. 48 express malicious satisfaction and hatred at the fate of Moab. The reason for this hatred may have been the things Israel had to endure from neighbouring peoples during her own tribulations under Nebuchadnezzar. Feelings of this sort are also articulated in other messages addressed to foreign nations which are included in the books of Isaiah and Jeremiah.

Particular interest is naturally reserved for the nations with which Israel had direct contact. Thus in Isa. 19 and Jer. 46 we find pronouncements about Egypt which go back in part to the neo-Babylonian period, but in part without doubt to the Persian period, as we can see from references to a Jewish Diaspora[1] and to internal troubles in the land.[2] The destruction of Egypt is foretold. But in addition the references to Egypt include some which look forward to the re-establishment of Egypt at least in the last days.[3] The sayings in Isa. 23: 1–14 probably allude to the conquest of Sidon by Artaxerxes III in 343 B.C.E. and to the conquest of Tyre by Alexander the Great; in these verses the events are interpreted as having been planned and instigated by Yahweh.[4]

Besides the texts referring to foreign peoples which were collected with others to form larger collections,[5] the books of Isaiah and Micah in particular contain a series of eschatological texts which must have originated after the Babylonian Exile. To these belong in the first instance four prophecies of redemption that conclude partial collections of utterances in Isaiah: Isa. 2: 2–4; 4: 2–6; 9: 2–7; 11: 1–9.[6]

Isaiah 2: 2–4 is an eschatological prophecy of the pilgrimage of the nations to Zion. In the last days the nations will assemble before Zion and receive the command of Yahweh, and thereby everlasting peace will descend upon the peoples of the earth. Behind this text, which Joel

---

[1] Isa. 19: 18.   [2] Isa. 19: 2.
[3] Isa. 19: 23, 24. Cf., for Moab, Isa. 16: 4, 5.
[4] Further utterances about the Philistines, Ammon, Edom, Damascus, Arabia and Elam can be found in Jer. 47 and 49, all clearly revealing the hostile attitude of Israel towards her neighbours.
[5] Isa. 13 to 23; Jer. 46 to 51.
[6] G. Fohrer, 'The Origin, Composition and Tradition of Isaiah I–XXXIX', *ALUOS*, 3 (1961–62), 3–38.

deliberately turns on its head,[1] lies a more strongly universalist eschatology which has no interest in the destruction and decline of other nations.

Isaiah 4: 2–6 awaits the protection of Yahweh's glory for Zion–Jerusalem; but the latter must first endure a purifying judgement before it is vouchsafed final redemption. If this text saw the catastrophe undergone by Jerusalem in 587 B.C.E. as the judgement of the Lord, then it doubtless originated in the early Persian period and looks forward to a Jerusalem whose inhabitants are dedicated to the sole worship of Yahweh.

Isaiah 9: 2–7 is a messianic prophecy announcing the coming of the last days. Therewith oppression and servitude will come to an end, war will be replaced by everlasting peace, and Yahweh will invest sovereignty in the messianic ruler who in his titles is described as the ideal king. The text certainly dates from the post-exilic period in the light of its eschatological orientation.[2]

The messianic prophecy in Isa. 11: 1–9 is more strongly influenced by the doctrine of Wisdom. Its starting point is that the dynasty of David is in human eyes extinguished; but in the last days it will be renewed once more, for from it shall emerge the messianic ruler who will reign over a world at peace, where primordial harmony prevails.

More comprehensive eschatological prophecies are to be found in the so-called apocalypse of Isaiah (Isa. 24 to 27) – which, however, could not have originated before the Hellenistic period[3] – and also in the poems Isa. 33 and Isa. 34 to 35. Both poems deal with the coming of the last days which are heralded by the destruction of secular power and the re-establishment of Zion–Jerusalem. In the case of Isa. 34 to 35 we notice a strong dependence on Deutero-Isaiah and a particular emphasis on the destruction of Edom. Of all the neighbouring peoples, Edom was the one most frequently and most vehemently singled out for threats by Israelite prophets.[4]

An issue much in debate among scholars is the evaluation of chapters 4 to 7 of the book of Micah. These will therefore merely be touched on in conclusion. Micah 4 to 5 contains a collection of promises of which 4: 1–5 are repeated almost word for word in Isa. 2: 2–4. In general these promises speak of the ultimate re-establishment of Israel after she has

---

[1] Joel 3: 10.
[2] J. Vollmer, in 'Zur Sprache von Jesaja 9: 1–6', ZAW, 80 (1968), 343–50, and 'Jesajanische Begrifflichkeit', ZAW, 83 (1971), 389–91, proved that the text does not derive from Isaiah.
[3] O. Plöger, Theokratie und Eschatologie (2nd edn. Neukirchen-Vluyn, 1962).
[4] Obadiah; Isa. 63: 1–6; Jer. 49: 7–22; Mal. 1: 2–5.

been threatened by the onslaught of hostile nations[1] and of a Messiah from the house of David who will come from Bethlehem. To attribute these prophecies to Micah would prove extremely difficult. They belong rather to the post-exilic period.

Scholars are fond of ascribing to the pre-exilic prophet the section Mic. 6: 1 to 7: 6 which contains a series of condemnatory pronouncements. Yet even these words probably stem from the post-exilic period. Above all the indictment of a wicked city (Mic. 6: 9–16) would match the period of the reforms of Ezra and Nehemiah; and the criticism of sacrifices expressed in Mic. 6: 1–8 would by no means stand alone during that period.[2]

Finally, the prophetic liturgy Mic. 7: 8–20, with which the book of Micah closes, announces the re-establishment of Israel and Zion–Jerusalem in the last days, whereby Zion–Jerusalem appears as the centre of the nations; but Israel, it is said, will achieve redemption only when Yahweh has forgiven its sins.

THEMES AND TENDENCIES IN THE PROPHECY OF THE PERSIAN PERIOD

If we survey once more the prophecy of the Persian period as a whole, we realize that there were essentially three main sets of problems that preoccupied these prophets: the expectation of the last days, relations with foreign nations and the evaluation of public worship and ritual. These three areas of concern naturally overlap, usually in the sense that the question of worship and of other nations is seen in the light of eschatological expectation. Only in a few places are worship and foreign peoples treated independently of the expectation of the last days.

The fact that it is these three problems which engage the attention of the prophets of the Persian period is connected with the history of the people of Israel and their particular situation during the period under review, above all with the interpretation of the Babylonian Exile and the consequences that ensued. For eschatological prophecy[3] developed during the years of Exile, in the light of historical experience and as the result of a particular interpretation of pre-exilic prophecy; thereafter it provided the essential impulses for the prophecy of the post-exilic period. The warnings of calamity uttered by the pre-exilic prophets were seen as having been fulfilled in the conquest of Jerusalem and in the

---

[1] Similarly Joel 3.
[2] Cf. Isa. 58: 1–12.
[3] For the terminology, see G. Wanke, '"Eschatologie", Ein Beispiel theologischer Sprachverwirrung', *KD*, 16 (1970), 300–12.

Babylonian Exile – indeed, in an all-embracing manner. This fulfilment of a major part of pre-exilic prophecy endowed it with a quality which enhanced its status. There was a commensurate intensification of expectancy with regard to those prophecies which in the view of the Israelites had not yet been fulfilled. This found a precipitate in the pronouncements of eschatological prophecies, beginning with Deutero-Isaiah and Ezekiel. What is extraordinarily important is that redemption was seen in the same all-embracing manner as the earlier pre-exilic warnings of calamity that had since been fulfilled; thus a new vision of history and a new dimension of time were revealed. For if the Exile was indeed the judgement upon Israel that had been foretold by the prophets, the impending salvation must be interpreted as equally comprehensive, even universal. Judgement already lay behind the Israelites but redemption was yet to come. It was a time of transition from one age to the next, and men awaited the dawning of the new era that would bring about a new heaven and a new earth, above all a new manifestation of God's favour to his people.

For Deutero-Isaiah the coming of the last days was linked with the return of the dispersed to Jerusalem. In fact, however, the return had been accomplished under very different circumstances from those foretold by the prophet. The Israelites had come back to their land, only to have to struggle against extremely adverse conditions even to scratch a bare living. The situation did not change, so people took it upon themselves to establish some sort of footing in the land. At this juncture it was one of the vital tasks facing the prophets of the Persian period to sustain their people's faith in impending salvation and the mercy of Yahweh. They listed reasons for the day of the Lord having remained in abeyance, and tried to explain the postponement. Haggai and Zechariah pointed to the lack of progress in rebuilding the Temple, others pointed to the neglect of religious duties (Mal.; Isa. 58 and 59), while Joel in all probability saw the ignoring of prophetic utterances as another reason.

In addition the prophets depict in fantastic and wonderful images the events that will occur when the day of the Lord dawns. In this connection there is almost always some reference to non-Israelite nations. The attitude to other peoples is an illuminating index of differences within eschatological prophecy, not only of the Persian period. A particularist, nationalist tendency assumes that the nations will be overtaken by judgement when the time comes, while Israel will be preserved as the favourite of Yahweh.[1] Besides this there is a universalist current which interprets salvation as something available

[1] Haggai; Joel; Mic. 4: 11–13.

to all nations,[1] although in some way or another this redemption remains tied to Israel and Zion–Jerusalem.[2]

These various tendencies in religious thinking are also documented in non-eschatological prophetic literature which deals with the question of public worship and the problem of foreign peoples. We find utterances directed at other nations which envisage their total destruction,[3] while in other passages compassion and help are extended to certain peoples.[4] If it is correct that in Hag. 2: 10–14 certain groups are to be excluded from taking part in the building of the Temple or in religious sacrifices in order to guarantee the purity of the Temple and public worship, this would indicate that groups of particularists and rigorists were making their presence felt at an early date within the Jerusalem congregation. However, these were censured by other voices which supported the idea of a generous participation by non-Israelites in public worship.[5] Here the split within the congregation pointed to an issue of principle which would have far-reaching consequences in the subsequent history of Judaism.

Finally, the Persian period saw the development of a prophetic theme which was again to play a significant role in the later history of the Jewish religion: the expectation of the Messiah. Admittedly this notion occurs rather rarely in the Old Testament. In general, eschatological prophecy anticipates that Yahweh himself will rule in the last days. Only a few texts foretell an earthly king as the representative of Yahweh; he is usually called Messiah even though in the Old Testament the expression itself is not linked with this figure. The handful of texts that speak of this include Hag. 2: 20–23; Zech. 4: 1–14; 6: 9–15; 9: 9–10; Isa. 9: 2–7; 11: 1–9, 10; 16: 5; Jer. 23: 5–6 (parallel 33: 15–16); Ezek. 17: 22–23; Mic. 5: 1–3. The first to mention the Messiah were probably Haggai and Zechariah who viewed Zerubbabel, or Zerubbabel and Joshua as the rulers of the last days. All the other texts listed are certainly later.

The idea of the Messiah presupposes that in the last days a new community will arise on Palestinian soil with Jerusalem as its centre and the new Israel as its people. According to traditional belief, however, such a community is inconceivable without a king; in fact, in Israel it is inconceivable without a king from the house of David which the prophecy of Nathan[6] had promised would endure for ever.

As far as his identity is concerned, then, the Messiah is simply a

---

[1] Zeph. 3: 9–10.
[2] E.g. Isa. 2: 2–4, par. Mic. 4: 1–5; Zech. 8: 20–23; Isa. 19: 24–25; and others.
[3] Jer. 46–49.   [4] Isa. 15–16.
[5] Isa. 56: 1–8.   [6] 2 Sam. 7.

descendant of the house of David who is entrusted by Yahweh with certain sovereign powers. Though Haggai and Zechariah had a particular person in mind, the dashing of their hopes meant that thereafter the Son of David was no longer identified with a particular historical figure. Instead we merely find general references to a Messiah from the house of David. His task is to maintain the peace of the last days in every respect, both within the community and in the outside world. It is important to note, however, that the Messiah of the Old Testament is never seen as a saviour or the bringer of salvation. He is only the preserver and defender of a redemption already manifest. It is Yahweh himself who is seen as the redeemer, as the one who vouchsafes salvation. The saviour is God himself, never the messianic ruler.

PSALMS IN THE PERSIAN PERIOD

The difficulties confronting anyone who attempts to provide a reasonably reliable dating for the Psalms have already been outlined in the introduction to this section.[1] However, it is not as if there were no evidence whatsoever to help us arrange them in chronological order. A number of Psalms contain more or less clear allusions to historical events or circumstances that can be dated; others are characterized by linguistic features typical of a particular period; or they are permeated with a religious attitude which might feasibly belong to one period but is barely conceivable in another. Such indications permit at least an approximate dating, although even here there may be a wide divergence of scholarly opinion.[2]

The most important clues as to whether Psalms date from the post-exilic period are as follows: (1) allusions to the destruction of Jerusalem and to captivity in Babylon, to the dispersal of the Jews and the return to Palestine; (2) similarities to and dependence upon texts which are acknowledged to belong to the Exile or post-exilic period, such as Deutero-Isaiah or the Priestly Code; (3) the influence of Wisdom; (4) a marked devotion to the religious law; (5) connections with the themes of eschatological prophecy; (6) linguistic evidence (for example, a noticeable accumulation of Aramaisms). Yet all these indicators would not in themselves tell us whether a Psalm of the post-exilic period belonged to the Persian or the Hellenistic age. Here it is well-nigh impossible to draw firm distinctions which would

---

[1] See above p. 162.

[2] Although some 70 years ago all the 'royal' Psalms were still attributed to the Hasmonean epoch, nowadays the mention of a king in the Psalms is taken to indicate that the Psalm in question originated before the Exile.

produce reliable results. At the same time, this means that we have to deal with essentially the same questions and themes in the case of the Psalm literature of both the Persian and the Hellenistic period. We can assume, however, that the Hellenistic period will display a stronger emphasis on Wisdom and observance of religious law, while the Persian period will place a stronger stress on questions of worship and ritual.

THE COMPOSITION AND COLLECTION OF PSALMS

Although we cannot trace in detail the lines of the Psalm tradition, this much is now clear: at the time when deportees returned to Palestine at the beginning of the Persian period, the community in Jerusalem could already hark back to a considerable Psalm tradition, one moreover which had not suffered interruption during the years of Exile. The destruction of Jerusalem, the deportation of Judeans and the desolate conditions in the land itself even after the return of the deportees had given rise to the composing of Psalms particularly of the kind known as 'lamentations'. These Psalms[1] are certain to have been used during the ceremonies of mourning that took place on the site of the ruined Temple during the Exile and the post-exilic period.[2]

With the rebuilding of the Temple and the introduction of a regular form of public worship, the central point of reference of Psalm literature was finally re-established in 515 B.C.E. and this greatly facilitated the continuance of the tradition. For irrespective of the fact that a large number of Psalms represented the creative expression of individual members of the Israelite people and were probably not written initially with a ritual purpose in mind, the life of the individual was so intimately bound up with public worship and the Temple, with the life and actions of the community as a whole, that a completely 'private' use of the Psalm remained the exception. Another factor is that the personnel of the Temple took it upon themselves to cultivate the use of Psalms more intensively; priests and Levites either themselves composed Psalms or collected older Psalms, thus preserving them for future generations.

In particular this systematic collecting of Psalms must have been instigated for the first time during the Persian period. For an analysis of the editorial history of the psalter reveals fairly clearly that some of the collections on which the psalter is based go back to the activities of groups of Levite Temple singers, who had established themselves in the Temple in the post-exilic period and, according to the testimony

---

[1] Pss. 44, 60, 74, 79, 85, 126, 137; Lam. 1–5.
[2] Zech. 7: 3.

of the Chronicler,[1] played an important role in organized worship. Thus the so-called Elohim-psalter[2] emerged from smaller, originally separate collections: (1) the song book of the Korahites to which Pss. 84, 85, 87 and 88 also once belonged;[3] (2) the song book of the Asaphites, Pss. 50 and 73 to 83, in which (3) a David-psalter (Pss. 51 to 71) was interpolated. Apart from these there are other collections in the psalter: Pss. 3 to 41, a David-psalter; Pss. 120 to 134, the 'pilgrimage songs';[4] and Pss. 138 to 145 (plus 108 to 110), another David-psalter.

The fact that independent smaller collections are associated with groups of temple singers, the Asaphites and the Korahites, indicates that these groups collected Psalms for their own purposes within the Temple worship,[5] and perhaps even wrote a few psalms themselves. The other collections are also certain to have been put together for cultic purposes.[6] These collections finally gave rise to the psalter which is frequently and with good reason called the 'hymn book of the post-exilic congregation', since it was assuredly used not only in the Temple worship but also in the synagogues. Moreover, we must assume that even eschatological and apocalyptic circles, and Wisdom circles characterized by devotion to the Law, also used the psalter as a book of edification. This is indicated by – among other things – the messianic interpretation of Ps. 2: 2b, the close similarities between the songs of Zion and eschatological prophecy,[7] and the inclusion of poems of Wisdom both at the beginning (Ps. 1) and at later points (for example, Ps. 119).

Although about a quarter of the songs that have come down to us in the psalter date from the pre-exilic period, the main achievement in creating the psalter as a collection of songs must be attributed to the post-exilic congregation. The priests and Levites of the Temple during the Persian period doubtless made the greatest contribution. The Asaphites, a Levite group who, according to Ezra 2: 41 returned with Ezra from the Exile, and the Korahites who did not gain importance

[1] 1, 2 Chron.; Ezra; Neh.; about the mid fourth century.

[2] Pss. 42–83: characterized by the almost invariable replacement of the name of Yahweh by the term 'Elohim'. Cf. Ps. 14 with 53; 40: 13–17 with 70; 57: 7–11 and 60: 6–12 with 108.

[3] See G. Wanke, *Die Zionstheologie der Korachiten in ihrem traditionsgeschichtlichen Zusammenhang*, BZAW, 97 (Berlin, 1966), p. 1ff.

[4] The meaning of '*šyr hm'lwt*', the title of these Psalms, is a bone of contention. Other suggested meanings are: 'step songs', 'songs in series', 'travel songs'.

[5] This is not to suggest anything about the dating of individual Psalms in these collections.

[6] An exception may be the collection of David-Psalms, Pss. 3 to 41, which was perhaps put together for private use.

[7] See Wanke, *Zionstheologie*, pp. 113ff.

as a guild of Temple singers until after the time of Ezra and Nehemiah,[1] certainly played a significant role in this development.

PRINCIPAL THEMES OF THE PSALMISTS IN THE PERSIAN PERIOD

The Psalm literature of the Persian period is determined by a series of factors closely connected with the history and traditions of the Israelites in Exile and in the period of the re-establishment of the community under Cyrus and Darius I. There are basically five factors that characterize the religious content of the Psalms of this period: (1) the focusing of Israel's hopes on Zion–Jerusalem which was induced by the loss of political independence and by the prophecies of Ezekiel, Deutero-Isaiah, Haggai and Zechariah; (2) a stronger orientation towards the Temple worship in Jerusalem as a result of the change from nation to congregation and the re-establishment of the congregation; (3) the development of traditions and adherence to an older set of ideas, caused by the abandonment of public worship during the Exile, a development which was to lead to the special position of the law in the subsequent period; (4) the addition of a transcendental and universal dimension to the image of God, occasioned by the hymnic tradition and by the separating of the conception of God from its close ties with the land of Palestine; (5) the strong dissemination of ideas associated with the doctrine of Wisdom as a result of the gradual integration of that doctrine with the religion of Yahweh. These factors occur, of course, not only in isolation; the various themes are interrelated, they overlap and thus contribute to a multiplicity of doctrinal opinion which is to be found in no other book of the Old Testament, apart from the psalter.

The God of these Psalms is present in the Temple, on his holy mountain, in his city: this is the relatively clear message of the pre-exilic Psalms, and the unambiguous message of many of the post-exilic Psalms. This is where one must turn if one wants to find Yahweh and experience his protection and his help. The status of *Zion–Jerusalem as the place where Yahweh is present* is enhanced in an unprecedented manner during the Persian period, above all because of the pronouncements of the eschatological prophets. The city is held to be the dwelling place of God from which issue forth salvation and blessing; all enemies are brought down by her, even the foreign nations who will assail her in the last days. The city becomes the very centre of the world. It is a great distinction to live within her walls and those who are far away think back with melancholy yearning to the days when they were privileged to tarry in the Temple. The city is the goal which all pilgrims long to

[1] 2 Chron. 20: 19.

attain. A particularly powerful impression of this attitude is conveyed by the Psalms of Zion and the songs of pilgrimage.[1]

Jerusalem with her Temple is also the place of *sacrificial rites* with which petitions and thanksgiving are connected. This is a long-established and self-evident view which still prevails in the post-exilic period. We observe, however, that in some Psalms, as in Isa. 58 and Mic. 6: 1–8, sacrifice is not accepted without demur. There are statements which reveal an inward-turning of the sacrificial rites, their replacement by prayer. Thus Ps. 141 interprets prayer as incense and Ps. 40: 1–12 puts in their place a public profession of faith. Psalm 50 invokes a rationalistic argument to reject the custom of sacrifice altogether; the only proper sacrifice which can be offered to God is a prayer of thanksgiving and obedience. Finally, Ps. 51 contrasts sacrificial rituals with a contrite heart which Yahweh will accept as a sacrifice.[2]

The extension of the idea of God's sovereignty[3] to include all the other nations of the earth is matched in the course of further developments by a radicalization of various other concepts. Thus the emphasis on the transitoriness and weakness of man grows ever stronger.[4] The distance between man and God increases. Between them comes the *law*. The law and its demands become a condition of salvation; whoever disregards it challenges Yahweh to punish him.[5]

Thus in the post-exilic period we find above all a more forceful distinction between the godless and the righteous, between the evil-doer and the just;[6] in connection with the increased influence of the doctrine of Wisdom we find a further development of the belief in punishment into a *doctrine of retribution*. The notion of divine justice grew into a rigorous system which established in each case a necessary relationship between deed and condition. According to the doctrine of retribution it was possible to discover the cause of a certain unhappy condition in some past offence – which immediately made a sick man or some other unfortunate into a sinner struck down by God. The victim ran the risk of being expelled from the community. There were attempts to break out of this vicious circle by seeking asylum in the Temple, hoping either for a confirmation of one's innocence or a miraculous rescue from one's misfortunes. In a large number of individual lamentations this situation is movingly expressed by righteous believers.[7]

---

[1] Pss. 42 and 43; 46; 48; 84; 87; 122; and others.
[2] This attitude was obviously not popular, as a correction of this Psalm through verses 18–19 clearly shows.
[3] Particularly clear in the hymns to Yahweh the King (Pss. 47; 93; 96 to 99).
[4] Pss. 90 and 103.   [5] Ps. 1; 19: 7ff; 119.
[6] Pss. 9 and 10; 12; 14; 36; 37; 58; and frequently elsewhere.
[7] Pss. 6; 22; 38; 39; 69; and frequently elsewhere.

Here again with the increasing remoteness of God from man we observe a radicalization of theological ideas, which did not go completely unchallenged. For it became manifest that the automatism of the doctrine of retribution could not do justice to reality. Even the doctrine of retribution could not provide valid and definitive answers to the problem of the suffering and distress of individuals. This insight found a precipitate in individual psalms whose authors were seeking answers which transcended the schematic doctrine of retribution. In Ps. 49 the psalmist acknowledges the existing state of affairs in that he confirms the prosperity of the wicked, but he simply transposes the problem on to the transcendental level: the rich man will not evade death, whereas the poor and the righteous will be delivered by God out of the power of death. Is this the first time an author consoles himself with the thought of a compensatory justice in the next world? Psalm 73 gives a rather different answer. Throughout numerous tribulations the psalmist finds salvation in total self-surrender to the will of Yahweh.

Finally we must refer to one other aspect which scarcely accords with the schematic doctrine of retribution. This is the faith in a merciful God which Ps. 51 in particular conveys so impressively. In the confession of sins and the plea for *forgiveness* the law and the will of Yahweh are of course taken quite seriously, so that the individual must abandon himself totally to God; but man does not restrict Yahweh's actions to a systematized doctrine of retribution – he allows God the freedom to forgive. From this belief emerges the possibility of a fresh beginning, not a facile new start in the sense of magical purification rituals, but one achieved through a radical acquiescence in the will of God.

These few remarks about the religious content of the Psalms of the Persian period reveal on the one hand a limited number of problems – Zion–Jerusalem, sacrifice, law, retribution – and on the other hand a multitude of answers that were sought by the faithful. In all these attempts, however, the fundamental issue is how one should live one's life in accordance with the will and the loving-kindness of God.

CHAPTER 9

WISDOM LITERATURE IN THE PERSIAN PERIOD

Although the concept of Wisdom is highly problematic, what is known as Wisdom literature – at least in the older Jewish tradition – is easily defined. It involves those literary works in the biblical tradition which have a didactic purpose, yet do not belong to the priestly tradition of the Torah which describes the revealed will of God. The books in question include therefore such texts as Proverbs, Job, Ecclesiastes (Qoheleth), Ecclesiasticus and Wisdom. A series of Psalms has also been regarded as belonging to Wisdom literature, and rightly. Here, however, the category becomes less distinct since the majority of Psalms display certain traits of Wisdom literature, while yet conforming as a whole to the usual patterns of psalmodic composition. As the Psalms are discussed in another chapter, the present essay will refer only to those Psalms which are wholly influenced by the didactic character of Wisdom literature proper. Not until the Hellenistic period do more extensive overlaps occur, so that in addition to the Psalms even those literary works which do not belong to the didactic tradition are strongly endowed with the features of Wisdom literature, for example, Tobit and Baruch.

The dating of Wisdom literature poses greater difficulty – unless it can be traced back to a clearly identifiable historical author such as Jesus, the son of Sirach. Even then the material incorporated in such a work will display a character which is in many respects timeless, so that it can often be identified with older traditions. The book of Job and the bulk of proverb literature doubtless belong to the Persian period, that is, the early post-exilic period up to the advent of Alexander in 332 B.C.E. (In the case of Job one might concede that the final additions, and they alone, were made as late as the Hellenistic period.) Even if the material collected in Proverbs 10 onwards originated predominantly in the pre-exilic period, whereas the composition of chapters 1 to 9 could easily date from the earliest Hellenistic period, the essential shaping of this work must nevertheless have occurred in the Persian period. We shall do well therefore to consider the book of Proverbs in this chapter. By contrast, Ecclesiastes is commonly assumed to date back to the

Hellenistic period, though the end of the Persian period is also a possibility. So we shall confine ourselves in the main to Proverbs and Job; but we must also discuss in some detail the literary and historical preconditions of both these works, since they are the oldest Wisdom books of Israel.

THE PRESUPPOSITIONS OF JEWISH WISDOM LITERATURE

The roots of Jewish Wisdom literature lie in the pre-exilic period. The book of Proverbs is attributed to Solomon. Whatever this 'authorship' may signify, at least it reveals that under Solomon Israel participated in that spiritual movement usually denoted by the biblical keyword 'Wisdom'. After Israel had unreservedly entered the historical world of Near Eastern antiquity under the reign of David, it was then enabled under Solomon to partake of the highly advanced Near Eastern culture in which this Wisdom represented an essential element.

THE COMMON LEGACY OF NEAR-EASTERN 'WISDOM'

Throughout the ancient world, wherever we possess adequate literary evidence, we come across signs of a spiritual movement that seeks to acquire empirically insight into the order determining the world of nature and the life of man, to collect these experiences and transmit them as a doctrine. The intention is that man should conform to this order and attain the good life which it entails, thus experiencing the redemptive truth which confronts man in the cosmos. This 'Wisdom' is the precursor of Greek and Hellenistic philosophy. In contrast to the latter, however, it refrains from systematically tracing phenomena back to abstract principles. Rather, the phenomena are captured in their most striking empirical form, and brought into relation to one another and illuminated through comparisons; they are then heightened by accumulation and comprehensiveness into a totality rich in contrasts. Of course, the later transition to philosophy is by no means clear and abrupt: the writings of the Sophists might be understood in large measure as an evolution of the Wisdom tradition, though we lack appropriate studies of them from this viewpoint. Since Wisdom does not go beyond describing the order manifest in empirical reality, since it deliberately conforms itself to experience and perception, and avoids reducing them to abstract principles, the order which it reveals always remains substantial, an opposing, challenging force to which man must subordinate himself. The world order is experienced as something divine.

This insight into order is less a means of acquiring 'dominion' over the world than a spiritual penetration of the world which is rendered possible by empirical experience. The phenomenal realm of which the individual has direct knowledge ensures that this penetration of the world occurs independently of the religious traditions of myth and worship and national cultural characteristics. Therefore Wisdom reveals a core of internationally-shared features, a universal human attitude. Influences between one culture and another are facilitated, although every culture in the ancient Near East displays certain national variations on this theme of Wisdom. Egyptian Wisdom developed pre-eminently the instructional genre, a comprehensive, systematic complex of admonitions which are commended as a whole to the 'Son', the disciple of Wisdom. This Wisdom is sustained by the concept of Maat, queen of the cosmic order, the 'truth' which 'he who hears' obediently fulfils in his own life. In his disciplined subordination he is the 'truly silent one'; his counterpart is the 'hot-headed' man who asserts himself even against the order that demands obedience. Egyptian Wisdom in its classical form is already fully developed in the Ancient Kingdom. From the Middle Kingdom onwards, however, so-called pessimistic tones can be heard – that is, there emerges a stronger sense of threat to this order and a stronger sense of its impenetrability. On the other hand the religious connections are more clearly elucidated in the later Wisdom, especially in the teachings of Amenemope (in the latter years of the Ramses dynasty) which formed the basis of Proverbs 22: 17 to 23: 11.

The Mesopotamian Wisdom literature had already been widely developed in Sumerian writings. In addition to the instructional form also common in Mesopotamian Wisdom literature, collections of proverbs are a characteristic feature. They represent elementary text-book material. The disputation too seems to have been very popular, though of course it is a basic element in any Wisdom literature. Mesopotamian Wisdom gives greater emphasis to the dark side of human existence, and order can often only emerge from the vanquishing of chaos. The problem of apparently unmerited human suffering was frequently formulated in a paradigmatic scenario showing how a patient and humble lament could move the gods to restore their saving grace. We also find examples of the dialogue form, as in the book of Job.

The Wisdom book of Ahikar deserves special mention. It is known in the Old Aramaic version from the Elephantine papyri of the fifth century B.C.E., but must go back to Assyrian traditions. For the alleged author, Ahikar, is said to have been a chancellor of Sennacherib and Esarhaddon, who was treacherously denounced by his own ungrateful adopted son Nadan, after he had persuaded King Esarhaddon to appoint Nadan his successor; he only narrowly escaped death. His Wisdom takes the form of a collection of aphorisms preceded by an autobiographical introduction. Tobit 14: 10 tells the story of Ahikar, though there he is regarded as a pious Jew and a nephew of Tobit (1: 21f.; 2: 10) (see volume 2, chapter 12). Doubtless several of the maxims in the book of Tobit derive from this source. A number of passages from Proverbs can also be traced back to the Wisdom of Ahikar. His material was disseminated far and wide and its influence can still be discerned in Aesop's *Fables* and *The Thousand and One Nights*.

Regrettably so little of Canaanite literature has survived that we can merely infer the existence of a Canaanite Wisdom (see Ezek. 27: 8; 28: 3, 17; Zech. 9: 2). However, in Syria Ugaritic, in association with the Akkadian scribal culture, displays a familiarity with Mesopotamian Wisdom;[1] but even in the absence of such evidence we would have to assume the existence of a Wisdom literature in Syria. There are noticeably strong references in Israel to Edomite Wisdom and to that of the 'children of the east country' (1 Kings 4: 30; Jer. 49: 7; Obad. 8); this Wisdom is the source of the story of the friends of Job, and similarly of the supplements to the book of Proverbs transmitted in Prov. 30: 1–14 and 31: 1–9. Probably the Wisdom of those who lived on the margins of the civilized world counted as particularly authentic and undistorted.

Finally, we must mention a special form of Wisdom whose objective, scholarly and thus fundamentally supranational character is particularly convincing: the science of lists. We read of Solomon in 1 Kings 4: 30ff, that his wisdom excelled that of all famous wise men: 'And he spake three thousand proverbs: and his songs were a thousand and five. And he spake of trees, from the cedar tree that is in Lebanon even unto the hyssop that springeth out of the wall: he spake also of beasts, and of fowl, and of creeping things, and of fishes.' Here the proverb and the song are named as the basic forms of Wisdom; then, however, it becomes clear that besides these there is another genre involving the drawing up of comprehensive lists which establish a taxonomy for all botanical and zoological species. Trees and shrubs are enumerated according to size, while animals are divided into four categories. Lists of this sort are attested in Egypt and especially in Mesopotamia, and also in the Syrian Ugaritic, in association with the Akkadian scribal culture. Not only do they serve as a means of training scribes and as vocabularies; they also represent the original form of scientific activity (known as the science of lists) which begins with the naming and categorizing of the enormous mass of phenomena. In the inventory of

[1] *Ugaritica*, ed. P. Geuthner (Paris, 1939), v, texts 162–6.

the world which thus ensues, the phenomena of human culture are no less important than those of nature; as always in Wisdom literature, man and nature are regarded as interdependent. Thus we find lists of human tools and other utensils, lists of human characteristics and so on. The existence of lists of omens shows that in the ancient world even augury was largely determined by empirical methods. The collating of empirical experience in the form of lists is also the underlying impulse behind the collections of proverbs such as are attested from Sumer up to the paroemiographs of Late Antiquity – and especially behind the collections of aphorisms which bulk large in Wisdom literature and stretch well into the latter years of Antiquity, indeed even into the foundations of our modern culture.

WHERE WISDOM WAS CULTIVATED AND TRANSMITTED

It is evident that a science of lists can only flourish in a political system which provides the external conditions for a cultural achievement of this kind, in the shape of scribes and administrators, archives and organizational skills. Similarly Wisdom is in general closely bound up with the institution of monarchy. Not only the book of Proverbs as a whole (1: 1), but also individual sections are attributed to Solomon (10: 1; 25: 1, where the editorial function of 'the men of Hezekiah' is specifically mentioned), who in legend and anecdote appears as the wise man *par excellence* (1 Kings 3: 4–13, 15 abβγ; 3: 16–28; 10: 1–10, 13). The instruction of Lemuel (Prov. 31: 1) is addressed to a king. This attribute, which is strongly attested in Egyptian Wisdom literature as well, derives both from the historical dependence of the Wisdom tradition upon a royal court and from the intrinsic role which the monarchical ideology plays within it. If the king is the representative and guarantor of communal order as a reflection of cosmic order, he must therefore stand in an intimate relation to Wisdom, which is founded entirely upon a concept of cosmic order. The high esteem in which Wisdom literature holds the monarch (see, for example, Prov. 16: 10–15) is connected not only with the enjoyment of a position at court but also with the idea of order common to both Wisdom and the monarchical ideology (compare the Yahweh proverbs, Prov. 16: 1ff, prior to the maxims on kingship). The relationship is impressively formulated in Prov. 25: 2: 'It is the glory of God to conceal a thing: but the honour of kings is to search out a matter.' That is to say, the king searches out and uncovers the concealed order of God.

The doctrine of Wisdom had an eminently practical significance for the education and training of royal officials, both scribes and high-ranking counsellors. Various Wisdom texts are even attributed to senior officials, for example Ahikar. Naturally enough the skilful speeches of such counsellors are informed by the spirit of Wisdom, as may be seen from the disputation between Ahithophel and Hushai in 2 Sam. 17: 1–14. In fact any higher education was generally moulded by Wisdom teaching. The title *ḥākām* 'wise man' acquires here too its technical meaning. Though, to begin with, it denotes in a general sense an expert, especially a trained craftsman and artisan (for example, Exod. 28: 3; 31: 6 etc.; Isa. 40: 20; Jer. 10: 9; Ezek. 27: 8 and elsewhere), in the polemic of Isaiah (29: 14; 31: 2) it encompasses the adviser at court who has had the necessary education to enable him to offer counsel to the king himself; the 'counsel' (*ʿēṣāh*) is after all what is expected of the 'wise man', as the Torah is expected of the priest and God's word of the prophet (Jer. 18: 18). Whether *ḥākām* first came to denote the educated man in general during the late pre-exilic period, or whether its meaning had already been widened at an earlier stage cannot be deduced with any certainty, but the earlier date is probable. At all events, even in old texts the term 'wise man' is not confined to a particular social group but expresses a certain ideal. In the post-exilic period, with the transforming of Wisdom into a comprehensive theology, the 'wise man' takes on the meaning of the pious individual who is suffused with the truth that Wisdom describes as the order inherent in the world and in human existence, and who conducts his life in accordance with its precepts. This does not preclude the professional scholar from being thus named: his ideal image occurs in Ecclus. 38: 34b to 39: 11.

It would be a fundamental misinterpretation of the older Wisdom, however, if one were to see in it first and foremost a means of courtly education. Even in Egypt, where the teachings of Wisdom show far stronger traces of being designed for the education of officials, the range of Wisdom literature is considerably wider. And when one considers the social background of the earliest Israelite aphoristic collections in the book of Proverbs, it is clearer than ever that a restricted interpretation of this kind is wholly inappropriate. The world of the court figures in only a small number of aphorisms, and even then in a form which allows of more widespread application. We must therefore assume that the place where Wisdom was cultivated was the school, which could be found not only in its most advanced form in the royal capital but also throughout the land. In a primitive form it existed as soon as someone other than the parents was charged with educating the young person through a particular series of instructional dialogues. The prerequisite was not so much a body of trained teachers as the existence of a 'doctrine' to be taught, which we should envisage as something still rudimentary – popular lore or what is known as 'tribal wisdom'.[1] Thus we may assume the existence of many varieties of 'school' even in pre-exilic Israel, although we cannot describe them in detail. We can merely identify a certain expression of human culture which was widely distributed, without having any more precise information about the pedagogic tradition which this advanced cultural phenomenon presupposed. In any case this mediation of knowledge, as almost everywhere in Antiquity, doubtless occurred in many different ways. Yet certain formal conventions throw some light on the usual pattern of instruction: the pupil being addressed as 'son', the catechism of question and answer, perhaps too the solemn invocation that preceded a didactic utterance (for example, Deut. 32: 1; Isa. 28: 23; Ps. 49: 1–5),[2] and the mnemonic arrangement of aphorisms.[3]

THE GENRES AND FORMS OF WISDOM LITERATURE

The basic form of Wisdom literature is the saying. The appropriate Hebrew concept of *māšāl* has a wide range of meaning, from the single proverb to the extended didactic poem, and it can be couched in a mocking, admonitory or homiletic tone. *Māšāl* has been construed as 'simile' (from *mšl* I 'to compare') or as 'word of authority' (from *mšl* II 'to rule', which could originally have been cognate with *mšl* I). What is certain is that a *māšāl* rests largely on an act of comparison which first permits a significant insight; in its function as proverb, it not only reflects reality but also discloses a concealed truth. It might be said that the *māšāl* orders reality through association and thus proclaims a truth. The fact that the individual saying may evolve into a lengthy poem, or that the act of association in the simile may be couched polemically or objectively, is of no consquence when we consider the basic form of the *māšāl*.

A genre which preceded Wisdom proper is the *popular saying*. By this is understood not so much a mere idiom or comparison, for example, 'wherefore it is said, Even as Nimrod the mighty hunter before the Lord (Gen. 10: 9)', as a completely formulated sentence, for example: 'As saith the proverb [*māšāl*] of the ancients, Wickedness proceedeth from the wicked' (1 Sam. 24: 13), or 'Tell him, Let not him that girdeth

[1] See J-P. Audet, 'Origines comparées de la double tradition de la loi et de la sagesse dans le Proche-Orient ancien', in *25th International Congress of Orientalists, 1960*, vol. 1, pp. 352–7 (Moscow, 1962); E. Gerstenberger, *Wesen und Herkunft des sogenannten 'apodiktischen Rechts' in A.T.* WMANT 20 (Neukirchen-Vluyn, 1965).

[2] H. W. Wolff, *Dodekapropheton 1, Hosea*, BKAT 14, 1 (Neukirchen-Vluyn, 1961), p. 122.

[3] On the composition of aphorisms, see also p. 196f.

on his harness boast himself as he that putteth it off' (1 Kings 20: 11). Both sayings attempt to capture ethical rules of human life in the form of an *asseveration* and an *admonition*. For the most part, however, this ethical aspect is lacking in the popular saying. What is articulated is merely the necessary order of things, often with a stress on the peculiar and the whimsical, even the absurd (Jer. 23; 28b; Ezek 18: 2b).

The basic genre of Wisdom literature is the artificially composed *proverb*, the *maxim*, the *aphorism* (*gnōmē, sententia*). The proverb is always poetic, formulated according to a *parallelismus membrorum*, and may occur in the form of a declaration or, less frequently, an admonition. More rarely one finds it taking the form of a rhetorical question (for example, Prov. 6: 27) or a first-person statement (for example, Prov. 24: 30ff) which underlines the empirical experience behind it (experiential saying). The form of the proverb as a literary composition leads to the subject-matter being presented in a highly artistic, cogent formulation whereby a simple observation often acquires a remarkable degree of nuance. The manner in which metaphors and similes are selected; or in which, with the aid of parallelism, the assertion is intensified, generalized, made more concrete, turned on its head or developed further and underpinned; the way in which, finally, the external form is rendered memorable by word-play (paronomasia) – all this betokens an artistry to which translation cannot really do justice. Above all we should note the function of the simile because of the character of the *māšāl*; the comparison is not just intended as depiction, it also enhances the self-evident nature of the insight and on occasion even discloses a hidden meaning, so that the aphorism may acquire unsuspected depth.

The simile makes possible the *riddle* (*ḥîdāh*). In the solving of riddles the process of apprehension, which the composer of the riddle has himself gone through, is once again repeated. In the contest of riddles one may witness an intellectual struggle for power. It is significant that Solomon in his wisdom could solve every riddle put to him (1 Kings 10: 1–3). Wisdom therefore includes the riddle, which could be described as a *māšāl* in reverse.

A special form of ancient Syrian Wisdom seems to have been the *numerical saying* (cf. Prov. 6: 16–19; 30: 15ff; Job 5: 19–22). What we find there is an enumeration of things compared; one less than the total number is announced by way of introduction, then raised in the parallelism to the full number according to the formula $x - 1 \| x$. The numerical saying presents in a memorable manner the ordered apprehension of essential truths, which, as in the *māšāl* and the riddle, consists in drawing comparisons.

A series of aphorisms on the same theme can produce a *didactic poem*. Thus in Ps. 37, for example, we find an unobtrusively structured composition which is moreover arranged acrostically; here every aphorism is given its due weight and internal cross-references do not dispel the impression of a simple succession. A very different impression is made by a didactic poem like Ps. 49 which has clear-cut divisions with an introduction (verses 1 to 4) and two strophes each rounded off with a refrain (verses 5 to 12, 13 to 20); the whole thing can be called a *māšāl* (verse 4). Proverbs 1 to 9 and the book of Job are rich in didactic poems of this kind.

A development of the comparison that is a basic constituent of the *māšāl* leads to the *parable*, but this does not appear until the later Wisdom literature which is no longer exclusively bound by strict poetic form. A related form is the *exemplary tale*, in which the comparison is extended into a paradigm. On the other hand the simile may also be pushed further, into *allegory*, if the comparison yields a whole series of corresponding features. If the comparison is derived from the animal or plant world and pursued through narrative in order to illuminate and covertly to criticize human conduct and institutions, the result is the *fable*. In these prose forms, or forms that are not primarily poetic (least of all the parable), the nature of the comparison inherent in the *māšāl* is modified; it performs not so much a noetic function as an expository one and is aimed more at the listener.

In various ways the doctrine of Wisdom impinged upon other forms, especially those of ceremonial worship in accordance with the later change from Wisdom to theology proper. Thus the hymn and the individual prayer, the private lament and the song of trust could be adopted from, or at least moulded by, the conventions of Wisdom literature.

Once Wisdom literature is fully developed, we often discover the dialogue form, which mirrors the scholarly discussion practised among the wise men. This form may be cultivated as a disputation or as a conversation with oneself. This kind of disputation plays a role in the book of Job, but it would be wrong to try and account for the Job text solely by reference to this form. The issue can only be resolved by reference to the history of the book's origins. We shall return to this point during our discussion of Job.

GENERAL CHARACTERISTICS OF THE OLDER ISRAELITE WISDOM

The Wisdom of the ancient Near East, in its efforts to interpret the world as an ordered cosmos on the basis of empirical experience, displays a thoroughly secular character owing little to specific religious traditions, apart from the fact that the reverential search for and apprehension of order are themselves proof of a basic religious attitude to the world. The secular character of Wisdom is initially evinced in Israel too. Indeed it makes possible the extensive borrowing from alien sources. To begin with, nothing distinguishes Israelite Wisdom from the common heritage of Antiquity, since it is the same world that confronts the Israelite, and he endeavours to divine the order behind the natural and the human world in the same way. But on the other hand this experience of the world could not be allowed to contradict that of Yahweh; rather, the order that was sought had to be the one established by Yahweh which the non-Israelite in his Wisdom text simply attributed to 'the god'. It was necessarily Yahweh's will that man should conduct himself in a manner befitting this order.

The order perceived in the world demanded that man should subordinate himself to it and humbly conform to what was 'right'. However much the secular nature of Wisdom entails a certain 'enlightened' attitude, it is far removed from the illusion of a free, autonomous humanity. On the contrary, humility becomes a prime virtue, expressed above all in the conquest of self. Silence is highly esteemed, as in Egypt, and declared to be better than speech, unless it is a question of the word of Wisdom at the appropriate moment. Every form of unbridled passion is condemned, the hothead and the man quick to wrath are fools, like the Egyptian 'man of hot blood'.

It is completely consistent with Wisdom literature's conception of order that proper obedience to the law leads to the experience of salvation. If man enters the sphere of the good and the just, he can himself experience justice and goodness. Ancient Wisdom knows nothing of the later ontology that distinguishes between appearance and reality and poses the question of Job – whether man is pious *in vain* (1: 9) – with the implication that the truly righteous man can be virtuous in himself without having justice vouchsafed to him in return. Rather, in the older teaching the deeds and the fortunes of man are inseparable, and reality is not yet split into its subjective and objective aspects. Scholars have talked of the 'synthetic attitude to life' or the 'relationship between conduct and condition' which is characteristic of this older ontology. It would therefore be an egregious error to ascribe eudemonism to the old Wisdom teaching; one would thereby invoke utterly inappropriate categories.

In the light of the correspondence between good deeds and salvation we can also see that the individual is still an integral part of his social environment, and that consequently he can mediate salvation to a wider circle. Conversely salvation would be unthinkable without the acknowledgement of society. 'Honour' is dependent upon one's fellow men and without them no redeemed existence would be possible.

The idea of a relationship between conduct and fortune that lies at the root of the old Wisdom does not, however, lead to the illusion that one can draw a simple inference of righteous behaviour from good fortune or vice versa. True, the temptation to draw such inferences is great, and the pauper may be blamed for his idleness if it is manifest. Yet Wisdom literature remains fully aware of the limits to its apprehension of order. No matter how eagerly it pursues its insights into cosmic order, it never forgets that ultimate knowledge is withheld from men. Here again the cardinal virtue of humility may be revealed; a complacent allusion to one's own good fortune is felt to be a blasphemous arrogance. This basic modesty is matched by a willingness to give succour to the weak. Succour and good deeds are an essential precondition of a redeemed societal existence and the 'righteous' man will always exert a beneficial influence on his neighbours.

Since in Israel the apprehension of order is necessarily equated with insight into the order established by Yahweh, the limits of the knowledge afforded by Wisdom, the impenetrability of order, mark the point in the old Wisdom at which a direct personal relationship with Yahweh is clearly postulated. And here traditional Wisdom undergoes modifications in the spirit of the Yahweh revelation, the more so as time goes on. The fact that it is Yahweh who determines the course of events, even against the will of the human agent, is emphasized again and again (Prov. 16: 1, 9, 33; 20: 24; 21: 31). It is thus inconceivable that the order divined by Wisdom could in any way circumscribe the will of Yahweh. This order never becomes a principle independent of Yahweh. Therefore the idea of a connection between conduct and condition can blend effortlessly into the notion of a requital of human behaviour by Yahweh, once the concept of a personal judgement on each individual gains prominence. For even this relationship between conduct and condition is thought of only as the form in which Yahweh institutes cosmic salvation. This Israelite Wisdom teaching does not lead into a sphere of experience independent of Yahweh, but leads through this experience of the world to the experience of Yahweh Himself: 'There is no wisdom nor understanding nor counsel against the Lord' (Prov. 21: 30).

THE BOOK OF PROVERBS

This is usually said to be the first of the Solomonic books: Proverbs, Ecclesiastes, the Song of Songs and Wisdom; or if the Song of Songs and Ecclesiastes are included among the Five *Megilloth*, while Wisdom is excluded, it is the only book of Solomon to be presented separately. It derives its name from the title (1: 1): 'The proverbs (*mišlê, paroimiai*) of Solomon the son of David, king of Israel'. This heading continues with a delineation of the book's purpose in verses 2 to 6, and finally states the Wisdom-literature 'principle' of the fear of the Lord (verse 7) as a *summa* of the contents of the whole. This lengthy heading is thus designed not only for an initial subsection but obviously as an introduction to the whole book.

THE STRUCTURE OF THE BOOK

In the light of headings and introductions and other formal characteristics the constituent collections of the book of Proverbs can easily be recognized.

I	1: 1 to 9: 18	With the general introduction mentioned above.
II	10: 1 to 22: 16	'Proverbs of Solomon'.
III	22: 17 to 24: 22	An instruction of thirty[1] aphorisms furnished with a prologue in 22: 17–21 and called 'the words of the wise' (verse 17).
IV	24: 23–34	'These things also belong to the wise'.
V	25: 1 to 29: 27	'These are also proverbs of Solomon, which the men of Hezekiah king of Judah copied out'.
VI	30: 1–14	'The words of Agur the son of Jakeh', the Massaite.[2]
VII	30: 15–33	Numerical sayings.
VIII	31: 1–9	'The words of King Lemuel', king of Massa, 'that his mother taught him'.
IX	31: 10–31	An acrostic paean to the ideal woman.

The Greek version arranges them in a different order: after I, II, III with an addition of eleven hemistichs come VI, IV, VII and VIII, while the concluding acrostic (IX) remains at the end of the whole book after V. How are we to interpret these different sequences in the Hebrew and the Greek versions? Their length alone shows that in the case of IV and VI to VIII, to say nothing of the final poem IX, we are dealing with additions. These are attached by the Septuagint to the complex I, II, III, according to the number of proverbs they comprise; after all, the instruction containing thirty aphorisms (III) itself constituted a

---

[1] In verse 20, read *šᵉlōšîm*.   [2] Read *hammaśśā'î*.

supplement to the extensive Solomonic collection II. On the other hand, the Masoretic text places the foreign, Massaite collections VI and VIII at the end of the book. (Since VI ends with a quasi-numerical saying in 30: 11–14, the other numerical sayings in VII are added to it.)

This history of its composition gives us an insight into the structure of the work. Two older collections, II and V, which are distinguished both by their length and by virtue of being specifically attributed to Solomon, form the two pillars of the book (the instruction containing thirty aphorisms was added at an early stage as a conclusion to II). An introduction was supplied by collection I which interpreted the book as a whole in the spirit of later theological Wisdom. Small supplementary collections could be integrated at various points, either at the end of the complex formed by II and III since there already existed one additional passage, or at the very end after V, which the Masoretic text preferred because foreign authors were involved. At the time when the Greek book of Proverbs was written (at the latest in the first half of the second century B.C.E., as the Sirach prologue shows), there was still a degree of flexibility in the composition but this clearly presupposes a knowledge of the basic structure. Collection IX as a conclusion had a theological significance in so far as the relationship to one's wife provided an analogy with one's relationship to Wisdom as it has been outlined in I.

INDIVIDUAL SECTIONS

(1) *Collection II (10: 1 to 22: 16)*, entitled the 'proverbs of Solomon' and forming with V the core of the whole book, numbers 375 proverbs and is thus the most extensive. (Since the name *Šelōmōh* has a numerical value of 375, scholars have tried to find similar correspondences in the rest of Proverbs.) They are aphorisms formulated in the main as asseverations which unfold the broad spectrum of ancient Israelite Wisdom: the agricultural nation; the high esteem in which they held their king, who is only conceivable as one of their number; the importance of the law; family life with a special appreciation of the woman; and frequent religious allusions. Scholars are inclined to assume that the section consists of two sub-collections: 10: 1 to 15: 33 and 16: 1 to 22: 16, because in the second part admonitions occur more often and antithetical parallelisms less often. It has been suggested that the second part, rather than the first, was destined for officials. Yet such subdivisions remain uncertain. We shall only be sure of our ground if the principle of composition has been grasped.

Although it is repeatedly maintained that this composition – with the

exception of a few short thematic sequences or an echoing of keywords –
is purely arbitrary, such a contention is utterly improbable. In Antiquity,
aphoristic collections of this kind, while lacking a logical arrangement
of their subject matter, are at least structured according to external
criteria (alphabetical order). What is striking is the frequent duplication
of the theme being treated, so that one very often observes separate
groups of two sections. Within this framework an argument may then
be developed along the lines of a statement followed by a contradiction,
objection or confirmation. This suggests that the composition is
inspired by the idea of a 'dialogue' in aphorisms.

We may safely assume that this collection was written in the pre-exilic
period, at least as far as its main parts or some individual subsections
are concerned. The use of certain Aramaic words does not necessarily
point to a post-exilic dating since the elevated language of the *māšāl* likes
to resort to unusual vocabulary.

(2) *Collection V (25: 1 to 29: 27)* is a counterpart to II. If 'the men
of Hezekiah' are said to have copied this out (25: 1), it could be the
result of the movement to restore the older traditions evident in the
seventh century; and the spread of northern Israelite traditions to Judah
may have been another impulse behind the collection. Perhaps too it
may simply have been the notable esteem in which Hezekiah was held
by posterity that led to the tradition preceding Deuteronomism being
thus described. At all events collection V doubtless dates from the
pre-exilic period, at least in its basic elements.

Here too there is a tendency to discern two subdivisions, 25: 1 to
27: 27 and 28: 1 to 29: 27, because in the first section antithetical
parallelism seldom occurs and other formal statistical differences can be
seen. In terms of content, the first half is rich in nature imagery, while
in the second political allusions predominate. The similarities between
collection V and collection II are, however, manifest and a series of
comparable aphorisms can be found in both. Moreover, in addition to
the sequence of keywords, the principle of duplication can be recognized
in the composition. Yet the structure is not so much reminiscent of a
'dialogue'; rather, it presumably attempts to classify the world according
to an objective order.

(3) *The instruction containing thirty proverbs: III (22: 17 to 24: 22)*. In
contrast to the aphoristic collections mentioned above, we are here faced
with a different form: a well-composed introduction (22: 17–21)
prefaces the complex, in which the teacher (speaking in the first person)
declares to his disciple that he has written down thirty[1] 'things in
counsels and knowledge'. In 22: 22 to 24: 22 there indeed follow thirty

[1] See note 1, on p. 200.

aphorisms. The majority, however, unlike those in the older collections, appear as admonitions and are even explained (whereby the reasons are sometimes merely implied in the particular formulation). Finally, the frequent use of the familiar second person singular and the addressing of the pupil as 'my son' are noteworthy. This is all typical of the instructional genre in which the aphoristic complex is transformed into a coherent teaching addressed by a wise man to his pupil.

Considerable interest was aroused by the discovery in 1924 that the first part of this instruction (22: 22 to 23: 11) was paralleled almost entirely, down to detailed verbal correspondences, by the instruction which the Egyptian Amenemope, a high-ranking official of the later Ramses dynasty, drew up for his youngest son. This work, in thirty numbered chapters, stands out from the general run of Egyptian instructions by virtue of its humble piety. There can be no doubt about the connection between the biblical and the Egyptian texts, even though it has occasionally been suggested[1] that the Egyptian text borrowed from the biblical one, a hypothesis which has been convincingly refuted (particularly by Couroyer).[2] The oldest manuscript of Amenemope's teaching dates back to the twentieth/twenty-first dynasty. But this instruction was handed down for a long period and still taught up to about 600 B.C.E., so that it could have influenced the Israelite wise man some time during the post-Solomonic, pre-exilic period. The author of the instruction containing thirty aphorisms in the book of Proverbs must have come to know and value this Egyptian teaching, and been impelled to create an Israelite equivalent. Thereby, of course, he not only effected external changes in accordance with the Palestinian environment and the social conditions in Israel; he also introduced different religious accents, especially in the latter two-thirds of his instruction, which are distinguished by a noble ethos (compare 24: 10–12 about giving succour or 24: 17f about the offence of malicious delight at the misfortunes of others, and 23: 17f; 24: 1, 19f, which are reminiscent of the overcoming of the theodicy problem in the Wisdom psalms of the Persian period – Pss. 37: 1, 7f; 73: 3: they also remind us of Prov. 3: 31). Furthermore they express that intimate personal relationship with Wisdom (in 23: 26–28 Wisdom itself seems to speak with the voice of a wife and mother; see also 23: 15f; 24: 13f) which anticipates the spirit of the post-exilic

---

[1] See W. O. E. Oesterley, 'The "Teaching of Amen-em-ope" and the Old Testament', *ZAW*, 45 (1927), 9–24; R. O. Kevin, 'The Wisdom of Amen-em-apt and its Possible Dependence upon the Hebrew Book of Proverbs', *JSOR*, 14 (1930), 115–57; E. Drioton, 'Le livre des Proverbes et la Sagesse d'Aménémopé', *Sacra Pagina*, 12 (1959), 229–41.

[2] B. Couroyer, 'L'origine égyptienne de la Sagesse d'Amenemopé', *RB*, 70 (1963), 208–24.

collection, Prov. 1 : 1 to 9 : 18. We must therefore think in terms of the pre-exilic period (compare the mention of the king in addition to Yahweh in the concluding admonition, 24: 21f).

This important instruction was attached at an early stage to the Solomonic collection II, under the heading 'words of the wise'.[1] It fused with II to form a complex which stood side by side with the Hezekianic collection V as a principal constituent in the origins of the book as a whole. Together they seem to have been the core of the Proverbs tradition and were held to date back to the pre-exilic period.

(4) The short *collection IV* (*24: 23–34*), comprising only seven proverbs, is rightly seen as a supplement to the thirty aphorisms – thus the Masoretic text – and the heading 'These things also belong to the wise' appears to point to this.

(5) *Collection VI* (*30: 1–14*) is attributed to Agur the son of Jakeh, from the northern Arabian tribe of Massa,[2] and gives the impression of being a late text. To begin with (verses 2 to 4) we are told humbly of the 'ignorance' of the author compared to the (divine) Wisdom that is in fact essential to man (compare Pss. 49: 10, 12, 13f, 20; 73: 22), in order that the authority of God's word may be emphasized the more strongly (verses 5f; compare Job 40: 5; 42: 6). In the subsequent observations of Wisdom, which can take on the form of prayer, one is struck by the sophisticated argument, while the parallels given put one in mind of the Persian period. In view of the fame of eastern Wisdom (1 Kings 4: 30f, and see especially Job and his friends) the inclusion of this collection in the book of Proverbs needs no explanation. Since the Wisdom of Agur ends with a disguised numerical saying (verses 11 to 14), the *collection of numerical sayings VII* (*30: 15–33*) which follows in the Masoretic text may perhaps be viewed as an original continuation of it. This supposition would be supported by the fact that in the concluding admonition (verses 32f) there is possibly a further allusion to Job (Job 40: 4).

(6) *Collection VIII* (*31: 1–9*), which contains words intended for the Massaite King Lemuel, is a short instruction composed by his mother. The wit and form point to a date similar to that which we must assume for the Wisdom of Agur. Hedonism (women and wine) is repudiated in favour of tending the needy, for whom wine and the oblivion it brings are more fitting; one should open one's mouth only to pass righteous judgement.

(7) Collections VI (VII) and VIII are chronologically perhaps even later than the great *introductory complex I* (*1: 1 to 9: 18*) which presupposes perhaps the existence of only II, III (IV?) and V, but which

---

[1] Compare LXX.   [2] See note 2, on p. 200.

at all events serves as a prologue to the whole book of Proverbs. It is our principal evidence for the changing interpretation of Wisdom in the post-exilic period up to the beginning of Hellenism (perhaps extending also to the latter part of the fourth century). In formal terms the main difference from the collections discussed above is the predominance of Wisdom poems. Though the latter can be compared with the instructional genre because of the regular stylization into an admonition and the frequent addressing of a 'son', they are not comprised of individual maxims arranged in a thematic sequence. Instead, didactic passages usually of a general and fundamental purport and in the form of sustained compositions follow one after the other.

After the heading, 1: 1–7, which refers to the book as whole, there ensues first a warning against consorting with sinners (verses 10–19), following the basic admonition to accept the teaching of one's parents (verses 8f). Then Wisdom appears as a penitential preacher and exhorts his listeners in a *prophetic* idiom to hearken to him (verses 20 to 33). The homily begins with a poem of six strophes on the blessings of Wisdom, a rhetorical masterpiece in a single sentence (chapter 2). Chapter 3: 1–12 describes, in a similarly well-composed poem (3 × 2 sections), the religious character of Wisdom by enumerating admonitions appertaining to the relationship with Yahweh as Torah and commandment, after the fashion of a *priest*. There follows an account of the significance of Wisdom for one's own life (verses 13 to 26) and, finally, we have admonitions concerning one's relationship with neighbours and sinners (verses 27–30; 31 to 35). The theme of the two paths, the path of Wisdom and the path of the ungodly, is treated in fatherly admonition in chapter 4, framed by the counsel to acquire and retain Wisdom (verses 1 to 9, 10 to 19, 20 to 27). By contrast we then find the first great warning against the strange woman (chapter 5), followed by four shorter warnings against standing surety (6: 1 to 5), idleness (verses 6 to 11), falseness (verses 12 to 15) and, finally, the seven things that are an abomination to the Lord (verses 16 to 19). The second great parental warning against the strange woman (6: 20 to 7: 27) is the background which brings into relief the climax of the prologue, the speech in which Wisdom commends herself to men, appearing in public places as in 1: 20ff and reaching all with her words. Framed by the admonitions to hearken to her voice (8: 4–11, 32–36), she shows her importance for human society (verses 12 to 21) and the cosmos (verses 22 to 31). In conclusion chapter 9 conveys the invitations of both Wisdom and folly to enter their homes.

The introductory complex in chapters 1 to 9 as a whole does not appear to be a single sustained composition; the individual sections were obviously written to a large extent as separate pieces, and some do not seem to have been inserted until later. But it is difficult to distinguish convincingly between the various strata. As far as the time-span is concerned, the penitential sermon of Wisdom, 1: 20ff, which being situated as early as chapter 1 is certainly no late addition, is itself evidence that we cannot go back as far as the pre-exilic period; for in adapting the proclamations of Wisdom literature to prophetic forms, this passage presupposes a familiarity with the Deuteronomizing stratum of the Jeremiah tradition. Reminiscences of the early post-exilic Isaiah tradition also point unequivocally to a post-exilic dating. Moreover, the poem about the transcendent power of Wisdom (Job 28), one of the additions to the book of Job in the Persian period, represents a preliminary form of Prov. 8: 22ff. On the other hand the instruction containing thirty aphorisms (III) which dates from the end of the pre-exilic period seems to anticipate Prov. 1 to 9, so that there is no need to go as far as the early Hellenistic period. It is therefore most probable that these chapters originated in the Persian period.

(8) At the end of the book of Proverbs (31: 10–31) there occurs an acrostic poem *in praise of the ideal woman*. This looks like a return to the erotic theme so often treated in chapters 1 to 9: the virtuous housewife prepares the flourishing happiness of Jewish family life like a representative of Wisdom. Thus the book is splendidly rounded off.

THE INTERPRETATION OF WISDOM IN THE PERSIAN PERIOD

The ancient Wisdom had endeavoured empirically to apprehend and portray in texts the order underlying the world, nature and human life, through a multi-faceted observation of phenomena. This Wisdom tradition, growing ever stronger, itself felt the need for a summary of its insights, and the concept of a world order inherent in Wisdom from the outset demanded the more strongly to be objectified, the more clearly it could be abstracted from the myriad empirical observations. The transformation of myth into nature philosophy in the Israelite world, which can be traced from the late Assyrian period, and the marked 'scientific' character of the priestly doctrine of creation in Israel, point to a development that can be summed up as a process of generalizing abstraction. At all events the concept of Wisdom, which may also be called 'understanding', 'knowledge', 'teaching', 'discipline' and so on, and which denotes the (acquiescent) apprehension of order or even this world order itself, acquires the greatest importance in the later Wisdom of Israel.

Since the ancient Wisdom regarded order as self-evidently established by Yahweh, even though its apprehension was a purely secular affair that had nothing to do with the Israelite concept of revelation, this idea of world order was synonymous with the idea of a cosmic order instituted in creation and sustained by Yahweh. This order governed the whole of human life as well, for the human and the natural worlds were basically one and the same. Thus the Creator could be praised in hymnic utterances: 'O Lord, how manifold are thy works! in wisdom [*bᵉḥokmāh*] hast thou made them all!' (Ps. 104: 24). Thus too in Prov. 3: 19f it is taught that 'The Lord by wisdom [*bᵉḥokmāh*] hath founded the earth; by understanding hath he established the heavens. By his knowledge the depths are broken up, and the clouds drop down the dew.' Creation reveals the supreme order, being its true cosmic substance, and testifies in and with it to the power of the Creator. Knowledge of the world order changes from being a knowledge of the world to a knowledge of God and an originally profane Wisdom becomes theological Wisdom.

That a confusion of God and the world, Creator and creation, is simply not possible, is shown by the very concept of *ḥokmāh* which gives Wisdom precedence over creation. In Job 28, a paean to Wisdom which was added to the book of Job before the end of the Persian period and is meant to form Job's last utterance before his concluding lamentation and apologia in chapters 29 to 31, the transcendent quality of Wisdom is discussed in response to the question as to where it can be found. The poem is divided into three parts identifiable by the refrain in verse 12 and verse 20. The first part (verses 1 to 11) treats of the transcendent location of Wisdom in relation to the world of nature: even in the bowels of the earth to which the miner penetrates, it cannot be found. The second part (verses 13 to 19) makes a similar point in relation to the world of man: Wisdom cannot be purchased even for the most costly riches or from the most remote lands. The third part (verses 21 to 28) begins with a summing-up: Wisdom's place is not in this world, and even Hades and death have only 'heard the fame thereof with our ears'. Then it proceeds to a positive asseveration. Wisdom has her place with God and with creation. 'Then did he see it, and declare¹ it, he prepared it, yea, and searched it out' (verse 27). Wisdom as a world order, as a cosmic law is thus portrayed almost mathematically. It is the prerequisite of the work of creation and is therefore 'perceived' and 'ascertained' by God for creation, not physically 'created'. God creates the world according to this pre-existent and, of course, transcendental order. Wisdom thus occupies an almost mediatory position between God and the world. The conclusion of this paean to Wisdom is

¹ Read *wayyispᵉrāh*.

particularly splendid: 'And unto man he said, Behold, the fear of the Lord, that is wisdom; and to depart from evil is understanding' (verse 28). Here the cosmic law is identified with the fundamental religious and ethical precept which God reveals to man.

This text finds a more developed counterpart in Wisdom's praise of herself in Prov. 8. After Wisdom as a spiritual principle (compare verse 12) has placed herself above any human order of salvation (verses 12 to 21), and has even laid claim to divine attributes (compare, with verse 14, Job 12: 13, 16), she portrays herself as the first thing in creation (verses 22 to 31). Brought forth before creation as a 'beginning' (compare Gen. 1: 1), she was there when the divine act of creation was performed; and this presence is then elucidated in the phrase 'Then I was by him *'mwn*' (verse 30a). The meaning of *'mwn* is a bone of contention.[1] Two principal explanations are offered:

(1) *'āmōn* or *'ommān* – 'foreman' (compare Jer. 52: 15 and Song of Songs 7: 2). Thus Wisd. 7: 21; 8: 6 can construe *sophia* as *technitis*. This interpretation is contradicted by the context according to which God Himself performed the creative act.

(2) *'āmūn* – 'held in the lap', 'nursed' (see Lam. 4: 4 where the 'sucking child' is denoted thus), with which the following lines seem to fit in particularly well: 'and I was daily his[2] delight, playing always before him, playing in the habitable part of his earth; and my delights [= the delight over me] was with the sons of men' (verses 30 to 31). According to this, the relationship between God and the cosmic order is the same as that between a father and his cherished child whom he nurses on his lap. (In the present writer's opinion, God is here envisaged as seated upon his throne, as the Creator who made the cosmos by setting boundaries and ordaining laws; thus the world order is allowed to share the throne, seated on his lap; compare Wisd. 9: 4 where Wisdom is described as 'sitting by thy throne'.[3] After the creation of the world the child celebrates cosmic existence before God, in play that arouses supreme joy. On the other hand, men who partake of this joy also perceive it, so that the knowledge of Wisdom becomes a form of communion with God and Wisdom itself mediates God to the world.

The strong influence of Egyptian models on this representation of Wisdom has been identified. Not only does the form of the text put one in mind of the self-portrayal of Egyptian gods: the figure of the

[1] An outline of the debate may be found in R. B. Y. Scott, 'Wisdom in Creation: The *'āmōn* of Proverbs VIII, 30', *VT*, 10 (1960), 213–23. The most recent discussion is in O. Keel, *Die Weisheit spielt vor Gott* (Freiburg–Göttingen, 1974).
[2] Read *šaᶜăšîᶜā(y)w*, as in LXX.
[3] Compare John 1: 18.

Egyptian 'just order', the Maat, who as the daughter of Re can embrace the creator god and 'quicken' him, and even the notion of the holy game points to the Egyptian tradition.[1] Admittedly the Egyptian influence on Prov. 8: 22ff would not have been possible unless the notions in question had already been anticipated within the Israelite tradition, as Job 28 shows, so that it was necessary to resort to Egyptian models only for the mythopoeic–poetic execution. Likewise the ground was prepared for the personification of Wisdom by the incipient hypostasization evident in Job 28. It did not come about as the result of adopting a myth – especially since this personification, so widespread in the late Wisdom texts, cannot have entered the Wisdom tradition through the present text alone. Finally, one can point to material differences from the Egyptian sources; for there neither is Maat portrayed as seated on a throne nor have we a precise example of her being said to play before God.

The importance of this text, Prov. 8: 22ff, lies in the fact that the tradition of Wisdom praising herself as a pre-existent essence provides the basis for the text of Ecclus. 24: 1–12, the conceptual horizons of which must date from as late as the third century. According to this, Wisdom is placed above all heavenly beings; it came forth from the mouth of God and is identical with God's epiphany. Ruling both creation and the human world as the creative *logos*, it seeks an abode in the world and finds it at God's behest in Israel. It then dwells in the holy place of Zion as *shekinah*, symbolized by the ark of the covenant. The cosmic order is here identified with Yahweh's revelation to Israel and develops through the adoption of the Sinai and Zion traditions into the Torah or *shekinah*.

It can be clearly shown that what here ensues is a completely consistent theological evolution. If Wisdom as a cosmic law has the task of mediating God to the world, this notion threatens to clash with the tradition of God's revelation to Israel to such an extent that the equating of the word of creation with the word of revelation which is evinced as early as Deutero-Isaiah necessarily leads to this expansion of the concept of Wisdom. An explicit attestation of this can be found in Ps. 19, the first part of which (verses 1 to 6) praises the silent *logos* of creation and illustrates it by reference to the sun; its second half, however, (verses 7ff) identifies this *logos* with Wisdom which is conceived of wholly as Torah and divine commandment.

If we date the editing of the Psalms in the first collection, of which

[1] See H. Donner, 'Die religionsgeschichtlichen Ursprünge von Prov. Sal. 8', *ZA*, 82 (1958), 8–18; C. Kayatz, *Studien zu Prov. 1–9* (Neukirchen-Vluyn, 1966); Keel, *Weisheit*.

Ps. 19 is one, before the end of the fourth century,[1] it must be assumed that this theology developed as early as the Persian period. This corresponds to the fact that in Prov. 1: 20ff the word of Wisdom becomes a prophetic speech, or that in Prov. 3; 1ff it becomes Torah and commandment (compare 6: 23 where again *tôrāh* means more than just the 'bidding' of Wisdom which it denotes elsewhere). The commandment associated with institutional worship can be taken over from Wisdom (3: 9). By contrast with Deut 4: 6 not only does the Torah appear as Israel's Wisdom in the sight of the nations – theological Wisdom itself acquires the character of Torah.

The new theological connotations of Wisdom are expressed in the custom, common at this period, of terming Wisdom (or its 'beginning') the fear of the Lord. Humble submission to the perceived order of things has ceded to Yahweh-piety, which is unthinkable without the counsel of Wisdom or obedience to the admonitions of Wisdom – and indeed shows itself in these very things. The old exhortation to obedience now becomes a choice of life or death (Prov. 8: 35f) comparable to the summons to obey the Torah in Deuteronomic theology.

The urgent nature of Wisdom's admonitions, which may take on a prophetic form as though they proceeded from Yahweh Himself (1: 24–33), and which pursue men ineluctably (1: 20f; 8: 1–3; 9: 3), is underlined by the personification of Wisdom. What is striking is its personification as a woman who can invite men into her house and to her table, personification that is paralleled by that of folly (Prov. 9: 13ff) as the 'strange woman' (Prov. 5; 6: 20 to 7: 27). To account for this, one can of course adduce the close bond, indeed love, which unites the Egyptian Maat and mankind; yet there one does not come across the same imagery. One can also point to the cult of Astarte which is presupposed above all in 7: 5ff.[2] Yet that does not make Wisdom a positive copy of the Syrian goddess. In Zech 5: 5–11, a text of the early Persian period, there appears a similar female personification – but of wickedness. Although the word is normally masculine, the feminine form is preferred. Here there may have been an allusion to Ishtar in Babylon, but why was wickedness or the principle of evil not presented as a male idol? If one bears in mind that these texts are directed at a male audience, the purpose of a female personification becomes clear: only thus can the ultimate personal bond which lies behind this personification be visualized, the spiritual *eros* that unites the wise man with Wisdom (Prov. 4: 6, 8; 7: 4, where 'sister' denotes mistress;

[1] H. Gese, *Vom Sinai zum Zion* (Munich, 1974), p. 165.
[2] G. Boström, *Proverbiastudien* (Lund, 1935); though for a counter-argument see B. Lang, *Die weisheitliche Lehrrede. Eine Untersuchung von Sprüche 1–7* (Stuttgart, 1972).

compare Song of Songs 4: 9f etc.; 8: 17, 21, 34; 9: 1ff); and similarly the total union with the misruled world of the dead (especially impressive in Prov. 7: 26f; 9: 18). In this context not only does marital fidelity, which had always been one of Wisdom's precepts, acquire a new meaning, but monogamy is also held in high esteem (Prov. 5: 18, see from the same period Mal. 2: 14, 15b, 16).

To sum up: in the Persian period the concept of world order is recognized as a transcendental force wherein God unites with the world, and through which the percipient man can attain a redeemed existence. Wisdom has become a theological force which acquires a stronger and stronger connection with the Israelite traditions of revelation. Similarly an extension of the concept of the Torah to encompass Wisdom can also be glimpsed. Piety as a whole must be fundamentally determined by these once separate but now combined traditions of theology and Wisdom, which fuse in the later Old Testament. Thereby the older, secular, 'scientific' tradition is also subsumed as knowledge of the empirical world.

THE BOOK OF JOB

The biblical book of Job, which is by an anonymous author and named after its protagonist, belongs to the best-known texts of Wisdom literature. The influence of the Jeremiah tradition and some allusions to contemporary Persian events suggest that it dates from the early post-exilic period. The core of the book belongs to the fifth rather than to the fourth century, since we can scarcely date the supplementary chapter, Job 28, which has already been mentioned, later than the first half of the fourth century. It most probably originated in Palestine because numerous details would only have been comprehensible there.

THE STRUCTURE OF THE BOOK OF JOB

The book consists of a prose framework (chapter 1 to 2 and 42: 7–17) and a series of poetic speeches (3: 1 to 42: 6). The prologue (chapters 1 and 2) narrates how at Satan's instigation the pious and blessed Job was subject to a twofold, progressively exacerbated temptation: first, the loss of all his property and children, and then grievous physical affliction; but Job resists temptation. The prologue ends with the introduction of the three friends. This twofold structure is reflected in the speeches. After the initial lament of Job in chapter 3, two different sequences can clearly be discerned when the three friends, alternating with Job, speak one after the other. In the first sequence, the friends endeavour to comfort Job and to persuade him to confess his guilt before God; but in the second sequence they treat him increasingly as a transgressor because Job refuses to make such a confession. In the first part Job's responses are each directed at his friends; in the second they are addressed to God. Here, too, marked differences in subject-matter can be seen between the first and the second sequence. Of a possible third sequence only fragments remain. For both thematic and formal reasons chapter 21 can scarcely be read as a complete speech by Job in response to the last speech made by his friends in the second sequence. And there have been many theories about the original order and the core passages of chapters 22 to 27. There is much to be said for the assumption that there was originally no third sequence, merely that several supplementary sections were added at the end. They covered a range of themes: the transition from Job's personal dilemma to the general problem of theodicy, the mitigation of Job's excessively harsh judgements, the emphasis of Job's profound knowledge, and so on. It is best to regard these as additions rather than as surviving fragments of a once complete whole, since even in terms of content the speeches are problematic where they now stand. We can perhaps assume that originally the second sequence terminated with the response of Job in chapter 21; 23; 27: 1–10. The Wisdom poem in chapter 28 on the transcendent power of Wisdom is generally acknowledged to be an addition designed to bring Job's speeches to a climax before the final judicial summing-up of Job's case in chapters 29 to 31. The latter is divided into the depiction of his erstwhile happiness and prosperity (chapter 29), his current state of wretchedness (chapter 30), and the oath of purification, the protestation of innocence (chapter 31). Thus God is finally challenged to debate the justice of the case (31: 35–37). Then in chapters 32 to 37 there follow the lengthy utterances of a new and younger wise man, Elihu, who disapproves of the speeches of the three older friends; yet he is no longer mentioned when the question of who spoke the right thing is subsequently decided (42: 7ff). It is generally accepted that this intervention too is a supplementary passage which 'reforms' the Wisdom teaching of the original friends in the spirit of the new viewpoint emerging from the book. God's answers, in chapters 38 to 41: 34, with the short avowals of submission by Job, again show that twofold structure common to the rest of the composition. One should not take exception to this, as often happens, and presume that there was once a single unified utterance by God at this point (sometimes it is also argued on the grounds of content alone that the original version of the book never contained any speeches by the Lord). After all, the pattern of duplication which moulds ancient Near Eastern and biblical thinking in so many ways is not confined to the book of Job. The epilogue, 42: 7–17, narrating the restoration of Job's good fortunes, closes the circle of the composition and links up with the prologue (friends, relations, property and children, corresponding to the prologue pattern of property and children, wife and friends). Even though the structure – apart from the obscurities in chapters 21 to 27 – is clear and comprehensible, including the obvious interpolations in chapter 28 and chapters 32 to 37, difficulties nevertheless arise when we come to consider the history of the book's origins.

THE PRELIMINARY HISTORY OF THE BOOK OF JOB AND ITS FORMAL PROBLEMS

Together with the Syrian hero of the Deluge, Noah, and King Daniel who features in the Ugaritic epic, Job is named in Ezek 14: 14, 20 as one of the famous just men of the pre-Israelite period. This testifies to the existence of a Job tradition which formed the basis of the biblical text. According to this Job dwelt in the land, or rather tribal territory, of Uz and belonged to 'the men of the East' (1: 1, 3). Uz is partly associated with Aram, partly with Edom; the most likely area is the northern part of the land to the east of the Jordan, though there are many pointers to Edom and northern Arabia (the friends' names). The traditional story of Job's piety on which the biblical account depends can be reconstructed with a fair degree of probability. At any rate the basic narrative content must have tallied; a pious and once happy Job is put to the test by God, subjected to grievous sufferings and finally restored to his original state of grace, indeed blessed with complete prosperity. Tales of this sort are familiar from Sumerian–Akkadian Wisdom literature in particular, where they deal with the problem of theodicy after their fashion. However much they differ in detail – and necessarily differ because of changing theological and cultural assumptions through the ages – they all have in common the object of showing how completely unexpected and inexplicable suffering must be borne humbly by the pious man; all he can do is trust in God and offer prayers of lament and petition – whereupon God will finally hear his plea. This produces a threefold structure: an account of apparently unmerited woe – lamentation – the hearing of the prayer and restoration of happiness. And in accordance with its paradigmatic character the lament is given verbatim. Of particular importance is the fact that the lament may also be couched in the form of a dialogue in which friends and relatives participate. This genre, depicting paradigmatically how God hearkens to a lament (though many dispute that it forms a distinct genre) must also have been familiar in Syria. On the one hand we can point to a discovery such as Ras Shamra 25.460[1] from Ugaritic, which attests an acquaintance with corresponding Akkadian literature; on the other hand we can adduce the didactic adaptation by Wisdom of private songs of gratitude such as Ps. 32. That the traditional story of Job must be seen in relation to such texts as these is clear from the subject matter and also from the basic formal structure, which can still be discerned in the biblical book and in which the lament is of central importance.

This older story of Job is of course fundamentally changed in the Bible narrative. Here, in contrast with the older tradition, Job does not play the role of a trusting, humble petitioner. On the contrary, this is precisely the attitude which his friends demand of him in vain. They are thus at odds with Job, and the speeches rendered in the book take on the function of a disputation. Job stresses his innocence and demands justice, whereas his friends demand that he profess his faith in God's righteous judgement (in what is called a judgement doxology). Although the disputation is a familiar genre in Wisdom literature, one would not be doing justice to the book as a whole if one were to argue that the book of Job was nothing more than a conventional Wisdom disputation about the meaning of suffering. Consider quite simply the lengthy lamentations of Job. The book of Job could be called a dramatized lament; but even this definition is not wholly satisfactory, since one cannot really describe the friends' utterances as lamentations at all. Scholars have also pointed to the numerous reminiscences of judicial forms and tried to interpret the whole thing as a kind of legal proceeding. There is no doubt that all these forms and others too, such as hymns, interact in the biblical book of Job, and one cannot ignore the diverse functions and different position of these forms. If the paradigm showing how God hearkens mercifully to human lamentation provides the basic structure of both the subject matter and the form, this accounts for the particular importance of the lament in the middle part of the book. The opposition between Job and his friends led to the function of the dialogues being determined by the traditional disputation (without the story of an event thereby developing into the discussion of a problem). Finally, the theological shaping of Job demanded the introduction of certain basic forms from legal practice.

The question how much of the text of the old Job 'chap-book' could still be contained within the present prose framework is hotly debated. It seems more or less impossible that the framework could have been derived wholly from the old tradition. Yet, on the grounds of tensions and contradictions in the subject matter, attempts have been made to

[1] *Ugaritica* v, no. 162.

identify not only the narrative legacy of the original source but even portions of the original text. Admittedly analyses of this kind are so hypothetical that no great degree of agreement has ever emerged. In fact it is far more likely that the poet formulated the whole framework himself, since here the problem is presented from the outset in the spirit of the theology informing Job's own speeches. For instance, the idea that a man should fear God *in vain* (1 : 9) presupposes a mental attitude which the older Wisdom simply could not share because it had a fundamental belief in the correlation between conduct and condition. Least of all can we accept that the speeches ever existed without the framework, for a knowledge of the prologue is essential if we are to understand Job's position correctly, whether it is a question of God's attitude towards him or of his ignorance of the true situation.

THE THEOLOGICAL CONTENT OF THE BOOK OF JOB

The book begins with the question raised by Satan, the heavenly accuser, whether Job is pious *for nought* (1 : 9; compare also 2 : 3) when his life is so blessed. Thereby a view of piety is postulated which has abandoned the relationship between conduct and condition as its basic tenet. Any question of theodicy is thus relativized. The trials which Job endures at God's hands serve to prove Job's piety and this in turn provides God with proof to confound Satan. The occurrence is dramatized when Job is visited by his three wise friends. After seven days of sympathetic silence, Job's despairing lament expressing only his desire for death moves them to attempt to interpret what has happened from the point of view of the older Wisdom. In the spirit of the old story they summon Job through humble lamentation and petition and by piously acknowledging the divine judgement (judgement doxology) to plead for the restoration of God's favour which he has obviously forfeited. And since Job steadfastly refuses to do so, they find themselves in the second sequence of dialogue compelled to attack him more and more openly as a transgressor. Thus Job's friends become accusing enemies.

Job cannot concede the demands of his friends, since they necessarily appear pointless to him. For one thing, he is not aware of having offended against the covenant with God and this subjective relationship with God has acquired a fundamental importance by comparison with the older piety which (for instance, in the idea of a connection between conduct and condition) does not draw any sharp distinction between subject and object. Secondly, in the face of God's absolute power, everything human seems to him paltry, so that even human sin becomes

insignificant before the infinite power of God. In defiance of his friends
and hard pressed by their reproaches, he asks God to explain to him
the meaning of his suffering and to show him where his guilt lies. At
the end of the first speech sequence he actually challenges God to a
debate about justice. Job is concerned not with happiness in this life
(like his friends) but solely with the relationship between himself and
God. He sees himself treated by God as an 'enemy' (a play on words,
'ôjēb) and cannot endure this enmity, the destruction of the bond
between him and God. He merely wants to die but cannot bear the
thought that he has been repudiated by God. The new conception of
piety no longer depends on human health and happiness, but is based
on a personal relationship with God that can bridge the gulf between
the infinity of God and the nullity of man through the idea of
justification. In the second sequence Job calls for a divine advocate who
can plead for him to God (16: 18–21); indeed he wins through to a faith
in his divine 'redeemer' even though his physical existence has been
destroyed (19: 25–27).

The theological Wisdom of the Persian period, therefore, achieves
a knowledge of transcendence, the awareness that an intimate, personal
relationship with God demands as a corollary a transcendent dimension
beyond physical existence. We can perceive this in two Wisdom Psalms
of the same period, Pss. 49 and 73.[1] Ps. 49: 15 expresses the deliverance
of the *nepeš*, individual existence, from the power of the underworld and
indeed voices the rapture of the speaker, while Ps. 73: 23–26 says the
same thing in words that are not unlike those of Job 19: 26f. Since these
Wisdom Psalms are also concerned with the question of theodicy –
which is answered to the effect that while all godless power perishes,
the personal relationship with God not only establishes a new reality
in this life but endures for ever – one can justifiably ascribe this
experience of transcendence to the theological Wisdom of the Persian
period.

God responds to Job's demand by revealing Himself in the whirlwind.
And from the split in his image of God (divine advocate and redeemer
standing over against the *deus absconditus*) Job attains an experience of the
wholly Other. The first speech refers to boundless cosmic sovereignty.
The negative experience of God's absolute power in contrast to the
nullity of man cedes to the experience of the unfathomable cosmic
mystery which is exemplified in the abundant richness of the *nepeš*, the

---

[1] Ps. 49 belongs to the Korahite collection (Pss. 42 to 49); Ps. 73 belongs to the Asaph
collection (Pss. 73 to 83). Both collections date back to the second half of the fourth
century, though the Psalms themselves must be older (see Gese, *Vom Sinai zum Zion*,
p. 165).

phenomenal world (as in the old 'scientific' Wisdom literature). The second speech refers to justice and shows how God banishes injustice and chaos, as represented by the creatures of the abyss, Behemoth and Leviathan. This experience of the transcendent God as the *deus revelatus* leads Job to recant. His struggle for communion with his God is over. 'I have heard of thee by the hearing of the ear; but now mine eye seeth thee' (42: 5; compare 19: 27). Those who sometimes take exception to the fact that the words of God reveal a certain similarity to the descriptions of the cosmic God in the speeches of Job's friends forget that this affinity is inevitable. How else should the cosmos and its redemption be depicted? The transcendental character of the divine epiphany cannot be fully articulated in human language.

The friends are humbled by God because they did not speak of Him '*the thing that is right*'. In view of Job's recantation this reproof is a necessary ingredient of the tale. But the fact that they did not speak 'the thing that is right' in Job's case does not mean that what they said is intrinsically false. It is clear that the author of Job makes the three comforters spokesmen for the older Wisdom, which he for his part has left behind. It is equally clear, in the light of the splendidly executed speeches of these friends, that the insights of the older tradition were never intended to be simply dismissed as invalid. We have seen how in the book of Proverbs an introductory section (chapters 1 to 9), written in the spirit of a new Wisdom theology, could be placed before the early collections of aphorisms that were redolent of an older view of things, without these older ideas being thereby invalidated. Similarly the Wisdom of Job's friends retains its relevance; it is merely qualified by a new and more profound understanding. In short, one can state that, according to the friends' Wisdom, reality by and large corresponds to truth; although the order of the world may sometimes remain hidden from men and the connection between conduct and condition remain obscured, God will once again reveal the truth to him who humbly submits to and accepts reality as he experiences it. Job on the other hand is led through his tribulations to postulate truth as lying beyond the reality of human life and to seek the transcendent salvation of personal communion with God. From the conception of an intrinsic piety emerges the transcendent salvation of the personal relationship.

It is particularly meaningful that Job's wretched lot should be terminated at the point when he prays for the friends who have become foes. Job has no *right* to be restored to health and happiness, as he himself admitted at the outset (2: 10), but God's *mercy* allows man to experience salvation in this life. Thereby the question of theodicy is completely reversed and ultimately too Satan's complaint is rejected.

Without doubt true human piety does only exist intrinsically, but unless he experiences God's redeeming mercy the weak man cannot endure on earth.

In the Jewish culture of the Persian period the way in which Wisdom assimilated a theological spirit and the notion of transcendence marked a development unparalleled in Antiquity. This development made it possible to retain the old tradition and yet to deepen it in an unprecedented manner. A truth emerged which was capable of withstanding even the challenges of the Hellenistic period – a truth which no one today would seriously claim to be able to fathom completely.[1]

---

[1] This chapter was completed in June 1975.

CHAPTER 10

JEWISH RELIGIOUS LIFE IN THE PERSIAN PERIOD

The 'Persian period' – roughly, the two centuries from Cyrus' capture of Babylon in 539 to Alexander's capture of Tyre in 332 B.C.E. – presents us with such variety in what may loosely be called 'Jewish religious life' that it raises the question, what is meant by 'Jewish'? The adjective derives from the noun 'Jews', *Yehudim* in Hebrew, *Yehudin* in Aramaic. For these terms there is on the one hand the territorial definition, 'residents of Judea', implied, for example, by the reference to the Persian 'governor of Judea' as 'governor of the Jews' (Ezra 6: 7, purportedly quoting a letter of Darius I); on the other hand, the ethnic 'descendants of Judeans', the members of the Persian garrison in Elephantine, settled there for well over a century,[1] still called themselves *Yehudin* although they had intermarried with Egyptians and worshipped a number of deities besides Yahweh.[2] A third definition is implied by the uses in Ezra 4: 12; 5: 4–5, which equate 'the Jews' with the exiles returned from Babylonia, excluding the population left in Palestine. These Jews worship only 'the God of heaven and earth' (that is, Yahweh), and explain their history in terms reminiscent of Deuteronomy (Ezra 5: 11). Other documents suggest other definitions – for example, Nehemiah's apology (notably 5: 1, 17) refers to 'the Jews' as if they were a privileged class in Jerusalem. If more texts were preserved we should probably have yet more variety. Did the worshippers of Yahweh in the province of Samaria call themselves 'Jews'? The 'Jews' of Elephantine got help from the Samaritans, but not from the priests of Jerusalem (*CAP* 32). Perhaps the publication of the Samaria papyri would help us.[3]

† This sign will be used throughout the chapter to indicate points on which additional material will be found in the terminal note.
[1] *CAP* 30. The priests of the temple of Yahweh in Elephantine, writing in 408 B.C.E., speak of themselves as Jews and claim that their temple was built 'in the days of the kings of Egypt', therefore at least before 525 B.C.E., and possibly long before.
[2] This could not be obscured by W. F. Albright, *Archaeology and the Religion of Israel* (4th edn., Baltimore, 1956), p. 174. Cf. B. Porten, *Archives from Elephantine* (Berkeley, 1968), pp. 160, 164, 173, 179, etc.
[3] The manuscripts have been awaiting publication by Professor F. M. Cross for twenty years. See *BA*, 26 (1963), 110–21.

Given this variety in the use of the term 'Jew' during the Persian period, we shall keep the bodies of evidence about them distinct, and see what each tells us. The evidence in the Old Testament will require discussion and subdivision, so we shall begin with the other, minor bodies, which are often of considerable value, especially as evidence of the extent and variety of our ignorance.

Good examples of this are the Hebrew names scattered through Mesopotamian documents.† Their increasing frequency during the late Babylonian and early Persian periods presumably reflects the arrival of Judean exiles in Babylonia and their gradual rise in social and economic life.[1] Professor Bickerman has calculated that in the published documents of the Murashu family – moneylenders of Nippur, whose archive runs from 455 to 403 – about eight per cent of the names are 'Jewish'.[2] Many persons with such names appear as relatives of persons with names expressing devotion to Mesopotamian deities. Presumably many of these relatives were also descendants of Judeans – that is, 'Jewish' in the ethnic sense of the term – and probably a number of other persons with pagan names were also of Judean background, since we know from Ezra and Nehemiah that some Judeans, even those devoted to the cult of Yahweh, bore pagan names (for example, Zerubbabel and Shesh-bazzar). On the other hand, an Egyptian named Eshor ('property of the god Horus') who married a Jewess in Elephantine appears in documents written after his marriage as 'Nathan'.[3] So at least a few of the persons with biblical or Hebraic names probably were of pagan ancestry.

In the ancient world anybody might appeal to any god for financial or political help, deliverance from sickness, the gift of a son, or whatever, and might name one of his children in honour of the god thought to have responded. Such a testimonial did not *prove* 'conversion' to exclusive worship of the god honoured, nor even 'adhesion' to some regular cult (though these might occur), but at the very least a name did testify to gratitude for a favour, and thus to a likelihood that, when another favour was needed, the beneficiary would again apply to the same deity.[4] 'Gratitude', said Voltaire, 'is the expectation of favours

---

[1] So already S. Daiches, *The Jews in Babylonia in the Time of Ezra and Nehemiah*, Jews' College Publications, no. 2 (London, 1910), p. 8.

[2] See chapter 10, 'The Babylonian Captivity', pp. 338–54.

[3] *CAP* 15, 20, 25. For the meaning of Eshor, I follow P. Grelot, *Documents araméens d'Egypte* (Paris, 1972), p. 470.

[4] For the distinction between 'conversion' and 'adhesion', see A. Nock, *Conversion* (Oxford, 1933), pp. 6ff.

yet to be received.' And closer adhesion to the benefactor's cult was possible.[1]

Such pious practices explain in part the gradual dissemination of names compounded with Yahweh through the pagan populations of Syria, Mesopotamia, and Egypt. Another partial explanation was intermarriage, and other factors (naming children for friends or benefactors etc.) can be imagined. Moreover, to name a child for a god gave no assurance that when the child grew up it would worship its namesake. Accordingly, when evaluating names we must allow for a number of cases in which the evidence is deceptive. Nevertheless we may suppose that the majority of names with biblical parallels, and particularly the majority of those compounded with forms of Yahweh (Yah, Yeho, Yahu, Ia, Iama etc.), were borne by Judeans and testified to their worship of their tribal god.

Beyond this they are not very informative. The majority of those in the Murashu documents are found chiefly in the post-exilic books of the Old Testament and argue for the connection of those books with their environment. The frequency of names compounded with Yahweh indicates the importance of his cult for the exiles and perhaps for their neighbours. Names like 'Yahweh built' (Baniyah), 'God built' (Banael), 'Yahweh redeemed' (Padiyah), 'Comforter' (Menahem) have been seen as references to the rebuilding of the Jerusalem Temple. These and the many variations of *hanan* ('He was gracious'), *barak* ('He blessed'), *tob* ('He is good') are thought to reflect the piety also expressed in the Psalms. Again the name Shabbetai which first appears in the exilic period has been thought to testify to the increasing importance of the Sabbath.[2] The notion is not improbable, but persons apparently pagan are also called Shabbetai and the name may have been originally neither Jewish nor connected with the Sabbath, but rather with the day of the full moon.[3]

'Shabbetai' is therefore a prime example of the primary problem that confronts us in attempting to use these names as evidence of religion,

---

[1] The question of the possibility of conversion is complicated; we shall return to it in discussing Ezra and Nehemiah.

[2] This and all the above from Daiches, *Jews*, pp. 32–5. Daiches' reference of Haggai to the time of the Exile overlooks the feminine, Haggith, wife of David, 2 Sam. 3: 4; 1 Kings 1: 5, 11; 2: 13; etc.; but the name becomes much more frequent in exilic times.

[3] For non-Jewish *Shabbetais* see Porten, *Archives*, p. 127; J. Teixidor, 'Bulletin d'épigraphie sémitique', *Syria*, 48 (1971), 462, no. 37. The history of the term is reviewed by A. Dupont-Sommer, 'Sabbat et parascève à Éléphantine', *MPAIBL* (1950), 82f; that of the week by J. Tigay, 'Notes on the Development of the Jewish week', *Eretz-Israel* 14 (Ginsberg Volume, 1978), pp. 111–21.

namely, when is a 'Jewish' name Jewish? The Semitic languages have
so many roots in common, and so many religious ideas and attitudes
were common throughout ancient near eastern culture[1] that names like
'(so and so) was gracious' can come from almost any part of the area.[2]
Similarly Haggai just means 'of the festival' (*Hag*). Consequently it
appears in Phoenician and Palmyrene, and probably was current in other
languages; it cannot be supposed 'Jewish' without other evidence.
Names derived from the proper names of gods, or compounded with
them, are better evidence, but we have seen the uncertainty of their
significance. They testify to somebody's reverence for the deities
specified, most often, doubtless, to that of the parents of the person who
bears the name, but beyond this, what?

Professor Bickerman has pointed out that in the Murashu tablets,
when pagan names and Yahwist names appear in the same family, the
pagan names are commonly those of the parents, the Yahwist names
those of the children. Hence he concludes that the century following
the fall of Jerusalem (586–486 B.C.E.) saw considerable adoption of
pagan cults by the Judean exiles, but after the rebuilding of the Temple
the advocates of the exclusive worship of Yahweh had more success and
many exiles abandoned the worship of pagan deities.[3] This is a possible
and plausible explanation of the facts; alternatively, we might suppose
that the parents who bore pagan names were not Judeans, and that their
imposition of Yahwist names on their children was due to the increasing
repute of Yahweh as a god of miraculous powers. (The rebuilding of
His Temple certainly helped his reputation; as 'Ezra' exclaimed – 7:
27 – it showed what He could do.)

That Yahweh's increasing fame also brought many exiles back to His
cult seems likely. But as to how they conceived and practised that cult,
the Babylonian documents tell us almost nothing and the possible
inferences from biblical material (most of it prior to the Persian
conquest) are to be found indicated in Bickerman's chapter (pp.
352–54). The best argument for thinking these names evidence of
conversion to the cult of Yahweh *alone* are the facts that: (1) from the
reports of events in Palestine we know that this form of Yahweh's cult
was influential in Persian court circles at this time, and (2) centuries later
we find in Babylonia a large community of exclusively Yahwist Jews,
but no comparable communities of Syrians, Phoenicians, Philistines and
so on, of whom equally numerous exiles had been deported to

[1] See M. Smith, 'The Common Theology of the Ancient Near East', *JBL*, 71 (1952),
135–47.

[2] Even names from uniquely north-west-Semitic roots may have been borne by
Canaanites, Edomites, Moabites, Ammonities, Phoenicians etc., as well as by
Israelites; they cannot be supposed peculiarly Judean.

[3] E. Bickerman, 'The Babylonian Captivity', below, chapter 13, pp. 338–54.

Mesopotamia. Presumably those who worshipped or came to worship Yahweh *alone* were preserved as a distinct social group, while those who worshipped other gods were assimilated into the surrounding society.[1]

A similar but fuller picture is given by the Persian-period Aramaic documents from Egypt. The largest group, the Elephantine papyri – more than two hundred pieces, of which 84 are recognizable documents – have already been mentioned.[2] Besides the papyri hundreds of ostraca were found at Elephantine, but only some four dozen have appeared.[3] Objects from other parts of Egypt – papyri, inscriptions, seals and so on[4] – contain occasional Yahwist or biblical names suggesting that persons we should call 'Jews', and who probably called themselves so, were found throughout the country.

As the Elephantine community is described in the chapters by Professors Bresciani and Porten,[5] we discuss only the evidence it affords for our special concern, the religious life of Judeans. 'Judean' here seems an ethnic rather than a religious designation: the same persons are called 'Judeans' in some documents and 'Arameans' in others;[6] probably 'Arameans' was a linguistic term for all speakers of Aramaic, as opposed to Egyptian, while 'Judean' was an ethnic (originally territorial) group within the larger class of 'Arameans'.[7] However, we begin by looking at the persons specifically said to be 'Judeans'.

The first is Mahsiyah son of Yedoniah ('Yah is my trust', son of 'Yah

[1] This has interesting corollaries: the north-Israelite exiles of the eighth century, who were assimilated, were therefore not worshippers of Yahweh alone; the exclusive form of the cult therefore became significant in the south, that is, Judea, and probably after the eighth century.

[2] Most are in *CAP*, of which nos. 1–59, 61, 76 (?), 79, 80, the Ahikar and Behistun papyri, and 98 fragments collected as nos. 62–69, come from Elephantine. Further, E. Kraeling, *The Brooklyn Museum Aramaic Papyri* (New Haven, 1953), contains 17 documents from Elephantine. N. Aimé-Giron, *Textes Araméens d'Égypte* (Cairo, 1931) prints 22 fragments which Kraeling, *Papyri* (p. 16, n. 59) thinks may contain some from Elephantine. Finally E. Bresciani, 'Papiri aramaici egiziani...di Padova', *RSO*, 35 (1960), 11–24 and plates I–V has published two Elephantine letters and a fragment of a third, bringing the totals to those given above.

[3] Most of the remainder – the collection of Clermont-Ganneau – has been in the hands of Professor A. Dupont-Sommer since about 1940, but remains unpublished. These figures do not include jar sealings, of which 83 were published by E. Sachau, *Aramäische Papyrus und Ostraka aus Elephantine* (Leipzig, 1911), pp. 244–57.

[4] A convenient translation of most of this material (including the Elephantine) is given in Grelot, *Documents*.† B. Porten and J. Greenfield, *Jews of Elephantine and Aramaeans of Syene* (Jerusalem, 1974) is a more recent presentation of the major groups of papyri, with English translations. See Porten's fine photographs in 'A New Look', *BA*, 42 (1979), 74–104.

[5] See pp. 354–68, and 368–96.

[6] See the alternations in Grelot, *Documents*, nos. 4, 43, 49; 32–38; 52, 53.

[7] So Porten, *Archives*, p. 33.

will judge').[1] A member of the garrison, he appears in 471 in real estate transactions, as the neighbour of two other 'Judeans' of the garrison, Qoniyah ('Yah is my owner'),[2] son of Zadok, and Yezaniah, son of Uriyah ('Yah will feed',[3] son of 'Yah is my light'); among their other neighbours were an Egyptian and a Khorazmian. They all went to court before Persian judges, but when Mahsiyah had to take an oath to satisfy the Khorazmian, he and his wife and son swore 'by Yaho, the god in the fortress of Elephantine'.[4] Mahsiyah had two sons, Yedoniah and Gemariah ('Yah completed'), and a daughter, Mivtahiyah ('my trust is Yah') who in 460 was the wife of Yezaniah, but some time before 440 married an Egyptian, Pia, son of Pahi (a nickname of Harpocrates). Their divorce was settled in 440[5] and in 435 she married another Egyptian, Eshor ('property of Horus'), son of Seha.[6] Apparently her devotion to Yahweh was not exclusive. When sued by her second husband she took an oath by the goddess Sati;[7] the oath would not have been deemed satisfactory unless there had been reason to believe she reverenced the goddess. However she named her sons (by Eshor) Yedoniah and Mahsiyah, after her father and grandfather, and they both became 'Judeans of the garrison'. In 420 we find them sued by two other 'Judeans', Menahem and Ananiah ('Yah answered'), the sons of Meshullam, son of Shelomam.[8] Their father Eshor appears in later documents as Nathan;[9] probably he changed his name. At marriage Mivtahiyah had not taken his practice of monogamy for granted; she had it required by the marriage contract, a caution common and therefore probably necessary.[10] Mivtahiyah died about 410 leaving, among other possessions, a slave named Petosiris ('given by Osiris').[11] Of her brothers, Yedoniah had a son called Shemaiah ('Yah heard') and Gemariah had three girls, one named for his sister Mivtahiyah, one called Meshullemet, and one Isiweri ('Great is Isis'). He also had a son

[1] The alternative explanation, 'Let Yah hear', Porten, *Archives*, p. 143, n. 115; Grelot, *Documents*, pp. 498f, overlooks the irregularity of spelling in these documents and the fact, noted by Porten, that the lists of Judeans 'include almost no Aramaic names and exhibit little Aramaic influence' (*Archives*, p. 147); accordingly Hebrew etymologies are to be preferred.†

[2] *CAP* 5, 'Yah is my creator', is possible, but less likely. There is no evidence that the Elephantine Jews thought of Yahweh as creator, while names identifying individuals as the property, slave etc., of one or another deity are common: Eshor, Pamut, Obadiah etc.

[3] Again the Hebrew etymology is preferable to the Aramaic, which would give 'Let Yah hear'.

[4] *CAP* 6; 464 B.C.E.; Grelot, *Documents*, no. 33. The following dates likewise come from Grelot.

[5] *CAP* 14.   [6] *CAP* 15.

[7] *CAP* 14, line 5.   [8] *CAP* 20.   [9] *CAP* 25, 28.

[10] *CAP* 15, cf. Kraeling, *Papyri*, no. 7.   [11] *CAP* 28.

whom he named for his grandfather Yedoniah, and who became one of the most important men in the Judean community; we shall come back to him.[1] The family seems to have had some gentile friends who appear as witnesses in its documents when Gentiles are involved,[2] but in documents concerning only Judeans all the witnesses commonly have names that seem Judean. This looks as if it were deliberate, not the result of random selection from a mixed circle of friends.

Another declared 'Judean' from whose family we have a dossier is Meshullam, son of Zakur,[3] a moneylender who in 449 B.C.E. married his Egyptian slave girl Tapamut ('property of the temple of the goddess Mut') to Ananiah, son of Azariah ('Yah aided'). Ananiah was an assistant (*lḥn*) in the temple of Yaho, but evidently not fussy about marriage with non-Judeans. Unlike Eshor, his wife kept her pagan name, but acquired her husband's Yahwist title, becoming '*lḥnh*' of the temple of Yaho.[4] He seems to have had two children by her, a boy called Pilti (probably short for Paltiyah, 'Yah delivered me') evidently born before their marriage,[5] and a girl, Yahoyishma ('Yaho hears'). Eventually in 427 B.C.E. Meshullam bequeathed freedom to Tapamut and Yahoyishma, specifying that they should be free 'to the sun' and probably referring to the sun as 'the god'.[6] Eventually Yahoyishma married an Ananiah, son of Haggai, son of Meshullam, son of one Besas who was named for the Egyptian god Bes.[7] This circle had many gentile friends, Medes and suchlike, who appear as witnesses to their legal documents,[8] but, again, principally to those involving Gentiles.

[1] I follow the reconstruction of the family by Porten, *Archives*, p. 238.

[2] *CAP* 5, 6, 14.

[3] Since it was customary to name boys for their grandfathers, Meshullam's father was presumably the 'Zekaryah' ('Yah remembered', for which Zakur may be short) 'son of Meshullam' who appears as a witness in slightly earlier documents; *CAP* 8–9.

[4] Kraeling, *Papyri*, no. 12.

[5] The marriage contract specified that Meshullam, who owned the child since he owned its mother, should not have the right to take him away; Kraeling, *Papyri*, no. 2.

[6] Kraeling, *Papyri*, no. 5. Addressing Tapamut, Meshullam speaks of Yahoyishma as 'your daughter whom you bore to me' perhaps because he was the owner of them both (but he freed only Yahoyishma, not her brother). As to the sun, I follow the interpretation of Kraeling and Rosenthal (as cited by Kraeling, *Papyri*) against that of Porten and Grelot. To the analogous material cited by Kraeling add F. Bömer, *Untersuchungen über die Religion der Sklaven in Griechenland und Rom. Teil II: Die sogenannte sakrale Freilassung*, (*Abhandlungen der Akademie der Wissenschaften Mainz, phil.-hist. klasse* 1960), no. 1, pp. 8off and 166f. But *mn tl' lšmš'* (in Kraeling's text, line 9) may be an expression meaning 'from the earth to the sun', that is, 'everything'. The land of Egypt is, in Egyptian, *kem(t)*, 'the dark', namely, the dark soil.

[7] Kraeling, *Papyri*, no. 7, 10, 12. On Besas see Grelot, *Documents*, p. 468.

[8] See the witnesses at the ends of Kraeling, *Papyri*, nos. 1, 3, 4, 5, 9, 10, 11; for the meanings of the names, see Grelot, *Documents*, pp. 460–502. Porten is often hasty in

These are the only Judean families of Elephantine whose histories are well documented. Although one was the family of an official of the temple of Yaho, the cult of Yaho plays little part in the documented history. It is the source of most of the names: Mahsiyah and his wife and son, when required to give an oath, swore by Yahweh; Ananiah worked at the temple of Yaho; both families lived near it (but so did Marduk, a priest of the gods Han (?) and Atti (?); Horus the gardener of the god Khnum; a couple of Egyptians; and two soldiers from the Caspian regions).[1] Both families intermarry with Egyptians, reverence other gods as well as Yahweh, and have gentile friends. If these letters were all that had been discovered we should take them as evidence of friendly assimilation which preceded absorption of the Judean community by the Egyptian environment.

But another collection of papers was found. These belonged to Mivtahiyah's nephew, Yedoniah the son of Gemariah. He was one of the leaders of the Jewish community (though given no official title) and these papers deal with community affairs. (Immediately after him in the community leaders stood 'the priests' of Yaho.)

Among the papers is a list, written in 419 (?), of the members of 'the Judean garrison' who 'gave money to Yaho the god, each 2 shekels of silver'; Yedoniah held the money.[2] 'The Judean garrison' was presumably an ethnic, not a religious, entity, and the need to list the names of those members who had contributed to Yaho suggests that some had not. Names of 121 persons were listed; about 95 names are preserved sufficiently so that one or other of their two elements (given and parental) can be discerned. At least 33 of the 95 were women – membership in 'the Judean garrison' was hereditary. About 40 of the 95 have some form of Yahweh as one of their components; presumably it was a component of many more; most have been abbreviated by omission of the divine element. Since the list is of those 'who gave money to Yaho', we may suppose the divine element was usually Yaho. But a number of other gods appear. Accepting Porten's restorations (which minimize this) we find among the donors Pamut ('property of

supposing that 'Yahweh' is to be supplied whenever a name implies relationship to a deity but does not specify which one. See above, pp. 221f.

[1] Porten, *Archives*, pp. 94f following Kraeling, *Papyri*, p. 78, n. 11. Kraeling's confidence that a man with a Babylonian name could not (in the Persian period!) have been a priest of Egyptian gods is surprising.

[2] *CAP*, 22, re-edited from photographs by Porten, *Archives*, pp. 320ff. I follow Porten. Since Yedoniah is in charge, the date, 'the fifth year', is that either of Darius II (419) or of Artaxerxes II (400). That the 'Passover Papyrus' (*CAP* 21) was written in 419 and addressed to Yedoniah and his associates suggests some connection between it and this list. 121 is Porten's figure, p. 162.†

Mut') and Bagaphernes, and among their parents persons with names expressing devotion to Eshem,† Herem, Bethel, Hadad, Neith ('of Sais'), Thoth ('the weigher of souls'), Sati (?), Horus, and Anath. An unsolved riddle is the absence of components with '*el*, frequent in the Old Testament. (If only we had a list of the names of those who did not contribute!) Also unknown is the purpose of the contribution; attempts to associate it with political events or religious festivals are ingenious but inconclusive.

Certain, however, is the names' account of the role of Yahweh in the minds of his worshippers: He is great and lofty, their splendour and their king; He is also dew (fertility) and mercy; and He is their trust, He is 'with' them. He hears, remembers, intervenes, helps, bestows, restores, shelters, judges, saves, blesses and completes. Therefore they also give names that ask 'Who is like Yah?', and that urge their children to turn to Yah, look to Him, and praise Him. Of the abbreviated names that were almost certainly Yahwist, the commonest declare that He answered, comforted, rewarded and gave. This vocabulary is that of many Psalms. No doubt similar psalms were sung in the Elephantine temple of Yaho and similar personal piety, centred on hopes of help and protection, was an important element of the religion. Although most names are Hebrew, while the documents are Aramaic, we should not think the names meaningless family hand-me-downs, as are Isidore and John at present. More likely they are evidence that Hebrew was used in the temple cult. Some fifteen years earlier Nehemiah complained of the use of Aramaic ('Ashdodite') in Jerusalem,[1] although Hebrew was used in the Temple.

Most surprising, although the list reflects such Yahwist piety, and the heading says the money was given 'to Yaho', a postscript says that a little over a third of it was for Yaho, a little over a third for Anathbethel, and a little less than a third for Eshembethel.[2] Anath, Eshem and Bethel are gods individually attested by references along the Palestine–Syrian coast; Anathbethel may appear in an Assyrian treaty,[3] but almost nothing is known of their cults, nor of how they were related to the Elephantine cult of Yaho.

The centre of Yaho's cult was his temple – probably, like most temples, located in a walled sacred area. The Judeans claimed that the complex – including a building with stone pillars, a cedarwood roof (therefore one spanning a room of considerable size; that was what

---

[1] Neh. 13: 23f, in the 430s.
[2] Porten, *Archives*, p. 326. The figures are, roughly, of 318 shekels, 126 for Yaho, 120 for Anathbethel, and 70 for Eshembethel.
[3] R. Borger, 'Anath-Bethel', *VT*, 7 (1957), 102ff; cf. *ANET Supplement* p. {534}.

necessitated the expensive timber), bronze hinges, gold and silver basins etc. – was built before the Persian conquest of 525 (the text suggests well before) and, unlike Egyptian temples, was spared by the Persians when they took the country.[1] (The Persians reverenced Yahweh as 'the God of the heavens' and this title is also used for him by Judeans, perhaps especially when writing to outsiders.[2]) Porten calculated the size of the temple enclosure as about 27 × 9 metres.[3] Within it, probably in front of the temple building, was at least one altar, whence the whole could be referred to as 'the altar house',[4] as well as 'the temple of Yaho',[5] and 'the house of Yaho'[6] – he is emphatically 'the god who dwells in the fortress of Elephantine'.[7] He was worshipped principally by sacrifice; we hear of grain offerings,[8] incense,[9] whole burnt offerings (of animals),[10] and other animal sacrifices.[11] However, when the temple was destroyed in 411, 'Yedoniah and his associates, the priests in Elephantine', in a petition to have it rebuilt, assured the Persian governor of Judea[12] that if he secured its rebuilding he would have more merit before Yaho than a man who brought a thousand talents' worth of holocausts and other animal sacrifices.[13] The animal sacrifices seem to have been a sore point, for when Yedoniah and his companions tried to bribe somebody to get a rebuilding permit they made a written undertaking that 'sheep, ox, and goat are not to be offered' in the restored temple, 'but incense, grain offering [and...only (?)]',[14] and when the governors of Judea and Samaria finally instructed somebody to ask the satrap of Egypt, in their name, to allow the rebuilding, they reportedly specified that grain offering and incense were to be offered on the altar, but said nothing of animal sacrifice.[15] From these facts it has been plausibly conjectured that the animal sacrifices (especially of

[1] *CAP* 30, 31, 32.

[2] Persian usage, *CAP* 32 (also exemplified in Ezra 1 : 2; 5 : 12; 6 : 9f; 7: 21, 23); Judeans to outsiders, *CAP* 30, 31; Judeans to each other, *CAP* 38, 40.

[3] *Archives*, p. 110. 1 cubit = 0.45 metre.

[4] *CAP* 32.

[5] The common expression, *CAP* 13, 25, 30, 31, 33 etc. Kraeling, *Papyri*, no. 12.

[6] N. Aimé-Giron, 'Trois ostraca araméens d'Elephantine,' *ASAE*, 26 (1926), 27f; A Dupont-Sommer, "Maison de Yahve" et vêtements sacrés a Elephantine', *JA*, 235 (1946–47), 80–7 first over-restores the text and then over-interprets it. His 'results' are uncritically repeated by Grelot, *Documents*, no. 90.

[7] Kraeling, *Papyri*, no. 12, cf. nos. 2, 4, 10; *CAP* 6.

[8] *CAP* 27 (text uncertain), 30.   [9] *CAP* 30, 31.

[10] *CAP* 30, 31.   [11] *CAP* 30, 31.

[12] Not only was his name Persian, but a tradition reported by Josephus remembered him as an alien not permitted to enter the temple, *Ant.* XI.297–301.

[13] *CAP* 30, 31.   [14] *CAP* 33.

[15] *CAP* 32.

sheep) were offensive to the Egyptian priests of Khnum, a ram god worshipped in the main Egyptian temple on Elephantine. Khnum's priests are said to have bribed the Persian commandant of southern Egypt to have the temple of Yaho destroyed by Egyptian and other troops under Persian command.[1] At all events it is clear that the Judeans of Elephantine did not think animal sacrifice essential for the cult of Yaho, and thought it worthwhile to have a temple even if nothing but grain and incense could be offered there. The merit of contributing to the cult was many times that of sacrifice.

Sacrifice was presumably accompanied and, when necessary, replaced by prayers. The petitioners have assured us that the prayers of the Judeans can secure Yaho's favour for their benefactors. They also report with pride that their prayers, reinforced by fasting, abstaining from wine, oil, and sex, and wearing sackcloth, persuaded 'Yaho the Lord of the heavens' to destroy their enemies.[2] Blessing may be a particular form of prayer. These writers never pray that the recipients may be blessed 'by Yaho' alone.[3] Once a certain Gedal (short for Gedaliah, 'Yahweh is great'?) writing to Micah ('who is like Yah?') began 'I bless you by Yaho and Hn(m)';[4] more often writers asked the blessing of 'the god of the heavens', without identifying him as Yahweh;[5] most often they simply expressed a hope that the recipient would be blessed by 'the gods' (unspecified plural).[6] Prayer in the temple was doubtless accompanied by prostration; 'the place of prostration', so holy that an oath by it might carry conviction, was probably the temple itself.[7] Pious writers began their letters by praying that the temple might be at peace, as did other pious Arameans for the temples of Nabu, Banit, Bethel, and the Queen of the Heavens (Anath?), all near Elephantine,[8] and the author of Ps. 122 for the Temple of Yahweh in Jerusalem.

We have seen that persons called 'Judeans' swore by Yahweh, but also by other gods. Similar oaths are sworn by other persons with Yahwist or biblical names. Malkiyah ('My king is Yah') undertook to

---

[1] *CAP* 30, 31.

[2] *CAP* 30, 31.

[3] In the prayer for blessing 'by Yaho the god' of Padua papyrus no. 1, the words 'by Yaho the god' have been supplied by editorial conjecture; see E. Bresciani, 'Padova', 18.

[4] I.e. 'Khnum'? Grelot, *Documents*, no. 87.

[5] *CAP* 30, 31, 38.

[6] Used with verbs in the plural. The rendering 'God', in Porten and Greenfield, *Jews* is indefensible. *CAP* 21, 37 (?), 56; Kraeling, *Papyri*, no. 13. (Clermont-Ganneau ostracon no. 277, Grelot, *Documents*, no. 88, cannot safely be supposed Judean).

[7] So *CAP* 44.

[8] Bresciani, 'Padova', no. 1; 'Le lettere aramaiche di Hermopoli', *Memorie*, Accademia Nazionale dei Lincei, Scienze morali VIII.XII.5 ; *Atti*, 363 (1966), nos. I–IV.

swear (?) 'by Herembethel the god among the four avengers' (whoever they were); Menahem, son of Shallum swore by the Place of Prostration and by Anathyahu, and possibly 'by Herem the god'.[1] On the other hand an unnamed writer in a private letter swears twice that, 'as sure as Yaho lives' he will punish the recipient unless his directions are followed.[2]

Finally religious festivals: a number of ostraca have been read as referring to the Sabbath and probably do so,[3] but are not clear enough to tell us how the day was observed. Another, referring to a cult banquet, may have nothing to do with Judeans.[4] Yet another refers to the Passover (*psḥ*),[5] but without significant context. Another mentions bread that may be eaten 'until tomorrow evening' or 'until tomorrow, the day of preparation' (for a festival).[6] If the former, the bread may have come from a sacrifice of which the elements had to be consumed within two days (days ended at sunset);[7] if the latter, it was probably leavened bread, use of which would be prohibited during the Passover and the following Feast of Unleavened Bread. *Non liquet.* Even more puzzling is an ostracon, sent to one Hoshayah ('Yah saved'), evidently a steward or the like in the household of the writer, who tells him how 'the children' are to be taken care of and then adds, 'Let me know when you will make the Passover',[8] as if the date were a matter to be decided by the person in charge of a household. Many ingenious legal hypotheses have been proposed to 'explain' (away) this evidence,[9] but even more have been called forth by the famous 'Passover Papyrus',[10]

---

[1] *CAP* 7 and 44. I accept the restoration, but not the translation, of Porten and Greenfield, *Jews*, pp. 122f. For another oath 'by Yaho the god' see *CAP* 45.

[2] A. Dupont-Sommer, 'L'ostracon araméen du Sabbat', *Semitica*, 2 (1949), 29–39.

[3] A. Dupont-Sommer, 'L'ostracon' and again in *MPAIBL* (1950), 67–88; Grelot, *Documents*, no. 91. Contrast Porten, *Archives*, p. 126. Clermont-Ganneau ostracon no. 44, published by A. Dupont-Sommer, 'Un ostracon araméen inédit', in *Hebrew and Semitic Studies presented to G. Driver* (Oxford, 1963), pp. 53–8; Grelot, *Documents*, no. 99.

[4] Grelot, *Documents*, no. 92, with bibliography.

[5] M. Lidzbarski, *Ephemeris füer semitische Epigraphik* (Giessen, 1902–1915), vol. II, pp. 229ff; Grelot, *Documents*, no. 93.

[6] Grelot, *Documents*, no. 95, with bibliography; the ambiguous word '*rwḥḥ* occurs also in Clermont-Ganneau ostracon no. 204 in a context that does nothing to define it more closely.

[7] Cf. Lev. 7: 16f, where the law speaks only of the flesh; 19: 5ff, where the law seems to apply to all elements of the sacrifice.

[8] Grelot, *Documents*, no. 94, with bibliography.

[9] For a sample see Porten, *Archives*, pp. 131f.

[10] Earlier publications are replaced by the studies of Porten, *Archives*, pp. 311ff and pl. 9, and Grelot, *Documents*, pp. 95ff.

a note written in 419 from one Hananiah ('Yah gave [him] graciously') a secretary of Arsames, the Persian satrap of Egypt, to 'my brothers' Yedoniah and the Judean garrison, tipping them off that an order 'from King Darius has been sent to Arsames'. Unfortunately the summary of the order is lost. The text resumes with Hananiah's advice as to what should be done in consequence: 'So now count four...and from day 15 to day 21...be pure and act carefully...do not (?) drink, and nothing fermented...sunset, to the twenty-first of Nisan...lock up in your chambers and seal between the days...'.

Reconstructions of this text must be conjectural, the more so because there is no telling how much has been lost at the end of each line. Most reconstructions and interpretations have supposed that the preserved text reported the gist of Darius' commands, but this is almost certainly false. We have only fragments of Hananiah's advice about what the Judeans should do in the situation resulting from the king's evidently laconic order. Hananiah seems to be advising them to keep the Feast of Unleavened Bread (*nothing* is said of Passover), but if 'lock up in your chambers and seal' refers to leaven, his advice flatly contradicts the command in Exodus 12:19. 'For seven days leaven shall not be found *in your dwellings.*'[1] The problems are to imagine and explain a royal command that would make a Judean secretary of the satrap of Egypt, when leaking it to his 'brothers', add such advice. Had they not kept the Feast of Unleavened Bread before, and did they not know how? Perhaps not. It may be that the royal command was simply 'Judeans must follow the rules of the Jerusalem Temple'. If such an order would soon arrive in the hands of an inspector sent by the satrap, the community at Elephantine might need a quick warning to get itself into shape, and advice about the observances necessary for the forthcoming feast of the Jerusalem calendar. As to the details, perhaps Hananiah just got them wrong. He certainly was not a member of the Yahweh-alone sect that had recently gained control of Jerusalem and had much influence in the Persian court[2] – on the contrary, he began his letter with a prayer that 'the gods' (plural) would take care of his brothers. He may have been cynical. There was no need for them to get rid of all their leaven. If they just locked it up out of sight and put on a show of purity, the inspector would go on his way and they could return to

---

[1] Cf. Exod. 13: 7; Deut. 16: 4. Rabbinic legal fictions to avoid literal observance of these commandments are of course irrelevant.

[2] On this see below and, for fuller treatment, M. Smith, *Palestinian Parties and Politics* (New York, 1971), pp. 126–47, 170–2. Hananiah's friendship for the Elephantine polytheists argues that he was not the brother of Nehemiah, the paladin of the Yahweh-alone party.

theirs. As to why the king should have sent such an order, various conjectures are possible but none can be confirmed.

Hananiah's concern for his 'brethren' appears again in a hasty letter to 'Yedoniah, Uriah, and the priests of the god Yaho', from a Yahwist who had been jailed as a jewel thief by the Persian commandant but released by the intervention of two Egyptians Seho and Hor (Horus), servants of 'Anani'.[1] His benefactors were now coming to Elephantine and he was anxious that they should be generously treated, not only for his sake, but also because 'Khnum has been against us as long as Hananiah has been in Egypt',...'and whatever you do for Hor you do for yourselves (?); Hor is the servant of Hananiah'. This might be dismissed as bluff if the Judean community did not testify that a few years later, in 411, the priests of Khnum did succeed in having the temple of Yaho destroyed.[2] In the correspondence consequent on that destruction, the appeals of the Elephantine community to 'Jehoḥanan the High Priest and his colleagues the priests' of Jerusalem and 'the nobles of the Jews' as well as to the governors of Judea and Samaria,[3] we see further expressions of the same ethnic feeling which appears in the letter of Hananiah to his 'brothers' – the trust (which might be disappointed) in brotherhood and the awareness of membership in a far-reaching community of which Judea was the source and the Temple of Jerusalem in some sense the centre. (Notice that no appeal was sent to the priests or nobles of Samaria!) This is the unexpected conclusion to the positive evidence from Elephantine as to Jewish religious life in the Persian period.

The negative evidence would be equally impressive if only we could be sure that what has not been found never existed in the community – an assumption often discredited in similar cases. In this case we have no evidence from Elephantine of any biblical books, nor of books that might be forerunners of our biblical books. Though most of the papyri are legal documents, 'the law of Yaho' is never mentioned. When Judeans go to law with each other they do so before Persian judges. There is no prophecy and no trace of any prophet. (Since the tradition of the Psalms is presupposed by the nomenclature, we observe its potential independence from the prophetic tradition.) There is no sign of a synagogue. Wisdom literature is represented by the *Words of Ahikar*, an Assyrian sage whose god was Shamash, the sun (whom some Judeans may have revered). But did the Ahikar manuscript belong to a Judean?

---

[1] *CAP* 38. 'Anani' is probably a mis-spelled abbreviation of Hananiah.
[2] *CAP* 30, 31.
[3] *CAP* 30, 31.

Persian religion is represented by a copy of the Behistun inscription of Darius I, but this may have been issued by the government to all garrisons. Even so the remains of these texts suggest that some members of the community read literature as well as letters and legal documents, and this makes the total absence of Israelite literature more surprising, especially when we compare Elephantine with the Jerusalem of its time, which we know almost exclusively from its literary fecundity. What of Judaism elswhere? How much was like that of Elephantine; how much like that of Jerusalem?

From the rest of Egypt we have little information – some names that might, but might not, belong to Judeans, a few compounded with Yahweh, most of these in contexts irrelevant to religion. One exception is Adyah ('Yah adorned') whose daughter, in 482 B.C.E. was given a proper burial in Saqqara with a gravestone representing her entry before Osiris.[1] Another stela from Saqqara, of the mid fourth century B.C.E, has lost most of its pictures but still shows mourners, an offering, and inscription: 'Blessed be Petesis ['gift of Isis'] son of Yh'...'. After completion of the name, this text would normally have concluded 'before the god Osiris'.[2] A scaraboid carnelian from Egypt shows a uraeus, emblem of the sun god, with an ankh (?) and the inscription '(this belongs) to Yrm (son of) Zimriyahu' ('Yah is my song').[3]† Such occasional pieces tell us nothing of general conditions, but they are all we have and, because of the spotty preservation of remains from the period, even the absence of other material cannot be used as evidence.

A third body of evidence is that provided by Palestinian archeology. Remains of the Persian period are most frequent along the coast and in the southern foothills, poorest in the hill country of Judea.[4] Those in Judea may be supposed to come from Judeans, but need not. There were always some aliens in the territory – if not the Persian governor, who was often a Jew, at least persons in his staff and garrison, agents of Persian nobles or officials who had financial interests in the area,

---

[1] *KAI* 267, with bibliography.

[2] N. Aimé-Giron, 'Adversaria Semitica', *BIFAO*, 38 (1939), 41–3. Aimé-Giron recognized the possibility that the broken name had been Yahwist, for instance, Yahor, but inclined, for no stated reason, to think it Egyptian.

[3] Ashmolean, N. 443. Lidzbarski, *Ephemeris*, vol. i, pp. 11f.

[4] E. Stern, *The Material Culture of Palestine in the Persian Period, Part i* (Jerusalem, 1968), p. vii. This is the English summary of Stern's dissertation. The dissertation has been published in Hebrew as *Hattarbut heḥomrit shel Ereṣ Yisra'el bitequfah happarsit* (Jerusalem, 1973). When possible, I cite the English as more widely readable.

merchants, pilgrims to Jerusalem and so on.[1] Most Persian-period
remains outside Judea presumably did not come from Judeans, but
some probably did, so the possibility can rarely be ruled out. Moreover,
many may have come from worshippers of Yahweh, and, as remarked
above (pp. 220f), such worshippers may have been called 'Judeans'
(*Yehudim*, that is, 'Jews') because of their religious affiliation. Given the
Elephantine evidence, we cannot be certain that apparently pagan
material in Palestine may not have come from syncretistic worshippers
of Yahweh. And since 'biblical' names might be carried by pagans, we
cannot be certain that such names on archeological material refer to
Jews.

How, then, can we hope to extract information about 'Judaism' from
the archeological material? We might locate temples of Yahweh and see
what they yield, or examine all objects that show traces of the cult of
Yahweh, or compare the finds from Judea with those from the rest of
the country – if marked differences are observable, these might provide
indications of religious practices.

Of these possible methods, the first yields little evidence. The 'solar
shrine' at Lachish may have been a temple of Yahweh and may date
from the Persian period; otherwise no temple of Yahweh from this
period has been recognized.[2] Archeologists have not been looking for
such temples (they usually find what they look for). Remains of the
Persian period are poor (they were exposed both to erosion and to
disturbance by Hellenistic and Roman building). Moreover, Yahweh's
cult was mainly out of doors, 'on every high hill, and under every green
tree' as biblical texts reiterate.[3] Archeological evidence has been
interpreted as indicating that the out-of-doors cult on the high place
at Dan continued until Hellenistic times.[4] Presumably the cult at
Gerizim did so; the building of a temple there in the Hellenistic period
was remembered as an innovation.[5] Evidence has been found for
continuation of Israelite cults without temples at Carmel, Hermon,

---

[1] See M. Bailey, 'Levitical Legend from the Persian Period', *JBL*, 46 (1927), 132–8;
cf. the evidence for pilgrimage at this time to Phoenician shrines, F. Abel, *Histoire
de la Palestine* (2 vols; Paris, 1952), vol. 1, p. 6 end. Further, S. Safrai, *Pilgrimage in
the Time of the Second Temple* (Jerusalem, 1965; in Hebrew).

[2] On the Lachish temple, see below; on the remains of other Palestinian temples of
the Persian period see Stern, *Hattarbut*, pp. 64ff. The other temples known from
remains do not seem to have been connected with the cult of Yahweh.

[3] 1 Kings 14: 23; 2 Kings 16: 4; 17: 10f; Jer. 2: 20; 3: 6; Ezek. 20: 28.

[4] *Ḥadashot 'Arkiologi'ot*, 31–32 (1969), p. 2.

[5] Josephus, *Ant.* xi.324. The temple on Gerizim seems, in fact, to have been built early
in the Hellenistic period; see R. Bull, 'The Excavations of Tell er-Ras', *BA*, 31 (1968),
70f.

Tabor, and Mambre (outside Hebron),[1] at high places outside Jerusalem etc.[2] Such worship was probably supported by primitive tradition. Part of the Israelite population remained rural and regarded cities and temples with hostility. We hear of pre-exilic and post-exilic sects whose members would not live in built houses,[3] and a series of biblical passages, continuing into the New Testament, either attacks temples as unworthy to house God,[4] or defends them from such attack.[5]

Yet there may have been temples of Yahweh in Persian Palestine. The 'solar shrine' at Lachish may have been – or been modelled on one of them.[6] Its resemblance to the temple at Arad is striking.[7] The cult at this temple must have been a matter of private devotions or the worship of small groups. The entire building measured about 27 × 17 metres, and the interior courtyard, the only place where a body of worshippers could assemble, was about 12 × 15⅓ metres. At the west side of this court, and somewhat south of centre, five steps led up to a broad, narrow antechamber, roughly 4 × 12 metres, and in the west wall of this, opposite the entrance, three steps led up to a tiny cella, about 3 × 3½ metres.[8] Doorways at the end of the antechamber led to storerooms flanking the cella and the north wall, a row of small storerooms and vestibules lined the east wall, behind the court. The smaller rooms were roofed, the court was not.

For the man in the court the focal object was probably a limestone altar, over thirty centimetres square and perhaps a metre high, that stood at the top of the steps in the centre of the entrance to the antechamber. It was decorated with bas-reliefs – one side showed a man, probably a

---

[1] Carmel, Hermon, and Tabor: R. de Vaux, *Ancient Israel*, tr. J. McHugh (London, 1961), p. 280; Mambre: ibid., pp. 292f; M. Smith, 'On the Wine God in Palestine', – *Salo Wittmayer Baron Jubilee Volume* (Jerusalem, 1975 title page '1974', but see corrigenda – 3 vols.), vol. 2, pp. 815–29.

[2] De Vaux, *Israel*, p. 285.

[3] Jer. 35: 7–10; Ascension of Isaiah 2: 10ff; Heb. 11: 36ff.

[4] 2 Sam. 7: 5–7; 1 Kings 8: 27; Isa. 66: 1; 2 Chron. 2: 5; 6: 18; Acts 7: 47–51; 17: 24; Mark 14: 58 and parallels; Rev. 21: 22.

[5] 2 Sam. 7: 13; 1 Kings 8: 10–21; Ps. 132.

[6] In the primary publication O. Tufnell, *Lachish III* (Oxford, 1953, 2 vols.), vol. 1, pp. 141ff; vol. 2, plate 121, hesitated between Persian and Hellenistic date. Stern, *Hattarbut*, pp. 65ff, dated it to the Persian period, by the associated artifacts. Y. Aharoni has argued strongly for a Hellenistic date, *Investigations at Lachish*...V, (Tel Aviv, 1975), pp. 3ff. However he goes on to argue that the many incense altars found at Lachish must have come from a Persian-period temple, and that this temple was the neighbouring building R/Q/S 15–16 (Tufnell) = 10 Aharoni of which the plan is 'virtually identical' to that of the 'solar shrine' (p. 9).

[7] And far closer than that of any of the temples adduced by Stern, *Hattarbut*, 67.

[8] These calculations are based on the plan in Aharoni, *Lachish V*, plate 56.

worshipper, with raised arms; another, the upright palm of a gigantic hand, most likely 'the hand of the Lord'. Worshipper and palm presumably symbolized prayer and answer. The remaining faces are worn beyond decipherment.[1] In the top was a shallow depression that may have served for incense or vegetable offerings, hardly for animal sacrifices, for which there seems to have been no provision. In the south-east corner of the antechamber was a small incense altar; nine more, each about eight centimetres square by twenty centimetres high, stood on a bench in the north storeroom (reserves for festivals?). In the centre of the entrance to the cella was a drain, suggesting libations; in the south wall of the cella, a small recess near which was another drain. In this drain was an undescribed fragment of a pottery figurine, and on the floor a small hawk amulet of the god Horus.[2] Since this was lost in the cella it was probably worn by the god's priest or priestess. The head of another figurine, found on the floor of the court, is undescribed.[3] A third figurine, of a horseman, in the antechamber, was found in accumulated rubbish almost 50 centimetres above the floor and may be intrusive.[4] A few bowls, jugs, dippers, strainers, storage jars and so on indicate that the cult involved food and especially liquids.

Since temples of Yahweh are rare and dubious, few objects can be connected with his cult unless they carry some form of his name or are clearly related to others that do so. The largest class of such objects is that of seals and seal impressions showing names compounded with Yahweh. These are tiny, light things that easily get into strata to which they did not originally belong, so even those from excavations may have been misdated, and many are chance finds, often of uncertain provenance. Those that have been assigned to the Persian period[5] all, so far as is known, come from Judea and the neighbouring foothills and plains.[6] Only three carry names of gods other than Yahweh (two

---

[1] Tufnell, *Lachish III*, vol. 2, pl. 42, nos. 8 and 9.

[2] Described as a 'schist hawk', Tufnell, *Lachish III*, vol. 1, p. 143, and vol. 2, pl. 36, no. 56. Both were overlooked in Aharoni's report, *Lachish V*, p. 5.

[3] Tufnell, *Lachish III*, vol. 1, p. 144.

[4] Ibid.

[5] See the lists in D. Diringer, *Le iscrizioni antico-ebraiche palestinesi* (*Pubblicazioni della R. U. degli Studi di Firenze, Facoltà di Lett. e Filos.* 3rd series, 2; Florence, 1934), pp. 111–261; S. Moscati, *L'Epigrafia ebraica antica 1935–1950* (*BibOr*, no. 15, Rome, 1951), and F. Vattioni, 'I sigilli ebraici', *Bib*, 50 (1969), 357–88, and 'I sigilli ebraici II,' *Augustinianum*, 11 (1971), 446–54. All these give bibliographies of the objects. Add the monograph of N. Avigad, *Bullae and Seals from a Post-Exilic Judean Archive* (*Qedem*, no. 4, Jerusalem, 1976).

[6] Finds are recorded at Gezer, Jericho (?), Jerusalem and its suburbs, Ramat Rahel, and Tells el-Judeideh, en-Nasbeh, es-Safi, Qasile and Sandahanna. The *Yh* and *Yhw* sealings from Jericho reported by Lidzbarski, *Ephemeris*, vol. III, p. 45 are to be read

of Horus, one of Shamash, but all three are of uncertain provenance and two of dubious interpretation).[1] Only one carries a picture of living creatures (a bearded man holding up some object, perhaps a rhyton).[2] The owner of this seal, Asaniyahu ('Yahweh made me') calls himself 'officer of the king'; his office and the peculiarity of his seal may be connected.

This evidence suggests that during the Persian period the Palestinian cult of Yahweh, if not absolutely limited to Judea and vicinity,[3] was far more frequent there than elsewhere and was commonly not associated with the cults of other gods, nor with images. Though the seals and sealings give us only about twenty Yahwist names, these, so far as they go, present substantially the same picture of self-interested devotion as do those of Egypt and Babylonia. Yahweh makes, hears, helps, fosters (?), adorns, holds, visits, gives children, exalts and completes; men are His creatures and should be His servants; He is their brother (protector) and their light. Here the notion of Yahweh as the maker of men (Maaseyah, Asaniyahu)[4] which did not appear in the Egyptian texts, may reflect post-exilic theological development. As in Egypt, the great majority of names are based on Hebrew roots, not Aramaic, and suggest that Hebrew continued to be used in the cult.

A particularly important class of seals were the dies used in striking coins. We have a fair number of coins carrying the inscriptions *Yehud* or *Yehudah* – the Aramaic or Hebrew name of the province of Judea – and another lot inscribed 'Yehezqiyah the governor' or simply 'Yeh-

by analogy with other stamps as abbreviations or imperfect impressions of *Yhwd*, i.e. 'Judea.' The reading of the *Yh'zr* stamp Lidzbarski reported from Jericho (ibid.) was formerly doubted but has since been supported by the discovery of impressions of other seals bearing the same name, Y. Aharoni, 'Excavations at Ramat Rahel', *BA*, 24 (1961), 110; 'Ramat Rahel', *RB*, 70 (1963), 573.

[1] *Horus*: '[Property] of Obadiah (son of) Sheharhor', Schlumberger collection, Lidzbarski, *Ephemeris*, vol. II, pp. 70f = Diringer, *Iscrizioni*, Sigilli, no. 35; and '[Property] of Sheharhor son of Zephaniah', British Museum, Diringer, *Iscrizioni*, Sigilli no. 39. *Sheharhor* probably means either 'Seek Horus', or 'Horus [is like] dawn', but the reference to the god was rejected by Lidzbarski as 'zu krass heidnisch' and by Diringer as unknown to Hebrew; both objections are answered by the Elephantine documents. 'Obadiah' and 'Zephaniah' are 'Servant of Yahweh' and 'Yahweh hid/protected [him]'. *Shamash*: '[Property] of Yehoyishmah, daughter of Shawashsarusur', de Clercq collection; see N. Avigad, 'Seals of Exiles', *IEJ*, 15 (1965), 228f; *Shawash* is Shamash.

[2] Moscati, *Epigrafia Sigilli*, no. 2. Photograph and discussion in Stern, *Hattarbut*, p. 208. The seal was found at Tell Qasile (near Tel Aviv).

[3] To suppose such limitation would require too much reliance on an argument from silence.

[4] *Ma'aseyah*, Jerusalem: N. Avigad, 'A Group of Hebrew Seals' (in Hebrew), *Eretz-Israel*, 9 (1969), Hebrew section, p. 4.

ezqiyah' ('Yahweh will strengthen [him]').[1] He has been plausibly identified with the High Priest 'Ezechias' placed by Josephus at the time of Ptolemy I's conquest[2] which probably occurred about the end of his career. Significantly, he had coined as 'Governor', not as 'High Priest', and had at first put on his coins debased forms of monetary symbols fashionable in his time (the facing head of Syracusan coins, the owl of Athens), later a male head (Alexander?; Antigonus I?) and the protome of a winged feline.[3] After his time the coins of Ptolemaic Judea showed the Ptolemies and their eagles, as the Ptolemies ordered. Before his time the coins of the governors had shown the Persian king, the Athenian owl, and floral motifs. A yet earlier series had shown Athena as well as her owl, and some unrecognizably botched birds, animals, and heads. The earliest of all, the famous British Museum drachma of about 370 B.C.E.,[4] had shown on one side a bearded male head in a Corinthian helmet, on the other a god in a Greek chiton, seated on a winged wheel, holding an Egyptian falcon on his outstretched hand, and confronted by a large mask of a satyr. The inscription on this side was at first read YHW (*Yaho* = Yahweh) instead of YHD, so the figure was supposed a representation of Yahweh and was much discussed. The upshot of the discussion[5] seems to be that, although the reading 'Judea' is correct,[6] and *assurance* as to further interpretation is unjustified, the figure *may*, in fact, have been intended as a representation of Yahweh. The whole composition seems an *ad hoc* creation; it was not taken from any known coins.[7] The winged wheel could reflect notions of Yahweh's chariot; they had been developing in Ezekiel's time (1: 5–24, n. 3 on

---

[1] The following account of the coinage summarizes the masterly analysis by L. Mildenberg, 'Yehud', in *Greek Numismatics and Archaeology* (Festschrift for Margaret Thompson), edd. O. Mørkholm and N. Waggoner (Wetteren, 1979), pp. 183–96 and plates 21 and 22.

[2] A. Kindler, 'Silver Coins Bearing the Name of Judea', *IEJ*, 24 (1974), 73ff, on Josephus, *Contra Apionem*, 1, 187.

[3] This is puzzling; I have not found the same figure elsewhere on coins, and for these coins it is unusually well cut. Can it have been adopted as a symbol of Yahweh – a lion god (Job 10: 16; Isa. 31: 4; Ezek. 1: 10; 10: 14; Hos. 5: 14; 11: 10; etc.), but of the heavens?

[4] G. Hill, *Catalogue of the Greek Coins of Palestine* (*A Catalogue of the Greek Coins of the British Museum*, vol. 27; London, 1914) p. 181 and pl. XIX.29. The date is Mildenberg's.

[5] Admirably summarized by H. Kienle, *Der Gott auf dem Flügelrad* (Wiesbaden, 1975) (*Göttinger Orientforschungen* R. VI, Bd. 7), an amazingly full, fair, and judicious presentation of the conflicting theories.

[6] 'Yaho' is epigraphically possible, as Kienle shows (*Gott*, pp. 6–12, vs. Cross). However, it is ruled out by the analogy of the later coins.

[7] Mildenberg's contention (*Yehud*, 184) that it represents 'not a specific god, but a general conception of deity easily comprehensible to many people in the...Persian Empire' is an amazing anachronism.

p. 240, 'the wheel within the wheel', carefully shown on the coin).[1] The satyr's mask would indicate the importance of wine in Yahweh's cult, as in the economy and private life of Judea.[2] The falcon would be the symbol of Yahweh's servant, the sun (Horus), whom he sends forth as the light of the world.[3] If such symbolism seems credible, the Athena–owl coins, too, may be supposed to represent Anat/Atargatis and her associated birds.[4] How far the Judaism expressed by such symbols would have been acceptable to the general population of Judea, is unknown. Silver coins were for the rich.

Some evidence as to popular religion in Palestine comes from the many Persian-period ostraca that have now been found. From Arad there are 45 on which some words are legible, from Beer-sheba, 54.[5] Those from Arad were mostly found together and seem to be chiefly orders for foodstuffs and transport animals, sent by a military quarter-master named Yaddu'a to a central store. Most of the Beer-sheba ones were found in many different pits and are thought to be labels identifying the persons who had sent in, as payments of their taxes, the grain stored in these pits.[6] If so, the Arad material, by naming the proposed recipients, reveals the make-up of a Persian garrison; the Beer-sheba texts, listing the taxpayers, show the make-up of the surrounding civilian population.

A striking characteristic of both lists is the rarity of explicitly theophoric names. Even in names which formerly specified some god ('Yah answered me', etc.), the divine element is now often omitted, leaving no indication of which god (if any) was meant. Beyond this the lists differ markedly. In the garrison, five names (of 34) were compounded with Yah. Yahweh gave, looked towards, was to be followed, added, and healed (the last three dubious readings). An equal number were compounded with Qos, the Edomite god, but only one is clear – he will avenge. El, missing in Elephantine, here appears twice (he will redeem and restore). Among the taxpayers, by contrast, there

---

[1] And not on the Greek winged wheels shown by Kienle, *Gott*, pl. IV. However, concentric circles were used on amulets for good luck, E. Stern, 'Bes Vases', *IEJ*, 26 (1976), 187.

[2] Yahweh would later be identified with Dionysus, see Smith, *Wine God*. To distinguish sharply between a satyr's mask and a head of Bes, is mistaken; the Bes–satyr equation was already old.

[3] See M. Smith, *Helios in Palestine*, to appear in the Orlinsky volume of *Eretz-Israel*.

[4] S. Cook, *The Religion of Ancient Palestine in the Light of Archaeology* (London, 1930) (*Schweich Lectures*, 1925), p. 173. Whether the male heads represent gods or humans is indeterminable.

[5] See the chapters by J. Naveh in Y. Aharoni's *Beer-sheba I* (Tel Aviv, 1973), and *Ketovot Arad* (i.e. *Arad Inscriptions*) (Jerusalem, 1975). Also J. Naveh, 'The Aramaic Ostraca from Tel Beer-sheba (Seasons 1971–76)', *Tel Aviv*, 6 (1979), 182–98 and plates 24–31.

[6] *Tel-Aviv*, 6 (1979), 193.

are almost no Yahwist names; El again appears two or three times; we find one 'Slave of El' and two of Baal. Qos, however, is frequent. Men named after him appear in almost half the documents. Arabic names are also common; there were few in the garrison. Evidently a local Edomite population, much infiltrated by Arabs, was held down here, as was the Egyptian population in Elephantine, by a composite garrison, under Persian or Mesopotamian commanders,[1] containing a considerable number of Judeans. In Elephantine the Judeans formed a separate detachment; in Arad they seem to have been mingled with the other troops, which must have made legal observance difficult and probably a matter of indifference.

The Edomite names give us a glimpse of the cult of Qos, Yahweh's southern neighbour and competitor. As we should expect, his functions and attributes are those of Yahweh in Elephantine and in the Psalms. Like Yahweh, Qos adorns, avenges, blesses, chooses (?), gives, has mercy, and rescues; He is King (?), is light, and is mighty; some of his worshippers are called 'Son of Qos' (cf. Beniyahu = Son of Yahweh) and 'My Qos' (cf. Eli = My El). If this sample is representative, as it would seem to be, we should conclude that the popular cults of Qos in Idumea and of Yahweh in Judea were motivated by like concerns and centred on equivalent images of their equally imaginary gods.

The same picture appears from the few other ostraca that have turned up elsewhere. One from Ashdod, for instance, has been thought to show that a certain Zebediah ('Yahweh bestowed [him]') had a vineyard there, but it tells us nothing more of Zebediah's religion.[2] The Samaria papyri, if published, will be more informative; the reports thus far circulated show that Yahwist names alternated in the ruling family with those expressing devotion to other gods (notably Sin). We are told that while the majority of the names are Yahwist 'there is also a sizeable number of foreign names', among them compounds of Baal, Qos, Kemosh (of Moab), Nabu, and Sahar.[3]

---

[1] A commander at Arad was 'Slave of Nana' (the Babylonian goddess). Naveh, *Arad*, p. 176, remarks that in Egypt, too, company commanders commonly had Persian or Babylonian names.

[2] J. Naveh, 'An Aramaic Ostracon from Ashdod', in M. Dothan, *Ashdod II–III* ('*Atiqot*, English series, 9–10, Jerusalem, 1971), pp. 200f. The reading of the name is questioned by J. Teixidor, 'Bulletin d'épigraphie sémitique', *Syria*, 50 (1973), 429, no. 152.

[3] F. Cross, 'Papyri of the Fourth Century B.C. from Dâliyeh', *New Directions in Biblical Archaeology*, ed. D. Freedman and J. Greenfield (New York, 1969), pp. 42ff; the quotation is from p. 47.

Next to ostraca should come graffiti and inscriptions, but the stone of Palestine is so soft and soluble that few have been preserved, and from the Persian period none of those few yields indisputable and important evidence as to Judaism. The one possible exception is an incense altar from Lachish that was found in a cave with about 160 similar altars,[1] apparently smashed and dumped there. The votive inscription on it may possibly declare it an offering to Yah,[2] and thus make it evidence of a local cult, independent (?) of that of Jerusalem. Unfortunately, the stone is broken and the reading disputed. Nevertheless Prof. Aharoni, although he accepted a non-committal reading, argued that the names of the donor were Levitical, therefore the altar must (?) have been used for the cult of Yahweh; moreover, the great dump of altars must have come from a temple, so there must have been a functioning temple of Yahweh in Lachish during the Persian period.[3] The pottery found with the broken altars was of the fifth century, roughly the period of Nehemiah's reforms,[4] so it is not improbable that the altars were broken and dumped when adherents of Nehemiah's 'Yahweh-alone' party took over the city. The opposite side of the inscribed altar carried a drawing of a palm tree; others were decorated with graffiti showing men, animals, birds, snakes, trees, the sun and so on.[5] Stern has shown such incense altars were originally Mesopotamian and appeared in Palestine in the sixth century as a result of Mesopotamian influence which led to their local manufacture, probably by Phoenicians.[6] Legend reported that worshippers of Yahweh turned to Phoenician craftsmen for their cult utensils already in Solomon's time (1 Kings 7: 13–46). Phoenician influence was particularly strong during the Persian period.[7] The increasing importance of incense in the cult of Yahweh

---

[1] Tufnell, *Lachish III*, vol. 1, p. 226, cf. p. 383.

[2] See the review of the discussion by R. Degen, 'Der Raeucheraltar aus Lachish', *Neue Ephemeris für Semitische Epigraphik*, 1 (1972), 39–48, which denies this. In defence of the translation, 'Incense altar of *'y.sh ben mḥ*. [dedicated] to Yah the (or, his) King' it may be said (1) that there is room enough in the second line for the names *Mahir* or *Mahli* written without vowel letters; (2) that the use of *lamed* to indicate the recipient of a gift is well attested at Lachish (Aharoni, *Lachish V*, 23f); (3) that none of the defenders of the translation espoused by Degen has explained why a man of Lachish, dedicating a votive offering in Lachish, where everybody must have known him, should identify himself as being 'from Lachish'.

[3] Aharoni, *Lachish V*, pp. 7ff.   [4] See below, pp. 242–6.

[5] Tufnell, *Lachish III*, vol. 2, plates 68–71; see the analogous examples in Stern, *Hattarbut*, pp. 184–94.

[6] *Hattarbut*, pp. 192f.

[7] Stern, *Hattarbut*; M. Smith, *Palestinian Parties and Politics that Shaped the Old Testament* (New York, 1971), pp. 69ff.†

during this period has often been remarked.[1] The importance of the notion of Yahweh as king is attested by names like Malkiyah, and by the many celebrations of his kingship in the Psalms.[2]

Theories about religion have been formed not only from the individual archeological sites and objects, but also from the differences between archeological finds generally in the different areas of the country. Reifenberg, for instance, from his lifelong study of Hebrew seals, once remarked that those showing only writing were more frequent in Judea, those with pictures in Galilee. Of what he believed a representative group he found 76 per cent of the Judean seals showed only inscriptions; 89 per cent of the Galilean showed pictures as well as writing.[3] Stern's study of all material remains of the period has led him to the conclusion that when it began there were two cultural spheres in Palestine. The older, eastern culture, native to the area and open to influences from Syria, Mesopotamia and Egypt, prevailed in the hills of Samaria and Judea; whereas in Galilee and along the coast a new, western culture, Cypriot and East Greek in origin and carried mainly by the Phoenicians, was well established. Through the Persian period this western culture steadily gained ground at the expense of the older one; by the end of the period it was dominant throughout all the country.[4] This cultural change has often been connected with religious problems. For instance, much Greek pottery carried pictorial decorations, including pictures of humans and gods. At first it was common only in Galilee and along the coast; eventually it was everywhere in Judea.[5] So were naturalistic Greek figurines (mostly of deities; finding places include Beersheba, Lachish, Gibeon, Engedi)[6] and Phoenician amulets in the form of human heads (recently found at Engedi).[7] Yahwist names are rarely associated with objects representative of this new culture, and the extension to Judea seems to have been slow. Nevertheless it occurred, and such cultural change forms the background of the evidence about Persian-period Judaism that appears in the literary

---

[1] A. Lods, *Histoire de la littérature hébraïque et juive* (Paris, 1950), p. 535. S. A. Cook, *The Religion of Ancient Palestine in the Light of Archaeology* (The Schweich Lectures, 1925; London, 1930), p. 62. There were nine incense altars in the storeroom of the Lachish temple, and one in its sanctuary.

[2] Pss. 10: 16; 24: 8ff; 47: 3, 7; 93: 1; 96: 10; 97: 1.

[3] A. Reifenberg, 'Some Ancient Hebrew Seals', *PEQ*, 71 (1939), 195.

[4] Stern, *Culture*, pp. xxxf.

[5] Stern, *Culture*, p. xvii, more fully in *Hattarbut*, pp. 140f, with an impressive map of finding places on p. 141.

[6] E. Stern, 'Maṭmon shel Ṣlamiyot', *Eretz-Israel*, 12 (1975), 91ff; Stern, *Hattarbut*, pp. 160–78.   [7] Stern, *Hattarbut*, pp. 153f.

material. Its relation to religion, however, is not so simple as commonly supposed. See the terminal note.†

Pagan literature tells us little about the Jews of the Persian period. Herodotus says that 'the Phoenicians and Syrians in Palestine admit that they learned (circumcision) from the Egyptians'.[1] But were these Jews? Hecateus of Abdera, according to Diodorus Siculus,[2] said that as a result of the Jews' association with strangers while under Persian rule many of their ancestral practices were changed. Clearchus of Soli, a pupil of Aristotle, put into the mouth of his master a story of meeting, in north-western Turkey, a Jewish 'philosopher' who not only spoke Greek, but had the soul of a Greek and sought out Greek scholars to enjoy their philosophical conversation.[3] This may have been the introduction to a story about magical feats performed by the Jew. The report is not incredible, but Clearchus' ignorance of the Jews (he says they are descendants of the Indian philosophers) suggests the yarn was made up.

The rest of our literary information about Judaism in the Persian period comes from the Judeo-Christian tradition. It is of two sorts: (1) works containing reports about the period and (2) works supposed to have been written or edited then, and evidence of the culture that produced them.

Of the reports only Ezra and 1 Esdras, Nehemiah, Haggai, Zechariah, Josephus, and 2 Macc. 1: 18–36 and 2: 13 contain material of importance for an historical account of Judaism in the Persian period. Esther may show some recollection of the Persian court and government – the magnificent parties, the enormous harems, the seven great nobles who might come into the presence of the king, the cut-throat competition of imperial officials each protecting and backed by his own ethnic group, various minor details; beyond this, however, it is a romance, of the ancient genre of romantic–religious novellae that revived in the

---

[1] Herodotus, *Histories* II.104.3. On this and the following classical texts see the commentary by M. Stern, *Greek and Latin Authors on Jews and Judaism*, I, *From Herodotus to Plutarch* (Jerusalem, 1974); II, *From Tacitus to Simplicius* (1980).

[2] Diodorus, *Bibliotheca Historica* XL.3.8. Diodorus' other reports may refer to times either before, during, or after the Persian period. A. Momigliano, *Alien Wisdom* (Cambridge, 1975), p. 84, observes that Hecateus' remark conformed 'with a well-known pattern of Greek ethnography'. This does not prove it false.

[3] Josephus, *Contra Apionem* I. 176–83; for the following comment see Stern, *Authors*, pp. 51f. The historians Pompeius Trogus (in Justin, XXXVI.3, end) and Tacitus, *Histories*, v.8 mention the Jews' subjection to the Persians, but say nothing of their religion at that time.

Hellenistic world.[1] Even less reliable are the apocalyptic legends of Daniel, 2 Esdras and so on, and the targumic and midrashic inventions of later Jewish literature.[2]

As to the works written and edited in Jerusalem during the Persian period there is less unanimity, but most scholars would agree that Ezra, Nehemiah, and 1 and 2 Chronicles, Isaiah 56 to 66, Jonah, Haggai, Zechariah, Malachi, many of the Psalms, Proverbs 1 to 9, Ecclesiastes and the Song of Solomon were written during this period; and many would add Ruth, Job, Joel, possibly Tobit, more of the Proverbs, and the later strata of many prophetic books and of the priestly material in the Pentateuch.[3] Besides these works, this period saw the copying and preservation of all the earlier Hebrew literature that has come down to us. Presumably the material copied was indicative of the copyists' religious interests and beliefs.

To describe these interests and beliefs it seems best to begin with the reported events of the period, hence infer the social structure of Jerusalem, and understand the different elements of the literary tradition as expressions of different groups.[4] These groups were distinguished not only by common social criteria (rich/poor, priestly/lay, urban/rural etc.) but also by a long-standing theological quarrel which now came to centre on the question of the permissibility of marriage with Gentiles. An important group of Judeans in Babylonia had evidently refrained from such marriages and prided themselves on their 'purity', but many left in Judea had contracted alliances with families of neighbouring provinces. Although many of these families also worshipped Yahweh, the self-segregated Babylonian Jews thought such marriages made those who contracted them impure. Consequently, when they returned to Jerusalem – either under Cyrus or later – they at first would not let 'the people of the land' participate in the cult now re-established on the site

---

[1] On Esther see E. Bickerman, *Four Strange Books of the Bible* (New York, 1967); on the genre see M. Braun, *History and Romance in Graeco-Oriental Literature* (Oxford, 1938). The first great example in Israelite literature is the Joseph romance, on which D. Redford, *A Study of the Biblical Story of Joseph*, VTSup 20 (Leiden, 1970). Esther is appropriately followed by a long train: Judith, Susannah and the Elders, the three pages of 1 Esdras, *The Lives of the Prophets* etc.

[2] On these see L. Ginzberg, *The Legends of the Jews* (Philadelphia, 1909–46), vol. 4, pp. 343–448, and vol. 6, pp. 430–81.

[3] Compare, for examples, the opinions of R. Pfeiffer, *Introduction to the Old Testament* (New York, 1948; 2nd edn 1953); O. Eissfeldt, *Einleitung in das alte Testament* (3rd edn., Tübingen, 1964); G. Fohrer, *Introduction to the Old Testament*, trans. D. Green (Nashville, 1968).

[4] The following account is based on Smith, *Palestinian Parties*, chs. 5 to 7, where justification of the details will be found.

of the former Temple.[1] This led to protests to the Persian government and the rebuilding of the Temple was held up until 520,[2] when, at the instigation of the prophets Haggai and Zechariah, the Persian governor of Judea, a Jew named Zerubbabel, took it in hand.[3] Some compromise was worked out with the High Priest Joshua[4] (who was in need of contributions from both sides), and although Zerubbabel presently disappeared – perhaps his admirers worried the Persian government by mistaking him for the Messiah[5] – the Temple was virtually completed with Persian assistance in 515 B.C.E., though work on its decoration, gateways and so on may have continued for another century.[6]

After 515 the moderates represented by Joshua probably remained in power until 458 – the prophetic writings from the period (that is, those preserved by the segregationist party which ultimately prevailed) attack the presence of 'Canaanites' in the Temple, intermarriage with Gentiles, 'misinterpretation' of the law by the priests and so on.[7] In 458,[8] the segregationist Ezra arrived in Jerusalem with a royal commission to reform the law; the first problem he attacked (after the introduction of his new law code and the festival intended to make it popular) was the question of intermarriage. He attacked it so vigorously, by attempting to compel divorce of all foreign wives, that he disappeared. Presumably he was recalled by the Persian government as a troublemaker. However, the segregationist party was strongly based in the Persian court, so fourteen years later another of its members, Nehemiah, got himself appointed governor of Judea, won the support of the Jerusalem plebs, and put through a series of reforms that made the city a stronghold of segregationist Judaism and secured the party's control even of the Temple until almost the end of the century.[9]

Nehemiah also rebuilt the walls of the city and increased its population by providing homes for settlers (doubtless his supporters) from the countryside.[10] Since he was repeatedly charged with plotting

---

[1] Ezra 4: 1–3, on which see Smith, *Palestinian Parties*, pp. 113 and 244, n. 22.

[2] Ezra 4: 4f.

[3] Ezra 5: 1ff; Haggai.

[4] Haggai 2: 10–19; Zech. 3 and 6: 9–15, on which see Smith, *Palestinian Parties*, pp. 109f.

[5] See the references in the preceding note, also Zech. 12: 2–10, and Smith, *Palestinian Parties*, p. 115f.

[6] Ezra 6: 14f; 2 Macc. 1: 18; Neh. 2: 18; Isa. 56: 5.

[7] Zech. 14: 21; Mal. 1; 2: 1–12.

[8] On Ezra and the date of his visit to Jerusalem see Smith, *Palestinian Parties*, pp. 120–5, on Ezra 7 to 8; Neh. 8; Ezra 9 to 10.

[9] Smith, *Palestinian Parties*, ch. 5, on Neh. 1 to 7: 5a and 13: 4–31.

[10] Neh. 7: 4; Ecclus. 6: 14; Josephus, *Ant.* XI.181.

revolt,[1] his success may have worried the Persians. At all events, the next governor seems to have been a Persian named Bagoses[2] who was anti-segregationist.[3] He probably succeeded in restoring the anti-segregationist party in control of the Temple. We know they regained power because their great work, the final edition of 'The Law' (that is, the Pentateuch) became the law of the Jerusalem Temple, and must be dated after Nehemiah: it contains provisions for conversion to Judaism which undercut Nehemiah's ban on marriage with aliens. Moreover, although a Jerusalem code, it was adopted with only minor modifications by the Yahwists of central Palestine for their centre at Samaria. This adoption can only have taken place during a period of good feeling, and probably close marital relations, between the leading families of Judea and Samaria. We have several reports of such intermarriage in the Persian period,[4] and we find that in the early third century Judeans and Samaritans formed a single 'ethnic' (that is, legal) group in Egypt.[5]

On the basis of historical events, then, we should say that the main concerns of Jewish religious life in the late sixth century were the return to Jerusalem, the rebuilding of the Temple, and the conflicts and messianic expectations it touched off; in the fifth century, the long fight over intermarriage, purity, control of the Temple, and a tangle of related questions that issued, early in the fourth century, in the great compromise of the present 'Law', the Pentateuch. The mid fourth century, from about 366 to 332, was a time of repeated political crises, as the Persian imperial structure in the west was shaken to its foundations by the satraps' revolt and the Egyptian invasion of the Syro-Phoenician coast, then restored by the recovery of the coast and ultimately of Egypt under Artaxerxes III, and finally destroyed by Alexander. Presumably the practical importance of these conflicts for the people of Jerusalem made them centres also of religious concern

---

[1] Neh. 2: 19; 6: 6-9.

[2] A change from what had hitherto been a line of Jewish governors; Avigad, *Bullae*, p. 35. 'Bagoses' is Josephus' Greek spelling of the Persian name.

[3] Josephus, *Ant.* XI.297-301; *CAP* 32 shows Bagoses (= Bigvai) acting in concert with the Yahwist governor of Samaria to secure the rebuilding of the syncretistic Jewish temple at Elephantine.

[4] Neh. 13: 28; Josephus, *Ant.* XI.306-12.

[5] Josephus, *Ant.* XII.10. Members of the group quarrelled as to whether some funds they had raised should be used for sacrifices for Jerusalem or for Gerizim. Josephus says this quarrel occurred among the descendants of settlers who had gone to Egypt in the time of Ptolemy I, i.e. after one of his conquests of Palestine, dated from 320 to 302 B.C.E. by M. Volkmann, 'Ptolemaios 18,' *RE*, 13, 2 (1959), 1603-45, dates in cols. 1612 and 1623. This would put the quarrel of the descendants between, roughly, 300 and 270.

and produced many of the political prophecies now attributed to earlier prophets.

Besides these political concerns, however, the continuing religious life of the Temple-centred province and Diaspora was complicated by the variety of the social structure. On top was the Persian governor, usually a Jew,[1] with his staff and his garrison (probably Gentiles). Barely beneath him, the high priest would have liked to be governor, and towards the end of the period attained that position.[2] Beneath him were priestly families who had either positions in the Temple or colonies, sometimes controlling entire towns, in the Judean countryside and farther afield.[3] These priestly families were a few of a larger clan of 'Levites' whose members had once been priests in high places throughout Israelite territory. When these provincial high places had been destroyed by foreign conquest or suppressed by internal reform, the priests of Jerusalem had refused to allow provincial Levites to function in the Jerusalem Temple.[4] Consequently by Nehemiah's time they had became a rural class. Nehemiah had called them to Jerusalem, established them in the Temple as guards, and given them, for support, the proceeds of a ten per cent tax on the agricultural products of the province.[5] As guards of the Temple their main function initially was doubtless to require the priests to observe Nehemiah's purity rules, which derived from a different legal tradition than that the priests had followed.[6] However, once established in the Temple, the Levites acquired other functions. They became gatekeepers and treasurers and took charge of all objects used for the cult (except those in the Temple's sanctuary and cella, which they were not allowed to enter, and the altar itself); in the public services they provided the choir and the band. Nehemiah had also used them as police in the city, to enforce his Sabbath laws, and they claimed, at least, to have been teachers, judges and prophets.[7] Beneath the Levites, in turn, came several classes of hereditary Temple servants and slaves.[8]

---

[1] Avigad, *Bullae*, p. 35.

[2] Kindler, *IEJ*, 24 (1974), 76; cf. Josephus, *Contra Apionem* 1.187.

[3] Such 'cities of the priests' existed already in David's time, if 1 Sam. 22: 19 is to be trusted. Presumably such were the basis for the wishful structure of Joshua 21.

[4] 2 Kings 23: 9; in defiance of Deut. 18: 6ff.

[5] Smith, *Palestinian Parties*, pp. 134f, 163–9. Neh. 13: 10–14.

[6] Smith, *Palestinian Parties*, pp. 133ff.

[7] Smith, *Palestinian Parties*, pp. 166ff. H. Vogelstein, *Der Kampf zwischen Priestern und Leviten* (Stettin, 1889) still deserves cautious attention.

[8] See B. Levine, 'The *Netînîm*', *JBL*, 82 (1963), 207–12, and 'Later Sources on the *Netînîm*', in *Orient and Occident*, C. Gordon Festschrift, ed. H. Hoffner (Neukirchen-Vluyn, 1973), pp. 101–7.

Besides the Temple personnel, the city had a substantial lay population. The landed families of Judea maintained houses there; so did
provincial officials. There were merchants and craftsmen organized in
guilds, some with considerable means. Beneath them came the free
labourers and the slaves of several sorts.[1] Yet more, the city always had
visitors and resident aliens, most of them from the outlying towns and
the rural population of Judea, but many from abroad. The ancient
practice by which all 'the countryside went up to the holy place for the
three annual festivals was now supplemented by occasional pilgrimage
from long distances.[2] Peasants and pilgrims brought gifts, Temple and
city became rich, and their wealth attracted foreign merchants and
craftsmen.

The variety of this population was matched by the variety of parties
and opinions that divided it. To judge from the preserved literature,
the long struggle between segregationists and assimilationists was the
main concern, with most of the priests and the local gentry on the
assimilationist side, which therefore was generally in control and able
to get rid of occasional segregationist leaders from the eastern Diaspora
(Zerubbabel and Ezra) until Nehemiah brought in the Levites, won over
the plebs, and so produced a balance of power that eventually forced
the priests to compromise. But another enduring division was that
between rich and poor, overlooked in most of the literature (which
expresses the opinions of its literate and leisured authors) but clear in
Nehemiah's story of his struggle for support,[3] and explosively expressed
in many Psalms:[4] establishment of the Levites as the Temple singers
gave an official medium of expression to the interests and feelings of
the poor. Political differences were also important. Palestine had long
been a battleground between Egypt and powers from the north or east,
its population divided by adherence to the different contestants. A further
factor was the profound cultural change already mentioned (see above,
pp. 242–3). Divisions produced by such cultural change are apt to widen
the perennial split between young and old. Add the rivalries of families
and individuals, the perennial plague of small communities, and the
complications of this 'little temple state' can be seen to correspond to
the variety of the literature preserved from it. (The more extreme
expressions were probably not preserved.)

Much of the preserved literature can be assigned to certain groups.
That material in the Pentateuch and Joshua which has long been
recognized as 'priestly' came at least in large part from the priests.

---

[1] On the social structure of Jerusalem see Smith, *Palestinian Parties*, pp. 151–4.
[2] On the growth of pilgrimage see p. 234, n. 1.
[3] Neh. 5.
[4] Pss. 10: 2; 14: 6; 18: 28; 22: 25; 34: 7; 35: 10; 37: 14; 69: 30; 70: 5; etc.

The Levites produced Psalms, Chronicles, Ezra and Nehemiah, and edited Haggai, Zechariah and perhaps other books. Wealthy laymen were the authors of Job, Ecclesiastes, Ruth, Jonah, Tobit and the Song of Songs (Judith and Esther show the continuance of the school and the novella form into Hellenistic times). Besides these, however, there is much material, especially additions to the prophetic books, roughly datable to the Persian period, but not clearly marked as the product of any of these groups.[1] And even the preceding assignments are accurate only in general. The dating of many of the minor books is more or less disputed, most of the major compilations contain important elements from earlier times, and a number of scholars have thought their remodelling continued into the Hellenistic age. Nevertheless it would generally be agreed that these compilations were given the essentials of their present structures in the Persian period, and that most of the minor works were produced at this time. We may therefore treat this whole body of literature as characteristic of the age, while recognizing that many of the components were older and that individual works may have been completed later.

Relation to the period is clearest in Haggai and the early (genuine) chapters of Zechariah; and in Ezra and Nehemiah, originally a single work of which the purpose was to recount the re-establishment of the cult, the rebuilding of the Temple, the refortification of the city, the introduction and acceptance of the Law, the reformation of both cult and city, the re-establishment of the Levites in the Temple, and the purge of the priesthood. These are achieved by the help of Yahweh and the consequent patronage of the Persian government.[2] The work assures Jewish readers that the pious practices it advocates are obligatory – acceptance of 'the law of God given by Moses' entails abstinence from intermarriage with Gentiles, from business transactions on the Sabbath, and from crops grown in the sacred seventh year, and acceptance of many financial obligations to support Temple, priests and Levites. But the work is also intended for gentile readers, who are to be convinced that the Temple and its rules are fully authorized and supported by the *Persian* government. It is hard to suppose such a work was produced in any period but the Persian; a likely occasion would be the reconquest of Palestine commonly supposed to have been carried out in the 350s by Artaxerxes III[3] when the Temple needed justification

---

[1] For justification of these assignments, see Smith, *Palestinian Parties*, pp. 161ff.

[2] Ezra 1: 1, 5, 7f; 3: 7; 4: 3; 5: 1, 13ff; 6: 1–14, 22; 7: 6, 9, 12–28; 8: 22f, 25, 36; 9: 8f. Neh. 2: 8, 18, 20; 4: 20; 7: 5; 8: 10; 9: 31; 12: 43.

[3] See Smith, *Palestinian Parties*, p. 185 and n. 191. For other suppositions see P. Schäfer on 'The Hellenistic and Maccabaean Periods', in J. H. Hayes and H. Maxwell Muller, eds., *Israelite and Judean History* (Philadelphia, 1977), pp. 501–2.

vis-à-vis the Persians. This explains why the legal documents reporting Persian investigation and authorization were written in Aramaic,[1] the international language that would have been used had they been genuine (as some perhaps were, at least in parts) and the language that Persian agents could readily read. By contrast, Ezra's confession of sins, with its off-colour conclusion, 'Behold we are now slaves, and slaves on the land you gave our fathers... and its produce is tribute to the kings you have put over us because of our sins',[2] was expressed in the holy obscurity of provincial Hebrew.

Antithetically related to Ezra–Nehemiah are the novellae in which the Judean gentry, leaders of the assimilationist party,[3] attack the theory of segregation. Jonah is a satirical portrait of a segregationist, a petty person devoid of human feeling, who would prefer the destruction of a city to the loss of his reputation, and be no less angry at the death of a vine than he was at Yahweh's refusal to·kill all the people of Nineveh. Ruth makes a heroine of a Moabite woman and ends happily with her marriage to an Israelite (contrast Deut. 23: 4) and the report that she became the great-great-grandmother of David.[4] By the time Judith, Tobit and Esther were written, the aristocratic authors had come closer to the position of their opponents. The books of Judith and Tobit teach the Law, but are also apologies for Ammonites and Samaritans,[5] Esther is a story of how the Jews were saved by the marriage of a Jewess to a Gentile. Closely related to these novellae, almost a novella in lyrics, the Song of Songs celebrates the love of Solomon for a girl from the Lebanon, *not* one of the 'daughters of Jerusalem'.[6]

These works may thus be seen as reactions to the controversy set off by the segregationist party. Their common *Tendenz* is more remarkable because of their differences in subject and style. Ruth, the Song and perhaps Judith are deliberately archaistic (a common trait of bucolic romances), while Tobit, Esther and Jonah have exotic settings (also common in romances). But beneath these differences lie other important similarities. All these works involve stories of deliverance in dire need,

---

[1] Ezra 4: 6 to 5: 16; 7: 11–26.
[2] Neh. 9: 36f. Perhaps a later addition.
[3] W. Rudolph, *Esra und Nehemia*, HAT 1.20; (Tübingen, 1949) on Ezra 2: 2ff; 10: 18–44.
[4] For further assimilationist argument in Ruth, and for elements that made these works acceptable to the tradition, see Smith, *Palestinian Parties*, pp. 161ff.
[5] Smith, *Palestinian Parties*, p. 162; J. Milik, 'La patrie de Tobie', *RB*, 73 (1966) 522ff; H. Kippenberg, *Garizim und Synagoge*, RGVV 30, Berlin, 1971, p. 88.
[6] S. of S. 1: 5; 2: 7; 3: 5; 4: 8, 15; 5: 8, 16; 8: 4; the epithet *Shulammit* in 6: 13 is of uncertain meaning: H. Ringgren, *Das Hohe Lied*, ATD 16.2. (Göttingen, 1958), p. 31. On the whole poem see the full commentary by M. Pope (New York, 1980).

the deliverer is always Yahweh,[1] all the stories glorify Him. He is either explicitly the sole god or ar least the only god considered, usually the god of heaven,[2] creator of heaven and earth;[3] He manages all that happens. Except in Jonah, those delivered are always the righteous; even in Jonah the Ninevites escape destruction by repentance, fasting, sackcloth, ashes and prayer.[4] These are the standard means of getting favours from Yahweh;[5] He likes to have people make themselves conspicuously uncomfortable.

The basic stories of a god who hears and saves, is moved by demonstrative 'penance' and answers fervid prayer, are developed in various ways and show various aspects of the religious life of their times. Usually, however, the information is skimpy. Ruth is most directly concerned with the question of intermarriage; its purpose was to picture the ideal proselyte[6] and to report her justification. In doing so it told a story of such psychological delicacy, charm, pathos and quiet humour as to make it one of the masterpieces of world literature. The machinery of religious law is incidental and probably misunderstood.[7] Jonah's assault on the priggish prophet uses the piety of the Gentiles only for contrast.[8] At most its description of Yahweh as 'a god gracious and merciful, slow to anger and of great goodness' (4: 2) echoed a familiar formula (Exod. 34: 6) as did the assurance that Yahweh might 'repent' of intended punishments.[9] Esther 'explains' the origin of Purim, but otherwise, except for references to penitential practices and prayer, says almost nothing of Jewish religious life.

Tobit and Judith are exceptional in giving us accounts of *dévots* whose practices present their authors' ideals. Tobit, in Palestine, made the annual pilgrimages to Jerusalem (1: 6), but did not think of doing so from the Diaspora. On his pilgrimages he took his first fruits and the several sorts of tithes (1: 6). He observed purity rules, and not only

---

[1] So even in Ruth, 4: 14.

[2] Jonah 1: 9; Tobit 10: 11; Judith 5: 8.

[3] Jonah 1: 9; Tobit 8: 5f; Judith 9: 12.

[4] Jonah 3: 6–10. The prophet originally may have been saved in spite of himself, for further instruction. As things stand, he too is saved by repentance and a prayer, the psalm in ch. 2.

[5] Jonah 3: 6–10; Judith 4: 10; 9: 1; Esther 4: 1, 16; Judith's perennial mourning – sackcloth, fasting etc. – after her husband's death, was evidence of her virtue.

[6] Essential is the speech of Ruth, 1: 16f.

[7] Cf. 4: 7f with Deut. 25: 7–10. The author had never heard of, or forgotten, or deliberately overlooked (?) Lev. 19: 9.

[8] Not only the Ninevites' repentance, but also the virtue of the sailors, 1: 15.

[9] Jonah 3: 10; Ex. 32: 14; 2 Sam. 24: 16; Jer. 26: 19; 1 Chr. 21: 15.

as regards food (1: 10f) – he would not sleep in his house after having performed a burial (2: 9) so as not to render the house impure; nor would he employ a man until assured of his Jewish ancestry (5: 10ff). The author was influenced by Wisdom literature – he invented Jewish ancestry for Ahikar (1: 21; 14: 10; etc.) – and was fond of moral exhortations in which he recommended prayer and fasting, giving to the poor, burying the dead,[1] marrying within Israel, paying workmen promptly, avoiding drunkenness, and asking advice from the wise and help from Yahweh (4: 12–19). Asceticism was creeping in; the story is of a marriage, but, safe in the bedroom, the groom begins by getting out of bed to assure Yahweh, in prayer, that he is not marrying because of lust, but as a moral duty and for companionship.[2] Another side of religious life is the greatly-increased role of demons and angels, another the intense devotion to Jerusalem expressed in the concluding chapters (probably expanded by additions predicting the conversion of all Gentiles and the reconstruction of Jerusalem in gold and precious stones: 13: 15–18; 14: 5b–7, contradicting 5a). Similar asceticism, concern for festivals and purity laws, and devotion to Jerusalem appear in Judith.[3]

Tobit and Judith also have in common a stylistic trait probably connected with contemporary liturgical developments – the frequency of long speeches, prayers and Psalms,[4] the speeches being often moral exhortations, the psalms, hymns of thanksgiving. Several are introduced by or made up of long reviews of sacred history reported as the great deeds of Yahweh. More and more various examples of such forms appear in Chronicles, Ezra and Nehemiah, and have close relations to Psalms and the later prophetic passages. In the novellae they are interesting as evidence of the increasing approximation of these authors to the style as well as the theology of the schools their predecessors had opposed.

To this tendency, however, there is one outstanding exception – the Song of Songs. It never refers to religion, not even when such a reference might have been expected. The hero, Solomon, was remembered as the builder of the Temple, and the author was fond of

[1] Tobit 1: 17; 4: 7; 12: 8ff.

[2] Tobit 8: 4–7; cf. the similarly ascetic rejection of remarriage which is represented as Judith's chief virtue (apart from murder).

[3] Judith 8: 5ff; 12: 25–9, 19. Note the expectation of eternal torment, 16: 17.

[4] Tobit 3: 1–8, 11–15; 12: 6–15 (moral exhortation); 13 (hymn of praise and prophecy); 14: 3–11 (moral exhortation and prophecy). Judith 2: 5–12 (speech by Nebuchadnezzar) 5: 5–21, Achior's speech (the Israelite legend); 6: 2–8 (Holofernes' reply); 8: 11–27 (Judith's prayer); 11: 5–19 (Judith's speech to Holofernes); 16: 2–17 (Judith's song of thanksgiving).

architectural comparisons: the nose of his fair one is like a tower of Lebanon overlooking Damascus (7: 4), her eyes like the fish pools in Heshbon (7: 4), her neck like the tower of David (4: 4) and so on; she is beautiful as Jerusalem (6: 4), but not as the Temple. Probably it was not an impressive building; the author of Tobit did not think much of it (14: 5). In any case the wholehearted sensuality of the Song resembles the original story of the three pages in 1 Esdras 3: 1 to 4: 32 which declared that wine is strong, the king stronger, but women are strongest. The editor sanctified this by adding an appendix, 4: 33–41: truth is yet stronger (which is true).

The editor's interest in truth, and the interest of the original text in platitudes, connect the story of the three pages with another form of literature cultivated by the gentry, the 'Wisdom' books. Collections of wise sayings had long functioned in the Near East as copybooks for children learning to write. Such collections are difficult to date, but one generally assigned to the Persian period and of particular value for our knowledge of Jewish life is Prov. 31: 10–31, the classic description of the good wife who manages the household (including a staff of slave girls), maintains it by their spinning and weaving, supports her husband in leisure, invests the surplus in vineyards, gives to the poor, and lectures to everybody. In the present Hebrew text she is described[1] as 'a woman who fears Yahweh', but nothing is said of her visiting any place of worship or participating in any worship at all.

Another outstanding passage is now the first section of Proverbs, probably one of the last to be written (chapters 1 to 9), which show this proverbial wisdom organized in a somewhat coherent structure by a moralist convinced that education should not only teach, but train; not only communicate knowledge, but produce skill, prudence and, above all, virtue. He therefore lays down, as his first principle, that 'the fear of Yahweh is the beginning of wisdom'. Hence his pupils should avoid association with wicked men and attend to Wisdom, who is personified and given the sort of speech attributed to Yahweh by the prophets and the deuteronomic tradition. What 'Wisdom' (that is, the author) has to say, is mainly abuse of those who will not listen to her (him) – they are fools and will soon suffer for their folly – and recommendation of herself, that is, of the author's teaching: it embodies the principles by which the world was created, and which underlie sound government.[2] But the actual teaching contains nothing relevant to cosmology, and approaches political science only by recommendation of 'justice'.[3] The few specific precepts of the section (avoid robbers and

[1] Perhaps by a textual corruption, cf. LXX.
[2] Prov. 3: 19f; 8: 15f, 22–31.   [3] Prov. 2: 6–9, 21f; etc.

loose women, keep to your own wife, be trustworthy and modest, pay
your debts promptly, do not be contentious, do not go bail for your
neighbour, be industrious, etc.) – all these, like the proverbs of the
earlier collections, pertain to private morality. Thus the proverb tradition is here recommended by a new, abstract rhetoric concerned with
cosmology (as were the priestly authors) and indebted to the prophets
and the deuteronomic school (as were the Levites). That it pays almost
no attention to the Temple – a single distich recommends the giving
of first fruits (3: 9) – is probably due not only to the character of the
tradition, but also to the interests of the editor. The gentry were willing
to adopt ideas from priests and Levites, but not to insist on scrupulous
payment of Temple taxes.

The laic character of the Israelite Wisdom tradition appears also in
its two masterpieces, Job and Ecclesiastes. In the original parts of
Job – most of the poetic dialogue, chapters 3 to 27 and 29 to 31[1] – a
lay aristocrat attacks the deuteronomic teaching that virtue will be
rewarded by prosperity, and vice punished by misfortune, in this world.
The hero is a man of great wealth, wholly concerned with himself and
his relations to his peers and to God. The problem, as in many Greek
tragedies, arises from the hero's pride (*hybris*). He demands justice, even
from God! His demand is made particularly outrageous by the author's
notion of God as creator and absolute ruler of the cosmos, therefore
great beyond human comprehension, to say nothing of human standards.
This notion is a consequence drawn from the monotheism of Second
Isaiah, whence came also much of the poetic language.[2] The rigour with
which the author forced monotheism to its conclusion in moral
nihilism, and the passion with which he perceived the human pre-
dicament implied by this conclusion, have made his work a unique
monument of the Judean religious life of its time – if it be of Judean
origin. It may have been written in Samaria, Idumea or Transjordan.

Perhaps the best argument for Judean origin is the book's dependence
on Second Isaiah. This also indicates its date: late sixth or early fifth
century. The indication is confirmed by various details[3] and jibes, with
the book's general indifference to Judaism. Apparently the gentry of
Palestine, who had acquired estates after the foreign conquests by taking
over properties of persons deported,[4] had transferred their loyalties to

[1] M. Pope, *Job*, 3rd edn. (New York, 1974), pp. xxiii–xxx.
[2] R. Gordis, *The Book of God and Man* (Chicago, 1966), pp. 216ff. The rejection of this
    argument by Pope, *Job*, pp. xxxviiiff is based on Albright's theory of 'primitive
    Israelite monotheism'.
[3] Smith, *Palestinian Parties*, pp. 158ff and notes 34–37, 41–45.
[4] Ezek. 11: 15, on which Smith, *Palestinian Parties*, pp. 99f.

the imperial regime that secured their holdings, followed Persian fashion in identifying Yahweh as 'the god of the heavens,'[1] and had little interest in his cult. At all events, the god of the original book of Job was not identified with Yahweh,[2] the hero was not said to be an Israelite, and the text never mentioned the special practices or festivals of Judaism, nor Israelite tradition. Copyists added a prose preface, like those for Greek tragedies, telling the myth to which the work referred; they gave Job a speech in praise of wisdom (beginning with the fear of Yahweh, chapter 28), deleted the original conclusion, added verbose speeches to justify the suffering of the righteous as educational and to defend the deity as inscrutable, and appended a prose conclusion to assert the doctrine of material reward and punishment in this world. In preface and conclusion the god is Yahweh, Job is assiduous in sacrificial worship, and the blame for Job's suffering is shifted to one of Yahweh's ministers, an angel. This way of exculpating the ruler was probably suggested by Persian practice, and the angel here introduced, the 'accuser' (Hebrew, *śaṭan*), may have been 'the king's eye', the royal prosecuting attorney who was supposed to have been also head of the intelligence bureau, an official peculiar, so far as is known, to the Persian court.[3]

Ecclesiastes was probably written as an answer to Job, though several generations may have elapsed between them. It expresses the same upper class attitude, is concerned with the same private problems, but shows the sophistication of one acquainted with the arguments of Job, who finds human speculation on such subjects pathetic. Instead of working himself into a fury about the injustice of the human condition, the wise man will relax and enjoy it. All men will soon die, so nothing human

---

[1] Above, p. 228, n. 5; p. 229, nn 2 and 5.

[2] Job 12: 9 is a gloss.

[3] For identification of 'the accuser' with 'the king's eye' see Pope, *Job*, pp. 10f, on Zech. 4: 10b. Mithra's 'ten thousand eyes' and 'spies' are also thought to be reflections of these officials, see I. Gershevitch, *The Avestan Hymn to Mithra* (Cambridge, 1959), pp. 26 and 36f, and *Yasht* 10.7 and 24. The oldest Greek evidence is in Aeschylus, *Persai*, 980; Herodotus 1.114; Aristophanes, *Acharnenses* 92 and scholium. (Against these Xenophon, *Cyropaedia* VIII.2.10ff; 6.16; is clearly apologetic and theoretical.) From the Greek evidence it would seem that the title referred to a corps of officials and *par excellence* to the great minister who headed the corps. Unfortunately the Persian and other evidence does not match the Greek. However, the conjecture advanced here is close to the position of R. Frye, *The Heritage of Persia* (Cleveland, 1963), pp. 97f, who believes that these officials functioned not only as informers, but as prosecuting attorneys of the crown. Pope's supposition that there were equivalent officials in more ancient near-eastern courts (*Job*) is unsupported, but not improbable. However, to account for the evidence he must hypothecate not only a similar function, but a similar title.

matters much. 'Vanity of vanities,...all is vanity...Live, therefore, with the woman you love all the days of your vain life...for this is your lot.'[1] Or, as Paul put it, 'Let us eat and drink, for tomorrow we die.'[2] This recalls Epicurus: the good life is that of tranquillity, which is happiness. But there is no reason to suppose either author influenced the other. In Palestine, as in Greece, the age of heroic drama and speculative philosophy was followed by one of elegiac tone and subjective concern.

This personal impiety was compatible with acceptance of established religion. As Epicurus advised his followers to keep on good terms with their neighbours – to ensure a tranquil life – the author of Ecclesiastes advises his reader to keep on good terms with his god (whom he does not identify as Yahweh,), to go to the Temple, pay his vows, and resign himself to the world this god has made and the rules he has made for it, but 'Be not righteous overmuch, and do not make yourself overwise, for why should you waste yourself?'[3] Pious readers loaded the text with comments recommending the fear of God and warning of ultimate judgement, or damning the author as a fool.[4] That the book survived is evidence of the survival in Jerusalem of a wealthy, literate and disillusioned circle whose gradual adjustment to the religion around them turned out to be, for western civilization, one of the most valuable aspects of the city's religious life.

All these works of the lay aristocracy (except Proverbs) resemble the Greek literature of these centuries, not only in content, literary form and tone, but also in being individual works of individual authors, each composed by a single man to say what *he* wanted to say. By contrast, the huge compilations left by the Levites and the priests – the Psalter, Chronicles–Ezra–Nehemiah, the Pentateuch, and Joshua – are like the mounds of ancient near-eastern cities, layer over layer of deposits from generation after generation of nameless persons who lived in these structures, added, destroyed, remodelled, and left the complex to their successors for further alterations. Often we cannot confidently distinguish work of the Persian period from earlier material or Hellenistic additions. We must do what we can with the usual datings[5]

---

[1] Eccles. 1: 1; 9: 9.
[2] 1 Cor. 15: 32, echoing Isa. 22: 13.
[3] Eccles. 2: 24ff; 3: 13ff; 5: 1ff etc.; 7: 16   [4] Eccles. 4: 5, 13; 9: 17; 10: 12ff.
[5] On Chronicles–Ezra–Nehemiah, see the magisterial commentary by W. Rudolph, *Esra und Nehemia*, HAT 1.20, (Tübingen, 1949) and *Chronikbücher*, HAT 1.21, (Tübingen, 1955); also K. Galling, *Die Bücher der Chronik, Esra, Nehemia*, ATD 12 (Göttingen, 1954). The variety of competent opinions can be judged from the review of this by S. Mowinckel, 'Erwägungen zum chronistischen Geschichtswerk', *TLZ*, 85 (1960), 2ff.

and hope that if somewhat earlier or later materials creep into our account, they may not greatly distort it.

The Levites who produced Chronicles and Ezra–Nehemiah wanted to justify and magnify their position in Temple and cult. They found the histories produced by the deuteronomic school unsatisfactory. Judges 17 to 21 told bad stories about Levites; Samuel and Kings probably never mentioned them. The silence they corrected, as copyists,[1] but the occasional references they could insert did not suffice for their purpose. They were forming a new concept of sacred history, to rival that of the priests. The deuteronomic history had been ethnocentric, the history of the holy people of Israel, to the destruction of their kingdoms. Despairing of kingdoms, the exiled priests had conceived of another holy history, that of the work of Yahweh through creation, selection and revelation, to constitute a holy congregation of his worshippers. This history led to the giving of the Law, establishment of sacrificial worship, and appointment of the priests as supreme authorities in these supreme subjects. To counter this the Levites produced a third holy history, that of the Temple and of the Levites who served it. Human existence, from creation to David, was abbreviated almost to a genealogical outline. David planned the Temple and appointed the Levites. To justify their position in the post-exilic Temple, the destruction of 587 was seen as an interruption; the history continued in an account of the second Temple, leading to its purification (from pollutions introduced by the high priest!) and to the re-establishment in it of the Levites, by their hero Nehemiah.

The characteristics of this levitic history are explained in part by its plan, in part by the history of the Levites during the Persian period.[2] Its plan explains omission of most accounts of the northern kingdom. (This is not the result of hostility to the northerners; the later strata would welcome them if they came to worship in Jerusalem.)[3] The same plan explains omission of the stories about Elijah and Elisha; they were admirable, but not relevant to the history of the holy Temple and its Levites. Building, ceremonies and reformations of the Temple fill almost three-quarters of the text. Yahweh's protection of his Temple, city, and people, so long as they trust, obey and worship him only, is emphasized by fantastic miracle stories intended for popular appeal. Levites guide the kings by prophecy and are the agents of salvation. Was not a countless army of Ammonites, Moabites and Edomites

---

[1] Levites now appear momentarily in 1 Sam. 6: 15; 2 Sam. 15: 24; 1 Kings 8: 4; 12: 31, but immediately vanish. All these are probably interpolations; only 1 Kings 12: 31 can possibly be original.

[2] For reconstruction of this history see Smith, *Palestinian Parties*, pp. 163–70.

[3] 2 Chron. 15: 9; 30: 1, 6ff, 11, 18; 31: 1; 34: 33; 35: 18.

annihilated when they burst into song?[1] Even prayer could do as much. The army of Sennacherib was destroyed at the prayers of Hezekiah and Isaiah, and more than a million Ethiopians at the prayer of Asa alone.[2]

Indication of date are given by the passages that describe the employments of the Levites. Those that show them 'mounting the guard' and having some sort of police power[3] reflect Nehemiah's initial use of them to enforce his purity and Sabbath rules.[4] Stories of their performing priestly functions (even 'helping their brothers the priests perform the sacrifices'! 2 Chron. 29: 34) reflect their attempt to assume these functions, probably under a high priest who owed his office to Nehemiah's expulsion of the legitimate successor, and who consequently depended on their support.[5] Defeat of this attempt is celebrated by the priestly authors of Num. 16. Presumably defeat entailed the Levites' loss of their police powers and decided them to turn to the lower Temple officials, the singers and gatekeepers, whom they eventually assimilated or replaced. Passages representing these groups as distinct from the Levites belong to the earlier strata of the Chronicler's history, those that call them Levites, to the later.[6] Hence came the Levites' connection with psalmody; psalms in Chronicles and references to Levites' singing reflect this development.

Along with these adventures in the Temple, the Levites seem to have played an even more important role outside it in the new form of worship now becoming common – worship in synagogues. As to the origin of synagogal worship we have no direct evidence. The long accepted opinion, that it began in Babylonia, when worship at the Temple was no longer possible, is plausible, but supported only by plausibility. Traces of it are commonly found in Neh. 8, where Ezra's reading of his law, not in the Temple, but in 'the street before the Water Gate' (of the city, 8: 1) has been supplemented by the levitic editors with traits appropriate to a synagogue service: 'Ezra...stood on a wooden pulpit' with attendants on either side. When he opened the book the congregation stood. He then blessed 'Yahweh, the great God' and they answered, 'Amen, amen',...'first lifting their hands and then prostrating themselves before Yahweh' (that is, before the book).

[1] 2 Chron. 20: 22f.
[2] 2 Chron. 32: 20f; 14: 11ff.
[3] 1 Chron. 9: 23, 28ff; 23: 28ff, 32; 26: 12 (?); 2 Chron. 8: 14; 31: 17 (?); G. von Rad, *Das Geschichtsbild des chronistischen Werkes*, BWANT 4.3 (Stuttgart, 1930), pp. 107ff.
[4] Neh. 13: 10–31.
[5] Neh. 13: 28; Josephus, *Ant.* XI.297–301.
[6] Von Rad, *Geschichtsbild*, pp. 102–18; G. Hölscher, 'Levi', RE 12.2 (1925), 2185.

Thirteen Levites 'made the people understand the law, while the people stayed in their place, and they read the book...with explanation' (? 8: 4–8). It is not certain whether the last verses refer to exegesis of the law (*midrash*) or to a translation (*targum*) into Aramaic, or both.[1] In any event both *targum* and *midrash* developed early.

The first reference to synagogues is commonly found in Ps. 74: 8 (the enemy 'have burned all the meeting places of God in the land'); the first certain evidence of their existence is in two Greek inscriptions from Egypt, of about 240 to 221 B.C.E.[2] But synagogal worship is not bound to any fixed architectural form; consequently rooms that served as synagogues may have gone unrecognized in excavations. Since it needed no sacrifice, it needed no priests, temples, courts, or altars; it was adapted to missionary propagation and survival as a private cult, centred in learning, prayer and praise. It was also fashionable; many circles of the fifth and fourth centuries B.C.E. were critical of sacrifice.[3] Moreover, it had the advantage of economy; thanks are the cheapest offerings. With these advantages it eventually brought about one of the major religious reformations of the western world – the conversion of Judaism, Islam and much of Christianity to non-sacrificial worship.

Among the Judeans this reformation probably progressed during Nehemiah's governorship; he was an adherent of the deuteronomic tradition hostile to sacrifices outside Jerusalem. There are reasons for thinking the Levites played a large part in the change. Chronicles makes them the interpreters in Ezra's reading of the law, and represents them as teaching the peasantry of Judea.[4] Chronicles, Ezra, and Nehemiah are full of parts of sermons that look like the remains of preaching[5] and are deuteronomic in style and content, as befits the adherents of Nehemiah. So are the many prayers in the same books. These are often echoed in later synagogal prayer for which they seem to have set the

[1] Nehemiah complains that many men of Jerusalem had married women from Ashdod, Ammon, and Moab, and their children spoke a Hebrew that was half Aramaic (13: 23f).

[2] *Corpus Papyrorum Judaicarum*, ed. V. Tcherikover and A. Fuks (Cambridge, Mass., 1957–64, 3 vols.), vol. 3, pp. 141 and 164 (appendix 1, nos. 1440, 1532A). Ptolemy III married Berenike in 246 so the dedications to them 'and their children' make the neighbourhood of 240 a *terminus post quem*. Berenike's first child was born in 244, H. Volkmann, 'Ptolemaios IV', *RE*, 23.2 (1959), 1678; Ptolemy III died in 221.

[3] Eusebius, *Praeparatio Evangelica*, IV.10–14, citing Empedocles and Theophrastus; J. Wettstein, *Novum Testamentum Graecum* (Amsterdam, 1751, 2 vols.), on Rom. 12: 1, citing Isocrates and many others.

[4] 2 Chron. 17: 7ff; cf. 35: 3.

[5] G. von Rad, 'Die levitische Predigt in den Büchern der Chronik', in *Festschrift Otto Procksch* (Leipzig, 1934), pp. 113ff.

tone. A function of the levitical priests in monarchic times had been to carry the sacred 'ark' of Yahweh – a box believed to be the seat of the deity. Similar processions seem to have been revived in synagogue services, a box containing a law scroll being used for the ark.[1] The prominence in Chronicles of stories about the ark has been taken as evidence that the Levites were important in this revival.[2] Above all, to suppose that the Levites played a large role in the spread of synagogal worship would explain the diversity of the Psalms, of which many serve the interests of the Temple or the 'national' religion – pilgrim songs, prayers for the people as a whole, etc. – but others have a sectarian tone better suited to conventicles of the self-righteous, hostile to the society around them.[3]

In the Psalter the Levites produced one of the most influential books of all history. It is the one book of the Bible from which, until recent times, selections were read in almost every Jewish and Christian service. Read through every week in medieval monasteries, it formed the minds of the teachers of the western world. Until the present century it was the daily companion of the pious, read morning and night. And it was read as the Word of God.

This the Levites did not foresee. They simply collected hymns which had come down to them and added more of their own.[4] In their own hymns, as in their history, the religion expressed is that of the deuteronomic tradition, as modified by the peculiar interests of the Levites: Yahweh is the god of Israel, Israel the people of Yahweh. Worship Yahweh alone and trust in him and he will deliver both his people and his trusting servant from all evils. This is occasionally proved by appeal to the national legend; from the Exodus or even from Abraham down,[5] but such references are rare: the story of Abraham appears only in Ps. 105,[6] which also contains the only reference to Isaac, and the only reference to 'Jacob' as a person, not merely an eponymous ancestor.[7] This recalls the Chronicler's near elimination of all history prior to the planning of the Temple; a major deviation from the

[1] Deut. 10: 1–5.
[2] Smith, *Palestinian Parties*, pp. 164ff.
[3] So Pss. 12; 35 to 38; 41; 52; 55; 58; 64; 69; 71; etc.
[4] Estimates as to the number of post-exilic psalms differ widely. Fohrer, *Introduction*, pp. 285–92, assigns 86 of the 150, either in whole or in large part, to the post-exilic period.
[5] Pss. 78; 80; 81; 105; 106; 114; 136; 10–22; etc.
[6] 'The God of Abraham' is mentioned in Ps. 47: 9.
[7] There are a dozen references to 'the God' or 'the mighty one' of Jacob, and about twenty-five to 'the seed' or 'children' 'of Jacob' or to 'Jacob', meaning the people.

deuteronomic line. Emphasis is no longer on the past history, but on the present God.[1]

A second deviation from Deuteronomy: this God is not primarily giver of the law, but protector and strengthener. Hence the attitude most emphasized is not obedience, but trust. A few Psalms – 9 of the 150 – do refer to the Law;[2] a very few of these, notoriously Ps. 119, insist on its importance. But these are understandably exceptional: the Law was the province of the priests, the Levites' rivals.[3] By contrast, more than half the psalms have some variation of the simple theme, 'Trust in Yahweh and He will save you' – usually 'from your enemies'. Often this is put in the perennially popular form of a confession ('I trusted...he saved'). Characteristic words for 'hope' and 'trust' occur some twenty and fifty times respectively in the Psalter, only once and eight times in the Pentateuch.[4] The expected salvation is commonly miraculous, sometimes it involves an epiphany complete with lightning, thunder, earthquake etc. (for example, Ps. 18), but usually the means are left to Yahweh's ingenuity and the reader's imagination; all that interests the author is the result. These psalms and the Chronicler's stories of miraculous deliverance are similar expressions of the same mentality. But Chronicles deals with national emergencies; the Psalms promise help to individuals as well as to the people. Consequently the enemies always at hand, whose destruction is eagerly anticipated, are often private enemies, especially the rich. Many psalms use 'the poor' as equivalent to 'the righteous'. Deuteronomy had been remarkable for its legislation on behalf of the poor; in these psalms the attitude of the poor finds direct expression; the two works are related as stimulus and response. But the appeal of these pictures of a world of enemies, from whom the isolated individual takes refuge in private converse with his God, goes beyond social antagonisms to the roots of those schizoid personalities whom the influence of the Psalter has done much to multiply.

Besides hope of deliverance, the other great theme of the book is celebration of Yahweh, His power, His glory, and the joy of His worship. This was the Levites' proper business; it is particularly

---

[1] Need it be said that the pseudo-historical headings of the psalms are secondary?

[2] Pss. 1; 19; 37; 40; 78; 89; 94; 105; and 119.

[3] The Chronicler's claim that the Levites had sometimes been judges (1 Chron. 23: 4; 26: 29; 2 Chron. 19: 8; etc.) probably derives from wishful thinking.

[4] *Qawah* and derivatives, meaning 'hope', only in Gen. 49: 18 – a psalm inserted into the pentateuchal text; *batah* and derivatives in Gen. 34: 25; Lev. 25: 18, 19; 26: 5; Deut. 12: 10; 28: 52; 33: 12, 28. All uses except Deut. 28: 52 are adverbial (*betah/labetah* = 'securely'), and Deut. 28: 52 does not refer to trust in Yahweh.

common in the last third of the collection (Pss. 95 to 150), but there are many earlier examples.[1] Yahweh is celebrated as creator and ruler of the world, victor over the monsters of chaos, the magnificent king who rules all peoples, but has chosen Israel and established Jerusalem and the Temple. He protects the righteous and will destroy the wicked (individuals immediately, nations eventually). He is celebrated by all the powers of nature: sun and moon, heavens and earth, and above all by His people in their festivals: a famous sequence is devoted to the fashionable pleasures of pilgrimage.[2]

All these themes were intertwined: Nehemiah's success in winning the support of the poor had enabled him to put through his (basically deuteronomic) reforms, and to establish the Levites in the Temple. The Levites had formerly been poor themselves and now depended, for protection against the priests, on continued support by the city populace. The poor were in turn dependent on Temple charities and on the reputation of Temple and city as holy places, that drew the continuous influx of pilgrims and funds, that supported both them and the Levites, who by their songs and 'history' spread the reputation of the city's and Temple's holiness and the greatness of their god. Hallelujah.

The priests of the restored Temple seem to have been, as to politics and opinions, a more mixed lot than the Levites. This is understandable. Almost all Levites owed their support from the tithe, and their positions in the Temple, to Nehemiah, hence their unanimity in following his party line. The priests were beholden to nobody; they got in by hereditary right. In the past there had been disputes as to which priestly families enjoyed this right, and questions about the purity of some priestly pedigrees. Later Nehemiah, as governor, drove out of the city a descendant of the high priest, and probably other priests, who had married women from outside Judea.[3] But his action was exceptional. Otherwise, priests seem to have been secure in their positions, and as a group showed the variety in opinions that often results from economic security.

This variety appears in both their political record and the pentateuchal material commonly attributed to them. As for record, Ezra had been a priest, but there had been priests among his opponents, the assimilationists.[4] When Nehemiah drove out some priests, others stayed, benefited from his measures on behalf of the Temple, and

---

[1] E.g. Pss. 8; 19; 24; 29; 33; etc.
[2] Pss. 120 to 134. See also the work of G. Wanke, *Die Zionstheologie der Korachiten, Beihefte, ZAW*, 97 (Berlin, 1966).
[3] Neh. 13: 28ff; cf. Josephus, *Ant.* XI.312.   [4] Ezra 7: 1–5; 10: 18ff.

supported those against intermarriage.[1] As for material, the final editors
of the Pentateuch, surely priests, put side by side with their own
traditions the deuteronomic code which often contradicted them.[2]
Moreover, the priestly material itself is not uniform; sometimes a single
passage shows a primary text, secondary expansion with segregationist
tendencies, and final 'corrections' by an assimilationist editor.[3] Unfortunately, it is often impossible to distinguish the strata, but the preserved complex of priestly materials shows what the final, assimilationist
editors of the Pentateuch, in the early fourth century, wished or
consented to preserve.

We begin with the contradictions. Is the Passover sacrifice to be
roasted (Exod. 12: 8f) or boiled (Deut. 16: 7)?[4] Is an Israelite slave girl
to go free after seven years (Deut. 15: 12) or is she not (Exod. 21: 7)?
Shall Levites begin to serve in the Temple at twenty-five (Num. 8: 24)
or at thirty (Num. 4: 2)? And so on. These practical questions cannot
have escaped the editors' notice. Inclusion of contradictory rules implies
some accepted exegetic method to settle what should be done. Such a
method (in fact, an 'oral law', as it later came to be called) was primarily
the province of the priests, but the deuteronomic requirement that each
Israelite learn the law[5] had created a body of informed adherents, at least
of that tradition. Conflicts between lay and priestly interpreters reached
a climax when Nehemiah threw out of the Temple the property of an
Ammonite whom the high priest had admitted, and had the Temple
purified from this 'pollution'.[6] We have seen something of the resultant
conflict;[7] the final compromise, expressed in the present Pentateuch, did
not satisfy a group of die-hard segregationists, headed by a few priests,
but mostly Levites and laity. They appealed to the memory of Nehemiah
and the deuteronomic tradition and formed a conventicle for observance
of their own, stricter law, at the head of which they put the articles: no
intermarriage with non-Judeans; strict observance of Sabbath and
Sabbath-year.[8] A list of rules for the support of the Temple followed.

---

[1] Neh. 13: 28ff; cf. Josephus, *Ant.* XI.309.

[2] For a fuller account of the various priestly parties and their relations to each other
and to outsiders, see Smith, *Palestinian Parties*, pp. 170–4.

[3] See G. von Rad, *Die Priesterschrift im Hexateuch*, BWANT 4. 13 (Berlin, 1934), pp.
21–8; A. Bentzen, 'Priesterschaft und Laien in der jüdischen Gemeinde des 5
Jahrhunderts', *AfO*, 7 (1930–31), 280ff; A. Gunneweg, *Leviten und Priester*, FRLANT
89 (Göttingen, 1965), pp. 141, 144, 152, n. 1 (on von Rad); K. Koch, *Die Priesterschrift
von Exodus 25 bis Leviticus 16* (Göttingen, 1959), pp. 102ff.

[4] The translation 'roast' in the King James' and derivative versions is harmonistic.

[5] Deut. 6: 6ff.   [6] Neh. 13: 4–9.

[7] Above, pp. 245–7.

[8] Neh. 10: 1–32. The appeal to deuteronomic tradition is clear in the deuteronomic
wording of 30b.

This code, with a list of the sponsors and report of their agreement, was inserted in Neh. 10, where it stands as the first monument of that sectarian legality so important in later Judaism.

By contrast to such sects, the priestly material in the Pentateuch shows the mind of the Temple 'establishment', and their peculiar professional jargon (a verbose legal language of which the first datable document is the work of the priest Ezekiel, *fl.* 590 to 560 B.C.E.). Like most hereditary aristocracies, they were much interested in genealogies and even invented a family tree of nations, to make Israel head of the family.[1] Genealogies were fashionable in the Persian period.[2] But these priests had minds of their own – many fashionable themes did not interest them, notably relief of the poor, speculations about the end of the world, stories of angels, demons and such, psalms, preaching and confession of sins (the Levites' side of the services).[3] They had a lively interest in their livelihood, and therefore in the rules of the sacrificial cult.

The cult was conceived, in the near-eastern way, as domestic service of the deity, whose 'dwelling place' was the Temple.[4] The cella was divided by a curtain. The inner area, 'the holiest place'[5] was Yahweh's private room; only the high priest might enter it, and he only on the Day of Atonement.[6] In the outer area was a table, on which there was always bread, a lamp stand with seven lamps always burning, and a little gold altar on which incense was burned night and morning. Outside in the Temple court was a large stone altar on which parts of sacrificed animals, flour and cakes, with some oil, wine, salt and incense were offered to Yahweh by burning – He liked the smell.[7] Offerings of wine and the blood of the victims were commonly poured at the base of the altar. The blood might also be sprinkled or smeared on the altars and other instruments, the building, the priests and the offerants, to sanctify them. The priestly texts speak of the sacrifices as 'the food of your god' and so on,[8] and the plain purpose of these arrangements was thus understood by the people of Jerusalem until the destruction of the Temple in 70 C.E.[9]

---

[1] Pfeiffer, *Introduction*, p. 197.   [2] Smith, *Palestinian Parties*, p. 271, n. 95.

[3] Von Rad, *Geschichtsbild*, pp. 9 and 84; *Priesterschrift*, p. 187; Pfeiffer, *Introduction*, 208.

[4] Lev. 17: 4; Num. 16: 9; 17: 28; 19: 13; etc. The cognate expressions in Zech. 2: 14f; 8: 3 show this expression continued in use to Persian times. The protests against it will be noticed below.

[5] Commonly translated 'holy of holies', Exod. 26: 33f; etc.

[6] Lev. 16: 11ff. R. de Vaux, *Ancient Israel*, trans. J. McHugh (London, 1961), pp. 507ff.

[7] Exod. 29: 18; Lev. 1: 9, 13, 17; 2: 2, 9; 3: 5; etc.

[8] Lev. 21: 6, 8, 17, 21, 22; 22: 25; Num. 28: 2, 24; cf. Lev. 3: 11, 16; etc.

[9] Josephus, *War* VI.99f.

Accordingly the sacrifices can be divided, roughly, into two classes: (1) the god's regular allowance, one lamb each day for breakfast and another for dinner, each with some flour, oil and wine, and additional offerings on festivals – up to thirteen bulls, seven rams, fourteen sheep, and a goat, with their appropriate meal and wine offerings;[1] (2) sacrifices brought as additional *douceurs* to the deity for various reasons, of which the commonest were: (a) petition, to accompany prayers; (b) thanksgiving; (c) payment of obligations, either of fixed dues – the Passover, the first-born of all animals, the first fruits of crops, etc. – or of vows, which were promises to pay if the deity did a specified favour; (d) expiation for sin or some other deviation from accepted behaviour, for instance, becoming impure (as with leprosy or childbirth), or undertaking special religious observances, or the like. While these classes of sacrifices differed theoretically, they overlapped in practice; for instance, sacrifices for sin were commonly offered at festivals, and so became part of the regular provisions. The god's rations, sacrifices obligatory on the priests, and expiatory sacrifices on behalf of priests or of groups in which priests were included (for example, the whole people) were commonly burnt entire. Some of the others might be, for instance one might vow a 'whole burnt offering' or bring one when making a prayer (as Rabba said, 'The whole burnt offering is a gift'[2]). But generally the priests got most edible parts of the expiatory offerings, most of the vegetable offerings, and a sizeable share (usually the chest and the right thigh) of most others. Consequently they worked out with loving detail the rules governing sacrifices, of which this paragraph has given a skimpy summary.[3]

Comparable attention was given to the festivals as occasions for sacrifices and pilgrimage. Hence came the calendars in Lev. 23 and Num. 28. These agree in putting first of all feasts the Sabbath, perhaps because of the importance it had acquired in the diaspora as a distinguishing mark. For the priestly authors it is the goal and completion of creation, the cause of the commandments, the sign of the eternal covenant between God and Israel.[4] It has thrown into shadow the old celebration of the new moons, which Leviticus omits. Surprisingly, Leviticus omits the Passover, an old festival of the nomads to avert evil spirits from their flocks[5], and instead of the Feast of Unleavened Bread, filling the

[1] Exod. 29: 38ff; Num. 28: 3ff; 29: 13–16.
[2] *Babli Zebaḥim* 7b.
[3] Fuller treatments will be found in de Vaux, *Israel*, Part 4, and especially pp. 415–56, and in the distinguished article by T. Gaster, 'Sacrifices and Offerings. OT', *IDB* 4, 147–59.
[4] Gen. 1: 1–2: 3; Exod. 19: 11 versus Deut. 5: 15.
[5] Cf. de Vaux, *Israel*, p. 489.

week after Passover, it has a feast of a single day to be celebrated when the first sheaf from the harvest of the new grain is offered to Yahweh. Numbers has the familiar feasts of Passover and Unleavened Bread. The two calendars come together in the Feast 'of Firstfruits' which Leviticus dates seven weeks and a day after the offering of the sheaf; this is the end of the harvest season, loaves made of meal from the new grain are the symbolic offering. The hot, dry summer, without agricultural events, was therefore without religious festivals. On the first day of the seventh month came the Day of the War Cry[1] when no labour might be done – an unexplained celebration, unknown to pre-exilic sources, and *not* said to be a new year's festival. On the tenth day of this month was the Day of Atonement, also unknown to pre-exilic sources and probably inspired by similar ceremonies in Babylonia.[2] The following fifteenth to twenty-second saw the seven-day 'Feast of Booths' celebrating the grape and fruit harvest, and an eighth day that closed the festal calendar for the year.

These two calendars must come from the latter half of the Persian period. What was done before that time is uncertain. Ezra 3: 4 claims that returned exiles in 538/7 celebrated the Feast of Booths 'as it is written', but Nehemiah 8: 14ff says that the commandments prescribing this feast were 'discovered' when the people came to read the law introduced by Ezra in 458, and the feast was then, for the first time since the days of Joshua, celebrated 'as it is written'. This same passage of Nehemiah goes from the first day of the seventh month to the Feast of Booths without any mention of an intervening Day of Atonement.[3] And the preceding story of Ezra's reading his law, on the first day of the seventh month, knows nothing of that day's being a festival. Evidently the assimilationist priesthood in the fourth century reorganized the religious year and amplified it by introduction of the autumn war festival and the Day of Atonement. Given the disintegration of Persian control, the satraps' revolt, and the Egyptian invasion, a war festival was appropriate. That assimilationists introduced the Day of Atonement is reasonably certain, not only because of the Babylonian parallel, but also because of the ritual prescribed in Lev. 16: the sins of the people are magically, by laying on of hands, transferred to a goat which is sent off to 'Azazel' – presumably a demon – in the wilderness. Such names compounded with '*el* (god) become familiar as names of angels and demons. The story of the fall of the angels, in Enoch 6 to 11, written about a century after Lev. 16, combines several accounts, in one of which Azazel was chief of the demons.

[1] Lev. 23: 24; Num. 29: 1; cf. de Vaux, *Israel*, pp. 254, 259.
[2] Cf. de Vaux, *Israel*, p. 508.   [3] De Vaux, *Israel*, 509f.

Besides directing the ceremonies and offering the sacrifices of the cult, the priests had many other functions. Some were connected with the ceremonies – for instance, they were the trumpeters who gave the signals not only in festivals, but also in public assemblies and war.[1] Understandably, it was they who inspected the animals offered for sacrifice – only perfect ones were acceptable – and who set the value of objects that had been vowed to Yahweh but, because of imperfections or for other reasons, could not be sacrificed and had to be bought back by payment of their value plus one-fifth.[2] It was their peculiar privilege to bless the people in the name of Yahweh.[3] In war they accompanied the armies and assured them of Yahweh's support.[4]

More functions derived from their authority in matters of law, especially on 'ritual purity' (something completely distinct from ordinary cleanliness). Questions on this subject were brought to them (for example, Haggai 2: 11ff) as later to rabbis. Their powers were frightening – if a priest said a man had 'leprosy' the man could no longer live in an observant community; a house or garment declared 'leprous' might have to be destroyed.[5] To the 'leprous' only a priest, by official pronouncement and prescribed rituals (including sacrifices), could restore cleanliness.[6] Only a priest could cleanse a woman after childbirth,[7] or a 'Nazirite' who had taken a vow to be 'holy to Yahweh' (and therefore to abstain from haircuts and grape products).[8] Only a priest could administer the ordeal and offer the sacrifices to convict or cleanse a woman suspected of adultery.[9] And only a priest could prepare the special water (mixed with the ashes of a red cow and other ingredients) necessary to remove defilement caused by a dead body.[10]

Besides their functions as authorities on ritual and purity, the priests are often spoken of as teaching 'the law' in general.[11] Deuteronomy had

---

[1] Num. 10: 1–10; 31: 6; 1 Chron. 15: 24; 2 Chron. 5: 12; 13: 12ff.

[2] Lev. 1: 3; etc.; Lev. 27: 8, 12, 14 etc.

[3] Num. 6: 22–27.

[4] Deut. 20: 2–4.

[5] Lev. 13: 45f, 52, 55, 57; 14: 45; Num. 5: 2ff. The Hebrew term translated by 'leprosy' refers to various skin and fungus conditions.

[6] Lev. 13; 14. [7] Lev. 12.

[8] Num. 6.

[9] Num. 5. *Utehorah* in verse 28 should probably be rendered: 'Then [as a consequence of the performance of this ceremony] she is [now] clean [for intercourse with her husband].'

[10] Num. 19: 3–7. By contrast, the priests in Deut. 2: 5 seem intruded. They do nothing; the ceremony, like those in the adjacent texts, is conducted by the elders.

[11] Deut. 33: 10; Hos. 4: 6; Micah 3: 11; 4: 2 = Isa. 2: 3; Jer. 2: 8 (?); Mal. 2: 4–7; Lev. 10: 11; Deut. 27: 14ff (but in the corresponding passage, Josh. 8: 30–34, the law is read by Joshua).

given them a large role in legal affairs,[1] but the priestly legal material includes little civil or criminal law, beyond moral precepts. The law taught by the priests was presumably like that preserved in the Pentateuch, 'codes' mainly of moral rules, with detailed teaching on rituals, cleanliness, obligations to the Temple, and so on.

Of this law the priests were not only the custodians but the 'unacknowledged legislators'.[2] How much of their legislation was produced in the Persian period is uncertain, as are the stages by which it was attached to the narratives that now frame it in the Pentateuch. The old peasant stories of the patriarchs and Joshua (heroes of Palestinian holy places at Bethel, Hebron, Beersheba and Shechem) had doubtless long been collected in cycles and may, before Persian times, have been connected with some or all of the other elements of the hexateuchal narrative, myths about the beginning of the world, the flood and so on, the Joseph romance, nomads' tales of Moses, and stories about the conquest of the country. These components are clear; how they were put together is hazy; but most scholars would agree that the Jerusalem priests of the Persian period were the final editors who gave the material substantially its present form, wrote as a prologue for it the account of creation in Gen. 1: 1 to 2: 3 (which a Greek critic cited as an example of sublimity),[3] connected the parts by a genealogical framework, and rewrote many stories to serve their own purposes, usually as legal precedents. The whole now has the form of a history, and expresses a theory of history, to wit: the world is the work of Yahweh, but the lower gods (Gen. 6: 2) and men have revolted from him. He does not destroy them because, after the flood, Noah's institution of sacrifice persuaded him to promise not to send another general destruction.[4] Thenceforth he has pursued, by selection and training of those he hoped would obey him, his goal: to get proper service. Neither the Davidic kingdom nor the Jerusalem Temple was essential for this. His worship could be properly performed in a tent in the wilderness. Essential are the ritual law, the law of purity, and the priesthood that knows, fulfils and teaches both.

The latent internationalism of this history reflects the thinking of assimilationist elements in the priesthood, and possibly of their in-laws in Samaria, Ammon, Moab and even Egypt.[5] Another example of this

[1] Deut. 17: 18; 31: 9ff (the elders of Israel were probably tagged on at the end of verse 9 by a glossator); Deut. 17: 8–13 (the judge may be an addition).
[2] From Shelley's description of poets, 'the unacknowledged legislators of mankind'.
[3] 'Longinus', *De sublimitate* ix.9.
[4] Gen. 8: 20ff, a masterpiece of priestly poetry.
[5] The Joseph romance made Joseph marry an Egyptian. On its date see D. Redford, *A Study of the Biblical Story of Joseph*, VTSup 20 (Leiden, 1970).

way of thinking appears in Genesis 17: 1–8, which insists that Abraham was to be the father of 'a multitude of nations' including all inhabitants of Palestine. Similarly, 17: 20, 23–27 emphasizes God's blessing on Ishmael, the father of the Arabs, and Ishmael's circumcision on the same day as Abraham, implying his inclusion in the covenant. Such tendentious narratives, of which many examples could be found,[1] were significant because they were parts of the framework of a collection of laws and might be used as legal precedents. Yet more important were changes in the laws, especially those governing relations between Israelites and aliens.

The segregationists' insistence that non-Judeans were impure had evidently been coupled with the assumption that nothing could be done to alter their status, Hence, as one of Ezra's collaborators put it, the only 'immersion pool for Israel', the only way by which the people could be cleansed from the pollution of marriage with aliens, was divorce.[2] Ezra's consequent demand for divorce led to his downfall while Nehemiah exiled priests married to aliens and resorted to tyrannical measures, including torture, to prevent further marriages.[3]

The priests met the difficulty by developing a new legal concept, that of conversion, a process by which a Gentile might become an Israelite. They concealed the novelty of this solution by using an old term, *ger*, to signify the new legal entity, convert.[4] And since they possessed the official texts of the laws, they wrote their new concept into the texts.[5] Thereby they effected probably the quietest and most far-reaching revolution in history. They changed fundamentally the character of Judaism, its offshoot Christianity, and its derivative Islam. 'Judaism' became, legally, a condition open to anyone able to satisfy the requirements for admission, and these requirements might be matters of practice or belief, not ancestry or territorial origin. Thus 'Judaism' could become a world religion, capable of indefinite extension by conversion of all peoples. The novelty of this concept can be seen by comparing the vision of (Second) Isaiah 60 to 61 with that of the author of Rev. 5: 9f, who echoes Isaiah's words, but has a radically different notion of the new Jerusalem. 'Isaiah' anticipated that all nations should

---

[1] Smith, *Palestinian Parties*, p. 177 and references there.

[2] Ezra 10: 2.

[3] Neh. 13: 25, 28.

[4] On the history of *ger* see Smith, *Palestinian Parties*, pp. 178f. The new concept came in between the books of Ruth and Judith. Ruth, the ideal proselyte, is never converted; she is married; that suffices. The ritual conversion of Achior the Ammonite is carefully recorded, Judith 14: 10.

[5] It appears in Exod. 12: 43–50; Num. 9: 14; 15: 1–31; 19: 10; 35: 15; Deut. 19: 10; Joshua 20: 9. On these see Smith, *Palestinian Parties*, pp. 181ff.

come to 'bring gold and frankincense, and...proclaim the praise' of Yahweh and offer sacrifice to Him (60: 6f) but *not* that they should become converts to Judaism. On the contrary they remain 'aliens' and become servants of the Israelites who are the peculiar 'people of priests' offering the sacrifices brought by all other peoples, and living in luxury on the proceeds (61: 5f). In Rev. 1: 6, on the contrary, the *converts* 'from every tribe and tongue and people and nation' have been 'made...a kingdom for our God, and priests, and they shall rule the earth'.

The immediate consequence of the new law was the more modest one for which it had been introduced: it provided a legal way to discredit objections against marriage with aliens. We have seen that it did not satisfy everyone. Obstinate segregationists made a law of their own (Neh. 10), so the gentry kept up propaganda in favour of intermarriage until Maccabean times.[1] But the law now provided a way to legitimize marital relations between Judeans and their neighbours. Relations presently became so close that the Samaritans accepted the Pentateuch. They may have made a few changes in the text (they made more later) but their chief difficulty in accepting it – Deuteronomy's limitation of sacrifice to 'the place Yahweh shall choose, to make his Name dwell there' – was probably eliminated by exegesis: the Hebrew could be made to mean 'any place', and the priestly law in the Pentateuch allowed for sacrifice in every village.[2] Thus, thanks to priestly edition, exegesis and policy, the sacral law of Jerusalem took the first step of its international career.

When we think of the works of genius and vast influence produced by the gentry, Levites and priests of Jerusalem during these two centuries – Ruth, Job, Ecclesiastes, the Song of Songs, most Psalms, Genesis 1, the edition of the Pentateuch, to mention the greatest – it is hard to believe that there should be more. But this age also saw the final flowering of Israelite prophecy, though the prophecies are often overlooked because attached to earlier books; they are dismissed as 'spurious' without consideration of their merits. Neglect has resulted, too, from the difficulty of recognizing interpolations, the differences between scholars as to which passages belong here,[3] the scattered condition of the material, the diversity of the viewpoints represented, and the difficulties of dating isolated prophecies and distinguishing them

---

[1] Above, pp. 249–50.

[2] J. Morgenstern, 'Supplementary Studies in the Calendars of Ancient Israel', *HUCA* 10 (1935), 1ff; p. 36 on Lev. 23. Cf. Lev. 17: 1–7 and 26: 31, and Smith, *Palestinian Parties*, p. 225, n. 248.

[3] This account follows mainly Pfeiffer, *Introduction*, Fohrer, *Introduction*, and Eissfeldt, *Einleitung*. Their agreements, however, do not yield a wholly adequate list.

from mere literary expansions (ranging from occasional comments to systematic editorial enlargement, as in Jeremiah).

Given these difficulties, it seems best to begin with the works that refer to recognizable situations. Of what is called 'Third Isaiah' (Isa. 56 to 66) the main body (Isa. 56: 9 to 65: 16) fits the period between the beginning of the exiles' return and the rebuilding of the city and Temple, still in ruins (63: 18; 64: 10f) but soon to be restored.[1] Continuing pagan practices of the Judean population are denounced, repentance is demanded as the condition for restoration,[2] the unrepentant are threatened with destruction, the righteous assured of success:[3] all in a style modelled on the Babylonian prophecies of Second Isaiah. This is the work of one of those returned exiles who would have nothing to do with 'the people of the land'.[4] Its superb picture of all nations bringing offerings to Jerusalem emphasizes the unique position of the Jews as the priests whom the rest will serve.[5]

This poem circulated separately for some time, and minor compositions were added to it: 56: 1–8 promises foreigners and eunuchs access to the Temple, provided they join themselves to Yahweh, love His name, serve Him and keep His Sabbaths. Nehemiah, leader of the segregationist party, was a eunuch; this equation of eunuchs and foreigners was polemic.[6] It dates the passage, as does the concern for the Sabbath, shared by Nehemiah, the levitic historians and the priestly legislators.[7] At the end of 'Third Isaiah' stands a cluster of additions, among them fragments from a prophet who foresaw an entirely new creation, a new heaven, new earth and new Jerusalem in which all creatures should live at peace, there should be no sacrifice, and all mankind should worship Yahweh by humility and reverence.[8] This combines the old prophetic principle, that Yahweh wants obedience, not sacrifice,[9] with the new notion of a new creation,[10] a concept equally important and unexplained. Such *nova* reveal how little is known of the intellectual and religious life of this age.

[1] Isa. 58: 12; 60: 7, 10, 13, 17; 61: 4; 62: 7, 10.
[2] Isa. 57: 13b–19; 58: 8, 10ff, 14; 59: 20; 65: 8–16.
[3] Isa. 57: 13a, 20f; 59: 18; 65: 6f, 8–16.
[4] Ezra 4: 1–5.
[5] Isa. 60: 12; 61: 5f.
[6] Smith, *Palestinian Parties*, p. 180 and n. 170.
[7] Above, pp. 247, 258 and 263. The same hand may have added 58: 13f.
[8] Isa. 65: 17–25; 66: 1–4, 7–13 (?), 22f.
[9] Amos 5: 21ff; Hos. 6: 6; Micah 6: 6ff; Isa. 1: 11–14; Ps. 1: 8ff.
[10] The prose gloss in Isa. 51: 6 may come from this author. It probably means 'For [even if] the heavens should melt away like smoke...my salvation would endure forever'. But it may have posed the problem that led to this answer.

Shortly after Third Isaiah come the prophecies of Haggai, from August to December of 520 B.C.E., and of Zechariah, from October 520 to December 518.[1] Haggai's were simple: Yahweh was angry because his Temple had not been rebuilt; consequently crops had been bad. If the Judeans would start building he would bless them. Though their building was inferior to the former Temple, Yahweh would make it splendid; he was about to overthrow the kingdoms and make the Persian governor of Judea (a Jew, Zerubbabel) his signet – that is, viceroy. Zechariah's prophecies were more complex. He demanded repentance; the people repented,[2] and he began to see symbolic objects that had to be interpreted – an ancient procedure[3] destined for development in apocalyptic. The interpretations revealed Yahweh's intent to have his Temple rebuilt, bless Jerusalem, and cut off the peoples that oppressed Judah. The city, though unwalled, would be populous; Yahweh would dwell among them as glory within and a wall of fire without.[4] The High Priest Joshua would be purified and confirmed in his authority (*provided* he would keep Yahweh's law)[5] but should expect the coming of the true Branch (from the tree of Jesse), the destined Davidic king. This Branch was soon identified as Zerubbabel, the Persian governor, who was equated with the high priest and eventually crowned.[6] Other visions promised internal security: Yahweh's curse as a winged scroll (of the law?) would fly about the city and strangle thieves and perjurers; 'Wickedness', worship of other gods, would be carried off to Babylonia where a 'house' was being prepared for her (chapter 5) – probably a syncretistic temple. Finally, peace, prosperity and joy would follow rebuilding of the Temple and re-establishment of justice (chapters 7 and 8). Such 'prophetic' words probably cost Zerubbabel his life.[7]

A probable reference to Zerubbabel's death dates the largest of the oracles now appended to the genuine prophecies of Zechariah. This oracle (Zech. 12: 1 to 13: 6) speaks of hostility between the people of

---

[1] Not November; see R. Parker and W. Dubberstein, *Babylonian Chronology, 626 B.C.–A.D. 75* (*Brown University Studies*, 19; Providence, 1956), p. 30.

[2] An editorial introduction?

[3] Amos 7: 1, 4, 7; 8: 1; 9: 1; etc.

[4] That many nations should join themselves to Yahweh *and be his people*, Zech. 2: 15, is an addition by some assimilationist.

[5] He had evidently been under fire from the segregationists. Zechariah was attempting a compromise to get support for rebuilding of the Temple and Zerubbabel's messianic putsch; see Smith, *Palestinian Parties*, p. 110.

[6] Zech. 4, and 6: 9–14; the texts have been garbled; see Smith, *Palestinian Parties*, pp. 109f.

[7] Smith, *Palestinian Parties*, pp. 116f.

Judea and the Jerusalemites, understandable as a reaction of 'the people of the land' to the exclusive claims of the returned exiles. The author foresees that Jerusalem will be attacked by all nations,[1] including the Judeans, but the Judeans will go over to the Jerusalemites; the nations will be destroyed; the victors will mourn 'for him whom they pierced'; idols, unclean spirits and prophets (!) will be removed from the land.[2] Evidently the assimilationists had their prophets, too. One of their prophecies is Zech. 9; 10: 3b–12, which predicts Judean conquest of all the Palestine–Phoenician coast, and the coming of a king who will rule the world (even the Greeks, though far off, will be cowed). Yahweh will save Judah *and Ephraim* in battle and gather the dispersed. The emphasis on the union of Judah and Ephraim indicates assimilationist origin; the antithesis between Egypt and 'Assyria'[3] points to a date in the fourth century after Egypt had regained its independence. More puzzling is a prophecy against 'the shepherds' (probably the Persian governors: 10: 3a; 11; 13: 7–9) which probably reflects Nehemiah's difficulties with the three governors of Samaria, Ammon, and north-west Arabia,[4] and his breaking off good relations with the neighbouring peoples, and particularly with the Samaritans. Detail and purpose are alike unclear. Finally, Zech. 14 contains a miscellany of pronouncements about 'that day' (namely, of Yahweh) showing the popularity of the theme and the variety of the fantasies in which it found expression.

The prophecies of 'my messenger' (Hebrew: *malachi*) are complaints of a segregationist from the half-century between the completion of the Temple and the coming of Ezra (515–458), when the assimilationist priesthood was in power. After celebrating Yahweh's love for Israel (demonstrated by his destruction of Edom) the author complains that the priests dishonour Yahweh by presenting blemished offerings, and corrupt his law by false teaching. Judah has been faithless and married the daughter of an alien god. (An assimilationist retorts: divorcing the wife of your youth is worse; Yahweh hates divorce. So much for Ezra.) Oblivious of the destined retort, the author proceeded to foretell Yahweh's coming to purify the priests, so that they would present pure offerings, and to destroy the wicked. A postscript (by the same author?) adds that now Yahweh is being robbed by those who skimp their tithes; bring full tithes and he will bless you. This is hardly compatible with

---

[1] Does this reflect the size and multinational make-up of the Persian army? Cf. Herodotus VII.60–99.

[2] On the whole section see Smith, *Palestinian Parties*, pp. 115ff.

[3] Zech. 10: 10f, understand 'Persia', which it was not safe to mention.

[4] Geshem, the Arabian ruler, was on a different level than the provincial governors, but probably had some nominal position in the Persian system.

expectation of an immediate judgement, but prophets were never notable for consistency. The collection closes with another eschato-logical blast – the day comes burning like an oven (is the final fire Persian?), evildoers will be burned up and the righteous saved. Remember the law of my servant Moses; I shall send Elijah to effect a last-minute reformation.

Latest of all the prophecies preserved as separate books may be that of Joel: the country has been wrecked by insect pests, drought and invasions; cereal and drink offerings at the Temple are cut off; the priests are wailing. Worse, the day of Yahweh is coming, in the form of an invasion by an army (of locusts?). To avert it, blow the trumpets, call a solemn assembly, declare a fast, and wail some more. Yahweh will hear, drive off the invaders, and send rain and food. So you shall know (in the words of Second Isaiah) 'that I, Yahweh, am your God, there is none else'. Then I shall pour out my spirit, cause prophecies, give portents, gather all nations for judgement into the valley of Jehoshaphat, darken the sun and moon, cause an earthquake, destroy Edom, and spare Judah and Jerusalem, which shall thenceforth prosper.[1]

Such eschatological effusions enable us to date approximately the similar passages, incompatible with their contexts, in the books 'of' earlier prophets. Thus in Isa. 4: 2–6, when Yahweh has purified Zion with a fiery wind all survivors in it shall be holy,[2] the city will be covered by cloud by day and fire by night.[3] In Isa. 11 to 12, we find again the Branch from the tree of Jesse, the total peace – even between hostile animals – in Jerusalem,[4] the return of the exiles, and the subjugation of Edom, Moab and Ammon. The promise that the earth shall be full of the knowledge of Yahweh is close to the promise that all nations shall come to Jerusalem to worship.[5] Isaiah 24 to 27 destines the earth and the host of heaven for desolation, if not complete replacement. (Leviathan, too, will be punished; a unique item.) Yahweh himself will reign in Zion, regather the exiles, and make a feast for all peoples. Similar alterations of the physical world are promised by Isa. 30: 18–33

---

[1] The accusation that the Philistines and Phoenicians have sold Judeans and Jerusa-lemites to the Greeks as slaves (3: 6) need not be Hellenistic. Trade with Greeks flourished throughout the Persian period, and Yahweh's revenge (to give Phoenicians and Philistines to the Judeans for sale as slaves to the Arabians, 3: 8), fits the loose government of the later Persian period better than Ptolemaic times. The distinction between Judeans and Jerusalemites probably reflects the schism of the early Persian period; see above on Zech. 12: 1 to 13: 6.

[2] Cf. Zech. 14: 4; Isa. 30: 27ff; 33: 12f; 66: 15f; etc.

[3] Zech. 2: 5.

[4] Isa. 11: 6–9; 65: 25.

[5] Isa. 11: 9; 56: 7; 60: 14; 66: 19ff; Jer. 12: 14ff; 16: 19ff; Zech. 2: 11; 14 end.

and 32 to 35, again culminating in purification by fire, destruction of the nations or the 'Assyrians' (Persians), and true knowledge of Yahweh. Jeremiah 17: 19–27, like the present preface to Third Isaiah,[1] makes observance of the Sabbath the criterion for salvation, and like Malachi threatens destruction of the wicked by fire. In 33: 1–4 the wicked shepherds are to be punished, as in Zechariah. In Micah 4 to 5 mount Zion will be raised above all other mountains, many nations shall come to learn the law and shall thenceforth live in peace. The exiles will be gathered in and Yahweh will reign in Zion forever. But also the nations assembled to profane Zion shall be defeated and a king from David's city (Bethlehem) shall rule the world including 'Assyria'.

These examples, and many more,[2] show the characteristics of the eschatological excitement evidently persistent in Jerusalem during the Persian period. Its background was the sudden collapse of Assyria (620–609 B.C.E.), Media (550), Lydia (546), Babylonia (539), and Egypt (525) in quick succession, then the usurpation of the Persian throne and attendant revolts in 522–520. The failure of the revolts and, in Judea, the fate of Zerubbabel probably cooled speculation for some time, but did not quench it. The great revolt in Egypt from 460 to 454 doubtless revived it; shortly after 444 Nehemiah was accused of messianic pretensions and of having hired prophets to proclaim him king (Neh. 6: 7). The successful revolt of Egypt, beginning about 410, and disintegration of Persian control of the western provinces during the fourth century, with the satraps' revolt, beginning in 366, and the Egyptian invasion of Palestine in 361 to 360, provided more occasions for such fantasies.

To this political background the prophetic reactions were primarily political and provincial. The hopes most often reiterated are for the rebuilding or glorification of Jerusalem and the Temple, the regathering of Israelite – especially Judean – exiles to form a strong military power, agricultural produce to support them, and conquest of their neighbours, most often of Edom, Moab, Ammon and the Philistine plain, but sometimes also of Phoenicia and Damascus. As leader of this imperialistic revival the prophets usually hope for a king from the Davidic dynasty, who will institute a reign of justice (for Israelites) and (once the neighbours are subjected) of perpetual peace.

These elements of the visions can thus be selected to make a picture

[1] Isa. 56: 1–8.
[2] Notably Isa. 1: 27ff; 15; 16; 19; 21: 11ff; 23: 1–14; 29: 5ff, 17–24; 31: 4–9; Jer. 9: 23f; 10: 1–16; 12: 14ff; 16: 19ff; 25: 15–38; 31: 29–37; 33; Ezek. 38 to 39; Amos 9: 8b–15; Obad. 1: 1–15b; Micah 7: 8–20; Nahum 1: 1–10; Hab. 3; Zeph. 3: 8 to end.

at least realistic, if not realizable. But besides we find themes of pure fantasy, and these are mixed with the realistic elements. The prophecies cannot be divided into two types, one realistic and the other fantastic; some stand closer to realism, others to fantasy, but most have some elements of both. However, if we put together most of the fantastic themes, they also yield a roughly coherent picture: the king will not be a Davidide, but Yahweh Himself. At His coming a new heaven and earth will be created or the old purified by fire; the wicked will be destroyed and the order of nature drastically changed. Sickness shall be no more, the blind shall see, the deaf hear. Peace shall be perfect; the wolf and the lamb shall lie down together. The king's rule shall be universal and eternal. The world shall be full of the knowledge of Yahweh; all nations shall come to worship at Jerusalem, and even be joined to Israel. Yahweh will pour out His spirit on all mankind, or write His law in their hearts, so that all shall know Him by nature, not by learning.

The roots of this vision are not in political events (though those may have encouraged its expression) but in the revolt of the human spirit against the conditions of humanity. The expressions of that revolt are necessarily nonsense, but the courage to express such nonsense as a vision of the future here found its fullest, if not its first, expression. Hence the unique power and joy of this pathetic poetry.

In conclusion: this chapter has been limited to what can be learned from the preserved evidence that speaks explicitly of 'Jews' or can be identified as 'Jewish', that is, mainly the archeological evidence connected with the name of Yahweh, the Elephantine papyri, and the literary material that subsequent generations of Jerusalem pietists chose to preserve. To suppose that the Jewish religious life of the Persian period was as limited as are these bodies of evidence, would be absurd. Connections with the cults of other gods besides Yahweh are clear at Elephantine and elsewhere in Egypt and Palestine, are implied by the nomenclature in Babylonia, and are attested by the polemics in Palestinian literature. So we have outlined only a portion of the Yahwistic nucleus. Around this was a body of Judean syncretism and paganism we can reasonably infer, but not reconstruct. A common error of historians is to suppose that what cannot be proved to have existed, did not exist. Perhaps no other supposition has done so much to distort the history of ancient Judaism. We must try to learn to be ignorant.

TERMINAL NOTE

The following comments on the points indicated by the lemmata deal with matters that have come to my attention during the years since the completion of this article.

Hebrew names in Mesopotamian documents. See M. Coogan, *West Semitic Personal Names in the Murašû Documents* (Missoula, 1976) (*Harvard Semitic Monographs* 7), the review of this by R. Zadok, *BASOR*, 231 (1978), 73–8, and Zadok's two monographs, *On West Semites in Babylonia during the Chaldaean and Achaemenian Periods* (Jerusalem, 1977), and *The Jews in Babylonia during* (etc.) (Jerusalem, 1978), both in Hebrew.

Grelot's documents. Notice Grelot's corrections in *RB*, 82 (1975), 288–92 and the comments of E. Lipiński, *Bibliotheca orientalis*, 31 (1974), 119–24, to which Grelot's judgments are sometimes preferable.

Meanings of Elephantine Jewish names. The conclusion here drawn from Porten's observation as to the prevalence of Hebrew names in the lists of Judeans is not affected by the arguments of M. Silverman for a prevalence in all the Jewish documents of what he calls 'Jewish Aramaic' names. By this he means names which 'most probably received their first coinage in Hebrew, but because of their structure suited the Aramaic language as well...(and) could easily pass into that tongue, their (Hebraic) significance still strong and apparent' (*Jewish Personal Names in the Elephantine Documents* (Waltham, 1967), p. 171 – a Brandeis dissertation). Silverman's theories as to the religious development of the community depend too much on dubious paleographic datings and question-begging concepts.

Elephantine contributors. An additional fragment of this list has been identified and published by R. Degen, 'Neue Fragmente aramaeischer Papyri aus Elephantine, I', *Neue Ephemeris für semitische Epigraphik*, 2 (1974), 71–8 and Abb. 21. It adds five names of which one is *Shabbetai*, one was probably compounded with *Eshem*, and the rest are uncertain.

Egyptian data. Add W. Kornfeld, 'Jüdisch–aramäische Grabschriften aus Edfu', *Anzeiger der Oester. Ak. d. W., Ph.-h. Klasse*, 110 (1973), 123–37, where we find a *Zebadyah bar 'Azgad* ('Yahweh gave [him], son of Gad is strong', or 'My strength is Gad' – so Teixidor, 'Bulletin', *Syria*, 53 (1976), § 164, who also would read *kbdyh*, 'My glory is Yahweh', instead of *zbdyh*. Gad was the god of chance). Another member of the family

was Shelemzion ('Peace [be on] Zion'). But an offering table of the type
used for Egyptian gods was inscribed 'Obadiah son of Simon'.
'Obadiah' means 'Slave of Yahweh'.

Phoenician influence. This has now been documented by recent publications
of finds at coastal towns, e.g. E. Stern, *Excavations at Tel Mevorakh*
(1973–76) I (Jerusalem, 1978) (*Qedem* 9). Notice page 82, Stern's
remarks on 'the extensive and concentrated Phoenician expansion
towards the northern coast of Palestine, which was led by the kings of
Tyre and Sidon under Persian encouragement and tutelage'. Cf. Stern's
review in *PEQ*, 104 (1972), 157f of J. Elgavish, *Archaeological Excavations*
at Shikmona...I (Haifa, 1968).

Greek culture. It is true that Greek artifacts were often more conspicuously
decorated with pictures of men and gods. However, ancient near-eastern
culture was far from aniconic. In Palestine, for instance, pre-exilic seals
carrying biblical names commonly carry pictures, and often pictures of
deities. In the post-exilic period such seals almost never carry pictures
(above, p. 237). This change must have resulted from deliberate reform.
An important section of the Judean upper class had now accepted the
deuteronomic ban on images. Therefore the incoming flood of imagery
(most of it religiously indifferent, mainly decorative) was met by an
expanding dyke of intolerance which attributed religious significance
to objects not hitherto prohibited, and thus made the use even of
indifferent imagery a matter, sometimes, of importance as evidence of
rejection of the requirements now being advanced. The difficulty is to
determine which finds are evidence of religious attitudes, which of
fashion.

CHAPTER 11

PERSIAN RELIGION IN THE ACHEMENID AGE

A key point in the study of Achemenid religion is the date of Zarathushtra, over which scholars have been long divided. One group judged the issue on the evidence of the Gathas, the seventeen hymns attributed to the prophet. These are composed in the oldest known stage of 'Avestan' (the eastern Iranian language of the Avesta or Zoroastrian holy texts), and have their closest linguistic affinities with the Rig-Veda. The social and world outlook implicit in them is correspondingly archaic, and so it was deduced that Zarathushtra must have lived about 1000 B.C.E. or even earlier.

The other group of scholars laid weight on a date to be derived from a late chapter of the Bundahishn. This is a composite Pahlavi work, that is, it belongs to the secondary Zoroastrian literature preserved in Pahlavi or Middle Persian, most of which was written down between the fourth and tenth centuries C.E. The chapter in question contains king-lists designed to fill out a schematized world-history; and it gives a place to Kavi Vishtaspa, Zarathushtra's royal patron, which sets the prophet's *floruit* at '258 years before Alexander'. This is the date expressly recorded, as that assigned by the Zoroastrians to their prophet, by the early Islamic scholars al-Mas^cudi and al-Biruni. Its modesty and apparent precision made it seem credible to some modern scholars, who accordingly assigned Zarathushtra to the sixth century B.C.E., supposing him thus to have been an eastern Iranian contemporary of the Achemenid Cyrus the Great.[1] This then made it impossible to regard Cyrus himself as one of his followers. Further, there is a tradition found in some Pahlavi books to the effect that there was no such thing as orthodox Zoroastrianism before the Sasanids established the second Persian empire (*circa* 224–651 C.E.); and this encouraged the supposition that even the later Achemenids had had only a vague knowledge of the prophet's teachings.

There were weighty objections, however, to this interpretation of the

---

[1] For references, and the names of some of the chief protagonists of the two schools of thought, see A. Sh. Shahbazi, 'The "traditional date of Zoroaster" explained', *BSOAS*, 40 (1977), 25–35.

history of the faith. The Gathas were orally transmitted down to at least the fourth, and possibly as late as the sixth century C.E., when the invention of the phonetically-precise Avestan alphabet (on the basis of the imperfect Pahlavi one) made it possible to set them down accurately. Writing is not likely to have been used even for secondary religious works in the various Iranian vernaculars before the Christian era. Hence an unbroken continuity must be assumed in Zoroastrian belief and worship, since the gap of even one generation would have meant the irrevocable loss of orally transmitted liturgies. It is generally agreed, moreover, that Sasanid Zoroastrianism was based essentially on the teachings of the Gathas; and yet Sasanid scholar–priests, as the existing Middle Persian translations show, had only an imperfect understanding of the meaning of these venerable texts. Sasanid orthodoxy must therefore have rested on something else – presumably an inherited tradition of doctrine and observance.

These apparent contradictions have been resolved by numerous discoveries made this century (mostly by archeologists), which shed more light on the religious history of the Iranian empires – the two Persian ones, Achemenid and Sasanid, and the intervening one of the Parthian Arsacids. It has thus become possible to trace, even if sketchily, the continual history of Zoroastrianism in Iran during these three epochs; and so it has grown clear that the accusations of heterodoxy and laxness levelled by the Sasanids at their predecessors were part of their propaganda against the Parthians, put out in an attempt to gain for themselves the adherence of pious Zoroastrians in eastern Iran (whose loyalties lay more naturally with the conquered Arsacids).[1] It has further been shown that the date '258 years before Alexander' was artificially arrived at by Persian priestly scholars after the establishment of the Seleucid era in 312/311 B.C.E., which gave an impulse to chronological calculations. This date never, it seems, gained currency among the Zoroastrians of eastern Iran, who continued to assign their prophet (though vaguely) to a much earlier epoch.[2]

With the calculated date shown to be spurious, it became possible to give due weight to the arguments for the antiquity of the Gathas; and indeed new assessments of the social picture which they convey suggest the necessity of setting Zarathushtra in an epoch before the Iranians invaded the land now called after them, probably, that is, at some time between 1500 and 1300 B.C.E., when his people would still have been pastoral nomads on the South Russian steppes.[3] His teachings were

[1] See M. Boyce, Zoroastrians, their religious beliefs and practices (London, 1979), chs. 5–8.
[2] See Shahbazi, BSOAS, 40 (1977).
[3] See M. Boyce, History of Zoroastrianism, vol. 1, ch. 1; vol. 2, ch. 1.

evidently carried with them by Iranian peoples who invaded their new land in the east, 1200+ B.C.E.; and were eventually brought from there to western Iran, which had been invaded and settled by the Medes (in the north) and Persians (in the south). The faith probably gained its first western Iranian converts in the Median trading city of Raga (modern Ray, to the south of Tehran),[1] perhaps as early as the eighth century B.C.E. From there it seems to have spread only slowly, meeting doubtless with hostility from (among others) members of the hereditary western Iranian priesthood, the magi, who are not likely to have welcomed a new teaching and a new scripture. At some point, however, the magi of Raga appear to have been converted. Raga became a holy city for western Iranian Zoroastrians, and the Median magi seem to have enjoyed a recognized seniority in the faith over their Persian brethren, even as late as the Sasanid period.

CYRUS THE GREAT AND THE ZOROASTRIAN FAITH

The records of ancient Iran are sparse; and the first piece of evidence for Zoroastrianism among the Persians comes from personal names among the Achemenids, who in the seventh century B.C.E. were ruling over Pars (Greek Persia, the modern Iranian province of Fars) as vassals of the Medes. Cyrus I was on the throne in 639; and he had a younger cousin, Arsames, who probably flourished about 600. This Arsames gave one of his sons the name Hystaspes or Vishtaspa, which was that of Zarathushtra's royal patron. In the next generation Cyrus II, grandson of the first Cyrus, called his eldest daughter Atossa, generally interpreted as a Greek rendering of Hutaosa, the name of Kavi Vishtaspa's queen; and thereafter names from Zoroastrian tradition recur among the Achemenids. Thus the grandson of the Achemenid Vishtaspa was again called Vishtaspa; and he had a son known to the Greeks as Pissouthnes, a rendering, it seems, of Avestan Pishishyaothna, the bearer of which name, according to Zoroastrian tradition, was one of Kavi Vishtaspa's sons.[2] This group of names thus provides evidence that members of two branches of the Achemenid family had accepted Zoroastrianism in the early sixth century B.C.E., and wished publicly to declare their allegiance to it.

In due course Cyrus II, known to history as Cyrus the Great, rebelled against the Median King Astyages and established the first Persian

---

[1] See H. S. Nyberg, *Die Religionen des alten Iran*, (Leipzig, 1938, reprint 1966), pp. 5–6, 46, 342–3, 396–7.

[2] On these names see F. Justi, *Iranisches Namenbuch* (Marburg, 1895, repr. 1976) and M. Mayrhofer, *Iranisches Personennamenbuch*, 1.2 (Vienna, 1979), s.v.

empire. A remarkable feature of that rebellion was that Cyrus was actively supported by members of the Median nobility, who thereby brought about the subjection of their own people to the Persians. Herodotus accounts for this by a folkloric tale of little historical likelihood;[1] but evidence for political and religious propaganda made on Cyrus' behalf before he risked his revolt suggests that one of the main factors may have been that Astyages held to the Old Iranian faith of his forefathers, whereas Cyrus put himself forward as a champion of Zoroastrianism, and so attracted support from Median adherents of the eastern religion.

The aim of this propaganda appears to have been to gain the neutrality, if not active support, of neighbouring kingdoms in the coming struggle; and it seems likely that the agents were Zoroastrian magi, both Medes and Persians, who were prepared to risk their lives for the advancement of their faith. In Ionia traces of Zoroastrian cosmological doctrines have been found in the philosophy of Anaximander of Miletus (*fl. circa* 550 B.C.E.);[2] and agents of Cyrus appear to have won over the priests of an Apollo-shrine near Magnesia on the Meander, who gave a favourable oracle for the Persian king when his armies finally reached Asia Minor.[3] In Babylonia the priests of Marduk were led to issue an oracle, presumably in 553, to the effect that the gods of Babylon would cause Cyrus, 'his petty vassal with his small army', to overcome Astyages and take him captive;[4] and other Persian agents evidently sought out the numerous peoples exiled in Babylonia, among them the Jews. Striking testimony to this comes from the verses of Second Isaiah, who was brought to hail Cyrus, with complete trust, as the coming deliverer of his people. That in Babylon, as in Ionia, Cyrus' agents blended religious teaching with political propaganda can be deduced from certain elements in the prophecies of Second Isaiah, which, it has been suggested, were not only relatively unfamiliar to Jewish ears, but were markedly Zoroastrian in character. One of the leading doctrines taught by Zarathushtra was that Ahuramazda (previously worshipped by the Iranians as one of their great gods) was God Himself, the one eternal beneficent Being, 'Creator of all things through the

---

[1] 1.107ff, especially 119ff, 129.

[2] See most recently M. L. West, *Early Greek Philosophy and the Orient* (Oxford, 1971), pp. 76ff.

[3] See the letter of Darius the Great to Gadatas, text (with bibliography) ed. F. Lochner-Hüttenbach, in W. Brandenstein and M. Mayrhofer, *Handbuch des Altpersischen* (Wiesbaden, 1964), pp. 91–8. For the above interpretation see Sidney Smith, *Isaiah Chapters XL–LV*, The Schweich lectures 1940 (London, 1944), p. 41.

[4] See Smith, *Isaiah*, pp. 32–3.

Holy Spirit' (Y.44.7). This doctrine, which pervades his utterances, finds particularly majestic expression in Yasna 44.[1] Striking parallels have been traced between verses in this Gatha and words uttered by Second Isaiah; and it has been suggested that the stress put by the Jewish prophet on the concept of God the Creator owes something to his contact with Zoroastrian teachings.[2] Acceptance of this interpretation depends on the date ascribed to certain of the Psalms; but it undoubtedly seems possible that Second Isaiah, listening to the nameless magus speaking of the might and majesty of Ahuramazda, and his power to accomplish his will through his instrument Cyrus, accepted both the message of hope and the new concept of God, but saw the Supreme Being according to his own faith as Yahweh. Jew and Zoroastrian would have found a minor bond in their rejection of images in worship – a theme which is prominent with Second Isaiah; but Zoroastrian dualism was wholly alien to Jewish thought, and appears to be explicitly rejected through the words: 'I am Yahweh, there is no other...author alike of prosperity and trouble' (Isa. 45:7).[3]

ZOROASTRIAN DUALISM

Zarathushtra's own dualism is expressed with characteristic force and concentration in the following Gathic verses:

Truly there are two primal Spirits, twins renowned to be in conflict. In thought and word, in action, they are two: the good and the bad. And those who act well have chosen rightly between these two, not so the evil-doers. And when these two Spirits encountered, they created life and not-life, and how at the end the Worst Existence [i.e. hell] shall be for the deceitful, but [the House of] Best Thought [i.e. heaven] for the just' (Y.30.3–4).[4]

Here is encapsulated the doctrine of two uncreated Beings, opposed, the one good, God the Creator, the other evil, the Hostile Spirit, Angra Mainyu (so named in Y.45.2), who is the source of all that is negative

---

[1] The Gathas are numbered Yasna 28–34, 43–51, 53, because they are preserved as part of the liturgy of the yasna, the main Zoroastrian act of worship. For translations see the bibliography.

[2] See Morton Smith, 'II Isaiah and the Persians', *JAOS*, 83 (1963), 415–21.

[3] Translation according to the New English Bible, but with 'Yahweh' substituted for 'the Lord'. On the word rendered as 'trouble', which in Hebrew 'embraces both woe and evil', see C. Westermann, *Isaiah 40–66, A Commentary*, English translation by D. M. G. Stalker (London, 1969), p. 162.

[4] Following the translation of S. Insler, *The Gāthās of Zarathustra*, Acta Iranica 8 (Leiden, 1975). Against modern attempts to understand the two Spirits as other than Ahuramazda and his Adversary see, with references, Boyce, *History*, 1, pp. 193–4; 2, p. 232.

and wrong; also the doctrine of individual judgement at the end of life, with each departed soul assigned to heaven or hell according to its deserts. Sharp antitheses such as these are ever present in the Gathas, with the principle of justice and truth (*aša*) constantly opposed to that of evil and falsehood (*drug*). This world is a place of conflict, and has been created to be such, for the overcoming of evil; and the struggle of opposites will be resolved only on the last day, and at the Last Judgement, when through 'blazing fire and molten metal' the deceitful will be destroyed, and the just for ever saved (Y.51.9). The tradition amplifies the words of the Gathas, making it clear that on the last day all souls will pass through a river of molten metal – an apocalyptic version of the judicial ordeal by molten metal practised by the ancient Iranians. In the earthly ordeals (so it was believed) liars and wrongdoers perished, while the just and truthful survived through the intervention of the divine powers. So it will be also at the Last Judgement. The wicked will be annihilated, the good saved to enjoy eternal bliss in the kingdom of Ahuramazda to come upon an earth restored to its original state of unmarred perfection.[1] It is then that the Supreme Being, having destroyed his Adversary and all his forces, will be not only wholly good and wise, but also all-powerful, ruling over a universe which he has set free from evil.

THE OTHER DIVINE BEINGS

Zarathushtra invokes other lesser divine beings in the Gathas, notably a great heptad which includes the Holy Spirit. These seven beings appear as hypostases of qualities of the Supreme Being, which are also qualities of the just and good man: Truth (or Justice), Good Thought, Dominion (rightfully exerted), Devotion, Wholeness and Immortality. They are invoked and supplicated as divinities; and the prophet expresses Ahuramazda's relationship to them in various ways, speaking of him as the Creator of one, the Father of another. They are said to be 'of one will' with him; and in a Pahlavi passage his bringing them into existence is compared to the lighting of torches from a torch.[2]

Zarathushtra invokes among other divinities Hearkening and Recompense; and the 'other Ahuras', that is Mithra and Varuna (the latter not named in Iranian tradition, but worshipped by titles such as 'the high Lord' and 'the Dispenser of Good').[3] The names Mithra and

[1] See H. Lommel, *Die Religion Zarathustras nach dem Awesta dargestellt* (Tübingen, 1930), pp. 219ff; Boyce, *History*, I, pp. 242–4. The stern doctrine of the destruction of the wicked was modified in later times, see ibid.

[2] See Boyce, *History*, I, pp. 194ff.   [3] See ibid., pp. 40ff; 2, pp. 15–17.

Varuna probably imply Fidelity and Truth (the Indo-Iranian religious tradition having a striking capacity for hypostatizing virtues and states); and although it is not explicit in the Gathas, his followers were presumably faithful to their prophet's profoundly coherent teachings in believing that these and all the other beneficent divinities recognized in the Avesta were brought into existence by Ahuramazda, to help him in the cosmic struggle against evil. So all are subordinate beings, acting in accord with their Creator's will. Collectively (together with the first great heptad) they are called the Amesha Spentas, 'Holy Immortals', or the Yazatas, 'those to be worshipped'. The word *spenta* is characteristic of Zarathushtra's revelation, and has a sense such as 'bounteous, beneficent, holy'. It is widely applied in his faith to what belongs to, or furthers, the good creation of Ahuramazda.

Opposed to the holy, beneficent powers were the Daevas, wicked, supernatural beings who demanded worship, but sought to lead men astray. They were 'the seed of Bad Thought, the Lie and Arrogance' (Y.32.3), cohorts of the Hostile Spirit, who 'have defrauded mankind of good life and immortality' (Y.32.5). Originally the Daevas were probably ancient, amoral gods of war;[1] and the prophet, loving justice and peace, utterly forbade his followers to venerate or propitiate them. To do so, he taught, was to become oneself wicked while living, and damned hereafter.

ARCHEOLOGICAL TESTIMONY TO THE ZOROASTRIANISM OF CYRUS

Cyrus duly fulfilled what his propagandists had foretold, overthrew Astyages in battle in 550, and founded the Achemenid empire. After making the last of his territorial acquisitions, Babylonia with her tributaries Syria and Palestine, in 539, he built himself a new capital at Pasargadae, in the north of Pars. Its ruins have by now been thoroughly explored; and among the surface finds were the fragments of two (or possibly three) objects of striking religious interest: elegant fire-holders, finely carved in stone, which can be reconstructed as consisting of a three-stepped top and base, joined by a square shaft. The whole probably stood about waist-high; and in the top was a hollow bowl, deep enough to hold a thick bed of ash for sustaining an ever-burning wood fire.[2]

The cult of the hearth fire was, it seems, general among the Indo-European peoples, and had undoubtedly been practised by the

[1] See Boyce, *History*, I, pp. 53-5.
[2] See D. Stronach, *Pasargadae* (Oxford, 1978), p. 141 with fig. 72 and pl. 107.

ancient Iranians; but its intention was to honour the divinity of fire, and its rites could be carried out by a single member of the household. Zarathushtra appointed fire as the symbol of justice and truth, and laid on all his followers the duty of praying in its presence at appointed times each day (compare Y.43.9). During these prayers wood and incense would be placed on the fire; and the fire-holders of Pasargadae appear to have been designed so that a Zoroastrian King of kings could say the obligatory prayers, and make the offerings, with appropriate dignity. A similar fire-holder, or 'fire-altar' as western scholars have termed it, appears in the funerary carvings of Darius the Great and all his successors; and it became a standard type of 'fire-altar' when a temple cult of fire was evolved in the late Achemenid period.

In the early period the Iranians still raised no buildings for worship, preferring to venerate the divine beings, in traditional manner, among the natural objects of their own creation. The ancient Iranian cosmogony divided the world into seven distinct creations, in order sky, water, earth, plants, animals, man, fire (the last being as it were the life-force within the rest, as well as visibly present in sun, moon and hearth fire). Zarathushtra apprehended the seven great Amesha Spentas to be the guardians of these seven creations, and moreover immanent in them, as well as transcendent; Dominion in the sky, Devotion in the earth, Wholeness or Health in water, Immortality in plants, Good Thought in cattle, and the Holy Spirit in the just man, while Justice or Truth itself resided in fire. At Zoroastrian acts of worship all seven creations are physically represented and blessed, and their guardian divinities are invoked and venerated. The places of worship are simple, essentially a small rectangular area ritually marked out on flat ground, and then purified and consecrated. These left no traces of old for the archeologist. However, at Pasargadae two noble stone plinths survive, standing in the open on a stretch of the plain;[1] and these were presumably set there for the king to take a conspicuous part in public acts of worship. Such open-air sanctuaries appear to have been called by the Old Persian word *āyadanā* 'places of worship'.

There also survives at Pasargadae the tomb of Cyrus. The Zoroastrian rite of exposure, for the corrupting flesh to be swiftly devoured by birds and beasts, spread only slowly, it seems, among the western Iranians (who had previously buried their dead); and it was never adopted by their kings. The rulers of all three imperial dynasties were entombed at death; but Cyrus, who set the precedent, made a serious concession to orthopraxy in that he had his tomb built in such a way that no impurity from the embalmed body within could reach the good

[1] See Stronach, *Pasargadae*, pp. 138–41, with pls. 103–6.

creations. (According to Zoroastrian doctrine, whatever is ritually or actually unclean belongs to the counter-creation of the Hostile Spirit, and is part of his physical assault on the originally unblemished world of Ahuramazda.) So the tomb chamber was made of stone, set high on a six-tiered plinth of solid stone; and it had a stone door and a double roof of stone. Over the door was carved its only ornament, a great flower, the symbol of immortality. At Cyrus' death his son Cambyses duly had his body laid in this tomb, royally clad, and in a gold coffin; and two hundred years later Aristobulus recorded that there was a small building nearby, made for the magi who 'ever since the time of Cambyses...had kept watch over the tomb, the duty passing from father to son throughout that period. They received from the king a sheep and fixed quantities of wheat-flour and wine every day, and every month a horse to be sacrificed for Cyrus'.[1] Except for the horse, similar offerings for the dead are recorded for the early Sasanid kings, and were still being regularly made in conservative Zoroastrian communities in Iran in the twentieth century C.E.[2] The custom undoubtedly originated in very ancient times, and survived under Zoroastrianism.

CYRUS AND OTHER RELIGIONS

Cyrus kept his word, as befitted a worshipper of Truth, in allowing the exiled peoples in Babylonia, including the Jews, to return to their own lands. In the words of the Cyrus-cylinder, discovered in the palace-ruins of Babylon in the nineteenth century:[3]

I am Cyrus, king of the world...whose rule Bel and Nebo love....Marduk, the great lord, rejoices at my pious acts, and extends the grace of his blessing upon me...From...Nineveh, Assur, and also from Susa, from Akkad, Eshnunna, Zamban, Me-Turnu, Der, up to the land of the Guti, to the cities beyond the Tigris...the gods who inhabit them, I returned them [that is, their images] to their place, and I made their habitation very great for ever. I gathered all their peoples and led them back to their abodes. And the gods of Sumer and Akkad...at the order of Marduk, the great lord, I had them installed in joy in their sanctuaries...May all the gods whom I have led back to their cities wish daily before Bel and Nebo for the length of my days.

The words of this declaration were clearly composed by Babylonian priests, but must have been approved by Cyrus; and the spirit of religious tolerance which they show appears also in his famous edict

[1] See Arrian, *Anabasis* VI.29.1.4ff.
[2] See M. Boyce, *A Persian Stronghold of Zoroastrianism* (Oxford, 1977), pp. 157–62.
[3] See (with bibliography) W. Eilers, 'Der Keilschrifttext des Kyros-Zylinders', *Festgabe deutscher Iranisten zur 2500 Jahrfeier Irans* (Stuttgart, 1971), pp. 156–66.

to the Jews, with the words: 'Yahweh, God of heaven , has given me all the kingdoms of the earth, and he has charged me to build him a house at Jerusalem, which is in Judah' (Ezra 1: 2). The Persian king also permitted the priests of Ur to state that it was the 'great gods' of their city who 'had delivered all the lands' into his power, while those of Sin proclaimed that it was the moon god who had brought about his conquests.[1] Such statements were plainly difficult to reconcile theologically with the worship of Ahuramazda as God, the sole ultimate source of all benevolent power; equally plainly they were diplomatically useful, and won Cyrus a general harvest of goodwill. In allowing them to be made he was following established tradition, in an area of ethnic faiths; and he probably did so the more readily because, whatever the logic of his beliefs, he would himself inevitably have felt that, despite the universal nature of Zarathushtra's revelation, nevertheless Ahuramazda, though Creator and Lord, was above all 'God of the Iranians',[2] to whom he had revealed himself through his prophet; and that his care for other peoples was naturally less. Perhaps it was possible for Zoroastrian theologians to regard the benevolent gods worshipped by non-Iranians as, remotely, also the evocations of Ahuramazda; but whatever doctrinal justification was found, the Achemenids in general showed a positive benevolence towards the established religions of their subject peoples.

Wanton destruction of Egyptian temples, it is true, together with other impieties, was traditionally imputed to Cambyses; but archeological discoveries have shown that this is historically unsound.[3] The tradition, it is suggested, was in all probability fostered by his cousin Darius, a usurper, and by the Egyptian priesthood, whose wealth and power he had curtailed. The slander therefore became firmly established, and was duly recorded by the Greeks, and is alluded to in a letter written by the Jews of Syene in 408 (some three generations after the supposed desecrations).[4]

[1] See E. J. Bickerman, *Studies in Jewish and Christian History*, part 1 (Leiden, 1976), p. 93.

[2] The phrase occurs in the Elamite version of Darius' inscription at Behistun, III.77 (L. W. King and R. C. Thompson, *The Sculptures and Inscription of Darius the Great* (London, 1907), p. 147).

[3] See G. Posener, *La première domination perse en Égypte, Recueil d'inscriptions hiéroglyphiques* (Cairo, 1936).

[4] Cowley, *Aramaic papyri*, no. 30: 12–14.

THE RELIGIOUS ELEMENT IN THE INSCRIPTIONS OF DARIUS

Darius the Great, son of Hystaspes, of the other branch of the Achemenid family, seized the throne after Cambyses' death in 522. He founded a new capital at Persepolis in Pars, and had many inscriptions carved there and elsewhere, in which orthodox Zoroastrian theology finds expression in lines such as the following: 'A great god is Ahuramazda, who created this earth, who created yonder sky, who created man, who created happiness for man.'[1] A likeness has been traced between lines such as these and verses from Second Isaiah, both possibly being of Gathic inspiration;[2] but Darius' particular praise of Ahuramazda as Creator of 'happiness for man' is significant, since for him as a Zoroastrian the supreme Lord was Creator only of what is good, hence of happiness but not of suffering (which is inflicted by the Hostile Spirit).

The corruptions of Ahuramazda's good creation by his Adversary are acknowledged by Darius through frequent references to *drauga* 'the lie, falsehood, disorder', a term corresponding to Avestan *drug*, and the opposite of *aša* (Old Persian *arta*). The king sets due emphasis on justice, so prominent in Zarathushtra's teachings, as when he declares: 'I am a friend to right, I am not a friend to wrong. It is not my desire that the weak man should have wrong done him by the mighty; nor is that my desire, that the mighty man should have wrong done him by the weak. What is right, that is my desire.'[3]

Although Darius' utterances are in harmony with the teachings of Zarathushtra, there is a lack of specific references to several of his leading doctrines: for example, the principle of falsehood is named, but not the Hostile Spirit: an Old Persian equivalent of the characteristic term *spenta* is absent; and the word used for a divine being is *baga*, which is not found in the Gathas and is rare in the later Avesta. Such divergences and omissions led some scholars in the past to doubt that Darius was a Zoroastrian; but by now more inscriptions of the Sasanid period have been studied, which show that, for instance, the term *baga* (Middle Persian *bay*) was still in common use among Persians then. Avestan, the holy tongue, must always have been the language of formal prayer and worship; but preaching and teaching would have taken place

---

[1] DNa 1–3, cf. DNb 1–3, DSs 1–4. (For the texts of the Old Persian inscriptions, with English translations, see R. G. Kent, *Old Persian, Grammar, Texts, Lexicon* (New Haven, 1950, 2nd ed. 1953).

[2] See E. J. Bickerman according to M. Smith, *JAOS*, 83 (1963), p. 420.

[3] DNb 7–12.

in the vernacular, with use necessarily being made of familiar Persian terms, which therefore evidently remained current. Further, the Achemenid inscriptions were given their literary form by scribes familiar with established near-eastern models; and this may account for the absence from them of Zarathushtra's own name (which is notably lacking from the Sasanid inscriptions also).

Darius invokes no divinity by name except Ahuramazda, to whom he attributes all his achievements. 'After Ahuramazda made me king in this earth, by the will of Ahuramazda all that I did was good.'[1] 'Unto me Ahuramazda was a friend, what I did, all that was successful for me'.[2] He acknowledges the existence of other divine beings simply by the phrases 'with all the gods',[3] and 'the other gods who are';[4] but he appears to make an explicit visual reference to the divine heptad in the carving which he had set above his own tomb.[5] The tomb itself was cut high in the rock-face of a mountain now known as Naqsh i-Rustam, not far from Persepolis, and so it held the corpse even more securely from polluting the creations, if that were possible, than the tomb of Cyrus. In a relief above the door Darius is shown standing on a three-stepped plinth, his right hand raised in a gesture of reverence as he looks towards a 'fire-altar' of the Pasargadae type, on which flames are leaping up. Above, between the king and the fire, hovers a figure in a winged circle, a modification ultimately of the ancient Egyptian symbol of the sun-god Horus, which the Achemenids made much use of in their carvings. For them it most probably represented the royal *khvarnah* or 'glory', the divine power which attends a rightful king;[6] and also it seems, as here, the sun itself. For on a level with this symbol is carved the moon-disk – and prayer, Zoroastrianism enjoins, should be said facing sun, moon or fire, the three natural manifestations of cosmic fire, the icon of righteousness. Darius is thus shown in an attitude of orthodox devotion. He is flanked by six smaller figures, three on each side, who represent the six Persian nobles who helped him gain the throne; but while the three on the left carry arms, the three on the right are weaponless, and stand in an attitude of ritual mourning; and it has been suggested[7] that Darius deliberately had himself represented

---

[1] DSi 2–4.
[2] DSj 4.
[3] DPd 14–15, 22, 24.
[4] DB iv 62–3.
[5] See E. F. Schmidt, *Persepolis* (University of Chicago Oriental Institute Publications), 3 (Chicago, 1970), pp. 87ff, with pls. 19ff.
[6] See A. Sh. Shahbazi, 'An Achaemenid Symbol I', *Archäologische Mitteilungen aus Iran*, N.F. 7 (1976), 135–44; P. Calmeyer, 'Fortuna – Tyche – Khvarnah', *Jahrbuch des deutschen Archäologischen Instituts*, 94 (1979), 347–65.
[7] By A. Sh. Shahbazi.

with the six in a way that implied an analogy with Ahuramazda and the six great Amesha Spentas, of whom three are regarded as dominant (Truth, Good Thought and Dominion), and three as God in action or God immanent, and more passive (Devotion, Wholeness and Immortality). The Holy Spirit is essentially one with Ahuramazda, whose earthly representative is here shown to be Darius. So the carving was a visual expression of the thought conveyed by him also in words: 'Unto Ahuramazda thus was the desire, he chose me as [his] man in all the earth; he made me king in all the earth'.[1] It was therefore a powerful religious and political statement, and as such was repeated over the tomb of every succeeding Achemenid, a testimony to the unchanging nature of the dynasty's creed. The perpetuation of the symbolism is also attested in an exquisite pair of Persian ear-rings attributed to the late fifth century, in which a royal central figure, rising from the sun-disk, is shown surrounded by six smaller ones, rising from moon-disks;[2] and in a Zoroastrian text preserved in Middle Persian the king in his palace, surrounded by his ministers, is expressly said to be the earthly counterpart of Ohrmazd in heaven, with the great Amashaspands.[3]

RITUAL OBSERVANCES UNDER THE EARLY ACHEMENIDS

It was, it seems, meditation upon the rituals of the Old Iranian faith which led Zarathushtra to apprehend the six great Amesha Spentas as immanent in the objects which he as priest, himself filled with the Holy Spirit, handled and blessed; and there is no evidence that he sought to abolish or change any of the ancient acts of observance.[4] Rather he appears to have taught his followers to imbue these with new meaning by giving them added spiritual and ethical significance. A seal discovered in the ruins of Persepolis appears to bear a stylized allusion to one of the main Zoroastrian ritual acts, the pressing of twigs of the *haoma* plant.[5] On this seal a man in the characteristic garb of an Achemenid magus (tunic, trousers, sleeved mantle, and 'tiara' or felt headgear) is shown standing before a fire-altar. Between him and it is a pestle and mortar upon a table. In his left hand he holds a long stick, in his right a bundle of rods, the *baresman* (Middle Persian *barsom*). In ancient

[1] DSf 15–18.
[2] See A. B. Tilia, *Studies and Restorations at Persepolis*, 2 (Rome, 1978), p. 39, n. 2 with pl. C.
[3] *Gošt-i Fryan* 11.55–9, see H. Jamaspji Asa and M. Haug, *The Book of Arda Viraf* (London, 1872), pp. 254–5.
[4] See Boyce, *History*, 1, pp. 214–19.
[5] See Schmidt, *Persepolis*, 2 (1957), p. 9 with pl. 7, seal no. 20.

Indo-Iranian usage the priest had held a bunch of grasses in his hand
while performing the high rituals; and it has been suggested that the
development of the grasses into the Zoroastrian rods (longer in imperial
times than in present usage) may owe something to the use of rods in
Urartian observance.[1] That the *baresman* appears in Ezekiel 8: 17 has
long been disproved.[2]

This seal-design does not, however, represent any enactment of a
haoma-ritual known to living Zoroastrianism; nor has it proved possible
to find religious significance in the numerous pestles and mortars
discovered in the Persepolis treasury, the Aramaic writings on which
have proved to be simply administrative dockets.[3] A more realistic
delineation of a religious rite appears intended in a carving from the
Achemenid satrapal capital of Daskylion, in Asia Minor. This carving,
now attributed to the reign of Darius the Great,[4] is the product of a
Greco-Persian artistic school, and shows two magi standing side by side,
each holding the *baresman* (correctly) in his left hand, the right being
raised in the ritual gesture of reverence. Each wears the lower fold of
the 'tiara' pulled up to cover both nose and mouth, in order to keep
the polluting breath from consecrated objects. Beside them are the heads
of an ox and a ram, and they appear to be about to consecrate sacrificial
animals to the *yazata* Haoma, a rite solemnized by the Parsis down to
the nineteenth, and by Irani Zoroastrians into the twentieth century
c.e.[5]

Zoroastrian observance of animal sacrifice meant that Zoroastrian
kings had no religious scruples about aiding those of other faiths to
make similar offerings. So Darius, upholding Cyrus' decree to the Jews,
commanded not only that funds for re-building the Temple should be
provided from the funds of the satrapy Beyond the River, but that
sacrificial animals, corn, wine and whatever else was necessary should
be given to the priests in Jerusalem (Ezra 6: 8–10). Cambyses and Darius
are also known to have provided for offerings to be made in Egyptian
temples.

[1] See P. Calmeyer, 'Barsombündel im 8. und 7. Jahrhundert v. Chr.', *Wandlungen,
Studien...E. Homann-Wedeking gewidmet* (Waldsassen–Bayern, 1975), pp. 11–15.
[2] See R. Gordis, 'The Branch to the Nose', *JTS*, 37 (1936), 284–8.
[3] See, with bibliography, W. Hinz, 'Zu den Mörsern und Stösseln aus Persepolis',
Monumentum H. S. Nyberg 1, Acta Iranica 4 (Leiden, 1975), 371–85.
[4] On it see Th. Macridy, 'Reliefs gréco-perses de la région de Dascylion', *Bulletin de
Correspondence Héllénique*, 37 (1913), 348–52 with pl. VII. The attribution to the late
sixth century has been made by D. Stronach, 'Notes on the relief of the magi from
Dascylion', *Festschrift K. Bittel* (Berlin, in the press).
[5] See M. Boyce, 'Haoma, priest of the sacrifice', *W. B. Henning Memorial Volume*
(London, 1970), pp. 72–9.

A name for what appears to be a place for the performance of Zoroastrian rituals occurs in an Aramaic inscription from Syene dated to 458 B.C.E., thàt is, to the reign of Darius' grandson, Artaxerxes I. What can be read of the relevant lines runs: '..., commander of the garrison of Syene, built this *brẓmdn'* in the month of Siwan, that is Meḥir, in the seventh year of Artaxerxes the king'.[1] The Old Persian word *braẓman* has been interpreted as meaning 'ritual, religious ceremony', and **braẓmadāna*, accordingly, as 'place of rituals', presumably, that is, a walled and possibly even roofed enclosure in which acts of worship could be performed in ritual purity. Such places must have been needed by the Iranians wherever they became city-dwellers, or lived among an alien people.

THE DAIVA-INSCRIPTION OF XERXES

The word *braẓman* is attested in a famous inscription of Artaxerxes' father, Xerxes, who succeeded Darius in 486. Early in his reign Xerxes put down a Babylonian revolt; and in order, it is thought, to extinguish all hopes of revival of an independent Babylonian kingdom he had the great temple of Esagila demolished, and Marduk's image, which had been the focal point for annual royal rites, destroyed. Subsequently he embarked on the war with the Greeks; and when in 479 his armies fought their way to Athens, he punished the Athenians for their long-standing resistance (which included the murder of heralds sent by Darius), by allowing his soldiers to plunder and burn the Acropolis. After this had been done, he ordered the Athenian exiles in his train to 'go up to the Acropolis and offer sacrifice after their manner'.[2] Persistent attempts have been made to identify one or other of these acts of destruction with that described by Xerxes himself in the afore-named inscription. After an enumeration of the countries over which he ruled, he there declares: 'And among these countries was (a place) where previously Daivas were worshipped. Then by the will of Ahuramazda I destroyed that Daiva-sanctuary, and I made proclamation, "Daivas shall not be worshipped!" Where previously Daivas were worshipped, there I worshipped Ahuramazda with due order and rites.'[3] From these words it is clear that this sanctuary cannot have been the Acropolis (which was in a land over which Xerxes did not rule, and where he actually ordered the continuance of Greek rites); and there

---

[1] On this inscription, first published in 1903, see M. Bogoliubov, 'An Aramaic inscription from Aswan' (in Russian), *Palestinski Sbornik*, 15 (1966), 40–6.

[2] Herodotus VIII.54.

[3] XPh 35–41.

is not the slightest reason to identify it with the Esagila, which remained in ruins while the priests of Marduk continued their own ancient rites of worship nearby. Persian tolerance of non-Iranian religions appears to have been the benevolent aspect of a basic indifference, tempered by pragmatism; and the destruction of the Acropolis and Esagila were political acts, whereas Xerxes' words make it clear that there was a strong religious motive for that of the Daiva-sanctuary. Old Persian *daiva* is equivalent to Avestan *daeva*; and the obvious explanation of Xerxes' statement is that he, as a Zoroastrian, had destroyed an Iranian sanctuary where those gods of war were still worshipped whom Zarathushtra had condemned as having 'afflicted the world and mankind' (Y.30.6). Whether Cyrus or Darius had launched any earlier persecution of adherents of the old faith is unknown; but plainly Persian kings would have wished their Iranian subjects to be of the same religion as themselves, if only for the strengthening and cohesion of the state; and, to judge from the evidence of later times, the Zoroastrian magi are likely to have urged strong measures to bring this about. Nevertheless, the physical nature of Iran, a huge country with great mountains and deserts, and remote valleys, doubtless made it possible for the old faith to survive locally for generations.

What the nature of the Daiva-sanctuary would have been remains a matter for surmise. There is still no evidence at this period for the building of temples by Iranians; but it could have been a sanctuary on a plain with altars such as those of Pasargadae, or an artificial hill enclosed by a wall, such as Strabo describes from the time of Cyrus at Zela in Pontus,[1] or possibly a sacred grove somewhere in the then-afforested land of Iran.

Xerxes' inscription continues in devout fashion: 'That which I did, all I did by the will of Ahuramazda. Ahuramazda bore me aid, until I completed the work. Thou who shalt be hereafter, if thou shalt think "Happy may I be when living, and blessed (*artavan-*) when dead", have respect for the law which Ahuramazda has established; worship Ahuramazda with due order and rites.'[2] Old Persian *artavan* is the equivalent of Avestan *ašavan*, 'possessed of *aša*, righteous'; and since the righteous are those who will be saved hereafter, this term can be used as a synonym also for 'blessed'. In an Avestan passage Xerxes' sentiment is expressed in negative terms, and with the adjectives reversed, in that it is said of a man who has committed an offence: 'Living, he is not *ašavan-*, dead, he does not enjoy the Best Existence [that is, heaven].'[3]

---

[1] *Geography*, XI.8.4.   [2] XPh 43–51.

[3] *Vendidad* v.61; see J. Kellens according to U. Bianchi, 'L'inscription "des daivas" et le zoroastrisme des Achéménides', *RHR*, 192 (1977), 7–8.

PERSIAN RELIGION ACCORDING TO HERODOTUS

Herodotus, born a Persian subject in Asia Minor, was only a child at the time of Xerxes' Greek war; but he is thought to have gained much of his information from Persians and Greeks who themselves took part in the campaigns. He mentions a number of religious observances carried out on both sides, some incidental, others in direct furtherance of military aims. The Greeks relied on lay seers and divines, and oracles sought from their great shrines, while the Persian army was accompanied by magi. Herodotus describes in impressive detail the ceremonial march of the Persian host out of Sardis, and tells how at its very centre came 'the sacred chariot of Zeus [that is, Ahuramazda], drawn by eight white horses, the charioteer on foot following the horses and holding the reins; for no mortal may mount into that seat'.[1] Thereafter, at Ilium, Xerxes viewed the ruins of Troy, 'and sacrificed a thousand kine to Athene of Ilium, and the magi offered libations to the heroes',[2] honouring thus the spirits of brave men of another race.

Subsequently there came the famous incident when waves destroyed the bridge built for Xerxes across the Hellespont, and he 'gave command that the Hellespont be scourged with three hundred lashes, and a pair of fetters be thrown into the sea'; and he ordered the scourgers to say: 'Thou bitter water...our master thus punishes thee, because thou didst him wrong albeit he had done thee none...It is but just that no man offers thee sacrifice, for thou art a turbid and a briny river.'[3] However unworthy this act, these words accord with the letter of evolved Zoroastrian doctrine, which is that salt water is sweet water tainted by the assault of the Hostile Spirit.

Later, when battle had been joined, both Greeks and sailors in the Persian fleet are said to have sacrificed captives to secure success for their arms.[4] Herodotus also states that at a place called 'Nine Ways' the Persians 'buried alive that number of boys and maidens, children of the people of the country'. He adds: 'To bury alive is a Persian custom; I have heard that when Xerxes' wife Amestris attained to old age she buried fourteen sons of notable Persians, as a thank-offering on her own behalf to the fabled god of the nether world.'[5] This sacrifice must have been made when that formidable woman was queen mother, when her will was with difficulty gainsaid by her son Artaxerxes; and, like the sacrifice at Nine Ways, it was presumably a propitiatory offering

---

[1] VII.40.   [2] VII.43.

[3] VII.35.

[4] See Herodotus VII.180; Plutarch, *Lives*, Themistocles, 13 (in Dryden's translation, Everyman's Library, vol. 1, p. 175).

[5] VII.114.

to Yama, the Old Iranian king of the dead.[1] Both acts thus represent survivals of pagan custom, occurring at times of communal or individual stress.

In general the religious picture which emerges from Herodotus' account of the war is no more edifying than is usual when humanity is at strife, with both sides importuning the divine beings for aid by every means in their power, which included prayers, hymns, libations, blood sacrifices and rich offerings. At another part of his great work the Greek historian gives a more general account of Persian beliefs and practices as he himself had learnt of them in the reign of Artaxerxes I (465–424). Widely travelled though he was, he appears never to have visited Iran itself, but to have acquired his information from Persians in Asia Minor, depending probably largely on verbal accounts, since it is unlikely that, as a non-Zoroastrian (and hence necessarily unclean in the eyes of the orthodox), he would have been allowed to be present at religious observances.

Generally, Herodotus says of the Persians:

It is not their custom to make and set up statues and images and altars...but they call the whole circle of heaven Zeus, and to him they offer sacrifice on the highest peaks of the mountains; they sacrifice also to the sun and moon and earth and fire and water and winds. These are the only gods to whom they have ever sacrificed from the beginning.[2]

This seems a very fair attempt by a Greek gentleman to render the Zoroastrian doctrine of Ahuramazda (described in Y.30.5 as wearing the sky as a garment) and the Amesha Spentas, immanent in their creations; and still today the Irani Zoroastrians make seasonal pilgrimages into the mountains to offer sacrifice in high places.[3]

Herodotus then describes the manner in which a Persian layman would himself make a sacrifice, in the open, attended by a magus, 'for no sacrifice can be offered without a magus'.[4] His account has been held to be un-Zoroastrian in character, partly because of an old misconception (originating in the eighteenth century) that Zarathushtra rejected blood sacrifice, partly because the rites which he describes were compared with the priestly ceremonies of the faith, and were found to be very different. In fact, apart from what appear to be some small misunderstandings on his part, Herodotus' description accords very well with what is now known of the lay offering of sacrifices by Zoroastrians (maintained by the Irani community to the present day).[5]

Elsewhere Herodotus observes that 'the Persians hold fire to be a

[1] See Boyce, *History*, 1, pp. 83–4.   [2] I.131.
[3] See Boyce, *Persian Stronghold*, pp. 240ff.   [4] I.132.
[5] See Boyce, *Persian Stronghold*, index s.v. 'sacrifice'.

god';[1] but he has nothing specific to say about the cult of fire. Of water he states: 'Rivers they chiefly reverence; they will neither make water nor spit nor wash their hands therein, nor suffer anyone so to do'.[2] This is Zoroastrian observance, out of respect for the pure creation of water and for the Amesha Spenta who guards and informs it; no natural source of water may be polluted in such ways.

With regard to the disposal of the dead, and the usages of priests, Herodotus says:

There are...matters concerning the dead which are secretly and obscurely told – how the dead bodies of Persians are not buried before they have been mangled by bird or dog. That this is the way of the magi I know for a certainty; for they do not conceal the practice...These magi are much unlike to the priests of Egypt, as to all other men: for the priests count it sacrilege to kill aught that lives, save what they sacrifice; but the magi kill with their hands every creature, save only dogs and men; they kill all alike, ants and snakes, creeping and flying things, and take much pride therein.[3]

These two Zoroastrian practices, the unusual manner of disposing of the dead, and the killing of creatures regarded as noxious, are ones which were to attract the attention of alien observers down the centuries. Harmful or hideous creatures were regarded as belonging to the counter-creation of the Hostile Spirit, and so to destroy them was a meritorious act, helping to reduce his forces. Herodotus naturally exaggerates when he says that the magi killed everything but dogs and men, but his words are accurate in that they indicate the characteristic Zoroastrian respect for the dog; and priests would have killed sacrificial animals as well as destroying baleful ones, so that some confusion was understandable. His comments on exposure of the dead suggest that the magi, having once embraced the eastern religion, accepted its observances unreservedly, with the discipline and logic characteristic of their fraternity, whereas the laity, with royal example before them, appear still in the mid fifth century to have practised exposure somewhat reluctantly.

On the ethical side Herodotus records the Persians' regard for truth,[4] and indicates the characteristic Zoroastrian morality whereby a man may outweigh bad acts by good ones, here as well as in the hereafter; for he observes that there is 'a praiseworthy law...which suffers not the king himself to slay any man for one offence, nor any other Persian for one offence to do incurable hurt to one of his servants. Not till reckoning shows that the offender's wrongful acts are more and greater than his services may a man give vent to his anger.'[5]

[1] III.16. [2] I.138. [3] I.140.
[4] I.138, cf. 136. [5] I.137, cf. VII.194.

Herodotus does not mention the name of Iran's prophet; but (if the attribution of the fragment is correct) this occurs in the work of his older contemporary Xanthos of Lydia, who wrote of Persian soldiers under Cyrus thinking upon 'the sayings of Zoroaster', and who also said: 'As for Zoroaster, the Persians claim that it was from him they derived the rule against burning dead bodies or defiling fire in any other way.'[1]

THE ACHEMENIDS AND EZRA AND NEHEMIAH

In the twentieth year of his long reign, that is, in 444, Artaxerxes I sent his cupbearer, the Jew Nehemiah, to govern in Jerusalem. The Achemenids regularly set local rulers over cities and small provinces, so that this appointment was not unduly remarkable; but the fact that Nehemiah had served the King of kings in this confidential capacity, while other Babylonian Jews also attained high places in government service, suggests that the Achemenids maintained good relations with the Jews in Mesopotamia, in particular with the 'Yahweh-alone' group among them, to which Second Isaiah, Nehemiah and Ezra all belonged.[2] This being so, the possibility undoubtedly exists of some influence having been exerted by the faith of these benevolent kings, with all their might and majesty, on this group among their subjects, who had good cause to be grateful to them, and so receptive. In the case of Nehemiah, a particular area in which such influence might well have been felt was the field of purity laws; for no man could have been cup-bearer to the King of kings without being obliged himself to keep the Zoroastrian purity laws, so as not to bring contamination on his royal master.

These laws (as we have been seeing) had their doctrinal basis in the belief that the good world created by Ahuramazda (which includes man himself) is under continual assault by the Hostile Spirit, whose weapons on the physical plane include dirt, rust, mould, stench, blight, decay, disease and death. To reduce, banish, or at least as far as possible avoid, any of these things is therefore to contribute, however humbly, to the defence of the good creation, and its ultimate redemption. Hence for a Zoroastrian cleanliness is not next to godliness, but a part of it; and every member of the community is involved in fighting the good fight through the ordinary tasks of daily life. Down the centuries priests elaborated rules in defence of both actual and ritual purity, and so created in time an iron code which raised an effective barrier between

---

[1] C. Müller, *Fragmenta Historicorum Graecorum* (Paris, 1841–72), 1, p. 42, fig. 19.
[2] See Morton Smith, *Palestinian Parties and Politics that Shaped the Old Testament* (New York, 1971), pp. 29ff, 82ff.

Zoroastrians and any unbeliever who did not also observe it. The existence of this code must have been a factor in preventing the spread of Zoroastrianism beyond the Iranian peoples themselves, since in its stringency it made demands of a kind to which it is best to grow accustomed in infancy. As it is said in a Zoroastrian text: 'A non-Zoroastrian is not naturally fit for observing the precautions about purity.'[1]

After years of necessarily keeping the Zoroastrian code (which has nothing in it repugnant to Jewish laws), it seems hardly surprising that Nehemiah, although a layman, should have concerned himself in Jerusalem with questions of purity among the Jews. Nor does it seem overbold to consider the possibility that it was Zoroastrian example, visible throughout the empire, which led to the gradual transformation of the Jewish purity code from regulations concerning cultic matters to laws whose observance was demanded of every individual in his daily life, their setting being not only the Temple, but 'the field and the kitchen, the bed and the street',[2] and the keeping of them being a matter which set the Jews in their turn apart from other peoples.

Scholarly opinion is still divided as to whether it was Artaxerxes I or his grandson, Artaxerxes II, who sent Ezra, the commissary for Jewish religious affairs in Babylonia, to Jerusalem with a letter of authority, and also with silver and gold 'freely offered by the king and his counsellors' with which to buy sacrificial animals, and with vessels to be delivered to the Temple 'before the God of Jerusalem...for why should there be wrath against the realm of the King and his sons?' The king conferred at the same time various privileges and exemptions on the priests of the Temple (which in character were very like those conferred by Cyrus on the priests of the Apollo-shrine in Asia Minor); and the intertwining of affairs of religion and state is made explicit in the final words of his letter: 'And whosoever will not do the law of thy God and the law of the King, let judgment be executed speedily upon him.'[3]

Jewish tradition has honoured Ezra by attributing to him the writing down of the canonical books of the Old Testament; and many modern scholars associate him specifically with the Priestly Code, that fourth strand of the Pentateuch which is regarded as a product of the exilic

---

[1] For the reference, and more details about Zoroastrian purity laws, see Boyce, *History*, I, pp. 295ff.

[2] J. Neusner, 'The idea of purity in the Jewish literature of the period of the Second Temple', *Monumentum H. S. Nyberg* 2, Acta Iranica 5 (Leiden, 1975), p. 137; see further his *The Mishnaic system of uncleanness, its context and history* (Leiden, 1977).

[3] Ezra 7: 11–26.

and post-exilic periods. Considering Ezra's own background, it is not surprising that those parts of the Pentateuch in which the possibility of Zoroastrian influence appears should all be assigned to P. One such section is Genesis 1:1 to 2:4a, with its account of creation which differs so entirely from that in Genesis 2:4bff, and which resembles the Zoroastrian cosmogony in two striking particulars. First there is the great declaration: 'In the beginning God created the heavens and the earth...and the Spirit of God was moving over the face of the waters.' This is the only place in the Old Testament where the Spirit of God is associated with creativity; and attempts have been made accordingly to give *rūᵃḥ* a special meaning here, such as wind or storm; but a recent commentator insists that 'to use modern terms, the Spirit is the active principle, which was wholly necessary in order to accomplish a creation. It was...the driving factor...Where God was, there too his Spirit was at work.'[1] It is precisely in such terms that scholars have sought to define Zarathushtra's teachings about the Holy Spirit through which Ahuramazda is 'Creator of all things'.[2] Secondly, there is the division of the acts of creation into seven stages. The biblical and Zoroastrian stages are not identical, and in particular the creation of fire, which is the culmination of the Zoroastrian creation story, is given a less conspicuous place in Genesis, with the luminaries being set between the plants and the birds and fishes. Yet there is a broad and noble likeness between the two cosmogonies; and since cosmogony was of such importance in Zoroastrianism, being linked with the doctrines of the seven Amesha Spentas, and God's purpose in creating the world, knowledge of the Zoroastrian account can be expected to have become known to theologians of other faiths throughout the empire.

As prominent in Zoroastrianism, because vitally important for each believer, were the Gathic teachings about fate after death (with individual judgement, heaven and hell), and at the last day (with the Last Judgement, and annihilation for the wicked but eternal bliss for the saved in fellowship with Ahuramazda). The contrast is dramatic between these beliefs and the oldest layer of Jewish ones concerning the hereafter, of which it has been said:

One of the most astonishing things about Israel's religious faith is the warmth and intensity of fellowship with God which was experienced against the sombre background of a belief in nothing but the most shadowy and unsatisfactory kind of survival after death. In Amos (chapter 9) and Psalm 139 we find the

[1] A. S. Kapelrud, 'Die Theologie der Schöpfung im Alten Testament', *ZAW*, 91 (1979), 165–6.

[2] Y.44.7 (see above), cf. Y.51.7. On the Holy Spirit see Lommel, *Die Religion*, pp. 18ff; Boyce, *History*, 1, pp. 193, 211, 221.

belief that Yahweh's writ extended even to the underworld of Sheol, but there is little evidence till near the end of the Old Testament period that there was any belief in a blessed existence after death.[1]

The earliest reference to such a belief has been seen in what is regarded as a post-exilic verse, Isaiah 26: 19: 'But thy dead live, their bodies will rise again. They that sleep in the earth will awake and shout for joy; for...the earth will bring those long dead to birth again.'[2] It is striking that this new hope of joy in the hereafter is expressly linked with the doctrine alluded to in Y.30.7, and a Zoroastrian article of faith,[3] that on the last day the earth will give up the dead. (This teaching was duly ascribed to Zoroaster by Theopompos, who was born in 380, in the reign of Artaxerxes II.[4]) With it and other elements of Zoroastrian apocalyptic finding their counterparts eventually in pharisaic beliefs, it seems once more difficult wholly to set aside the possibility of influence by the Iranian religion on the development of Jewish salvation-faith in the post-exilic period.

The Zoroastrians linked their eschatological hopes with belief in a world Saviour, the Saoshyant of the Avesta, who will be born of the prophet's seed by a virgin mother. He will appear to lead the forces of good in a last conflict with those of evil, and, triumphant, will bring about *Frašokereti*. This Avestan term probably means 'the making wonderful'; and it refers to the transformation which will take place when, the Last Judgement having been enacted, the kingdom of Ahuramazda will be established on an earth once more made perfect, as at its first creation. The belief in the world Saviour, adumbrated perhaps in the Gathas,[5] had been developed in eastern Iran before the faith reached Persia;[6] and the expectation has always been that the Saoshyant will appear from the east.

DARIUS II AND THE JEWS OF ELEPHANTINE

Darius II, the son of Artaxerxes I, evidently maintained the Achemenid tradition of benevolent patronage towards the Jews, for in 419 he sent an order to the Egyptian satrap through the Jew Hananiah, bidding the

---

[1] N. W. Porteous, 'The Theology of the Old Testament', *Peake's Commentary on the Bible* (London, 1962), p. 159.

[2] Translation according to the New English Bible.

[3] See Boyce, *History*, 1, pp. 235–6.

[4] According to Aeneas of Gaza, see C. Clemen, *Fontes Historiae Religionis Persicae* (Bonn, 1920), p. 95.

[5] See Lommel, *Die Religion*, pp. 228–9.

[6] See Boyce, *History*, 1, p. 293.

Jews of Elephantine to keep the Festival of Unleavened Bread for seven days. The reason for this order, it is suggested, was to ensure that the Egyptians allowed the Jewish soldiers time off to observe this festival.[1]

In 410, while the Persian satrap was away from Egypt, the Jewish temple in Elephantine was destroyed by Egyptian priests in collusion with the Persian governor of the fort. The motives behind this collusion are obscure; but eventually Bagoas, the Persian governor of Judea, requested the Persian satrap in Egypt to have the temple 'rebuilt in its place, as it was formerly'.[2]

AN OSSUARY AND A TOMB FROM THE TIME OF ARTAXERXES II

The earliest archeological evidence for adoption of the rite of exposure of the dead by the Persian nobility comes from Asia Minor about 400 B.C.E., in the reign of Artaxerxes II, son of Darius II.[3] A rock-cut sepulchre near the Lycian town of Limyra has an Aramaic inscription stating that 'Artim son of Arzifiy made this ossuary (astodana)'. A longer Greek inscription records that 'Artimas' had constructed the tomb 'for himself and his kindred'. Within it are two small chambers, each with a rectangular cavity in the rock floor, intended, it seems, to hold the disarticulated bones of the family dead after exposure elsewhere. The maker of the ossuary has been identified in all likelihood as the Artimas who in 401 was appointed governor of Lydia by Cyrus the Younger (Artaxerxes' brother); and his father Arzyphius was apparently a son of Amytis, daughter of Xerxes and Amestris. Once the rite of exposure had been adopted by Persians of such rank, it probably quickly became general. It is certainly attested as the common funerary rite in western Iran under the two later empires.

The body of Cyrus the Younger himself, it has been suggested, may have been given royal burial by the queen mother, Parysatis, in a tomb in the valley of Buzpar in Pars. This tomb is a smaller, humbler copy of the tomb of Cyrus the Great,[4] and like it would have contained the pollution of the body securely.

---

[1] See E. G. Kraeling, *The Brooklyn Museum Aramaic Papyri* (New Haven, 1953), pp. 92–6; B. Porten, *Archives from Elephantine* (Berkeley, 1968), pp. 279–82.

[2] *CAP*, nos. 31, 32; Kraeling, *Papyri*, pp. 100–10. [For Bagoas, see n. 3 on p. 246. Eds.]

[3] See A. Sh. Shahbazi, *The Irano-Lycian Monuments* (Tehran, 1975), ch. 4.

[4] See Stronach, *Pasargadae*, pp. 300–2 with pls. 182–5.

CULTIC DEVELOPMENTS

Zoroastrianism underwent certain cultic developments in the later Achemenid period. During pre-Zoroastrian times the Persians appear to have adopted to a large extent the Babylonian cults of Ishtar and Nabu, assimilating these two beings to stellar divinities of their own worship: *Anahiti, goddess of the planet Venus, and *Tiri, god of the planet Mercury, who both accordingly became hugely popular. The cult of Mithra, lord of justice who was associated with the sun, was also, it seems, influenced by that of Babylonian Shamash, god of the sun and of justice, with the result that Mithra had become more of a sun-god, and had gained even greater popularity than before, thus beginning to overshadow his brother Ahura, Varuna.

With the coming of Zoroastrianism, these developments evidently caused difficulties. The Avesta was then already virtually a fixed canon, in which direct innovation was not possible; and although Mithra is prominent in it, the names of *Anahiti and *Tiri do not occur. The liturgical worship of these two divinities was therefore not possible. (All Zoroastrian acts of worship have an Avestan liturgy.) Veneration of them must nevertheless have continued popularly in Persia; and in the end their recognition appears to have been imposed on the whole Zoroastrian community by Artaxerxes II. He presumably demanded of leading magi that they should find some means of receiving them into orthodox observance; and this they managed to do by identifying *Anahiti with the Avestan Aredvi Sura Anahita, *yazata* of the mythical river which is the source of all the waters of the world; and *Tiri with Avestan Tishtrya, *yazata* of the star Sirius. These identifications were plainly awkward and contrived; but they served their purpose, and 'Nahid' and 'Tir' are venerated by Zoroastrians to this day together with 'Ardvisur' and Tishtar.

Artaxerxes further broke with the precedent established by Darius the Great by invoking Mithra and Anahita in his inscriptions, after Ahuramazda.[1] Also the Babylonian historian Berossus, who wrote in the third century B.C.E., is cited as recording that 'after a long period of time they [the Persians] began to worship statues in human form, this practice having been introduced by Artaxerxes son of Darius...who was the first to set up statues of Aphrodite Anaitis, at Babylon, Susa, Ecbatana, Persepolis, Bactria, Damascus and Sardis, thus enjoining on those communities the duty of worshipping them'.[2] Bactria (Balkh) was an ancient centre of eastern Zoroastrianism, and a sense of outrage is likely to have been particularly strong there at this departure from

[1] A²Sa 4–5; A²Sd 3–4; A²Ha 5–6.
[2] Clement of Alexandria, *Protrepticus* 5.65.3 (Clemen, *Fontes*, p. 67).

orthopraxy; but it must also have been felt by many of the western Iranians, who had for so long, despite the example of their neighbours, maintained a tradition of worship without images. The prime mover in this radical innovation may well have been the queen mother, Parysatis, another of the formidable Achemenid queens, who was half-Babylonian by blood, and who may have learnt from her mother to worship Ishtar/*Anahiti through a cult-statue. According to Plutarch,[1] her influence over her son was strong, and she was singularly persistent in her aims.

Later references to the Ecbatana temple (plundered by the Seleucids) show that wealth was lavished on the 'Anahit' shrines; and the splendour of the new cult, and the royal favour it enjoyed, may well have brought many worshippers to them. Temples thus became established in Zoroastrian devotional life; and probably it was not long before some of the orthodox, accepting this, made a counter-move by founding other temples in which there was no cult-image, but instead a consecrated fire, the only permissible icon for a true follower of Zarathushtra. This could not have been done without royal assent; but there is no reason to suppose that Artaxerxes would have withheld this. The fact that he had himself felt the need to gain recognition for the *Anahiti cult shows that he was an observant Zoroastrian; and the arguments for establishing a temple cult of fire were doubtless strong and persuasive.

The scarcity of sources makes it impossible to trace the growth of this cult during the remainder of the Achemenid period; but references from after the downfall of the empire show that fire-temples had by then been founded very widely, in both Iranian and non-Iranian satrapies (in the latter to serve the local Persian communities). In these temples an ever-burning wood fire was set on a raised 'altar' (probably usually of the Pasargadae type) within an inner sanctuary, where its purity was strictly guarded. It was tended by priests with the rites of the traditional fire-cult, and worshippers came to say their own prayers in its presence. Once established, the temple cult of fire seems to have gained importance rapidly; and it was probably embers from a temple fire which were carried on a 'silver altar' by priests as a palladium before the army of Darius III when he marched against Alexander. This was innovation; but behind the fire came the empty chariot sacred to Ahuramazda, drawn by white horses as in the days of Xerxes.[2]

[1] See his *Life of Artaxerxes*.
[2] Curtius Rufus, *History of Alexander* III.3.9 (Clemen, *Fontes*, p. 38). Xenophon, *Cyropaedia* VIII.3.12, earlier described a procession of sacrificial animals followed by sacred chariots, behind which there came 'men carrying fire in a large brazier'; but this was presumably for the practical purpose of cooking the flesh.

The establishment of temples had many consequences. Till then Zoroastrianism had been rich in doctrine and observance, but had made, it seems, relatively few material demands on its followers. Now sacred buildings had to be constructed and maintained, and priests employed to serve in them. This gave new scope for the wealth of imperial Persia to be lavished on the faith; and it brought into being a new branch of the ecclesiastical hierarchy. It was perhaps in connection with the temples and their attendant priests that a new title was created, *magupati, 'master of magi', which became widely known (as Parthian magbed, Middle Persian mowbed) in later epochs as a title for a Zoroastrian high priest.

THE CALENDAR AND FESTIVALS

At some time in the later Achemenid period a convocation of priests from east and west must have been held to create a religious calendar for use throughout the community. The traditional Iranian calendar was retained, of twelve months with thirty days each; but each month and each day was now dedicated to a divine being. Ahuramazda himself received the dedication of a month and four separate days (each devoted to him as Creator); and each of the six great Amesha Spentas received that of a month and a day. There are slight signs in some of the remaining dedications of controversy and compromise, for plainly full agreement on all points of doctrine and observance could not be expected between the older communities in the east and the western ones, nor between the king's men and orthodox traditionalists. The calendar dedications were important, for from that time on at all Zoroastrian religious services the priests invoked the yazata of the day, so that the 'calendar yazatas' came to be the most regularly venerated of the divine beings.

The western Iranian feasts of *Mithrakana and *Tirikana (Middle Persian Mihragan and Tiragan), which had been established evidently in the pre-Zoroastrian period, found a place in this calendar; but although their celebration was held to be meritorious, and they were in fact maintained with great joyfulness and splendour, their observance was not obligatory. The only Zoroastrian feasts of obligation are the seven (in Middle Persian No Roz and the gahambars) which, according to tradition, were founded by the prophet himself. These, scattered through the twelve months, are celebrated in honour of Ahuramazda the Creator and the six great Amesha Spentas; and they constitute the framework of the Zoroastrian devotional year.

After the overthrow of the Achemenid empire this Zoroastrian calendar continued in use throughout the Zoroastrian community, and (with modifications) remains so still today.

ZURVANISM

Colleges of Zoroastrian priests must have existed from early times, for the preservation and study of the Avesta, and the teaching of doctrine. In the Achemenid period individual Persian scholar–priests evidently sought knowledge too at Babylonian centres of learning, and elsewhere. At some stage – it is usually thought late in the period – some heterodox thinkers among them evolved the heresy of Zurvanism. Worship of a god of Time (perhaps as a local development of one aspect of Egyptian sun-worship) has been traced in Phoenicia in the seventh or sixth century B.C.E.;[1] and Babylonian religion in the first millennium had a strong astral element, with developments in astronomy being matched by evolving astrological ideas about the stars controlling man's fate. One of the most striking elements in Zarathushtra's own teachings was his apparently wholly original concept that history would have an end, a concept which was embodied in his doctrine of the Three Times: the epoch of original cosmic separation of good and evil; the present limited epoch of 'mixture', in which good and evil contend in this world; and the last eternal epoch of perfect goodness. These teachings imprinted on his followers' minds the idea of a linear development of history, and of events taking place within a chronological framework. Comparing these doctrines of their own, it seems, with other ideas which they encountered, certain Persian priests pondered their holy texts afresh, and evolved a new exegesis of the Gathic verse Y.30.3, with its declaration that there were 'two primal Spirits, twins'. Fastening on the word 'twins' – a metaphor for coevity – they postulated that as twins the two Spirits must have had a father, who could be none other than Time, for which the Avestan word is *zurvan*. Originally 'Zurvanism' was perhaps no more than intellectual speculation; but it grew into a full-blooded heresy, although its doctrines and myths are not attested before the Sasanid period, and even then there are variants in the accounts.[2] According to one of these relatively late sources, Zurvanites believed that in the beginning Zurvan alone existed. Then he begot a son; but before that son was born, he doubted whether he would be perfect, and from that doubt the Hostile Spirit was engendered and came first into the world, before Ahuramazda, a black and hideous creature who horrified his sire. This myth gave scope for further speculation (in whose womb, for instance, had the twins been conceived?), and opened the way for philosophical reflections on the power of time and hence predestination. Zurvan was seen as lord of the Three

[1] See West, *Philosophy*, p. 35ff.
[2] For the texts, see R. C. Zaehner, *Zurvan, a Zoroastrian dilemma* (Oxford, 1955), pp. 419–43.

Times, but also as a remote First Cause, who entrusted his powers to his second son, Ahuramazda. Ahuramazda then created this world as an arena for the struggle with his wicked brother. Zurvan does not intervene in this struggle, and so adherence to Zurvanism produced no change in the objects and manner of regular Zoroastrian worship, or in moral or spiritual goals. Zurvanites could still call themselves 'Mazda-worshippers' (the usual term used then by Zoroastrians for themselves), and so could live in outward harmony with the orthodox.

Yet theirs was in fact a grievous heresy, which betrayed Zarathushtra's fundamental doctrine that good and evil are utterly separate and distinct by origin and nature. It also diminished the dignity of Ahuramazda, God and Creator, who had been proclaimed by Zarathushtra as the only divine Being worthy of worship who exists eternally; and it confused the clear teachings of the faith with tedious speculations and ignoble myths. Further, the Zurvanite preoccupations with time and fate obscured the basic Zoroastrian doctrine of free-will, with the power of each individual to shape his own destiny through the exercise of choice. Indeed, so deep is the doctrinal gulf separating Zurvanism from orthodox Zoroastrianism that it only seems possible to account for the tolerance shown it in Persia by assuming that it early gained influential adherents. The Sasanid royal family was Zurvanite, and consciously maintained Achemenid tradition in a number of ways. So it is possible that one of the late Achemenid kings – most probably Artaxerxes II – adopted the heresy and established it firmly in western Iran. This would help to account for the enormous influence which it came to exert on gnostic thought in Jewish and other communities (in which the concepts of the Three Times, the remote First Cause, and the lesser Creator of this world, were often fundamental). Orthodox Zoroastrians continued to denounce the heresy, however, as some of them must have continued to struggle against image-worship, and in the end they triumphed over both, despite royal example and the encouragement given to the image-cult through the spread of Hellenism in Alexander's wake.

This double, though hard-won, triumph is a testimony to the essential strength of orthodox Zoroastrianism, which its founder, a priest and thinker as well as a prophet, endowed both with coherent and clearly defined doctrines, and with observances (in the form of daily prayers and seasonal communal celebrations) which imprinted these on the minds and consciousness of his followers. It was evidently this inner strength, combined with its prestige as the imperial religion, which gave Zoroastrianism so much influence in the Near East under the Achemenids – an influence which persisted even after the downfall of the dynasty.

CHAPTER 12

IRANIAN INFLUENCE ON JUDAISM: FIRST CENTURY B.C.E. TO SECOND CENTURY C.E.

INTRODUCTION: THE PROBLEM AND THE METHOD

The fact that in the latter part of the Second Temple period Judaism was undergoing far-reaching changes and developing new aspects, trends, themes and ideas, which were to be retained in part as belonging to the permanent stock of Jewish life and thought, has long attracted the attention of students of Judaism. The most obvious of these changes was in the use of language – the structure, syntax, morphology and lexicon of the later writings in Hebrew display differences which put them apart from the earlier books, and a new language was added to the range of sacred expression, which figures already in some of the later biblical books. These outward changes reflect some of the adjustments made necessary by the new situation of the world: the creation of the world empire of the Persians, their adoption of Aramaic as an official language for purposes of international communication, and the fact that both Hebrew and Aramaic absorbed a great number of Persian words and coined certain expressions under the influence of Persian, as they also did subsequently under that of Greek. Many of these words and expressions were, naturally, in the field of government and administrative practice, but this was by no means the only field in which this linguistic impact was present. We have some words belonging to general civilian life, as well as some which became part of the Jewish religious terminology, although they were not exclusively of religious significance in their original linguistic background (for example, *raz,* *pardes, naḥśir*).

Given such an impact by the Persians on Jewish linguistic expression (an impact felt also by other users of Aramaic, apart from the Jews, and by other linguistic groups), one may wonder whether the prolonged contact with Persian civilization did not leave its mark in other fields as well, notably that of religious life and thought. The question has been asked whether the changes in Jewish religious thought and sensitivity which were taking place in the period under consideration were not at least partly moulded and fashioned as a result of contacts between Jewish and Persian cultures.

It is possible to exclude as unlikely two extreme positions which have been adopted in the course of scholarly discussions around these problems. One of these emphatically denies the actual existence or possibility of Persian cultural influence on Judaism as a factor affecting Jewish thought in the period under consideration (and even goes so far as to suggest exclusive influence in the opposite direction);[1] the other position is the one which would explain almost everything in the development of post-biblical Judaism as stemming directly from Iran.[2]

Between these two positions, it is important to try and establish the precise areas in which the effect of contacts between Jews and Iranians is likely to have taken place and borne fruit, and to define as far as possible what we mean by postulating such influence. It is also necessary to answer the historical question which has been raised about the effect of Persian influence on Judaism being noticeable, not in the period of Persian domination over Palestine, but in the subsequent period, when Palestine was under Greek and Roman rule.

The difficulties in approaching this subject with some detail and precision are considerable. The various new developments in the latest books of the Bible and the literature of the Apocrypha and of the Dead sea sect have from time to time been quite plausibly shown to be developments of certain trends inherent in earlier Jewish writings, and thus not to necessitate, in a compelling manner, foreign intervention for their explanation. While this position has much to commend it, it nevertheless misses the point of the argument. If contact with Iran is postulated as a contributing factor in the development of these ideas in Judaism, this does not imply that a set of concepts entirely alien to Jewish thought was introduced suddenly. What is suggested is that the new developments, probably stimulated by internal factors and prepared for by a set of indigenous ideas, no less than by the effect of pressure from without, took the direction and character which they did, not by mere accident, but as a result of the fact that the Iranian pattern was at hand and quite well known. It must however be admitted that if our

---

[1] Cf. for example M. Gaster, 'Parsiism in Judaism', *Encyclopaedia of Religion and Ethics*, (Edinburgh, 1908–26) 9, pp. 637–40; J. Darmesteter, *Le Zend Avesta*, III, Annales du Musée Guimet, 24 (Paris, 1893), pp. v–cvii.

[2] Cf. for example L. H. Mills, *Zarathushtra, the Achaemenids and Israel* (Chicago, 1906), and other works by the same author. A succinct survey of the scholarly discussion is given by J. Duchesne-Guillemin in *La religion de l'Iran ancien* (Paris, 1962), pp. 257ff, and *The Western Response to Zoroaster* (Oxford, 1958).

position is stated in these rather flexible terms, it is much less capable of direct and detailed proof or rebuttal.[1]

While we possess a wealth of literature which represents Jewish writings of the period around the beginning of the Common Era, our knowledge of Iranian religion in the corresponding period and before is sadly deficient. It depends to a large extent on hypothesis, reconstruction and reading back from a body of literature belonging to a much later period.

It would naturally be difficult for someone who is not a specialist in Iranian matters to evaluate the evidence adduced from Iranian writings, and it must be admitted that such evidence has been used from time to time in a manner which cannot arouse confidence. As a result, some scholars have tended to view the whole of this field of discussion with some mistrust. Nevertheless, it seems possible to establish by reconstruction certain elements of the earlier faith, even though they are not explicitly present in the Avesta. The methods to be used in attempting such a reconstruction should include the study of the evidence of the later books in an attempt to discover a clear line of development leading from an early period to later practice and faith. In addition, fragmentary references in Greek, Armenian, Syriac, Babylonian, Aramaic and later Arabic writings can be used as supplementary evidence for various points which were observed or reported by strangers. These would more often be points of observance than matters of faith. In addition, it may be permissible, in an attempt to evaluate the antiquity of some aspect of religious faith which is attested only in late sources, to resort to an argument by which the function of that item of faith is examined within the wider context of the structure of the religion, to see whether it can be identified as an old motif. A combination of all these methods may from time to time prove useful, but it is always necessary to bear in mind that they are used in the absence of firm and positive evidence which would place them in their proper historical setting, and that they are always open to the charge of subjectivity.

[1] For a general treatment of the problems one may single out the following publications: W. Bousset, *Die Religion des Judentums im spät-hellenistischen Zeitalter*, 3rd edn., rev. H. Gressmann (Tübingen, 1926); E. Stave, *Über den Einfluss des Parsismus auf das Judentum* (Harlem, 1898); D. Winston, 'The Iranian component in the Bible, Apocrypha and Qumran: A Review of the Evidence', *HR*, 5 (1965–66), 183–216; J. R. Hinnels, 'Zoroastrian Influence on the Judaeo-Christian tradition', *JCOI*, 45 (1976), 1–23.

IRANIAN LITERATURE AND ITS PROBLEMS

In order to appreciate the problems involved, a brief discussion of the relevant Iranian literature may be in order.[1] The earliest layer of religious literature in Iran, the group of hymns known as the Gathas, are quite commonly accepted to be a composition of the founder of the religion, Zarathushtra, whose date is not unanimously agreed upon. While some scholars would place him before the beginning of the first millennium B.C.E., others would bring him down to the sixth century B.C.E.[2] The opinion accepted by most scholars to be most reasonable is that Zarathushtra lived in the north-eastern regions of Iran, although according to the surviving Zoroastrian tradition he was in the north-western part of the country. The contents of the Gathas are imperfectly known, and they have been interpreted in different ways. The difficulties inherent in the text of the Gathas have given it the reputation of being one of the most obscure texts in religious literature. Two extreme approaches have tended to influence the interpretation of the Gathas: one would give a great deal of credence to the indigenous tradition of exegesis, although in many instances it seems clear that the tradition was faulty and did not always reflect the original meaning of the text; the other would disregard the Zoroastrian tradition altogether and would attempt to reconstruct the meaning of the text by a close study of it in conjunction with the closest literary monument available, the Rig-Veda, combined with a study of the Indo-Iranian and Indo-European etymologies of the words in the text. While some scholars tend to use one method more than the other, most scholars today would agree that it is necessary to find the right balance by combining the two approaches in a manner which makes it possible for the one to supplement the deficiencies of the other.

Subsequent portions of the sacred Zoroastrian scripture, known, in contrast to the Gathas, as the Younger Avesta, present fewer problems of interpretation, though they are not free from difficulties and textual corruptions. However, as the history of Iran has known two major breaks in cultural continuity – the conquest of Alexander the Great and the conquest of Islam – much of the text of the original canon of the Avesta is known to have been lost. The surviving Avesta is but a small

[1] More detailed information can be obtained from *Grundriss der Iranischen Philologie* (Strassburg, 1896–1904), II, pp. 1–129 (articles by K. F. Geldner, F. H. Weissbach, E. W. West); J. C. Tavadia, *Die mittelpersische Sprache und Literatur der Zarathustrier* (Leipzig, 1956); *Handbuch der Orientalistik, I, IV: Iranistik, 2. Abschnitt: Literatur, Lieferung 1* (Leiden, 1968), 1–66 (articles by I. Gershevitch and M. Boyce).

[2] Cf. M. Boyce, *A History of Zoroastrianism*, (Leiden, 1975) I, p. 190; W. B. H. Henning, *Zoroaster, Politician or Witch-Doctor?* (London, 1951).

portion of a much larger body of literature which once constituted the canon; although in talking of an ancient Avestan canon, it is by no means certain that a body of *written* literature was necessarily in existence. The portions that we possess are essentially those that were used for liturgical purposes, or that contained ritual prescriptions, and were thus in constant use. Almost the whole of the Avesta dealing with questions of doctrine, cosmology, cosmogony, eschatology, as well as the majority of the text which dealt with questions of law, is lost. Some portions of the lost books of the Avesta are imperfectly reflected in brief summaries given in Middle Persian, in Pahlavi books.

In addition to the sacred canon, the Avesta, in the fragmentary and somewhat corrupt form in which it is preserved, circumspect use can be made of the old layers of tradition preserved in the late Middle Persian, or Pahlavi, books. The latest redaction of these writings was, for the most part, in the period following the conquest of Iran by the Arabs, and some are several centuries more recent, but various considerations make it certain that much of what they contain stems from an older period. It is by no means easy to establish with complete confidence that an individual point goes back to an ancient tradition, and if it does, to date the period in which the ancient tradition was first formulated. In many cases, the judgement on these questions can only be based on a hunch. This is true even of those passages in Pahlavi literature which are explicitly presented as translations or summaries of the Avesta. Middle Persian renderings of Avestan texts are usually a combination of exegesis with straightforward translation, the latter sometimes being philologically suspect. It may thus be assumed that the Zoroastrian interpreters of a later period often read into the sacred text ideas which were not explicit in it, but belonged to their own period.

The two most important compositions in the fields of cosmology, eschatology and theology are the Bundahishn, available in two versions, a longer and a shorter one, and the Dinkard, an enormous compilation available for the most part in a single manuscript only, with two of its original nine books lost. Both books, compiled in the ninth century C.E., have been printed and partly translated into English, but they bristle with difficulties, textual and otherwise.

The incriptions of the Achemenid kings in Old Persian provide a glimpse into some notions of their faith, though only a tantalizingly defective one.

Our knowledge of early Iranian religious customs and faith can be supplemented by the study of foreign reports, such as those given by Greek historians, the most prominent among whom are Herodotus, Strabo and Plutarch; and for a somewhat later period, we may make use of references to Iranian religious practices as described or alluded to in the acts of the Persian martyrs in Syriac, in some anecdotes and references in the Babylonian Talmud, in the writings of the Armenian historians, and in the scattered fragments of Sasanid writings preserved in Arabic compilations of historical, edifying or entertaining character.

The Manichean, Buddhist and Christian writings which were discovered in some of the dialects belonging to the Middle Iranian group (Middle Persian, Parthian, Sogdian and Khotanese) sometimes afford an indirect glimpse into some points of Iranian religion in the Sasanid period, chiefly through their use of the Zoroastrian vocabulary.

Archeological excavations conducted in Iran have greatly enhanced the understanding of various aspects of life in ancient Iran. Their bearing on our understanding of the religious life has, however, so far proved to be rather limited.

It is thus only by making judicious use of information gained from the diverse sources at our disposal that certain points can be elucidated, but some central problems in the religious history of Iran are still unresolved. The uncertainty as to various points in the reality and experience of 'official' Zoroastrianism, and even more with regard to the popular religion of Iranians in antiquity, has made it possible to fit the known facts into more than one hypothesis, and has greatly encouraged speculation by scholars.

TRACES OF CONTACT WITH IRAN IN THE LATER BOOKS OF THE BIBLE

Certain books in the Hagiographa section of the Hebrew Bible were written during the Persian period and were subject to some external Persian influence.[1] The background of Persian court administration and official management of the state is clearly noticeable in the chronicles of Ezra and Nehemiah, while the books of Daniel and Esther, which have been conjectured to belong to a somewhat later period, are explicitly set in the Persian court (in Daniel in a somewhat confused manner).

The earliest attestation of reaction to Iranian ideas is found in Deutero-Isaiah. An admonition is addressed to certain Jews making them 'fire-lighters, girders of fire-brands' (Isa. 50: 11), presumably taking them to task for holding fire in veneration, though it is impossible to tell what particular practice is being followed. Some other references in Deutero-Isaiah are much less certain, though chapters 40–48 seem

---

[1] Cf. for what follows Winston, HR, 5 (1965–66).

to contain some quite explicit allusions to Iranian religious terminology, as in 45: 7.[1]

The theory of the Four Monarchies which are said to have held world rule, coupled with the view that the world is to undergo four different ages before it comes to its end, is well attested in late Iranian sources, and it has been argued that this is an old Persian idea, which was taken up also in Greek literature. This applies possibly also to the conception of the four ages as symbolized by four metals.[2]

The descriptions of the end of times abound in various details which conform to what we find in Iranian, Greco-Iranian (that is, writings in Greek and Latin which are believed to be derived from an Iranian source, such as the Oracles of Hystaspes) and Jewish sources. Among such themes the levelling of mountains, the shortening of the years, the young turning old, the young having no respect for the old, and so on, have been mentioned as possibly deriving ultimately from an Iranian source.[3]

COGNATE THEMES AND PARALLELS BETWEEN IRANIAN WRITINGS AND THE JEWISH APOCRYPHA, PSEUDEPIGRAPHA, AND THE QUMRAN SCROLLS

Of the numerous new themes and trends which came to the fore in the period under consideration, it may be possible to single out the following: dualistic tendencies; a complex demonology in contrast with and parallel to an elaborate angelology; predestination on a cosmic as well as on an individual level; a conception of a predetermined succession of periods of the universe, leading to a well-developed and quite intricate scheme of eschatology, again both universal and individual; eschatological descriptions consisting of judgements, ordeals, resurrection and salvation, following a set of signs heralding the end. All this is sometimes associated with speculations about time.

These innovations in Judaism stand parallel to close counterparts in Iranian literature (though it should be remembered that many Iranian themes are not attested until a fairly late date). The idea has naturally suggested itself that these ideas were formulated as a result of contacts with Iranian culture. Despite the diversity of the Jewish writings

---

[1] Cf. M. Smith, 'II Isaiah and the Persians', *JAOS*, 83 (1963), 415–21.

[2] J. W. Swain, 'The Theory of the four Monarchies: Opposition History under the Roman Empire', *ClassPhil*, 35 (1940), 1–21; D. Flusser, 'The Four Empires in the Fourth Sibyl and in the Book of Daniel', *IOS*, 2 (1972), 148–75.

[3] D. Flusser, 'Hystaspes and John of Patmos', in *Irano-Judaica*, Jerusalem (to be published).

mentioned in the heading of this section, it would be simplest to treat them as one block, selecting the major themes pertinent to our subject one by one. It will be evident that the material relating to Iran is mostly concentrated in a limited number of books. Problems and doubts with regard to the antiquity of the Iranian material will be indicated, though it is impossible to justify here in detail the contention that a given theme is sufficiently old to have been at least contemporary with the corresponding Jewish literature.

Certain literary themes have been recognized in the apocryphal literature as reflecting a Persian background. The story of the three youths in 1 Esdras 3: 1 to 5: 6, in which each one says before King Darius what the strongest thing is and the winner is the one who upholds the power of truth, can be quoted as one example.[1] The book of Tobit has been claimed as an adaptation of an Iranian (Median) story, but this seems doubtful.[2] It does, however, contain certain references to Iranian customs.

DUALISM

The notion of dualism, which finds strong expression particularly in the Testaments of the Twelve Patriarchs, the Manual of Discipline of Qumran, and the Judeo-Christian Didache, quite naturally brings to mind the classic dualistic religion, Zoroastrianism.

A common misconception has bred an argument against a comparison of Jewish dualism with the Iranian type of faith. It stresses the fact that in the Jewish writings under consideration, even those demonstrating the strongest dualistic tendencies, there is never a departure from the underlying monotheism, and whatever conflict develops between good and evil powers, they are always subordinate to God, who is in a sense above the antagonism (though He clearly sides with the good). This argument implies that in Iran we have 'pure' dualism, with a pair of deities on an equal footing poised against each other, representing the two opposing principles. This is not an entirely accurate description of the Iranian dualism.

In Zarathushtra's Gathas we have one deity, Ahuramazda, 'the lord wisdom', with a host of entities representing abstract notions assisting him designated as *mainyu*, that is, non-tangible, invisible, non-sensual, intelligible entities. One of these entities, which tends to be identified with 'the lord wisdom' himself, is Spenta Mainyu (or Spenishta Mainyu), 'the Bounteous (or the Most Bounteous) Spirit'. The Evil

[1] R. H. Pfeiffer, *History of New Testament Times* (New York, 1949), p. 67.
[2] J. H. Moulton, *Early Zoroastrianism* (London, 1913), pp. 332ff.

Spirit, or Angra Mainyu, is seen to be not in direct opposition to Ahuramazda, but to Spenta Mainyu, with whom he shares the title *mainyu* 'spirit'. (Ahuramazda is of course also a *mainyu*, a spirit, but one which is designated as Lord.) For Angra Mainyu to be in opposition to Spenta Mainyu is basically the same as for him to be in opposition to Ahuramazda himself, but it does not seem to be the same in terms of the structural conception of early Zoroastrianism. In the later literature the two terms, Ahuramazda and Spenta Mainyu, are totally identified, and the dualistic conflict thus runs neatly between the two figures, Ahuramazda/Spenta Mainyu and Angra Mainyu. They are described in the theological literature, which was possibly elaborated during the Sasanid period (third to seventh centuries C.E.), as two eternal principles, immutable, without beginning or end. Even so, the dualistic confrontation is not based on equality. Ahuramazda exists, while Angra Mainyu does not, and faith in the existence of the one and the non-existence of the other is an essential part of the Zoroastrian credo, to be explicitly uttered daily. The theological non-existence of Angra Mainyu is possibly to be understood as reflecting the position that Angra Mainyu is said to be existing only in non-material, or *mēnōg*, form, and to have no real presence in the material world, known as *gētīg*. It is, however, difficult to assign a definite date to this doctrine, which is attested in a late form only. These elaborations do show, however, that the doctrinal supremacy of Ahuramazda over Angra Mainyu is always maintained, and that Angra Mainyu is conceived of throughout as a negative force, and as such is doctrinally secondary to the divine power of Ahuramazda, against whose existence and creation he sets out to fight. Destructiveness is the *raison d'être* of Angra Mainyu, and his nature, which is secondary and, in this sense, derivative, implies the primary existence and creative power of Ahuramazda.

It can thus be maintained that the contrast between the relative dualism of sectarian Judaism of the period under consideration and the more boldly pronounced dualism of the Iranian religion is not as deep as may be imagined from a cursory comparison. The type of dualism present in these Jewish books is also akin to Iranian dualism in that in both the division cuts across the material and the spiritual universe, unlike gnostic dualism, where the spiritual was identified with the divine. The similarity in structure, on the other hand, does not by itself require the assumption of influence. Unless one can show definite correspondence in details which would be unlikely to develop in the two cultures on their own, the argument in favour of the contention that Judaism was helped in shaping certain of its ideas by the proximity of Iran would rest on shaky grounds.

ANGELOLOGY AND DEMONOLOGY

An interesting feature of the dualism in Iran as well as in the Jewish writings under consideration is the highly involved conception of a heavenly host set against a demonic one. Each one of the two contenders, the deity and his antithesis, has a camp of supporters.[1] These are spirits which derive from the main protagonist and represent his power, and which make it possible for him to conduct the cosmic battle waged between them.

It seems significant that the term used for these minor divine and demonic powers is closely similar in content in Israel and Iran.[2] The Iranian term *mainyu* (later form *mēnōg*), is commonly translated 'spirit'. It basically denotes a non-material entity. It should be noted that the non-material aspect of the universe does not represent in Iranian usage a higher value as compared with the material world, expressed by the Avestic term *astvant* (later called *gētīg*). The term *mēnōg*, known to us as a fully developed notion only in the late Pahlavi writings, represents, when analysed in modern terms, at least three distinct notions: (*a*) an abstract idea of quality, such as Truth, Untruth, Wisdom, Generosity; (*b*) a quality or psychological urge, operating within the individual person – the same examples, truth(fulness), deceit(fulness), wisdom, generosity, could be used again to illustrate their subjective, inherent, sense; (*c*) finally, a personified entity, conceived of as a divine or demonic power, active both within the individual and on a cosmic scale. It is scarcely necessary to emphasize that the distinctions made here are not explicitly made in the original texts, and most probably were not felt to be present. For the authors of the Zoroastrian texts, the three aspects defined here are probably a single concept. The 'subjective' force operating within the individual person is the same as the cosmic or 'abstract' idea, which is essentially a modern way of describing what to Zoroastrians is a real entity.

A similar analysis could be made of the corresponding notion in the Jewish writings of the period under consideration, whether it is expressed by the Hebrew term *ruaḥ* or by the Greek *pneuma*. The resemblance in the semantic structure and in the application of the notion is quite striking. The contrast between *mēnōg* and *gētīg*, and the complex meaning of the former term, as analysed above, seems to be deeply rooted in Iran, and can be said to belong to an early layer of

---

[1] Cf. a survey of the subject by D. S. Russell, *The Method and Message of Jewish Apocalyptic* (Philadelphia, 1964), pp. 257–62.

[2] Cf. S. Shaked, 'The notions *mēnōg* and *gētīg* in the Pahlavi texts and their relation to Eschatology', *AcOr*, 33 (1971), 59–70; 'Qumran and Iran', *IOS*, 2 (1972), 433–46.

Iranian thinking. Since the notion of *mainyu*, with all its complexity of meaning, is already present in the Gathas, and as the contrast between the two ideas of *mēnōg* and *gētīg* is a key to understanding the religious terminology of Zoroastrian Iran, it can quite safely be assumed to have been a feature of the religious thinking of Iran at the time of the prophet Zarathushtra. Under gnostic influence, the corresponding Judeo-Christian term *ruaḥ/pneuma* also developed, at a somewhat later date, the additional connotation of a higher level of existence, akin to divinity, as opposed to matter, which signifies corruption and depravity. All this seems to be alien to the layers of the Jewish literature of the period which we are discussing.

There are analogies not only on the level of the conceptual framework between the notion of 'spirit' in Judaism and in the Zoroastrian writings; there is also a similarity in the literary treatment of the theme. In both literatures there is the tendency to arrange these spirits, which are also psychological concepts, in lists, sometimes in parallel fashion, good spirits against evil ones. The tendency to arrange spirits in this manner has no close parallels in the ancient Near East, though some parallels may be adduced from Buddhist India.

As a point of detail, one name of a demon in Jewish writings seems to be borrowed from Zoroastrianism: it is the Iranian Aešma, who might be called by his generic designation Aešma-daeva 'the demon of wrath', though this combination is not actually attested. He has been identified in the Greek text of the book of Tobit under the form Asmodaios, and he also survives in the popular layer of the rabbinic literature under the form Ashmedai.

PREDESTINATION, DIVISIONS OF THE WORLD, AND TIME

It is often said that, in contrast with the strong spirit of predestination which possesses the Jewish writings most suspected of Zoroastrian influence, the Zoroastrian religion itself is based on a doctrine of free will and the free choice of the individual. This is true in so far as the Gathas and the Younger Avesta contain verses in which the verb 'to choose, to make a choice' is prominently used, indicating adherence to or acceptance of the faith. However, this usage need not necessarily imply *freedom* of choice. The two eternal spirits, eternally committed from the beginning (in the later, Sasanid, writings, they are specifically said to have no 'beginning') to the two absolute principles they represent, each 'chose' its own particular way: the one chose truth, the other falsehood. It may however be suggested that the verb 'to choose' does not imply, in such a context, an act which follows deliberation and weighing of possibilities as we understand the terms. It would rather seem to denote a whole-hearted adoption of the attitude which each one actually fulfils, a willing commitment, as opposed to doing one's duty under constraint or in an equivocal frame of mind. Neither in the Avesta nor in later Zoroastrian literature is there any indication that it might be possible to hope for the conversion of the utterly wicked, or for a change of choice on the part of demons, wicked people or obnoxious animals. Sinners within the good religion of Zoroastrianism should be exhorted and reprimanded and made to change their ways; and adherents of the faith are called to constant exertion, so as to become entirely righteous and worthy of reward, and to fulfil their crucial task in the fight against the demons and the evil powers. It is in this context that the idea of choice makes sense, and it is applied with equal validity to the two arch-spirits themselves, who not only are what they are, but also 'chose' to be that. In the same way, the bull, a major figure in the Avesta, is said to have 'chosen' its protector, and this usage again seems to indicate primarily its willingness, its heartfelt acceptance of the protection given to it. It would make little sense to assume that the bull carefully weighs the merits of its protector against the harm caused by its enemy, and comes to the conclusion that the former is preferable. From the Middle Persian texts, where questions of free will and predestination are explicitly discussed, it becomes clear that the area of free will is extremely limited. A division of human functions is made into five categories: fate, action, habit, nature and heredity. Man would seem to have no control over 'fate' (which determines livelihood, wife and children, etc.), 'habit' (where the natural bodily functions belong), 'nature' (which determines man's inherent qualities), and 'heredity' (from which the intellectual powers are derived). There remains 'action', which determines how one fulfils one's religious duties – whether one is righteous or wicked – and the duties of one's social class. A man's action, it would seem, makes it possible to grade him from the point of view of religious adherence and of faithfulness to his social obligations.[1] It seems that this idea need not go against the view of the Qumran sectarians, despite the strong emphasis on predestination in the Manual of Discipline and in the Thanksgiving Scroll. If it is accepted that the views of the Qumran sectarians on the problem of individual freedom differed from those of official Zoroastrianism in emphasis rather than in substance, we merely remove a point which has been used as an argument against the assumption that the Qumran sectarians were close to some Zoroastrian views.

---

[1] Cf. S. Shaked, *Wisdom of the Sasanian Sages* (Boulder, Colorado, 1979) commentary on *Dēnkard* vi, D1a.

There is, however, a related theme on which it is possible to point out a fairly substantial area of agreement – the destiny of the world. In the Zoroastrian view, the world's destiny is determined by the very act of creation, by the function allotted to the world at its creation, by the intention of its Creator, and by the circumstances of the battle between the two powers which brought about the creation. An important part of the initial scheme which establishes the destiny of the world is the conception of a definite succession of periods. The duration of this world's existence, as well as the length of each major period, is strictly established in advance. The duration of the world is fixed at 12,000 or 9,000 years, and this sum is made up of units of 3,000 years each, with the present era placed in the final group of 3,000 years. The Jewish views are not as well-defined or as unequivocal as those expressed in the Iranian writings, but we do have a division of universal history into twelve parts (2 Baruch 56: 3 ; 4 Ezra 14: 11), and other divisions of world history are also quite well known, such as the notion of the four periods of the world.

Here we have a pattern of thought which seems to be not only typical of Iran, but also logically associated with other Iranian ideas. The material world, having been created for a specific function – for serving as the battleground between Ahuramazda and his rival – is bound to reach its end when the work for which it was created is completed. It is one aspect of a double creation, the other aspect being represented by the invisible world (*mēnōg*). Eschatology brings about not only the ultimate victory, but also a new harmony between the two in the reconstitution of the world. Although this set of notions is only given explicit expression in the late Zoroastrian literature, which is not earlier in its present form than the post-Sasanid period, there is strong reason to assume that it was present in Iran at a much earlier date. The eschatological function here is not an independent idea, to which figures can be attached in a more or less arbitrary manner, but part of the scheme of creation, eschatology bringing the cycle to its close.

The ideas are closely associated with the Zoroastrian thinking about time, a major theme in the Middle Persian accounts of the creation. We learn from these accounts that before the process of creation began, there was no time in our common usage of the term, only 'unlimited time' (*zamān ī a-kanārag*). For the purpose of creation, Ohrmazd brought forth 'limited time' (*zamān ī kanāragōmand*), which has internal divisions, and this is the entity which is known also as 'Time of the Long Dominion' (*zamān ī dērang-xwadāy*). The creation of this entity was necessary not only because the existence of the material universe is temporal (that is, it exists in time) as well as temporary, but also because the very creation of the material world was conceived so as to provide a battleground for good and evil. The function of this battleground was to make it possible to conclude the war and achieve victory over evil within a time-limit set by the Creator. The alternative would have meant an endless war without conclusion.

This curious notion of double time, parallel as it is in Iran to the notion of the two aspects of existence, the material and the invisible, as well as to two notions of space, was also borrowed by Jewish literature, although it seems not to have enjoyed wide popularity and is only attested in the so-called Slavonic book of Enoch.[1] As this is one of the clearest cases of borrowing, it may also provide us with a welcome opportunity of dating this idea in Iran to an earlier period than its attestation in Iran itself, where again it does not occur before the Middle Persian books. The Slavonic book of Enoch contains a number of other motifs borrowed from Iran, such as the creation of the world by stages from invisible (= *mēnōg*) to visible (= *gētīg*), and making man a composite of the two elements; and the idea of the soul of the beast (2 Enoch 58: 3ff).

ESCHATOLOGY

In the field of eschatological ideas, we encounter some of the most striking points of similarity between Iran and the Jewish writings. The chronological difficulties are present here in all their weight, since we have an explicit statement of the structure of Zoroastrian eschatology only in the late Middle Persian texts, the Avesta containing only some scattered hints about a limited number of eschatological notions.

It is, however, not very likely that such a complex and interwoven set of ideas would come to exist in two religious cultures independently of each other. It would indeed be desirable to find a method by which to establish with a reasonable degree of clarity which of the two first evolved its eschatological structure, and in what follows a suggestion will be made concerning this.

The complexity, lack of coherence, and apparent contradictions in the eschatological schemes, both in Iran and in Judaism, are quite considerable. Many of the events which the individual experiences after death, such as confronting a bridge, a weighing of his deeds, a judgement, are repeated in the accounts of universal eschatology. While

---

[1] Cf. S. Pines, 'Eschatology and the Concept of Time in the Slavonic Book of Enoch', in *Types of Redemption*, Studies in the History of Religions, Supplements to *Numen*, 18, ed. R. J. Z. Werblowsky and J. C. Bleecker (Leiden, 1970), pp. 72–87, and Winston, *HR*, 5 (1965–66), 197–8.

it may be natural for such ideas to evolve in a somewhat inconsistent manner by transposing certain motifs from one area to another and by repeating them in both places, it is nevertheless striking that the similarities between the eschatology of Judaism and that of Iran are apparent not only in the use of the themes, but also in their seeming incoherence.

The Iranian view of the two aspects of the world, the invisible, non-sensual or ideal (*mēnōg*), and the material (*gētīg*), helps here, too, in understanding the structure of eschatology. *Mēnōg* precedes *gētīg* both temporally and logically, but also exists side by side with it. They coexist separately, as two different modes of existence on two separate planes, but they are also combined in the perceptible world in which we live. This view provides an explanation for many of the details of Iranian eschatology. Creation, according to the Pahlavi books, was done in two (or three) stages: the world was first created in *mēnōg*, then as *gētīg* in *mēnōg*, and then in *gētīg*, the former serving as a model for the latter. On the plane of individual human existence, it seems correct to say that people exist in *mēnōg*, as individual spirits (called *fravaši*), before they are born into the material world. In individual eschatology, at the death of a person he returns to his *mēnōg* existence, where an account, a judgement, is made of his earthly existence. With the universe, a somewhat similar process is envisaged: the world 'dies' in its present constitution, and the subject-matter of the final time of the world is recorded by apocalypse. When the end comes, it does not dissolve, and does not return to its *mēnōg* existence; its material existence is continued in a modified form. Its former inhabitants return to it by resurrection, there is a final accounting and purification through judgement and ordeals, and humanity remains constant by the abolition of death and birth. An ultimate phase of ideal existence sets in, in which the earth rises and approaches the luminaries, the two planes of *mēnōg* and *gētīg* come close to each other, and the dichotomy introduced by the presence of evil is removed forever.

In this simplified account of the events of eschatology, the interpretation of the events was presented as part of the narrative. This is not the case in the original texts. By this interpretation, however, one can see the structure and coherence of the main themes of Iranian eschatology, and how they are closely tied to the interplay between the twin notions of *mēnōg* and *gētīg*. Although the events, and the elements required for the interpretation, are mostly attested in the Middle Persian books, it may be argued that such coherence indicates the origin in Iran of this eschatological structure. The constituent elements may have conceivably not originally belonged together, but may have received their coherence through their function as part of a structure. In Jewish writings many of the same elements are found, while the overriding structure is lacking; and it may well be a valid conclusion that we have a case of an organic development of a system in Iran, as against Judaism, where the same elements are present in a more or less haphazard manner. These eschatological motifs certainly answered a need and fitted in with a current mood in Judaism, but they may not have developed there organically. This comparison could well serve as an argument that certain elements of the eschatological system in Iran, where they formed part of a larger conception, were borrowed and adapted to the requirements of Judaism.

Several detailed parallels, some of which are very close, have been shown to exist between eschatological themes in Judaism and in Iran. It can however be shown that certain eschatological themes were partly available in biblical verses which could be developed in an eschatological sense; and thus the process must have been one by which an existing tradition was adapted to express a new mood, rather than an alien tradition arbitrarily grafted. The Zoroastrian idea that the soul of a dead person does not depart from the vicinity of the body for three days and nights following death is echoed in the Testament of Abraham (Recension A, 20) and elsewhere in Jewish literature. Certain details of the resurrection, such as the notion that the separate components of the body will be retrieved from specific elements of the universe (compare 2 Enoch) are a major theme in Zoroastrian literature. The dramatic scenes of the meeting of those risen from the dead are also elaborated upon in Iranian as well as in Jewish literature.

The idea of a general resurrection of the whole of mankind, in which all people will be put to judgement in their physical bodies for deeds performed while they were alive, seems to have been moulded by contact with Iran. An earlier idea (Isa. 26: 19; Dan. 12: 2–3) seems to have envisaged a selective resurrection – and that idea may or may not have been originally Jewish.

The origins of the doctrine associated with the figure of the Man or Son of Man have been the subject of much speculation. Although some affinities have been pointed out with the Iranian figure of Gayomard, the Primal Man of Zoroastrian mythology, these seem to be imprecise and are somewhat equivocal. If foreign elements have here been blended with Jewish traditional ideas, they are not easy to identify.[1] Some other

[1] Cf. Russell, *Jewish Apocalyptic*, pp. 315ff, 346ff. Of the extensive literature on the subject one may mention only R. Reitzenstein, *Die hellenistischen Mysterienreligionen nach ihren Grundgedanken und Wirkungen*, 3rd edn.; (Leipzig and Berlin, 1927); O. G. von Wesendonk, *Urmensch und Seele in der iranischen Überlieferung* (Hannover, 1924); C. H. Kraeling, *Anthropos and Son of Man* (New York, 1927); a critical summary of the discussion in C. Colpe, *Die religionsgeschichtliche Schule* (Göttingen, 1961).

aspects of Jewish eschatology, especially in 1 Enoch, may very well have been derived from Greek ideas of Orphic origin (which in its turn may have absorbed some Persian influence at an earlier period). This seems to be the case with the idea of Sheol, the abode of the dead, where punishment and reward are given to the wicked and the righteous respectively; and the intermediate state after death and before resurrection. Certain aspects of the doctrines of fallen angels and the marriage of angels and human beings seem also to have been borrowed from Greek ideas.[1] The idea of the eschatological conflagration is probably not of Persian origin.

CONCLUSION

It seems useless to debate the question whether or not the religious developments in Judaism of the late Second Temple period were partly fashioned by contacts with one of the prevailing cultures of the period, that of Iran. Opinions may, of course, differ as to the extent and significance of these contacts, and whether more weight should be given to the local development of a given theme or to the adoption of a foreign trait of culture. It does not seem at all likely that so many similarities could have been formed in parallel independently, and, despite the chronological difficulties of the documentation, in most of the parallel points one may feel quite confident that the ideas were indigenous to Iran. It is much more difficult to establish how contacts between Jews and Iranians took place in such a way as to bring about the awareness of common religious concerns evidenced by compositions which were perhaps for the most part written in Palestine and its environment, and not in Iran. A parallel question which may be raised in the same context is how we should explain the fact that the religious developments in Judaism, which allegedly imply contact with Iran, are attested to a period considerably later than the period of Persian rule and administration in Palestine, since they are in fact products of the Hellenistic period in Palestine.

It is possible to suggest an answer to these questions by assuming that the Achemenid Persian administrators in Palestine and elsewhere were probably not the most likely carriers of Persian religious ideas among other peoples. It is certainly true that it never was the official policy of the Persian government in Achemenid times to impose Zoroastrianism or other attributes of Persian culture on the alien population. The best locale for the creation of a Jewish response for Persian culture may have been Persia and Mesopotamia, where Jews lived among a predominantly Persian population; and the most likely

[1] Cf. T. F. Glasson, *Greek Influence in Jewish Eschatology* (London, 1961), p. 1.

carriers of this new set of ideas may have been Jews from that Diaspora who had constant communication with their brethren in Palestine through pilgrimage and immigration. Asia Minor, which since the Achemenid period had substantial groups of Persian colonists, may be considered a possible alternative. The most likely period for this development to take place seems to have been the Hellenistic era, since it was in this period that the general cultural mood was open to the absorption of ideas from the East and to oriental exotica. It may be assumed that the new Jewish expression was achieved in Palestine and its vicinity, but that some of the impetus for using the themes which come up in that layer of Jewish literature for the first time may have been transmitted by Jews who had come from Iran or Mesopotamia. It seems quite significant in this context that the specific Iranian religious themes encountered in the Jewish books discussed above tend to be concentrated in a number of compositions, such as the Testaments of the Twelve Patriarchs (particularly Levi, Dan, Naphtali, Asher and Benjamin), 2 Enoch (Slavonic Enoch), and the Manual of Discipline, while other books seem to share certain ideas ultimately derived from Iran in a secondary manner.

A further question which has to be dealt with is this: granted that the religion of Israel as it developed in the Hellenistic period in Palestine absorbed (or at least certain groups or circles in it did) elements of Iranian faith, can these elements be identified as deriving from any particular brand of Iranian religion? There have been some attempts to answer this question, either by referring vaguely to popular religion, or, particularly in the wake of the discovery of the Dead sea scrolls, by identifying the Iranian component believed to be found there as specifically 'Zurvanite'. The complication here is twofold. In the first place, despite the valiant attempts made by Iranists to reconstruct a whole system of theological thinking around the notion of Zurvan, the Time god, it still seems quite doubtful whether Zurvanism ever existed as a separate religious entity, with a set of beliefs and practices of its own. All we know for certain is that a certain myth of creation, in which the Time god figures as primordial and as originator of the duality of gods, was in circulation in the Sasanid period. It may have been merely a popular variant of the Zoroastrian myth. The second complication is that, if it is accepted that the Iranian elements in Jewish writings of the Hellenistic period are indeed the result of a process of adaptation and absorption into an existing framework of beliefs, and that they primarily helped to mould ideas which were vaguely there, the shape they would have in the texts available would necessarily be modified in a Jewish way, and it is unlikely that any deductions could be made from them about their supposed originals.

CHAPTER 13

THE DIASPORA

A. BABYLONIA IN THE PERSIAN AGE

POLITICAL HISTORY

By the end of the seventh century B.C.E. only four major powers were left on the political map of the Near East: Egypt, Babylonia, Media and Lydia. In 550 the Persians, led by their king, Cyrus II, seized Media and over the next three years invaded Elam, Parthia, Hyrcania on the Caspian sea, and the whole of Asia Minor including Lydia and the Greek colonies. Between 545 and 539 B.C.E. Cyrus II conquered all the regions of Central Asia and Eastern Iran as far as the borders of India.

Following this, in the spring of 539 B.C.E. the Persian army attacked Babylonia and began to advance down the Diyala river valley. At this critical point, Ugbaru, the governor of Gutium (a Babylonian province to the east of the middle course of the Tigris) went over to Cyrus.[1]

All the efforts of Nabonidus, the king of Babylonia, to resist the Persian advance proved doomed to failure. It was in the interests of Babylonia's merchants for an enormous empire to be created which would guarantee them a market and safe trading routes to Egypt,[2] Asia Minor and other countries of the east, and they were therefore prepared to collaborate with the invaders. Influential priestly groups were also dissatisfied with Nabonidus. Although he continued to worship the ancient Babylonian gods Marduk, Nabu and their companions, he gradually began to promote the cult of the Moon god, Sin. Moreover, the Moon god whom Nabonidus patronized was not the traditional god Sin, but one whose symbols and forms of worship were more reminiscent of Aramaic deities.

With the help of religious reforms and military campaigns, Nabonidus sought to unite around him the numerous Aramaic tribes of Western Asia and ward off the approaching threat from Iran.[3] Unfortunately,

---

[1] W. W. Hallo, 'Gutium', RLA, 3 (1971), 717–19.

[2] See M. Lambert, 'Le destin d'Ur et les routes commerciales', RSO, 39 (1964), 103–4.

[3] On Nabonidus, see H. Tadmor, 'The Inscriptions of Nabunaid', in Studies in Honor of Benno Landsberger (Chicago, 1965), pp. 351–63. Contains references to previous works on the subject.

however, his reforms brought him into conflict with the priesthood and the general population of Babylon, Borsippa, Nippur, Uruk and the other ancient cities of Babylonia.

In the various regions of Babylonia there lived thousands of foreigners, including many Jews, whom the Babylonian kings had deported from their homelands by force. These people never lost hope of returning home, and were therefore ready to assist any enemy of Nabonidus and awaited the Persians as their liberators. As for the Babylonian artisan and peasant class, who were, in terms of numbers and significance, the staple population of the country, these took no part in, and were indifferent to, Nabonidus' military preparations, and had no qualms about exchanging their old rulers for new ones. The Babylonian army was exhausted from its perennial wars in the Arabian desert and it is difficult to imagine it being in a state to hold back an enemy that was both numerically superior and better armed.

In August 539[1] the Persians completely routed the Babylonian army, commanded by Nabonidus' son Bel-shar-uzur (the Belshazzar of the book of Daniel), at the town of Opis close to the Tigris. They then outflanked the powerful line of defences erected as early as Nebuchadnezzar II's reign to shield such major towns as Sippar, Cutha, Babylon and Borsippa, and crossing the river south of Opis laid siege to Sippar. The town offered only feeble resistance and on 10 October fell to the Persians. Two days later the invaders were in Babylon. On 29 October 539 Cyrus II himself entered Babylon and was given a triumphant welcome.

Cyrus' policy towards the conquered races was considerably different from that of the Assyrian and Babylonian kings before him. The idols that had earlier been removed from Susa, the region of Gutium[2] and the towns of northern Mesopotamia were restored to their original temples. Cyrus also permitted those peoples who were living in captivity in Mesopotamia to be repatriated. His decision to let the Jews return to their homeland and rebuild their Temple was only one aspect of the general policy of government he pursued.[3]

Formally, Cyrus preserved the Babylonian kingdom as it was, and did not change its social structure or traditional methods of government in any way. Babylon became one of the royal cities. Cyrus adopted the official title of 'king of Babylon, king of the lands', which his successors retained until the time of Xerxes. No substantial changes occurred in the country's economic life. Babylonian officials kept their places in the

---

[1] See S. Smith, *Isaiah Chapters XL–XV. Literary Criticism and History* (London, 1944), pp. 42–8.
[2] See n. 1, p. 326.
[3] See G. G. Cameron, *Ancient Persia*, AOS, vol. 38 (1955), pp. 71ff.

administrative machine. The priesthood was allowed to revive its ancient cults, which Cyrus did everything to patronize. Nevertheless, from being an autonomous state Babylonia had been turned into a satrapy of the Achemenid Empire and deprived of all independence in foreign policy. In fact, internally as well, the highest administrative authority rested with the Persian vicegerent.

In 538 Cambyses, Cyrus' son, was appointed king of Babylon and the northern part of the country, whilst central and southern Babylonia remained under the rule of Cyrus and his governors. In documents of this period Cambyses is referred to as king of Babylon, and his father as king of the lands. Cambyses remained king of Babylon for only about nine months, however, as in 537, for reasons unknown, Cyrus removed him from office.[1]

After the conquest of Babylonia, Cyrus at first left the Babylonian Nabu-ahhe-bullit in charge of the country as his representative. The latter had held the post before under Nabonidus. Four years later, however, in 535, Cyrus merged Mesopotamia and Beyond the River (*eber nāri*), that is, the lands to the west of the Euphrates (Phoenicia, Syria and Palestine) into one province and appointed as governor the Persian Gubaru, who remained in the post for at least ten years, until 525, and possibly until the beginning of 520.[2] This province, comprising the territory of the former neo-Babylonian kingdom, was given the name of 'Babylon and Beyond the River'.

The reign of Cambyses (530–522 B.C.E.) saw no significant changes in the Persians' policy towards Babylonia. When in 522 the throne was seized in Iran by the Magian Gaumata, who claimed to be Cyrus' youngest son Bardiya, the Babylonians recognized him immediately. But in the same year Darius I killed Gaumata and himself became king. When this news reached Babylonia an uprising took place headed by Nebuchadnezzar III, who claimed to be the son of the last Babylonian king, Nabonidus (according to the official Persian version he was a pretender by the name of Nidintu-Bel). He was acclaimed king in Babylon, Sippar and several other towns. Darius led the campaign against the insurgents in person. On 13 December 522 the Babylonians were defeated on the banks of the Tigris and five days later Darius won a decisive victory in the Zazana region on the banks of the Euphrates. The Persians then entered Babylon and the leaders of the rebellion were

---

[1] See M. San Nicolò, 'Beiträge zu einer Prosopographie neubabylonischer Beamten der Zivil- und Tempelverwaltung', *Sitzungsberichte der Bayerischen Akademie der Wissenschaften*, Philos. hist. Abteilung (1941), 51–4; A. Lee Oppenheim, 'A New Cambyses Incident', in *A Survey of Persian Art*, vol. 15 (1974), pp. 3497–502.
[2] San Nicolò, 'Beiträge', 54–63.

executed. In August 521, while Darius was busy putting down rebellions in Persia, Media, Elam and other satrapies of his extensive empire, the Babylonians rose again. This time, according to the official version, they were led by an Armenian called Arakha, who declared himself to be Nebuchadnezzar, son of Nabonidus. On 27 November 521 this rebellion was also crushed.

A few years after the pacification of the empire, Darius began to implement his famous administrative and financial reforms. These led to the creation in Babylonia and the other imperial lands of a fundamentally new administrative system, which underwent no significant alterations for the rest of the Achemenids' reign. By March 520 Babylonia had been divided from Beyond the River and turned into an independent satrapy, at the head of which was placed the Persian Ushtani.

The next changes in Babylonia's political status took place under Xerxes, when the Babylonians made a new attempt to regain independence. In 484 B.C.E., under the leadership of Belsimanni, they rose against Persian rule. After this rebellion had been quelled, another broke out in 482, this time led by one Shamash-riba. The rebels succeeded in gaining control of Babylon, Borsippa and Dilbat at least. Xerxes dealt with them unmercifully. While the rebellion was being suppressed, Babylon suffered heavily, its chief temple, Esagila, was razed, and the image of the god Marduk deported to Persia.[1] After this, Babylonia never again tried to revolt or achieve political independence. In fact, this was now impossible: one could only become king of Babylon after performing an ancient religious ceremony and receiving power from the hands of Marduk, but the latter was no longer in Babylon. The Babylonian kingdom, which had hitherto been regarded as existing on a level of union with the Achemenid kings, was liquidated and reduced to the status of an ordinary satrapy. Babylon succeeded in recovering its importance as the economic centre of the country, however, and also remained one of the capital cities of the realm. In 331 Babylonia was overrun by the army of Alexander the Great.

The Achemenid empire was the first in the world to occupy extensive areas of the globe from the Indus valley as far as Egypt. In its system of administration it bore a certain resemblance to the neo-Assyrian kingdom, since the Persians borrowed many of the features of their system of regional government from the Assyrians, probably through the agency of Median rule. But unlike the Assyrian kings, who attempted to spread the worship of their tribal god Ashhur in the

[1] See F. M. Th. de Liagre Böhl, 'Die Babylonischen Prätendenten zur Zeit Xerxes', BO, 19 (1962), 110–14.

countries they conquered, the Achemenids were far from wanting to impose on their subjects the cult of Ahuramazda, the supreme deity in the Iranian pantheon. In Babylonia the Persian kings worshipped Marduk, Sin and so on; in Egypt, Amon, Ra and others; in Jerusalem Yahweh; in Asia Minor the Greek gods; and in the other conquered countries they paid homage to the local deities. They did this not merely from political considerations. Although the Persian kings considered their Ahuramazda the most powerful god, they also believed in the gods of the subjugated peoples, worshipped them, and sought their assistance.[1]

SOCIETY AND THE ECONOMY

The Persian period in Babylonia's history is exceptional for its wealth of written source material, mainly thousands of domestic, administrative and private legal documents. Their contents are extremely varied: they include receipts of debts, contracts of apprenticeship, contracts for the sale and rent of land, receipts for the payment of state taxes, statements from law cases, correspondence of an official and personal nature, and so forth. On the basis of these texts, the socio-economic structure of this period can be described as follows.

Society in each Babylonian city consisted of fully-fledged citizens (*mār-banī*, literally 'sons of the fair'); various free classes of the population who were, however, dependent and without civic rights (that is, semi-free); and finally slaves.

Fully-fledged citizens were members of the popular assembly (*puhru*) attached to one or other of the temples, which had jurisdiction in the settling of family and property matters. The citizens took part in the rites of the particular temple and were entitled to a certain share of its income. Fully enfranchised citizens of this type included officials of the state and temples, priests, scribes, merchants, artisans and farmers. Legally they were all considered to have equal rights and their status was hereditary. All these persons lived in the cities and owned land within the agricultural district adjoining the particular city, which was controlled by the local popular assembly.

The free persons without civic rights consisted of the king's military colonists, as well as Persian and other foreign officials in the king's service, and generally all aliens living in Babylonia for one reason or another (although sometimes such people could form their own organization of self-government, see pages 333–4). All these groups

[1] See E. J. Bickerman, 'The Edict of Cyrus in Ezra 1', *JBL*, 65 (1946), 262ff; E. J. Bickerman, *The Seleucids and the Achaemenids*, Accademia Nazionalei dei Lincei, Quaderno N. 76; Atti del convegno sul tema: La Persia e il Mondo Greco-Romano (Rome, 1966), p. 97.

were without civic rights, since they did not own lands within the communal fund of a town and therefore could not become members of a popular assembly.

The dependent sections of the population consisted of farmers who were without their own land and worked from generation to generation on land belonging to the state, the temples and private individuals. From the legal point of view, they did not count as slaves and were not allowed to be sold. These farmers lived in the agricultural district, which was not part of the structure of self-government of the town and where, apart from military colonists, there were no freemen at all.

Slaves were the property of their master and *vis-à-vis* him had no rights, only obligations. Hundreds of slaves worked on the temple estates, and wealthy citizens possessed between three and five each. Large business houses owned a few dozen and sometimes even several hundred. On the whole, however, the number of slaves was several times smaller than that of all the freemen put together. The basis of agriculture was the labour of free farmers and leaseholders, and handicrafts were also dominated by the labour of free artisans, whose profession was handed down in the family.[1]

When landowners could not use slave labour on their own estates or considered it unprofitable to do so, quite often the slaves were left to work for themselves, as long as they paid a certain quitrent from the *peculium* in their possession. This varied with the size of the slave's plot, but on average amounted to twelve silver shekels a year, which was also the average annual wage of an adult hired labourer irrespective of whether he was a freeman or slave. For comparison, it might be mentioned that a slave was worth about 60 to 90 shekels and a shekel of silver bought 150 litres of barley or figs. In Babylonia there was a comparatively large number of slaves with families, their own houses and considerable personal property. They were allowed to dispose of the latter fairly freely, for example, mortgage it, lease it, or sell it. Slaves could not only take part in the economic life of the country, but also possess their own signets and act as witnesses in all kinds of business transactions between freemen or slaves. Legally, slaves could appear in court like freemen and bring suits against other slaves or freemen; though not, of course, against their masters.[2]

[1] See I. Mendelsohn, *Slavery in the Ancient Near East* (New York 1949), pp. 111–12; M. San Nicolò, 'Der neubabylonische Lehrvertrag in rechtsvergleichender Betrachtung', *Sitzungsberichte der Bayerischen Akademie der Wissenschaften*, Philos. hist. Klasse (1950), part 3, p. 6.

[2] See M. A. Dandamayev, 'The Economic and Legal Character of the Slaves' *Peculium* in the Neo-Babylonian and Achaemenid Periods', *Bayerische Akademie der Wissenschaften*, Philos. hist. Klasse, Abhandlungen. N.F., part 75 (1972), 35–6.

Already by the beginning of the Persian period the practice of enslaving debtors had been considerably modified. A creditor could arrest an insolvent debtor and have him put in prison, but he could not sell him into slavery to a third person. Usually the debtor liquidated his debt by *antichresis* (unpaid labour for the creditor), retaining his freedom. The practice of offering oneself as surety or selling oneself into slavery had completely disappeared by the Persian period.[1]

Babylonian private law did not change at all fundamentally under the Achemenids, although many public institutions gradually underwent Iranian influence.[2] In particular, by the end of the reign of Darius I the reforms in the system of government had brought with them a number of changes in the sphere of private law as well.[3] Supreme judicial power in the land was wielded by the satrap. The most important cases, however, were decided by the king's judges, manslaughter falling particularly within their scope. Under the Achemenids the long-drawn-out tussle between the royal lawcourt and the Popular Assembly ended in the defeat of the latter, and now only property suits and individual crimes of a local nature came under their jurisdiction. In private legal documents the expression 'the king's *dāta*' (an Iranian word meaning law) occurs. It is not yet clear, however, whether this refers to a code of laws drawn up by Darius I, or is being used in the sense of 'the king's laws' in general.[4]

Although after the Persian conquest the local administrative traditions of Babylonia continued uninterrupted, gradually considerable changes took place both within the structure of government and in the titles of the various state officials. In particular, many terms appeared that were borrowings from the Ancient Persian vocabulary of administration, for example, *dātabara* (judge), *ganzabaru* (treasurer), *ḫamarakara* (bookkeeper), *iprasakku* (investigator), and so on.[5] After the reforms of Darius I the Persians occupied a special position in the state apparatus and all the most important military and civil posts were concentrated in their hands. Nevertheless, the Persian administration gladly appointed representatives of other nations to responsible positions as well. In

---

[1] See H. Petschow, 'Neubabylonisches Pfandrecht', *Abhandlungen der Sächsischen Akademie der Wissenschaften zu Leipzig*, Philol. hist. Klasse, vol. 48, part 1 (1956), 63, 66.

[2] See G. Cardascia, *Les Archives des Murašû* (Paris, 1951), pp. 5–8.

[3] See M. San Nicolò, 'Neubabylonische Urkunden aus Uruk', *Or*, 19 (1950), 218 n. 1.

[4] See H. Petschow, 'Gesetze', *RLA*, vol. 5, 3 (1971), 279.

[5] See W. Eilers, *Iranische Beamtennamen in der keilschriftlichen Überlieferung*, part 1 (Leipzig, 1940), pp. 5ff.

Babylonia and other countries, judges, governors of towns, heads of state arsenals and managers of the king's construction projects were generally Babylonians, Arameans, Jews, Egyptians, Greeks and others, with their many centuries of technical and administrative experience. One such administrator was Nehemiah, who was a personal counsellor of Artaxerxes I.

The official language of the Persian civil service in Babylonia ever since Cyrus II was Aramaic. Under Darius I it was used for communication between government departments throughout the Persian state. Official documents went out in Aramaic from the administrative capital in Susa to all the corners of the empire. Scribes, who knew two or more languages, translated these documents on arrival into the native language of the governors of the regions, who did not know Aramaic. In addition to Aramaic, the common language of the whole empire, in various countries the scribes also drew up official documents in the local languages, and in this way correspondence was conducted in two languages. More particularly, in Babylonia private legal documents were written in cuneiform Akkadian. In the capital of Persia itself, Persepolis, for administrative purposes the Elamic language was also widely used alongside Aramaic, until it was finally ousted by the latter in the second half of the fifth century B.C.E. As for Ancient Persian, this was not used as an administrative language at all.

The Achemenids confiscated part of the land of the Babylonian nobility and divided it into large estates which passed into the full hereditary ownership of the royal family, members of the Persian nobility, high-ranking officials and so on. The Persian nobility gradually began to settle in Babylon, becoming great land and slave owners. Like their Babylonian counterparts, they generally leased their land out.

A considerable proportion of the land also belonged to temples and large business houses. Small landowners (including artisans) usually had plots ranging from a third of a hectare to several hectares in area. Such landowners worked their strips themselves with members of their families and sometimes with the help of slaves and hired labourers, who were generally taken on for the duration of the harvest. Hired labourers were widely used on large estates – especially ones belonging to temples – where they would work either the whole year round or just at harvest time.

Finally, under the Achemenids a system of land tenure was practised in Babylonia whereby the king settled his troops on a patch of ground and these cultivated the allotments apportioned to them collectively, in brigades, as their military service, and paid a cerain tax in money and kind. Allotments of this kind were termed holdings of the bow, the horse, the chariot and so forth, and their owners were liable to service as archers, cavalrymen and charioteers.[1]

This system of farming was called *ḥatru* (the exact meaning and origin of the word are not clear). In addition to military colonists, it was carried on by various groups of artisans, for example, carpenters, tanners, ferrymen and shepherds, as well as merchants, scribes and so on, who of course worked side by side with shepherds, merchants and scribes who were independent of the imperial administration. It also included various ethnic groups (Scythians, emigrants from Tyre in Phoenicia and the region of Haraiva in present-day Afghanistan, etc.), as well as workers on the king's estates and estates belonging to members of the royal family. The latter workmen were called *gardu*. The *ḥatru* were headed by officials called *šaknu*, who governed the land that went with it, collected the king's taxes, and paid them into the treasury. In Nippur and its districts this was done through the Murashu trading house.

The *ḥatru* system arose in the Persian period and is known to us mainly from the documents of the second half of the fifth century B.C.E. from the Murashu archive in Nippur. Judging from some texts, though, it was typical of Babylonia as a whole and began to form as early as the reign of Cambyses, that is, in the third decade of the sixth century.[2] As for the royal estates, on the whole these were not of major significance. The biggest farms were either privately owned or belonged to temples.

In the Persian period important changes took place in the policy of the imperial administration towards the temples. Whereas the neo-Babylonian kings and members of their families had paid the temples an annual tithe in gold, silver and livestock and so on, the Achemenids kept the tithe as an obligatory tax on their subjects, but did not pay it themselves. In the majority of cases the inhabitants of Babylonia paid the temple's tithe in barley and figs, but sometimes also in silver, sesame, wool, livestock and poultry. The tithe roughly corresponded to a tenth of the taxpayer's income.

Further, the neo-Babylonian kings had rarely interfered in temple affairs and the temples' contribution to the state's income was negligible; the temples, indeed, received gifts of land, slaves, and other commodities from the kings. Under the Achemenids, however, the temples were obliged to pay the state considerable taxes in kind, in oxen and sheep, barley, figs, wool and so forth, as well as to provide state officials with

---

[1] See G. Cardascia, 'Le fief dans la Babylonie Achéménide', *Recueils de la Société Jean Bodin*, vol. 1: *Les Liens de Vassalité* (Brussels, 1958), pp. 55–88.

[2] See G. Cardascia, 'Ḥaṭru', *RLA*, 4 (Berlin, 1973), 150–1.

foodstuffs and to supply provender for the king's cattle. In addition, the temples paid dues by sending their slaves (farmers, shepherds, gardeners, carpenters etc.) to work on the royal estates in Babylon and other cities.

To ensure that the obligations of the temples to the state were carried out, fiscal agents and royal representatives with full powers were introduced into their organization. These supervised the prompt and accurate payment of taxes and performance of duties. The king's officials were also entrusted with keeping a check on the temple's goods and property, of which they made regular inspections. Finally, they organized the work of the temple slaves when this formed part of the temples' obligations to the state.[1]

No sudden changes came about in the economic life of Babylonia after the Persian invasion. At first the prices of the various goods and products remained the same. By the end of the Achemenid period they had risen approximately one and a half times.[2] A gradual increase of this kind is typical of Babylonia throughout its history. Contrary to common belief, in itself it does not imply that the economy or standard of living were in decline, since it was chiefly the result of an increase in the circulation of silver, which served as currency.

As before, under the Achemenids payment in internal trade was made not in minted coin, but in silver ingots, rods, wire and so on. These ingots contained various alloys. The kinds most frequently mentioned are 'white' and 'refined' silver, and silver with one-eighth alloy. Ingots bore carat marks and were weighed every time they changed hands.[3] Gold was an article of trade and not employed as money. The relative value of gold to silver was roughly 1 : 13 1/13.

Thus, although minting had been invented as early as the second half of the seventh century in Lydia, and Darius I had introduced a single monetary gold unit for the whole empire, called the daric and weighing 8.4 grams, coins were not in use in Babylonia or the other countries of the empire, with the exception of Asia Minor and the Phoenician–Palestinian world. When they found their way into circulation in Babylonia they were treated as unminted money and valued by weight.

Babylonia was one of the richest satrapies of the Persian empire. From the period of Darius I's administrative and financial reforms onwards

[1] See M. A. Dandamayev, 'Politische und wirtschaftliche Geschichte', *Historia*, Einzelschriften, part 18: *Beiträge zur Achämenidengeschichte* (Wiesbaden, 1972), 52–4.

[2] See W. H. Dubberstein, 'Comparative Prices in Later Babylonia', *AJSL*, 56 (1939), 20–43.

[3] See W. Eilers, 'Akkadische *kaspum* "Silber, Geld" und Sinnverwandtes', *WO*, 2 (1957), 329.

it paid annual taxes of 1,000 talents (about 30 tons) of silver, the combined total of money levies from all the conquered peoples being 7,740 talents. On top of this, the Babylonians were obliged to provide 500 eunuchs a year for the king's court. Judging from documents in the Murashu archive, with the possible exception of the urban population the inhabitants of Babylonia paid levies in kind (grain, livestock, beer etc.) as well as monetary taxes, but it is difficult to establish the overall amount of these for the country as a whole. These taxes in kind were designed for the maintenance of the troop garrisons and the satrap's court. Since the alluvial soil of Babylonia contained no silver deposits, its inhabitants were eventually forced to acquire silver from other countries by selling the products of their land and handicrafts.

The money remitted as taxes to the state was stored away for many decades in the royal treasure houses and thus went out of circulation. Only a small fraction of it returned to Babylonia and the other satrapies in the form of wages to hired workers and to finance the administration. For trade, therefore, there was a shortage of silver, which often meant resorting to barter.

During the Achemenid period regular trading relations were established between Babylonia and its neighbouring countries. Babylonia began to act as a trading link between the Phoenician–Palestinian world and the countries to the south and east of Mesopotamia. Trade with Egypt, Syria, Elam and Asia Minor, where Babylonian merchants bought iron, copper, tin, building timber, wine and other goods, became particularly active.[1] From Egypt the Babylonians imported alum, which was used for bleaching wool and fabrics, as well as in medicine and the manufacture of glass.[2] Together with Egypt, Babylonia supplied grain to the lands of the Achemenid empire. At any rate, Babylonian merchants exported barley to Elam.[3] In addition, the Babylonian cities were major producers of woollen clothes, which were much in demand in other countries, notably Elam.[4] There was also a notable increase in internal trade between the various regions of Babylonia. For the most part this was carried out along the rivers and canals.

Of great importance in foreign and home trade, and to the economy as a whole, were the powerful business houses, which controlled considerable tracts of land. The oldest of these was the house of Egibi. It had been in existence before the Persian invasion and continued to

[1] See A. L. Oppenheim, 'Essay on Overland Trade in the First Millenium B.C.', *JCS*, 21 (1969), 236–54.
[2] See D. J. Wiseman, 'Some Egyptians in Babylonia', *Iraq*, 28 (1966), 155.
[3] See M. A. Dandamayev, 'Connections between Elam and Babylonia in the Achaemenid Period', in *The Memorial Volume of the Vth International Congress of Iranian Art and Archaeology*, vol. 1 (Teheran, 1972), p. 259.
[4] See Dandamayev, 'Connections', p. 259.

operate throughout the reigns of Cyrus, Cambyses and Darius I, buying
and selling land, slaves and so forth. At the same time, the house of
Egibi managed professional banking operations, acting as a creditor,
banking deposits, issuing and receiving bills of exchange, meeting its
clients' debts, and founding and financing commercial companies.[1]

As regards the house of Murashu, which was engaged in trading and
money-lending in central and southern Babylonia in the fifth century
B.C.E., the nature of its activity was determined by the changes which
the Persians introduced into the system of land tenure in Babylonia. The
house of Murashu rented plots of land belonging to Persian dignitaries,
administrators and bodies of soldiers, and paid their owners' taxes into
the exchequer in money and in kind. Usually, it sublet such land,
supplying leaseholders with draught animals, seed, farm implements,
and water for irrigation. In other words, the house of Murashu was,
generally speaking, an institution of agricultural credit, which managed
the distribution of land plots, and acted as mediator between landowners
and agricultural workers. Unlike the house of Egibi, Murashu played
no part in international trade. It did, however, sell the produce of the
land it leased, such as figs and barley, inside the country.[2]

As the thousands of cuneiform religious, astronomical, mathematical
and literary texts show, the ancient Babylonian culture continued to
flourish and develop throughout the Persian era. The Babylonians took
a lively interest in their history, and in the temple schools they studied
and made copies of their ancient works of literature, the Laws of
Hammurapi, and the like. Although Aramaic became the language of
conversation all over Babylonia, Akkadian continued to be the language
of science, religious liturgy and to a considerable extent of legal
documents.

Judging from numerous texts, the Babylonians remained true to their
ancient religion and no noticeable changes occurred in their beliefs.[3]
As for literary works, at the moment it is difficult to determine which
of them were written in Persian times.

During the Persian period the Babylonians made particularly important advances in mathematical astronomy. On the basis of systematic
observations of lunar eclipses and summer solstices, a calendarial cycle
was worked out by which seven extra fixed months were added over
every nineteen years. At first the choice of when to include these months
varied randomly, but from 367 (or about 380) B.C.E. onwards they were

---

[1] See A. Ungnad, 'Das Haus Egibi', *AfO*, 14 (1941), 57–64; R. Bogaert, *Les Origines
    antiques de la banque de dépôt* (Leiden, 1966), pp. 105ff, 122ff.
[2] See Cardascia, *Archives*, pp. 195ff.
[3] On religion, see H. W. F. Saggs, *The Greatness that was Babylon* (New York and
    Toronto, 1968), pp. 288ff.

added in a strict sequence of years. As a result, the variations in the date of the beginning of the new year (the first day of the month of Nisannu), which fell in early spring, were reduced to 27 days. The Achemenids adopted the Babylonian lunisolar calendar as the official one for the whole of of the Persian empire.

From the accounts of ancient authors, we are familiar with the name of the Babylonian astronomer Nabunanus, who is credited with discovering a method of calculating the phases of the moon, although we cannot be entirely sure of this. Another Babylonian astronomer mentioned by ancient authors, Kidenas, is apparently identical with Kidinnu, the writer of many astronomical treatises that have come down to us.[1]

ETHNIC MINORITIES

As early as the reign of the Chaldean kings, Babylonia had been overrun by Aramaic tribes, who lived side by side with the original local population. Many thousands of Jews had also been deported to Babylon, along with Cilicians, Elamites and members of other nations. Thus, by the middle of the sixth century B.C.E., ethnically the population of Babylonia was already fairly mixed.

The period of Achemenid rule is notable for a sharp increase in intermarriage between the races, and syncretization of their cultures and religious beliefs. The main reason for this was that contact between the various lands had become more regular. In particular, after the Persian invasion of Babylonia this fertile country became open to immigrants. Moreover, the Achemenids formed military colonies in Babylonia from members of various races, or not infrequently appointed persons of foreign origin to posts in the administration. Hence Persians, Elamites, Lydians, Phrygians, Egyptians, Medes and others began to settle in the country. For example, about a third of all proper names in the documents of the Murashu archive from Nippur are not of Babylonian origin. They include dozens of Iranian names whose bearers were Persians, Medes, Sakas, Areioi and representatives of other Iranian races. In Nippur and its neighbouring districts in the fifth century B.C.E. there were military colonies composed of Phrygians, Lydians, Carians, Armenians, Syrians, Arabians and others.[2]

In a number of cases these aliens were accommodated in quite large

---

[1] For information on Babylonian astronomy, see O. Neugebauer, *The Exact Sciences in Antiquity* (Providence, 1967), chs. 2 and 5. On the calendar see E. J. Bickerman, *Chronology of the Ancient World* (2nd edn. London, 1979), pp. 18ff.

[2] See E. Unger, *Babylon. Die heilige Stadt nach der Beschreibung der Babylonier* (Berlin, 1970), p. 40.

communities in special quarters of the cities and even had their own popular assembly. In Nippur and its neighbouring districts, for instance, each ethnic group was guaranteed a particular territory on which to live. In Babylon itself there was a special Egyptian quarter. A document of the time of Cambyses mentions an 'assembly of the elders of the Egyptians' which passed judgement in a case involving the land allotted to Egyptians.[1] Texts also mention *bīt āl miṣirāja*, 'the Egyptians' settlement', *nāru ša amēl miṣirāja*, 'the canal of the Egyptians', and so on. One quarter in Babylon in the Achemenid period bore the name Shushan, from the capital of Elam, Susa.[2] Evidently this was inhabited mainly by Elamites.

Egyptians are quite often mentioned in documents from Ur, Uruk, Babylon, Nippur, Sippar, Borsippa and other towns, from which one may conclude that they were dispersed all over Babylonia. Frequently the Egyptian nationality (*miṣirāja*) is referred to. In other cases, the Egyptian origin is revealed by their proper names, which are often theophorous and contain the names of the gods Amon, Isis, Hapi or Horus (for example, Patan-Esi, and Hapishballa, son of Pishamish). It is interesting to note that the Babylonian scribes knew that these names, as well as Iranian ones containing the elements Baga, Mitra, and so on, were theophoric, since they often prefaced them with the determinative sign for a god. In some cases, elements of Egyptian and Babylonian names were used to form double-barrelled names such as Amat-Esi, Rahim-Esi and so forth, where the first half is Babylonian, the second Egyptian.

In the majority of cases, however, as a result of mixed marriage and in an attempt to assimilate themselves into the population, the Egyptians in Babylonia gradually began to give their children Babylonian names. In such cases their descendants retained the sign of nationality (*miṣirāja*) as their generic name. Quite frequently it was used as a proper name too.

A certain number of Egyptians became administrators, such as tax collectors, overseers of the king's workmen and the like. Sometimes scribes were of Egyptian origin. On the other hand, a proportion of the Egyptian prisoners of war in Babylonia was enslaved. A soldier who had taken part in Cambyses' campaign of 525 B.C.E. against Egypt, for instance, sold 'an Egyptian girl, the spoils of his bow' in Babylon in 524, together with her three-month-old daughter.[3] Documents also

---

[1] See J. N. Strassmaier, *Inschriften von Cambyses, König von Babylon* (Leipzig, 1890), no. 85.
[2] See Unger, *Babylon*, pp. 81–2.
[3] See Strassmaier, *Cambyses*, no. 334.

mention other slaves belonging to the temples or privately owned, who
had been brought out of Egypt.[1]

According to a text from the time of Darius I, in 505 B.C.E. a native
of Asia Minor, one Megibarshu, made a loan of 50 shekels of silver to
a representative of the business house of Egibi in Babylon. The
witnesses to this transaction were several other natives of Asia Minor
living in Babylon, namely Utiya, Umarzana and others of the tribe of
the Shibucians and Charzibayans, and the 'Cimmerian' Sakita.[2] Another
contract of the time of Darius I mentions one Samannapir, an Elamite,
judging by his name, who gave his daughter in marriage to an
Egyptian.[3]

A series of economic documents from the end of the sixth century
B.C.E. records the distribution of a large quantity of figs, sesame and
silver from the temple storehouses in Sippar to 'workmen from Elam',
who came to Babylonia to do seasonal work on the farms in return for
board and wages, returning home after the harvest. One letter mentions
that 'all the workmen from Susa (that is, the capital of Elam) had arrived
in Babylon'.[4] Judging from another document, 'the Elamite
Ummanshibir' (the name itself is also Elamite) was a workman in one
of the Babylonian temples.[5] In a document from the time of Cambyses
reference is made to 'the Elamite Niriabignu',[6] although the name itself
is Iranian.

Iranians appear so frequently in documents from Babylonia that
merely to list their names would take up many pages. For example, in
523 the Iranians Razararma, son of Razamumarga, and Aspumitanu, son
of Asputatik, sold two slave girls in Babylon with Iranian names. Then,
when some sort of dispute arose out of this transaction, the Iranian
Artarush, 'a chief of merchants', maintained that both of them had
already received payment from the contractor.[7] In 429 an Iranian named
Bagamiri, son of Mitridata, leased his field and one he had inherited from
his father's brother Rushundata to the house of Murashu for 60 years.

[1] See Wiseman, *Iraq*, 28 (1966), 154–8; M. A. Dandamayev, 'Egyptians in Babylonia
  in the Sixth and Fifth Centuries B.C.', *Drevnii Egipet i drevnaya Africa* (Moscow, 1967),
  pp. 15–26 (in Russian).
[2] See J. N. Strassmaier, *Inschriften von Darius, König von Babylon* (Leipzig, 1897), no. 458.
[3] Strassmaier, *Darius*, no. 301.
[4] Strassmaier, *Darius*, nos. 516, 530; *Cuneiform Texts from Babylonian Tablets in the British
  Museum*, vol. 22 (London, 1906), no. 59.
[5] See F. M. T. Böhl, *Assyrische en Nieuw-Babylonische oorkonden* (Amsterdam, 1936), p.
  49, no. 878.
[6] See p. 339, n. 1.
[7] See Strassmaier, *Cambyses*, no. 384.

Both fields were situated near Nippur on the banks of two canals next to the field of another Iranian, called Rushunpati.[1]

According to documents from the Murashu collection, several Jews owned land in the neighbourhood of Nippur, and some worked as agents for Persians and Babylonians or were servants of the Crown. A certain Hannani, for instance, son of Minahhim, held the post of *ša ana muhhi issur-hia ša šarri*, 'one who is over the birds of the King', that is Darius II.[2] Many Jews also feature in documents as parties to contracts, and witnesses.[3]

It was during the Achemenid period, as well, that the Greeks borrowed several major cultural achievements from Babylonia. The historian Herodotus, who visited Babylon around 450 B.C.E. and left a detailed description of it, wrote in his great work (II.9) that the Babylonians were the Greeks' teachers in astronomy.[4]

Even the Persians themselves, the ruling nation, fell under the influence of Babylonian traditions. For example, the son of the Persian Gubaru, who was satrap of Babylon under Cyrus and Cambyses, was called by the Babylonian name of Nabu-gu. The Persians Bagana, Artabarri, Ushtabuzana and others, living in Nippur in the fifth century B.C.E., gave their children the purely Babylonian names Nidintu-Bel, Bel-ibni and Belittannu. By the second half of the fifth century, the military colonists from the remote Iranian province of Haraiva (in modern Afghanistan) and Scythian settlers living around Nippur as a rule bore purely Babylonian names. On the other hand, Babylonians also gave their children Iranian, Aramaic and other foreign names.[5] For instance, Ninurta-etir gave his son the Iranian name Tiridata. Such a mixture of names was often the result of intermarriage. Thus, for

---

[1] See H. V. Hilprecht, 'Business Documents of Murashû Sons of Nippur', in *The Babylonian Expedition of the University of Pennsylvania*, vol. 9 (Philadelphia, 1898), no. 48.

[2] See A. T. Clay, 'Business Documents of Murashû Sons of Nippur', in *The Babylonian Expedition of the University of Pennsylvania*, series A: *Cuneiform Texts*, vol. x (Philadelphia, 1904), no. 128.

[3] See S. Daiches, *The Jews in Babylonia in the Time of Ezra and Nehemiah according to Babylonian Inscriptions*, Jews College Publications, no. 2 (London, 1910); E. Ebeling, 'Aus dem Leben der jüdischen Exulanten in Babylonien. Babylonische Quellen', *Wissenschaftliche Beilage zum Jahresbericht des Humboldt-Gymnasiums* (Berlin, 1914); L. Gry, 'Israélites en Assyrie, Juifs en Babylonie', *Le Muséon*, 35 (1922), 153–85; 36 (1923), 1–26.

[4] See W. Röllig, 'Griechen', *RLA*, vol. 3, part 9 (1971), 644–7.

[5] See H. V. Hilprecht and A. T. Clay, 'Business Documents of Murashû Sons of Nippur', *The Babylonian Expedition of the University of Pennsylvania*, series A: *Cuneiform Texts*, vol. IX (Philadelphia, 1898), 28–9.

example, the Persian Mitradata married the Babylonian girl Ekur-belet, daughter of Bel-belatu ittannu, and they gave their son the Iranian name Bagamiri. Since all the names just quoted – both Babylonian and Iranian – are theophoric ('by the grace of the god Ninurta', 'given by the god Mitra', etc.), it is safe to assume that their owners worshipped both their traditional gods and foreign ones.

For various reasons, then, quite a large number of foreigners found their way into Babylonia in the Achemenid period. Some of those settlers lived more or less closely together in special areas. The majority, however, were scattered throughout the country, lived side by side with the native population, were completely integrated into the socio-economic life of the country, owned their own houses and land, and some served in their country's administration. Foreigners were gradually assimilated into the local population, took Babylonian names, spoke in Aramaic, which had become the customary language of conversation in Mesopotamia, and in their turn exerted a certain cultural influence on the Babylonians.

Gradually, the synthesis of scientific knowledge, artistic techniques and religious beliefs of the various peoples brought about what was essentially a new material and spiritual culture.[1] Later, this contributed to the triumph of Hellenism, which was the product of a synthesis of Greek culture with that of the peoples of the East.[2]

This benevolent and tolerant treatment of the customs, traditions and culture of neighbouring and remote nations was the logical outcome of the existence of the Achemenid empire, in which the language of the civil service was Aramaic and the leading political role was played by Persians, whilst the ancient culture of the Babylonians, Elamites, Jews, Egyptians and other peoples continued to exist and develop further.

B. THE BABYLONIAN CAPTIVITY

Little is known of the eastern Diaspora. Sons of Abraham returned to Mesopotamia and came to Iran mostly as deportees. First, they came from the northern kingdom, carried away by Tiglath-pileser in 734–733 B.C.E., by Shalmaneser in 724, and by Sargon in 721. The latter settled the exiles of Samaria in northern Mesopotamia, at Halah, a place or district not identified as yet, and on the upper Habor river, the modern Khabur, an eastern tributary of the upper Euphrates, in the district of

[1] See Hilprecht and Clay, 'Business Documents', 28.
[2] Cf. Bickerman, *Seleucids and Achaemenids*, p. 103.

Gozan, that is east of Haran (Carrhae). They were also sent to cities of Media (2 Kings 17: 6).

An Aramaic sherd containing a list of persons, many of whom bear biblical names, a reference to a 'Samaritan' in an official Assyrian letter written from Gozan, and a number of Israelite personal names found in Assyrian documents are the only extant records of the northern *gôlâh*.[1] This scarcity of documentation is merely the result of the law of chance that governs archeological discoveries. We know in fact that the men of Jerusalem expected the redemption of Samaria. 'He who scattered Israel will gather him', and Israel shall again plant vineyards on the mountains of Samaria (Jer. 31: 5). Even after the restoration of Jerusalem, a prophet continued to speak of two 'prisoners of hope', Judah and Ephraim (Zech. 9: 12–13). Yet, there is no trace of contact between the exiles of Samaria and the exiles of Jerusalem. The former did not migrate to the Holy City after the rebuilding of the Temple to worship their common Deity, the God of the patriarchs and of Moses.

We can guess the reason for this estrangement: when the Jerusalemites, in the name of God, promised the redemption of the deportees from Samaria, they imposed a condition: conversion to the cult of Jerusalem. Israel must acknowledge the guilt of her defection from the house of David and from the Temple on Zion (Jer. 31; 2 Kings 17: 22). Moreover, the new nation will be ruled by a king of David's house and will worship at Zion (Ezek. 37; Jer. 33: 14). It is understandable that the exiles of Samaria were not delighted by such promises. As did the Samaritans, they refused to recognize the pre-eminence of Jerusalem. On the other hand, how could Jeremiah and Ezekiel visualize a redemption that would again separate Israel from Judah and thus lead them to new fratricidal wars?

What happened to the ten tribes in Assyria and Media? Did they build temples and high places to the Lord on foreign soil? Did they continue a syncretistic kind of worship? Were they through intermarriage absorbed into the native population? We do not know. The only book preserved by the Jews that refers to the life of the exiles from Israel is the book of Tobit, which represents the hero, a Galilean, as a faithful worshipper at the Temple of Jerusalem.

Thus, in our historical tradition, and because of the accident of archeological discovery, in our documentary evidence the Diaspora is reduced to the exiles of Judah and Benjamin.

[1] W. F. Albright, 'Aramaic Ostracon from Calah', *BASOR*, 149 (1958), 33–6; A. Malamat, *EncJud* (New York, 1971), 6, pp. 1034–5. Nabonidus may have settled some Jews as military colonists in Arabian oases. C. J. Gadd, 'The Harran Inscriptions', *Anatolian Studies*, 8 (1958), 87.

The first deportation from the southern kingdom was that ordered by Sennacherib, in 701 B.C.E.; one of his palace reliefs in Nineveh depicts the transportation of captives from Lachish. This was followed by the Babylonian captivity, the deportations of 597, 587 and 582 B.C.E. (Jer. 52: 29). The Hebrew and Aramaic records of the Babylonian captivity, written on leather or on other perishable material, have disappeared without a trace. Some ten thousand cuneiform clay tablets from Babylonian and Persian Mesopotamia have come down to us, but with some exceptions, such as Daniel and his companions (Dan. 1: 4), the Jews in Babylonia did not learn cuneiform script. We might hope to find some references to the exiled Jews in administrative records, business letters, and other documents written on clay tablets, but the difficulty is that cuneiform scribes only rarely and haphazardly indicate the nationality of the persons they mention. We do not know, for instance, why a certain Tilapa, son of Minna, who owned a plantation of date-palms in a village near Nippur, was styled Lycian in a receipt.

Therefore, to identify Jews or Persians or Egyptians in the cuneiform records, we must rely primarily on proper names. This tool, however, is often unreliable, as we shall presently see. Nevertheless, the discovery of over six hundred and fifty cuneiform tablets from the archives of the business houses of Murashu, written between 455 and 403 B.C.E., in a room at Nippur, has shed some light on life of the Babylonian Diaspora in the second half of the fifth century B.C.E., inasmuch as Jewish names occur in approximately eight per cent of all published Murashu documents.[1]

Nippur was a very old, originally Sumerian city, situated on 'the river Chebar' (Ezek. 1: 1), that is, on the 'grand canal' of the Euphrates. Faithful to the Assyrians, the city for several years resisted Nabopolossar of Babylon, and the king, in all probability, confiscated a great part of her territory.[2] Therefore Nebuchadnezzar, his son, could settle the Jewish exiles deported in 597 on the new crown land. Among them was the prophet Ezekiel, who with his companions lived at Tel Abib (Ezek. 3: 15), near Nippur, and had his vision of God on the 'grand canal' east of Nippur. It is probable that the captives of Nebuchadnezzar's later deportations were also settled near Nippur. Afterwards, the Achemenids distributed some tracts of the royal land around Nippur to members of the royal house and Persian grandees, such as Arsames, the satrap

[1] G. Cardascia, Les Archives des Murašû (Paris, 1951), p. 2, n. 2.
[2] A. L. Oppenheim, 'Siege Documents from Nippur', Iraq, 17 (1955), 69–89; W. Eilers, Iranische Beamtennamen in der keilschriftlichen Ueberlieferung, Abhandlungen Deutscher Morgenländischen Gesellschaft, 25 (1940), 12.

of Egypt in the latter part of the fifth century, who is often mentioned in the Elephantine papyri, and whose mail-pouch with his letters in Aramaic to his bailiffs in Egypt has been found there.[1]

The house of Murashu in Nippur loaned money, held mortgages, leased and subleased land, collected taxes and rents, and was engaged in other operations related to the management of land property, the mainstay of the Babylonian economy; the Murashu records only exceptionally deal with real estate in the city, and we learn nothing from them about the Jews in the city of Nippur itself.

As to the territory of Nippur, the allodial land, held in absolute ownership, with two exceptions, does not appear in the Murashu records. The house of Murashu obviously concentrated its attention on the more profitable dealings with tenants of the crown land. The latter was held by its occupants at the pleasure of the sovereign on consideration of services and payment of taxes and dues, and could be subleased or mortgaged, but not alienated. The big estates probably returned to the crown after the death of the grantee, as was the rule for the *dorea* (grant) of royal land in Ptolemaic Egypt. The fiefs were in reality hereditary, but a great part of the land in fief was attributed to corporations (*ḫatru*), the members of which exploited their lots individually with the usual rights of possessors. The self-governing *ḫatru* (presided over by a prefect who in all probability was appointed by the government) was, however, responsible for the discharge of the obligations of its members to the king. It is obvious that this system facilitated the task of the royal administration.[2]

Some corporations were ethnic and, probably, military formations, as for instance a colony of Cimmerians. There were also similar professional bodies of the same type; for instance, that of carpenters, which in all probability was attached to the service of the royal court. Again, certain social groups were settled on land and in return for that had to serve as a labour force at the call of the government.[3] Men belonging to the category *shushanu* constituted several bodies of this kind, for instance a *ḫatru* of the *shushanu* of the royal treasury. They were free men, but like the later Roman *coloni*, could be imprisoned, for their compliance with the demands of the government was secured by the

[1] G. R. Driver, *Aramaic Documents of the Fifth Century B.C.* (London, 1957), pp. 88–96; I. M. Diakonov, 'Estates of Persian Grandees', *VDI*, no. 4, (1959), 70–92 (in Russian); M. A. Dandamayev, 'The Domain Lands of Achaemenes in Babylonia', *Schriften zur Geschichte und Kultur des Alten Orients*, 11 (1974), 123–7 (Berlin, 1974).

[2] G. Cardascia, *RLA*, 4 (1973), 150, s.v. *ḫatru*.

[3] M. A. Dandamayev, *Slavery in Babylonia in the 7th to 4th centuries* (Moscow, 1974), pp. 365–75 (in Russian).

device of collective responsibility: a fief was ceded to a man and his co-feudatories, who mostly were his relatives.[1]

Jews are attested in twenty-eight settlements (out of about 200) distributed over the whole region of Nippur.[2] To our knowledge, there was no Jewish *ḥatru*. Individual Jews belonged to various groups mentioned above. Some Jews held military fiefs. Their owners were obliged to go to war when ordered, or to furnish substitutes. Thus in 422 B.C.E. a certain Gadalyaw Gedaliah, himself the son of a feudatory, volunteered to serve as a mounted and cuirassed archer in place of a son of Murashu.[3] This Gedaliah was the earliest, individually known predecessor of medieval mailclad and mounted knights. Other Jews received their land tenures as members of less distinguished groups, as for instance, of the above mentioned *shushanu* or of the *gardu*.[4] There were Jewish shepherds who, like the Patriarch Jacob of old, leased stock and prospered, or fewer who made their living as irrigation experts. In 434 B.C.E., one Jedaiah mortgaged his land to the house of the Murashu and rented it from his creditor at a yearly rental of some 30,000 litres of barley. Three years later, he with his sons and some other partners could enlarge their holding considerably at three times the rent. A certain Peliah became associated with the then principal of the house of Murashu in leasing some land from the temple of Bel.[5]

Some Jews became agents of the Persian government or of Persian grandees who possessed domains around Nippur.[6] Out of fourteen canal

[1] G. Cardascia, 'Le fief dans la Babylonie Achéménide', *Recueils de la Société Jean Bodin* I (Librairie Internationale, Brussels; 2nd edn. 1958), pp. 55–88; M. A. Dandamayev, 'Die Lehnsbeziehungen in Babylonia unter den ersten Achaemeniden', in *Festschrift W. Eilers* (Wiesbaden, 1967), pp. 37–42.

[2] R. Zadok, 'Nippur in the Achaemenid Period: Geographical and Ethnical Aspects' (dissertation, Hebrew University, 1974), pp. xiii, xxi, xxxiii.

[3] Cardascia, *Archives*, pp. 179–82, and *Recueils*; G. Widengren, 'Recherches sur le féodalisme iranien', *Orientalia Suecana*, 5 (1956), 150–3.

[4] See for example, H. V. Hilprecht and A. T. Clay, *The Babylonian Expedition of the University of Pennsylvania* (Philadelphia, 1904), 10, p. 92 = D. Sidersky, 'L'onomastique hebraique des tablettes de Nippur', *REJ*, 87 (1929), 177–200, no. 18; Dandamayev, *Slavery*, pp. 330–40.

[5] A. T. Clay, *The University of Pennsylvania, The Museum* (publication of the Babylonian Section, Philadelphia, 1912), 2, p. 148 = J. Augapfel, *Babylonische Rechtsurkunden* (Denkschriften of the Wien Academy), 59, 3 (1917), p. 85; Hilprecht and Clay, *Expedition*, 9, p. 3 = Cardascia, *Archives*, p. 170; Hilprecht and Clay, *Expedition*, 9, p. 25 and 9, p. 45 = Augapfel, *Rechtsurkunden*, p. 77; J. Kohler and A. Ungnad, *Hundert ausgewaehlte Urkunden aus der Spaetezeit des babylonischen Schriftums* (Leipzig, 1911), p. 36; Sidersky, *REJ*, 87 (1929), 188; Hilprecht and Clay, *Expedition*, 9, p. 14 = Kohler and Ungnad, *Urkunden*, p. 51, Sidersky, *REJ*, 87 (1929), 188.

[6] See, for example, Hilprecht and Clay, *Expedition*, 10, p. 127 = Cardascia, *Archives*, p. 89.

managers known by name, these key workers of the irrigation economy were Jews. One Hanani managed the royal poultry farm. Eliada, a son of the above-mentioned Jedaiah, together with a Persian colleague, were agents of Artabara, the steward of royal domains in the region of Nippur in 419 B.C.E. Sherebiah, the son of Peliah, was the head of the organization (*ḥatru*) or '*shushane* of the royal treasure' in 421 B.C.E.[1] Certainly among the known officials only six per cent were Jews, but this percentage more or less corresponds to their number in the population around Nippur.[2] At the other end of the social scale we find a small number of Jewish slaves. In Persian Babylonia a slave remained a person with recognized rights and duties. For instance, two slaves, one of them a Jew, were ordered by the head of the house of Murashu to repair the dam of the irrigation canal passing through their lots; otherwise they were to be responsible for damages. This order became formulated as a contract between the master and his two slaves.[3] Our documentation deals with Murashu's business in the countryside around Nippur, and the references to transactions outside this region or to the business activity of other firms and persons are incidental.[4] By chance we learn of a mortgagee named Jedaiah. He had lent one mine of silver to a fief-holder, received this amount from the house of Murashu, and assigned the pledged field to this new creditor. A man named Zechariah guaranteed the repayment of the debt of one Belittannu, the son of Ardi-gula, to a creditor who also had a Babylonian theophoric name.[5] Integrated into the agricultural economy of Persian Babylonia, often working with native Babylonians side by side (for instance, a fisherman called Zebadiah and four non-Jewish men leased five nets for catching fish for twenty days), the sons of exiles followed the advice of Jeremiah

[1] Hilprecht and Clay, *Expedition*, 9, p. 14; 9, p. 15 = Augapfel, *Rechtsurkunden*, p. 34, Sidersky, *REJ*, 87 (1929), 188; Clay, *University*, p. 205 = Augapfel, *Rechtsurkunden*, p. 41. Cf. M. W. Stolper, 'Management and Politics in Later Achaemenid Babylon' (dissertation, University of Michigan, 1974), pp. 63 and 71–5; Hanani: Hilprecht and Clay, *Expedition*, 9, p. 28 = Kohler and Ungnad, *Urkunden*, p. 29; Eliada: Clay, *University*, p. 84 = Cardascia, *Archives*, p. 93; Sherebiah: Hilprecht and Clay, *Expedition*, 10, p. 65 = Sidersky, *REJ*, 87 (1929), 192. On his position, cf. Stolper, *Management*, pp. 132–6.

[2] R. Zadok, *The Jews in Babylonia in the Chaldean and Achaemenian Periods in the Light of the Babylonian Sources* (Tel Aviv, 1976), p. 20.

[3] Hilprecht and Clay, *Expedition*, 9, p. 55 = Augapfel, *Rechtsurkunden*, p. 96. Cf. Dandamayev, *Slavery*, p. 228.

[4] Hilprecht and Clay, *Expedition*, 10, p. 94 (cf. ibid. p. 33) = Kohler and Ungnad, *Urkunden*, p. 68 = Sidersky, *REJ*, 87 (1929), 14. Cf. Cardascia, *Archives*, p. 185; THMC, 123. M. Dandamayev kindly translated this document for me. It is not certain that the tablet comes from Nippur.

[5] Hilprecht and Clay, *Expedition*, 9, p. 45 = Kohler and Ungnad, *Urkunden*, p. 53.

(29: 5–7), and built houses, planted gardens and sought the welfare (*šālôm*) of the land whither their ancestors had been carried away. Some Jews even named their sons Shulum-babili, that is, 'welfare of Babylon'. They also, as Jeremiah had told them, multiplied and did not decrease: when we have information about Jewish families, they comprise several sons. As a rabbinic interpreter put it, despite the efforts of Ezra the Jews in Babylonia were rather reluctant to go up to the Eretz Israel. According to Josephus, they clung to their properties.[1]

Most Jews who appear in the Murashu documents, as we have seen, belonged to the lower classes. The life and manners of the well-to-do Jews in the Diaspora towards the end of the Persian empire about 350 B.C.E are mirrored in the book of Tobit. Tobit and his nephew, Ahikar, were royal purveyors. Ahikar rose to the post of chief of financial administration. As in the case of Nehemiah, the road to success was royal favour. But Raguel, Tobit's relative, was an opulent landowner, whose fortune consisted of slaves, oxen, sheep, asses and camels, clothing, money and utensils. Just as in the Murashu documents, there was no hint of commercial or financial dealings by the Jews. Tobit made a deposit of money not for investment, but for safe custody, and this very substantial deposit of ten talents of silver, equal to the wages of 60,000 workers for one day, brought no interest for years. We are still in a society where assistance to needy brethren meant giving a 'piece of bread' or 'a handful of barley' (Ezek. 13: 19). The modern idea, expressed originally by Voltaire, that the Jews became tradesmen and usurers in the Babylonian captivity, belongs to the professional mythology. The ordinary Jew, the Jew of the Murashu documents, appears in the book of Tobit anonymously, as one among the brethren who receive succour from the aristocracy. But, we catch a glimpse of a Jewish guide hired for a journey. He receives a daily wage and expenses, and in addition a bounty at the end of the voyage. We also hear of an impoverished Jewish woman who spins at home and sells her work. As in Athens in the same period, this was the sole means of making a living that befitted a lady without resources.

The Jewish aristocracy intermarried within their kin and, like Ezra and Nehemiah, made much of lineage. A deed of marriage was written, after the oral betrothal, by the father of the bride as proof that he had given his daughter to wife. It is noteworthy that in giving his daughter away, Raguel uses the sacramental expression 'according to the Law of Moses', which is still a part of Jewish nuptial ritual, although it is now addressed by the bridegroom to his bride.[2]

[1] *b. Kidd.* 69b. Cf. J. Marshak, *Die Restoration der Juden nach dem Babylonischen Exil* (dissertation, Bern 1908), pp. 50–6; Josephus, *Ant.* xi.8.

[2] Cf. E. Volterra, 'Intorno a Pap. Ent. 23', *Journal of Juristic Papyrology*, 15 (1965), 25.

But except for such picturesque details, the book of Tobit provides no information about the constitution and life of the Jewish community. While the author stresses the piety of his heroes and Tobit's concern for his brethren, we hear nothing about any communal institution. Did Tobit ever go to a synagogue? The author of his story passes over such matters.

In point of fact, the question of Jewish self-government in Persian Babylonia is difficult. As we have seen, there was apparently no Jewish military colony at Nippur. The Jews were settled at random in Babylonian villages. Yet, when Ezra noticed the absence of Levites in his caravan, he knew that they and the *n^ethînîm* were to be found at Casiphia (Ezra 8: 17). Further, the secular clans, with their genealogies, also survived the captivity. One hundred and thirty years after the fall of Jerusalem, Ezra's caravan, for instance, included 200 men 'of the sons of Pahat-Moab' under their own chieftain (Ezra 8: 4).

On the other hand, even dispersed among the Babylonians, the Jews could have communal institutions. Accordingly, biblical writers speak of 'elders' (*z^eqênîm*) of the captivity.[1] It records the decision of the 'elders of the Egyptians' in the city of Babylon about a dispute concerning some fiefs.[2] These 'elders' therefore, just as did the elders of the Jews, represented a total body of sojourners and, again as the elders of the Susanna tale, they judged litigation between their co-nationals. Such corporations of foreigners existed in Babylonian cities alongside the assembly of citizens, which also exercised jurisdiction in civil matters. For instance, the case of a Jew against the house of Murashu was tried in the citizens' assembly of Nippur. It appears that the structure of the late Babylonian city anticipated in some ways that of the Hellenistic *polis* where, too, foreign *politeumata*, such as the Jewish community in Alexandria, coexisted with a civic body within the same city.[3]

We cannot check the claims of the story of Susanna that the Jews in the city of Babylon enjoyed complete judicial autonomy within the community, including criminal jurisdiction. But an authentic document shows that at Sippar Jews adopted some Babylonian legal customs even within the family life.[4] Thus, the daughter of Yasheyaw (Joshua) was

---

[1] H. Zucker, *Studien zur juedischen Selbstverwaltung im Altertum* (Berlin, 1936), pp. 173–91.
[2] M. Dandamayev, 'Egyptian Settlers in Babylonia', in *Drevnii Egipet in drevniaia Afrika* (Moscow, 1967), a volume in honour of V. V. Struve, pp. 15–27 (in Russian).
[3] G. Ch. Sarkisyan, 'The Self-governing City of Seleucid Babylonia', *VDI*, 1 (1952), 68–83 (in Russian); *idem*, 'Social role of cuneiform notarial law system in Hellenistic Babylonia', *Eos*, 48, 3 (1956), 29–44 (in Russian).
[4] Dandamayev, *Slavery*, p. 12. Cf. V. Mark, 'Die Stellung der Frau in Babylonien', *Beiträge zur Assyrologie* 4, (1902), 11. Cf. also J. J. Finkelstein, 'On Some Recent Studies in Cuneiform Laws', *JAOS*, 90 (1970), 244.

warned, with the assent of her mother, that she would be marked as a slave if she should surrender to her boy-friend. The document, written in 531 B.C.E. and certified by several witnesses, among them two Babylonian priests, was drafted by some (to us) anonymous authority. It parallels another document of the same year where the marriage of a young Babylonian woman, concluded with the agreement of her brother but without the authorization of her father, was dissolved by the court, and she was informed that she would be marked as a slave if she should meet her lover again. The punishment strikes the girl and not her seducer because her misbehaviour deprives her family of a valuable piece of property, her body. And the parents are justified in expecting some return on the capital invested in bringing up a female who invariably abandons her family for that of a man.

The internal life of Babylonian Jewry however, remains completely closed to us. What we know comes from the prophets of the Exile, Jeremiah, Ezekiel, and Second Isaiah, and their data, chronologically and psychologically, bear on particular situations. Moreover, they do not reveal anything that we could not imagine without their testimony. Do we need Ezekiel or Deutero-Isaiah to believe that the hearts of the exiles were set on their gains (Ezek. 33: 31)? And that they pursued gain even on the Sabbath (Isa. 58: 13)? Or that among them were hungry Jews (Isa. 58: 7)?[1]

We are not surprised that the exiles mourned their homeland (Isa. 61: 3; 66: 10), fervently expected the soon-to-come Return, and relied on the words of their prophets, who were obviously predicting the impending fall of Babylon. The second chapter of Daniel has preserved one of these 'dreams', as Jeremiah (29: 8) calls them, that comforted the Captivity. But these wishful tales sustained the will to return. The stubborn optimism of the Babylonian Diaspora was neither unique nor exceptional. The refugees from Harran, devastated by the Assyrians, spent 54 years in Babylonia until the day of return. The Messenian exiles had to wait a century to come back in 369 B.C.E.

What was singular was, rather, the religious situation of the Babylonian Captivity. The emigrant carried with him the protection of his ancestral gods. An Aramean who died at Daskyleion in north-western Anatolia, placed his grave under the protection of Nabu and Bel, his gods. On the other hand, the emigrants also tried to win the favour of the gods of the new country. A Babylonian in the Ammonite land inscribed his seal with the Aramaic words: '*Mannu-ki-Inurta*' (blessed by Milkom), the god of the Ammonites. He needed double insurance

[1] Here and elsewhere I follow the translation given in *The Book of Isaiah*, introduced by H. L. Ginsberg (Philadelphia, 1973).

against evil, for he was outside his land and far from his ancestral gods.[1]
For this reason, Naaman, having been healed by the prophet Elisha, and
wanting to worship the Deity of Elisha in Damascus, took with him
from Israel as much soil as two mules could carry, that he might be
able to pray to the God of Israel on Israelite soil (2 Kings 5: 17).
Likewise, Sennacherib of Assyria placed a clod of Babylonian soil in
the foundation of the temple of Ashur, which was to be a replica of a
Babylonian sanctuary.[2] Conversely, on foreign soil one bowed to its
gods. When David was driven out of 'the inheritance of the Lord', his
enemies mocked him: 'Go, serve other gods' (1 Sam. 28: 19). The king
of Assyria commanded Babylonian settlers in Samaria to learn how they
should fear Yahweh (2 Kings 17: 28), and King Sargon ordered that
the deportees to Assyria be given instruction on how to worship the
Assyrian gods and to serve the king.[3] Men of Jerusalem said of the
deportees in 597 B.C.E.: 'They are far away from Yahweh; to us this
land is given as our possession' (Ezek. 11: 15). For this reason, the
Torah never considers as sin the idolatry of the Gentiles. Deuteronomy
rather wants it to be more enlightened and, several centuries before
Plato's astral religion, states that worship of the stars is allotted to the
nations outside the Holy Land (Deut. 4: 19; 29: 26).[4]

Consider now the situation of Babylonian Jewry. They were not
emigrants, but captives forsaken by their own deity (Ezek. 37: 11; Isa.
62: 4), because of their sins (Ezek. 33: 10). They believed that God had
rejected both Israel and Judah (Jer. 33: 24). Accordingly these outcasts,
almost 50 years after the fall of their city, were still scorned by the
nations (Isa. 49: 7; 51: 7). Their fate blackened the reputation of their
God, Who was unable to rescue His city. Jeremiah, predicting the fall
of Babylon, says that therefore Marduk-Bel, her tutelary god, would be
put to shame. But in the meantime it was Jerusalem that had been taken
by Nebuchadnezzar of Babylon, and the name of the Lord was,
therefore, despised 'all the day' (Isa. 52: 5). Ezekiel derived his theorem
of redemption from this situation. The nations, he says, pretend that
the exile of the people of YHWH from His land has demonstrated His
weakness. But this claim profanes God's Holy Name. Therefore, for
the sake of His own reputation, He will bring the exiles again to their
homeland (Ezek. 36: 22–32).

[1] F. M. Cross, Jr., 'An Aramaic inscription from Daskyleion', *BASOR*, 184 (1966),
7–10; N. Avigad, 'Seals of Exiles', *IEJ*, 15 (1965), 222–8.
[2] B. Landsberger, 'Brief des Bischofs von Esagila an Koenig Esarhaddon', *Medede-
elingen* of the Netherlands Academy, N.R. 28, no. 6 (1955), 18.
[3] Cf. S. Paul, 'Sargon's Administrative Diction', *JBL*, 88 (1969), 73–4.
[4] Cf. M. Weinfeld, *The Book of Deuteronomy and the Deuteronomic School* (Oxford
University Press, 1972), pp. 27–35.

The exiles could hope; they could not hasten the Redemption. In the meantime they saw two ways, each complementing the other, to solve their religious problem. First, as the other emigrants, they could turn to the gods of the new country, without abandoning the ancestral worship, just as the Assyrian colonists in Samaria had learned the right way to worship Yahweh (2 Kings 17: 27). The oath in the Egyptian assembly in Babylon (see above, p. 350) was sworn by the names of Bel and Nabu. Why should not the Jews do likewise in the land of Bel? Ezekiel himself (11: 16) conceded that outside the Holy Land, the Deity was only a 'diminished sanctuary', and could only promise to the exiles that after the Return, God will be their God and they His people (Ezek. 11; 20; 37: 26–28).

Thus it was rather a matter of course, predicted by the biblical writers, that in the Diaspora, the Jews would worship gods of wood and stone (Deut. 4: 28). Jeremiah announced in advance that in a land which neither the exiles nor their fathers have known, they will 'serve other gods day and night' (Jer. 5: 12; 16: 13), just as they will serve their enemies in the foreign lands (Jer. 17: 4). For the ancients, to be compelled to seek favours of an alien god in an alien land, a god who would naturally prefer his own flock, was a part of the sad lot of exiles; 'Forasmuch as I will show you no favour' (Jer. 17: 13).

These dire predictions were fulfilled almost immediately. The Temple of the Lord stood still when the Elders of the deportation of 597 B.C.E. came to Ezekiel, saying that they wanted to be like the nations around them, and worship their gods. At least Ezekiel (20: 32) ascribed to them these thoughts. It did not mean that these Jews became apostates. On the contrary, they came to obtain the Lord's approval for their plan (Ezek. 14: 3). They listened to the prophets of the Lord (Ezek. 14: 9), but in a foreign land they needed and desired to complement His worship with that of the gods of this land. The power of this motive is shown by a passage in Deutero-Isaiah (48: 5). The prophet states that God had revealed the coming events leading to the Redemption so that the exiles, who swear by the name of the Lord, would be prevented from attributing the deliverance to false gods, by boasting: 'My idols did it.' As the Jews could hardly participate in the public worship of Marduk or Nabu, they probably had private shrines for their alloy of cults.

The other way to obtain a better divine protection in a foreign land was to transplant there one's ancestral deity. Once a denizen, a god would be able to protect this flock in any alien territory. Examples of such transfer are innumerable. For instance, the Arameans built altars of Nabu, Banit, Bethel, and the queen of heaven in their colony at

Syene.[1] Jewish military colonists had the temple of YHW at Elephantine. In Babylonia some Jews did likewise. In Ezekiel (20: 39) God says to the Jews of the Captivity: serve your idol, if you do not listen to Me, but do not profane My Name with your gifts and your idols. God, says the prophet, will demand and accept these offerings only on the holy mountain in the land of Israel, meaning after the restoration of Jerusalem. But the voice of Ezekiel was in all probability not strong enough to be obeyed by the Jewry in Babylonia. Zechariah's vision of wickedness carried from the land of Judea to the land of Babylonia, where a 'house' (that is, temple) was to be established, probably refers to some plan of building a sanctuary of the God of Jerusalem in Babylonia.[2]

Public worship of an ancestral deity in a foreign country, however, weakened and in due course loosened the bonds between the emigrant and the original seat of his cult. A deity was inseparable from his or her abode. The god of the new temple, perhaps, was a double of but not identical with the god of the mother-country. One and the same godhead theologically, they were separate beings functionally, in the same way that Notre Dame de Lourdes is not the patron saint of Barcelona and Nuestra Senora de Merced does not perform the healings of Lourdes. Ishtar of Accad, Ishtar of Uruk, and 'Our Lady of Nineveh' were, similarly, three separate divine beings. Accordingly, the true zealots of the ancestral deity were reluctant to transfer their homage to another idol of the same name. Sin, the divine crescent, angry with Haran, his city, went up to heaven, and Haran was conquered by the Medes in 610 B.C.E. A votaress of Sin's, the mother of the future King Nabonidus of Babylon, did not transfer her devotion to Sin of Uruk, nor was she satisfied with worshipping the idols of Haran that had been transported to Babylon. Rather, for 54 years she continued to supplicate Sin to return to his abode in Haran so that the people of his city might worship the great deity. Again, when enemies carried away the idol of Marduk from his temple in Babylon, the Babylonians did not switch their adoration to Marduk in neighbouring Borsippa. Transferred to Ashur, the idol blessed the Assyrians, while his absence caused affliction in Babylon. Returned to his temple in Babylon, he called all countries to bring tribute to Babylon,[3] just as the good tidings

---

[1] B. Porten, *Archives from Elephantine* (University of California Press, 1968), pp. 165–70.

[2] Morton Smith, *Palestinian Parties and Politics that Shaped the Old Testament* (Columbia University Press, 1971), p. 90. But there is no evidence that shrines or altars were built by the exiles in Babylonia.

[3] *ANET*, 560; R. Borger, 'Gott Marduk and Gott-könig Sulgi als propheten', *BO*, 28 (1971), 18.

'of Isaiah' (60: 5) promised that after the return of the Lord to Zion, 'the wealth of the nations shall come' there.

Conversely, the allegiance to a sanctuary in the new country alienated the worshippers from the god of their fathers. The Jews at Elephantine, the Jews in Jerusalem, and the Samaritans praised the same God of Heaven in their respective temples. But in Elephantine He was 'YHW who dwells in Elephantine, the fortress', and in Jerusalem He was 'YHW Who dwells in Jerusalem'. Accordingly, the Jews in Elephantine did not care for Jerusalem, and the Samaritans opposed the restoration of the Temple on Zion after the return of Jews from the Exile. Thus, the Jews in the Babylonian Exile had to choose between equally disastrous alternatives: to build altars to their God in the new country and forget Jerusalem, or to live as outcasts without their own protective deity. 'How shall we sing the Lord's song on alien soil? If I forget you, O Jerusalem...' (Ps. 137: 4). Yet, they knew that in Babylonia they were separated from the Lord in Jerusalem. In 597 B.C.E., men of Jerusalem said of the first deportees to Babylonia: 'They are far away from Yahweh; to us this land is given for a possession' (Ezek. 11: 15). Several centuries later, the rabbis in Babylonia, who again lived in the shadow of the destroyed Temple, understood the psychological situation of their remote ancestors. The prophets told them: 'Repent'. But they answered: 'We had been handed over to Nebuchadnezzar and a sold slave, or a divorced wife, and the former master or husband have no longer any rights over the other party.'[1]

How did these Jews survive as Jews in Babylonia? How did they maintain themselves spiritually as part of 'the people of Israel,' deprived as they were of the Lord's grace-giving presence and unable to offer sacrifices that appeased the Deity and cleansed from sin? How could they resist the appeal of the genius of heathenism, of the gods who displayed their might and splendour?

We should not underestimate this temptation. These idols were revered with fervour and with great magnificence. The believers lavished on them praise which used the same expressions as the Hebrew Psalms and prayers. They spoke of Bel, who grasped the hand of the fallen, and of Belit, his spouse, who released the captives. These idols could impoverish the rich and make the poor wealthy; they were both terrible and merciful. 'Who except for you is Lord,' asked the Babylonian priest addressing Marduk, 'god of heaven and earth.' The inscription drawn on above (p. 353), of the mother of Nabonidus, manifests the truly pious and moving devotion to Sin, the moon god.

[1] *b. Sanh.* 105a. Rashi on Ezek. 20: 1 uses this rabbinic legal argument to explain the enquiry of the Elders reported by the prophet. See above, p. 352. I owe both references to Mosche Greenberg of the Hebrew University.

A pamphlet written in the Persian or the Hellenistic Age, the apocryphal Epistle of Jeremiah to the exiles in Babylonia, documents the feelings of an average Jew who, awestruck, observed the multitudes before and behind the ritual procession, worshipping the idols in gold and silver borne upon priests' shoulders. 'Fear them not,' the author warns him, for they are no gods, and he repeats this slogan ten times in some 70 verses of his message. 'Say in your heart: Lord, we must worship you.' And answering Babylonian religious propaganda, he tries to prove again and again that the idols are powerless: they cannot give riches, deliver a man in distress, help the weak, redress a wrong, set up a king or put him down, nor give rain. The violence of this attack which falsely identifies god and his image proves the danger of the polytheistic contagion in the Babylonian Diaspora. Later, when the Jews had become immunized against this danger, the rabbis disdained such argumentation. For them 'there was not the slightest need to argue and to preach' against idolatry.[1]

The author of the Epistle of Jeremiah ends by asserting that 'better is a just man, who has no idols, for he will be far from reproach'. It appears that such righteous men began to win the struggle against the lure of polytheism in the age of Ezra and Nehemiah. To establish this point, we must turn to Jewish nomenclature at Nippur.[2]

As we have stated, to identify the Jews, or men of any other nationality, in Babylonian records we are compelled to rely with rare exceptions on proper names, a device, we must note again, that is not always reliable. An Egyptian or a Jew living among the Babylonians might very well give his son the Babylonian name Apla, that is 'heir'. With regard to names of religious import, the situation is different. Just as the names glorifying the god Ashur, to a large extent at least, suggest the descendants of the Assyrians exiled to Babylonia in 612 B.C.E., so the name Jonathan – 'Yahweh gave (him)' – would in all probability indicate a Jew. Likewise, an Egyptian named Patesi, who names his son Belshunu, and a Jew, who names his son: 'May Bel protect the father' (Bel-abu-usur), suggest that they recognize the might of Bel. Similarly, when the son of Pharaoh Necho, or when Daniel and his companions receive Babylonian theophoric names, the change placed them under the protection of Babylonian gods. A relationship to the deities asserted in theophoric names was obvious to the Babylonians, and scribes often drew the cuneiform sign indicating a divine name before the personal names that referred to some foreign deity, be it Yahweh, Isis or Mitra.

Starting from these premises, let us examine Jewish nomenclature in the Murashu records. In these documents every free person, as a rule,

---

[1] S. Lieberman, *Hellenism in Jewish Palestine* (New York, 1950), p. 121.
[2] E. J. Bickerman, 'The Generation of Ezra and Nehemiah', *PAAJR*, 44 (1977).

is described by his personal name and that of his father. Almost a third of the patronymics of persons with familiar biblical names or names compounded with Yahweh are compounds that acknowledge Babylonian gods. Yet these fathers, who bear idolatrous names, almost without exception invoke Yahweh when naming their sons. Beluballit ('the god Bel called me into life') names his son Nathania, that is 'gift of Yahweh'. A certain Nana-iddima (gift of the goddess Nana) names his son Igdaliah, that is, 'Yahweh is great.' Out of twenty persons whose names proclaim the graciousness of Yahweh (Hananiah, etc.), half had fathers whose given names invoked the favour of the idols of Babylon. Certainly, secular Babylonian names continued to be given to Jewish boys. Yet, a man called 'peace of Babylon' (Shulum-babili) named his son 'Who is mighty like Yahweh' (Mannù-danni-iama).

This change in nomenclature, which according to the extant evidence begins about 480 B.C.E., is remarkable. We should rather expect that after a century of quiet life in Babylonia, the Jews would have largely accepted Babylonian onomastic practice as, for instance, the Assyrian and the Egyptian exiles did. As a matter of fact, the house of David did it too. Sheshbazzar, 'the prince of Judah', who in 538 B.C.E. brought back to Jerusalem the sacred vessels which Nebuchadnezzar had carried away from the Temple and who was probably identical with Shenazzar, son of the king Jehoiachin (1 Chr. 3: 18), bore a name marking him as a worshipper of the Babylonian moon god, Sin. Shealtiel, father (or uncle) of Zerubbabel, had a name which sounds Babylonian, and Zerubbabel himself was named 'Offspring of Babel'. When he went to Jerusalem to rebuild the Temple, two out of six members of his staff bore names referring to Bel-Marduk (Neh. 7: 7). Two generations later, in 458 B.C.E., not even one among the companions of Ezra bore a pagan theophoric name.

How is this psychological change to be explained? In the first place, we have to remember that, as stated above, no more than a third of the Jews bore names of Babylonian religious connotation, and the Yahwist families naming their sons proclaimed their trust in Yahweh.

Still under the Babylonian kings, a Jew named Shamashsharusur, 'the god Shamash may protect the king', named his daughter Jehoishma, 'May Yahweh hear', a name also popular at Elephantine. Later a man bearing a Yahwist name called his son Zechariah. A document of 430 shows that a certain Jedahia named his sons Jonathan, Simeon and Ahiah.

This 'Yahweh-alone' group,[1] as its spokesman Ezekiel and later

[1] I borrow this definition from the illuminating book of Morton Smith, *Palestinian Parties*, p. 90.

Second Isaiah show, was unyielding in the demand that the Jews worship only Yahweh. For them, the gods of the nations were idols of wood and stone and their cult vanity and delusion. On the other hand, the Jews who put their trust in Bel or Ninurta also trusted Yahweh and, perhaps, relied upon Him even more than upon their idols. The intolerant party, naturally, prevailed, for its partisans were absolutely convinced of the absolute truth of their faith: 'They shall be turned back, they shall be put to shame, who trust in carved idols, who say to molten images, "You are our gods"' (Isa. 42: 17). So dared to speak a prophet, though the Temple of his God still lay in ruins.

Furthermore the monotheists, again owing to their intolerance, won the ear of the Persian court. The Achemenids, heirs of the Babylonian kings and of the pharaohs, and thus of the house of David, freely used the royal prerogative to control the temples and to regulate the religion of their subjects. Cambyses, for instance, approved a new scheme of rations for the temple servants of Ishtar of Uruk, just as a later Persian king regulated the daily allowances of the Temple singers in Jerusalem (Neh. 11: 23) and a Persian satrap in 358 B.C.E. confirmed a cultic statute of the city of Xanthos.[1]

Similarly, in 419 B.C.E. the Persian court sent instructions to the satrap of Egypt concerning the feast of unleavened bread in the Jewish military colony at Elephantine. The royal mandate to Ezra empowered him to appoint persons, 'who know the law of thy God' as magistrates and judges to judge 'His (the God of Jerusalem's) people' in the satrapy beyond the Euphrates, and to make known the Law to those (among the Jews) 'who do not know it' (Ezra 7: 25).[2] We may suppose that a similar measure, earlier or later, was enacted for Babylonia.

Such orders or, for instance, Darius' command concerning the election of administrative heads of Egyptian temples,[3] presuppose specialized bureaux for dealing with the temples and the worship of the nations within the Persian empire. Accordingly, we hear of a certain Petahia, who was 'at the king's hand in matters concerning the people' of Israel (Neh. 11: 24).

The strict monotheists were the only ones who had sufficient ideological interest in penetrating and manipulating the 'desk' of Jewish affairs. The Jews who worshipped Yahweh and Nabu with equal

[1] M. Dandamayev, 'The Temples and the State in the Late Babylonian Period', *VDI*, 4 (1968), 20 (in Russian). Cf. M. San-Nicolò, 'Beiträge zu einer Prosopographie neubabylonischer Beamten', *S. B. Bayer. Akad.*, (1941), 66. The trilingual inscription from Xanthos is in A. Dupont-Sommer, E. Laroche, H. Metzger and L. Robert, 'La stèle trilingue récemment découverte', *CRAIBL* (1974), 82, 119, 281.

[2] H. L. Ginsberg, 'A Strand in the cord of Hebrew Hymnody', *Eretz-Israel*, 9 (1969), 49.

[3] E. Bresciani, 'La satrapia d'Egitto', *SCO*, 7 (1958), 167.

fervour, or indifference, would hardly care to run this bureau except
for personal advantage. They were adherents of no particular ideology
and would not have risked royal displeasure, as Nehemiah did for the
sake of Zion. And so, the weight of royal favour shifted the balance
of power within the Babylonian Jewry to the party of Ezra and
Nehemiah. Those who were really attached to Bel or Nana by family ties,
by some miraculous help, or by some other circumstance, became cold
to Yahweh and desisted from inquiring of Him. Those whose faith in
Yahweh was hot saw their cause triumph. And the lukewarm, the
'Laodiceans', sided with the winner as usual.

The new attitude of the Babylonian Diaspora became paradigmatic.
From everywhere, the Diaspora turned to Zion and to Zion alone.
Abominating the idols of their neighbours, yet themselves lacking
sacrificial worship, the essence of religion to both the average Jew and
the average heathen, the Jews in the Diaspora naturally appeared
'godless' to their neighbours. And so the Diaspora came to be a peculiar
people, without parallel among the nations. For this reason the Jew was
now a magnet attracting both the 'joiners' (Isa. 56: 3) and the hate of
those who, perhaps rightly, cannot stand singularity.

C. EGYPT, PERSIAN SATRAPY

The conquest of Egypt clearly fitted into the policy of imperialistic
expansion followed by Cyrus the Great, the founder of the Achemenid
empire, since the valley of the Nile represented the most important – and
probably the only – economic and political power in Africa. It was
Cambyses, son and in 530 B.C.E., successor of Cyrus, who defeated the
last pharaoh of the twenty-sixth dynasty, Psammetichus III, and
annexed the country as a satrapy of the Achemenid empire.[1] The year
of Cambyses' conquest, 525 B.C.E., marks the beginning of the so-called
'first Persian domination' (also called, with Manetho, the twenty-seventh
dynasty), which ends around 401 B.C.E. Cambyses remained in Egypt
until 522, conducting an 'African' policy with expeditions against
Carthage, against the oases of the Libyan desert and against Nubia.
From the point of view of an Asiatic Persian, a policy to enlarge the
Egyptian province – already peripheral and difficult to control – appears
a dangerous action, that can only be explained on the assumption that

[1] For the general history of Persia see A. T. Olmstead, *History of the Persian Empire*
(Chicago, 1948). For studies on Egypt in the Persian era see G. Posener, *La première
domination perse en Egypte* (Cairo, 1936); F. K. Kienitz, *Die politische Geschichte
Ägyptens vom 7. bis zum 4. Jahrhundert vor der Zeitwende* (Berlin, 1953);
E. Bresciani, 'La satrapia d'Egitto', *SCO*, 7 (Pisa, 1958), 132ff, and 'Egypt and the
Persian Empire', in *The Greeks and the Persians*, ed. H. Bengtson (Delacorte Press:
New York, 1968), pp. 335ff.

Cambyses wanted to be considered a pharaoh. As an Egyptian sovereign he followed an Egyptian policy, the normal policy of Saitic sovereigns. This inspired him particularly in the Nubian campaign: he followed in the footsteps of Psammetichus II. The three campaigns were a failure; the Phoenician allies refused to march against Carthage, a fraternal colony. Fifty thousand men sent against the Libyan oases disappeared – if we can believe Herodotus – in a sandstorm. The expedition against Napata, badly and hastily organized, resulted merely in the acknow-ledgement of northern Nubia alone (for a century under Egyptian influence and sovereignty) as tributary of Persia (Herodotus III.97–98).

It appears that Cambyses wanted the Egyptian people to consider him the legitimate descendant of the Saitic dynasty, come to revenge the throne which the 'usurper' Amasis had taken from Apries, the legitimate pharaoh. Significant for this subject is the legend which regarded Cambyses as a son of the daughter of Apries,[1] and in this light the report of Herodotus about the posthumous persecution of Amasis, whose mummy was burned by Cambyses, seems likely. If we have no way to prove the truth of this event, we have none the less proof of a defamation of the memory of Amasis during the years of Cambyses' invasion, of a *damnatio memoriae* attested by numerous Egyptian monu-ments showing the intentional chiselling out of Amasis from the royal cartouche.[2] As a matter of fact a series of Greek witnesses all agree in attributing to Cambyses deranged, impious and cruel behaviour (Herodotus, III.27–38; Diodorus, 1.46; Strabo, XVII.27; Plutarch, *De Iside et Osiride* 44c). Fortunately, however, direct Egyptian sources and contemporary Egyptian monuments allow us to reassess and sometimes, indeed, to refute such witnesses.[3] Undoubtedly some units of the Persian occupation in the first throes of a military conquest in Egypt gave themselves to violence and impudence, even against the temples and their treasures. This is admitted even by contemporary Egyptian sources. But Cambyses is not held responsible for this. On the contrary, it appears that, when informed of the abuses, he tried to stop them. A demotic papyrus informs us, however, of a decree promulgated by Cambyses concerning 'the revenues granted to the temples of the Egyptian Gods at the time of the Pharaoh Amasis'.[4] Under this

---

[1] The three versions of the legend differ in detail, but they are identical in their essential meaning; see Herodotus, I.1–3; Atheneus, XIII.10; Ctesias, fragment 13a.

[2] See E. Bresciani, 'A statue of the XXVIth dynasty with the so-called "Persian Dress"', *SCO*, 16 (Pisa, 1967), 277, 279, with bibliography on the problem.

[3] See Posener, *La première domination*, pp. 171ff; A. Klasens, 'Cambises en Egypte', *Ex Oriente Lux* (1946), 339ff.

[4] W. Spiegelberg, *Die sogennante demotische Chronik des Pap. 215 der Bibliothèque National zu Paris* (Leipzig, 1914), pp. 32, 33; J. H. Johnson, 'The demotic Chronicle as an historical Source', *Enchoria*, 4 (1974), 1–19.

ordinance the revenues, in the same amount as before, were left to three temples only. As for the others even though they were left free to provide for the cult ('the priests themselves ought to raise their own geese and offer them to their Gods'), there were drastic reductions. But this decree, interpreted without prejudice, appears as a wise economic measure, reducing the enormous financial expenditure which Amasis had thought it good policy to assume, and not a decision dictated by 'impiety'. Naturally a decree of this character was not likely to bolster the popularity of the foreign conqueror and provoked in the Egyptian priesthood an implacable hatred, from which surely stems the tradition of impious atrocities attributed to Cambyses.

While in Egypt Cambyses was acting out his role as pharaoh, in Persia his ruin was under way, through the contrivance of the Magush Gaumata who, presenting himself as Smerdis, the brother put to death by Cambyses, claimed the throne of Cyrus. Cambyses left Ariandes in charge as satrap of the Egyptian province and hastened to return but died in Syria at the beginning of 522 B.C.E. Darius, son of Hystaspes, restored order, eliminating the false Smerdis. In Egypt also his intervention was necessary to subdue the tendencies towards independence of Ariandes, the satrap left behind by Cambyses. Darius based his rule on a policy of pacification and a wise policy of toleration. As for Egypt, Darius visited it, it seems, in the fourth year of his reign. The country had an important status (the sixth) among the twenty satrapies into which he divided the empire. He established its administrative and tax organization and codified its laws. Diodorus (1.95) names Darius I as Egypt's sixth and final legal codifier,[1] and this is confirmed by a demotic papyrus – the one mentioned above with reference to the decree of Cambyses on the Egyptian temples. The text reports that in the third year of his reign, Darius I sent his satrap to Egypt to convoke wise men chosen from the warriors, the priests and the scribes to put down in writing the former laws which had been in force up to the forty-fourth year of Amasis.

The commission worked at the collection of these laws for sixteen years. It was then transcribed on papyrus 'in Aramaic (literally, Assyrian) writing and in Demotic writing'. Darius I, then, was not so much a legislator as a *codifier* of Egyptian law which had been in force up to the end of the reign of Amasis. Thanks to the translation of the legal 'corpus' of Egyptian laws into Aramaic as well, he furnished a

---

[1] See N. Reich, 'The codification of the Egyptian Laws by Darius and the origin of the "Demotic Chronicle"', in *Mizraim*, 1 (1933), pp. 78ff; also E. Seidl, *Aegyptische Rechtsgeschichte der Saiten und Perserzeit* (Glückstadt, N.Y., 1956), p. 60. See now E. Bresciani, 'La morte di Cambise ovvero dell'empietà punita: a proposito della "Cronaca demotica"', Verso Col. C. 7–8, in *EVO*, 4 (1981), 222–7.

written and well-defined guide to the indigenous laws in the language of the officials of the empire – beginning with the satrap – the administrative language of the Achemenid Empire, the Aramaic. It is probable that Darius I would have made provision to restore the 'laws of the temples' as they were at the time of Amasis, which were in a state of crisis because of the decree of Cambyses. Darius I surely decided that he could not do without the approval of the priests, if he wanted a durable union of Egypt and his empire; certainly the king received maximum support from the Egyptian priesthood and from the whole country. The protection provided by the great king for the cult and for the Egyptian priesthood was expressed also in the construction of a grandiose temple for Ammon-Ra in the oasis of El-Kharga. We have proof of the king's building activities in Egypt from the inscriptions of the stone quarries at wadi Hammamat, while blocks with his name belonging to temples have been found at El Kab in Upper Egypt and at Busiris in the Delta region. A very great number of steles of the Serapeum at Memphis are dated in the reign of Darius I, between his third and his thirty-fourth year as king. We know from the statue of the chief doctor Wedjahorresnet[1] that Darius I ordered the restoration of the 'House of Life' at Sais, the cradle of the twenty-sixth dynasty. Nevertheless Darius did not renounce the right to ratify (either by himself or through his representative in the satrapy, the satrap) the choice – proposed by the electoral college of the priests – of the administrator of the temples, the *lesonis*.

The opening of the navigable canal joining the Nile and the Red sea, from Bubastis to lake Timsah through the Bitter lakes, which took place under Darius I, was of extreme importance for commercial relations between Egypt and the Persian gulf.[2] This undertaking – conceived and probably at least partly realized already by Pharaoh Necho of the twenty-sixth dynasty – was commemorated by hieroglyphic and cuneiform steles erected along the banks of the canal, and rediscovered there.

Towards the end of the reign of Darius I there seems to have been a slackening of Persian control over the Egyptian colony, probably because of the Persian engagement with the Greeks, who had successfully resisted the great king at Marathon (490 B.C.E.). It is a fact that a little before the death of Darius I in 486 B.C.E., Egypt rebelled. There is no proof that the satrap Pherendates was involved;[3] but the fact that

---

[1] See Posener, *La première domination*, n. 1; G. Botti and P. Romanelli, *Le sculture del Museo Gregoriano greco-egizio* (Vatican City, 1951), p. 33, pl. 28. For the building activity of the Persian kings, see Bresciani, *Satrapia*, pp. 177ff.

[2] See Posener, *La première domination*, pp. 180–1; Kienitz, *Geschichte*, p. 65.

[3] Demotic documents of the satrap Pherendates are published by W. Spiegelberg, 'Drei dem. Schreiben aus der Korrespondenz des Pherendates des Satrapen Darius I mit dem Chnum Priestern von Elephantine', *SAW* (Berlin, 1928), p. 604.

Xerxes, son and successor of Darius from 486 to 465/4 B.C.E., quickly tamed the Egyptian rebellion, installing his brother Achemenes as satrap in Egypt, confirms this suspicion.

In 460 B.C.E., in the first years of the reign of Artaxerxes I, successor of Xerxes (465/4–424/3 B.C.E.), Egypt suffered another insurrection led by the Libyan Inaros, son of Psammetichus (Thucydides, 1.104) who was backed by the Athenian fleet. Two hundred ships on their way to Cyprus, turned towards Egypt and went up the Nile in the direction of Memphis. (The classical sources do not mention this, but I have reason to believe that they went up along the Canopic branch, the westernmost and thus the closest to Mara, the sphere of action of Inaros, and besides well-known for a long time to the Greeks because the fluvial port of Naucratis had been reserved for the Greeks, for whom the Saitic sovereigns had reserved the Canopic river front of Naucratis.) In a battle between Inaros and the Persian troops at Papremis in the western Delta,[1] the satrap Achemenes (son of Darius I) was defeated and killed. When Herodotus about 450 B.C.E. travelled to Egypt, he visited the battlefield of Papremis and examined the remains of the soldiers who had perished in action. He there found confirmation of his theory as to why the Egyptians, who were going bareheaded in the sun, had strong and resistant skulls, while the Persians, who covered their heads with tiaras, had weak skulls (III.12). Megabyzus, satrap of Syria, was sent to Egypt, and so securely recovered Memphis that the Greek fleet, barricaded in the island of Prosopitis, was defeated. A few Greeks succeeded in saving themselves by fleeing to Cyrene. And so the Greek intervention in favour of Egyptian liberty ended in disaster. Inaros was handed over to the Persians and was crucified by them in 454 B.C.E. But the uprising had been limited to the zone of the delta, and some Egyptian documents furnish proof that during the years of the rebellion of Inaros, southern Egypt had remained in Persian hands; a hieroglyphic inscription left in wadi Hammamat by the Persian official Ariyawrata is from the fifth year of Artaxerxes;[2] two Aramaic papyri from Elephantine are of the sixth year, one of the ninth and one of the tenth year of Artaxerxes. The peace restored in Egypt – let us remember that the peace of Callias, 449 B.C.E., forbade Athens to interfere or intervene against Persia in political matters concerning Cyprus and Egypt – was not broken for a long time, following the reign of Artaxerxes. After the death of Achemenes, the post of satrap went to Arsames, who remained in charge during the whole reign of Darius II (424–404 B.C.E.). Arsames is known

---

[1] For a new etymology and a new localization of the site of Papremis in the western delta, see E. Bresciani, 'Ancora su Papremi', *SCO*, 21 (1972), 299ff.

[2] See Posener, *La première domination*, p. 178; Bresciani, *Satrapia*, p. 139.

also from Greek sources (Ctesias, *Persica* XIV, XV, XVIII; Polyenus, *Stratagemata* VII. 28), from seven Aramaic papyri at Elephantine, and from letters on leather published by Driver in 1955 and probably found in Memphis.[1]

Persian policy towards Egypt during the reign of Darius II is not well known to us; but we do know that during the last years of his reign there were agitations against the Persian government. There are references to unrest in the delta between 411 and 408, while the satrap Arsames was in Susa.[2] It is not impossible that this subversive activity arose at the instigation of Amyrteus, who a few years later freed Egypt from Persian domination. During the absence of Arsames there occurred episodes of rebellion at the southern border as well, in the Egyptian military detachments situated at Syene. These were accompanied by episodes of violence, perpetrated by the Egyptians, directed against the Hebrew settlers living on the island of Elephantine. These episodes were instigated by the priests of the god Khnum, and with the help of high local officials of the Persian government. They culminated in the destruction of the temple of Yahu on the same island.[3]

Notwithstanding the uprisings and disorders, the Persian authority was recognized, at least up to the southern borders of Egypt, up to 404 B.C.E. After this date, in the whole of Egypt, including Elephantine, Amyrteus was the recognized pharaoh, with whom started a period of 60 years during which three indigenous dynasties follow (the twenty-eighth, twenty-ninth and thirtieth). Thereafter Egypt knew a new, very brief, second Persian domination (342–332 B.C.E.) beginning with the conquest by Artaxerxes III Ochus, who left Pherendates as satrap of

---

[1] G. R. Driver, *Aramaic Documents of the Fifth Century B.C.* (Oxford, 1954).

[2] Driver, *Documents* v.6; VII.1–4; VIII.2.

[3] See E. Kraeling, *The Brooklyn Museum Aramaic Papyri. New Documents of the Fifth Century B.C. from the Jewish Colony at Elephantine* (New Haven, 1953), pp. 100ff; B. Porten, *Archives from Elephantine* (Berkeley–Los Angeles, 1968), pp. 278–89; P. Grelot, *Documents araméens d'Egypte* (Paris, 1972), pp. 386ff. For the origin of the colony and the construction of the temple of Yahu, see pp. 367–9 and nn. 1, 2, 3 (pp. 367–8).

The responsibilities of the priesthood of Khnum, god of Elephantine, in the destruction of the temple of Yahu are well ascertained. It is noteworthy that a letter (*CAP*, no. 38.7) sent to the authorities of the Jewish Colony at Elephantine by a co-religionist who was in Memphis affirms that Khnum (that is, his priests) is against the Jews 'since the time Hananiah came to Egypt'. Should we think, then, of a Machiavellian plan by the religious authorities in Jerusalem, who wanted to remove from the temple of Elephantine the privilege of celebrating holocausts, reserved only to the Temple in Jerusalem; and who therefore, through the work in Egypt of Hananiah, who took there the new rules for Passover, fomented a latent uneasiness in the Egyptian priesthood?

the reconquered province, and continuing through the short reign of his son Arses and the reign of Darius III, whose first satrap in Egypt, Sabaces, died in the battle of Issus, and whose second, Mazakes, ceded the country to Alexander the Great in 332 without offering any resistance. With this cession the Achemenid domination of Egypt came to an end. The valley of the Nile became a province of the empire of Alexander, whose inheritance was taken up by the Ptolemies, who in their turn passed the country on to the Romans. From then on Egypt knew only foreign domination.

At this point it is opportune to examine the administrative and economic aspects of the Persian domination in Egypt, and to try also to understand its intellectual and religious life.[1] In the valley of the Nile, organized as a satrapy, the satrap – the representative of the great king for his subjects – resided in Memphis, the most ancient capital. The Imperial Chancery (the records office) of Memphis, a faithful copy of the great king's at Susa, employed numerous officials and scribes, including Egyptian scribes, for correspondence and reports in the native language. As a matter of fact, although Aramaic was the official language of the Achemenid Empire, in official communications with the natives the satrap could use the demotic language in which they answered. We have both Aramaic and demotic documents coming from the chancery of the satrap. There was a distinction between the scribe who was the amanuensis, the manual redactor of the text, and the royal scribe, who was the functionary, the responsible head of the satrapal chancery.

The entire country retained the administrative division into large 'districts', which were at the same time administrative and juridical, and which had already existed in the preceding epoch. In comparison with the older Egyptian *nomoi*, it seems, however, that the districts of the Persian period were fewer in number and hence larger in territory. In this and in other respects, the Persian government did not bring particular innovations to the Egyptian satrapy, but limited itself to substituting its own officials for Egyptian ones, especially at the beginning of the domination. At the head of each district was a governor, called by Egyptian Aramaic documents *fratarak*. For the district of Tascetres, 'the southern district', which stretched from Assuan to Hermontis, where the district of Thebes started, the *fratarak* in the years around 410 was the Persian, Waidrang. With his son, the head of the army, he participated in the destruction of the temple of Yahu at Elephantine. His predecessor had been Damadin, while Waidrang was head of the army. The seat of the *fratarak* of the southern district

[1] For all this part see n. 1 on p. 368, especially Bresciani, *Satrapia*, pp. 132ff.

was at Syene, 'the Market', on the bank of the Nile facing the island of Elephantine. The administration of the districts employed numerous 'provincial scribes', together with other officials who were called in the Aramaic papyri *Azdakaya*. The lesser administrative units, cities and towns, had their own governors of inferior rank, who depended upon the *fratarak*. Hieroglyphic inscriptions found in the stone quarries of wadi Hammamat give the names of two Persians, the brothers Attiyawahi and Ariyawrata, sons of Arsames and Qanju (an Egyptian woman?).[1] The first was governor of Coptus in the district of Thebes, and besides this title he bore constantly that of 'saris of Persia'. His inscriptions are dated between 486 and 473 B.C.E., while the inscriptions of his younger brother, Ariyawrata, run from 461 to 449 B.C.E. It is interesting to note that in the later inscriptions, those of Ariyawrata, the title of 'saris of Persia' is translated by two terms in Egyptian between which it wavers (*r Prs*, 'prefect of Persia,' and *ḥrj Prs*, 'head of Persia') showing the ever stronger influence of the Egyptian ambience of the conquered people over the conquerors.

The state treasury was situated in Memphis, under the patronage of the god Ptah. The expression 'of the weight of Ptah' referring to a sum of *šeqâlîn* in an Aramaic papyrus of Elephantine is the equivalent, I believe, of the expression 'of the house of the treasure of Ptah', used by contemporary demotic papyri to assure the legality of the *deben* and of its tenth, the *kedet*, the most common of the monetary-weight measures used by Egypt. In the demotic documents of the Persian Era, there are indications of the value of metal according to its weight in pounds; in Aramaic documents, money is computed in *kerâsin*, *šeqâlîn* and *hallûrîn*, while greater values are calculated by weight, based on the official standard, 'the weight of the king'. It is interesting to find the term *sttry*, 'stater', in Aramaic papyri between the end of the reign of Darius II and the reign of Amyrtaeus (two *šeqâlîn* are considered equal to a stater). Greek money had begun to circulate in Egypt during the Saitic era, but the Egyptians accepted it by weight. Up till now Median silver shekels have not been found in Egypt. But Herodotus' information on silver coins (minted by the unfaithful satrap Ariandes) which rivalled the golden daric of Darius for purity and which, at the time of his trip, the Greek historian says were still in circulation (IV.166), leads us to believe that there was at least a limited circulation of coins minted in Egypt. The *šeqâlîn* said to be 'of the weight of Ptah' in the above-mentioned Aramaic papyrus were different from the ones named in other documents, and these were Median shekels and not Phoenician–Hebrew shekels.

[1] See Posener, *La première domination*, p. 178.

Towards the end of the reign of Darius I, the head of the treasury of Ptah at Memphis was the Egyptian Ptahhotep. His naophoros statue, which presents him in the so-called 'Persian dress' with a necklace of Achemenid type (possibly a decoration granted him by the 'Great King'), is at the Brooklyn Museum.[1] A stele with his name, now at the Louvre Museum, is dated in the thirty-fourth year of Darius I and comes from the Serapeum of Memphis.

Officials in great numbers were attached to the administration of the treasury. The central treasury was in Memphis, but every district had its own 'treasury' with 'treasurers' and 'accountants'; Aramaic documents of Elephantine also mention the 'scribes of the treasury' connected with the 'house of the king', evidently the governmental storehouse where the reserves of tributes in kind were kept. From these came the 'rations' that the mercenary soldiers of the Persian government received, besides wages in money (Aramaic *prs*). And some officials (called by the title *pakhuta* in an Aramaic papyrus)[2] sent from Migdol in the Delta to Elephantine, were also officials of the treasury, since they had to decide on the disbursement of the wages in money to individuals belonging to the Hebrew military colony.

A special aspect of the satrapic administration in Egypt concerns the administration of personal property that the satrap owned, as is proved by letters on leather published by Driver in 1955.[3] This group of letters – written when Arsames went to Susa between 411 and 408 B.C.E. – refers to the estate that the satrap owned in Lower Egypt (he also owned one in Upper Egypt) which was in the care of a *peqid*. This official (we know from the letters on leather the names of two functionaries with this position, both of them Egyptian, Psamtik and Nekhtihur, who succeeded Psamtik) had troops under his command to maintain order and defend the possessions of his master. He also held the charge of 'treasurer' of the personal wealth of the satrap which came from the revenues of the estate entrusted to him and which he administered with colleagues, 'accountants'. Through this group of documents we are informed that other Persian personages also possessed estates in Egypt – Widdaps and his wife, Prince Warohi, and also Artawant, substitute for and representative of Arsames during his absence from Egypt. The estate mentioned in the letters on leather was located very probably in the western delta – famous for its vineyards – because one of the letters mentions the 'wine of Papremis'.[4]

---

[1] Published by J. D. Cooney, 'The Portrait of an Egyptian Collaborator', *Bulletin of The Brooklyn Museum*, 15 (1953), 1–16.

[2] E. Bresciani, 'Papiri Aramaici Egiziani di epoca persiana presso il Museo Civico di Padova', *RSO*, 35 (1960), 11.   [3] See n. 2, p. 362.

[4] Bresciani, 'Ancora su Papremi', 300.

The Achemenid government established in Egypt a strong military contingent for the defence of the borders and for internal security. For knowledge of military organization and for the localization of military detachments and colonies in the valley of the Nile in the Persian era, we must essentially draw upon the papyri and other Aramaic documents which Egypt has restored to us. The fullest documentation comes from the group of Aramaic documents from Elephantine and from Assuan, which illuminates in a special way the life of the Hebrew military colony, which was part of the Persian garrison on the southern border.[1]

The Jews of the colony of Elephantine – the oldest dated document is an Aramaic papyrus of 495 B.C.E., the latest a papyrus of 398 B.C.E. – call themselves *yahwdîn*.[2] They originated from Judea and were worshippers of Yahu, for whom they built a temple on the island itself. Concerning the Judeo-Egyptian Diaspora of the Saitic–Persian epoch there are grave problems, not yet solved in a definitive way. When and from where did the Jews of Elephantine arrive in Egypt? Why do the Jewish Egyptian settlers write and speak only Aramaic and never Hebrew? When was the temple of Yahu built on the island? Jeremiah (44: 1), while reproaching his compatriots in Egypt for having forsaken the God of their fathers and given themselves to idolatry, does not mention a temple of the God of the Jews in Upper Egypt at all. One wonders whether, if he did know of the temple's existence at Elephantine, he would not have mentioned it and if he would not have added the reproach of its existence to the other reproaches of meagre orthodoxy which he addressed to the residents of Egypt. The silence of the redactor of the book of Jeremiah cannot be over-estimated, and leads us to exclude the possibility that around 580 B.C.E. the temple of Yahu at Elephantine had already been built. On the other hand, great importance attaches to the testimony of Aramaic documents of Elephantine,[3] deriving from around the end of the fifth century B.C.E. (part of the remains of the Jewish community) which explicitly affirm that the construction of the temple on the island preceded the coming of Cambyses to Egypt (525 B.C.E.). But by how many years is not mentioned. The Jewish construction of a temple before 586, that is, before the destruction of the Temple of Jerusalem, certainly has very little probability. If we add the 'pre-exilic, pre-Deuteronomic' character of the Hebrew religion of this remote garrison post, the problem

---

[1] See n. 3, p. 363; and the chapter by B. Porten, 'The Jews in Egypt' below (pp. 372–400), and pertinent bibliography.

[2] See E. Volterra, '*yhwdy* and *rmy* nei papiri aramaici del V secolo provenienti dall' Egitto', *RAL*, Classe di Scienze morali, Ser. 8, 18 (1963), 131–73.

[3] A. E. Cowley, *Aramaic Papyri of the Fifth Century B.C.* (Oxford, 1923), nn. 30 and 31.

becomes much more complex. Many and varied have been the proposals
and the opinions of scholars. But not one is definitive, because of the
lack of documents that can decide the question with absolute certainty.
I ask whether I, too, could not advance an hypothesis on the origin and
the date of the Hebrew colony of Elephantine? My hypothesis is first
that the settlement in Elephantine of the Jewish colony which built the
temple of Yahu could not be much more ancient than the coming of
Cambyses (the documents which treat the subject come from the end
of the fifth century B.C.E., and in any case at the distance of a few
generations an antiquated style may have been used on purpose to give
the impression of remoteness!); and secondly that the settlers could
have been Judeans who had lived in exile and after 538 B.C.E., in
consequence of the edict of Cyrus, returned from the regions of
Babylonia to their own country. But instead of staying in Judea,
possibly because of disagreements with local chiefs or for other reasons,
these Jews preferred to take refuge in the hospitable country of
Egypt – where, as we know, other Jews had already been living for
generations. These new settlers were located at the southern border
under the then sovereign, Amasis. This could explain the construction
of a temple without regard for the one that was being built in Jerusalem,
and the separation from the authorities in Jerusalem.

As for Cambyses, his respect for the temple of Yahu at Elephantine
(affirmed by the Aramaic papyri mentioned above) is in keeping with
the spirit of toleration of his father Cyrus. If we accept the 'Mesopotamian' origin of the Jewish group, we can then find a highly likely
explanation for the already cited 'Aramaic character' of the Jewish
settlers who in the very oldest documents speak – and write! – Aramaic
without Hebraic idioms. This fact cannot be explained only through
contacts with the Aramaic elements already present in Egypt during the
Saitic era, and even less can it be explained as a requirement of the
Achemenid government that its mercenaries were to use the language
of the empire. The fact is that between the Jewish settlers and the other
'Aramaic' Semites of Egypt, there existed a unity not only of language,
but of culture. The Aramaic and the Phoenician non-Jewish documents
are already attested during the seventh and sixth centuries B.C.E., and
then during the first Persian domination, by both official and private
documentation from various zones of Egypt (Daphne, Memphis,
Hermopolis, Oxyrhynchus, Thebes, Assuan, Elephantine). In Syene
there were temples of the Semitic divinities worshipped by foreigners
who were settled in Egypt; the Letters of Hermopolis locate in Syene
the temples of Nabu, Banit-Syene, Bethel and Melkat-Shemin.[1] As for

---

[1] E. Bresciani and M. Kamil, *Le lettere aramaiche di Hermopoli* (Rome, 1966) (= *Mem-*
orie, Accademia Nazionale Lincei, Series 8, vol. 12, 5).

these sanctuaries (which had in common, because of the identity of the divinities to whom they were dedicated, the devotion of Babylonians, Arameans, Phoenicians and also Hebrews drawn by the 'queen of heaven'), we do not know if they existed before the conquest of Egypt by Cambyses (as is the case with the temple of Yahu at Elephantine). But it seems probable that they were built after the Achemenid conquest, and in consequence of the reinforcement and enlargement of the Semitic colony at the southern border of the country. The cemetery of the Semites in Syene was not at all far from the Ptolemaic temple of Isis in Assuan.[1]

Memphis, the capital, and its citadel 'the white wall', were fortified (Herodotus III.91); the presence of Semitic soldiers, of *ḥaila* (the army), in Memphis is well documented; so soldiers were also employed in the arsenal at Memphis, the 'house of the ships'.[2] From a zone of the Semitic necropolis at Saqqara, which has furnished quantities of Aramaic material from the Persian era, comes also a funereal stele which is bilingual, hieroglyphic and Aramaic, dated in the fourth year of Xerxes (482 B.C.E.).[3] Semitic units were deployed in the delta in Daphne and Migdol; and in Tell Maskhuta there was a group of Arabs worshipping the Goddess Ilat (Han-Ilat).[4]

The Egyptian military class appears to be recognized as having a position of authority in the decree of Darius I, in which the Great King ordered the Egyptian law, in force prior to the conquest of the country, to be collected and written down.[5] As a matter of fact, along with the scribes and the priests, the 'warriors' are also considered competent in this undertaking. The presence of Egyptian detachments in Syene, alongside Semitic ones, is attested. Hieroglyphic documents bring to our knowledge in the Persian era Egyptian 'Heads of the Army', like Ahmosis, of whom we have two steles, both from Memphis.[6] In one of them he affirms that he engendered respect for the sacred bull Apis 'in the heart of the people and also of the foreigners of all the alien countries who were in Egypt'. Also the architect Khnumibre, active during the reign of Darius I, bears the titles of 'chief of the army' and 'chief of the troops'.[7] The Persian army – actually Persian only because it was at the service of Persia – was formed of a mosaic of elements from

---

[1] See Kornfeld, 'Aramäische Sarkophage in Assuan', *WZKM*,61 (1967), 10–16.
[2] N. Aimé-Giron, *Textes araméens d'Egypte* (Cairo, 1931), pp. 12ff.
[3] *CIS*, 2, 122; Grelot, *Documents*, p. 341, n. 85.
[4] J. Rabinowitz, 'Aramaic inscriptions of the Fifth Century B.C.E. from a North Arabian Shrine in Egypt', *JNES*, 15 (1956), 1–9.
[5] See above, note 1, p. 360.
[6] Posener, *La première domination*, nn. 6 and 7.
[7] Posener, *La première domination*, nn. 11–23.

the various provinces of the Achemenid empire: Persians, Babylonians, Phoenicians, Cilicians, Ionians, Carians, Greeks were, after all, present in Egypt in the Persian era not only as military men, but also in the exercise of various trades, for the needs of the civil population and of the soldiers of the garrisons. These elements, and the Semitic military colonies, established themselves solidly in the country and there survived the Persian domination.

The satrap was the supreme authority in Egypt, not only for administrative and military affairs but also for the administration of justice;[1] the demotic papyrus Rylands IX and Aramaic documents show that a petition to the satrap represented the final appeal.[2] The respect for indigenous rights and laws on the part of Darius I is shown by the above-mentioned decree, which ordered the transcription of the juridical 'corpus' of Egyptian laws not only in demotic but also in Aramaic. However, for the administration of justice and for the organization of tribunals, we owe our knowledge essentially to Aramaic Egyptian documents, especially to those of the military colony of Elephantine. We know that in the districts, the governor, the *fratarak*, presided over a civil tribunal in which rights and laws were applied according to the nationality of the man to be judged, and hence according to the Egyptian rights and laws for the natives. The 'chief of the army' (*rab-haila*) had judiciary functions limited to military personnel. Aramaic documents name also 'judges' and 'royal judges' (they could be the same as 'judges of the province'), *tiftaya*, police functionaries, and *gaskaya*, informers or spies. The examination of juridical demotic documents of the Persian era, regarding private laws on contracts, show that the formulae relative to this law do not present direct continuity with those of the period immediately preceding. Elements of law and legal formulae in certain cases appear to have passed over into the usage of the Jewish mercenary troops of Elephantine. Some legal elements (as, for example, the obligation to furnish documents proving the right to possess or to alienate, or the exact description of property of buildings sold or ceded) were common to Egyptian private law and to the neo-Babylonian private law. I have already spoken of the policy of the Achemenid sovereigns, and particularly of that of Cambyses and

[1] For the code of laws in Egypt during the Persian era, and especially for laws and the administration of justice, as it appears from contemporary Aramaic documents, see R. Yaron, *Law of the Aramaic Papyri*, (Oxford, 1961); Porten, *Archives*, pp. 189ff; Seidl, *Rechtsgeschichte*, pp. 86ff; Y. Muffs, *Studies in the Aramaic Legal Papyri from Elephantine* (Leiden, 1968); and A. Verger, *Richerche giuridiche sui papiri aramaici di Elefantina* (Rome, 1965), with ample bibliography.

[2] F. Ll. Griffith, *Catalogue of the Demotic Papyri in the John Rylands Library*, III (1909), IX.

Darius I towards the temples and the Egyptian priesthood.[1] After the revocation of the restrictive decree of Cambyses, life in the temples does not seem to have immediately suffered interruptions or special modifications; and the only substantial change was the disappearance, in Thebes, of the figure and the function of the 'divine consort' or 'consort of Amon', a function which had been politically very important under the twenty-fifth and twenty-sixth dynasties. The great possessions she owned and administered were probably absorbed into the 'domain of Amon'. Darius I ordered an imposing temple to be built in the oasis of El Kharga, which reflected in architecture and decoration the purest Saitic tradition. The influence of the Egyptian ambience in religion as well as in artistic themes is notable in the steles and in the sarcophagi belonging to Semites established in Egypt, even though there are some corruptions and interpretations of the Egyptian stylistic elements. A certain number of monuments, statues, reliefs, show male subjects wearing clothes of a special style, a long skirt knotted on the breast, worn over a short jacket, with sleeves of varying length, with a V-neck. Interpreted as a Persian style of clothing and, as such, an element suggesting its chronological attribution to the twenty-seventh dynasty, it has been recently demonstrated by this writer to have been a motif of a fashion already diffused in Egypt during the twenty-sixth dynasty, so that it could denote Assyrian influence. During the Persian domination, however, it appears that this sort of dress acquired a new vogue. We also find these clothes worn by personages certainly active during the Persian era, like the doctor-in-chief, Wedjahorresnet and the 'chief of the treasury', Ptahhotep.

Various objects of Persian make, executed in Egypt by Persian artists, or imported from Asia, have been found in Egypt. Fortunately, the presence of Persian artists in Egypt is confirmed by one of the letters on leather sent by the satrap Arsames from Susa to his *peqid* Nekhtihur.[2] In this he requests that the sculptor Hanzani execute a sculpture of 'a horse with its rider, as he already did for me, and other sculptures', and that the sculptures be brought to Susa.

On the other hand, Egyptian monuments were found in Susa. We know that Egyptian labourers and architects took part in the construction of the palace of Darius I at Persepolis, and the influence of Egyptian art and architecture on those of Persia is well known.[3] The

---

[1] See n. 1, p. 360.   [2] See n. 2, p. 369.

[3] See J. D. Cooney, 'The Lions of Leontopolis', *Bulletin of The Brooklyn Museum*, 15 (1953), p. 17; A. Roes, 'Achemenid Influence upon Egyptian and Nomad Art', *ArtAs*, 15 (1953), 21; Posener, *La première domination*, p. 190; M. A. Dieulafoy, *L'art antique de la Perse* (5 vols. Paris, 1884–99).

composition of a rather interesting literary text, written in demotic, 'the teachings of Anekhsheshoni',[1] should probably be dated in the Persian era. The setting out of the 'teachings' within an historic framework followed by a series of moral maxims, very closely resembles the structure of the Wisdom of Ahikar, of Assyrian origin. The Aramaic version of Ahikar circulated in Semitic Egyptian circles, since a copy of a papyrus dated in the fifth century B.C.E. was found at Elephantine.[2] That the proverbs of Ahikar were known to Egyptian culture is proved, after all, by the mention of the name of the Assyrian sage in a demotic text of the Roman era.[3]

The memory of the Persian conquest of Egypt, and of the military colonies of the Persian government in the country, persisted and is indicated throughout the fourth and third centuries B.C.E. by the term *Mtj*, 'Mede' or 'Persian', borne by individuals who belonged to the military colonies of the Achemenid age. This word *Mtj* probably corresponds to the Greek term *Persaigyptios*. The original ethnic meaning was preserved in Coptic proper names, while the Coptic *matoi*, 'soldier', perpetuated in the national consciousness of the Egyptians and in their native language the memory of the Persian military conquerors; just as in Syriac *romaja*, 'Romans', usually signifies 'soldiers'.[4]

D. THE JEWS IN EGYPT

EARLY IMPRESSIONS AND CONTACTS

Egypt played a formative role in shaping the experience and moulding the mentality of early Israel. On the one hand, she served as a haven for the hungry (Gen. 12: 10ff; 26: 1f, 42–46), provided opportunity for the rejected (Gen. 39ff), and offered sanctuary to the political dissident (1 Kings 11: 40). On the other hand, she was the house of bondage (Exod. 13: 3, 14), and the symbol of abominable sexual practices (Lev. 18); the offspring of a mixed Egyptian–Israelite marriage was likely to curse God (Lev. 24: 10ff). Still Israel's sojourn there taught solicitude for the stranger (Exod. 22: 21) and acceptance of the Egyptian, after the third generation, into the community of Israel (Deut. 23: 8f), even as

---

[1] S. R. K. Glanville, *The Instructions of Onchsheshonqy* (London, 1955).
[2] See the new studies and translation of Grelot, *Documents*, pp. 427–52.
[3] See W. Spiegelberg, 'Achikar in einem demotischen Texte der römischen Kaiserzeit', *OLZ*, 37 (1930), 962.
[4] See E. Bresciani, 'Annotazioni demotiche ai Περσαι της Επιγονης', *La parola del passato*, CXLII–CXLIV (Naples, 1972), 128.

reflection upon the Exodus was meant to inculcate consideration for the widow and orphan, the poor debtor and resident alien (Lev. 25: 35ff; Deut. 24: 17f).

Egyptian sources make an invidious distinction between Asiatics and Egyptians. The latter are 'people' while the former are 'foreigners'.[1] Syro-Palestine might be a good place to live when one was beset by troubles at home, as Sinuhe discovered, but Egypt was the only place to die and be buried.[2] The only explicit reference to Israel in contemporary Egyptian sources appears at the conclusion of a lengthy hymn of victory over the Libyans by Merneptah (c. 1219) where it is said that 'Israel is laid waste, his seed is not.'[3] In the third century B.C.E. Greek History of Egypt by the Egyptian priest Manetho, as excerpted by the Jewish historian Josephus (first century C.E.), the inhabitants of Jerusalem were descendants of the impious Hyksos who had terrorized Egypt for 511 years until forced out by King Thutmose (Thummosis) (Josephus, Contra Apionem 1.14, 73ff). They occupied Egypt again 518 years later and, in alliance with a band of leprous slaves led by a Heliopolitan priest Osarseph-Moses, polluted the people, mutilated idols, and pillaged temples for thirteen years until expelled by Ameno-phis and his son Ramses. Meanwhile, Moses had enjoined upon his group many laws opposed to Egyptian custom (Contra Apionem 1.26, 228ff). As the Egyptians retold Israelite history, Joseph was not a benefactor but a plunderer, and Moses not a leader of oppressed slaves but of sacrilegious lepers. The Exodus was not a divine deliverance but an ignominious expulsion. Though it is not possible to ascertain the antiquity of Manetho's account, the antipathy toward the Israelities is not surprising given the general Egyptian bias against Asiatics.

Despite the negative sentiments that existed on either side, Israel and Egypt usually appeared as allies during the 400 years or so of Israelite monarchy. Solomon secured his western border through marital alliance with the Pharaoh (Siamun?), who gave a dowry to his daughter of the recently sacked city of Gezer (1 Kings 3: 1; 9: 15f).[4] During the reign of Ahab, Egypt (Musri) sent a 1,000-man contingent to the Syro-Palestinian coalition which stopped Shalmaneser III of Assyria at

---

[1] 'The Instruction for King Meri-ka-Re', ANET, p. 416, lines 90ff; 'The Admonitions of Ipuwer', ANET, p. 441ff (cf. iff).
[2] 'The Story of Sinuhe', ANET, pp. 18ff.
[3] 'Hymn of Victory of Mer-ne-Ptah', ANET, 376ff.
[4] A. Malamat, 'Aspects of the Foreign Policies of David and Solomon', JNES, 22 (1963), 19ff; A. Malamat, 'The Kingdom of David and Solomon in its Contact with Egypt and Aram Naharaim', BAR, 2 (1964), 89–98; Y. Aharoni, The Land of the Bible (Philadelphia, 1967), p. 272.

Qarqar in 853.[1] Jehoram son of Ahab was suspected of having hired
the 'kings of the Hittites and the kings of Egypt' to relieve the Aramean
siege of Samaria (2 Kings 7: 6).[2] In 724 Hoshea, king of Israel, sought
the aid of Tefnakhte, ruler of Egypt, at Sais, against Shalmaneser V (2
Kings 17: 3f)[3] and later Tirhakah, king of Ethiopia, came to Hezekiah's
aid against Sennacherib (2 Kings 19: 9; Herodotus, II.141).[4] Towards
the end of 588, Apries (589–570) came to the aid of Zedekiah,
besieged in Jerusalem by Nebuchadnezzar (Jer. 37: 5ff; Ezek. 17: 15,
29: 1ff, 30: 20ff, 31: 1ff; Lachish letter III, lines 13ff).[5] On only two
occasions did a pharaoh attack Israel – Shishak harboured the fugitive
Jeroboam (1 Kings 11: 40) and in the fifth year of the reign of his rival
Rehoboam (c. 924) embarked upon a plundering campaign of both
Judah and Israel (1 Kings 14: 25f; 2 Chron. 12: 2ff)[6] and Necho slew
Josiah at the mountain pass of Megiddo for attempting to thwart his
northward passage to aid Assyria against Babylonia (2 Kings 23: 29f;
2 Chron. 35: 20ff).[7]

As an ally, Egypt proved to be a 'broken reed' and the prophets
looked askance at any reliance upon her. Hosea mocked northern
Israel's oscillation between Assyria and Egypt (Hos. 7: 11, 12: 1) –
probably referring to the diplomatic courting by Menahem before 738
when the 'patron king' (Hos. 5: 13, 10: 6) Tiglath-pileser III extended
his protection (2 Kings 15: 19).[8] Jeremiah castigated Judah for similar
pursuit, now of Egypt, now of Assyria, prior to Josiah's reform of 622
(Jer. 2: 18).[9] Both Hosea and Jeremiah asserted that this chase after
lovers would end in shame (Hos. 8: 13 to 9: 6; Jer. 2: 33–37). Isaiah
condemned Israel, and Jeremiah and Ezekiel denounced Judah for their
expectations of deliverance through Egyptian military assistance (Isa.
30: 1ff, 31: 1ff, 36: 4ff; Jer. 37: 5ff; Ezek. 17: 11ff), while all three
prophets pronounced oracles of doom against Egypt, Ezekiel citing her

[1] Shalmaneser III's 'Monolith Inscription', *ANET*, p. 278f; H. Tadmor, 'Que and Muṣri', *IEJ*, 11 (1961), 143ff.
[2] Tadmor, *IEJ*, 11 (1961), 149.
[3] H. Goedicke and W. F. Albright, 'The End of "So, King of Egypt"', *BASOR*, 171 (1963), 64ff.
[4] J. Bright, *A History of Israel* (2nd edn; Philadelphia, 1972).
[5] A. Malamat, 'The Last Kings of Judah and the Fall of Jerusalem', *IEJ*, 18 (1968), 151f. K. S. Freedy and D. B. Redford, 'The Dates in Ezekiel', *JAOS*, 90 (1970), 470ff, 481.
[6] B. Mazar, 'The Campaign of Pharaoh Shishak to Palestine', *VTSup*, 4 (1957), 57ff; Aharoni, *Land of the Bible*, pp. 283ff.
[7] D. J. Wiseman, *Chronicles of Chaldaean Kings (626–556 B.C.)* (London, 1956), pp. 19f, 63; Malamat, *IEJ*, 18 (1968), 139.
[8] H. L. Ginsberg 'Hosea, Book of', *EncJud*, 8 (1971), 1917.
[9] J. Milgrom, 'The Date of Jeremiah Chapter 2', *JNES*, 14 (1955), 65ff.

especially for failure to aid Judah effectively (Isa. 19 to 20; Jer. 43: 8ff, 44: 30, 46: 1ff, Ezek. 29 to 32, especially 29: 6ff). Despite their denunciations, all three prophets foretold the restoration of Egypt subsequent to her punishment (Isa. 19: 18ff; Jer. 46: 26; Ezek. 29: 13ff). Thus even the prophets who condemned Egypt preserved for her a special place in the divine plan.

JEWISH SETTLEMENT

The Egyptian orientation of both Israel and Judah resulted not in the independence of those states before the onslaught of Assyria and Babylonia respectively but in the migration of fugitives after the collapse of both rebellions. Isaiah spoke of the ingathering of exiles from 'Lower Egypt, from Pathros, from Ethiopia' (Isa. 11: 11), while Jeremiah paired the Jewish community in Egypt with that of Judah even before the Destruction (Jer. 24: 8). Not every fugitive received asylum; the prophet Uriah, son of Shemaiah, was extradited at the behest of King Jehoiakim and subsequently executed (Jer. 26: 20ff). Nor did every émigré migrate voluntarily; the young King Jehoahaz was deposed after only three months, apparently after indicating an anti-Egyptian orientation, and sent captive to Egypt (2 Kings 23: 29ff; 2 Chron. 36: 1–3). But on the whole the Jews received a ready welcome. Fearful for their lives after the assassination of the Babylonian-appointed governor, Gedaliah, son of Ahikam, the remnant Jewish community, under the leadership of Johanan, son of Kareah, fled to Egypt, forcefully taking the prophet Jeremiah with them (Jer. 43: 1ff). The dominant group among these refugees consisted of soldiers (Jer. 40: 13, 43: 5) and in lower Egypt they settled at sites known for their military garrisons, namely Migdol, Tahpanhes (= Daphnae; compare Herodotus II.30, 152ff) and Memphis (Herodotus II.30, 112, 152ff). They also found their way into Pathros (= upper Egypt), though no sites there are singled out (Jer. 44: 1). The wrath of Jeremiah pursued these settlers in their new homes as he prophesied their total destruction (Jer. 44: 13f). In an oracle delivered against Egypt he foretold its capture by Nebuchadnezzar: 'her mercenaries... shall turn and flee' (Jer. 46: 13, 21, 25f). In a similar oracle delivered from Babylonian exile in 571 B.C.E., the prophet Ezekiel foresaw complete destruction of Egypt by Nebuchadnezzar: 'from Migdol to Syene they shall fall within her by the sword' (Ezek. 29: 10, 17ff, 30:6). Nebuchadnezzar may have campaigned in 568/67 against Pharaoh Amasis,[1] but he failed to capture Egypt. As for the Jews there, Deutero-Isaiah singled out 'the land of

[1] Freedy and Redford, *JAOS*, 90 (1970), 472f, 483.

Syene' as the southernmost point from which they would be redeemed and restored to Zion (Isa. 49: 12 according to 1QIsa*a*).

DOCUMENTATION

Extra-biblical knowledge of Jewish settlement in Egypt derives from the Persian period and centres around the southern border posts of Syene and the adjacent island of Elephantine. This knowledge stems basically from Aramaic texts – papyri, parchments and ostraca. Isolated and fragmentary texts were discovered during the nineteenth century and published in volume two of *Corpus Inscriptionum Semiticarum* (Paris, 1888). Three great discoveries made at the turn of the century were published in 1906,[1] 1911[2] and 1953[3] respectively. Subsequent finds were published in 1931,[4] 1936,[5] 1954,[6] 1960[7] and 1966.[8] Several dozen ostraca have been published over the years but the promised corpus of all the texts has still to appear.[9] Still unpublished are recently discovered papyrus fragments from Saqqara,[10] as well as papyri from wadi Daliyeh in the Jordan valley,[11] which will shed indirect light on Jewish life in Egypt. Study of the material has been extensive and has yielded

---

[1] A. H. Sayce and A. E. Cowley, *Aramaic Papyri Discovered at Assuan* (London, 1906).

[2] Ed. Sachau, *Aramäische Papyrus und Ostraka aus einer jüdischen Militär-Kolonie zu Elephantine* (Leipzig, 1911). The papyri in the Sayce–Cowley and Sachau collections were republished by A. E. Cowley, *Aramaic Papyri of the Fifth Century B.C.* (Oxford, 1923; photographic reproduction by D. Zeller, 1967).

[3] E. G. Kraeling, *The Brooklyn Museum Aramaic Papyri. New Documents of the Fifth Century B.C. from the Jewish Colony at Elephantine* (New Haven, 1953).

[4] N. Aimé-Giron, *Textes araméens d'Égypte* (Cairo, 1931).

[5] H. Bauer and B. Meisner, 'Ein aramäischer Pachtvertrag aus dem 7. Jahre Darius I', *SPAW*, 72 (1936), 414–24.

[6] G. R. Driver, *Aramaic Documents of the Fifth Century B.C.* (Oxford, 1954; photographic reproduction by D. Zeller, 1968. Abr. and rev., 1957).

[7] E. Bresciani, 'Papiri aramaici egiziani di epoca persiana presso il Museo Civico di Padova', *RSO*, 35 (1960), 11–24. See, too, the papyrus published by her: 'Un papiro aramaico da El Hibeh del Museo Archeologico di Firenze,' *Aegyptus*, 39 (1959), 3–8.

[8] E. Bresciani and M. Kamil, 'Le lettere aramaiche di Hermopoli', *Atti della Accademia Nazionale dei Lincei, Classe di Scienze Morale, Memorie*, ser. VIII, 12 (1966), 357–428.

[9] Some ostraca were published by Sayce–Cowley and Sachau. Those discovered in the French expedition have been entered into the Clermont-Ganneau collection and are being published by A. Dupont-Sommer.

[10] See the notice in *Orientalia*, 37 (1968), 103.

[11] Preliminary reports of these fourth century B.C.E. papyri have been given by their editor, F. M. Cross, Jr.: 'The Discovery of the Samaria Papyri', *BA*, 26 (1963), 110–21; F. M. Cross, 'Aspects of Samaritan and Jewish History in Late Persian and Hellenistic Times', *HTR*, 59 (1966), 201–11; *idem*, 'Papyri of the Fourth Century B.C. from Daliyeh', in *New Directions in Biblical Archaeology*, ed. D. N. Freedman and J. C. Greenfield (New York, 1971), pp. 45–69.

numerous articles, as well as monographs in German (1910–12),[1] French (1915–37),[2] Dutch (1928),[3] Hebrew (1948)[4] and Italian (1965).[5] A comprehensive study in English was published by the author in 1968.[6] A corpus, in a French translation, of 108 entries appeared in 1972[7] and one of 51 entries, with Hebrew, and English translation by the author, in 1974.[8] Recent research has been dominated by legal[9] and epigraphic[10] investigations. When studied against the background of Persian, Babylonian, biblical, Egyptian, Greek and Talmudic sources, the Aramaic texts vividly illuminate many aspects of the life of Jewish soldiers at Elephantine.

The Aramaic documents consist of letters, lists, legal contracts and literary or historical texts. The best-preserved texts are those acquired on the antiquities market; they consist of the eleven contracts of the family archive of Ananiah son of Azariah (Kraeling, 1–7, 9–12), the ten contracts of the family archive of Mibtahiah daughter of Mahseiah (*CAP* 5, 6, 8, 9, 13–15, 20, 25, 28) and the thirteen parchment letters of the satrap Arsames and other Persian officials (Driver 1–13). Most of the papyri discovered in the 1907 excavations of Otto Rubensohn are either damaged or have lines or parts of lines missing. They consist of the communal archive of Jedaniah, son of Gemariah, which comprised eight letters (*CAP* 21, 27, 30, 31, 33, 34 plus 56, 37, 38), one memorandum (*CAP* 32), one (*CAP* 22) and perhaps at least three more lists of names (*CAP* 12, 19, 23; compare *CAP* 24, 51–53); three (*CAP* 39, 40, 42) and perhaps four (*CAP* 41) letters of Hoshaiah, son of Nathan;

---

[1] N. Peters, *Die jüdische Gemeinde von Elephantine-Syene und ihr Tempel* (Freiburg i.B., 1912); H. Anneler, *Zur Geschichte der Juden von Elephantine* (Berne, 1912); E. Meyer, *Der Papyrusfund von Elephantine* (Leipzig, 1911; 2nd edn., 1912).

[2] A. van Hoonacker, *Une communauté judéo-araméenne à Éléphantine*, The Schweich Lectures, 1914 (London, 1915); A. Vincent, *La Religion des judéo-araméens d'Éléphantine* (Paris, 1937).

[3] C. G. Wagenaar, *De joodsche Kolonie van Jeb-Syene in de 5de Eeuw voor Christus* (Gröningen, 1928).

[4] P. Korngrun, *Jewish Military Colonies in Ancient Times* (Tel Aviv, 1948; in Hebrew).

[5] A. Verger, *Ricerche giuridiche sui papyri aramaici di Elefantina* (Rome, 1965).

[6] B. Porten, *Archives from Elephantine: The Life of an Ancient Jewish Military Colony* (Berkeley, 1968).

[7] P. Grelot, *Documents araméens d'Egypte* (Paris, 1972).

[8] B. Porten in collaboration with J. C. Greenfield, *Jews of Elephantine and Arameans of Syene (Fifth Century B.C.E.): Fifty Aramaic Texts with Hebrew and English Translations* (Jerusalem, 1974).

[9] R. Yaron, *Introduction to the Law of the Aramaic Papyri* (Oxford, 1961); A. Verger, *Ricerche*; Y. Muffs, *Studies in the Aramaic Legal Papyri from Elephantine*, Studia et Documenta ad Iura orientis antiqui pertinentia, 8 (Leiden, 1969).

[10] J. Naveh, *The Development of the Aramaic Script*, Proceedings of the Israel Academy of Sciences and Humanities, v/1. (Jerusalem, 1970).

miscellaneous legal texts (*CAP* 1–4, 7, 10, 11, 18, 29, 35, 36, 43–49); the *Words of Ahikar* and fragments of the Behistun inscription; administrative texts and letters of the Persian authorities (*CAP* 16, 17, 24, 26; compare *CAP* 51–53); and memoranda written on the back of texts of the Behistun inscription (*CAP* 61–63). Thirteen ostraca mention the woman Ahutab[1] and the seven intact letters discovered at Hermopolis were destined for members of an Aramean family residing at Syene (Bresciani and Kamil 1–4) and at Luxor (Bresciani and Kamil 5–7). Another group of three letters was written from Migdol to their relatives at Elephantine (Bresciani 1–3). The earliest contract (515 B.C.E.) is a land-lease between the west-Semite Padi and an Egyptian (Meissner papyrus).

ESTABLISHMENT OF THE COLONY AT ELEPHANTINE

The earliest Elephantine contract is a deed of exchange dating from 495 B.C.E. (*CAP* 1), while the latest document is a letter of the year 399 (Kraeling 13). A letter of 407 B.C.E. reported that the Jewish community at Elephantine, with a temple to its God, YHW, was well established before the Persian conquest in 525 (*CAP* 30: 13f; 31: 12f). There have been numerous suggestions regarding the date and origin of the Elephantine colony, some tracing its inhabitants to north Israelites or Samaritans,[2] others to the allegedly Jewish colony of Yadi in southern Anatolia,[3] and one scholar to the Hebrews who remained in Egypt at the time of the Exodus.[4] The most informative notice on the subject is the statement in *The Letter of Aristeas* about the migration of Jews to Egypt under the Ptolemies and under the Persians which adds 'and even before this others had been *sent out* [italics mine] as auxiliaries to fight in the army of Psammetichus against the king of the Ethiopians' (line 13). Psammetichus II did campaign against Nubia in 591 B.C.E. and his mercenary forces left their graffiti on the colossus of Ramses II at Abu Simbel. The names indicate Carians, Ionians, Rhodians, and Phoenicians but no Jews.[5]

[1] Cf. the references in Porten, *Archives*, p. 136, n. 82.
[2] C. van Gelderen, 'Samaritaner und Juden in Elephantine-Syene', *OLZ*, 15 (1912), 337ff; F. Nau, 'Juifs et Samaritains à Éléphantine', *JA*, 10th series, 18 (1911), 66off; Vincent, *Religion*, pp. 357ff. [See above p. 364 for E. Bresciani's views. Eds.]
[3] C. H. Gordon, 'The Origin of the Jews in Elephantine', *JNES*, 14 (1955), 56ff.
[4] E. C. B. Maclaurin, 'Date of the Foundation of the Jewish Colony at Elephantine', *JNES*, 27 (1968), 89ff.
[5] S. Sauneron and J. Yoyotte, 'La campagne nubienne de Psammétique II et sa signification historique', *BIFAO*, 50 (1952), 200f; *idem*, 'Sur la politique palestinienne des rois saïtes', *VT*, 2 (1952), 131ff; N. Slouschz, *Thesaurus of Phoenician Inscriptions* (Tel Aviv, 1942), nos. 53–4 (Hebrew). A. Bernand and O. Masson, 'Les inscriptions grecques d'Abou-Simbel', *REG*, 70 (1957), 1–46.

It is more likely that the ruler referred to in *The Letter of Aristeas* was the founder of the Saitic dynasty, Psammetichus I. To establish his position over the other local dynasts, to unite Egypt under his rule and overthrow the Assyrian yoke he relied on foreign mercenaries.[1] King Manasseh of Judah had earlier been forced to send a military contingent to aid Ashurbanipal in his conquest of Egypt.[2] Now, around the year 650 B.C.E. when Assyria was preoccupied with rebellion nearby, Manasseh sought independence from Assyria and committed his troops to Psammetichus to aid him in his campaign against the Ethiopians.[3] These forces would have been subsequently stationed at Elephantine (compare Herodotus II.30) to replace the Egyptian soldiers there who had earlier fled to Nubia because of their dissatisfaction with the new state of affairs in Egypt.[4] Allusions in the Book of Deuteronomy, discovered in the Jerusalem Temple under Josiah (2 Kings 22 to 23; 2 Chron. 34 to 35), support the assumption of a migration under Manasseh. The book forbade the king to return the 'people' (= soldiery [see 2 Kings 13: 7]) to Egypt in exchange for horses (Deut. 17: 16) and objected to worship of the heavenly bodies (Deut. 4: 19). The first as well as the second injunction may echo the activity of Manasseh, who was known to have introduced worship of the heavenly bodies into the Temple itself (2 Kings 21: 5ff, 23: 4; 2 Chron. 33: 1ff). This paganization did not go unopposed (2 Kings 21: 10ff), and it is possible that alienated priests fled to Elephantine and there established a new temple.

No Egyptian documents explicitly mention the Jews in Elephantine or elsewhere in Egypt but two texts may refer to them. Under Apries, the 'Governor of the Door of the Southern Countries', Nesuhor, dissuaded the mercenaries at Elephantine from desertion to Nubia. In addition to Greeks these included '*zmw*-Asiatics and *Sttyw*-Asiatics.[5] One term may refer to Jews and the other to Arameans. Similarly, a fragmentary demotic papyrus from Elephantine (529 B.C.E.) shortly before the Persian conquest, recorded two different Semitic groups – 60 *rmt n Ḥr* ('Palestinians') and 15 *rmt n 'Išwr* ('Syrians') – in a caravan to Nubia.[6]

[1] F. K. Kienitz, *Die politische Geschichte Ägyptens vom 7. bis zum 4. Jahrhundert* (Berlin, 1953), pp. 9ff.

[2] J. B. Pritchard, *ANET*, pp. 294ff.

[3] For the Nubian campaign of Psammetichus I, cf. Sauneron and Yoyotte, 'Campagne'.

[4] Kienitz, *Die politische Geschichte*, p. 40.

[5] J. H. Breasted, *Ancient Records of Egypt. Historical Documents from the Earliest Times to the Persian Conquest* (Chicago, 1906), vol. 4, p. 508, and discussion in Porten, *Archives*, p. 15, n. 55.

[6] W. Erichsen, 'Erwägung eines Zuges nach Nubien unter Amasis in einem demotischen Text', *Klio*, 34 (1941), 56–61.

GARRISONS AT ELEPHANTINE–SYENE

None of the Elephantine Aramaic documents refers to Greeks or Phoenicians. Instead we find Babylonians (*CAP* 6: 19), Caspians (Kraeling 3: 2, 23f, 4: 11, 12: 4), Khorazmians (*CAP* 6: 2, 8: 23), Medes (Kraeling 5: 17), and of course Persians. The garrison at Elephantine must have been predominantly Jewish and was known as 'the Jewish force' (*ḥayla'*) (*CAP* 21, 22), while the one on the mainland must have been mixed, since it was simply known as the 'Syenian force' (*CAP* 24: 33). In the legal contracts, individual Jews were variously designated 'Aramean of (the fortress of) Syene' (*CAP* 5: 2, 13: 2 etc.), 'Aramean of [the fortress of] Elephantine' (*CAP* 25: 2, 35: 2 etc.) or 'Jew of (the fortress of) Elephantine' (*CAP* 6: 3, 9: 2 etc.). In petitions the Jews called themselves 'citizens (*ba'alē*) of Elephantine' (*CAP* 30: 22) and their leaders were designated 'Syenians who [ho]ld [prop]erty in the fortress of Elephantine' (*CAP* 33: 6). Classical sources reported that Egypt had a warrior class devoted exclusively to military training and bequeathing its profession to its children (Herodotus, II.164ff; Xenophon, *Anabasis* 1.8.9; Diodorus 1.73). This situation foreshadowed the Greek cleruchy of the Hellenistic period and may serve as a model for understanding the condition of the Jewish soldiers at Elephantine–Syene during the Persian period.

The organization of the Jews was a socio-military one. Individuals, whether men or women, not associated with the Temple, were members of a detachment (*degel*), apparently equivalent to the Persian chiliarchy, which was further subdivided into centuries. Jews and non-Jews served together in the same detachment (Kraeling 11: 1f), but all the century and detachment leaders were non-Jews. Names such as the Persian Varyazata (*CAP* 6: 3, 13: 2) and Haumadata (*CAP* 8: 2, 9: 2), the Babylonian Iddinnabu (Kraeling 5: 2, 14: 2, 7: 1f; *CAP* 20: 2ff) and Nabukudurri (*CAP* 7: 3, 29: 1f, 35: 2; Kraeling 11: 1f, 12: 2f), and the Aramean Nabuaqab (*CAP* 22: 20) were borne by these leaders. The garrison commanders were all Persians: Ravaka at the beginning of the fifth century (*CAP* 1: 3), and, toward the end, Vidranga (*CAP* 20: 4f, 25: 2ff; Kraeling 8: 2f) and, later, his son Naphaina (*CAP* 30: 7), both of whom were attached to Syene but appeared to control the Elephantine garrison as well.

The Elephantine documents contain virtually no information on the military tasks of its soldiers. These were imposed by the natural features of the region and must have been similar throughout the ages. The first cataract above (that is, south of) Assuan marked the limits of deep water navigation in Egypt. Special cataract boatmen were employed to navigate the rapids and the area beyond (Herodotus II.29; *CAP* 5: 13, 6: 10f, 8: 7f, 26: 1, 7; Kraeling 12: 20). Elephantine was thus necessarily a point of trans-shipment, and the garrison there would probably be entrusted with the maintenance of the Nile boats (*CAP* 26, compare Aimé-Giron 5–24), supervision of commerce and the collection of tribute from the Nubians (Herodotus III.97). It was also a staging-point for expeditions into Nubia[1] and for caravans into Egypt (Papyri Loeb 1).[2] The Elephantine soldiers would have accompanied both (see *CAP* 38: 3f; Bresciani 1: 2). Demotic papyri and the inscription of the Aramaic word *by* ('house') indicate that quarrying activity at Elephantine and Syene continued to be carried on during the Saitic–Persian period.[3] The prominent Jewish woman, Mibtahiah, was married in succession to two Egyptians, Pia son of Pahi and Eshor son of Seho, respectively designated 'builder' (*CAP* 14: 2) and 'royal builder' (*CAP* 15: 2). As soldiers, the Jews may have worked in the quarries, supervised the work, or served as military escort on distant quarrying expeditions. Another activity of theirs might have been involved with supervision of the Nilometer. One from Roman times is preserved on the south-east end of the island. The rise of the Nile was carefully charted to serve as a guide for water distribution and canal work and to forecast crop yield and government revenues (Strabo, XVII.1.148, 817).

In pursuit of their duties the Elephantine soldiers had contact with numerous officials at the local and provincial level. The province of which the Elephantine–Syene garrisons may have been the main sites was Tshetres, 'the Southern District' (*CAP* 24: 39, 43; 27: 9), corresponding to, if not identical with, the term 'Pathros, southern land', known from the Bible (Isa. 11: 11, Jer. 44: 1, 15) as a place of Jewish settlement. The chief official at Elephantine bore the title *frataraka*, 'the foremost' (compare the title *fratama* underlying biblical *partĕmim* [Esther 1: 3, 6: 9; Dan. 1: 3]) and, like the garrison commander under his jurisdiction there (*CAP* 25: 2ff; Kraeling 8: 2f) exercised both civil–judicial (*CAP* 20: 4) and military functions (*CAP* 30: 5ff; 31: 5ff). Here, too, the individuals holding the post bore Persian names, Ramandaina (*CAP* 20: 4) and Vidranga (*CAP* 27: 4, 30: 5; 31: 5). So

---

[1] Erichsen, *Klio*, 34 (1941).

[2] W. Spiegelberg, *Die demotischen Papyri Loeb* (Munich, 1931), pp. 1ff.

[3] W. Erichsen, 'Ein Bericht über Steinbrucharbeiten auf der Insel Elephantine in demotischer Schrift', in *Studi in memoria di I. Rosellini* (Pisa, 1955), 2, 75ff; *idem*, 'Zwei frühdemotische Urkunden aus Elephantine', in *Coptic Studies in Honor of Walter Ewing Crum* (Boston, 1950), pp. 272ff; A. H. Sayce, 'An Inscription of S-ankh-ka-Ra, Karian and other inscriptions', *PSBA*, 28 (1906), 174ff, pls. 2, 10; *idem*, 'An Aramaic Ostracon from Elephantine', *PSBA*, 30 (1908), 41.

did one of the leading judges, Damidata (*CAP* 6: 6). We may conjecture that the other provincial officials, the *typty*', 'police' and the *gauša-ka*, 'spies' (*CAP* 27: 9)[1] were likewise Persians. The only person with a Hebrew name holding an administrative position was 'Anani the Scribe (and) Chancellor' at the court of the satrap Arsames in Memphis (*CAP* 26: 23). In their difficulties with the Egyptian priests, who won the support of the *frataraka* and his son the garrison commander (*CAP* 30: 5ff; 31: 5ff), the Elephantine Jews looked to their co-religionist at court for backing (*CAP* 38: 4ff).

Unfortunately most of the documents referring to administrative matters are damaged (*CAP* 2–3, 16–17, 24, 37) or difficult to interpret (*CAP* 26), so that the precise role of other officials is not always clear. Since most of the documents are legal contracts there are numerous references to judges, once to 'royal judges', who, together with the garrison commander, distributed 'portions' to some Jewish women (*CAP* 1), once to 'provincial judges' who investigated the actions of the Egyptians against the Jewish force (*CAP* 27: 9f). A complainant was entitled to take his case, not only to a judge, but to a *šĕgan* or lord (Kraeling 12: 28). Did the *šĕgan* refer to the garrison commander or the *frataraka*? Did 'lord' refer to the *frataraka* or the satrap (compare *CAP* 17: 1, 5)? Might a complainant appeal directly to the top authority or did he have to take his case first to local judges (compare *CAP* 16)?

The need to go through well-defined channels may be seen from a twenty-three-line letter sent in the name of the satrap, Arsames, by his scribe and chancellor, Anani, and written by an Aramean, Nabuaqab (*CAP* 26). It reviews the procedures necessary to secure the repair of a boat and authorizes that repair. Two boatmen, the Egyptian Psamsineith and his colleague, reported to their Persian superior, the (chief-)boatman, Mithradates, that the boat needed repair (*CAP* 26: 2–3). Mithradates ordered the treasurers to take the Aramean (Phoenician?), Shemshillech, and his companions, the foremen (*framanakara*), together with the Egyptian chief carpenter Shamou son of Kenufi and inspect the boat (*CAP* 26: 3–6). The foremen and carpenter drew up for the treasurers a precise list of all the materials necessary for the repair (*CAP* 26: 6–21), and the latter authorized disbursement of the material. The report, inspection, and approval were all recounted to Arsames by Mithradates, and the former now responded with a letter to the Egyptian Wahpremahi (*CAP* 26: 1, 24) to implement the repair immediately. The recipient scribbled two lines in Aramaic and one in demotic at the end of the letter. The need to write to the satrap's office at Memphis in order to secure approval for repair of a boat at

[1] For the etymology of these Persian titles cf. Porten, *Archives*, pp. 44, 5of.

Elephantine may shed light on the complaint of a Jewish father, Osea, to his son, Shelomam, on caravan escort to Elephantine: 'Since the day you left (Lower) Egypt salary has not been given to us and when we complained to the governors here at Migdol about your salary, we were told thus, saying, "About this, [complain] to the scribes and it will be given to you"' (Bresciani 1–5).

STANDARD OF LIVING

The Elephantine–Syene colonists, both men and women, received a monthly ration (*ptp'*) in grain and legumes (*CAP* 2, 43: 8; Kraeling 11: 4), and a monthly payment in silver (*prs* [*CAP* 2: 16, 11: 6; Bresciani and Kamil 1: 5, 8f]). Of Egypt's three major grains, wheat was the most expensive and is rarely mentioned (*CAP* 49: 2). The cheapest grain was emmer (*kntn*) (*CAP* 10: 10; Kraeling 11: 3ff; Aimé-Giron 87 [*k'* = *kntn* *'rdb*, 'an ardab of emmer']) and the most common was barley (*CAP* 2: 3ff, 10: 10, 24: 38, 33: 14, 45: 8, 49: 2; Kraeling 17: 3 [*šp/š/// = s'rn prs/š'n///*, '1 *peras* 3 *seahs* of barley']; compare Kraeling 17: 4, *CAP* 61: 2, 3). A loan contract was drawn up between the Jew, Anani, son of Haggai, son of Meshullam, and the Egyptian-named Aramean, Pakhnum, son of Besa, whereby the Jew borrowed 2 *peras* 3 *seahs* of emmer from the Aramean and agreed to return the same amount (*kp//š'n/// = kntn prsn//*etc.)[1] out of the grain ration he would receive from the royal storehouse (Kraeling 11: 1–4). A *peras* was apparently a very large measure, a vat or storage cubicle, since the area beneath the stairway in a private house might be designated '*peras-container*' (*byt prs'* [Kraeling 9: 4, 7f]). An official account of disbursement of barley to members of the Syenian garrison indicates a three-scale payment of one ardab (roughly a bushel), one and one-half ardabs and two and one-half ardabs (*CAP* 24: 27–30). There is no indication as to the amount of silver paid per month. The Elephantine shekel was the equivalent of one-half of an Athenian stater (tetra-drachm) (*CAP* 29: 3, 35: 3f; Kraeling 12: 5, 14). The monthly wage of the Greek mercenary at the time was one gold daric (= $12\frac{1}{2}$ silver shekels) (Xenophon, *Anabasis* 1.3.21, etc.) and it has been estimated that the minimum annual cost of living for an Athenian worker with wife and child was 136 shekels.[2]

If the Elephantine soldier earned what the Athenian worker did, how

[1] H. L. Allrik, 'The Lists of Zerubbabel (Nehemiah 7 and Ezra 2) and the Hebrew Numeral-Notation', *BASOR*, 136 (1954), 23f, which must modify what I wrote in *Archives*, pp. 71f.

[2] H. Michel, *The Economics of Ancient Greece* (2nd edn.; New York, 1957), pp. 132f.

much could he buy? Prices in marriage contracts and conveyance documents provide some data:

Woman's dowry (less *mohar*) – 60½–68½ shekels (*CAP* 15: 14; Kraeling 7: 15f)
Expensive woollen garment – 28 shekels (*CAP* 15: 7f)
House – 14–18¼ shekels (Kraeling 3: 6, 12:.5, 14)
Average woollen garment – 7–12 shekels (*CAP* 15: 9ff; Kraeling 2: 4f, 7: 6ff)
Linen garment – 1 shekel (Kraeling 7: 10ff)
Bronze utensil – ½–1½ shekels (*CAP* 15: 11ff; Kraeling 7: 13ff)

The *mohar* varied between five and ten shekels (*CAP* 15: 4f; Kraeling 7: 4f) and the cost of divorce was 7½ shekels (*CAP* 15: 24; Kraeling 2: 8, 10, 7: 26). An average loan was four shekels (*CAP* 10: 3f, 11: 2f), though a well-to-do woman might, on occasion, supply her father with 50 shekels' worth of goods (*CAP* 13: 5f). The estimated price of a slave would vary between 25 and 50 shekels.[1]

The fertile land at the first cataract was meagre but some gardening and shepherding were practised. The government staples were supplemented by beans, cucumbers, gourds, and other vegetables. The date- and dom-palms, which grew on the island, also yielded edible fruit as well as material for weaving baskets (*CAP* 15: 16; Kraeling 7: 17). Other wickerwork baskets came from willow (*slk*) branches and papyrus reed (*gm'*) (*CAP* 15: 15f; Kraeling 7: 17f).[2] Sheep supplied wool, and cheese was made from goat's milk. Animal skins from Nubia provided leather garments and sandals (*CAP* 15: 16 supralinear, 37: 10; Kraeling 2: 5, 7: 20 ['a pair of Persian leather (sandals)']; Bresciani and Kamil 3: 7f). According to Herodotus, men in Egypt wore 'linen tunics with fringes hanging about the legs...and loose white woollen mantles over these' (II.81). The letters contain frequent requests for hides (*CAP* 37: 10; Bresciani and Kamil 3: 7f) and tunics (Bresciani and Kamil 2: 11; *CAP* 42: 8; Bresciani 1: x+1 seq.), and the marriage contracts indicate that women possessed both linen (Kraeling 7: 11ff) and large woollen garments (8 × 5 cubits and 6 × 4 cubits), usually dyed throughout or simply along the edges (*CAP* 15: 7ff; Kraeling 7: 6ff; compare *CAP* 42: 9, Bresciani and Kamil 3: 10). A product for the toilet, as well as the table, was oil and at least four different kinds, including (imported) olive oil, castor oil and probably sesame oil are known (Kraeling 7: 20f). The letters contain frequent requests for castor oil

---

[1] W. H. Dubberstein, 'Comparative Prices in Later Babylonia (625–400 B.C.),' *AJSL*, 56 (1939), 34ff; M. Malinine, 'Un jugement rendu à Thèbes sous la XXVᵉ dynastie', *RE*, 6 (1951), 171, n. 1.
[2] P. Grelot, 'Études sur les textes araméens d'Éléphantine', *RB*, 78 (1971), 517ff.

(Bresciani and Kamil 2: 13, 3: 12, 4: 7; *CAP* 37: 10), and there may have been a castor grove at Syene (Aimé-Giron 99).

The dwellings were of sun-dried mud brick (*CAP* 10: 9; Kraeling 11: 11). Rectangular in shape, they often contained more than one room, and an outer staircase leading to the roof, indicating either a second storey or an upper living area. The house might also contain a courtyard or entryway and a beamed roof (Kraeling 3, 4, 6, 9, 10, 12). Local wood was scarce, however, and the roofs in most of the excavated houses were brick barrel vaults.[1] Jews dwelt next to their temple (*CAP* 13: 13f, 25: 6; Kraeling 3: 9f, 4:9f, 12: 18f), but also next to the district of the Egyptian god, Khnum (Kraeling 3: 8, 4: 10), and their neighbours included Caspians (Kraeling 3: 2, 7f, 4: 11), Khorazmians (*CAP* 6: 7f, 8: 5f), Egyptians (*CAP* 5: 12f, 6: 10f, 8: 7f; Kraeling 6: 7f, 9: 10, 10: 6, 12: 20f) and other foreigners (*CAP* 13: 15). In fact, the construction of an Egyptian shrine in the midst of the Jewish community (Kraeling 9: 8f, 10: 3ff) seems to have been a factor leading to the destruction of the Jewish temple.

RELIGION

The possession of a temple to the God YHW was one of the most fascinating features of the Elephantine Jewish community. The shrine was usually designated *'egōrā* < Akkadian *ekurru*, 'temple' < Sumerian *é.kur*, 'mountain house' and was probably enclosed within a courtyard since it possessed five carved stone gateways with bronze hinges (*CAP* 30: 9ff; 31: 8ff; compare the six gateways in Ezekiel's Temple [Ezek. 40]). Its cedarwood roof (*CAP* 30: 11; 31: 10) indicates a rectangular structure and this is confirmed by a calculation of the dimensions of the adjacent buildings. It is likely that the outer dimensions of the courtyard were 60 by 20 cubits, reminiscent of those given for Solomon's Temple (1 Kings 6: 2).[2] The woodwork (? *'šrn*) in the Elephantine temple (*CAP* 30: 11) may refer to logs alternating with brick or stone layers in the walls (compare 1 Kings 6: 36; Ezra 5: 8, 6: 4) or to interior wainscoting (compare 1 Kings 6: 15ff).

In concept and cult the Elephantine temple bore striking resemblance to the temple of ancient Israel. It was the 'House of YHW' (Bresciani 1: 1) and He was 'YHW The God who dwells in the fortress of Elephantine' (Kraeling 12: 2; compare Ps. 135: 21; Isa. 8: 18; Joel 4: 17, 21; Ps. 74: 2), the 'God of Heaven' (*CAP* 30: 2, 27f; 31: 2, 26f,

---

[1] W. Honroth, O. Rubersohn and F. Zucker, 'Bericht über die Ausgrabungen auf Elephantine in den Jahren 1906–1908', *ZA*, 46 (1909–10), 18.

[2] B. Porten, 'The Structure and Orientation of the Jewish Temple at Elephantine – A Revised Plan of the Jewish District', *JAOS*, 81 (1961), 38ff.

32: 3f, 38: 5; compare Ezra 1: 2, 5: 12, Neh. 1: 4f etc.) and 'Lord of hosts' (*YHW ṣb't*; compare 1 Sam. 4: 4; 2 Sam. 6: 2).[1] These four terms express the immanence–transcendence theology of ancient Israel: God is both far and near.[2] His house is an 'Altar House' (*CAP* 32: 3) where meal-offering, incense and holocaust were offered up daily – in Israel (Exod. 29: 38ff; Num. 28: 3ff) as, probably, at Elephantine (*CAP*, 30: 21f; 31: 21). This daily cult was designed to guarantee the presence of God in the midst of His people (Exod. 29: 45). The welfare sacrifice (*dbḥ* [*CAP* 30: 28; 31: 27]) established a merit before God intended to induce His blessing upon the offerer (compare Gen. 8: 20 to 9: 1; Lev. 9: 22f; Num. 6: 22ff). The communal leader Jedaniah gave expression to this idea in his letter to Bagohi governor of Judah; if he responded favourably he 'would have merit (*ṣdqh*) before YHW the God of Heaven more than a person who offers Him holocaust and welfare sacrifices worth a thousand talents of silver and (about) gold' (*CAP* 30: 27f; 31: 26f). In their terminology the Elephantine Jews made the same distinction between Jewish priest (*khn* [*CAP* 30: 1, 18, 38: 1, 12]) and pagan priest (*kmr* [*CAP* 13: 5, 27: 3, 8, 30: 5]) as did their Israelite forebears (compare 2 Kings 23: 5ff; Zeph. 1: 4).[3]

Though the cult itself may not have been heterodox the very existence of the temple is surprising. From earliest times (Josh. 22; 1 Sam. 26: 19, 27: 1f) the idea persisted (2 Kings 5: 15ff; Jer. 16: 13; Ezek. 4: 13) that foreign soil was ritually unclean precluding erection thereon of a temple. Still, even after the Deuteronomic reformation concentrated worship in Jerusalem (2 Kings 22 to 23; 2 Chron. 34 to 35), three temples were erected outside the city of David: the Samaritan temple on mount Gerizim, the Qasr el-Abd of Hyrcanus at Araq el-Emir in Transjordan, and the temple of Onias IV at Leontopolis in Egypt. The military character of each of these sites and the feature of priestly disaffection present at their establishment support a dating in the reign of King Manasseh for the founding of the Elephantine temple. Shechem was rebuilt and strongly fortified at the same time that the Samaritan temple was erected under the high-priesthood of Manasseh, who broke with his brother Jaddua, high priest in Jerusalem (Josephus, *Antiquities* XI.7.2, 302ff).[4] Rebuffed by the High Priest Simon II, Hyrcanus son of

[1] A. Dupont-Sommer, 'Yahô' et 'Yahô-Seba'ôt' sur des ostraca araméens inédits d'Eléphantine', *CRAIBL* (1947), 175–91.
[2] Porten, *Archives*, pp. 107ff.
[3] Cf. J. A. Montgomery, *A Critical and Exegetical Commentary on the Book of Kings*, ICC (New York, 1951).
[4] Cross, *BA*, 26 (1963), 120f; *idem*, *HTR*, 59 (1966), 203ff; G. E. Wright, *Shechem: The Biography of a Biblical City* (New York, 1965), pp. 172ff.

Joseph, of high-priestly lineage, retired to the ancestral fortress in Transjordan where he erected the Qasr el-Abd, now considered to have been a temple.[1] Onias IV, passed over for the high-priesthood in favour of Alcimus, descended into Egypt and erected a temple in the fortress of Leontopolis.[2] Like the Elephantine temple, this one resembled that in Jerusalem (*War* I.I.I, 33; *Antiquities* XII.9.7, 388; XIII.3.1, 63, 67; 10.4, 285; XX.10.3, 236; but compare *War* VII.10.3, 427f).

Analogy from the Leontopolis temple may further illuminate the foundation of the Elephantine shrine. The former was said to have been inspired by the prophecy of Isaiah: 'In that day there will be an altar to the Lord in the midst of the land of Egypt, and a pillar to the Lord at its border' (Isa. 19: 19), and erected under a permit of Ptolemy VI, who hoped thereby to foster Jewish loyalty toward himself (*Antiquities* XIII.3.1., 62ff; compare Babylonian Talmud Menahoth 109b). The Jewish priests who, in the present writer's view, fled from Manasseh's paganization, might likewise have been moved by Isaiah's prophecy, which for them would have been of most recent origin. Similarly the permit granted by Psammetichus I might have had political motivation – to guarantee the loyalty of his Jews to him and not to Manasseh, who failed in his attempted revolt against Assyria (2 Chron. 33: 10ff) and consequently might have been forced into an anti-Egyptian posture.[3]

Evidence for the Sabbath at Elephantine derives from four ostraca and five occurrences of the name Shabbetai. Rather than clarifying the question of Sabbath observance, these data merely serve to obscure it. The identity of the five names, whether Jewish or not, is unclear. One lacks a praenomen (*CAP* 58: 3), while one is a son of Kibda (*CAP* 2:21), probably a Hebrew name. The other three all appear in non-Jewish contexts: father of the Babylonian Sinkishir (Kraeling 8: 10); son of Shug (Bresciani and Kamil 4: 10), and of 50 non-Jews recorded in the Hermopolis letters; an individual buried in a sarcophagus at Syene along with two others bearing non-Hebrew names.[4] Though it is possible that these individuals owe their names to parents who were attracted by the Sabbath and chose to 'join themselves to the Lord' (compare Isa. 56: 6ff), it is more likely that they were not full proselytes

---

[1] P. W. Lapp, 'Soundings at 'Arâq el-Emîr (Jordan)', *BASOR*, 165 (1962), 24ff; *idem*, 'The second and third campaigns at 'Araq el-Emir', *BASOR*, 171 (1963), 39ff. (1963), 39ff.

[2] Josephus, *War* I.I.I, 33; 9.4, 190ff; *Ant.* XIV.8.1, 127ff; *War* VII.10.2–3, 420ff; *Ant.* XII.9.7, 287f; XIII.3.1–3, 62ff; 10.4, 284ff; XX.10.3, 236; *Contra Apionem* II.5, 49ff.

[3] E. L. Ehrlich, 'Der Aufenthalt des Königs Manasse in Babylon', *ThZ*, 21 (1965), 285f.

[4] W. Kornfeld, 'Aramäische Sarkophage in Assuan', *WZKM*, 61 (1967), 9ff.

and resembled the many Sambathions in Egypt during the Roman period.[1] The reference to the Sabbath (*šbh*) in one ostracon is obscure (Clermont-Ganneau 44),[2] while two suggest observance of the day itself since they indicate something being done before the Sabbath (Clermont-Ganneau 186, 204).[3] The fourth ostracon is addressed to Islah and reads, 'Now, behold I shall send vegetables tomorrow. Meet the boat tomorrow on the Sabbath (*bšbh*). Otherwise, if it be lost, by the life of YHW, I shall surely take yo[ur] life. Do not rely upon Meshullemeth or upon Shemaiah' (Clermont-Ganneau 152).[4] Were the Elephantine Jews as lax in their Sabbath observance as their brethren in Judah, rebuked by Nehemiah for treading grapes, transporting produce, and trading on the Sabbath (Neh. 13: 15ff)? Or did the threat to take Islah's life indicate some extraordinary circumstance and indirectly attest regular Sabbath observance?

We are somewhat better informed about observance of the Passover than we are of the Sabbath, but here, too, the documents raise more questions than they answer. One ostracon makes passing reference to the Passover (*psḥ*); a second possibly alludes to Passover eve (*ʿrwbh*), suggesting, if so, the non-eating of leaven on that day (compare Pesahim 1: 4); a third asks, 'Inform me when you will keep/perform the Passover'.[5] Did this question mean that the date of the festival was unfixed? That the celebrant was ritually impure? That a second Adar might be intercalated? Did it refer to the paschal sacrifice or to the celebration of the festival? The question is found in a private note and asked in such an off-hand manner that it is hard to decide what information it was seeking.

Equally difficult to grasp is the import of a letter written to the Jewish leader Jedaniah, son of Gemariah, and his colleagues by Hananiah in 419 (*CAP* 21). The letter is fragmentary and the preserved text mentions neither the Passover nor the Feast of Unleavened Bread

---

[1] Cf. V. A. Tcherikover and A. Fuks, *Corpus Papyrorum Judaicarum* (Cambridge, 1964), vol. 3, pp. 43ff.

[2] A. Dupont-Sommer, 'Un ostracon araméen inédit d'Éléphantine (Collection Clermont-Ganneau Nᵒ 44)', in *Hebrew and Semitic Studies Presented to G. R. Driver*, ed. D. W. Thomas and W. D. McHardy (Oxford, 1963), pp. 53ff.

[3] Dupont-Sommer, *CRAIBL* (1947), 178ff; *idem*, 'Un ostracon araméen inédit d'Éléphantine', *RSO*, 32 (1957), 403ff; *idem*, 'Sabbat et parascève à Éléphantine', *MPAIBL*, 15 (1960), 68ff; 74.

[4] A. Dupont-Sommer, 'L'ostracon araméen du Sabbat', *Semitica*, 2 (1949), 29–39; *idem*, 'Le sabbat dans les ostraca araméens inédits d'Éléphantine', *CRAIBL* (1945), 260–2; *idem*, *MPAIBL*, 15 (1960), 71ff; F. Rosenthal, ed., *An Aramaic Handbook*, Parta Linguarum Orientalium, x (Wiesbaden, 1967), 1/1, 12f. Translation based in part on conversation with H. L. Ginsberg.

[5] Grelot, *Documents*, pp. 376ff; E. L. Sukenik and E. Y. Kutscher, 'A Passover Ostracon from Elephantine,' *Qedem*, 1 (1942), 53ff (in Hebrew).

explicitly. Its biblical terminology, however, permits a relatively certain restoration of the greater part of the letter. If correctly restored, it would have called upon the Elephantine Jews to keep both feasts; to observe ritual purity; to abstain from work on the fifteenth and twenty-first days of Nisan; to abstain from eating leaven and drinking beer; to eat unleavened bread during the seven days of the festival; and to seal all leaven in special chambers. The beginning of Hananiah's letter to his 'brothers' reported a brief message of Darius II to the Egyptian satrap Arsames. Although the message may not be confidently restored, the brevity of the letter, as well as the paleographic dating of the third Passover ostracon cited above, indicates that the festival was practised prior to Hananiah's letter. Whatever its purpose, Hananiah's mission aroused the animosity of the Elephantine Khnum priests against the Jews (*CAP* 38: 7). Any emphasis of a festival commemorating Egyptian defeat at the hands of the Jews' ancestors was likely to antagonize (see *Contra Apionem* 1.14, 73ff; 26–31, 227ff), and the Khnum priests may have prevented the Jews from celebrating their festival until Hananiah received renewed royal permission.[1]

Private contracts shed further light on this conflict between the Jews and the Khnum priests. Some time after 437 (Kraeling 3) and perhaps already by 420 (Kraeling 6) an Egyptian 'divine chapel' (*qnḥnty* = *knḥ ntr*) displaced the Caspian Satibar on the north-west side of the house of the temple official, Ananiah, son of Azariah (Kraeling 9: 9, 10: 5). The south-eastern border, known earlier as 'the district of the god Khnum' (Kraeling 3: 8, 4: 10), became inhabited by 420 by the Khnum officiant, Hor son of Peteisi (Kraeling 6: 8, 9: 10, 10: 6), and subsequently, by the Egyptian boatmen Pehi and Pemet sons of Tawi (Kraeling 12: 20). In 410 when Arsames had departed for a visit to the king, the Khnum priests bribed the Persian governor at Elephantine, Vidranga, to allow them to destroy the temple of YHW and part of the royal storehouse and erect a wall (*CAP* 27: 2ff, 30: 4ff; 31: 4ff). This was probably the Egyptian-built wall referred to in Ananiah's contracts of 404 and 402. Where formerly the royal storehouse bordered on his property to the northeast (Kraeling 3: 9, 6: 6f) now 'the wall of the shelter which the Egyptians built, that is, the way of the god' (*tmw'nty* = *tꜣ my . t ntr*)[2] cut between the two properties (Kraeling 9: 8f, 10: 3f) to provide an approach road to the chapel. It would seem that the expansion of the interests of the god Khnum brought his priests into conflict with the Jewish temple. The conflict had long been

---

[1] Porten, *Archives*, pp. 128ff, 279ff; Grelot, *Documents*, pp. 378ff; B. Porten, 'Aramaic Papyri and Parchments: A New Look', *BA*, 42 (1979), 88ff.

[2] Cf. B. Couroyer, 'Le temple de Yaho et l'orientation dans les papyrus araméens d'Eléphantine', *RB*, 68 (1961), 524–40.

simmering; both sides were bribing the Persian officials; and the Jews had taken their case to the investigators at Memphis (*CAP* 37) – ultimately to no avail.

Upon the destruction of the temple, the Jews went into mourning and reported the events to the Jewish authorities in Jerusalem, namely the governor Bagohi, the High Priest Johanan, Ostanes brother of Anani, and the nobles of Judah (*CAP* 30: 18ff; 31: 17ff). Their prayers were partially answered when Vidranga and others responsible were punished, some by death (*CAP* 30: 16f; 31: 15f), but permission to rebuild was not forthcoming. A letter was sent to Delaiah and Shelemiah, sons of Sanballat, governor of Samaria (*CAP* 30: 29; 31: 28), and a second letter dispatched to Bagohi on 25 November 407 (*CAP* 30: 30; 31: 29) urging intercession for the full restoration of their temple and its sacrificial cult. Bagohi and Delaiah withheld the requested letter, but they did instruct the Elephantine messenger to report to Arsames that the temple be rebuilt and meal-offering and incense be offered as formerly (*CAP* 32). The right to offer animal sacrifices was omitted, apparently as the exclusive prerogative of the Jerusalem sanctuary. The Elephantine Jews accepted the limitation and on the basis of the messenger's memorandum appealed once more to the Persian authorities, promising money and grain (*CAP* 33). Ananiah's sale contract of 12 December 402 indicated that southwest of his property lay the 'Temple of YHW' (Kraeling 12: 18f) – the site still sacred to the Jewish God and perhaps already rebuilt.

Shortly thereafter, on 1 June 400, at the time of the Feast of Weeks, Jedaniah recorded two-shekel contributions from some 122 persons, including more than thirty women (*CAP* 22).[1] The overwhelming majority of Hebrew names indicates onomastic conservatism and little intermarriage. The list, however, does pose two problems. One is mathematical and is known to us from contemporary biblical lists (of temple vessels [Ezra 1: 9–11] and of repatriates [Ezra 2; Neh. 7]), namely the non-congruence between the recorded total and the running total. In our text the recorded total of 31 *karsh* 8 [error for 6] shekels = 316 shekels does not accord with the running total of 244 shekels = 2 shekels × 122 contributors. The second problem involves the apparent contradiction between the opening and closing of the list:

'These are the names of the Jewish garrison who gave silver to YHW the God' (line 1)
'The silver which was that day in the hand of Jedaniah son of Gemariah.... silver, 31 *karsh* 8 shekels;

[1] Porten, *Archives*, pp. 128ff, 279ff; Grelot, *Documents*, pp. 378ff; Porten, 'Aramaic Papyri and Parchment: A New Look', *BA*, 42 (1979), 88ff.

12 k. 6 sh. of this are for YHW;
7 *karsh* are for Eshembethel;
silver, 12 *karsh* are for Anathbethel.'   (lines 118–123)

The 72-shekel difference between the two tallies may be explained on the assumption that two columns are absent from our papyrus; each column would have contained eighteen names ($36 \times 2 = 72$). But what are we to make of the diversion of funds collected for YHW to Eshembethel and Anathbethel? Since the Elephantine documents also record the existence of a Herembethel (*CAP* 7: 7) and an AnathYHW (*CAP* 44: 3), it has been customary to consider all four divinities as part of the YHW cult at Elephantine.[1] While the evidence for considering AnathYHW as a syncretistic combination is strong, that for Bethel and affiliates suggests that these were part of the cult of the Arameans at Syene.

The Hermopolis letters addressed to Syene indicate the presence there of temples to the queen of heaven (Bresciani and Kamil 4: 1), Bethel (Bresciani and Kamil 4: 1), and Nabu (Bresciani and Kamil 1: 1). Bethel appears in an Aramaic religious text in demotic,[2] while one Sheil, priest of Nabu, was buried near Memphis.[3] Diversified evidence shows Bethel and Nabu at home in Syro-Phoenicia for a millenium and at one location even linked together. Bethel was mentioned in a treaty between Esarhaddon and Baal of Tyre (*circa* 675),[4] included in the pantheon of Philo of Byblos (11.16), and worshipped in the third century C.E. along the Orontes and at Dura-Europas:[5] Nabu was popular among the Arameans at Haran in the seventh century B.C.E.[6] and during the Christian era was worshipped at Edessa and elsewhere in the Jebel Seman,[7] as well as at Dura-Europas.[8] Anathbethel may also appear in the Esarhaddon–Baal treaty[9] while the deity Symbetylos on a Kefr Nabu

---

[1] W. F. Albright, *Archaeology and Religion of Israel* (4th edn. Baltimore, 1956), pp. 168ff; A. Vincent, *La religion des judéo-araméens d'Eléphantine* (Paris, 1937), pp. 562ff; *CAP* VIII seq.; Kraeling, *Papyri*, pp. 87ff.

[2] R. A. Bowman, 'An Aramaic Religious Text in Demotic Script', *JNES*, 3 (1944), 226.

[3] Aimé-Giron, pp. 99f; *idem*, 'Adversaria Semitica', *BIFAO*, 38 (1939), 35f.

[4] R. Borger, 'Anath-Bethel,' *VT*, 7 (1957), 102ff.

[5] P. C. Bauer, M. I. Rostovtzeff and A. R. Bellinger, *The Excavations at Dura-Europas* (New Haven, 1933), pp. 68ff.

[6] C. H. W. Johns, *Assyrian Doomsday Book* (Leipzig, 1901), p. 16.

[7] Cf. R. Duval, 'Histoire politique, religieuse et littéraire d'Édesse jusqu'à la première croisade', *JA*, 8th Series, 18 (1891), 228f; Aimé-Giron, *loc. cit.*

[8] C. B. Welles, R. O. Fink and J. F. Gilliam, *The Excavations at Dura Europas; Final Report V*, Part 1; *The Parchment and Papyri* (New Haven, 1959), pp. 61ff.

[9] See above n. 4.

inscription[1] is probably identical with Eshembethel. Kefr Nabu is located in the Jebel Seman, formerly called Jebel Nabu,[2] ancient Bit Agusi with its capital at Arpad. The beginning of Aramean settlement in Egypt may go back to the destruction of Arpad in 740 by Tiglath-pileser III.[3] In any event, Arameans settling there brought with them their deities as did the Jews theirs. In the sixth to fifth centuries the worship of Bethel, Herem, Eshem, and Nabu in Egypt and Babylonia is widely attested by their appearance in personal names. The first three appear in forty-six names, of which twenty-seven are or have patronymics. Of these latter only three are joined with Hebrew names.[4] In the Egyptian Aramaic papyri more Aramean names are compounded with Nabu than with any other non-YHWistic theophoric element; at Nippur he is the most represented deity in West-Semitic names next to El and YHW (written *ya-a-ma*).[5] The biblical figure Bethel, scornfully compared by Jeremiah to the pagan deity Chemosh (Jer. 48: 13), was a local angel who had protected Jacob (Gen. 31: 11ff, 48: 16) and continued to be venerated thereafter. The identity of name with the Aramean Bethel is a case of nominal congruence but functional distinction. The communal funds collected for YHW and distributed to Him as well as to Eshembethel and Anathbethel may have been a goodwill gesture, or may have derived from Arameans whose names appeared on the lost columns.[6]

While the evidence for a syncretistic communal cult of the Jewish deity at Elephantine dissipates upon close inspection, that for individual Jewish contact with paganism remains. The latter evidence is of two kinds: greetings in letters and judicial oaths. The plural form *'lhy'* in

[1] W. K. Prentice, *Syria: Greek and Latin Inscriptions, Northern Syria* (Leiden, 1907), III/B, pp. 180ff.

[2] H. C. Butler, *Syria: Geography and Itinerary* (Leiden, 1930), I, map facing p. 60, 68ff.; Aimé-Giron, pp. 99f.

[3] E. G. H. Kraeling, *Aram and Israel* (New York, 1918), p. 109; A. Dupont-Sommer, *Les Araméens* (Paris, 1949), p. 61.

[4] Cf. Porten, *Archives*, pp. 328ff.

[5] H. V. Hilprecht, *Business Documents of Murashû sons of Nippur*, Babylonian Expedition of the University of Pennsylvania, series A: *Cuneiform Texts*, 9, (Philadelphia, 1898), nos. 23: 8, 65: 25(?), 67: 1(?), 70: 4, 82: 6, 85: 22, 86: 18; ibid., 10: 31: 2 L. E., 64: 6 U. E., 67: 15, 109: 3, 110: 4, 120: 3, 126: 11 U. E. (?); A. T. Clay, *Business Documents of Murashu sons of Nippur*, University of Pennsylvania Museum, Babylonian Section II/1 (Philadelphia, 1912), 31: 9, 42: 2, 53: 14, 79: 1. 108: 12, 203: 6, 221: 1, 10. See also M. D. Coogan, 'West Semitic Personal Names in the Murašû Documents' (unpublished Ph.D. Diss., Harvard University, 1971; corrected, 1973), 73ff.

[6] U. Cassuto, 'The Gods of the Jews at Elephantine', *Biblical and Oriental Studies*, II (Jerusalem, 1975), pp. 240ff.

greetings to Jews by Jews (*CAP* 21: 2, 39: 1, 56: 1, compare 37: 1f) may be the equivalent of Hebrew *Elohim*, with singular meaning, or a frozen formula used unconsciously; alternatively the letters may have been drawn up by non-Jewish scribes. On two ostraca non-Jews wrote to Jews and blessed them by pagan deities: Yarho greeted Haggai (Clermont-Ganneau 277) by invoking Bel, Nabu, Shamash, and Nergal;[1] the tailor Giddel (compare Ezra 2: 47, 56; Neh. 7: 49, 58 for the non-Jewish use of the name) blessed Micaiah (Clermont-Ganneau 70) by YHW and *Ḥn* [= Han?, Khnum?].[2] There are three judicial situations in which a Jew takes, or promises to take, an oath by a pagan deity. In one, and perhaps two, of the cases the reason may be the non-Jewish identity of the person to whom the oath is being rendered. Mibtahiah, divorced from the Egyptian Pia, swears to him by the Egyptian goddess Sati (*CAP* 14); Malchijah son of Jashobiah promises to a person whose name is missing that he will 'call' to the god Herembethel (*CAP* 7). In the third case Menahem, son of Shallum, son of Ho[shaiah/daviah], swore (or: will swear) to Meshullam, son of Nathan, 'by Ḥ[erem?] the [god] in/by the place of prostration and by AnathYHW' (*CAP* 44). This latter deity appears to be a clear example of Jewish syncretism. Anath's title in Egyptian was *nbt pt*, 'Lady of Heaven' appearing on a stela from Bethshan and a jar of Prince Psammetichus.[3] The Semitic equivalent was 'Queen of Heaven' and, as noted, under this epithet she had a temple at Syene (Bresciani and Kamil 4: 1). In pre-exilic Judah individual Jews, particularly women, worshipped the Queen of Heaven and continued to do so after their migration to Egypt (Jer. 7: 16ff, 44: 15ff). To them she provided prosperity and security and so AnathYHW would be that aspect of YHW which assured man's well-being.

LEGAL DOCUMENTS AND SCRIBAL CRAFT

The largest single group of texts, some forty in all, consists of legal contracts. Broadly speaking, we may divide these into deeds of conveyance, obligation, marriage and adoption. Conveyance documents

---

[1] A. Dupont-Sommer, 'Bêl et Nabû Šamaš et Nergal sur un ostracon araméen inédit d'Éléphantine', *RHR*, 128 (1944), 28ff.

[2] A. Dupont-Sommer, 'Le syncrétisme religieux des juifs d'Éléphantine d'après un ostracon araméen inédit,' *RHR*, 130 (1945), 17ff; *idem*, *CRAIBL*, (1947), 177f.

[3] A. Rowe, *The Topography and History of Beth-shan* (Philadelphia, 1930), pp. 32f, pl. 50, no. 2: *idem*, *The Four Canaanite Temples of Beth-shan* (Philadelphia, 1940), pp. 33f, pl. 65A, no. 1; B. Grdseloff, *Les débuts du culte de Rechef en Égypte* (Cairo, 1942), pp. 28ff.

are the most frequent; six categories may be differentiated, of which the first three were common: (1) house-sale (Kraeling 3, 12); (2) house-gift (*CAP* 8, 9, 13, 46, 47; Kraeling 4, 6, 9, 10); (3) withdrawal, usually subsequent to litigation (*CAP* 6, 14, 20, 25, 43; Kraeling 1, 5 [emancipation]); (4) exchange of shares (*CAP* 1); (5) wall-building (*CAP* 5); (6) slave assignment (*CAP* 28). Six marriage contracts, or parts thereof (*CAP* 15, 18, 36; Kraeling 2, 7, 14), and perhaps a seventh (*CAP* 48), have been preserved. Since the endorsements from several deeds of obligation are missing (*CAP* 2, 3, 7, 11, 29, 35, 45, 49) or non-existent (*CAP* 44), classification is according to content rather than official terminology. Four kinds of text appear: loan of money (*CAP* 10, 11) or of grain (Kraeling 11); promise to pay a balance, whether on a house (*CAP* 29) or of dowry to a *divorcée* (*CAP* 35); promise to deliver entrusted grain (*CAP* 2, 3); and obligations of payment (*CAP* 45) or oath (*CAP* 7, 44) attendant upon judicial proceedings. One text is too fragmentary for classification (*CAP* 49). There is only one adoption text (Kraeling 8) and its endorsement is missing; perhaps it was called 'deed of sonship'.

The variegated kinds of text as well as the fixed legal formulae therein testify to diverse social and economic activity on the one hand and to a developed scribal craft on the other. In about thirty texts the name of the scribe is preserved or may be inferred. Thirteen such names have survived and the interesting fact is that seven were non-Jewish: Itu son of Abah (*CAP* 6: 16 [464 B.C.E.]), Atarshuri son of Nabuzeribni (*CAP* 8: 27f, 9: 16 [460/459]), Bitia, son of Mannuki (Kraeling 1: 10 [451]), Peteisi son of Nabunathan (*CAP* 14: 11 [440]), Rawhshana, son of Nergalshezib (Kraeling 8: 9 [416]), Nabutukulti, son of Nabuzeribni (*CAP* 28: 14f [440]), and Shewahram son of Eshemran (Kraeling 11: 12 [402]). Most of the eight texts by these scribes bear certain features in common: at least six were drawn up in Syene, residence of the Arameans (*CAP* 6: 17, 8: 28, 9: 16, 14: 12; Kraeling 8: 1, 11: 1, 12), and only one in Elephantine (*CAP* 28: 1, 15); all or several of the witnesses in four documents (*CAP* 6, 14; Kraeling 1, 8) were Arameans, that is, local residents; the scribal hand is either extreme (Kraeling 1) or semi-extreme (*CAP* 6, 8, 9, 28; Kraeling 8, 11) with only one specimen of the more conservative semi-formal (*CAP* 14). Recourse to an Aramean scribe of Syene rather than a Jewish one from Elephantine is explicable in three cases: the adoption proceedings took place in the presence of Vidranga, garrison commander resident at Syene (Kraeling 8: 2f); the loan of grain was made from one resident at Syene (Kraeling 11: 2); the builder who was party to the contract was resident at Syene

(*CAP* 14: 2). Why the Jewish parties in the remaining documents turned to Aramean scribes is not apparent.[1]

Of the six Jewish scribes three appear in the early part of the century and two of these draw up their own documents: Hosea, son of Hodaviah (*CAP* 2: 1f, 18 [484; compare *CAP* 3]), and Gemariah, son of Ahio (*CAP* 11: 1, 16 [479]),[2] while Pelatiah, son of Ahio (*CAP* 5: 15 [471]), was commissioned by Mahseiah son of Jedaniah. With the same patronymic, Pelatiah and Gemariah may have been brothers. Two Aramean scribes with the same patronymic, but separated by fifty years, may have been grandfather and grandson: Atarshuri, son of Nabuzeribni (*CAP* 8: 27f, 9: 16 [460/459]), being the elder and Nabutukulti, son of Nabuzeribni (*CAP* 28: 14f [410]), being the younger. Two of the three remaining Jewish scribes were most certainly father and son: Nathan, son of Ananiah, wrote four (*CAP* 10: 20 [456]; Kraeling 2: 14 [449]; *CAP* 13: 17 [446], 15: 37 [435?]) and possibly six (*CAP* 47, 48) of our texts; while his son Mauziah may have begun his scribal activity during the lifetime of his father (Kraeling 14 [446?]):[3] he wrote six of our texts (Kraeling 4: 22 [434]; *CAP* 20: 16 [Elul, 420]; Kraeling 7: 42 [Tishre, 420]; *CAP* 25: 17 [416], 18: 3 [date?], 45: 9 [so restore![4] 413]) and one (*CAP* 38: 12) and perhaps two of the letters (*CAP* 41). A contemporary of Mauziah was Haggai, son of Shemaiah, who drew up five, maybe six, of our texts (Kraeling 3: 23sl [437], 5: 15f [simply 'Haggai', 427], 9: 22 [404], 10: 17 [Adar, 402], 12: 32 [December, 402]; *CAP* 35 [? 400]). Mauziah and Shemaiah were two of the five Jewish communal leaders during the temple crisis (*CAP* 33: 2f). Their scribal hand, as well as that of the other Jewish scribes except for Pelatiah, was semi-formal; the latter's was semi-extreme. Thus, though we know more Aramean scribes than Jewish, the latter, judging by their scribal hand, were, with one exception, 'professional' while the former, likewise with one exception (Peteisi), were 'occasional'. At least eight of the ten contracts drawn up by the Temple servitor Ananiah, son of Azariah, were written by the three Jewish scribes: Nathan (Kraeling 2), Mauziah (Kraeling 4, 7), and Haggai (Kraeling 3, 5, 9, 10, 12).

---

[1] For discussion of the epigraphic style of the scribes from Elephantine cf. J. Naveh, *The Development of the Aramaic Script*, Proceedings of the Israel Academy of Sciences and Humanities, v/1 (Jerusalem, 1970), pp. 31ff.

[2] For reconstruction of line 1, cf. R. Yaron, 'The Schema of the Aramaic Legal Documents', *JSS*, 2 (1957), 42f; Porten, *Jews*, p. 108.

[3] Cf. B. Porten, 'The Restoration of Fragmentary Aramaic Marriage Contracts' in *Gratz College Anniversary Volume* (Philadelphia, 1971), pp. 244ff.

[4] Cf. Naveh, *Aramaic Script*, p. 23, n. 72.

Despite the schematic and formulaic nature of the legal contracts, individual scribes developed personal peculiarities of use and spelling, and we may call attention to five such features of Haggai as distinct from Mauziah: preference for the form *'m*, 'still' (Kraeling 3: 16, 19, 9: 21, 10: 11, 14) rather than *'pm* (*CAP* 20: 15, 25: 16; Kraeling 4: 16); use of the Persian words *'drng*, 'guarantor', *hnbg*, 'partner', *hngyt*, 'associate' (Kraeling 5: 5, 9: 18, 10: 12, 12: 27), first appearing in 427 (Kraeling 5) and used by other scribes (*'drng* [Kraeling 11: 8f]; *hngyt whnbg'* [*CAP* 43: 9]), but not by Mauziah where expected (*CAP* 20: 10f; 25: 9ff); use of the expression *qbl 'l...l*, 'complain against...to' (Kraeling 9: 19f, 10: 12f, 12: 28), found in other scribes (*CAP* 8: 13, 10: 12, 18, 47: 7; Kraeling 1: 5f; compare *CAP* 6: 16), but not in Mauziah where possible (Kraeling 4: 12ff; *CAP* 20: 10ff, 25: 9ff); the monetary precision *ksp ṣr(y)p*, 'pure silver' (Kraeling 5: 15, 9: 20, 10: 11, 12: 30) likewise used by other scribes (*CAP* 5: 7, 28: 11; Kraeling 11: 6), but never by Mauziah; distinct form or spelling of foreign names – *tpmt* (Kraeling 5: 2, 11, 18, 12: 1, 3, 11, 24, 35), *bgzšt* (Kraeling 3: 2, 10, 23, 25, 12: 4, 12, 31) and *štbr* (Kraeling, 3: 2, 8) rather than Mauziah's *tmt* (Kraeling 4: 2, 6), *bgzwšt* (Kraeling 4: 3) and *štybr* (Kraeling 4: 3, 11) respectively. On the other hand we may single out at least two forms of expression favoured by Mauziah: the expanded genitive with *zy*, 'of' rather than the simpler construct or apposition, as in the expressions *tkwnh zy ksp*, 'cash of silver' (Kraeling 7: 5f; contrast *ksp tkwnh*, 'silver cash' [*CAP* 15: 6]) and *'bygrn' zy ksp*, 'indemnity of silver' (*CAP* 20: 14f, 25: 15; Kraeling 7: 31) rather than *'b(y)grn(')* *ksp*, 'indemnity, silver' (*CAP* 28: 10, 43: 6; Kraeling 5: 8, 14, 6: 17, 8: 7, 9: 20, 10: 10, 14, 12: 30) or *ksp 'bgrn*, 'silver indemnity' (Kraeling 11: 6) used by other scribes; and the formula 'from this day forever' (*CAP* 20: 9f; Kraeling 4: 5, 7: 4, 14: 4) rather than the common 'from this day *and* for ever' (*CAP* 8: 9, 14: 7, 15: 4, 28: 7, 43: 4, [8], Kraeling 2: 4) used by the other scribes (Haggai twice has the unique plural form *'lmn* [Kraeling 3: 11, 12: 23] rather than the singular *'lm* and once a dittography and no conjunction: 'from this this day forever' [Kraeling 10: 8]).

The existence of individual stylistic peculiarities did not mean stylistic rigidity. Not only did the three professional scribes vary their formulation of stereotyped phrases and clauses from document to document, but even within the same text a repeated expression would be varied. Haggai wrote four documents regarding Ananiah's house, a sale contract in 437 (Kraeling 3); two gift contracts, one in 404 (Kraeling 9) and the other in March 402 (Kraeling 10); and a sale contract in December 402 (Kraeling 12). Three examples may be cited as illustrative of variations from document to document: (1) The formula for introducing the boundaries has five variations, appearing in two different forms in the final sale contract: 'And behold these are the boundaries' (Kraeling 3: 7); 'And behold the boundaries' (Kraeling 9: 8); 'And this (*sic*!) are its boundaries' (Kraeling 10: 3); 'And behold this (*sic*!) are the boundaries' (Kraeling 12: 8f) and in the same document, 'This (*sic*!) are its boundaries' (Kraeling 12: 16f). (2) The order in which the boundaries are listed varies three times in four texts: above–below–east–west (Kraeling 3: 7–10); east–above–below–west (Kraeling 9: 8–11); east–west–above–below in the two texts written during the same year (Kraeling 10: 3–6, 12: 17–21). (3) The thought chain 'you – your children – a donee' has various formulations; moreover, there are three variations of the third link in the chain: 'he to whom you desire to give (it)' (Kraeling 3: 12, 14ff); 'you may give it to whomever you wish' (Kraeling 10: 21); 'anyone to whom you give (it) as a gift' (Kraeling 12: 23, 26, 31).

In addition to distinctive features and variations a third scribal characteristic should be noted – symmetry or patterning. Just as the documents have formulaic expressions, so they have a schema and that for the deeds of conveyance, marriage, and loan respectively has been worked out.[1] But no more than formulae meant verbal rigidity did schema mean structural rigidity. Each text, even within the same category, had its own structure and balance of clauses. We may cite three different kinds of examples to illustrate this principle of structural variation. (1) Non-suit clauses: each conveyance contract has a double clause restraining the donor/vendor/claimant or his dependants from further contesting the transaction and imposing a penalty should such an attempt be made. When expressed in full, well-balanced form such clauses might either take on an *abab* pattern, twice favoured by Haggai (Kraeling 3: 12–19, 10: 9–15), or an *aabb* pattern favoured by Mauziah (Kraeling 4: 12–16). The former pattern is 'we shall not be able to sue' – 'should we sue' (*ab*); 'children shall not be able to sue' – 'should they sue' (*ab*). The latter pattern is 'we' – 'children' (*aa*); 'should we' – 'should children' (*bb*). But both scribes might reduce the four elements to two, either by elimination – 'children' – 'should they' (Kraeling 9: 18–21 [Haggai]) – or combination – 'we and children shall not be able to sue' – 'should we and children sue' (*CAP* 20: 10–16 [Mauziah]) – thus creating a simple *ab* pattern. Or both scribes might create an imbalanced pattern of *aab* – 'we...sue you' – 'we...sue your children' – 'should we sue you and your children' (*CAP* 25: 9–17 [Mauziah]) – or one of *aaab* – 'I...sue you' – 'I...sue children' – 'children...sue' – 'whoever sues' (Kraeling 12: 24–31 [Haggai]). (2) Repetition and interweaving of key words in a sevenfold pattern of

[1] Cf. Porten, *Archives*, pp. 334ff with bibliography.

aa-bb-aba: 'released' – 'released' (*aa*); 'not have right to' – 'not have right to' (*bb*); 'released' – 'not have right to' – 'released' (*aba*) (Kraeling 5: 3–10 [Haggai]). This sevenfold repetition and the interplay of the positive 'you are released' and negative 'no one has right to you' link together, in this unique emancipation document, three sections – transaction, non-investiture, guarantees for future. (3) A sixfold chiastic symmetry which links up seven clauses in two non-adjacent sections; each of four clauses in the transaction section is marked by the word 'sold' and each of three double clauses in the guarantees-for-future section is marked by the word 'sue' (Kraeling 3 [Haggai]):

A	1	We SOLD house of *Ippuliya* whose *condition* is....	(3–5)
	2	We SOLD for *price*....	(5–7)
B	3	*Boundaries* of house we SOLD....	(7–10)
C	4	We SOLD and *withdrew*	(10–11)
C	5	We cannot SUE for house we sold...*withdrew*	(12–16)
B	6	Children cannot SUE for house whose *boundaries*....	(16–19)
A	7	If stranger SUE...house *like* yours unless *Ippuliya*...*price*....	(19–23)

Despite the various niceties and individual finesses of which the professional scribes were capable, the legal contract was not a polished text. It abounded in erasures and supra-linear additions, apparent grammatical and spelling errors, and occasional incongruencies between the Babylonian and Egyptian dates at the head of most documents (*CAP* 10; compare *CAP* 8, 9). The numerous erasures and additions in a marriage contract drawn up by Mauziah enable us to sense the dickering that went on between the proprietor of the bride and groom up to the last minute (Kraeling 2). A sale contract drawn up by Haggai breaks off in the middle of line 10 and starts over again from the beginning, leaving the rejected text intact and enabling us to trace the inaccuracies which led him or one of the parties to insist on a new start (Kraeling 12). That the scribe could produce a polished piece when necessary may be seen from the two drafts of the letter to Bagohi (*CAP* 30, 31), where the second draft (*CAP* 31) contains some forty corrections in twenty-nine or thirty lines of text. A legal contract, tied and sealed so as not to be opened except in case of legal dispute, did not require the same precision and external appearance as a letter to be read by the governor of Judah.

FAMILY ARCHIVES

Over a period of some 50 or 60 years a family would accumulate an archive of ten or eleven legal contracts safeguarding personal or property rights. Two archives have been preserved, one of the Jewish temple official Ananiah, son of Azariah, married to the Egyptian slave girl Tamut; and the other of the woman Mibtahiah, aunt of the communal leader Jedaniah, son of Gemariah. Ananiah's much-emended marriage contract (Kraeling 2) indicates the equilibrium established in his triangular situation and incidently informs us that the couple already had a son named Pilti. Tamut had full rights as wife; Ananiah had full rights as father; and Tamut's master Meshullam, son of Zaccur, retained full rights as slave owner. There was no *mohar* and the dowry was negligible. Both parties enjoyed the right of divorce, while Pilti reverted to Meshullam should Ananiah exercise that right. Meshullam could apparently snatch Pilti away from Ananiah upon payment of 50 shekels. In case of death, the surviving spouse took control of the joint property.

A dozen years after their marriage contract was drawn, Ananiah purchased a run-down house for fourteen shekels from the Caspian couple, Bagazushta and Ubil. It adjoined the royal storehouse and lay across from the temple of YHW. The deed (Kraeling 3) accorded Ananiah the right to dispose of the property as he saw fit, and over the next thirty-five years he ceded part to his wife, part to his daughter, and the remainer to his son-in-law. The gift to Tamut (Kraeling 4) was possibly made after the birth of their daughter, Jehoishma; upon death of either spouse, his or her portion was to devolve upon the two children. The gift to Jehoishma (Kraeling 6) was apparently first made at the time of her betrothal to Ananiah, son of Haggai, and was twice reconfirmed in revised form in later documents (Kraeling 9, 10). Jehoishma had been born a handmaiden to Meshullam, and in his old age he emancipated and adopted mother and daughter (Kraeling 5). Thus Jehoishma's marriage contract was drawn up between the groom and her legal brother Zaccur, son of Meshullam, who provided her with a handsome dowry, including the refunded *mohar*, of $78\frac{1}{8}$ shekels. Both parties enjoyed freedom of divorce[1] but in certain circumstances the $7\frac{1}{2}$ shekel divorce penalty fell not on the initiating party but on his opposite number: on Ananiah, if he took another wife; on the party denying the other conjugal rights. Should Ananiah die before Jehoishma, and the couple be childless, she was to succeed to his possessions as long as she did not remarry. Should she, being childless, predecease him, he would inherit her possessions (Kraeling 7). Eighteen years after their marriage, Ananiah, son of Haggai bought the unceded part of his in-laws' house for thirteen shekels (Kraeling 12) and about the same time took a loan of emmer from Pakhnum, son of Besa (Kraeling 11).

---

[1] The woman's right of divorce, evident in all three Elephantine contracts, was common in Egypt, found elsewhere in the Near East and may not have been absent from Israel; cf. Porten, *Archives*, pp. 209ff, 261f. [The *mohar* was a price paid for a wife. Eds.].

The family archive of Mibtahiah reveals a woman of means. During her lifetime she acquired three houses (*CAP* 8, 13, 25), three husbands (*CAP*, 9, 14, 15), and at least three slaves (*CAP* 28). Her first house she acquired upon the death of her first husband (compare *CAP* 25), the Jewish soldier Jezaniah, son of Uriah. Her second husband was the Egyptian builder Pia, son of Pahi, from whom she was divorced. Her third marriage was likewise with an Egyptian builder, Eshor, son of Seho. Ezra (9 to 10), Nehemiah (13: 23ff) and Malachi (2: 10ff) condemned intermarriage, which pervaded all strata of the post-exilic community in Judah (Ezra 10: 18–44), and it was eventually outlawed in the pact subscribed to by the whole community (Neh. 10: 31). What kind of feelings it aroused at Elephantine is unknown, but judging from the paucity of mixed names it was not a serious problem numerically. The onomastic and/or marital assimilation of the neighbouring Arameans was much greater. Apparently Eshor was absorbed into the Jewish community, as was the handmaiden Tamut since all their children bore Hebrew names, and Eshor himself is later known as Nathan (*CAP* 25: 3, 28: 2). Mibtahiah followed the prevalent practice of papponymy and named one son after her father, Mahseiah, and the other after her grandfather, Jedaniah. Upon their mother's death the two boys inherited her property, including the house she took over from her first husband (*CAP* 25) and four slaves (*CAP* 28). The brothers divided two of the slaves between them in a document drawn up just five months before the destruction of the temple (*CAP* 28). Unlike the Ananiah archive, the Mibtahiah family archive does not extend into the post-destruction period and we wonder how that event affected these brothers, whose houses also lay adjacent to the temple (*CAP* 13: 13ff, 25: 4ff).

FINALE

As indicated, the Jewish temple was probably restored after considerable diplomatic activity and financial expenditure, though without the right to offer up animal sacrifices as before. Not long afterwards, however, the Jewish community disappears from our eyes. Persian rule in Egypt was ended by the rise of the local ruler Amyrteus. The change at Elephantine took place some time between 18 January 401 (*CAP* 7: 1) and 19 June 400 (*CAP* 35: 1). The reign of Amyrteus was short-lived and a fragmentary letter to the Jew, Islah, at Elephantine of 1 October 399 reported the seizure of power by Nepherites (Kraeling 13). This is the latest dated document and comes almost 100 years after the earliest Elephantine contract (495 [*CAP* 1]). And so stands revealed before us a century of Diaspora Jewish life from the time of Ezra and Nehemiah which, but for these papyri, would have vanished forever.

BIBLIOGRAPHIES

GENERAL BIBLIOGRAPHY ON THE PERSIAN PERIOD

For earlier work see *The Cambridge Ancient History*. Vol. 4. *The Persian Empire and the West*. Edited by J. B. Bury, S. A. Cook, and F. E. Adcock. Cambridge, 1926, p. 613.

Ackroyd, P. R. *Exile and Restoration*. Philadelphia/London, 1968.
Israel under Babylon and Persia. Oxford, 1970.
Alt, A. *Kleine Schriften zur Geschichte des Volkes Israel*. Vol. 2. Munich, 1953.
Baron, S. W. *A Social and Religious History of the Jews*. Vol. 1. 2nd edn. Philadelphia, 1952.
Bengtson, H. (ed.). *Fischer Weltgeschichte*. Vol. 5. *Griechen und Perser*. Frankfurt, 1965.
Griechische Geschichte. 5th edn. Munich, 1977.
Ben-Sasson, H. H. (ed.). *History of the Jewish People*. Vol. 1. *The Ancient Times*. Tel-Aviv, 1969 (in Hebrew). ET: Cambridge, Mass. 1976.
Boyce, M. *Zoroastrians: Their Religious Beliefs and Practices*. London, 1979.
Bright, J. *A History of Israel*. 2nd edn. Philadelphia/London, 1972.
Bury, J. B., Cook, S. A. and Adcock, F. E. (eds.). *The Cambridge Ancient History*. Vols. 3–5. Cambridge, 1924ff.
Cameron, G. C. *History of Early Iran*. Chicago, 1936.
Cathedra, 4 (1977), 4–50 (in Hebrew; various authors).
Culican, W. *The Medes and Persians*. London, 1965.
Dandamayev, M. A. *Persian unter den ersten Achämeniden (6. Jahrhundert v. Chr.)*. Trans. from Russian by H.-D. Pohl. Wiesbaden, 1976.
Forrer, E. *Die Provinzeinteilung des assyrischen Reiches*. Leipzig, 1921.
Frye, R. N. *The Heritage of Persia*. London, 1962.
Galling, K. *Studien zur Geschichte Israels im persischen Zeitalter*. Tübingen, 1964.
Ghirshman, R. *Iran*. London, 1954.
Grelot, P. *Documents Araméens d'Égypte*. Paris, 1972.
Hayes, H. J. and Miller, J. M. *Israelite and Judaean History*. Philadelphia–London, 1977.
Heichelheim, F. M. *Geschichte Syriens und Palästinas von der Eroberung durch Kyros II bis zur Besitznahme durch den Islam (547 v. Chr.–641/2 n. Chr.)*, in *Handbuch der Orientalistik, 12. Band, 4. Abschnitt, Lieferung 2*, pp. 99–290. Ed. B. Spuler. Leiden, 1966.
Hengel, M. *Judentum und Hellenismus. Studien zu ihrer Begegnung unter besonderer Berücksichtigung Palästinas bis zur Mitte des 2. Jh.s v. Chr.* 2nd edn. WUNT 10. Tübingen, 1973. ET: *Judaism and Hellenism. Studies in their Encounter in Palestine during the Early Hellenistic Period*. Philadelphia, 1974.
Herrmann, S. *Geschichte Israels in alttestamentlicher Zeit*. Munich, 1973. ET: *A History of Israel in Old Testament Times*. London 1975.

Herzfeld, E. *Iran in the Ancient East.* London, 1941.

The Persian Empire. Wiesbaden, 1968.

Huart, C. and Delaporte, L. *L'Iran Antique.* Paris, 1952.

Janssen, E. *Juda in der Exilszeit.* Göttingen, 1956.

Junge, P. J. *Darius I, König der Perser.* Leipzig, 1944.

Klausner, J. *History of the Second Temple* (in Hebrew). 5 vols. 6th edn. Jerusalem, 1963.

Kreissig, H. *Die sozialökonomische Situation in Juda zur Achämenidenzeit.* Berlin, 1973.

Maier, J. *Das Judentum von der biblischen Zeit bis zur Moderne.* Munich, 1973.

Meyer, E. *Die Entstehung des Judenthums.* Halle, 1896; repr. Hildesheim, 1965.

Momigliano, A. *Hochkulturen im Hellenismus. Die Begegnung der Griechen mit Kelten, Römern, Juden und Persern.* Munich, 1979.

Myers, J. M. *The World of the Restoration.* Englewood Cliffs, 1968.

Noth, M. *Geschichte Israels.* Rev. edn. Göttingen, 1954. ET: *A History of Israel.* 2 vols. Rev. edn. London–New York, 1960.

Oesterley, W. O. E. and Robinson, T. H. *A History of Israel.* 2 vols. London, 1932.

Olmstead, A. T. *History of the Persian Empire.* Chicago, 1948.

Osten, H. H. von der. *Die Welt der Perser.* Stuttgart, 1956.

Parker, R. A. and Dubberstein, H. *Babylonian Chronology, 625 B.C.–A.D. 75.* New York, 1956.

Sacchi, P. *Storia del mondo Giudaico, 1.* Turin, 1976.

Smith, M. *Palestinian Parties and Politics that Shaped the Old Testament.* New York, 1971.

Snaith, N. H. *The Jews from Cyrus to Herod.* New York, 1956.

Stern, E. *The Material Culture of the Land of the Bible in the Persian Period* (in Hebrew). Jerusalem, 1973. ET forthcoming.

Toynbee, A. J. *A Study of History,* vol. 7. Oxford, 1955.

Walser, G. (ed.). *Beiträge zur Achämenidengeschichte.* Historia, Einzelschriften, 18. Wiesbaden, 1972.

Wiseman, D. J. (ed.). *People of Old Testament Times.* Oxford, 1973. Chapter 13, 'The Persians', by G. Widengren.

Zadok, R. *The Jews in Babylonia during the Chaldean and Achaemenian Periods (according to the Babylonian Sources).* Haifa, 1979.

CHAPTER 1 THE GEOGRAPHY OF PALESTINE AND THE LEVANT IN RELATION TO ITS HISTORY

Atlases

Aharoni, Y. and Avi-Yonah, M. *The Macmillan Bible Atlas.* New York, 1968. Rev. edn. New York, 1979.

Atlas of Israel. Jerusalem: Survey of Israel, Ministry of Labour; Amsterdam, 1970.

Avi-Yonah, M. *Carta's Atlas of the Period of the Second Temple, the Mishnah and the Talmud* (in Hebrew). Jerusalem, 1966.

Baly, D. and Tushingham, A. D. *Atlas of the Biblical World.* New York, 1971.

Grollenberg, L. H. *Atlas of the Bible.* New York, 1957.

May, H. G. (ed.). *Oxford Bible Atlas.* 2nd edn. New York, 1974.

Wright, G. E. and Filson, F. W. (eds.). *The Westminster Historical Atlas to the Bible.* Rev. edn. Philadelphia, 1956.

Maps

Bordure Orientale de la Méditerranée: Carte Lithologique. 1:500,000. 2 sheets. Paris: Délégation Général au Levant de la France combattante, Service des Travaux Publics, 1942.

Carte Géologique du Liban. 1:200,000. Prepared by Louis Dubertret. Beirut: Ministère des Travaux Publics, République du Liban, 1955.

Carte Géologique: Liban, Syrie, et Bordure des Pays Voisins. 1:1,000,000. Prepared by Louis Dubertret. Paris: Musée Nationale de l'Histoire Naturelle, 1962.

Carte Pluviométrique du Liban. 1:200,000. Prepared by J. Rey, S.J., Observatoire de Ksara: Lebanon, 1954.

Geological Map of Jordan (East of the Rift Valley). 1:250,000. Prepared by A. Quennell. Amman: Government of the Hashemite Kingdom of the Jordan, 1959.

Geologische Karte von Jordanien. 1:250,000. 5 sheets. Prepared by F. Bender. Amman: Government of the Hashemite Kingdom of the Jordan, Natural Resources Authority, 1968.

The Hashemite Kingdom of the Jordan. 1:100,000. 15 sheets. In Arabic. Amman: Department of Lands and Surveys of the Hashemite Kingdom of the Jordan, 1951.

Israel. 1:100,000. 16 sheets. In Hebrew. Jerusalem: Department of Surveys, Israel, 1962.

Levant. 1:200,000. 28 sheets. Paris: Institut Géographique Nationale, 1949.

General

Abel, F. M. *Histoire de la Palestine depuis la Conquête d'Alexandre jusqu'a l'Invasion Arabe.* 2 vols. Paris, 1952.

    Géographie de la Palestine. 2 vols. 1933–38. Reprint, Paris, 1967.

Ackroyd, P. R. *Exile and Restoration.* Philadelphia, 1968.

Aharoni, Y. *The Land of the Bible: A Historical Geography.* Trans. by A. F. Rainy. Philadelphia, 1967. Rev. and enlarged edn. Philadelphia, 1979.

Avi-Yonah, M. *The Holy Land from the Persians to the Arab Conquest: A Historical Geography.* Grand Rapids, Michigan, 1966.

Baly, D. *Geographical Companion to the Bible.* New York, 1963.

    The Geography of the Bible. Rev. edn. New York, 1974.

Beaumont, P., Blake, G. H. and Wagstaff, J. M. *The Middle East: A Geographical Study.* London, 1976.

Birot, P. and Dresch, J. *La Méditerranée et le Moyen-Orient*; vol. 2: *La Méditerranée Orientale et le Moyen Orient.* Paris, 1955.

Brice, W. C. *South-West Asia: A Systematic Regional Geography.* London, 1966.

Cressey, G. G. *Crossroads: Land and Life in Southwest Asia.* Philadelphia, 1960.

Du Buit, M. *Géographie de la Terre Sainte.* 2 vols. Paris, 1958.

Fisher, W. B. *The Middle East: A Physical, Social, and Regional Geography.* 6th edn. New York, 1971.

Geography, compiled from material originally published in the *Encyclopaedia Judaica.* Jerusalem, 1971.

Hitti, P. K. *History of Syria, including Lebanon and Palestine.* New York, 1951.

Karmon, Y. *Israel: A Regional Geography.* New York, 1971.

Noth, M. *The Old Testament World.* Trans. by V. I. Gruhn. Philadelphia, 1966.

Orni, E. and Efrat, E. *Geography of Israel.* 3rd rev. edn. New York, 1971.

Smith, G. A. *The Historical Geography of the Holy Land.* 25th edn., 1931. Rev. edn. with introduction by H. H. Rowley, New York, 1966.

Structure

Blake, G. S. *The Stratigraphy of Palestine and Its Building Stones.* Jerusalem: The Crown Agent for the Colonies, 1928.

Blake, G. S. and Goldschmidt, M. G. *Geology and Water Resources of Palestine.* Jerusalem: Government Printer, 1947.

Burdon, D. J. *Handbook of the Geology of Jordan.* Amman: Government of the Hashemite Kingdom of the Jordan, 1959.

Ionides, M. G. *Report on the Water Resources of Transjordan and their Development.* London: Crown Agents for Overseas Governments and Administrations, 1939.

Kallner-Amiran, D. H. 'Geomorphology of the Central Negev Highlands', *IEJ*, 1 (1950–51), 107–20.

Picard, L. *Structure and Evolution of Palestine.* Jerusalem: Geological Department of the Hebrew University, 1943.

Vaumas, E. de. *Le Liban: Etude de Géographie Physique.* 3 vols. Paris, 1954.

'Structure et Morphologie du Proche-Orient', *Revue de Géographie Alpine*, vol. 49 (1961), 225–74, 433–509, 645–739.

Climate

Ashbel, D. *Bio-climatic Atlas of Israel.* Jerusalem: Meteorological Department of the Hebrew University, 1950.

Regional Climatology of Israel. In Hebrew. Jerusalem: Meteorological Department of the Hebrew University, 1951.

Atlas Climatique du Liban. 3 vols. Beirut: Service Météorologique du Liban, 1966.

Clerget, M. *Matériaux pour une etude climatologique de la Méditerranée orientale: types de temps.* Cairo, 1934.

Plassard, J. *Notice explicative de la carte pluviométrique du Liban au 1/200,000.* Beirut: Service Météorologique du Liban, 1972.

al-Shalash, A. H. *Rainfall Atlas of the Hashemite Kingdom of Jordan.* Amman, 1964.

CHAPTER 2. NUMISMATICS

The following list is a selection from the vast literature on the subject. Additional references for Jewish numismatics will be found in the bibliographies of B. Kanael and L. A. Mayer, listed below.

Works which were written both in Hebrew and in a European language are cited in their non-Hebrew version. Some preference is given to works which do not appear in the bibliographies mentioned, especially publications about non-Jewish coinage in Palestine, very recent publications, and some which are less accessible.

Introduction

General works and surveys

Avi-Yonah, M. *Prolegomenon* to the reprinted edn. (New York, 1967) of F. C. Madden, *History of Jewish coinage and of money in the Old and New Testament.* London, 1864, pp. xv–xlvi.
  in *Compendia Rerum Judaicarum*, ed. S. Safrai, M. Stern, D. Flusser and W. C. van Unnik, vol. 1, 1, pp. 58–62. Assen and Philadelphia, 1974.
Guépin, J. P. 'East Greek Numismatics, Syria to India'. *A Survey of Numismatic Research, 1960–1965*, ed. O. Mørkholm, especially pp. 62–76. Copenhagen, 1967.
Hill, G. F. *Catalogue of the Greek Coins of Palestine.* Catalogue of the Greek Coins in the British Museum. Vol. 27. London, 1914; repr. Bologna, 1965.
Kadman, L. 'The Development of Jewish Coinage', in *The Dating and Meaning of Ancient Jewish Coins and Symbols*, Publication of the Israel Numismatic Society, 1, (1954), pp. 98–103.
Kanael, B. 'Ancient Jewish Coins and Their Historical Importance', *BA*, 26 (1963), 38–62 = *BAR*, no. 3, pp. 279–303. New York, 1970.
Kindler, A. *The Coins of the Holy Land, Bank of Israel Collection.* Jerusalem, 1974.
Le Rider, G. 'Les Ateliers monétaires de la côte syrienne, palestinienne, égyptienne et cyrénéenne', *Congresso internazionale di Numismatica*, vol. 1: *Relazioni*, pp. 67–109. Rome, 1961.
Madden, F. W. *History of Jewish Coinage and of Money in the Old and New Testament.* London, 1864; repr., with prolegomenon by M. Avi-Yonah, New York, 1967.
  Coins of the Jews. London, 1881.
Meshorer, Y. *Jewish Coins of the Second Temple Period.* Tel Aviv, 1966.
Mørkholm, O. 'Syria–Palestine', *A Survey of Numismatic Research, 1972–1977*, pp. 80–5. Wetteren, 1979.
Reifenberg, A. *Ancient Jewish Coins.* 2nd edn. Jerusalem, 1947.
Romanoff, P. *Jewish Symbols on Ancient Jewish Coins.* Philadelphia, 1944; repr. New York, 1971.
Sylloge Nummorum Graecorum, especially: *The Royal Collection of Coins and Medals*, Danish National Museum, part 36: *Syria: Cities* (Copenhagen, 1959); part 37: *Phoenicia* (Copenhagen, 1961); part 38: *Palestine–Characene* (Copenhagen, 1961); vol. 4, part 8: *Syria–Nabathaea* (Fitzwilliam Museum, London, 1971); vol. 6, part 1: *The Greek and Hellenistic Coins* (The Lewis Collection, London, 1972).
Westermark, U. 'Syria, Phoenicia and Palestine', *A Survey of Numismatic Research, 1966–1971*, vol. 1, pp. 177–98. New York, 1973.

Collected Essays

Kadman, L., Kindler, A., Klimovsky, E. W., Meyshan, J., Mildenberg, L. and Cohn, G. (eds.). *The Dating and Meaning of Ancient Jewish Coins and Symbols*, Numismatic Studies and Researches, vol. 2. Jerusalem, 1958.
Kindler, A. (ed.). *International Numismatic Convention, Jerusalem, 1963: The Patterns of Monetary Development in Phoenicia and Palestine in Antiquity.* Tel Aviv–Jerusalem, 1967.

Klimowsky, E. W. *On Ancient Palestinian and Other Coins, Their Symbolism and Metrology*, Numismatic Studies and Researches, vol. 7. Tel Aviv, 1974.

Meyshan, J. *Essays in Jewish Numismatics*. Numismatic Studies and Researches, vol. 6. Tel Aviv, 1968.

Denominations

Ben-David, A. 'Jewish and Roman Bronze and Copper Coins: Their Reciprocal Relations in Mishna and Talmud from Herod the Great to Trajan and Hadrian', *PEQ*, 103 (1974), 109–29.

Kindler, A. 'Monetary Pattern and Function of Jewish Coins', *International Numismatic Convention, Jerusalem, 1963*, pp. 180–205. Tel Aviv–Jerusalem, 1967.

Sperber, D. 'Palestinian Currency Systems During the Second Commonwealth', *JQR*, 56 (1965–66), 273–301.

Bibliographies

Kanael, B. 'Literaturüberblicke der griechischen Numismatik: Altjüdische Münzen', *Jahrbuch für Numismatik und Geldgeschichte*, 17 (1967), 154–298.

Mayer, L. A. *A Bibliography of Jewish Numismatics*. Jerusalem, 1966.

Thompson, M., Mørkholm, O. and Kraay, C. M. *An Inventory of Greek Coin Hoards*, pp. 200–24. New York, 1973.

Periodicals

Alon HaHevra HaNumismatith LeIsrael (in Hebrew), 1 (1966); 6, 3 (December, 1978).

Israel Numismatic Bulletin, nos. 1–5. Jerusalem, 1962–63.

Israel Numismatic Journal, 1 and 2: Tel Aviv, 1963–64; 3: Jerusalem, 1965–66.

History of Research

Kanael, B. 'Literaturüberblicke der griechischen Numismatik: Altjüdische Münzen', *Jahrbuch für Numismatik und Geldgeschichte*, 17 (1967), 161–89.

Meyshan, J. *Essays in Jewish Numismatics*, Numismatic Studies and Researches, vol. 6, pp. 13–26. Tel Aviv, 1968.

The Persian Period

Balmuth, M. 'The Monetary forerunners of Coinage in Phoenicia and Palestine', *International Numismatic Convention, Jerusalem, 1963*, pp. 25–32. Tel Aviv–Jerusalem, 1967.

Kindler, A. 'The Mint of Tyre – The Major Source of Silver Coins in Ancient Palestine', *Eretz-Israel*, 8 (1967), 318–24.

'A New "Yehud" Coin-Type', *Bulletin of Museum Haaretz*, 14 (1972), 107–12.

Loewe, R. 'Biblical Allusions to Money', *PEQ*, 87 (1955), 141–50.

Mildenberg, L. 'Yehud: A Preliminary Study of the Provincial Coinage of Judea', *Essays in Honor of M. Thompson*, pp. 183–96. Wetteren, 1979.

Naster, P. 'Le développement des monnayages phéniciens avant Alexandre d'après les trésors', *International Numismatic Convention, Jerusalem, 1963*, pp. 3–24. Tel Aviv–Jerusalem, 1967.

Rahmani, L. Y. 'Silver Coins of the Fourth Century B.C. from Tel-Gamma', *IEJ*, 21 (1971), 158–60.

Rappaport, U. 'The First Judean Coinage', *JJS*, 32 (1981), 1–17.

Spaer, A. 'Some More "Yehud" Coins', *IEJ*, 27 (1977), 200–3.

'A Coin of Jeroboam?', *IEJ*, 29 (1979), 218.

Stern, E. *The Material Culture of the Land of the Bible in the Persian Period*, pp. 213–25 (in Hebrew). Jerusalem, 1973.

Under Alexander and the Hellenistic Dynasties

See also the previous section, 'The Persian Period' for source items on Yehud coins, some of which were struck in the early Hellenistic period.

Bellinger, A. R. 'The End of the Seleucids', *Transactions of the Connecticut Academy of Arts and Sciences*, 38 (June, 1949), 51–102.

Brett, A. B. 'Seleucid Coins of Ake–Ptolemais', *ANS Museum Notes*, 1 (1945), 17–35.

'The Mint of Ascalon under the Seleucids', *ANS Museum Notes*, 4 (1950), 43–54.

Kindler, A. 'Silver Coins Bearing the Name of Judea from the Early Hellenistic Period', *IEJ*, 24 (1974), 73–6.

Jenkins, G. K. 'The Monetary Systems in the Early Hellenistic Time with Special Regard to the Economic Policy of the Ptolemaic Kings', *International Numismatic Convention, Jerusalem, 1963*, pp. 53–74. Tel Aviv–Jerusalem, 1967.

Jeselsohn, D. 'A New Coin Type with Hebrew Inscription', *IEJ*, 24 (1974), 77–8.

Merker, I. L. 'Notes on the Abdalonymos and the Dated Alexander Coinage of Sidon and Ake', *ANS Museum Notes*, 11 (1964), 13–20.

Mørkholm, O. 'The Monetary System of the Seleucid Kings until 129 B.C.', *International Numismatic Convention, Jerusalem, 1963*, pp. 75–87. Tel Aviv–Jerusalem, 1967.

Rahmani, L. Y. 'A Hoard of Alexander Coins from Tel Tsippor', *Schweizer Münzblätter*, 16 (1966), 129–45.

Rappaport, U. 'Gaza and Ascalon in the Persian and Hellenistic Periods in Relation to Their Coins', *IEJ*, 20 (1970), 75–80.

Rostovtzeff, M. 'Some Remarks on the Monetary and Commercial Policy of the Seleucids and Attalids', in *Anatolian Studies presented to W. H. Buckler*, pp. 277–98. Manchester, 1939.

Spaer, A. 'A Hoard of Alexander Tetradrachms from Galilee', *INJ*, 3 (1965–66), 1–7.

The Hasmoneans

Bachmann, H. G. 'The Metallurgical Composition of Hasmonean Coins', *Museum Haaretz*, 15–16 (1972–73), 82–90.

Barag, D. and Qedar, S. 'The Beginning of the Hasmonean Coinage', *INJ*, 4 (1980), 8–21.

Ben-David, A. 'When did the Maccabees begin to strike their First Coins?', *PEQ*, 104 (July–December, 1972), 93–103.

Fischer, Th. 'Johannes Hyrkan I. auf Tetradrachmen Antiochos' VII?', *ZDPV*, 91 (1975), 191–6.

Hanson, R. S. 'Toward a Chronology of Hasmonean Coins', *BASOR*, 216 (December, 1974), 21–3.

Jeselsohn, D. 'Hever Yehudim – A New Jewish Coin', *PEQ*, 112 (January–June, 1980), 11–17.

Kanael, B. 'The Beginning of Maccabean Coinage', *IEJ*, 1 (1950–51), 170–5.

'The Greek Letters and Monograms on the Coins of Jehohanan the High Priest', *IEJ*, 2 (1952), 190–4.

Kindler, A. 'The Jaffa Hoard of Alexander Jannaeus', *IEJ*, 4 (1954), 170–85.

'The Coinage of the Hasmonaean Dynasty', in *The Dating and Meaning of Ancient Jewish Coins and Symbols*, Numismatic Studies and Researches, vol. 2, pp. 10–28. Jerusalem, 1958.

'Addendum to the Dated Coins of Alexander Janneus', *IEJ*, 18 (1968), 188–91.

'Hoard from the Second Half of the Second Century B.C.E.', *AHHI*, 4 (1970), 41–6 (in Hebrew).

'The Hellenistic Influence on Hasmonean Coins', in *The Seleucid Period in Eretz Israel*, ed. B. Bar-Kochva, pp. 289–308 (in Hebrew). Tel Aviv, 1980.

Meshorer, Y. *Jewish Coins of the Second Temple Period*, pp. 41–63. Tel Aviv, 1967.

'The Beginning of the Hasmonean Coinage', *IEJ*, 24 (1974), 59–61.

Minc, H. 'Yehohanan, The High Priest', *SAN, Journal of the Society for Ancient Numismatics*, 8 (1977), 30–3.

Naveh, J. 'The Dated Coins of Alexander Janneus', *IEJ*, 18 (1968), 20–6.

Rappaport, U. 'Pure Numismatics', *Beth Mikra*, 31 (1967), 112–18 (in Hebrew).

'On the Meaning of Hever HaYehudim'. *Mehkarim – Studies in the History of the Jewish People in the Land of Israel*, vol. 3, pp. 59–67 (in Hebrew). Haifa, 1974.

'The Emergence of Hasmonaean Coinage', *AJS Review*, 1 (1976), 171–86.

Sperber, D. 'A Note on a Coin of Antigonus Mattathias', *JQR*, 54 (1963–64), 250–7.

Herod and Archelaus

Kanael, B. 'The Coins of King Herod of the 3rd Year', *JQR*, 42 (1952), 261–4.

Meyshan, J. 'The Symbols on the Coinage of Herod the Great and their Meaning', *PEQ*, 91 (1959), 109–21 = *Essays in Jewish Numismatics*. Numismatic Studies and Researches, vol. 6, pp. 85–97. Tel Aviv, 1968.

Rappaport, U. 'Note sur la chronologie des monnaies Hérodiennes', *RN*, 10 (1968), 69–75.

Under Roman Governors

Bammel, E. 'Syrian Coinage and Pilate', *JJS*, 2 (1950–51), 108–10.

Kindler, A. 'More Dates on the Coins of the Procurators', *IEJ*, 6 (1956), 54–7.

Meshorer, Y. *Jewish Coins of the Second Temple Period*, pp. 102–6. Tel Aviv, 1967.

Stauffer, E. 'Zur Münzprägung und Judenpolitik des Pontius Pilatus', *La Nouvelle Clio*, 9 (1950), 495–514.

Herod Antipas and Philip

Kindler, A. 'A Coin of Herod Philip – the Earliest Portrait of a Herodian Ruler', *IEJ*, 21 (1971), 161–3. Cf. also J. Meyshan, *Essays in Jewish Numismatics*, Numismatic Studies and Researches, vol. 6. Tel Aviv, 1968.

Agrippa I and Agrippa II

Barag, D. 'The Palestinian "Judaea Capta" Coins of Vespasian and Titus and the Era on the Coins of Agrippa II minted under the Flavians', *NC*, 18 (1978), 14–23.
Lifschitz, B. 'Une monnaie du roi Agrippa I', *Scripta Classica Israelica*, 2 (1975), 105–6.
Meshorer, Y. 'A New Type of Coins of Agrippa II', *IEJ*, 21 (1971), 164–5.
Meyshan, J. *Essays in Jewish Numismatics*, Numismatic Studies and Researches, vol. 6, pp. 105–34. Tel Aviv, 1968.
Seyrig, H. 'Les ères d'Agrippa II', *RN*, 6 (1964), 55–65.

Currency in Palestine (to 70 C.E. approx.)

Ben-David, A. *Jerusalem und Tyros, Ein Beitrag zur palästinensischen Münz- und Wirtschaftsgeschichte (126 a.C.–57 p.C.)*. Basel and Tübingen, 1969.
Hamburger, H. 'The Coin Issues of the Roman Administration from the Mint of Caesarea Maritima', *IEJ*, 20 (1970), 81–91.
Klimowsky, E. W. 'Monetary Function of City Coins', *International Numismatic Convention, Jerusalem, 1963*, pp. 129–73. Tel Aviv–Jerusalem, 1967.

For more on city coinage see below.

The Coins of the First Revolt

Kadman, L. *The Coins of the Jewish War of 66–73*, Corpus Nummorum Palaestinensium, vol. 3. Jerusalem, 1960.

The Coins of the Second Revolt

Kanael, B. 'Notes on the Dates Used During the Bar Kokhba Revolt', *IEJ*, 21 (1971), 39–46.
Kindler, A. 'The Coinage of the Bar-Kokhba War', in *Dating and Meaning of Ancient Jewish Coins and Symbols*, publication of the Israel Numismatic Society, 1 (1954), pp. 62–80.
Mildenberg, L. 'The Eleazar Coins of the Bar Kochba Rebellion', *Historia Judaica*, 11 (1949), 77–108.
'Bar Kokhba Coins and Documents', *HSCP*, 84 (1980), 311–35.
Muehsam, A. *Coin and Temple*. Leiden, 1966.
Philonenko, M. 'Observations sur des monnaies juives de la Seconde Révolte (132–135)', *CRAIBL*, (1974), 183–9.
Sperber, D. 'Iyunim be-Matbeot Bar-Kochba', *Sinai*, 55 (1964), 37–41 (in Hebrew).
Spijkerman, A. *Herodium*, vol. 3: *Coins*. Jerusalem, 1972.

Municipal Coinage and Currency in Palestine (approx. 70–250 C.E.)

Carson, R. A. G. 'The Inflation of the Third Century and its Monetary influence in the New East', *International Numismatic Convention, Jerusalem, 1963*, pp. 231–250. Tel Aviv–Jerusalem, 1967.

Hamburger, H. 'A Hoard of Syrian Tetradrachms and Tyrian Bronze Coins from Gush Halav', *IEJ*, 4 (1954), 201–26.

'Minute Coins from Caesarea', *Atiqot*, 1 (1955), 115–38.

'The Coin Issues of the Roman Administration from the Mint of Caesarea Maritima', *IEJ*, 20 (1970), 81–91.

Kadman, L. *The Coins of Aelia Capitolina*, Corpus Nummorum Palaestinensium, vol. 1. Jerusalem, 1956.

The Coins of Caesarea Maritima, Corpus Nummorum Palaestinensium, vol. 2. Jerusalem, 1957.

The Coins of Akko-Ptolemais, Corpus Nummorum Palaestinensium, vol. 4. Jerusalem, 1961.

Kindler, A. *The Coins of Tiberias*. Tiberias, 1961.

Kleiman, E. 'Bi-Metalism in Rabbi's Time, Two Variants of the Mishna "Gold Acquires Silver"', *Zion*, 38 (1973), 48–61 (in Hebrew).

Levine, L. 'Some Observations on the Coins of Caesarea Maritima', *IEJ*, 22 (1972), 131–40.

Meshorer, Y. 'The Coins of Tiberias', *All the Land of Nephtali*, 192–4 (in Hebrew). Jerusalem, 1967.

'Monnaies de Raphia', *RN*, 18 (1976), 57–68.

'Sepphoris and Rome', *Essays in Honor of M. Thompson*, pp. 159–71. Wetteren, 1979.

Rosenberger, M. *City-Coins of Palestine*, The Rosenberger Israel Collection, 1 (1972); 2 (1975); 3 (1977).

Seyrig, H. 'Irenopolis–Neronias–Sepphoris', *NC*, 10 (1950), 284–9; and 'An additional note', *NC*, 15 (1955), 157–9.

'Temples, cultes et souvenirs historiques de la Décapole', *Syria*, 36 (1959), 60–78 (= *Antiquités syriennes*, vol. 6, pp. 34–53. Paris, 1966).

'Le monnayage de Ptolemais en Phénicie', *RN*, 4 (1962), 25–49.

'Divinités de Ptolémaïs', *Syria*, 39 (1962), 193–207 (= *Antiquités syriennes*, vol. 6, pp. 100–14. Paris, 1966).

'Alexandre le Grand, fondateur de Gerasa', *Syria*, 42 (1965), 25–34 (= *Antiquités syriennes*, vol. 6, pp. 141–4. Paris, 1966).

Sperber, D. *Roman Palestine 200–400, Money and Prices*. Ramat-Gan, Israel, 1974.

Spijkerman, A. 'A Supplemental Study of the Coinage of Aelia Capitolina (Jerusalem)', *Liber Annuus*, 7 (1956–57), 145–62.

'A Hoard of Syrian Tetradrachms and Eastern Antoniniani from Capharnaum', *Liber Annuus*, 9 (1959), 283–329.

'An Unknown Coin-type of Pella Dacapoleos', *Liber Annuus*, 20 (1970), 353–8.

'The Coins of Eleutheropolis Judaea', *Liber Annuus*, 21 (1971), 367–84.

The Coins of the Decapolis and Provincia Arabia, Studii Biblii Franciscani Collectio Maior 25, ed. M. Piccirillo. Jerusalem, 1978.

Sutherland, C. H. V. 'The Pattern of Monetary Development in Phoenicia and Palestine during the Early Empire', *International Numismatic Convention, Jerusalem, 1963*, pp. 88–105. Tel Aviv–Jerusalem, 1967.

The Currency of Palestine in the Late Roman and Byzantine Periods

Bellinger, A. R. *Coins from Jerash, 1928–1934*, Numismatic Notes and Monographs of the American Numismatic Society, no. 81, pp. 11ff. New York, 1938. Bellinger's comments are still valuable.

Grierson, P. 'The Monetary Reforms of Anastasius and their Economic Consequences', *International Numismatic Convention, Jerusalem, 1963*, pp. 283–310. Tel Aviv–Jerusalem, 1967.

Meshorer, Y. 'An Enigmatic Arab-Byzantine Coin', *INJ*, 3 (1965–66), 32–6.

Metcalf, D. M. 'Some Byzantine and Arab-Byzantine Coins from Palaestina Prima', *INJ*, 2, 3–4 (1964), 32–46.

Rahmany, L. Y. 'Two Hoards of Byzantine Coins from Khirbet Deir Dassawi', *INJ*, 2, 1–2 (1964), 19–21.

Sperber, D. *Roman Palestine 200–400, Money and Prices*. Ramat-Gan, Israel, 1974. About a hoard of some 3,000–4,000 Byzantine gold coins see E. Semmelman, in *Shekel* 7, 4 (winter, 1974), 6–8.

CHAPTER 3. CALENDARS AND CHRONOLOGY

General

Bickerman, E. J. *Chronology of the Ancient World*. London–Ithaca, 1968; 2nd edn. 1979.

The present Jewish calendar

Maimonides, *Sanctification of the New Moon*, ch. 6–10, trans. S. Gandz. New Haven, Conn., 1956.

The history of the Jewish calendar

The empirical calendar of the rabbis: Maimonides, *Sanctification*, chs. 1–4.

Zuckermann, B. 'Materialen zur Entwicklung der altjuedischen Zeitrechnung im Talmud,' *Jahresbericht des juedisch-theologisch. Seminar in Breslau*, 1882. This is an excellent antiquarian work.

Mahler, E. *Handbuch der juedischen Chronologie*. Leipzig, 1916: repr. Hildesheim, 1967.

Finegan, J. *Handbook of Biblical Chronology*. Princeton, N.J.; 1964. Cf. E. J. Bickerman's review in *BibOr*, 22 (1965), 184.

Frank, E. *Talmudic and Rabbinical Chronology*. New York, 1956.

Sidersky, D. 'Etude sur l'origine astronomique de la chronologie juive', *Mémoires présentés par divers savants à l'Académie des Inscriptions et belles lettres*, 12, 2 (1913), 595–683.

Dead Sea Scrolls calendar

Finegan, J. *Handbook of Biblical Chronology*, pp. 44–9. Princeton, N.J., 1964.

CHAPTER 4. THE PERSIAN EMPIRE

Sources

Aharoni, Y. 'Three Hebrew Ostraca from Arad', *BASOR*, 197 (1970), 16–28.

Avigad, N. 'Bullae and Seals from a Post-Exilic Judean Archive', *Qedem*, 4. Jerusalem, 1976.

Cooke, G. A. *A Text-book of North-Semitic Inscriptions*, p. 346. Oxford, 1903.

Cowley, A. E. *Aramaic Papyri of the Fifth Century B.C.* Oxford, 1923, and in J. L. Starkey and G. Lankester Harding, *Beth-Pelet II*, p. 29. London, 1932.

Cross, F. M. 'The Papyri and their Historical Implications', *AASOR*, 41 (1974), 17–29.

Driver, G. R. *Aramaic Documents of the Fifth Century B.C.* Oxford, 1954.

Dunand, M. 'Remarques Epigraphiques', *BMB*, 5 (1941), 74–8.

   'Nouvelles Inscriptions Phéniciennes du Temple d'Echmoun à Boston Ech-Cheikh, près Sidon', *BMB*, 18 (1965), 105–9.

Galling, K. 'Die Syrisch–palästinische Kuste nach der Beschreibung bei Pseudo-Skylax', in his *Studien zur Geschichte Israels in Persischen Zeitalter*, pr. 185–209. Tübingen, 1964.

Glueck, N. 'Ostraca from Elath', *BASOR*, 80 (1940), 3–10.

   'Ostraca from Elath', *BASOR*, 82 (1941), 3–11.

Grintz, Y. M. *The Book of Judith* (in Hebrew). Jerusalem, 1967.

Kraeling, E. G. *The Brooklyn Museum Aramaic Papyri*. New Haven, 1953.

Landau, W. V. 'Die Inschrift von Achoris, König von Ägypten', *MVAG*, 9 (1904), 342–7; pl. II.

Lapp, P. W. and Lapp, N. L. *Discoveries in the Wâdī-el-Dâliyeh*. *AASOR*, 41. Cambridge, Mass., 1974.

Macalister, R. A. S. *The Excavation of Gezer*, vol. II. London, 1912.

Naveh, J. 'Hebrew Texts in Aramaic Script in the Persian Period?', *BASOR*, 203 (1971), 27–31.

   'The Aramaic Ostraca', in *Beer-Sheba* I, ed. Y. Aharoni, pp. 79–82. Tel Aviv, 1973.

   'The Aramaic Ostraca from Tel Arad', in *Arad Inscriptions*, ed. Y. Aharoni, pp. 167–204 (in Hebrew). Jerusalem, 1975.

Rabinowitz, I. 'Aramaic Inscriptions of the Fifth Century B.C.E. from a North-Arab Shrine in Egypt', *JNES*, 15 (1956), 1–9.

Rowe, A. *A Catalogue of Egyptian Scarabs in the Palestine Archaeological Museum*, p. 295; pl. xxxviii. Cairo, 1936.

Tcherikover, V. A. 'Palestine in the light of the Zenon Papyri', in *The Jews in the Greco-Roman World* (in Hebrew). Tel Aviv, 1961.

General works

Babelon, E. *Les Perses achémenides, les satrapes et les dynasties tributaires de leur empire: Chypre et Phénicie*. Paris, 1893.

Culican, W. *The Medes and Persians*. London, 1965.

Ehtecham, L'Iran sous les Achemenides. Fribourg, 1946.

Frye, R. N. *The Heritage of Persia*, pp. 119–37. London, 1966.

Ghirshman, R. *Iran*, pp. 106–205. Harmondsworth, 1954.

Herzfeld, E. *Iran in the Ancient East*. London, 1941.
  The Persian Empire, Studies in Geography and Ethnography of the Ancient Near East, chs.
    14–15, pp. 288–347. Wiesbaden, 1968.
Huart, C. and Delaporte, L. *L'Iran Antique, Elam et Perse et la Civilization Iranienne*, pp.
    231–77. Paris, 1952.
Junge, P. J. *Darius I, König der Perser*. Leipzig, 1944.
Olmstead, A. T. *History of the Persian Empire, Achaemenian Period*. Chicago, 1948.
Rostovtzeff, M. *The Social and Economic History of the Hellenistic World*, vol. 1, ch. 1.
    Oxford, 1953.
Toynbee, A. J. *A Study of History*, vol. 7, pp. 580–689. Oxford, 1955.
Osten, H. H. von der. *Die Welt der Perser*, pp. 59–102. Stuttgart, 1956.

Outline of history

Barag, D. 'The Effects of the Tennes Rebellion on Palestine', *BASOR*, 183 (1966),
    6–12.
Cross, F. M., Jr. 'The Discovery of the Samaritan Papyri', *BA*, 26 (1963), 110–21.
  'Aspects of Samaritan and Jewish History in the Late Persian and Hellenistic Times',
    HTR, 59 (1966), 201–11.
  'Papyri of the Fourth Century B.C. from Daliyeh', in *New Directions in Biblical
    Archaeology*, ed. D. N. Freedman and J. C. Greenfield, pp. 45–69. Garden city, New
    York, 1971.
Dumbrell, W. J. 'The Tell el Maskhuta Bowls and the Kingdom of Qedar in the Persian
    Period', *BASOR*, 203 (1971), 33–44.
Liver, J. *The House of David from the Fall of the Kingdom of Judah to the Fall of the Second
    Commonwealth and After*, pp. 72–116 (in Hebrew). Jerusalem, 1959.
Porten, B. *Archives from Elephantine*. Berkeley–Los Angeles, 1968.
Stern, E. 'Archaeological Aspects of the History of the Coastal Regions of Palestine
    during the Fourth Century B.C.E.', in *Bible and Jewish History. Studies dedicated to
    the memory of Jacob Liver*, ed. B. Uffenheimer, pp. 207–21. Tel Aviv, 1971.
Tadmor, Miriam. 'Fragments of an Achaemenid Throne from Samaria', *IEJ*, 24 (1974),
    35–43.
Talmon, S. 'Biblical Tradition on the Early History of the Samaritans', in *Eretz
    Shomron*, The Thirtieth Archaeological Convention of the Israel Exploration
    Society, pp. 19–33 (in Hebrew). Jerusalem, 1973.
Wright, G. E. 'The Samaritans at Shechem', *HTR*, 55 (1962), 357–66.

The satrapy of *Abar Nahara* and the place of Palestine in the political organization of the Persian Empire

Avi-Yonah, M. *The Holy Land from the Persian Period to the Arab Conquest*, ch. 1. Grand
    Rapids, 1966.
Clermont-Ganneau, C. H. 'Le Paradeisos royal Achéménide de Sidon', *RB*, 30 (1921),
    106–9.
Contenau, G. 'Sculptures provenant de la ville', *Syria*, 4 (1923), 276–8.
Dothan, M. 'An Archaeological Survey of Mt. Casius and its Vicinity', *Eretz-Israel*,
    9 (1969), 47–54 (in Hebrew).

Eilers, W. *Iranische Beamtennamen in der Keilschriflichen Überlieferung* in *Abhandlungen für die Kunde des Morgenlandes*, 25. Leipzig, 1940.

Forrer, E. *Die Provinzeinteilung des assyrischen Reiches*. Leipzig, 1921.

Galling, K. 'Syrien in der Politik der Achamenidar', *AfO*, 28 (1929).

Hölscher, G. *Palästina in der persischen und hellenistischen Zeit*. Berlin, 1903.

Kleemann, I. *Der Satrap-Sarkophag aus Sidon*. Berlin, 1958.

Leuze. O. *Die Satrapieneinteilung in Syrien und im Zweistromlande von 520–330*. Halle, 1935.

Mazar, B. 'The Kingdom of Aram and its Relation to Israel', in *The Kingdom of Israel and Judah*, ed. A. Malamat, p. 156 (in Hebrew) Jerusalem, 1961.

Rainy, A. F. 'The Satrapy "Beyond the River"', *AJBA*, (1969), 51–78.

Shalit, A. 'Koile Suria from the Mid-Fourth Century to the Beginning of the Third Century B.C.', *Scripta Hierosolymitana*, 1 (1954), 64–77.

The province of Judah

Aharoni, Y. *Excavations at Ramat Raḥel (1959–1960)*. Rome, 1962.
  The Land of the Bible, pp. 356–65. London, 1968.
  'Tel Beersheba', *IEJ*, 21 (1971), 231; *idem*, *IEJ*, 22 (1972), 170.

Albright, W. F. 'Ostracon no. 6043 from Ezion Geber', *BASOR*, 82 (1941), 11–15.
  The Archaeology of Palestine. Harmondsworth, 1960.

Alt, A. 'Die Rolle Samarias bei der Entstehung des Judentums', *Festschrift Otto Procksch zum 60. Geburtstag*, pp. 5–28. Leipzig, 1934. = *Kleine Schriften II*, pp. 316–37. Munich, 1953.

Avigad, N. 'New Light on the MṢH Seal-Impressions', *IEJ*, 8 (1958), 113–19.
  'Hebrew Inscriptions on Wine Jars', *IEJ*, 22 (1972), 1–9.

Biran, A. and Cohen, R. 'Aroer 1976', *IEJ*, 26 (1976), 130.

Cross, F. M., Jr. 'The Aramaic Script of the Late Persian Empire and the Rise of the National Script', in *The Bible and the Ancient Near East. Essays in Honor of W. F. Albright*, ed. G. E. Wright, pp. 174–213. Garden City, 1965.
  'Judean Stamps', *Eretz-Israel*, 9 (1969), 20–7.
  'A Reconstruction of the Judean Restoration', *JBL*, 94 (1975), 4ff.

Galling, K. 'Verbannung und Heimkehr', in *Festschrift für Wilhelm Rudolph*, ed. A. Kuschke. Tübingen, 1961.

Glueck, N. 'Some Edomite Pottery from Tell El-Kheleifeh', *BASOR*, 188 (1967), 8–38.

Hill, G. F. *Catalogue of the Greek Coins of Palestine*. London, 1914.

Jeselsohn, D. 'A New Coin Type with Hebrew Inscription', *IEJ*, 24 (1974), 77–8.

Kallai, Z. *The Northern Boundaries of Judah* (in Hebrew). Jerusalem, 1960.

Kaufmann, Y. *The History of Israelite Religion*, pp. 177–9 (in Hebrew). Jerusalem–Tel Aviv, 1969.

Kindler, A. 'The Greco-Phoenician Coins struck in Palestine in the time of the Persian Empire', *INJ*, 1 (1963), 2–6; 25–7.
  'Silver Coins Bearing the Name of Judea from the Early Hellenistic Period', *IEJ*, 24 (1974), 73–6.

Kochavi, M. (ed.) *Judea, Samaria and Golan: Archaeological Survey 1967–68* (in Hebrew). Jerusalem, 1972.
  'The First season of Excavations at Tell Malhata', *Qadmoniot*, 3 (1970), 22–4 (in Hebrew).

Kutscher, E. Y. '"PHW" and its cognants', *Tarbiz*, 30 (1960–61), 112ff (in Hebrew).

Liver, J. 'The Return from Babylon, its time and scope', *Eretz-Israel*, 5 (1958), 114–19 (in Hebrew).

Meshorer, *Jewish Coins of the Second Temple Period*, pp. 15–18 (in Hebrew). Tel Aviv, 1966.

'Means of Payment Prior to Coinage and the First Coinage', *Qadmoniot*, 9 (1976), 56 (in Hebrew).

Morgenstern, J. 'Jerusalem 485 B.C.', *HUCA*, 27 (1956), 101–78; *idem, HUCA*, 28 (1957), 14–46; *idem, HUCA*, 31 (1960), 1–20.

Myers, J. M. *Ezra–Nehemiah*. New York, 1965.

'Edom and Judah in the Sixth–Fifth centuries B.C.', in *Near Eastern Studies in Honor of W. F. Albright*, ed. H. Goedicke, pp. 377–92. Baltimore and London, 1971.

Rahmani, L. Y. 'A Partial Survey of the Adulam Area', *BIES*, 28 (1964), 209–31, (in Hebrew).

'Silver Coins of the Fourth Century B.C.E. from Tel Gamma', *IEJ*, 21 (1971), 158–60.

Rappaport, U. 'Gaza and Ascalon in the Persian and Hellenistic Periods', *IEJ*, 20 (1970), 75–80.

Rosental, F. 'The Script of Ostracon 6043', *BASOR*, 85 (1942), 8–9.

Rudolph, W. *Esra und Nehemia*. Tübingen, 1949.

Schürer, E. *Geschichte des juedischen Volkes im Zeitalter Jesu Christi*. 3 vols. Leipzig, 1909.

Smith, M. *Palestinian Parties and Politics that Shaped the Old Testament*, pp. 193ff; Appendix: 'Alt's account of the Samaritans'. New York, 1971.

Stern, E. *The Material Culture of the Land of the Bible in the Persian Period, 538–332 B.C.E.* (in Hebrew). Jerusalem, 1973.

'Seal Impressions in the Achaemenid Style in the Province of Judah', *BASOR*, 202 (1971), 6–16.

'The Province of Yehud', in *Cathedra* 4 (1977) (in Hebrew).

Weinberg, S. S. 'Post Exilic Palestine, An Archaeological Report', *The Israel Academy of Sciences and Humanities Proceedings*, vol. 4, no. 5. Jerusalem, 1969.

Summary

Boardman, J. *The Greeks Overseas*, pp. 3–4. Harmondsworth, 1964.

Naveh, J. 'The Excavations at Mesad Hashavyahu', *IEJ*, 12 (1962), 89–99.

Riis, P. J. 'The First Greeks in Phoenicia and their settlements at Sukas', *Ugaritica*, 6, 435–50. Paris, 1969.

Sukas I, The North-East Sanctuary and the First Settling of Greeks in Syria and Palestine. Copenhagen, 1970.

CHAPTER 5. THE ARCHEOLOGY OF PERSIAN PALESTINE

Classification of the material

Avigad, N. *Qedem*, 4. Jerusalem, 1974.

Broshi, M. 'Tel Megadim – A Phoenician City and Roman–Byzantine Road-Station', *Qadmoniot*, 2 (1969), 124–6 (in Hebrew).

Cowley, A. E. *Aramaic Papyri of the Fifth Century B.C.* Oxford, 1923.

Cross, F. M., Jr. 'The Discovery of the Samaritan Papyri', *BA*, 26 (1963), 110–21.
  'Jar Inscriptions from Shiqmona', *IEJ*, 18 (1968), 226–33.
  'Papyri of the Fourth Century B.C. from Dâliyeh', in *New Directions in Biblical Archaeology*, ed. D. N. Freedman and J. C. Greenfield, pp. 45–69. Garden City–New York, 1971.
Dumbrell, W. J. 'The Tell el-Maskhuṭa Bowls and the "Kingdom" of Qedar in the Persian Period', *BASOR*, 203 (1971), 33–44.
Dunand, M. 'Remarques épigraphiques', *BMB*, 5 (1941), 74–85.
  'Nouvelles inscriptions phéniciennes du Temple d'Echmoun A Bostan Ech-Cheikh, près Sidon', *BMB*, 18 (1965), 105–9.
Elgavish, J. *Archaeological Excavations at Shikmona; The levels of the Persian Period, Seasons 1963–1965* (in Hebrew). Haifa, 1968.
Frye, R. N. *The Heritage of Persia*. London, 1966.
Galling, K. 'Syrien in der Politik der Achämenider', *AfO*, 28 (1929).
  'Die Syrische–Palästinische Küste nach der Beschreibung bei Pseudo-Skylax', *ZDPV*, 61 (1938), 66–96.
Kraeling, E. G. *The Brooklyn Museum Aramaic Papyri*. New Haven, 1953.
Lapp, P. W. and Lapp. N. L. *Discoveries in the Wâdī-el-Dâliyeh. AASOR*, 41 (Cambridge, Mass. 1974), 17–29.
Leuze, O. *Die Satrapieneinteilung in Syrien und im Zweistromlande*. Halle, 1935.
Macalister, R. A. S. *The Excavation of Gezer, I–III*. London, 1912.
Mazar, B. and Dunayevsky, I. 'En-Gedi. Fourth and Fifth Season of Excavations (Preliminary Report)', *IEJ*, 17 (1967), 133–43.
Naveh, J. 'Hebrew Texts in Aramaic Script in the Persian Period?', *BASOR*, 203 (1971), 27–32.
Olmstead, A. T. *History of the Persian Empire (Achaemenid Period)*. Chicago, 1948.
Pope, A. U. (ed.) *A Survey of Persian Art*. Vols. I–IV. Oxford, 1938.
Porten, B. *Archives from Elephantine*. Berkeley and Los Angeles, 1968.
Rabinowitz, I. 'Aramaic Inscriptions of the Fifth Century B.C.E. from a North-Arab Shrine in Egypt', *JNES*, 15 (1956), 1–10.
Rainy, A. F. 'The Satrapy "Beyond the River"', *AJBA*, 1 (1969), 51–78.
Rowe, A. *A Catalogue of Egyptian Scarabs in the Palestine Archaeological Museum*. Cairo, 1936.
Stern, E. *The Material Culture of the Land of the Bible in the Persian Period, 538–332 B.C.E.* (in Hebrew). Jerusalem, 1973; English translation: *The Material Culture of the Bible in the Persian Period*. Warminster, 1982.
Toynbee, A. J. *A Study of History*, vol. 7, pp. 580–689. Oxford, 1955.
Weinberg, S. S. 'Post Exilic Palestine, An Archaeological Report', *The Israel Academy of Sciences and Humanities Proceedings*, vol. 4, no. 5. Jerusalem, 1969.
Yadin, Y. *Hazor*, The Schweich Lectures of the British Academy, 1970. London, 1972.

Architecture

Aharoni, Y. 'The "Persian Fortress" at Lachish – An Assyrian Palace?', *BIES*, 31 (1967), 80–91 (in Hebrew).
Albright, W. F. *The Archaeology of Palestine*. Harmondsworth, 1960.
Amiran, R. B. K. and Dunayevsky, I. 'The Assyrian Open-court Building and its Palestinian Derivates', *BASOR*, 149 (1958), 25–32.

Avigad, N. 'Two Hebrew Inscriptions on Wine-Jars', *IEJ*, 22 (1972), 1–9.

Clermont-Ganneau, C. H. 'Le Paradeisos royal Achéménide de Sidon', *RB*, 30 (1921), 106–9.

Guy, P. L. O. 'Ayelet Hashahar', *Bulletin of the Department of Antiquities of the State of Israel* 5–6 (1957), 19–20 (in Hebrew).

Hamilton, R. W. 'Excavations at Tel Abu-Hawam', *QDAP*, 4 (1935), 2–5.

Iliffe, J. H. and Mitford, T. B. 'New Light on Ancient Siege-Warfare from Unique Cyprus Discoveries', *ILN* (April, 1953), 613–16.

Kelso, J. L. 'The Second Campaign at Bethel', *BASOR*, 137 (1955), 5–10.

Kenyon, K. M. *Archaeology in the Holy Land*. London, 1960.

Lamon, R. S. and Shipton, G. M. *Megiddo. I: Seasons of 1925–34*, OIP 42. Chicago, 1939.

Lapp, P. W. 'Tell el-Fûl', *BA*, 28 (1965), 2–10.

Malamat, A. 'The Last Wars of the Kingdom of Judah', *JNES*, 9 (1950), 218–27.

Petrie, W. M. F. *Gerar*. London, 1928.

Sinclair, L. A. 'An Archaeological Study of Gibeah (Tell el-Fûl)', *AASOR*, 34–5 (1960), 3–52.

Stern, E. 'Excavations at Gil'am (Kh. Er.-Rujm)', *Atiqot*, 6 (1970), 31–55 (Hebrew series).

'The Architecture of Palestine in the Persian Period', *Eretz-Israel*, 11 (1973), 265–76 (in Hebrew).

Sukenik, E. L. 'Tell esh Shûni (Tell el-Kudâdi)', *QDAP*, 8 (1938), 167–8.

Tufnell, O. *Lachish III. The Iron Age*. Oxford, 1953.

Watzinger, C. *Denkmäler Palästinas*, I–II. Leipzig, 1935.

Woolley, C. L. *A Forgotten Kingdom*. Harmondsworth, 1953.

Burials

Abel, A. and Barrois, A. G. 'Fouilles de l'Ecole Archéologique Française de Jérusalem, effectuées à Neirab', *Syria*, 9 (1928), 187–206; 303–19.

Culican, W. *The Medes and the Persians*. London, 1965.

Gjerstad, E. *The Swedish Cyprus Expedition*, vol. III: *Results of the Excavations in Cyprus 1927–1931*. Stockholm, 1937.

Grant, E. and Wright, G. E. *Ain Shems Excavations*, vol. 5. Haverford, Pennsylvania, 1939.

Hamdey-Bey and Reinach, T. *Une Nécropole Royale à Sidon*. 2 vols. Paris, 1892.

Iliffe, H. J. 'A Tell Far'a Tomb Group Reconsidered; Silver Vessels of the Persian Period', *QDAP*, 4 (1935), 182–6.

Johns, C. N. 'Excavations at 'Atlit 1930–1931; The South-Eastern Cemetery', *QDAP*, 2 (1933), 41–104.

Kukahn, E. *Anthropoide Sarkophage in Beyrouth*. Berlin, 1955.

Macalister, R. A. S. 'Some Interesting Pottery Remains', *PEFQS*, 5 (1915), 35–7.

Speiser, E. 'Reports on the Tell Billah and Tepe Gawra Excavations', *BASOR*, 46 (1932), 8–9.

Stern, E. 'A Burial of the Persian Period near Hebron', *IEJ*, 21 (1971), 25–30.

Thureau-Danjin, F. and Dunand, M. *Til Barsip*. Paris, 1936.

Torrey, C. C. 'A Phoenician Necropolis at Sidon', *AASOR*, 1 (1920), 1–27.

Woolley, C. L. 'A North Syrian Cemetery of the Persian Period', *AAA*, 7 (1914–16), 115–29.

Pottery

Amiran, R. *Ancient Pottery of the Holy Land from its Beginnings in the Neolithic Period to the end of the Iron Age*. Jerusalem, 1969.

Boardman, J. *The Greeks Overseas*. Harmondsworth, 1964.

Clairmont, C. 'Greek Pottery from the Near East', *Berytus*, 11 (1954–55), 85–139.

'Greek Pottery from the Near East, II: Black Vases', *Berytus*, 12 '1956–58), 1–34.

Crowfoot, J. W. *Samaria-Sebaste, III: The Objects*. London, 1957.

Hesterin, R. and Stern, E. 'Two "Assyrian" Bowls from Israel', *IEJ*, 23 (1973), 152–5.

Iliffe, J. H. 'Pre-Hellenistic Greek Pottery in Palestine', *QDAP*, 2 (1932), 15–26.

Lapp, P. W. 'The Pottery of Palestine in the Persian Period', in *Archäologie und Altes Testament, Festschrift für Kurt Galling*, pp. 179–97. Tübingen, 1970.

Naveh, J. 'The Excavations at Meṣad Ḥashavyahu – Preliminary Report', *IEJ*, 12 (1962), 89–113.

Oats, J. 'Late Assyrian Pottery from Fort Shalmaneser', *Iraq*, 21 (1959), 130–46.

Petrie, W. F. M. *Naukratis I*. London, 1886.

Tanis II. London, 1888.

Riis, P. J. *Sukas I, The North-East Sanctuary and the first Settling of Greeks in Syria and Palestine*. Copenhagen, 1970.

Wampler, J. C. 'Triangular Impressed Design in Palestinian Pottery', *BASOR*, 80 (1940), 13–16.

Woolley, C. L. 'Excavations at Al-Mina, Sueida', *JHS*, 58 (1938), 1–30; 133–70.

Objects of metal, alabaster and faience

Amiran, R. 'Achaemenian Bronze Objects from a Tomb at Kh. Ibsan in Lower-Galilee', *Levant*, 4 (1972), 135–8.

Avigad, N. 'Excavations at Makmish, 1960: Preliminary Report', *IEJ*, 11 (1961), 97–100.

Ben-Dor, I. 'Palestinian Alabaster Vases', *QDAP*, 11 (1945), 93–112.

Dothan, M. 'Ashdod II–III, The Second and Third Seasons of Excavations 1963, 1965', *Atiqot*, 9–10 (1971).

Fassing, P. 'Drinking Bowls of Glass and Metal from the Achaemenian Time', *Berytus*, 4 (1937), 121–9.

Frankfort, H. 'A Persian Goldsmith's Trial Piece', *JNES*, 9 (1950), 111–12.

Hamilton, R. W. 'A Silver Bowl in the Ashmolean Museum', *Iraq*, 28 (1966), 1–17.

Kantor, H. J. 'Achaemenid Jewelry in the Oriental Institute', *JNES*, 16 (1957), 1–23.

Lefebre, J. *Le Tombeau de Petasiris*. Cairo, 1923–24.

Luschey, H. *Die Phiale*. Bleicherode am Hatz, 1939.

Petrie, W. F. M. *Beth Pelet*, vol. 1. London, 1930.

Radan, G. 'Helmet Found Near Ascalon', *IEJ*, 8 (1958), 185–8.

Roes, A. 'Achaemenid Influence upon Egyptian and Nomad Art', *ArtAs*, 15 (1952), 17–30.

Schmidt, E. F. *Persepolis, vol. II: Contents of the Treasury and other Discoveries*. Chicago, 1957.

Sanctuaries and cult objects

Aharoni, Y. 'Trial Excavation in the "Solar Shrine" at Lachish', *IEJ*, 18 (1968), 157–64.
Albright, W. F. 'Some Recent Publications', *BASOR*, 98 (1945), 28.
 'Some Recent Publications', *BASOR*, 132 (1953), 46–7.
Avigad, N. 'Excavations at Makmish 1958', *IEJ*, 10 (1960), 90–6.
Bowen, R. L. and Albright, F. P. *Archaeological Discoveries in South Arabia, Part I: Archaeological Survey of Beihan*. Baltimore, 1958.
Breitenstein, N. *Danish National Museum, Catalogue of Terracottas, Cypriot, Greek, Etruscan, Italian and Roman*. Copenhagen, 1941.
Caton-Thompson, G. *The Tombs and Moon Temple of Hureidha*. Oxford, 1944.
Chehab, M. H. 'Les Terres cuites de Kharayeb', *BMB*, 10 (1951–52); 11 (1953–54).
Ciasca, A. 'Un deposito di statuette di Tell Gat', *OrAnt*, 2 (1963), 45–63.
Cleveland, R. L. *An Ancient South Arabian Necropolis; Objects from the Second Campaign (1951) in the Timna' Cemetery*. Baltimore, 1965.
Dunand, M. 'Encore la stèle de Yehavmilk Roi de Byblos', *BMB*, 5 (1941), 57–73.
 'Les Sculptures de la Favissa du Temple d'Amrit', *BMB*, 7 (1944–45), 99–107.
Forte, M. 'Sull 'origine di alcuni tipi di altarini sud-arabici', *AION*, 17 (1967), 97–120.
Galling, K. 'Gerar', *ZDPV*, 52 (1929), 242–50.
Gjerstad, E. *The Swedish Cyprus Expedition*, vol. 4, part 2: *The Cypro-Geometric, Cypro-Archaic and Cypro-Classical Periods*. Stockholm, 1948.
Glueck, N. 'Incense Altars', *Eretz-Israel*, 10 (1971), 120–5 (in Hebrew).
Iliffe, J. J. 'A Hoard of Bronzes from Askalon', *QDAP*, 5 (1935), 61–8.
Legrain, L. *Terracottas from Nippur*. Philadelphia, 1930.
Negbi, O. 'A Contribution of Mineralogy and Palaeontology to an Archaeological Study of Terracottas', *IEJ*, 14 (1964), 187–9.
 'A Deposit of Terracottas and Statuettes from Tel Sippor', *Atiqot* 6 (1966).
Pritchard, J. B. 'The Palace of Tell es Sa'idiyeh', *Expedition*, 11 (1968), 20–2.
Pryce, F. N. *Catalogue of Sculpture in the Department of Greek and Roman Antiquities of the British Museum*. 2 vols. Vol. 1, part 3: *Cypriot and Etruscan*. London, 1931.
Stern, E. 'Limestone Incense Altars', in *Beer-Sheba 1, Excavations at Tel Beer-Sheba, Seasons 1969–1971*, ed. Y. Aharoni, pp. 52–3. Ramat–Gan, 1973.
Woolley, C. L. *Ur Excavations*, vol. IX. *The Neo-Babylonian and Persian Periods*. London, 1962.
Ziegler, L. 'Tonkästchen aus Uruk, Babylon und Assur', *ZA*, 47 (1942), 224–40.

Seals and seal impressions

Aharoni, Y. *Excavations at Ramat Rahel (1961–1962)*. Rome, 1964.
Avigad, N. 'A New Class of Yehud Stamps', *IEJ*, 7 (1957), 146–53.
 'New Light on the MSH Seal-Impressions', *IEJ*, 8 (1958), 113–19.
 'Yehûd or Ha'ir', *BASOR*, 158 (1960), 23–7.
Bliss, F. J. and Macalister, R. A. S. *Excavations in Palestine 1898–1900*. London, 1902.
Cross, F. M., Jr. 'Judean Stamps', *Eretz-Israel*, 9 (1969), 20–7.
Dajani, R. 'A Neo-Babylonian Seal from Amman', *ADAJ*, 6–7 (1962), 124–5.
Eitan, A. (ed.). *Inscriptions Reveal, Documents from the time of the Bible, the Mishna and the Talmud; Israel Museum Catalogue no. 100*. Jerusalem, 1973.

Garbini, G. 'The Dating of the Post-Exilic Stamps', in Y. Aharoni, *Excavations at Ramat Raḥel, Seasons of 1959–1960*, pp. 61–8. Rome, 1962.

Kutscher, E. Y. '"Pḥw" and its cognants', *Tarbiẓ*, 30 (1960–61), 112ff (in Hebrew).

Lapp, P. W. 'Ptolemaic Stamped Handles from Judah', *BASOR*, 172 (1963), 22–35.

Porter, B. and Moss, R. L. B. *Topographical Bibliography of Ancient Hieroglyphic Texts, Reliefs and Paintings*, vol. 7. Oxford, 1951.

Richardson, H. N. 'A Stamped Handle from Khirbet Yarmuk', *BASOR*, 192 (1968), 12–16.

Stern, E. 'Seal Impressions in the Achaemenid Style in the Province of Judah', *BASOR*, 202 (1971), 6–16.

Tohus, C. N. 'Excavations at Atlit 1930–1931; The South-Eastern Cemetery', *QDAP*, 2 (1933), 104.

Wright, G. E. *Shechem, The Biography of a Biblical City.* New York–Toronto, 1965.

Weights and coins

Hill, G. F. *Catalogue of the Greek Coins of Palestine.* London, 1914.

Kindler, A. 'The Greco-Phoenician Coins struck in Palestine in the times of the Persian Empire', *INJ*, 1 (1963), 2–6; 25–7.

'The Mint of Tyre – The Major Source of Silver Coins in Ancient Palestine', *Eretz-Israel*, 8 (1967), 318–24 (in Hebrew).

Lambert, C. 'Egypto-Arabian, Phoenician and other Coins of the Fourth Century B.C. found in Palestine', *QDAP*, 2 (1932), 1–10.

Meshorer, Y. 'An Attic Archaic Coin from Jerusalem', *Atiqot*, 3 (1961), 185.

'A New Type of YHD Coin', *IEJ*, 16 (1966), 217–19.

Noe, S. P. 'A Bibliography of Greek Coin Hoards', *NNM*, 78 (1937).

Rahmani, L. Y. 'Silver Coins of the Fourth Century B.C. from Tel Gamma', *IEJ*, 21 (1971), 158–60.

Zayadine, F. 'Samaria-Sebaste Clearance and Excavations', *ADAJ*, 12–13 (1967–68), 77–80.

The character of the material culture

Aharoni, Y. 'The Second Season of Excavations at Tel Arad', *BIES*, 28 (1964), 153–75.

Alt, A. *Kleine Schriften zur Geschichte des Volkes Israel.* 3 vols. Munich, 1953.

Outline of history

Barag, D. 'The Effects of the Tennes Rebellion on Palestine', *BASOR*, 183 (1966), 6–12.

Stern, E. 'Archaeological Aspects of the History of the Coastal Regions of Palestine during the Fourth Century B.C.E.', in *Bible and Jewish History. Studies dedicated to the Memory of Jacob Liver*, ed. B. Uffenheimer, pp. 207–21 (in Hebrew). Tel Aviv, 1971.

Wright, G. E. 'The Water Systems of Gibeon', *JNES*, 22 (1963), 210–11.

CHAPTER 6. HEBREW AND ARAMAIC IN THE PERSIAN PERIOD

Selected Aramaic Sources of the Persian Period

Aimé-Giron, N. *Textes araméens d'Égypte*. Cairo, 1931.

'Adversaria Semitica nos. 113–121', *BIFAO*, 38 (1939), 1–63.

'Adversaria Semitica nos. 122–124', *ASAE*, 39 (1939), 39–63.

Bowman, R. A. *Aramaic Ritual Texts from Persepolis*. Chicago, 1970. Cf. the review article by J. Naveh and S. Shaked, 'Ritual Texts or Treasury Documents?', *Or*, n.s., 42 (1973), 445–57.

Bresciani, E. 'Papiri aramaici egiziani di epoca persiana presso il Museo Civico di Padova', *RSO*, 35 (1960), 11–24.

Bresciani, E. and Kamil, M. *Le lettere aramaiche de Hermopoli*. Rome, 1966. Most recent bibliography in B. Porten and J. C. Greenfield, 'Hermopolis Letter 6', *IOS*, 4 (1974), 14.

Cowley, A. E. *Aramaic Papyri of the Fifth Century B.C.* Oxford, 1923.

Degen, R. 'Zum Ostrakon CIS II 138', *Neue Ephemeris für Semitische Epigraphik*, 1 (1972), 23–37. A list of the Aramaic ostraca is provided.

Delaporte, L. *Épigraphes araméens*. Paris, 1912.

Driver, G. R. *Aramaic Documents of the Fifth Century B.C.* Abridged and revised, Oxford, 1965.

Dupont-Sommer, A. 'La stèle trilingue récemment découverte au Lêtôon de Xanthos: le texte araméen', *CRAIBL* (1974), 132–49.

Fitzmyer, J. A. 'The Padua Aramaic Papyrus Letters', *JNES*, 21 (1962), 15–24.

Hanson, R. S. 'Aramaic Funerary and Boundary Inscriptions from Asia Minor', *BASOR*, 192 (1968), 3–11.

Kornfeld, W. 'Jüdisch–aramäische Grabinschriften aus Edfu', *Anzeiger der phil.-hist. Klasse der Österreichischen Akademie der Wissenschaft* 110, pp. 123–37. Vienna, 1973.

Kraeling, E. G. *The Brooklyn Museum Aramaic Papyri*. New Haven, 1953.

Segal, J. B. 'The Aramaic Papyri (from Saqqara)', in *Proceedings of the 14th Congress of Papyrologists*, pp. 252–5. London, 1975.

Collections of Aramaic texts

Donner, H. and Röllig, W. *Kanaanäische und aramäische Inschriften* I–III. 2nd edn. Wiesbaden, 1968.

Gibson, J. C. L. *Text Book of Syrian Semitic Inscriptions*, vol. 2: *Aramaic Inscriptions*. Oxford, 1975.

Koopmans, J. J. *Aramäische Chrestomathie*. Leiden, 1962.

Lipiński, E. *Studies in Aramaic Inscriptions and Onomastics*, I. Louvain, 1975.

Porten, B. and Greenfield, J. C. *Jews of Elephantine, Aramaeans of Syene: 50 Aramaic Texts from Egypt*. Jerusalem, 1974.

Rosenthal, F. *An Aramaic Handbook*. Wiesbaden, 1967.

Studies on the Aramaic language

Altheim, F. and Stiehl, R. *Die aramäische Sprache unter den Achämeniden*, I. Frankfurt, 1963.

Bauer, H. and Leander, P. *Grammatik des Biblisch-Aramäischen*. Halle, 1927.

Degen, R. *Altaramäische Grammatik der Inschriften des 10–8 Jh.v.Ch.* Wiesbaden, 1969.

Garbini, G. *Le lingue semitiche, studi di storia linguistica.* Napoli, 1972.

Greenfield, J. C. 'Dialect Traits in Early Aramaic', *Leš*, 32 (1968), 359–68 (in Hebrew). English translation: 'The Dialects of Ancient Aramaic', *JNES*, 37 (1978), 93–9.

'Standard Literary Aramaic', *Actes du Premier Congrès International de Linguistique sémitique et chamito-sémitique*, pp. 280–9. The Hague, 1974.

Kutscher, E. Y. 'The Hermopolis Papyri', *IOS*, 1 (1971), 103–19.

'Aramaic', in *Current Trends in Linguistics*, 6, pp. 347–412. The Hague, 1971.

A History of Aramaic, part 1 (in Hebrew). Jerusalem, 1972.

Leander, P. *Laut- und Formenlehre des Ägyptisch-Aramäischen.* Göteborg, 1928.

Morag, S. *The Vocalization Systems of Arabic, Hebrew and Aramaic.* The Hague, 1962.

Moscati, S. (ed.). *An Introduction to the Comparative Grammar of the Semitic Languages: Phonology and Morphology.* Wiesbaden, 1964.

Rosenthal, F. *Die aramaistische Forschung seit Th. Nöldeke's Veröffentlichungen.* Leiden, 1939.

A Grammar of Biblical Aramaic. 2nd rev. edn. Wiesbaden, 1962.

Segert, S. *Altaramäische Grammatik.* Leipzig, 1975.

Dictionaries

Jean, C. and Hoftijzer, J. *Dictionnaire des inscriptions sémitiques de l'ouest.* Leiden, 1965.

Vinnikov, I. M. *Slovar arameyskikh nadpisey*, in *Palestinskiy Sbornik*, pp. 3–13. Leningrad, 1958–65.

Vogt, E. *Lexicon linguae Aramaicae Veteris Testamenti Documentis Antiquis Illustratum.* Rome, 1971.

Aramaic in contact with other languages and scripts

Benveniste, E. 'Termes et noms achéménides .en araméen', *JA*, 225 (1934), 177–94.

'Elements perses en araméen d'Égypte', *JA*, 242 (1954), 297–310.

Couroyer, B. 'Termes égyptiens dans les papyrus araméens du Musee de Brooklyn', *RB*, 61 (1954), 251–3; 554–9.

Eilers, W. *Iranische Beamtennamen in der keilschriftliche Überlieferung.* Leipzig, 1940.

Henning, W. B. 'Mitteliranisch', in *Iranistik, Handbuch der Orientalistik*, I:4:1, pp. 20–130. Leiden, 1958.

'Ein persischer Titel im Altaramäischen', in *Gedenkband Kahle*, *BZAW* 103, Berlin, 1968, pp. 138–45.

Hinz, W. *Neue Wege im Altpersischen.* Wiesbaden, 1973.

Kaufman, S. A. *The Akkadian Influences in Aramaic*, *AS* 19. Chicago, 1974.

Kent, R. G. *Old Persian Grammar, Texts, Lexicon.* 2nd edn. New Haven, 1953.

Leibovitch, J. 'Quelques égyptianismes contenus dans les textes araméens d'Égypte', *BIE*, 18 (1935–36), 19–29.

Lewy, J. 'The Problems inherent in Section 70 of the Bisutun Inscription', *HUCA*, 25 (1954), 169–208.

Menasce, J. de. 'Mots d'emprunt en noms propres iraniens dans les nouveaux documents araméens', *BO*, 1 (1954), 161–2.

Paper, H. H. 'The Old Persian /L/ Phoneme', *JAOS*, 76 (1956), 24–6.

Polotsky, H. J. 'Aramäisch *prš* und das *Huzvaresch*', *Le Muséon*, 45 (1932), 273–83.

Schaeder, H. H. *Iranische Beiträge*. Halle, 1930.

von Soden, W. 'Aramäische Wörter in neuassyrischen und neu- und spätbabylonischen Texten', *Or*, 35 (1966), 1–20; 37 (1968), 261–71.

Elephantine–General

Muffs, Y. *Studies in the Aramaic Legal Papyri from Elephantine*. New York, 1969.

Porten, B. *Archives from Elephantine*. Berkeley and Los Angeles, 1968.

Yaron, R. *Introduction to the Law of the Aramaic Papyri*. Oxford, 1961.

Hebrew in the Persian period

Ben-David, A. *Biblical Hebrew and Mishnaic Hebrew* (in Hebrew). 2 vols. Tel Aviv, 1967, 1971.

Driver, S. R. *An Introduction to the Literature of the Old Testament*. Repr. New York, 1956.

Ginsberg, H. L. *Studies in Daniel*. New York, 1948.

Studies in Koheleth. New York, 1960.

Hurwitz, A. *The Transition Period in Biblical Hebrew* (in Hebrew). Jerusalem, 1972.

'The Date of the Prose-Tale of Job Linguistically Reconsidered', *HTR*, 67 (1971), 17–34.

Rabin, C. 'Hebrew', in *Current Trends in Linguistics* 6, pp. 304–46. The Hague, 1970.

Wagner, M. *Die lexikalischen und grammatikalischen Aramäismen in alttestamentlichen Hebräisch*, *BZAW* 96. Berlin, 1966.

Post-Persian period

Ben-Hayyim, Z. *Studies in the Traditions of the Hebrew Language*. Madrid–Barcelona, 1954.

Fitzmyer, J. A. 'The Language of Palestine in the First Century A.D.', *CBQ*, 32 (1970), 501–31.

The Genesis Apocryphon of Qumran Cave 1. A Commentary. 2nd rev. edn. Rome, 1971.

'The Contribution of Qumran Aramaic to the study of the New Testament', *NTS*, 20 (1974), 382–407.

Goshen-Gottstein, M. H. 'Linguistic Structure and Tradition in the Qumran Documents' in *Aspects of the Dead Sea Scrolls*, SH, 4 (1958), pp. 101–37.

Kutscher, E. Y. *The Language and Linguistic Background of the Isaiah Scroll (1QIsaᵃ)*. Leiden, 1974.

'The language of the Genesis Apocryphon – a preliminary study' in *Aspects of the Dead Sea Scrolls*, SH, 4 (1958), pp. 1–35.

'The Languages of the Hebrew and Aramaic Letters of Bar Cochba and his Contemporaries', *Leš*, 25 (1961), 119–33; 26 (1962), 7–23 (in Hebrew).

Rabin, C. 'Historical Background of Qumran Hebrew', in *Aspects of the Dead Sea Scrolls*, SH, 4 (1958), pp. 144–61.

Segal, M. H. 'Mishnaic Hebrew and its relation to Biblical Hebrew and to Aramaic', *JQR*, o.s., 20 (1908), 647–737.

Epigraphic finds in Palestine

Aharoni, Y. *The Excavations at Ramat Raḥel. Seasons 1959–1960*: Rome, 1962; *Seasons 1961–1962*: Rome, 1964.

'Horvat Dorban', *IEJ*, 13 (1963), 337.

Avigad, N. 'A New Class of *Yehud* stamps', *IEJ*, 7 (1957), 146–53.

'New Light on the MṢH Seal Impressions', *IEJ*, 8 (1958), 113–19.

'Seals of the Exiles', *IEJ*, 15 (1965), 222–32.

Bullae and Seals from a post-exilic Judaean Archive, Qedem 4. Jerusalem, 1976.

Cross, F. M., Jr. 'An Ostracon from Nebi Yunis', *IEJ*, 14 (1964), 108–10.

'Judaean Stamps', *Eretz-Israel*, 9 (1969), 20–7.

'Papyri of the Fourth Century B.C. from Daliyeh', in *New Directions in Biblical Archaeology*, ed. D. N. Freedman and J. C. Greenfield. Garden City, New York, 1969.

Jeselsohn, D. 'A New Coin Type with Hebrew Inscription', *IEJ*, 24 (1974), 77–8.

Kaplan, J. 'Excavations at Tell Abu Zeitun', *BIES*, 22 (1958), 97–9 (in Hebrew).

Kindler, A. 'Silver Coins Bearing the Name of Judea from the Early Hellenistic Period', *IEJ*, 24 (1974), 73–6.

Kutscher, E. Y. 'PḤW' and its Cognates', *Tarbiz*, 30 (1961), 112–19.

Mazar, B. 'Archaeological Excavations near the Temple Mount', in *Jerusalem Revealed*, ed. Y. Yadin, pp. 25–40. Jerusalem, 1975.

Meshorer, Y. *Jewish Coins of the Second Temple Period*. Tel Aviv, 1967.

Naveh, J. 'The Scripts of Two Ostraca from Elath', *BASOR*, 183 (1966), 27–30.

'An Aramaic Ostracon from Ashdod', *Ashdod II–III, Atiqot*, 9–10 (1971), 200–1.

'Hebrew Texts in the Aramaic Script in the Persian Period?', *BASOR*, 203 (1971), 27–32.

'Two Aramaic Ostraca from the Persian Period', in *Bible and Jewish Studies Dedicated to the Memory of Jacob Liver*, ed. B. Uffenheimer, pp. 184–90 (in Hebrew). Tel Aviv, 1972.

'An Aramaic Tomb Inscription written in Palaeo-Hebrew Script', *IEJ*, 23 (1973), 82–91.

'The Aramaic Ostraca', in *Beer-Sheba* I, ed. Y. Aharoni, pp. 79–82. Tel Aviv, 1973.

'Aramaic Inscriptions from Arad', in *Ketobot 'Arad*, ed. Y. Aharoni, pp. 165–205 (in Hebrew). Jerusalem, 1975.

'The Aramaic Ostraca from Tel Beer Sheba (Seasons 1971–1976)', *Tel Aviv*, 6 (1979), 182–98.

Peckham, J. B. 'An Inscribed Jar from Bat-Yam', *IEJ*, 16 (1966), 11–17, pl. 4 A–B.

Rahmani, L. Y. 'Silver Coins of the Fourth Century B.C. from Tel Gamma', *IEJ*, 21 (1971), 158–60, pl. 31.

Rosenthal, E. S. 'The Giv'at ha-Mivtar Inscription', *IEJ*, 23 (1973), 72–81.

Rosenthaler, M. 'A Palaeo-Hebrew Ossuary Inscription', *IEJ*, 25 (1975), 138–9.

Script

Albright, W. F. 'A Biblical Fragment from the Maccabaean Age: the Nash Papyrus', *JBL*, 56 (1937), 145–67.

Avigad, N. 'The Palaeography of the Dead Sea Scrolls and Related Documents', in *Aspects of the Dead Sea Scrolls*, SH, 4, pp. 56–87. Jerusalem, 1958.

Cross, F. M., Jr. 'The Development of the Jewish Scripts', in *The Bible and the Ancient Near East*, ed. G. E. Wright, pp. 133–202. Garden City, New York, 1961.

Hanson, R. S. 'Palaeo-Hebrew Scripts in the Hasmonaean Age', *BASOR*, 175 (1964), 26–42.

Naveh, J. *The Development of the Aramaic Script*. Jerusalem, 1970.

'The Palaeography of the Hermopolis Papyri', *IOS*, 1 (1971), 120–2.

Nylander, C. 'Assyria Grammata, Remarks on the 21st Letter of Themistokles', *Opuscula Atheniensia*, 8 (1968), 119–36.

Purvis, J. D. *The Samaritan Pentateuch and the Origin of the Samaritan Sect*, pp. 18–52. Cambridge, 1968.

CHAPTER 7. THE JEWISH COMMUNITY IN PALESTINE IN THE PERSIAN PERIOD

Reference should also be made to the bibliographies to the other chapters in this volume.

Sources

The biblical text, primarily Ezra, Nehemiah, 1 Esdras, Haggai, Zechariah 1–8. Josephus, *Antiquities of the Jews*, book XI.

The Elephantine Papyri: see ch. 13.

The Samaria Papyri: see F. M. Cross, 'Aspects of Samaritan and Jewish History in Late Persian and Hellenistic Times', *HTR*, 59 (1966), 201–11.

Bullae, seals, coinage etc.: see N. Avigad, *Bullae and Seals from a post-exilic Judaean Archive*, *Qedem*, Monographs of the Institute of Archaeology, the Hebrew University of Jerusalem, 4 (1976).

Commentaries on the biblical texts

Fuller information may be found in the standard Introductions to the Old Testament, e.g. O. Eissfeldt, *The Old Testament: an Introduction*. Oxford, 1965; Brevard S. Childs, *Introduction to the Old Testament as Scripture*. Philadelphia, 1979, 2nd printing, 1980.

Ackroyd, P. R. *I and II Chronicles, Ezra, Nehemiah*. Torch Series. London, 1973.

Brockington, L. H. *Ezra, Nehemiah and Esther*. The Century Bible, n.s. London, 1969.

Coggins, R. J. *Ezra and Nehemiah*. Cambridge Bible Commentary. Cambridge, 1976.

Coggins, R. J. and Knibb, M. A. *1 and 2 Esdras*. Cambridge Bible Commentary. Cambridge, 1977.

Michaeli, R. *Les Livres des Chroniques, d'Esdras et de Néhémie*. Commentaire de l'Ancien Testament, 16. Neuchâtel, 1967.

Myers, J. M. *Ezra, Nehemiah*. AB, 14. New York, 1965.

I and II Esdras. AB, 42. New York, 1974.

Petitjean, A. *Les oracles du Proto-Zacharie. Un programme de restauration pour la communauté juive après l'exil*. Paris–Louvain, 1969.

Rudolph, W. *Esra and Nehemia*, HAT 1, 20. Tübingen, 1949.

Talmon, S. 'Ezra and Nehemiah', *IDBSup*, 317–28, with valuable bibliography. Nashville, 1976.

General works and special studies

Ackroyd, P. R. *Exile and Restoration*. London, Philadelphia, 1968.

Israel under Babylon and Persia. New Clarendon Bible. Oxford, 1970.

The Age of the Chronicler. Selwyn Lectures 1970. Supplement to *Colloquium* – The Australian and New Zealand Theological Review, 1970.

'History and Theology in the Writings of the Chronicler', *CTM*, 38 (1967), 501–15.

'God and People in the Chronicler's Presentation of Ezra', in *La Notion Biblique de Dieu*, ed. J. Coppens, pp. 145–62. BETL 41. Louvain, 1976.

'The Chronicler as Exegete', *JSOT*, 1/2 (1977), 2–32.

'The History of Israel in the Exilic and Post-Exilic Periods', in *Tradition and Interpretation*, ed. G. W. Anderson, ch. 12 (written 1974, slightly revised 1975). Oxford, 1977.

Ahlström, G. W. *Joel and the Temple Cult of Jerusalem*, *VTSup* 21. Leiden, 1971.

Barag, D. 'The Effects of the Tennes Rebellion on Palestine', *BASOR*, 183 (1966), 6–12.

Beuken, W. A. M. *Haggai–Sacharja 1–8*. Studia Semitica Neerlandica, 10. Assen, 1967.

Beyse, K. M. *Serubbabel und die Königserwartungen der Propheten Haggai und Sacharja*, *AVTR*, 52. Berlin, 1971.

Cross, F. M., Jr. 'A Reconstruction of the Judean Restoration', *JBL*, 94 (1975), 4–18 = *Int*, 29 (1975), 187–203.

Emerton, J. A. 'Did Ezra go to Jerusalem in 428 B.C.?', *JTS*, 17 (1966), 1–19.

Freedman, D. N. 'The Chronicler's Purpose', *CBQ*, 23 (1961), 436–42.

Galling, K. *Studien zur Geschichte Israels im persischen Zeitalter*. Tübingen, 1964.

Hanson, P. D. *The Dawn of Apocalyptic. The Historical and Sociological Roots of Jewish Apocalyptic Eschatology*. Philadelphia, 1975.

In der Smitten, W. T. *Esra: Quellen, Ueberlieferung und Geschichte*, Studia Semitica Neerlandica, 15. Assen, 1973.

'Die Gründe für die Aufnahme der Nehemiaschrift in das chronistische Geschichtswerk', *BZ*, N.F. 16 (1972), 207–21.

Japhet, S. *The Ideology of the Book of Chronicles and its Place in Biblical Thought*. In Hebrew, Jerusalem, 1973.

'The Supposed Common Authorship of Chronicles and Ezra-Nehemiah investigated anew', *VT*, 18 (1968), 330–71.

Kellermann, U. *Nehemia: Quellen, Ueberlieferung und Geschichte*, *BZAW*, 102 (1967).

'Erwägungen zum Esragesetz', *ZAW*, 80 (1968), 373–85.

Koch, K. 'Ezra and the Origins of Judaism', *JSS*, 19 (1974), 173–97.

Mosis, R. *Untersuchungen zur Theologie des chronistischen Geschichtswerkes*, Freiburger theologischer Studien, 92. Freiburg, 1973.

Myers, J. M. *The World of the Restoration*. Englewood Cliffs, 1968.

Petitjean, A. 'La mission de Zorobabel et la reconstruction du Temple', *ETL*, 42 (1966), 40–71.

Pohlmann, K.-F. *Studien zum dritten Esra. Ein Beitrag zur Frage nach dem ursprünglichen Schluss des chronistischen Werkes*. FRLANT, 104. Göttingen, 1970.

Smith, M. *Palestinian Parties and Politics that Shaped the Old Testament*. New York London, 1971.

Stern, E. *The Material Culture of the Land of the Bible in the Persian Period*. Warminster, 1982.

'The Province of Yehud: the Vision and the Reality.' *The Jerusalem Cathedra–1981*, 9–21, who promises a fuller discussion of the chronology and favours a late fifth century date.

Tuland, C. G. 'Ezra-Nehemiah or Nehemiah-Ezra? An investigation into the validity of the van Hoonacker theory', *AUSS*, 12 (1974), 47–61.

Vaux, R. de. 'Les decrets de Cyrus et de Darius sur la reconstruction du temple', *RB* 46 (1937), 29–57 = *Bible et Orient* (Paris, 1967), 83–113; ET: 'The Decrees of Cyrus and Darius on the Rebuilding of the Temple' in *The Bible and the Ancient Near East*, ed. G. E. Wright, pp. 63–96. London–Garden City, 1971.

Vink, J. G. 'The date and origin of the Priestly Code in the Old Testament', *OTS*, 15 (1968), 1–144.

Vogt, H. C. M. *Studie zur nachexilischen Gemeinde in Esra–Nehemia*. Werl, 1966.

Welten, P. *Geschichte und Geschichtsdarstellung in den Chronikbüchern*, WMANT, 42. Neukirchen, 1973.

Widengren, G. 'The Persian Period', in *Israelite and Judaean History*, ed. J. H. Hayes and J. M. Miller; ch. 9, with very full bibliography. Philadelphia, London, 1977.

Willi, T. *Die Chronik als Auslegung. Untersuchungen zur literarischen Gestaltung der historischen Ueberlieferung Israels*, FRLANT, 106. Göttingen, 1972.

Williamson, H. G. M. *Israel in the Books of Chronicles*. Cambridge, 1977.

Reference should also be made to the following histories of Israel:

Bright, J. *A History of Israel*. Philadelphia, 1959.

Herrmann, S. *Geschichte Israels in Alttestamentilicher Zeit*. Tübingen, 1973.

Noth, M. *History of Israel*. Rev. trans. P. R. Ackroyd. New York, 1960.

CHAPTER 8. PROPHECY AND PSALMS IN THE PERSIAN PERIOD

Ackroyd, P. R. *Israel under Babylonia and Persia*. The New Clarendon Bible, Old Testament, vol. 4. London, 1970.

Anderson, G. W. *A Critical Introduction to the Old Testament*. London, 1962.

Bentzen, A. *Introduction to the Old Testament*, vol. 2. 2nd edn. Copenhagen, 1952.

Bertholdt, L. *Historischkritische Einleitung in sämmtliche kannonische und apokryphe Schriften des Alten und Neuen Testamentes*. Erlangen, 1812–1819.

Eissfeldt, O. *Einleitung in das Alte Testament*, 3rd edn. Tübingen, 1964.

Kaiser, O. *Einleitung in das Alte Testament*. Gütersloh, 1969, 4th edn. 1978.

Oesterley, W. O. E. and Robinson, T. H. *Introduction to the Books of the Old Testament*, 3rd edn. New York, 1958.

Robert, A. and Feuillet, A. *Introduction à la Bible*. Vol. 1 : *Introduction générale, Ancien Testament*, by P. Auvray *et al.* 2nd edn. Tournay, 1959.

Sellin, E. and Fohrer, G. *Introduction to the Old Testament*. Nashville–New York, 1968.

Smend, R. *Die Entstehung des Alten Testaments*. Stuttgart, 1978.

Weiser, A. *Einleitung in das Alte Testament*, 6th edn. Göttingen, 1966.

Prophecy in the Persian period

Beuken, W. A. M. *Haggai–Sacharja 1–8*. Assen, 1967.

Beyse, K.-M. *Serubbabel und die Königserwartungen der Propheten Haggai und Sacharja*. Stuttgart, 1972.

Elliger, K. *Das Buch der zwölf kleinen Propheten II*, ATD 24, 7th edn. Göttingen, 1975).

Fohrer, G. 'Zehn Jahre Literatur zur alttestamentlichen Prophetie (1951–1960)', *TRu*, 28 (1962), 301–74.

Haller, M. *Das Judentum, Die Schriften des Alten Testaments II/3*, 2nd edn. Göttingen, 1925.

The Interpreter's Bible. Vol. 6. New York–Nashville, 1956.

Koch, K., *Die Profeten II*, Urban–Taschenbuch 281. Stuttgart, 1980.

Mitchell, H. G., Smith, J. M. P. and Bewer, J. A. *A Critical and Exegetical Commentary on Haggai, Zechariah, Malachi and Jonah*, 3rd edn. Edinburgh, 1951.

Plöger, O. *Theokratie und Eschatologie*. 3rd edn, Neukirchen-Vluyn, 1968.

Robinson, Th. H. and Horst F. *Die zwölf kleinen Propheten*, HAT 1, 14, 3rd edn. Tübingen, 1964.

Smith, J. M. P., Ward, W. H. and Bewer, J. A. *A Critical and Exegetical Commentary on Micah, Zephaniah, Nahum, Habakkuk, Obadiah and Joel*, 3rd edn. Edinburgh, 1948.

Weiser, A. *Das Buch der zwölf kleinen Propheten, I*, ATD 24, 16th edn. Göttingen, 1974.

Prophets and prophetic texts

Haggai

Ackroyd, P. R. 'Studies in the Book of Haggai', *JJS*, 2 (1951), 163–76; 3 (1952), 1–13.

Galling, K. 'Serubbabel und der Wiederaufbau des Tempels in Jerusalem', *Rudolph-Festschrift*, pp. 67–96. Tübingen, 1961.

Koch, K. 'Haggais unreines Volk', *ZAW*, 79 (1967), 52–66.

May, H. G. '"This People" and "This Nation" in Haggai', *VT*, 18 (1968), 190–7.

North, F. S. 'Critical Analysis of the Book of Haggai', *ZAW*, 68 (1956), 25–46.

Rothstein, J. W. *Juden und Samaritaner*, BWANT I/3. Leipzig, 1908.

Steck, O. H. 'Zu Haggai 1: 2–11', *ZAW*, 83 (1971), 355–79.

Zechariah

Galling, K. 'Die Exilswende in der Sicht des Propheten Sacharja', *VT*, 2 (1952), 18–36.

Jeremias, Chr. *Die Nachtgesichte des Sacharja*. FRLANT 117. Göttingen, 1977.

May, H. G. 'A Key to the Interpretation of Zechariah's Visions', *JBL*, 57 (1938), 173–84.

Rignell, L. G. *Die Nachtgesichte des Sacharja*. Lund, 1950.

Seybold, K. *Bilder zum Tempelbau. Die Visionen des Propheten Sacharja*. Stuttgart, 1974.

Trito-Isaiah

Duhm, B. *Das Buch Jesaja*, HKAT, 3, 1. Göttingen, 1892; 4th edn. 1922.

Elliger, K. *Die Einheit des Tritojesaja*. BWANT, 3, 9. Stuttgart, 1928.

Fohrer, G. *Das Buch Jesaja*. Vol. 3, Zürcher Bibelkommentare. Zürich–Stuttgart: 3rd edn. 1967.

Kraus, H.-J. 'Die ausgebliebene Endtheophanie', *ZAW*, 78 (1966), 317–22.
Maass, F., 'Tritojesaja?', *Rost-Festschrift*, BZAW, 105 (1967), pp. 153–63.
McCullough, W. St. 'A Re-Examination of Isaiah 56–66', *JBL*, 67 (1948), 27–36.
Westermann, C. *Das Buch Jesaja. Kapitel 40–66*. ATD 19. Göttingen, 1966.

Malachi

Boecker, H. J. 'Bemerkungen zur formgeschichtlichen Terminologie des Buches Maleachi', *ZAW*, 78 (1966), 78–80.
Pfeiffer, E. 'Die Disputationsworte im Buch Maleachi', *EvT*, 19 (1959), 546–68.
Wallis, G. 'Wesen und Struktur der Botschaft Maleachis', *Rost-Festschrift, BZAW*, 105 (1967), 229–37.

Joel

Ahlström, G. W. *Joel and the Temple Cult of Jerusalem*, *VTSup* 21. Leiden, 1971.
Bic, M., *Das Buch Joel*. Berlin, 1960.
Bourke, J. 'Le jour de Yahvé dans Joël', *RB*, 66 (1959), 5–31, 191–212.
Duhm, B. 'Anmerkungen zu den Zwölf Propheten. X. Buch Joel', *ZAW*, 31 (1911), 184–8.
Kapelrud, A. S. *Joel Studies*. Uppsala, 1948.
Kutsch, E. 'Heuschreckenplage und Tag Jahwes in Joel 1 und 2', *ThZ*, 18 (1962), 81–94.
Wolff, H. W. *Dodekapropheton 2. Joel und Amos*. BKAT, 14, 2nd edn. Neukirchen-Vluyn, 1975.

Anonymous prophetic texts

Anderson, G. W. 'A Study of Micah 6, 1–8', *SJT*, 4 (1951), 191–97.
Bardtke, H. 'Jeremia der Fremdvölkerprophet', *ZAW*, 53 (1935), 209–39; 54 (1936), 240–62.
Bright, J. *Jeremiah*. AB 21. New York, 1978.
Cannawurf, E. 'The Authenticity of Micah IV: 1–4', *VT*, 13 (1963), 26–33.
Fohrer, G. *Das Buch Jesaja*, vols. 1–2. Zürcher Bibelkommentare, 2nd edn. Zürich–Stuttgart, 1966–67.
'The Origin, Composition and Tradition of Isaiah I–XXXIX', *ALUOS*, 3 (1961–2), 3–38.
Gunkel, H. 'Jesaja 33, eine prophetische Liturgie', *ZAW*, 42 (1924), 177–208.
Hyatt, J. Ph. 'On the Meaning and Origin of Micah 6, 8', *ATR*, 34 (1952), 232–9.
Kaiser, O. *Das Buch Jesaja 13–39*. ATD 18. 2nd edn. Göttingen, 1976.
Renaud, B. *Structure et attaches littéraires de Michée IV–V*. Paris, 1964.
Rietzschel, C. *Das Problem der Urrolle*. Gütersloh, 1966.
Scott, R. B. Y. 'The Relation of Isaiah, Chapter 35, to Deutero-Isaiah', *AJSL*, 52 (1935–36), 178–91.
Vollmer, J. 'Zur Sprache von Jesaja 9: 1–6', *ZAW*, 80 (1968), 343–50.
'Jesajanische Begrifflichkeit?', *ZAW*, 83 (1971), 389–91.
Wildberger, H. *Jesaja*, I: *Jesaja 1–12*, BKAT, 10, 1. 2nd edn. Neukirchen-Vluyn, 1980.
Jesaja 13–27. BKAT, 10, 2. Neukirchen-Vluyn, 1978.

Themes and tendencies in the prophecy of the Persian Period

Browne, L. E. *The Messianic Hope in its Historical Setting*. London, 1951.
Eschatologie im Alten Testament, ed. by H. D. Preuss. Wege der Forschung 480. Darmstadt, 1978.
Freedman, D. N. 'History and Eschatology', *Int*, 14 (1960), 143–54.
Fohrer, G. *Geschichte der israelitischen Religion*. Berlin, 1969.
   'Die Struktur der alttestamentlichen Eschatologie', *BZAW*, 99 (1967), 32–58.
Gross, H. 'Der Messias im Alten Testament', *Trierer Theologische Zeitschrift*, 71 (1962), 154–70.
Herrmann, S. *Die prophetischen Heilserwartungen im Alten Testament*. Stuttgart, 1965.
Lindblom, J. 'Gibt es eine Eschatologie bei den alttestamentlichen Propheten?', *ST*, 6 (1952), 79–114.
Mowinckel, S. *He That Cometh*. Oxford, 1956.
Rad, G. von. *Theologie des Alten Testaments II*. 7th edn. Munich, 1980.
Ringgren, H. *The Messiah in the Old Testament*. London, 1956.
Schmidt, W. H. *Alttestamentlicher Glaube in seiner Geschichte*, 3rd edn. Neukirchen-Vluyn, 1979.
Wanke, G. '"Eschatologie". Ein Beispiel theologischer Sprachverwirrung', *KD*, 16 (1970), 300–12.
Wolff, H. W. 'Herrschaft Jahwes und die Messiasgestalt im Alten Testament', *ZAW*, 54 (1936), 168–202.
Zimmerli, W. *Grundriss der alttestamentlichen Theologie*. 3rd edn. Stuttgart, 1978.

Psalms in the Persian period

Buss, M. J. 'The Psalms of Asaph and Korah', *JBL*, 82 (1963), 382–92.
Dahood, M. *Psalms I*. AB 16. New York, 1966.
   Psalms II. AB 17. New York, 1968.
   Psalms III. AB 17A. New York, 1970.
Gunkel, H. *Die Psalmen*. Göttinger Handkommentar zum Alten Testament, 4th edn. Göttingen, 1926.
The Interpreter's Bible. Vol. 4. New York–Nashville, 1955.
Kraus, H.-J. *Psalmen*. BKAT 15, 5th edn. Neukirchen-Vluyn, 1978.
Mowinckel, S. *The Psalms in Israel's Worship* I/II. Oxford, 1962.
Pinto, B. de. 'The Torah and the Psalms', *JBL*, 86 (1967), 154–74.
Wanke, G. *Die Zionstheologie der Korachiten in ihrem traditionsgeschichtlichen Zusammenhang*, *BZAW*, 97. Berlin, 1966.
Weiser, A. *Die Psalmen*. ATD, 14–15, 9th edn. Göttingen, 1979.

CHAPTER 9. WISDOM LITERATURE IN THE PERSIAN PERIOD

General

Alt, A. 'Die Weisheit Salomos', *TLZ*, 76 (1951), 139–44 = *Kleine Schriften*, vol. 1, pp. 90–9. Munich, 1953.
Audet, J.-P. 'Origines comparées de la double tradition de la loi et de la sagesse dans le Proche-Orient ancien', in *Proceedings of the 25th International Congress of Orientalists, 1960*, vol. 1, pp. 352–7. Moscow, 1962.

Bauer-Kayatz, C. *Einführung in die alttestamentliche Weisheit.* Neukirchen-Vluyn, 1969.

Baumgartner, W. 'The Wisdom Literature', in *The Old Testament and Modern Study*, ed. H. H. Rowley, pp. 210–37. London, 1961.

Bea, A. 'Der Zahlenspruch im Hebräischen und Ugaritischen', *Bib*, 21 (1940), 196–8.

Beaucamp, E. *Des sages d'Israël ou le fruit d'une fidélité.* Quebec, 1968.

Bissing, F. W. von. *Altägyptische Lebensweisheit.* Zurich, 1955.

Boström, G. *Paronomasi i den äldre Hebreiska Maschalliteraturen.* Lund, 1928.

Brunner, H. *Altägyptische Erziehung.* Wiesbaden, 1947.

  'Lehren', in *Handbuch der Orientalistik*, ed. B. Spuler, I, vol. 1, 2, pp. 113–39. Leiden–Cologne, 1970.

Cazelles, H. *Sagesses antérieures aux 'Proverbes'.* Paris, 1967.

  'Bible, Sagesse, Science', *RSR*, 48 (1960), 40–54.

Couturier, G. P. 'Sagesse babylonienne et Sagesse israélite', *ScEccl*, 14 (1962), 293–309.

Cowley, A. E. *Aramaic Papyri of the Fifth Century B.C.*, pp. 204–48. Oxford, 1923.

Crenshaw, J. L. 'Wisdom', in *Old Testament Form Criticism*, ed. J. H. Hayes, 226–64. San Antonio, 1974.

Dahood, M. 'The Phoenician Contribution to Biblical Wisdom Literature', in *The Role of the Phoenicians in the Interaction of the Mediterranean Civilizations*, ed. W. A. Ward, pp. 123–52. Beirut, 1968.

Dijk, J. J. A. van. *La sagesse suméro-accadienne.* Leiden, 1953.

Dubarle, A. M. *Les sages d'Israel.* Paris, 1946.

Duesberg, H. and Frensen, I. *Les scribes inspirés.* Maredsous, 1966.

Eissfeldt, O. *Der Maschal im Alten Testament.* Giessen, 1913.

Fichtner, J. *Die altorientalische Weisheit in ihrer israelitisch-jüdischen Ausprägung.* Giessen, 1933.

  Gottes Weisheit. Stuttgart, 1965.

Fohrer, G. 'Sophia ktl., B. Altes Testament', *TWNT*, vol. 7, pp. 476–96.

Gemser, B. 'The Spiritual Structure of Biblical Aphoristic Wisdom', *HomBib*, 21 (1962), 3–10 = *Adhuc loquitur B. Gemser*, pp. 138–49. Leiden, 1968.

Gerstenberger, E. *Wesen und Herkunft 'apodiktischen Rechts'.* Neukirchen-Vluyn, 1965.

  'Zur alttestamentlichen Weisheit', *VF*, 14 (1969), 28–44.

Gese, H. *Lehre und Wirklichkeit in der alten Weisheit.* Tübingen, 1958.

Ginsberg, H. L. 'The Words of Ahiqar', *ANET* (1955), 427–30.

Godbey, A. H. 'The Hebrew Mašal', *AJSL*, 39 (1922–23), 89–108.

Gordis, R. 'The Social Background of Wisdom Literature', *HUCA*, 18 (1943–44), 77–118.

Gordon, E. I. 'A New Look at the Wisdom Literature of Sumer and Akkad', *BibOr*, 17 (1960), 122–52.

Grelot, P. 'Les proverbes araméens d'Aḥiqar', *RB*, 68 (1961), 178–94.

Gressmann, H. *Israels Spruchweisheit im Zusammenhang der Weltliteratur.* Berlin, 1925.

Harrington, W. 'The Wisdom of Israel', *ITQ*, 30 (1963), 311–25.

Heaton, E. W. *Solomon's New Men, the Emergence of Ancient Israel as a National State.* London, 1974.

Herbert, A. S. 'The "Parable" (mašal) in the Old Testament', *SJT*, 7 (1954), 180–96.

Hermisson, H. J. 'Weisheit und Geschichte', in *Probleme Biblischer Theologie*, Festschrift von Rad, ed. H. W. Wolff, pp. 136–54. Munich, 1971.

Herner, S. 'Erziehung und Unterricht in Israel', in *Oriental Studies Published in Commemoration of P. Haupt*, ed. C. Adler and A. Ember, pp. 58–66. Baltimore–Leipzig, 1926.

Hubbard, D. A. 'The Wisdom Movement and Israel's Covenant Faith', *TynBull*, 17 (1966), 3–33.

Humbert, P. *Recherches sur les sources égyptiennes de la littérature sapientiale d'Israël*. Neuchatel, 1929.

Jolles, A. *Einfache Formen*. 2nd edn. Halle, 1956.

Kramer, S. N. 'Sumerian Wisdom Literature', *BASOR*, 122 (1951), 28–31.

Lambert, W. G. *Babylonian Wisdom Literature*. Oxford, 1960.

McKenzie, J. L. 'Reflections on Wisdom', *JBL*, 86 (1967), 1–9.

Mettinger, T. N. D. *Solomonic State Officials*. Lund, 1971.

Murphy, R. E. *Introduction to the Wisdom Literature of the Old Testament*. Collegeville, 1965.

  Wisdom Literature. The Forms of Old Testament Literature, Vol. 13. Grand Rapids, 1981.

  'The Concept of Wisdom Literature', in *The Bible in Current Catholic Thought*, Festschrift Gruenthaner, ed. J. L. McKenzie, pp. 46–54. New York, 1962.

  'The Wisdom Literature of the Old Testament', *Concilium*, 1 (1965), 68–75.

  'Assumptions and Problems in Old Testament Wisdom Research', *CBQ*, 29 (1967), 407–18.

  'Form Criticism and Wisdom Literature', *CBQ*, 31 (1969), 475–83.

  'The Interpretation of Old Testament Wisdom Literature', *Int*, 23 (1969), 289–301.

  'Israel's Wisdom: A Biblical Model of Salvation', *Studie Missionalia*, Gregorian University, Rome, 30 (1981), 1–43.

Pfeiffer, R. H. 'Edomitic Wisdom', *ZAW*, 44 (1926), 13–25.

  'Wisdom and Vision in the Old Testament', *ZAW*, 52 (1934), 93–101.

Pirot, J. 'Le "Māšāl" dans l'Ancien Testament', *RSR*, 37 (1950), 565–80.

Preuss, H. D. 'Erwägungen zum theologischen Ort alttestamentlicher Weisheitsliteratur', *EvT*, 30 (1970), 393–417.

  'Das Gottesbild der alteren Weisheit Israels', *VTSup*, 23 (1972), 117–45.

Priest, J. F. 'Where is Wisdom to be Placed?', *JBR*, 31 (1963), 275–82.

Rad, G. von. *Wisdom in Israel*. London, 1972.

Rankin, O. S. *Israel's Wisdom Literature*. 2nd edn. Edinburgh, 1964; repr. New York, 1969.

Richter, W. *Recht und Ethos. Versuch einer Ortung des weisheitlichen Mahnspruches*. Munich, 1966.

Rost, L. 'Bemerkungen zu Ahiqar', *MIO*, 15 (1969), 308–11.

Roth, W. M. W. *Les sagesses du Proche-Orient ancien. Colloque de Strasbourg 17–19 mai 1962*. Paris, 1963.

  'The Numerical Sequence x/x + 1 in the Old Testament', *VT*, 12 (1962), 300–11.

  'Numerical Sayings in the Old Testament. A Form-critical study', *VTSup*, 13 (Leiden, 1965).

Schmid, H. H. *Wesen und Geschichte der Weisheit*. Berlin, 1966.

  Gerechtigkeit als Weltordnung. Tübingen, 1968.

  'Hauptprobleme der altorientalischen und alttestamentlichen Weisheitsliteratur', *SchTU*, 35 (1965), 68–74.

Schmidt, J. *Studien zur Stilistik der alttestamentlichen Spruchliteratur*. Münster, 1936.

Scott, R. B. Y. *Studies in Israelite Poetry and Wisdom*. Washington, 1971.

  The Way of Wisdom in the Old Testament. New York–London, 1971.

  'The Study of Wisdom Literature', *Int*, 24 (1970), 20–45.

  'Wise and Foolish, Righteous and Wicked', *VTSup*, 23 (1972), 146–65.

Westermann, C. 'Weisheit im Sprichwort', in *Schalom*, Festschrift Jepsen, ed. K. H. Bernhardt, pp. 72–85. Berlin, 1971.

Whybray, R. N. *The Intellectual Tradition in the Old Testament*. Berlin, 1974.

'Wisdom in Israel and in the Ancient Near East', Festschrift Rowley, ed. M. Noth and D. W. Thomas, *VTSup*, 3 (Leiden, 1955).

Wood, J. *Wisdom Literature: An Introduction*. London, 1967.

Zimmerli, W. 'Zur Struktur der alttestamentlichen Weisheit', *ZAW*, 51 (1933), 177–204.

'Ort und Grenze der Weisheit im Rahmen der alttestamentlichen Theologie', in *Gottes Offenbarung*, pp. 300–15. Munich, 1963.

The book of Proverbs

Previously mentioned titles are not repeated.

Barucq, A. *Le Livre des Proverbes*. Paris, 1964.

Boström, G. *Proverbiastudien*. Lund, 1935.

Bridges, C. *A Commentary on Proverbs*. 4th edn. London, 1968.

Buchanan, G. W. 'Midrashim pré-tannaïtes. A propos de Proverbes I–IX', *RB*, 72 (1965), 227–39.

Conrad, J. 'Die innere Gliederung der Proverbien', *ZAW*, 79 (1967), 67–76.

Couroyer, B. 'L'origine égyptienne de la Sagesse d'Amenemopé', *RB*, 70 (1963), 208–24.

Dahood, M. *Proverbs and Northwest-Semitic Philology*. Rome, 1963.

'Prov. 8, 22–31. Translation and Commentary', *CBQ*, 30 (1968), 512–21.

Donner, H. 'Die religionsgeschichtlichen Ursprünge von Prov. Sal. 8', *ZA*, 82 (1958), 8–18.

Drioton, E. 'Le livre des Proverbes et la Sagesse d'Aménémopé', *Sacra Pagina*, BETL 12–13 (Paris–Gembloux, 1959), 229–41.

Emerton, J. A. 'Notes on Some Passages in the Book of Proverbs', *JTS*, 20 (1969), 202–20.

Erman, A. 'Eine ägyptische Quelle der "Sprüche Salomos"', in *SPAW*, vols. 15–16, 86–93. Berlin, 1924.

'Das Weisheitsbuch des Amen-em-ope', *OLZ*, 27 (1924), 241–52.

Fox, M. V. 'Aspects of the Religion of the Book of Proverbs', *HUCA*, 39 (1968), 55–69.

Gemser, B. *Sprüche Salomos*. HAT, 1, 16. 2nd edn. Tübingen, 1963.

Gressmann, G. 'Die neugefundene Lehre des Amen-em-ope und die vorexilische Spruchdichtung Israels', *ZAW*, 42 (1924), 272–96.

Habel, N. C. 'The Symbolism of Wisdom in Proverbs 1–9', *Int*, 26 (1972), 131–57.

Hermisson, H. J. *Studien zur israelitischen Spruchweisheit*. Neukirchen-Vluyn, 1968.

Hulsbosch, A. 'Sagesse créatrice et éducatrice', *Augustinianum*, 1 (1961), 217–35, 433–51; 2 (1962), 5–39; 3 (1963), 5–27.

Humbert, P. 'La "femme étrangère" du livre des Proverbes', *RES* (1957), 49–64.

Irwin, W. A. 'Where shall Wisdom be Found?', *JBL*, 80 (1961), 133–42.

Jensen, K. L. *Wisdom, The Principal Thing: Studies in the Book of Proverbs*. Seattle, 1971.

Kayatz, C. *Studien zu Prov. 1–9*. Neukirchen-Vluyn, 1966.

Keel, O. *Die Weisheit spielt vor Gott*. Freiburg–Göttingen, 1974.

Kevin, R. O. 'The Wisdom of Amen-em-apt and its Possible Dependence upon the Hebrew Book of Proverbs', *JSOR*, 14 (1930), 115–57.

Kidner, D. *The Proverbs*. London, 1964.

Koch, K. 'Gibt es ein Vergeltungsdogma im Alten Testament?', *ZTK*, 52 (1955), 1–42.

Lang, B. *Die weisheitliche Lehrrede. Eine Untersuchung von Sprüche 1–7.* Stuttgart, 1972.

Mack, B. L. *Logos und Sophia.* Göttingen, 1973.

'Wisdom Myth and Mytho-logy', *Int*, 24 (1970), 46–60.

Marbök, J. *Weisheit im Wandel.* Bonn, 1971.

'Menschenweisheit und Offenbarung', *TPQ*, 118 (1970), 28–34.

Marcus, R. 'On Biblical Hypostases of Wisdom', *HUCA*, 23 (1950–51), 157–71.

McKane, W. *Proverbs.* Philadelphia and London, 1970.

Murphy, R. E. 'Kerygma of the book of Proverbs', *Int*, 20 (1966), 3–14.

Oesterley, W. O. E. 'The "Teaching of Amen-em-ope" and the Old Testament', *ZAW*, 45 (1927), 9–24.

Pfeifer, G. *Ursprung und Wesen der Hypostasenvorstellungen im Judentum.* Stuttgart, 1967.

Ploeg, J. van der. *Spreuken*, BOT 8, 1. Roermond, 1952.

Plöger, O. 'Zur Auslegung der Sentenzensammlung des Proverbienbuches', in *Probleme Biblischer Theologie*, Festschrift von Rad, ed. H. W. Wolff, pp. 402–16. Munich, 1971.

Ringgren, H. *Word and Wisdom.* Lund, 1947.

Sprüche, ATD 16, 1. Göttingen, 1962.

Sauer, S. *Die Sprüche Agurs.* Stuttgart, 1963.

Savignac, J. de. 'La sagesse en Proverbes VIII, 22–31', *VT*, 12 (1962), 211–15.

Schmitt, E. *Leben in den Weisheitsbüchern Job, Sprüche und Jesus Sirach.* Freiburg, 1954.

Scott, R. B. Y. *Proverbs. Ecclesiastes.* AB 18. Garden City, New York, 1965.

'Wisdom in Creation: The *'āmōn* of Proverbs VIII, 30', *VT*, 10 (1960), 213–23.

Skehan, P. W. 'The Seven Columns of Wisdom's House in Prov. 9, 1', *CBQ*, 9 (1947), 190–8.

'A Single Editor for the Whole Book of Proverbs', *CBQ*, 10 (1948), 115–30.

'Wisdom's House', *CBQ*, 29 (1967), 468–86.

Skladny, V. *Die ältesten Spruchsammlungen in Israel.* Göttingen, 1962.

Stecher, R. 'Die persönliche Weisheit in den Proverbien Kap. 8', *ZKT*, 75 (1953), 411–51.

Story, C. I. K. 'The Book of Proverbs and Northwest-Semitic Literature', *JBL*, 64 (1945), 319–37.

Thomas, D. W. 'Notes on Some Passages in the Book of Proverbs', *VT*, 15 (1965), 271–9.

Tournay, R. 'Buch der Sprüche 1–9', *Concilium*, 2 (1966), 768–73.

Vischer, W. 'Der Hymnus der Weisheit in den Sprüchen Salomos 8, 22–31', *EvT*, 22 (1962), 309–26.

Wallis, G. 'Zu den Spruchsammlungen Prov. 10, 1–22, 16 und 25–29', *TLZ*, 85 (1960), 147–8.

Weiden, W. A. van der. *Le Livre des Proverbes.* Rome, 1970.

Whybray, R. N. *Wisdom in Proverbs*, SBT 1, 45. 2nd edn. London, 1965.

The Book of Proverbs. Cambridge, 1972.

'Prov. 8, 22–31 and its Supposed Prototypes', *VT*, 15 (1965), 504–14.

'Some Literary Problems in Prov. 1–9', *VT*, 16 (1966), 482–96.

The book of Job

Alt, A. 'Zur Vorgeschichte des Buches Hiob', *ZAW*, 55 (1937), 265–8.

Anderson, H. 'Another Perspective on the Book of Job', *Glasgow University Oriental Society Transactions*, 18 (1961), 53–6.

Barr, J. 'The Book of Job and Its Modern Interpreters', *BJRL*, 54 (1971), 28–46.

Baumgärtel, F. *Der Hiobdialog*. Stuttgart, 1933.

Bič, M. 'Le juste et l'impie dans le livre de Job', *VTSup*, 15 (1966), 33–43.

Blommerde, A. C. M. *Northwest-Semitic Grammar and Job*. Rome, 1968.

Brandon, S. G. F. *The Book of Job, Its Significance for the History of Religions*. New York, 1969.

Brandwein, C. 'The Legend of Job According to its Various Stages', *Tarbiz*, 35 (1965), 1–17.

Buttenwieser, M. *The Book of Job*. London, 1922.

Crenshaw, J. L. 'Popular Questioning of the Justice of God in Ancient Israel', *ZAW*, 82 (1970), 380–95.

Dahood, M. 'Some Northwest-Semitic Words in Job', *Bib*, 38 (1957), 306–20.

'Northwest Semitic Philology in "Job"', in *The Bible in Current Catholic Thought*, Festschrift Gruenthaner, ed. J. L. McKenzie, pp. 55–74. New York, 1962.

Dhorme, E. *A Commentary on the Book of Job*. London, 1967.

Eerdmans, B. D. *Studies in Job*. Leiden, 1939.

Ellison, H. L. *A Study of Job. From Tragedy to Triumph*. 2nd edn. Grand Rapids, 1972.

Feinberg, C. L. 'The Poetic Structure of the Book of Job and the Ugaritic Literature', *BSac*, 103 (1946), 283–92.

Fohrer, G. *Das Buch Hiob*. KAT 16. Gütersloh, 1963.

Studien zum Buche Hiob. Tübingen, 1963.

Fullerton, K. 'The Original Conclusion to the Book of Job', *ZAW*, 42 (1924), 116–35.

Gibbs, P. T. *Job and the Mysteries of Wisdom*. Nashville, 1967.

Ginsberg, H. L. 'Job the Patient and Job the Impatient', *Conservative Judaism*, 21 (1966–67), 12–28 = *VTSup*, 17 (1969), 88–111.

Gordis, R. *The Book of God and Man*. Chicago, 1965.

'Wisdom and Job', in *Old Testament Issues*, ed. S. Sandmel, pp. 213–41. London, 1969.

Gray, J. 'The Book of Job in the Context of Near Eastern Literature', *ZAW*, 82 (1970), 251–69.

Guillaume, A. *Studies in the Book of Job*. Leiden, 1968.

'The Unity of the Book of Job', *ALUOS*, 4 (1962), 26–46.

Hempel, J. 'Das theologische Problem des Hiob', *ZST*, 6 (1929), 621–89 = *Apoxysmata*, 114–73. Berlin, 1961.

Herz, J. 'Formgeschichtliche Untersuchungen zum Problem des Hiobbuches', *WZLeipzig* (1953–54), 157–62.

Hölscher, G. *Das Buch Hiob*. HAT, 1, 17. 2nd edn. Tübingen, 1952.

Horst, F. *Hiob. 1 Teilband*. BKAT, 16, 1. Neukirchen-Vluyn, 1968.

Irwin, W. A. 'Poetic Structure in the Dialogue of Job', *JNES*, 5 (1946), 26–39.

'Job's Redeemer', *JBL*, 81 (1962), 217–29.

Jastrow, M., Jr. *The Book of Job*. Philadelphia–London, 1920.

Jepsen, A. *Das Buch Hiob und seine Deutung*. Berlin, 1963.

Johnson, L. D. *Out of the Whirlwind. The Major Message of Job*. Nashville, 1971.

Kissane, E. J. *The Book of Job*. Dublin, 1939; New York, 1946.

Kraeling, E. G. *The Book of the Ways of God*. London, 1938.

Kramer, S. M. 'Sumerian Literature and the Bible', *SBO*, 3 (1959), 185–204.

Kuhl, C. 'Neuere Literarkritik des Buches Hiob', *TRu*, 21 (1953), 163–205, 257–317.

'Vom Hiobbuche und seinen Problemen', *TRu*, 22 (1954), 261–316.

Kuschke, A. 'Altbabylonische Texte zum Thema "Der leidende Gerechte"', *TLZ*, 81 (1956), 69–76.

Kutsch, E. 'Hiob: leidender Gerechter – leidender Mensch', *KD*, 19 (1973), 197–214.

Laurin, R. 'The Theological Structure of Job', *ZAW*, 84 (1972), 86–9.

Lévéque, J. *Job et son dieu.* 2 vols. Paris, 1970.

Lindblom, J. *La composition du Livre de Job.* Lund, 1945.

MacKenzie, R. A. F. 'The Purpose of the Yahweh speeches in the book of Job', *Bib*, 40 (1959), 435–45.

McKeating, H. 'The Central Issue in Job', *ExpTim*, 82 (1971), 244–7.

Möller, H. *Sinn und Aufbau des Buches Hiob.* Berlin, 1955.

Müller, H.-P. *Hiob und seine Freunde. Traditionsgeschichtliches zum Verständnis des Hiobbuches.* Zurich, 1970.

Pope, M. H. *Job.* AB 15. Garden City–New York, 1965.

Richter, H. *Studien zu Hiob.* Berlin, 1959.

'Erwägungen zu Hiobproblem', *EvT*, 18 (1958), 202–24.

'Die Naturweisheit des Alten Testaments im Buche Hiob', *ZAW*, 70 (1958), 1–20.

Rowley, H. H. *Job.* London, 1970.

'The Book of Job and its Meaning', *BJRL*, 41 (1958), 167–207 = *From Moses to Qumran*, pp. 139–83. London, 1963.

Sanders, P. S. (ed.). *The Book of Job. A Collection of Critical Essays.* Englewood Cliffs, N.J.–Hemel Hempstead, 1968.

Sarna, N. M. 'Epic Substratum in the Prose of Job', *JBL*, 76 (1957), 13–25.

Sekine, M. 'Schöpfung und Erlösung im Buche Hiob', in *Von Ugarit nach Qumran*, Festschrift Eissfeldt, ed. J. Hempel and L. Rost, pp. 213–23. Berlin, 1958.

Skehan, P. W. 'Strophic Patterns in the Book of Job', *CBQ*, 23 (1961), 125–42.

'Job's Final Plea (Job 29–31) and the Lord's Reply (Job 38–41)', *Bib*, 45 (1964), 51–62.

Snaith, N. H. *The Book of Job. Its Origin and Purpose.* London, 1968.

Soden, W. von. 'Die Frage nach der Gerechtigkeit Gottes im Alten Orient', *MDOG*, 96 (1965), 41–59.

Stamm, J. J. *Das Leiden des Unschuldigen in Babylon und Israel.* Zurich, 1946.

Steinmann, J. *Le Livre de Job.* Paris, 1955.

Stevenson, W. B. *The Poem of Job.* 2nd edn. London, 1948.

Stockhammer, M. 'The Righteousness of Job', *Judaism*, 7 (1958), 64–71.

Thompson, K., Jr. 'Out of the Whirlwind. The Sense of Alienation in the Book of Job', *Int*, 14 (1960), 51–63.

Tournay, R. J. 'L'ordre primitif des chapitres xxiv–xxviii du Livre de Job', *RB*, 64 (1957), 321–34.

Tsevat, N. 'The meaning of the Book of Job', *HUCA*, 37 (1966), 73–106.

Tur-Sinai, N. H. *The Book of Job. A New Commentary.* 2nd edn. Jerusalem, 1967.

Vischer, W. 'God's Truth and Man's Lie. A Study of the Message of the Book of Job', *Int*, 15 (1961), 131–46.

Weber, J.-J. *Le Livre de Job.* Paris, 1947.

Weiser, A. *Das Buch Hiob.* ATD 13. 4th edn. Göttingen, 1963.

Westermann, C. *Der Aufbau des Buches Hiob.* Tübingen, 1956.

Williams, J. G. '"You have not spoken Truth of Me". Mystery and Irony in Job', *ZAW*, 83 (1971), 231–55.

Würthwein, E. 'Gott und Mensch in Dialog und Gottesreden des Buches Hiob', in *Wort und Existenz*, pp. 217–95. Göttingen, 1970.

CHAPTER 10. JEWISH RELIGIOUS LIFE IN THE PERSIAN PERIOD

Abel, F. *Histoire de la Palestine*. 2 vols. Paris, 1952.

Aharoni, Y. 'Excavations at Ramath Rahel', *IEJ*, 6 (1956), 445f.

'The Excavations at Tel Arad', *IEJ*, 17 (1967), 244.

'Trial Excavation in the "Solar Shrine" at Lachish', *IEJ*, 18 (1968), 157–64.

Aimé-Giron, N. *Textes Araméens d'Égypte*. Cairo, 1931.

'Trois ostraca araméens d'Éléphantine', *ASAE*, 26 (1926), 27f.

'Adversaria Semitica', *BIFAO*, 38 (1939), 41–3.

Albright, W. F. *Archaeology and the Religion of Israel*. 4th edn. Baltimore, 1956.

Avigad, N. *Bullae and Seals from a Post-Exilic Judean Archive*. *Qedem*, 4. Jerusalem, 1976.

'A Group of Hebrew Seals', *Eretz-Israel* 9 (1969) (in Hebrew). Hebrew section, p. 4.

Bailey, M. 'Levitical Legend from the Persian Period', *JBL*, 46 (1927), 132–8.

Bentzen, A. 'Priesterschaft und Laien in der jüdischen Gemeinde des fünften Jahrhunderts,' *AfO*, 6 (1930–31), 280–6.

Bickerman, E. *Four Strange Books of the Bible*. New York, 1967.

Borger, R. 'Anath-Bethel', *VT*, 7 (1957), 102ff.

Braun, M. *History and Romance in Graeco-Oriental Literature*. Oxford, 1938.

Bresciani, E. 'Papiri aramaici egiziani...di Padova', *RSO*, 35 (1960), 11–24 and plates I–V.

'Le lettere aramaiche di Hermopoli', *Memorie*, Accademia Nazionale dei Lincei, Scienze morali VIII.XII.5; *Atti*, 363 (1966), nos. I–IV.

Bull, R. 'The Excavations of Tel er-Ras', *BA*, 31 (1968), 70f.

Cook, S. *The Religion of Ancient Palestine in the Light of Archaeology*. The Schweich Lectures, 1925. London, 1930.

Cowley, A. *Aramaic Papyri*. Oxford, 1923.

Cross, F. M., Jr. 'Judean Stamps', *Eretz-Israel*, 9 (1969), 20ff.

'Papyri of the Fourth Century B.C. from Dâliyeh', in *New Directions in Biblical Archaeology*, ed. D. N. Freedman and J. C. Greenfield, pp. 42ff. London, 1969; New York, 1971.

'Postscript', *BASOR*, 193 (1969), 24.

Daiches, S. *The Jews in Babylonia in the Time of Ezra and Nehemiah*. Jews' College Publications, no. 2. London, 1910.

Diringer, D. *Le iscrizioni antico-ebraiche palestinese*. Pubblicazioni della R. U. degli Studi di Firenze, Facoltà di Lett. e Filos. 3rd series, 2. Florence, 1934.

Donner, H., and Röllig, W. *Kanaanäische und aramäische Inschriften*. Wiesbaden, 1962.

Dupont-Sommer, A. 'Maison de Yahvé et vêtements sacrés à Élephantine', *JA*, 235 (1946–47), 80–7.

'L'ostracon araméen du Sabbat', *Semitica*, 2 (1949), 29–39.

'Un ostracon araméen inédit', in *Hebrew and Semitic Studies Presented to Godfrey Rolles Driver*, ed. D. W. Thomas and W. D. McHardy, pp. 53–8. Oxford, 1963.

'Sabbat et parascève à Élephantine', *MPAIBL* (1950), 67–88.

Eissfeldt, O. *Einleitung in das Alte Testament*. 3rd edn. Tübingen, 1964. (ET: *The Old Testament: An Introduction*, by P. R. Ackroyd. New York, 1965.)

Fohrer, G. *Introduction to the Old Testament*. Trans. D. Green. Nashville, 1968.

Frye, R. *The Heritage of Persia*. Cleveland, 1963.

Galling, K. *Die Bücher der Chronik, Esra, Nehemia.* ATD 12. Göttingen, 1954.

Ginzberg, L. *The Legends of the Jews,* vols. IV and VI. Philadelphia, 1909–46.

Gordis, R. *The Book of God and Man.* Chicago, 1966.

Grelot, P. *Documents araméens d'Égypte.* Paris, 1972.

Gunneweg, A. *Leviten und Priester,* FRLANT 89. Göttingen, 1965.

Hill, G. *Catalogue of the Greek Coins of Palestine. A Catalogue of the Greek Coins in the British Museum,* vol. 27. London, 1914.

Hölscher, G. 'Levi', *RE,* 12, 2 (1925), 2185.

Kindler, A. 'Silver Coins Bearing the Name of Judea', *IEJ,* 24 (1974), 73ff.

Kippenberg, H. *Garizim und Synagoge,* RGVV 30. Berlin, 1971.

Koch, K. *Die Priesterschrift von Exodus 25 bis Leviticus 16.* Göttingen, 1959.

Kraeling, E. *The Brooklyn Museum Aramaic Papyri.* New Haven, 1953.

Levine, B. 'Later Sources on the *Netînîm*', *Orient and Occident,* C. Gordon Festschrift, ed. H. Hoffner, pp. 101–7. Neukirchen-Vluyn, 1973.

'The *Netînîm*', *JBL,* 82 (1963), 207–12.

Lidzbarski, M. *Ephemeris für semitische Epigraphik.* 3 vols. Giessen, 1902–15.

Lods, A. *Histoire de la littérature hebraique et juive.* Paris, 1950.

Milik, J. 'La patrie de Tobie', *RB,* 73 (1966), 522ff.

Morgenstern, J. 'Supplementary Studies in the Calendars of Ancient Israel', *HUCA,* 10 (1935), 1ff.

Moscati, S. *L'Epigrafia ebraica antica 1935–1950, BibOr,* 15. Rome, 1951.

Mowinckel, S. 'Erwägungen zum chronistischen Geschichtswerk', *TLZ,* 85 (1960), 2ff.

Naveh, J. 'An Aramaic Ostracon from Ashdod', in M. Dothan, *Ashdod II–III, Atiqot,* English Series 9–10, pp. 200ff. Jerusalem, 1971.

Nock, A. *Conversion.* Oxford, 1933.

Parker, R. and Dubberstein, W. *Babylonian Chronology, 626 B.C.–A.D. 75. Brown University Studies* XIX. Providence, 1956.

Pfeiffer, R. H. *Introduction to the Old Testament.* New York, 1948.

Pope, M. *Job.* 3rd edn. New York, 1974.

Porten, B. *Archives from Elephantine.* Berkeley, 1968.

Porten, B. and Greenfield, J. *Jews of Elephantine and Aramaeans of Syene.* Jerusalem, 1974.

Rad, G. von. *Das Geschichtsbild des chronistischen Werkes,* BWANT 4, 3. Stuttgart, 1930.

'Die levitische Predigt in den Büchern der Chronik', *Festschrift Otto Procksch,* pp. 113ff. Leipzig, 1934.

Die Priesterschrift im Hexateuch, BWANT 4, 13. Berlin, 1934.

Rahmani, L., 'Silver Coins of the Fourth Century B.C. from Tel Gamma', *IEJ,* 21 (1971), 158ff.

Ringgren, H. *Das Hohe Lied,* ATD 16, 2. Göttingen, 1958.

Rosenthal, F. (ed.). *An Aramaic Handbook* I.1. Porta Linguarum Orientalium, N.S. 10. Wiesbaden, 1967.

Rudolph, W. *Esra und Nehemia,* HAT 1, 20. Tübingen, 1949.

Chronikbücher, HAT 1, 21. Tübingen, 1955.

Sachau, E. *Aramäische Papyrus und Ostraka aus Elephantine.* Leipzig, 1911.

Safrai, S. *Pilgrimage in the Time of the Second Temple* (in Hebrew). Jerusalem, 1965.

Sellers, O. *The Citadel of Beth Zur.* Philadelphia, 1933.

Smith, M. *Palestinian Parties and Politics That Shaped the Old Testament.* New York, 1971.

'The Common Theology of the Ancient Near East', *JBL,* 71 (1952), 135–47.

'On the Wine God in Palestine', in *Salo Wittmayer Baron Jubilee Volume,* 3 vols., vol. 2, pp. 815–29. Jerusalem, 1975 (title page '1974', but see corrigenda).

Stern, E. *The Material Culture of Palestine in the Persian Period*. Jerusalem, 1968.
   Hattarbut heḥomrit shel Ereṣ Yisra'el bitequfah happarsit. Jerusalem, 1973.
Stern, M. *Greek and Latin Authors on Jews and Judaism*. 1. *From Herodotus to Plutarch*.
   Jerusalem, 1974.
   'Maṭmon shel Ṣlamiyot', *Eretẓ-Israel*, 12 (1975), 91ff.
Tcherikover, V. and Fuks, A. (eds.). *Corpus Papyrorum Judaicarum*. 3 vols. Cambridge,
   Mass., 1957–64.
Teixidor, J. 'Bulletin d'épigraphie sémitique', *Syria* 48 (1971).
Tufnell, O. *Lachish III*. 2 vols. Oxford, 1953.
Vattioni, F. 'I sigilli ebraici', *Bib*, 50 (1969), 357–88.
   'I sigilli ebraici II,' *Augustinianum*, 11 (1971), 446–54.
Vaux, R. de. *Ancient Israel*. Trans. J. McHugh. London, 1961.
Vogelstein, H. *Der Kampf ẓwischen Priestern und Leviten*. Stettin, 1889.

CHAPTER 11. PERSIAN RELIGION IN THE ACHEMENID AGE

Translations of primary sources

Bartholomae, C. *Die Gāthā's des Awesta*. Strasbourg, 1905.
Darmesteter, J. *Le Zend-Avesta*. Annales du Musée Guimet. 3 vols. Paris, 1892–93; repr.
   Paris, 1960.
Duchesne-Guillemin, J. *Zoroastre, étude critique avec une traduction commentée des Gāthā*.
   Paris, 1948. English translation of his rendering of the Gathas (without the notes)
   by Maria Henning: *The hymns of Zarathustra*. London, 1952.
Gershevitch, I. *The Avestan hymn to Mithra*. University of Cambridge Oriental Publi-
   cations 4. Cambridge, 1959; repr. 1964.
Humbach, H. *Die Gathas des Zarathustra*. 2 vols. Heidelberg, 1959.
Insler, S. *The Gāthās of Zarathustra*, Acta Iranica 8. Leiden, 1975.
Kent, R. G. *Old Persian, Grammar, texts, lexicon*. New Haven, 1950; rev. edition, 1953.
Lommel, H. *Die Yäšt's des Awesta*. Göttingen and Leipzig, 1927.
   Die Gathas des Zarathustra, ed. B. Schlerath. Basle–Stuttgart, 1971.
Mayrhofer, M. *Iranisches Personennamenbuch*, I.2. Vienna, 1979.
Smith, M. W. *Studies in the syntax of the Gathas of Zarathushtra, together with text, translation
   and notes*. Language dissertations published by the Linguistic Society of America,
   4. Philadelphia, 1929.
Taraporewala, I. J. S. *The Divine Songs of Zarathushtra*. Bombay, 1951.
Wolff, F. *Avesta, die heiligen Bücher der Parsen, übersetẓt auf der Grundlage von Chr.
   Bartholomae's Altiranisches Wörterbuch*. Strasbourg, 1910; repr. 1960.
   See also J. H. Moulton (below), whose *Early Zoroastrianism* contains a complete
   English translation of the Gathas.

Translations of important works representing the tradition

Anklesaria, B. T. *Zand-Ākāsīh, Iranian or Greater Bundahišn*. Bombay, 1956. A general
   work.
   Zand-ī Vohuman Yasn. Bombay, 1957. Representing the prophetic soteriological
   literature.
Dhabhar, B. N. *The Persian Rivayats of Hormaẓyar Framarẓ*. Bombay, 1932. Late
   material, but valuable for the purity laws, ceremonies and customs.

West, E. W. *Pahlavi Texts, Sacred Books of the East*, V, XVIII, XXIV, XXXVII, XLVI, Delhi, 1882–1901; repr. Delhi, 1965. Out of date, but still useful, with detailed indices.

General

Benveniste, E. *The Persian religion according to the chief Greek texts*. Conférences Ratanbai Katrak. Paris, 1929.

Bianchi, U. *Zamān ī Ohrmaẓd*. Storia e Scienza delle Religioni. Turin, 1958.

Bickerman, E. J. *Studies in Jewish and Christian History*, part 1. Leiden, 1976.

Bidez, J. and Cumont, F. *Les mages hellénisés*. 2 vols. Paris, 1938.

Boyce, M. 'Middle Persian Literature', *Handbuch der Orientalistik* (ed. B. Spuler, 1.4.2.1), pp. 31–66. Leiden, 1968.

  A history of Zoroastrianism. Handbuch der Orientalistik (ed. B. Spuler, 1.8.1.2), vol. 1: *The early period*, Leiden, 1975; vol. 2: *The Achaemenian period* (in the press).

  A Persian Stronghold of Zoroastrianism. Oxford, 1977.

  Zoroastrians, their religious beliefs and practices. London, 1979.

Clemen, G. *Fontes Historiae Religionis Persicae*. Bonn, 1920.

Dandamayev, M. A. *Persien unter den ersten Achämeniden (6. Jahrhundert v. Chr.)*, transl. from Russian by H.-D. Pohl. Wiesbaden, 1976.

Dhalla, M. N. *History of Zoroastrianism*. New York, 1938; repr. 1977.

Duchesne-Guillemin, J. *The western response to Zoroaster*. Oxford, 1958.

  La Religion de l'Iran ancien. Paris, 1962.

Frye, R. N. *The heritage of Persia*. London, 1962.

Geldner, K. F. 'Awestalitteratur', *Grundriss der iranischen Philologie*, ed. W. Geiger and E. Kuhn, 2, 1–53. Strasbourg, 1896–1904.

Gray, L. H. 'The foundations of the Iranian religions', *JCOI*, 15 (1929), 1–228.

Jackson, A. V. W. *Zoroastrian Studies*. New York, 1928.

Jamaspji Asa, H. and Haug, M. *The Book of Arda Viraf*. London, 1872.

King, L. W. and Thompson, R. C. *The Sculptures and Inscriptions of Darius the Great*. London, 1907.

Kraeling, E. G. *The Brooklyn Museum Aramaic Papyri: New Documents of the Fifth Century B.C. from the Jewish Colony at Elephantine*. New Haven, 1953.

Lommel, H. *Die Religion Zarathustras nach dem Awesta dargestellt*. Tübingen, 1930; repr. 1971.

Modi, J. J. *The religious ceremonies and customs of the Parsees*. Bombay, 1922; 2nd edn. 1937.

Moulton, J. H. *Early Zoroastrianism*. London, 1913; repr. 1972.

Neusner, J. *The Mishnaic system of uncleanness, its context and history*. Leiden, 1977.

Nyberg, H. S. *Die Religionen des alten Iran*. German translation by H. H. Schaeder. Leipzig, 1938; repr. 1966.

Olmstead, A. T. *History of the Persian Empire*. Chicago, 1948; repr. 1959.

Pavry, J. C. *The Zoroastrian doctrine of a future life*. New York, 1929.

Porten, B. *Archives from Elephantine*. Berkeley, 1968.

Posener, G. *La première domination perse en Egypte, Recueil d'inscriptions hiéroglyphiques*. Cairo, 1936.

Schippmann, K. *Die iranischen Feuerheiligtümer*. Berlin and New York, 1971.

Schlerath, B. (ed.). *Zarathustra*. Wege der Forschung, vol. 169. Darmstadt, 1970.

Schmidt, E. F. *Persepolis*. University of Chicago Oriental Institute Publications. Chicago: vol. 1, 1953; vol. 2, 1957; vol. 3, 1970.

Shahbazi, A. S. *The Irano-Lycian Monuments*. Tehran, 1975.

Smith, M. *Palestinian Parties and Politics that Shaped the Old Testament*. New York, 1971.

Smith, S. *Isaiah Chapters XL–LV*, The Schweich Lectures, 1940. London, 1944.

Spiegel, F. *Erânische Alterthumskunde*. 3 vols. Leipzig, 1871–78.

Stronach, D. *Pasargadae*. Oxford, 1978.

Tilia, A. B. *Studies and Restorations at Persepolis*, 2. Rome, 1978.

West, M. L. *Early Greek Philosophy and the Orient*. Oxford, 1971.

Zaehner, R. C. *Zurvan, a Zoroastrian dilemma*. Oxford, 1955.

CHAPTER 12. IRANIAN INFLUENCE ON JUDAISM

Bertholet, A. *Das Religionsgeschichtliche Problem des Spätjudentums*. Tübingen, 1909.
Persischer und jüdischer Auferstehungsglaube, Festschrift für F. C. Andreas, pp. 51–62. Leipzig, 1916.

Böklen, E. *Die Verwandtschaft der jüdisch-christlichen mit der persischen Eschatologie*. Göttingen, 1902.

Bousset, W. *Die Religion des Judentums im spät-hellenistischen Zeitalter*. 3rd edn., rev. H. Gressmann, Tübingen, 1926.

Boyce, M. *A History of Zoroastrianism*. Leiden, 1975.

Duchesne-Guillemin, J. *The Western Response to Zoroaster*, Oxford, 1958.

Dupont-Sommer, A. *Nouveaux aperçus sur les manuscrits de la Mer Morte*, pp. 123–36; 157–72. Paris, 1953.

Flusser, D. 'The Four Empires in the Fourth Sybil and in the Book of Daniel', *IOS*, 2 (1972), 148–75.
'Hystaspes and John of Patmos', in *Irano-Judaica*, Jerusalem (to be published).

Frye, R. N. 'Qumran and Iran: The State of Studies', in *Christianity, Judaism and Other Greco-Roman Cults*, ed. J. Neusner, vol. 3, pp. 167–73. Leiden, 1975.

Gall, A. F. von. *Basileia tou theou*. Heidelberg, 1926.

Gaster, M. 'Parsiism in Judaism', *Encyclopaedia of Religion and Ethics 9*, pp. 637–40. Edinburgh and New York, 1925.

Gressmann, H. *Der Ursprung der israelitisch-jüdischen Eschatologie*. Göttingen, 1905.
'Das Religionsgeschichtliche Problem des Ursprungs der Hellenistischen Erlösungsreligion', *ZKG*, 40 (N.F. 3; 1922), 178–91; 41 (N.F. 4; 1922), 154–80.

Hinnels, J. R. 'Zoroastrian Influence on the Judaeo-Christian tradition', *JCOI*, 45 (1976), 1–23.

Kohut, A. *Jüdische Angelologie und Dämonologie in ihrer Abhängigkeit vom Parsismus*, Abhandlungen für die Kunde des Morgenlandes, 4. Leipzig, 1866.

König, F. *Zarathustras Jenseitsvorstellungen und das Alte Testament*. Vienna–Freiburg–Basle, 1964.

Kuhn, G. 'Die Sektenschrift und die iranische Religion', *ZTK*, 49 (1952), 296–316.

Mayer, R. *Die biblische Vorstellung vom Weltenbrand. Eine Untersuchung über die Beziehungen zwischen Parsismus und Judentum*. Bonn, 1956.
'Monotheismum in Israel und in der Religion Zarathustras', *BZ*, N.F. 1 (1957), 23–58.

Michaud, H. 'Un mythe zervanite dans un des manuscrits de Qumran', *VT*, 5 (1955), 137–47.

Mills, L. H. *Zarathushtra, the Achaemenids and Israel*. Chicago, 1906.

Moulton, J. H. *Early Zoroastrianism*. London, 1913.

Pines, S. 'Eschatology and the Concept of Time in the Slavonic Book of Enoch', in *Types of Redemption*, ed. R. J. Z. Werblowsky and J. C. Blecker, Studies in the History of Religions, Supplements to *Numen*, 18 (Leiden, 1970).

Reitzenstein, R. *Die hellenistischen Mysterienreligionen nach ihren Grundgedanken und Wesendonk Wirkungen*. 3rd edn. Leipzig and Berlin, 1927.

Scheftelowitz, I. *Die altpersische Religion und das Judentum. Unterschiede, Übereinstimmungen und gegenseitige Beeinflussungen*. Giessen, 1920.

Schweizer, E. 'Gegenwart des Geistes und eschatologische Hoffnung bei Zarathustra, spätjüdischen Gruppen, Gnostikern und den Zeugen des Neuren Testamentes', in *The Background of the New Testament and Its Eschatology*, ed. W. D. Davies and D. Daube, pp. 482–508. Cambridge, 1956.

Shaked, S. *Wisdom of the Sasanian Sages* (forthcoming).

     'The Notions *mēnōg* and *gētīg* in the Pahlavi Texts and their relation to Eschatology', *AcOr*, 33 (1971), 57–70.

     'Qumran and Iran', *IOS*, 2 (1972), 433–46.

Smith, M. 'II Isaiah and the Persians', *JAOS*, 83 (1963), 415–21.

Söderblom, N. *La vie future d'après le mazdéisme à la lumière des croyances parallèles dans les autres religions. Étude d'eschatologie comparée*, Annales du Musee Guimet, 9. Paris, 1901.

Stave, E. *Über den Einfluss des Parsismus auf das Judentum*. Harlem, 1898.

Swain, J. W. 'The Theory of the four Monarchies: Opposition History under the Roman Empire', *ClassPhil*, 35 (1940), 1–21.

Tavadia, J. C. *Die mittelpersische Sprache und Literatur der Zarathustrier*. Leipzig, 1956.

Widengren, G. *Iranisch–semitische Kulturbegegnung in parthischer Zeit*. Köln and Opladen, 1960.

Winston, D. 'The Iranian Component in the Bible, Apocrypha and Qumran: A Review of the Evidence', *HR*, 5 (1965–66), 183–216.

CHAPTER 13. THE DIASPORA

A. BABYLONIA IN THE PERSIAN AGE

Böhl, F. M. Th. de Liagre. 'Die babylonischen Prätendenten zur Zeit Xerxes', *BO*, vol. 19 (1962), 110–14.

Cardascia, G. *Les Archives des Murašû*. Paris, 1951.

     'Le fief dans la Babylonie Achéménide', *Recueils de la Société Jean Bodin*, vol. 1: *Les Liens de Vassalité*, pp. 55–88. Brussels, 1958.

Daiches, S. *The Jews in Babylonia in the Time of Ezra and Nehemiah according to Babylonian Inscriptions*, Jews' College Publications, no. 2. London, 1910.

Dandamayev, M. A. 'Connections between Elam and Babylonia in the Achaemenid Period', in *The Memorial Volume of the Vth International Congress of Iranian Art and Archaeology*, vol. 1, pp. 258–64. Tehran, 1972.

     'Politische und wirtschaftliche Geschichte', *Historia*, Einzelschriften, Part 18: *Beiträge zur Achämenidengeschichte*, pp. 15–58. Wiesbaden, 1972.

Dubberstein, W. H. 'Comparative Prices in Later Babylonia', *AJSL*, 56 (1939) 20–43.

Ebeling, E. 'Aus dem Leben der jüdischen Exulanten in Babylonien. Babylonische Quellen', *Wissenschaftliche Beilage zum Jahresbericht des Humboldt-Gymnasiums*. Berlin, 1914.

Eilers, W. *Iranische Beamtennamen in der keilschriftlichen Überlieferung*. Part 1. Leipzig, 1940.

Gry, L. 'Israélites en Assyrie, Juifs en Babylonie', *Le Muséon*, 35 (1922), 153–85; 36 (1923), 1–26.

Petschow, H. 'Neubabylonisches Pfandrecht', *Abhandlungen der Sächsischen Akademie der Wissenschaften zu Leipzig*, Philol.-hist. Klasse, vol. 48, part 1, 1956.

San Nicolò, M. 'Beiträge zu einer Prosopographie neubabylonischer Beamten der Zivil- und Tempelverwaltung', *Sitzungsberichte der Bayerischen Akademie der Wissenschaften*, Philos.-hist. Abt., 1941.

Smith, S. *Isaiah Chapters XL–LV. Literary Criticism and History*. London, 1944.

Unger, E. *Babylon. Die heilige Stadt nach der Beschreibung der Babylonier*. Berlin, 1970.

Weisberg, D. B. *Guild Structure and Political Allegiance in Early Achaemenid Mesopotamia*. New Haven–London, 1967.

Wiseman, D. J. 'Some Egyptians in Babylonia', *Iraq*, 28 (1966), 154–8.

B. THE BABYLONIAN CAPTIVITY

Sources

Besides the biblical data, the almost exclusive source is the Murashu archives. See Hilprecht, H. V. and Clay, A. T. *The Babylonian Expedition of the University of Pennsylvania*, 9 (Philadelphia, 1898) and 10 (Philadelphia, 1904); Clay, A. T. *The University of Pennsylvania, The Museum*, Publication of the Babylonian Section 2, 1 (Philadelphia, 1912).

Some documents from the same archives came into other collections. Cf. G. Cardascia, *Les Archives des Murašû* (Paris, 1951), p. 11. For translation of these documents, see the references in Cardascia, *Archives*, pp. 208–32; and R. Borger, *Handbuch der Keilschriftliteratur* (Berlin: de Gruyter, 1967).

Further texts have been published in M. W. Stolper, *Management and Politics in Later Achaemenid Babylonia*. Dissertation, University of Michigan, 1974.

Studies

The basic work is G. Cardascia, *Les Archives des Murašû* (Paris, 1951). See, further, the dissertations of Stolper, *Management* and of R. Zadok, *Nippur in the Achaemenid Period. Geographical and Ethnical Aspects* (The Hebrew University, Jerusalem, 1974). English summary 27 pp.

53 cuneiform tablets which mention Jews, or men who could be Jews, have been translated in E. Ebeling, 'Aus dem Leben der juedischen Exulanten in Babylonien', *39 Bericht des Humboldt-Gymnasium zu Berlin Ostern 1914*. 25 of them have been translated again by D. Sidersky, 'L'onomastique hébraique des tablettes de Nippur', *REJ*, 87 (1929), 177–200.

50 'Jewish' tablets are transliterated and translated in Wallis (see below).

Jews in Babylonia

The only easily accessible work on the topic is E. Klamroth, 'Die juedischen Exulanten in Babylonien', *Beihefte zur Zeitschrift fuer die alttestamentliche Wissenschaft*, no. 10 (1912). It is very superficial and completely out of date. The essential work now is R. Zadok, *The Jews in Babylonia in the Chaldean and Achaemenian Periods in the Light of the Babylonian Sources* (Tel Aviv, 1976). See also Dandamayev, M. 'Egyptian Settlers in Babylonia', in *Drevnii Egipet in drevniaia Afrika*. Volume in honour of V. V. Struve, 15–27 (in Russian). Moscow, 1967.

G. Wallis, *Die soziale Situation der Juden in Babylonien zur Achaemenidenzeit* (Dissertation, Free University, Berlin, 1963) gives a valuable survey, which has been thankfully used in the section on economic activity of the Jews at Nippur (see pp. 344–8). Unfortunately, this thesis has not been published. The present writer is much obliged to the author for sending him a microfilm on the thesis. (The microfilm is deposited at the Library of the Jewish Theological Seminary in New York.)

C. EGYPT, PERSIAN SATRAPY

Editions and translations of Aramaic texts

Aimé-Giron, N. *Textes araméens d'Egypte*. Cairo, 1931.

Bresciani, E. 'Papiri aramaici egiziani di epoca persiana presso il Museo Civico di Padova', *RSO*, 35 (1960), 11–24.

Bresciani, E. and Kamil, M. 'Le lettere aramaiche di Hermopoli', *Atti Accademia Nazionale Lincei* (1966), *Memorie*, ser. 8, vol. 12, fasc. 5. Rome, 1966.

Cowley, A. E. *Aramaic Papyri of the Fifth Century B.C.* Oxford, 1923.

Driver, G. R. *Aramaic Documents of the Fifth Century B.C.* Oxford, 1954; repr. 1957.

Grelot, P. *Documents araméens d'Egypte*. Paris, 1972.

Kraeling, E. *The Brooklyn Museum Aramaic Papyri. New Documents of the Fifth Century B.C. from the Jewish Colony at Elephantine*. New Haven, 1953.

Sachau, E. *Aramäische Papyrus und Ostraka aus einer jüdischen Militär-Kolonie zu Elephantine*. Leipzig, 1911.

Sayce, A. H. and Cowley, A. E. *Aramaic Papyri discovered at Assuan*, with appendices by W. Spiegelberg and Seymour de Ricci. London, 1906.

General studies on the Persian period in Egypt and its Aramaic documents

Berger, A. *Ricerche giuridiche sui papiri aramaici di Elefantina*. Rome, 1965.

Bresciani, E. 'La satrapia d'Egitto', *SCO*, 7 (1958), 132–88.

　　'La morte di Cambise ovvero dell'empietà purita: a proposito della "Cronaca demotica"', verso, Col. C. 7–8, in *EVO*, 4 (1981), 222–7.

Elgood, P. G. *Later Dynasties of Egypt*. Oxford, 1951.

Kienitz, F. K. *Die politische Geschichte Ägyptens vom 7 bis zum 4 Jahrhundert vor der Zeitwende*. Berlin, 1953.

Meyer, E. *Der Papyrusfund von Elephantine*. Leipzig, 1912.

Muffs, Y. *Studies in the Aramaic Legal Papyri from Elephantine*. Leiden, 1969.

Posener, G. *La première domination perse en Egypte*. Cairo, 1936.

Porten, B. *Archives from Elephantine*. Berkeley–Los Angeles, 1968.

Vincent, A. *La religion des Judéo-araméens d'Elephantine*. Paris, 1937.

Yaron, R. *Introduction to the Law of the Aramaic Papyri*. Oxford, 1961.

D. THE JEWS IN EGYPT

Texts

Aimé-Giron, N. *Textes araméens d'Égypte*. Cairo, 1931.

Augapfel, J. *Babylonische Rechtsurkunden*. Denkschriften der Wiener Akademie, 59, 3 (1917).

Bresciani, E. and Kamil, M. 'Le lettere aramaiche di Hermopoli,' *Atti della Accademia Nazionale dei Lincei, Classe di Scienze Morale, Memorie*, ser. VIII, 12/5 (1966), 357–428, plus 10 plates.

Cowley, A. E. *Aramaic Papyri of the Fifth Century B.C.* Oxford, 1923.

Driver, G. R. *Aramaic Documents of the Fifth Century B.C.* Oxford, 1954; abr. and rev. 1957.

Grelot, P. *Documents araméens d'Égypte*. Paris, 1972.

Kohler, J. and Ungnad, A. *Hundert ausgewaehlte Urkunden aus der Spaetezeit des babylonischen Schrifttums*. Leipzig, 1911.

Kraeling, E. G. *The Brooklyn Museum Aramaic Papyri: New Documents of the Fifth Century B.C. from the Jewish Colony at Elephantine*. New Haven, 1953.

Porten, B. in collaboration with Greenfield, J. C. *Jews of Elephantine and Arameans of Syene (Fifth Century B.C.E.): Fifty Aramaic Texts with Hebrew and English Translations*. Jerusalem, 1974.

Sachau, Ed. *Aramäischen Papyrus und Ostraka aus einer jüdischen Militär-Kolonie zu Elephantine*. 2 vols, texts and plates. Leipzig, 1911.

Sayce, A. H. and Cowley, A. E. *Aramaic Papyri Discovered at Assuan*, with appendices by S. W. Spiegelberg and Seymour de Ricci. London, 1906.

Ungnad, A. *Aramäische Papyrus aus Elephantine*. Leipzig, 1911.

Studies

Anneler, H. *Zur Geschichte der Juden von Elephantine*. Bern, 1912.

Cassuto, U. 'The Gods of the Jews of Elephantine', *Biblical and Oriental Studies*, 2, (Jerusalem, 1975), 240ff.

Coogan, M. D. *West-Semitic Personal Names in the Murašu documents*. Missoula, 1974.

Greenfield, J. C. 'A New Corpus of Aramaic Texts of the Achaemenid Period from Egypt', *JAOS*, 96 (1976), 131–5.

Hoonacker, A. van. *Une communauté judéo-araméenne à Éléphantine, en Égypte, aux vie et ve siècles av. J.-C.*, The Schweich Lectures, 1914. London, 1915.

Meyer, Ed. *Der Papyrusfund von Elephantine*. 2nd edn. Leipzig, 1912.

Muffs, Y. *Studies in the Aramaic Legal Papyri from Elephantine*. Studia et Documenta ad Iura orientis antiqui pertinentia, VIII. Leiden, 1969.

Naveh, J. *The Development of the Aramaic Script*. Proceedings of the Israel Academy of Sciences and Humanities, V/1. Jerusalem, 1970.

Porten, B. *Archives from Elephantine: The Life of an Ancient Jewish Military Colony*. Berkeley, 1968.

'Aramaic Papyri and Parchments: A New Look', *BA*, 42 (1979), 74–104.

'Structure and Chiasm in Aramaic Contracts and letters', in J. W. Welch, ed., *Chiasm in Antiquity*, pp. 169–82. Hildesheim, 1981.

Verger, A. *Ricerche giuridiche sui papiri aramaici di Elefantina*. Università di Roma, Centro di Studi Semitici, 16. Rome, 1965.

Vincent, A. *La Religion des judéo-araméens d'Éléphantine*. Paris, 1937.

Wagenaar, C. G. *De joodsche Kolonie van Jeb-Syene in de 5ᵈᵉ Eeuw voor Christus*. Gröningen, 1928.

Yaron, R. *Introduction to the Law of the Aramaic Papyri*. Oxford, 1961.

INDEX

Abar Nahara, satrapy of, 72f, 75f, 78–82, 88, 144, 152, 154–6, 328f, 357
Abarim, 13
Abrocamus, satrap of Abar Nahara, 75f
Abu Simbel, 378
Achemenes, son of Darius I, satrap of Egypt, 362
Achemenids, 281, 286, 370
Achoris, king of Egypt, 75, 112
Adam (Damiyeh), 21
Adulam, 86
Adyah of Saqqara, 233
Aegae, coins of, 110
Aelia Capitolina (Jerusalem), coins of, 57
Aešma, 318
agriculture, 17f
Agrippa I, 46; coins of, 46f
Agrippa II, 46; coins of, 46f
Agur, son of Jakeh, 204
Ahab, king of Israel, 373
Ahikar 252, 348; Proverbs of, 117, 191f, 232, 372, 378
Ahmosis, head of Egyptian army, 369
Ahuramazda, 282–5, 287–91, 293f, 296, 298, 300f, 304–7, 315f, 320, 330
Ahutab of Elephantine, 378
Ahzai, governor of Judah, 157
Aijalon, valley of, 7
Akkadian, partly replaced by Aramaic, 115; continued in use, 337
Akko (Ptolemais), 4, 8, 11, 71, 80; Egyptian steles at, 89; inscription of Achoris, 75, 114; mint of, 29–31, 48, 56, 76; war and destruction in time of Alexander, 114
alabaster vessels, 101
alabastra, 101
Aleppo, 14

Alexander the Great, 9, 29f, 76f, 89, 153, 160, 178, 304, 307, 311, 329, 364
Alexander Janneus, king of Judea, coins of, 33, 36, 38f
Alexandria, Jews of, 67
Alexandrium, fortress of, 5
al-Jauf, 14
al-Mina, port on Orontes, 91, 99
allegory, 197
Allonim hills, 21
altars, incense, 106f, 241
Amasis, king of Egypt, 359f, 368, 375
Amenemope, instruction of, 191, 203f
Amenophis, king of Egypt, 373
Amesha Spentas, 285f, 291, 296f, 305
Amestris, wife of Xerxes, 295, 302
Amman, see Philadelphia
Ammon, 80; governor of, 273
Ammonites, 250; Ammonite language, 115
amulets, glass, 102
Amyrteus, king of Egypt, 75, 363, 400
Anani, scribe and chancellor, 382
Anani, son of Haggai, 383
Ananiah, son of Azariah, 225f, 377, 389, 395, 399
Ananiah, son of Haggai, 225, 399
Ananiah, son of Meshullam, 224
Anat(h), goddess, 227; Anat/Atargatis, 239
Anathbethel, goddess, 227, 391f
Anathyahu, goddess, 230, 391, 393
Anaximander of Miletus, 282
Anekhsheshoni, teachings of, 372
Angaraland, platform of, 3
angelology, 314, 317f
angels, 252, 255
Angra Mainyu, 283, 316
Anthedon, mint of, 57

Antigonus, *see* Mathathya Antigonus
Antioch, 9; coins of, 48, 58f
Antiochus IV Epiphanes, Seleucid king, 32, 63
Antiochus VII, Seleucid king, coins of, 31f
Antipater, vizier of John Hyrcanus II, 37
Antipatris, 14; mint of, 57
Apries, king of Egypt, 374, 379
Arab desert tribes, 87
Arabah, 12–4
Arabia, province of, 23, 57
Arabs, tribal system of, 80f
Arad, military fortress of, 81, 84; ostraca, 84, 113, 124; temple at, 235
Aradus, coins of, 110
Aramaic: epigraphic materials, 122–5; in use among Jews, 117–19, 128f, 227, 308, 342, 368; Jewish, Christian and Samaritan dialects, 118; official Aramaic, 116–18, 333; papyri in Egypt, 116; in Persian empire, 115–18; script, 115; Standard Literary Aramaic, 117f
Aramaisms, 183
Arbela, 14
Archelaus, son of Herod, ethnarch, 42
Ardh as-Suwan (desert), 13
Ariandes, satrap of Egypt, 360, 365
Aristeas, Letter of, 378f
Aristobulus II, king of Judea, 39
Aristobulus, son of Herod king of Chalcis, 46
Aristotle, story attributed to, 243
Ariyawrata, Persian official, 362
Arnon, canyon (gorge) of, 13, 17
Aroer, excavations at, 84
arrowheads, 102
Arsames, cousin of Cyrus I, 281
Arsames, satrap of Egypt, 73f, 231, 344f, 362f, 365, 371, 377, 382, 389f; letters of, 117, 126
Arses, king of Persia, 77, 364
Artabanus, vizier of Xerxes, 73
Artawant, representative of Arsames, 366
Artaxerxes I Longimanus, king of Persia, 73f, 142, 149, 151, 153, 160, 293, 295f, 298f, 333, 362

Artaxerxes II Memnon, king of Persia, 75, 160, 299, 302–4, 307
Artaxerxes III Ochus, king of Persia, 76f, 154, 175, 178, 249, 363
Artimas (Artim), governor of Lydia, 302
Arzyphius, grandson of Xerxes, 302
Asaphites, 185
Ascent of Blood, 7
Ashdod, 80; province of, 86–8
Asher, region of, 8
Ashkelon, city of, 79; coins of, 56f; figurines found at, 105; mint of, 31, 41, 48
ash-Shaghur fault, 16
Ashur, city of, 313
Ashurbanipal, king of Assyria, 379
Asmodaios, demon in Book of Tobit, 318
Assuan, temple of Isis at, 369
Astarte, cult of, 210
astronomy, mathematical, in Babylonia, 337
Astyages, king of Media, 281f, 285
Athens: assists Egyptian rebels, 73; coins of, 25, 27, 110; war with Persia, 71, 293
Atonement, Day of, 65f, 147, 264, 266
Atossa, daughter of Cyrus II, 281
Avesta, 303, 306, 310f, 318
Avestan, 279f, 289
Azazel, 266
Azeka, 86

Baal, names compounded in, 240
Baalbek, 16
Babylon, 353; rebellion in 483 B.C.E., 73, 293
Babylonia: aliens in, 330; culture, 337; ethnic minorities 338–42; farmers, 331; farming, 334, 347; free persons without civic rights, 330; full citizens, 330; land ownership, 333f; law, private, 332; in Persian period, 326–42; political history, 326–30; satrap of, 332, 341; slaves in, 331; society and economy, 330–8; taxes, 334–7; temples, 334f; trade, 336f
Babylonian: calendar, 62; empire, fall of, 70, 326f, 350; Jewry, 66f, 244, 341–58; names of months, 62

Bagaphernes, 227

Bagoas, satrap, 76f

Bagohi, Bagoas, Bagoses or Bigvai, governor of Judah, 74, 79, 155, 157, 160, 302, 386, 390, 398

Bagoses, general of Artaxerxes II's army, 160

Baqa'a (central valley), 12f

Banit, deity, temple of at Elephantine, 229, 352, 368

Bar Kochba (Shimeon ben Kosba), revolt of, 42, 51–3, 55; documents of from Judean desert, 63

Barada river, 13

Baruch, Book of, 189

basalt layers, 20

Batania, plateau of, 13f, 16, 20, 23

Bat Yam, jar inscription, 124

Beersheba, 11, 84; depression of, 5, 7; military fortress, 81; ostraca, 84, 124, 239

Behistun inscription of Darius I, 5, 78; copy of at Elephantine, 233, 378

Beithar, possible mint, 55

Bel, god, 350–2, 354, 356–8, 393

Belit, goddess, 354

Bel-shar-uzur (Belshazzar), son of Nabonidus, 327

Belsimanni, leader of Babylonian revolt, 329

Belsys, satrap of Abar Nahara, 76

Beluballit, 356

Benjamin, excavations in, 114; saddle of, 7, 11; territory of, 86, 91

Berossus, 303

beth-din, rabbinic, 64f

Bethel, deity, 227, 391f; temple of, at Elephantine, 229, 252, 368, 391

Beth-horon, ascent of, 7

Bethlehem, 18

Beth-shean, see Scythopolis

Beth-zur, 11, 32, 86; coin found at, 122

Beyond the River, satrapy or province of, see Abar Nahara, satrapy of

Bigvai, see Bagohi

Biq' at Zin, 12

bit-ḥilani building plan, 92

Bitter lakes, 361

Booths, Feast of, 266

Borsippa, 353

Bostra, 23f

bowls, bronze and silver, 100

Bubastis, 311

buildings, remains of in Palestine from Persian period, 90–3

bullae, 157

Bundahishn, 279, 312

burials: in Palestine, 93–5; Cist type, 93f; intermediate type, 93; Shaft type, 93f; of Persians, 302

Caesarea (Maritima), port of, 18, 20, 42, 47; mint of, 43, 47f

Caesarea Philippi (Panias), 47; mint of 46f, 56

calendar, Babylonian, 62, 337f

Cambyses II, king of Persia, 70f, 116, 143, 164, 287f, 292, 328, 357–9, 367–70

Canaanite (language), 118

Canatha, 23

caravan routes, 1, 17; trade 23; caravans, Nabatean, 17

Carmel, mount, fault scarp of, 11; headland of, 8; Israelite cult at, 234; range, 21; ridge, 11

Carthage, 359

Casiphia, abode of Levites and nᵉthînîm in Babylonia, 349

Casius, mount, in Cilicia, 9

Casius, mount, in delta area, 9, 79

Caspians, at Elephantine, 395, 399

cedar forests, of Lebanon, 16

cement, 93

Cenomanian limestone, 3f, 9, 18, 21

Charachmoba (Kir-hareseth), 13

Chemosh, Moabite god, 392; names compounded with, 240

Chronicler, the, 143, 147, 153, 160, 185; writings of, 131–3, 139, 256, 259f

Chronicles, Book of, Hebrew of, 121

chronology, 60–9

Cilicia, 9

Claudius, emperor, 47

Clearchus of Soli, 243

climate, 15–18; fluctuations in, 18

coastal plain of Palestine, 91

Coele-Syria, 78

Coinage 25–59, 257–9; in archeological discoveries, 110–12; of: Aegae, 110,

Coinage (cont.)
Aelia Capitolina, 57, Agrippa I and II, 46f, Akko-Ptolemais, 29–31, 56, Alexandrian empire, 29f, Anthedon, 57, Antioch, 58f, Antipatris, 57, Arabic–Byzantine, 59, Aradus, 110, Ashkelon, 56, Athens, 21–5, 110, Caesarea, 56, Capitolias, 56, Constantinople, 59, Cyprus, 111, Diospolis-Lydda, 57, Dora, 57, Egypt, 111, Eleutheropolis, 57, Gaza, 27, 31, 56f, Gerasa, 56, Hasmoneans, 32–40, 125, Herod and Archelaus, 41f, Herod Antipas and Philip, 43–6, Herodians, 48, Jaffa, 57, Jewish revolt, first, 48f, 51, 125, Jewish revolt, second, 51–3, 55, 125, Judea, 27, 85, 111, municipal, 56–8, Neapolis, 56f, Nicopolis, 57, Palestine, 26, 81, Panias (Caesarea Philippi), 56, Persian, 111, Philisto-Arabian, 27, 110; Phoenician, 25, Ptolemaic, 30f, Raphia, 57, Roman governors of Judea, 42f, 48, Scythopolis, 57, Sebaste, 57, Seleucids, 30, 33, Sepphoris, 56, Sidon, 110, Thasos, 25, 110, Tiberias, 56, Transjordan, cities of, 57, Tyre, 30f, 47f, 58, 110; denominations of: antoninianus, 58, Alexandreis 29, daric, 72, 111, 335, 365, 383, denarius, 48, 52, 58, didrachm, 48, dilepton, 36, drachm, 48, 238, half-peruta, 36–8, 41, half-shekel, 48f, lepton, 36, peruta, 36–8, 41, quarter-shekel, 49, shekel, 48f, 365, 383, sigloi, 111, stater, 365, tetradrachm, 30, 48, 52, 58, trilepton, 36f
Constantinople, coins of, 59
conversion, 220f, 269f
cornucopia on coins, 36–8, 40f, 43
cosmetic utensils, 100
creator, Persian concept of, 320–2
Crocodile river and marshes, 8
cult objects found in Palestine, 103–7
cyclones, 16
Cyprus, coins of, 111
Cyrene, 362

Cyrus I, 281
Cyrus (II); king of Persia, 70, 78, 116, 135, 142, 163, 279, 358, 368; cylinder of, 138, 287; edict of, 70, 72, 136, 138, 142, 281f, 285–8, 292, 299, 302, 326, 328, 333
Cyrus, younger brother of Artaxerxes II, rebel, 75, 302

Daivas, 285, 293
Daliyeh, wadi, papyri of, 81, 89, 113, 117, 122, 125, 219, 240, 376; seals of, 109
Damascus, city of, 1, 12–14, 17; district of, 17; rainfall, 16
Dan, 2; high place of, 234
Daniel, Book of, 118, 313
Daphnae in Delta, see Tahpanhes
Darb as-Sultan, 12
Darius I, king of Persia, 71f, 78, 88, 135, 137, 141f, 162, 232, 288–93, 303, 328, 332, 360f, 369–71; inscriptions of at Persepolis, 78, 89, 116, 289, 291
Darius II, king of Persia, 74f, 231, 301f, 362
Darius III Kodomanus, king of Persia, 77, 304, 364
Daskylion, carving from, 292; grave at, 250
'day of the Lord', 176
Dead sea, 12–14
Dead sea sect, see Qumran sectarians
Decapolis, 13; cities of, 23; coins of cities of, 57
Deliah son of Sanballat, governor of Samaria, 74, 155, 390
Demetrius II Nicator, Seleucid king, coins of, 31
demonology, 314, 317f
demons, 252, 266
desert, 17–19
Deutero-Isaiah (Isaiah 40–55), 163–5, 169f, 174, 179, 181–3, 209, 254, 282, 298, 313
Deuteronomic history, 131–4, 147, 257
Diadochi, 29; wars of, 114
Diaspora, 66; Jews of the, 325–400; of Babylonia, 342–58; of Egypt, 372–400

Didache, 315
didactic poem, 197
'difficulty, regions of', 19–21
Dinkard, the (ninth-century Zoroastrian sacred book), 312
Diocletian, 23; visit to Tyre (reported), 69
Diospolis-Lydda, mint of, 57
divorce, frequent, 173; woman's right of, 399
Docus, fortress of, 7
Dog river, 8
Dor, destruction of, 114; province of, 81, 97f
Dora, mint of, 57
dualism, gnostic, 316; Zoroastrian, 283f, 315f; and Judaism, 314–6

Ebal, 11
Ecbatana, temple at, 304
Ecclesiastes, Book of, 189, 200, 254–6
Edom, destruction of, 179
Edomite province around Hebron, 80; settlements, 84f; 'wall', 16
Edomites, 86f, 173
Edoraim, 85
Egibi, business house in Babylonia, 336f, 340
Egypt, coins of, 111; conquered by Cambyses, 70f; grain prices in, 383f; Jews in, 372–400; laws codified by Darius, 360f; laws, corpus of, 370; military organization, 367–70; as Persian satrapy, 358–72; prophecies concerning, 178; rebellion against Persians, 72f, 275, second rebellion, 75f, 246; reconquered by Persians, 73, 76, 246; satrap of, 228, 302, 344f, 357, 360–4, 370
Egypt, lower, 375
Egyptians, 9; in Babylonia, 338–40
El, divine name in compound names, 239f
Elamite language, 333
Elamites, 339f
Elath, Phoenician ostracon at, 124
Elephantine (Yeb), Jewish community and garrison at, 74, 138, 146, 158, 219, 226, 252f, 357, 363f, 368, 379,
381f, 390; dwelling at, 385; papyri from, 81, 89, 117, 126, 155, 191, 223, 234, 276, 288, 367, 375–400; family archives, 398–400; legal documents, 393–8; ostraca, 126, 223, 375; products at, 384; temple at, see Yahu, temple of
Eleutheropolis (Beit-Govrim), mint of, 57
Eleutherus river, 5, 9
Eliada son of Jedaiah, Jew in Babylonia, 347
Eliashib, high priest, 151, 159f
El-Kharga, oasis of (temple at), 371
Elnathan, 'the official', 123f, 'the governor', 157
Elohim psalter, 185
Emesa (Homs), 5, 12
Engedi, 86; archeological finds at, 90; ostraca, 123; Phoenician amulets, 242; springs of, 12
I Enoch, Book of, and calendar, 68
II Enoch, 321, 325
Eocene limestone, 3f, 21
Ephraim, 11
Epicurus, 256
Epistle of Jeremiah, see Jeremiah, Epistle of
eras: 'of freedom', 60; Seleucid, 61f, 64
eschatological texts, 178–81; 273–6
eschatology, Persian and Jewish, 314, 320–4
Esdraelon, winter marshes of, 20
I Esdras, 133f, 136, 143, 145
Eshem, god, 227, 392
Eshembethel, god, 227, 391f
Eshmunazar II, king of Sidon, 81
Eshor, son of Seho or Seha (later called Nathan), 220, 224, 381, 400
Esther, Book of, 243, 250f, 313; Hebrew of, 121
ethrog, on coins, 49, 52
Euphrates, 16
exemplary tale, 197
exilarch, 66f
Ezechias, High Priest, possibly = Yehezqiyah the governor, 238
Ezion-geber, 2

Ezra, Book of, 118; Aramaic and Hebrew of, 121

Ezra, priest and scribe, 73f, 143–7, 150, 153, 160, 173, 245, 248, 262, 298–300, 348, 356–8; date of, 135f, genealogy of, 159; narrative of, 143, 153, 159, 161; and foreign marriages, 143

Ezra and Nehemiah, Books of, 133f, 249f, 256, 259, 313

faience jewellery, 101

Faria, wadi, 4, 13

Felix, Antonius, governor of Judea, coins of, 43

Fertile Crescent, 1

festivals, Jewish, in Persian period, 265f

fire, divinity of for Zoroastrians, 286; symbol of justice and truth, 286

fire-holders, Persian, 285f, 291

fire-temples, 304

Firstfruits, feast of, 266

forgiveness in Psalter, 188

four ages, four monarchies, theory of, 314

fratarak, Persian governor in Egypt, 364f, 370, 381f

Galilee: lake of, 5, 12, 14, 23; Lower, 11, 21, 23, basin of, 20; Upper, 11, 21

Galilee–Bashan depression, 16

Galilee–Hauran depression, 5; region, 5, 13

Gathas, 279f, 284f, 300f, 311, 315, 318

Gaulanitis, 5

Gaumata (claimant to Persian throne), 328, 360

Gayomard, Primal Man, 323

Gaza, 8, 14, 80; coins of, 27, 29, 56; mint of, 31, 57; resists Alexander, 77; siege by Alexander and destruction of 91, 114

Gaza, province of, 88

Gazara, see Gezer

Gedaliah son of Ahikam, governor, 131, 157f, 375

Gedaliah, archer, in Murashu records, 346

Gemariah son of Ahio, scribe of Elephantine, 395

Gemariah son of Mahsiyah, 224

Gerizim, mount, 11; image on coins of Neapolis, 56; cult at, 234; temple built on, 160, 234, 386

Geshem 'the Arabian', or 'King of Qedar', 75, 81, 150, 158, 273

gētīg, 'the material', 316–18, 321f

Gezer (Gazara), 14, 86, 373; Egyptian steles, 89; inscription of Nepheritis, 114; tombs, 113

Ghab, the, 12

Gibeon, area of, 156

Gilead 17, 21; dome of, 13

Ginae (Jenin), 14

Gischala, 23

Giv'at ha-Mivtar, funerary cave inscription, 128

Gobryas (cf. Gubaru), satrap of Abar-Nahara, 78

Golan heights, see Gaulanitis

governors, Roman, of Judea, see Judea

Gozan, 343

Greek merchants and soldiers in Palestine, 87, 112

Gubaru (cf. Gobryas) satrap of Abar-Nahara, 328, 341

Hadad, deity, 227

Haggai, 72, 141, 163–7, 181, 245, 272; book of, 141, 164–8

Haggai of Elephantine, 393

Haggai son of Shemaiah, 395–8

Haifa bay, 5, 11

Halah, in northern Mesopotamia, 342

Hamath steppe, 7, 16

Hammamat, wadi, inscription at, 361f, 365

Hanani, Jew in Babylonia, 347

Hananiah, secretary of Arsames, 231, 301, 363, 388f

Hananiah son of Sanballat (II), 155

Hapi, deity, 339

Har Meron (or Jabal Jarmaq), 11

Haran, city, 353

Hasmonean state and coinage, 32–40

ḥatru (farming system in Babylonia), 334, 345–7

Hazor, archeological discoveries, 90

Hebrew language: Classical Biblical, 120; in continued spoken use among Jews, 115, 118–24, 127; epigraphic

Hebrew language (*cont.*)
material, 122; Late Biblical, 119f, 122, 308; Mishnaic, 120–2; Persian borrowings in, 308
Hebron, 11f, 18, 84f
Hecateus of Abdera, 243
Hejaz railway, line of, 14
Hellenization of Palestine, 23
Herem, deity, 223, 392
Herembethel, deity, 230, 391, 393
Hermon, mount, 16; Israelite cult at, 234
Hermopolis letters, 117, 378
Herod, coinage of, 41f
Herod Agrippa (I and II), *see* Agrippa
Herod Antipas, tetrarch, coins of, 43f, 46
Herod, king of Chalcis, 46
Herodotus: picture of Persian religion, 295–8, 312; picture of Babylon, 341
Hezekiah, king of Judah, 374
highland zone, 3
high places, 235, 247
high priest, 247, 264
Hillel II, patriarch, 67
Hinnom, valley of, 84
Homs–Palmyra corridor, 5, 7, 13
Hor son of Peteisi, Khnum officiant, 389
Horus, gardener of god Khnum, 226
Horus, god, 227, 236, 239, 290, 339
Hosea son of Hodaviah, scribe at Elephantine, 395
Hoshaiah son of Nathan, of Elephantine, 377
Hoshayah, steward of Elephantine, 230
Hoshea, king of Israel, 374
house-plan in Palestine in Persian era, 91–3
Huleh, lake (lake Semechonitis), 5, 12, 14, 20
Hyksos, 373
Hyrcania on Caspian sea, 77
Hyrcanus son of Joseph, 387
Hystaspes son of Arsames, 281

iconoclasm, 52
idols, idolatry, 351–5
Idumea, 7; province of, 42
Igdaliah, Jew in Babylonia, 356
Ilat, goddess, 369

images, prohibition of, not applied on coins, 23, 29, 32
Inaros son of Psammetichus, Egyptian rebel, 73, 362
incense in cult of Yahweh, 241f
incense altars, 106f, 241
incense trade, Arabian, 27
indiction, year of, 64
intercalation, 63, 66
intermarriage, *see* marriages, foreign
Iranian, *see* Persian
Iraq al-Amir, 13
Isaiah 40–55, *see* Deutero-Isaiah; 56–66, *see* Trito-Isaiah
Ishtar, goddess, 303f, 353, 357
Isis, goddess, 339
Isiweri daughter of Gemariah, 224
Islah, Jew of Elephantine, 388, 400
Israel, Egyptian reference to, 373
Issus, battle of, 77

Jabal Druze, 5, 16, 21, 23
Jabbok (Zerqa), 13
Jaddua, high priest, 160, 386
Jaffa (Joppa), 2, 8; mint of, 31, 57
Jarmaq, *see* Har Meron
Jedahia, Jew of Babylonia, 356
Jedaiah, Jew of Babylonia, 346
Jedaniah son of Gemariah 225f, 228, 231f, 377, 386, 388, 390, 399
Jedaniah son of Eshor, grandson of Jedaniah, 224, 400
Jedaniah (Jedoniah) son of Mahseiah (Mahsiyah), 224
Jehezekiah, governor of Judah, named on coins, 27, 80f, 122, 157, 237
Jehoahaz, king of Judah, 375
Jehohanan, *see* Johanan
Jehoiachin, king of Judah, 131, 356
Jehoiakim, king of Judah, 375
Jehoishma daughter of Ananiah, 356, 399
Jehoram, king of Israel, 374
Jeremiah, prophet, 375
Jeremiah, Epistle of, 355
Jericho, city, 86; possible destruction in 340s, 77
Jeroboam I, king of Israel, 374
Jerusalem, 18, 86, 273; devotion to, 252; destruction by Babylonians, 140;

Jerusalem (*cont.*)
    mint of, 43, 47, 55; name on coins of
    Bar Kochba, 53, 55; walls rebuilt,
    148–50, 245, 249
Jeshimon, wilderness of, 11, 18, 21
Jeshua son of Jozadak, high priest, 72,
    157
Jesus son of Sirach, 189
Jewish community in Palestine: history
    in Persian period, 130–61; religious
    life in Persian period, 219–78
Jezaniah son of Uriah, Jewish soldier at
    Elephantine, 400
Jezreel, valley of, 11, 14
Job, Book of, 189–91, 197, 211–18,
    254f; prehistory of, 213–15; structure
    of, 211–13; theological content of,
    215–18
Joel, Book of, 135, 174–7, 274
Joel, prophet, 163, 174–7, 181
Johanan grandson of Eliashib, high
    priest, 159f, 232, 390
Johanan son of Kareah, 375
John Hyrcanus I, coins of, 32, 35–7
John Hyrcanus II, no coins issued, 39
Jonah, Book of, 250f; Hebrew of, 121
Jordan river, 13f; valley, 11, 13, 20f, 86;
    badlands and jungle of, 21
Joseph, 373
Joshua, high priest, 137, 140, 164f,
    167–9, 182, 245, 272
Joshua brother of Johanan, 160
Josiah, death of, 374; reforms of, 145,
    147, 379
Judas Maccabeus, 63; rebuilds Beth-zur,
    86
Judah: as political unit, 79–81, 155;
    kingdom, collapse of, 130f; province
    of, 82–8
Judah the Prince, Rabbi, 127
Judah Aristobulus I, coins of, 36–8
Judea, 17, 42; coinage of, 27; coinage of
    governors of, 42, governor (*peḥa*) of,
    27, 42, 219, 228, 232, 247, 352;
    independent, 32; plateau of, 11;
    wilderness of, 18
Judean hills, 86
judgement day of, 174, 284, 308f;
    Iranian and Jewish views of, 321;
    personal, 199

Judith, Book of, 250–2
Jurassic limestone, 9

Kadesh-Barnea, military fortess, 81
Kavi Vishtaspa, king, 279, 281
Kemosh, *see* Chemosh
Kerak (Kir-hareseth), 13
Khabasha, Egyptian rebel, 71, 73
Khirbet at-Tubeiqeh, *see* Beth-zur
Khirbet el-Qatt, 86
Khirbet el-Zewiyye, 86
Khnum, Egyptian god, 226, 229, 232,
    385, 393; priests of, 229, 232, 363,
    389
Khnumibre, Egyptian architect, 369
Khorazmians, at Elephantine, 385
Kidenas (Kidinnu), Babylonian
    astronomer, 338
Kinah, fortress of, 84
'king's highway', 14
Kir-hareseth (Kerak), 13
Kishon, 11; valley, 20
Korahites, 185

Lachish, 84; altar, 107; city gates, 91;
    inscription on small altar, 125, 241;
    the Residence, 92; temple, 102, 234f
Law, the, 246–57, 261, 267f; reading of,
    145–7, 249, 266; and the psalter, 186f;
    and wisdom, 210f
Lebanon: forests of cedar, cypress and
    pine, 16, 20; the high, 9; mountains
    of, 9
Leontopolis, temple at, 386f
Levant: climate of, 15–18; geography
    of, 1–24; structural pattern of, 3–14
Levites, 247, 249, 257–64, 349; and
    psalmody, 184, 258
limes Palaestinae, 7
Litani river, 11
Lod, incorporated in Judah, 85f
lowland zone, 3
lulab on coins, 49, 52

Maan, 14
Maat, Egyptian deity, 191, 209f
Maccabean revolt, 23, 32
Macedonia, 29
Magdala, 14
magi, 287, 291, 294–7, 305

Mahseiah (Mahsiyah) son of Jedaniah (Yedoniah), 223f, 226, 395, 400

mainyu, 315, 317f, 320–2

Makmish: temple at, 102, 107; seal found at, 122

Malachi, Book of, 135, 163, 172–4, 273f

Malchijah (Malkiyah) son of Jashobiah, 229, 393

Mamre, Israelite cult at, 235

Manasseh, king of Judah, 379, 386f

Manasseh brother of Jaddua the high priest, 160, 386

Manetho, Egyptian priest, 373

Mannu-danni-iama, Jew in Babylonia, 356

Manual of Discipline, 315

maquis, 20f

Marduk, deity, 326, 329f, 352–4

Mareshah, near Lachish, 85

Marj-ayoun, 16

Marnas, deity on coin of Gaza, 56

marriages, foreign (mixed), 145f, 150, 244–6, 251f, 259, 263, 269–70, 273, 400

marshland, 20

Masoretic text-forms, 132, 201

Mathathya (Mattathias) Antigonus, coins of, 33, 39f; and royal title, 40

Mauziah son of Nathan, scribe at Elephantine, 395–8

Mazakes, satrap of Egypt, 364

Mazeus, satrap of Abar Nahara, 76, 79

Mediterranean climate belt, 15

Megabyzus, satrap of Abar Nahara, 73, 154, 362; rebels against Persians, 73

Megiddo, 11, 14, 80; destroyed under Alexander, 114; fortified area, 91; mountain pass of, 374; province of, 88

Memphis 364f, 369; chancery at, 364; investigators at, 390; Jewish settlement at, 375; state treasury, 365f

Menahem, king of Israel, 374

Menahem son of Meshullam, 224

Menahem son of Shallum, 230, 393

menog, see *mainyu*

menorah, seven-branched, on coins, 40

Merneptah, 373

Mesad Hashavyahu, 98f

Meshullam son of Nathan, 393

Meshullam son of Shelomam, 224

Meshullam son of Zakur (or Zaccur), 225, 399

Meshullemet daughter of Gemariah, 224

Meshullemet, 388

Messiahs, two, priestly and secular, 169

messianic expectations, 182; prophecies, 179

Mibtahiah daughter of Mahseiah, 224, 377, 381, 393, 399f

Micaiah of Elephantine, 393

Michmash, 7

midbar, 19–21

Midian, mountains of, 14

Migdol, in delta, 369, 375, 378

mirrors, 100

Mishru, tableland, 13, 17

Mithra, god, 284f, 303

Mithradates, Persian, chief boatman at Elephantine, 382

Mithredath, in Ezra narrative, 151

Mivtahiyah, *see* Mibtahiah

Mizpah, area of, 156

Moab, territory of, 13, 80; prophecies concerning, 177f

Moabite language, 115

Moreh, plateau of, 5, 14, 20

Moses, 373

Mozah, name stamped on jug, 123

Murashu tablets found at Nippur, 220, 222, 334, 336, 338, 340, 345, 347f, 355; trading house, 334, 337, 345–7, 349

Nabatean kingdom, 7, 13, 17, 23; annexed by Rome, 57

Nabateans, 5, 12, 87

Nablus, *see* Neapolis

Nabonidus, king of Babylon, 155, 326, 328; his mother, 353f

Nabu, god, 303, 326, 350, 352, 368, 391–3; temple of, at Elephantine, 229, 391; names compounded with, 240

Nabu-ahhe-bullit, governor of Babylonia, 328

Nabuaqab, 382

Nabunanus, Babylonian astronomer, 338

Nana, deity, 358

Nana-iddima, Jew of Babylonia, 356

Napata in Nubia, 359

nari (cap of limestone accretions), 21
Nathan son of Ananiah, scribe of Elephantine, 395
Nathania, Jew of Babylonia, 356
Naucratis, 99, 362
Nazirite, 267
Neapolis (Nablus), 11; coins of, 56
Nebi Yunis, ostracon, 124
Nebuchadnezzar II, king of Babylon, 374, 395; regnal years of, 60
Nebuchadnezzar III, son of Nabonidus, revolt of, 71f, 328
Nebuchadnezzar IV, revolt of, 72, 329
Necho II, king of Egypt, 361, 374
Nectanebo II, king of Egypt, 76
Negeb, 1–5, 7, 9, 11; destruction in, 114; low uplands, 16
Nehemiah governor of Jerusalem, 74, 79, 82f, 143, 145f, 148–53, 156f, 173, 175, 227, 231, 241, 245, 248, 257–9, 262f, 271, 275, 298f, 333, 348, 358, 388
Neith, deity, 227
Nekht-har-hebi nephew of king Tachos of Egypt, 76
Nekhtihur, *peqid* of Arsames, 366, 371
Nepherites I, king of Egypt, 75, 400; inscription of at Gezer, 114
Nergal, god, 393
Nesuhor, 'Governor of the Door of the Southern Countries', 379
Nicopolis (Emmaus), mint of, 57
Nile–Red Sea canal reopened, 361
Nilometer at Elephantine, 381
Ninurta, deity, 357
Nippur, 338f, 341, 344–7, 349, 355, 392
Nubia, 378; expeditions to, 381; tribute from, 381
Nubian sandstone, 3f, 12, 17
numerical sayings, 196, 204
numismatics, 25–59, 237–9
Nuseiriyeh mountains, 5, 9, 12, 16
Nysa, *see* Scythopolis

Oboda, city of, 12
Ohrmazd, *see* Ahuramazda
Onias IV and temple at Leontopolis, 386
Ophra, incorporated in Judah, 85
Opis, town by the Tigris, 327

Orontes river, 12, 91; valley, 9
Orphic concepts, influence of, 324
Osarseph-Moses, priest of Heliopolis, 373
Osea, Jew at Elephantine, 383
Ostanes brother of Anani, 390

Padi, a west Semite at Elephantine, 378
Pakhnum son of Besa, an Aramean at Elephantine, 383, 399
Palestine, archeological finds in: architectural, 90–3, burials, 93–5, inscriptions and graffiti, 241, metal, alabaster and faience, 99–102, ostraca, 239f, pottery, 95–9, sanctuaries and cult-objects, 102–7, seals and stamp impressions, 82, 90, 107–9, 236f, 242, weights and coins, 109–12; archeology of, under Persians, 88–114, 233–43; coins of, 26; geography of, 1–24
Palestinian highlands, 9, 17
palm-tree, palm-branch on coins, 41f, 44, 49, 53
Palmyra 1, 17; route from, 14; expansion of, 23
Pamut, 226
Panias, *see* Caesarea Philippi
papponymy, 159
Papremi in western Delta, 362, 366
parable, 197
Parthians, 40
Parysatis, queen mother, 302, 304
Pasargadae, 285f, 294
passover, 265f, date of, 64f, 67; at Elephantine, 230f, 388f
Passover papyrus, 230–2
pastoralism, 17
Pathros (Upper Egypt) as place of Jewish settlement, 375, 381
patriarchs, 65–7
pehah, term for governor 27, 155–7
Pelatiah son of Ahio, scribe, 395
Peliah, Jew in Babylonia, 346
Pentateuch, 246, 256, 263, 268
Perea, administrative district, 13
Persepolis, 289, 296, 333; inscriptions 89, 279–91
Persian empire, 88; coins of, 111; and Palestine, history, 70–87; organization

Persian empire (*cont.*)
in satrapies, 71, 78, 88; 'revolt of the satraps', 76, 246, 275
Persian literature, 311f; nobility, 333
Persians in Babylonia, 338, 340
Pethahiah (Petahia), 357
Petra, 1, 14, 16f, 23
Pharnabazus, satrap, 76
Pherendates satrap of Egypt, 361, 363f
Philadelphia (Amman), 2, 13
Philip, tetrarch, coins of, 43, 46
Philippopolis, 23
Philisto-Arabian coins, 27, 110
philosophy, Greek and Hellenistic, 190
Phoenician: cities on coast, 80; merchants, 25; script, 32
Phoenicians, coins of, 25; in Galilee and coastal plain, 87; and Shaft tombs 94; as transmitters of Greek material culture, 112
Pia son of Pahi of Elephantine, 224, 381, 393, 400
pilgrims to the Holy Land, 59
Pilti son of Ananiah of Elphantine, 225, 399
Pissouthnes (Pishishyaothna) son of Vishtaspa, Achemenid, 281
plateau, eastern, 3
Pompey, 9
Pontius Pilate, coins of, 42
population growth, 70
Poseideion (al-Mina or Basit), 79, 88
pottery in Palestine, 95–9; Assyrian, 97; Attic, 98; Cypriot, 98; Eastern Greek, 98; Greek, 96; Persian (Achemenid), 97, 99
predestination, 314, 318–21
prefects of Judea, *see* Judea, governor of
Priestly Code, 131f, 134f, 183, 248, 299f
priests of Jerusalem, 262–7, 299
Primal man, 323
proselytes, 251
Prosopitis, island in Egypt, 362
proverbs, 196
Proverbs, Book of, 189f, 200–6, 253
Psalms, 163; dating of, 183; of lament, 184, 187; in the Persian period, 183–8, 260–2; of Zion, 187; and wisdom influence, 183, 186, 189
psalter, collection of, 184f

Psammetichus I, king of Egypt, 379, 387
Psammetichus II, king of Egypt, 359, 378
Psammetichus III, king of Egypt, 358
Psamtik, *peqid* of Arsames, 366
Ptah, deity, 365
Ptahhotep, head of treasury of Ptah at Memphis, 366, 371
Ptolemais, *see* Akko
Ptolemies, 8f, 364
Ptolemy V, king of Egypt, 31
Ptolemy VI king of Egypt, 387
Punon (Feinan), copper mines, 14, 17; embayment, 14

Qainu bar Geshem king of Qedar, 75
Qarqar, 374
Qasr el-Abd at Araq el-Amir, 387
Qedar, king of, 27, 75
Qedorites, 87
Qoniyah son of Zadok, 224
Qos, Edomite god, 240; in compound names, 239f
Queen of Heaven, temple of at Elephantine, 229, 252, 368, 391, 393
Qumran sectarians, 68; views on predestination and freewill, 319
Qumran text-forms, 132
Quruntul, scarp of, 7

Raga, Median city, 281
Raguel, in story of Tobit, 348
rain, winter, 15
rainfall, 15–17
Ram, wadi, 14
Ramandaina, *fratarak* at Elphantine, 381
Ramath-Negeb, fortress of, 84
Ramathaim, incorporated in Judah, 85
Ramses, king of Egypt, 373
Raphia, mint of, 57
Ras an-Naqb, 14
Red sea, 14
regnal years, 60f
Rehoboam king of Judah, 374
Rehum, official in Samaria, 152, 155
resurrection, Persian and Jewish beliefs, 301, 323
return from Babylon, history of, 135, 165, 327, 350
retribution, doctrine of in psalms, 187f

Revolt, Jewish: of 66–70 C.E., 42, 48f,
  51, 61; of Bar Kochba (132–135 C.E.),
  42, 61
riddle, 196
rift-valley, central 3f, 12, 16f
Rig-Veda, 279, 311
road network, 20
ruaḥ, spirit, 317
Ruth, Book of, 250f

Sabaces, satrap of Egypt, 364
sabbatical year, 64
sabbath, observance of, 68, 150, 249,
  263, 265, 271, 350, 388; at
  Elephantine, 230, 387f
sacrifice, 259, 264f; at Lachish, 236; to
  Yahu at Elephantine, 228f
Safad, 23
Sahar, deity, names compounded with,
  240
Saharo-Arabian platform, 3
Sais, in Egypt, 374
Salome Alexandra, queen of Judea, 39
salvation: prophetic promise of, 163,
  165–72, 174, 176, 180, 183; in wisdom
  literature, 199
Samaria, city, 246, destroyed under
  Alexander, 114; siege of, 374; as
  political unit, 80f, 88; governors of,
  155, 158, 228f, 232, 273; province of,
  42; state, exiles from, 342f
Samaritan papyri of wadi Daliyeh, 89,
  113, 117, 122, 125, 219, 240, 376
Samaritans, 87, 219, 250, 354, 378;
  breach of Jews with, 74; rebellion
  under Alexander, 77, 114
Sanballat 'the Horonite', governor of
  Samaria, 74, 80, 150f, 155, 158, 390
Sanballat (II), 155
Sanballat (III), possible, 155
sanctuaries in Palestine, in Persian
  period, 102f, 107
Saoshyant, world saviour, 301
Sasanid royal family, 307
script, Aramaic, 125–7; Hebrew, old,
  126f; Hebrew, revival of old, 85, 125,
  128; 'Jewish', 126, 128f; Phoenician,
  126
Scythopolis (Beth-shean), 4, 11f, 14;
  coins of, 56f; mint of, 48

seals and seal impressions 82, 90, 107–9,
  113, 157, 236f, 242
Sebaste, mint of, 57
Sejanus, 42
Seleucids; coins of, 31, 33; dynasty of,
  8f; empire, 31; era 61f, 64
Semechonitis, lake, *see* Huleh, lake
Sennacherib, king of Assyria, 374
Senonian chalk, 3f, 11, 17f, 21
Sepphoris, mint of, 48, 56
Septuagint text-form, 132, 200f
Seraiah the high priest, 144, 159
settlement, regions of, 19
sexual rites attacked, 171
Shabbetai, name, 221
Shalmanesar III, king of Assyria, 373
Shalmaneser V, king of Assyria, 375
Shamash, deity, 232, 393
Shamash-riba, leader of Babylonian
  revolt, 329
Shamashsharusur, Jew of Babylonia, 356
Sharon, 18; forests of, 8; marshes of, 8,
  14; plain of, 20
Shealtiel, 356
Shechem, rebuilt, 386
Shelemiah son of Sanballat, 74, 155, 390
Shelomam son of Osea, 383
Shelomith (Shlomit) archive of, 123f,
  157
Shemaiah, 388
Shemaiah, son of Jedoniah, 224
Shenazzar son of Jehoiachin, 70, 138,
  356
Shephelah, 21, 86
Sherebiah son of Peliah, Jew of
  Babylonia, 347
Sheshbazzar, prince of Judah, 70, 79, 82,
  136–8, 141, 155f, 356; narrative of,
  141
shewbread, table of on coins?, 40
Shikmona, archeological finds at, 90f;
  destruction of, in wars of Diadochi,
  114
Shimshai, official in Samaria, 152
Shishak, king of Egypt, 374
Shulum-babili, Jewish name in
  Babylonia, 348, 356
shushanu, Babylonian category, 345–7
Siamun, king of Egypt, 373
Sidon, 8, 11, 25; coins of, 110;

Sidon (*cont.*)
   destruction of, 76, 175, 178;
   inscriptions, 75, 89; king of, 80;
   rebels against Persia, 76, 114; stele of
   Achoris at, 114; Tennes, king of, 76
Sidon–wadi Sirhan depression, 11, 16
Simon Maccabeus, 37
Simon II, high priest, 386
Simon bar Giora, leader of first Jewish
   revolt, 49
Sin, god, 326, 330, 353f, 356; in names,
   240
Sinai, border of, 11
Sinuhe, 393
Sippar, Jew of Babylonia, 349
Sirach, *see* Jesus son of Sirach
Sirbonis, lake (lake Bardawil), 79, 88
Smerdis brother of Cambyses, 360
Solomon, king of Israel, 373; in
   Proverbs, 200f; in Song of Songs,
   252; and wisdom, 190, 192
Son of Man, 323
Song of Songs, 250, 252
songs of pilgrimage, 187
'Sown', the, 17
Spenta Mainyu, 315f
spirit, concept of, 317f
statuettes and figurines, 103–5
Susa, capital of Elam, 339f
Susanna and the elders, 349
Syene, 365, 368f, 394f; land of, 376;
   inscriptions, 293
Symbetylos, name of god, 391
synagogues, 258f
Syrian desert, 23

Tabeel, 151
Tabernacles, feast of, 13
Tabor, mount, 11, 14; Israelite cult at,
   235
Tachos, king of Egypt, 76
Tahpanhes (Daphnae) in Delta, 99, 369,
   375
Tamut, wife of Ananiah, 399f
Tapamut, Egyptian slave at Elephantine,
   225
Tapsahes (unknown), 79
Tascetres, district, *see* Tshetres
Tattenai, governor of Abar Nahara, 72,
   155

taxes, Persian, 113
Tefnakhte, ruler of Egypt, 374
Tel Ashdod, ostracon from, 124
Tel Malhata, finds at, 84
Tel Megadim, archeological finds, 90f,
   98
Tel Sippor, destruction in time of
   Diadochi, 114; figurines from, 104f
Tell Abu Hawam, 91; destruction under
   Alexander, 114
Tell Abu Zeitun, 124
Tell el-Fara, military fortress, 81;
   ostracon from, 124
Tell el-Kheleifeh, excavation at, 84;
   military fortress, 81
Tell el-Maskhuta, colony of Arabs in
   Egypt, 75, 369; inscriptions from, 81,
   89, 369
Tell en-Nasbeh, 86
Tell es-Saidiye, altar, 107; Aramaic
   ostraca, 124
Tell es-Sukas, 99
Tell Jemmeh, military fortess, 81; find
   of coins, 111, 122
Temple of Jerusalem, 229, 257, 262–4,
   275, 379; destruction of first, 70; and
   presence of God according to psalms,
   186; rebuilding of, 72, 135–43, 152,
   164f, 170, 244f, 249, 272, 292;
   reorganized by Nehemiah, 149;
   representation on coins, 56; and
   sacrificial rites, 187, 386; vessels
   returned, 136–8, 141, 356; worship,
   exclusiveness of, 182; worship and
   Levites, 247f
Temple mount, monumental inscription
   from, 128
temples, 162
Tennes, king of Sidon, rebels against
   Persia, 76
terra rossa, 21
Testament of Twelve Patriarchs, 315,
   325
Tethys, (former) sea of, 3
Thasos, coins of, 25, 110
Thoth, deity, 227
Thutmosis (Thummosis), king of Egypt,
   373
Tiberias, 43f, mint of, 44, 47f, 56
Tiberius, emperor, 43

Tiglath-Pileser III, king of Assyria, 374
Time, god of, 306, 325; periods of, 320
Tirhakah, king of Ethiopia, 374
Timsah, lake, 361
tiršātā, term used of Nehemiah, 155f
Tithraustes, satrap, 76
Tobiads, territory of, 13
Tobiah, 150f, 158
Tobit, Book of, 189, 192, 250–2, 315, 343, 348f
Trachonitis 5, 7, 12f, 21, 23
Transjordan, development of, 23; plateau edge of, 16; structural pattern of, 3
tribal organization, 18
Tripolis, 8
Trito-Isaiah (Isaiah 56–66), as collection, 135, 169–73, 271
Tshetres or Tascetres, 'the southern district' of Egypt, 364, 381
Tyre, 18, 25; coins of, 31, 58, 110; mint of, 30, 41; resists Alexander, 77, 114; siege and conquest by Alexander, 31, 91, 178

Ugbaru, governor of Gutium (possibly cf. Gobryas, Gubaru), 326
Umm al-Fahm, section of Carmel range, 21
universalism, 171, 181f
Unleavened Bread, Feast of, 265f; at Elephantine, 230f, 302, 357, 388f
urbanization, 20
Uriah of Elephantine, 232
Uriah son of Shemaiah, prophet, 375
Ushtani, satrap of Babylonia, 329

Valerius Gratus, governor of Judea, coins of, 43
Varuna, deity, 284f, 303
Vidranga, *see* Waidrang
Vishtaspa, *see* Hystaspes

Waidrang, *fratarak* of Tshetres, 364, 381, 389f, 394
Wedjahorresnet, Egyptian doctor, statue of, 361, 371
weights in archeological finds, 109f
wisdom: in the ancient Near East, 196; Canaanite, 192; Edomite, 192;

Egyptian, 191, 198; forms of, 195–7; and higher education, 193f; hypostatization (personification) of, 209f, 253; influence in psalms, 183, 186, 189; and kingship, 193; literature in Persian period, 189–218, 253; Mesopotamian (Babylonian), 191; older Israelite, 198f; and order of the world, 206–9

Xanthos, city of, trilingual inscription, 357
Xanthos of Lydia, 298
Xerxes I, king of Persia, 72f, 78, 142, 151, 153, 160, 293–5, 302, 329, 362; inscription of, 293f

ya'ar, 19–21
Yadi, supposed Jewish colony in southern Anatolia, 378
Yah, form of Yahweh, 227
Yahu, name of God at Elephantine, 224, 226, 229, 232, 354, 367, 385, 392f; cult of, 226; priests of, 226; temple of, 225–7, 229, 232, 353, 363f, 367f, 378, 385, 387, 389f
Yahoyishma daughter of Ananiah of Elephantine, 225
Yahweh, 219, 221f, 226–8, 251, 255, 257, 261f, 272–4, 276, 283, 330, 351; cult of, 234, 239, 241
'Yahweh-alone' party, 223, 231, 241, 298
Yama, Old Iranian king of the dead, 290
Yarkon, 8; river, 14, valley, 14
Yarmuk gorge, 13
Yarmuth, 86
Yasheyau (Joshua), Jew in Babylonia, 350
Yedoniah, *see* Jedaniah
Yazatas (or Amesha Spentas), 285, 292, 303, 305
Yehezqia, *see* Jehezikiah
Yehoezer, governor of Judah, 157
Yehud coin-legend (= Judah), 27, 29f, 111, 122, 237f; as seal legend, 108f
Yehudah, coin-legend, 30, 237
Yeshayahu son of Sanballat (II), 155
Yezaniah, *see* Jezaniah

Zaccur son of Meshullam of
Elephantine, 399
Zarathustra, 284–91, 294, 298, 301, 306f,
311, 318; date of, 279f
Zebadiah, fisherman in Babylonia, 347
Zebediah, on ostracon from Ashdod,
240
Zechariah, Jew in Babylonia, 347
Zechariah, prophet, 72, 142, 163, 166–9,
181, 245, 272
Zechariah 1–8, 142, 166–9;
night-visions of, 167f
Zechariah 9–14, 135, 272f
Zedekiah, king of Judah, 374; regnal
years of, 60

Zenon papyri, 85
Zered valley (in Transjordan), 5; gorge
of, 15
Zerqa, see Jabbok
Zerubbabel son of Shealtiel, governor
of Judah, 72, 79, 82, 137f, 140–2,
155–8, 164–9, 182, 245, 248, 272, 275,
356
Ziklag, 84
Zoroastrianism, 279–307, 313, 315f,
318f, 324; calendar and festivals, 305;
and sacrifices, 296
Zurvan 306f, 325
Zurvanism, Zurvanites, Zoroastrian
heresy, 306f.

CHRONOLOGICAL TABLE[1]

B.C.E.	BABYLON AND PERSIA	EGYPT	LAND OF ISRAEL (PALESTINE)	GREECE	ROME
	BABYLON				
605	605 NEBUCHADNEZZAR II reigns. Battle of Carchemish: Egypt defeated by Nebuchadnezzar I	609 NECHO II (609–593)			
600					
597			597 Expedition of Nebuchadnezzar to Judah: Jehoiakin deported. Zedekiah		
593		593 PSAMMETICHUS II (593–588)			
588		588 APRIES (HOPHRAH) (588–570/69)	587 Jerusalem destroyed; mass deportation of Judeans to Babylon. 585 Murder of Gedaliah		
580					
570		570 AMASIS (AHMOSE) (569–525)		AGE OF TYRANTS (seventh and sixth centuries)	
560					
559	c. 559 CYRUS II (c. 559–530) rules Persia				
550	PERSIA				
540					
539	539 Cyrus takes Babylon. 538 Edict of Cyrus		538 Edict of Cyrus: First return of Jews under Sheshbazzar — Rebuilding of Temple		
530	530 CAMBYSES II OF PERSIA (530–522)	526 PSAMMETICHUS III (526–525). 525 Egypt conquered by Cambyses II	c. 522 Zerubbabel Governor?		
522	522 DARIUS I (522–486). Darius organizes satrapies		515		

520		
510	514 Conquest of Macedonia by Persia	
	509 Birth of the Roman Republic	
500		
490	490 Battle of Marathon: Persia defeated	
	486 AHASUERUS (XERXES) (486–465)	
480	480 Xerxes invades Greece: battles of Artemisium, Thermopylae, Salamis; Xerxes withdraws fleet	
470		
465	465 ARTAXERXES I (465/4–424/3)	
460	460 Rebellion of Inaros	
	458 Second return under Ezra?	
	454 Persians annihilate Athenian army on the Nile	
450	449 Peace of Callias (or Cimon)	
	441 Walls of Jerusalem reconstructed by Nehemiah; Ezra reads the Torah to the people	
440		
	431–404 PELOPONNESIAN WAR	
430	428 Second return under Ezra?	
424/3 DARIUS II (424/3–404)		

B.C.E.	BABYLON AND PERSIA	EGYPT	LAND OF ISRAEL (PALESTINE)	GREECE	ROME
420					
410		411/10 Destruction of temple at Elephantine	410 Sanballat Governor of Samaria; followed by Delaiah; Sanballat II; Yeshayhu and Hananiah		
			408 Bagohi (Bagoas?) Governor of Judah		
400	404 ARTAXERXES II (404–358)	c. 404–400 Egypt gains independence		404 Surrender of Athens ends war Sparta supreme in Greece	
				400 399 } Sparta and Persia at war	
			398 Second return under Ezra?		
390					
380				386 Peace concluded between Sparta and Persia Autonomy of Greece proclaimed	
370					
360					
350	358 ARTAXERXES III (358–338)				
340		343/2 Reconquered by Persia	348? Deportation of a number of Jews by Artaxerxes III		
	338 ARSES (338–336)				
	336 DARIUS III 336–330				
	333 Battle of Issus	332 Conquest by Alexander	332? Sanballat III Samaritan Governor?		
330	330 Death of Darius III		332 Conquest of Palestine by Alexander the Great		
		323 PTOLEMY I (323–285/3?)	323 Death of Alexander the Great		
320					

1 Strict accuracy in dating is not always possible. Question marks in the chart indicate uncertainties.